THE
Multi-Boot
CONFIGURATION
HANDBOOK

THE
Multi-Boot
CONFIGURATION
HANDBOOK

Roderick Smith

A Division of Macmillan USA
201 West 103rd Street, Indianapolis, Indiana 46290

The Multi-Boot Configuration Handbook

Copyright © 2000 by Que® Corporation

International Standard Book Number: 0-7897-2283-6

Library of Congress Catalog Card Number: 99-068221

Printed in the United States of America

First Printing: April, 2000

02   01   00   4   3   2

Trademarks

Warning and Disclaimer

ASSOCIATE PUBLISHER
Jim Minatel

SENIOR ACQUISITIONS EDITOR
Jenny L. Watson

DEVELOPMENT EDITORS
Todd Brakke
Rick Kughen

MANAGING EDITOR
Matt Purcell

PROJECT EDITOR
Tonya Simpson

COPY EDITOR
Michael Dietsch

INDEXER
Mary SeRine

PROOFREADER
Benjamin Berg

TECHNICAL EDITOR
Dan Maker, Keylabs
Tom McHugh

TEAM COORDINATOR
Vicki Harding

MEDIA DEVELOPER
Michael Hunter

INTERIOR DESIGNER
Anne Jones

COVER DESIGNER
Anne Jones

COPYWRITER
Eric Borgert

EDITORIAL ASSISTANT
Angela Boley

PRODUCTION
Tim Osborn
Mark Walchle

Contents at a Glance

Table of Contents

V Data Exchange   295

12 Filesystems for Assorted OSs   297

13 Tools for Accessing Foreign Filesystems   329

About the Author

Roderick W. Smith has years of experience running a wide variety of OSs, often in multi-boot configurations. He has run, on Intel x86 hardware alone, MS-DOS, DR-DOS, FreeDOS, Windows 3.1, Windows 95, Windows 98, Windows NT 4.0, Windows 2000, OS/2 2.1 through 4.0, assorted Linux distributions, and FreeBSD 2.2 through 3.3. Rod has publications in several computer magazines, most notably *Linux Journal*, and maintains several Web pages devoted to Linux and OS/2. He is author of two previous books, *Special Edition Using Corel WordPerfect 8 for Linux*, published by Que, and *Linux: Networking for Your Office*, published by Sams. He holds a Ph.D. in cognitive psychology from Tufts University and has completed post-doctoral research in that field at various institutions. He currently resides in Malden, Massachusetts, just outside Boston.

Rod can be contacted at rodsmith@rodsbooks.com or http://www.rodsbooks.com/multiboot/.

Dedication

To David, Amy, and Theo, for friendship, support, and laughter. May we share many more good times in the new century.

Acknowledgments

I'd like to thank acquisitions editor Jenny Watson, development editors Rick Kughen and Todd Brakke, and project coordinator Vicki Harding, all of whom worked with me before and during the book-writing process to ensure that the result would be worth the effort. Without their contributions this book would not have been possible.

A book like this doesn't just slide through the works without being checked for accuracy. Tom McHugh and Dan Maker deserve thanks for doing this generally thankless job. Any errors that remain are, of course, my own.

David King provided me with many useful leads and tips concerning information presented in this book. I would also like to thank all the many companies and individuals who have made multi-OS functions not just possible, but usable—the people who produce partition resizers, boot loaders, foreign filesystem drivers, and so on. Without their efforts, it would be much harder than it is to do productive work on a multi-OS computer. Unfortunately, listing them all would take a chapter unto itself.

Tell Us What You Think!

As the reader of this book, *you* are our most important critic and commentator. We value your opinion and want to know what we're doing right, what we could do better, what areas you'd like to see us publish in, and any other words of wisdom you're willing to pass our way.

As an associate publisher for Que, I welcome your comments. You can fax, email, or write me directly to let me know what you did or didn't like about this book—as well as what we can do to make our books stronger.

Please note that I cannot help you with technical problems related to the topic of this book, and that due to the high volume of mail I receive, I might not be able to reply to every message.

When you write, please be sure to include this book's title and author as well as your name and phone or fax number. I will carefully review your comments and share them with the author and editors who worked on the book.

Fax: 317-581-4666

Email: opsys@mcp.com

Mail: Associate Publisher
         Que Corporation
         201 West 103rd Street
         Indianapolis, IN 46290 USA

Introduction

Computer users at the turn of the millennium are increasingly faced with the possibility—and desirability—of running several operating systems (OSs) on a single computer. The explosive growth of Linux in the late 1990s, the interest in "real" UNIX versions that goes with this growth, the increasing usability of Windows NT (now called Windows 2000) as an alternative to Windows 9x, and the availability of "oddball" OSs such as BeOS and OS/2—these all make for a very dynamic OS marketplace. This dynamic marketplace is often hidden by the prevalence of Windows 9x in terms of total units shipped, but for a person who looks a bit farther than what's preinstalled on a computer, plenty of alternatives merit investigation.

Unfortunately, no one OS can be all things to all people. Indeed, it's unlikely that any one OS perfectly fills the needs of even a single person. By using multiple OSs, you can fill in the gaps, as it were. One OS might be slow and bloated but run a particular program you need, and another might be quick and sleek but might lack a few critical applications. You can get the best of both worlds by using both OSs.

Unfortunately, the range of available OSs, constantly changing standards, and differences in fundamental features of available OSs make it difficult to use multiple OSs on a single computer. In most cases, non-dominant OSs (currently meaning anything that's not Windows 9*x*) try to get along well with the dominant OS, but even so there are challenges for you to overcome. What's the best way to share files between Windows 98 and BeOS 4.5? How can you clear up enough disk space to install Windows 2000 without damaging Windows 95? What applications are good for enabling you to work in either Windows NT or Linux? Add two or more unusual OSs into the mix and the questions don't just add up, they explode.

In sum, although maintaining a multi-OS computer provides many benefits, it can also be challenging. Most people who try it manage to muddle through, slowly accumulating tidbits of information on integrating OS *x* with OS *y*. When the time comes to add OS *z*, the process begins anew. Some people run into one problem too many and give up before accumulating many tidbits.

As a long-time user of several OSs on x86 hardware, I've accumulated more than my fair share of multi-OS tidbits. In the interests of sharing (and because I thought it would be a fun project), I wrote this book. You'll find within these pages the accumulated knowledge of close to a decade running x86 PCs with multiple OSs. (I've run other computers with multi-OS configurations earlier than that, too—my first such experience was running both TOS and Mac OS 6 on an Atari ST! Today I run Mac OS 8.6 and Linux on an iMac, and I expect to add the UNIX-based Mac OS X as soon as it's released. I've restricted this book to a discussion of OSs for x86 PCs, however, in order to narrow the scope to a manageable level.)

Who Should Buy This Book?

This book is aimed toward an audience that's familiar with x86 PCs or at least with computers in general. You should be reasonably familiar with at least one OS but find that you want to experience something more. Chapter 1, "The Trials and Triumphs of a Multi-OS Computer," covers the many reasons you might have for wanting to run multiple OSs on your computer—curiosity, need for additional or specialized software, and so on. Suffice it to say, though, that I assume you're serious about this endeavor. Running multiple OSs on your computer takes work and dedication. I'm not talking about a volunteering-for-the-Peace-Corps level of dedication, of course, but you will invest many hours in the project—or give up in disgust.

What this book can do is to help reduce the amount of time it takes you to configure and effectively use a multi-OS system. It might even prevent you from throwing in the towel if you encounter a problem. Whether you've never installed more than one OS on a computer before or you're an old hand at it but need help adding a third, fourth, or subsequent OS, this book can help you find your way in the often intimidating realm of multi-OS computing. You'll find within these pages tips on sharing data (including foreign OSs' filesystems, common file formats, and cross-platform applications), information on partitioning and OS installation, advice on OS customization with an eye to easing multi-OS use, tips on emulators to run one OS's programs within another, and advice on the purchase and configuration of hardware.

This book is not intended as an introductory text on any specific OS. Although I do include plenty of material for specific OSs—including Windows 9*x*, Windows NT, Windows 2000, OS/2, BeOS, Linux, and FreeBSD—this book does not include the sort of day-to-day operations information you need to use a new OS. For that, you should read the manuals and online help files that come with your OS, or purchase a book specific to your OS. (Chapter 11, "Finding Help," can help point you toward many specific sources of information about a new or old OS.)

There are points in the book where I assume you have some knowledge of the basic tools available in an OS. For example, I assume you know how to start the X Window System in a UNIX-like OS and how to browse for files in Windows, OS/2, or BeOS. When two OSs I discuss do something differently, though, I try to point out these differences. For example, Chapter 12, "Filesystems for Assorted OSs," discusses the differences in filesystem features required by the various OSs available for x86 hardware today.

How This Book Is Organized

This book is divided into eight parts of from two to four chapters each. Each part covers a broad topic of interest in a multi-OS environment, and each chapter covers one particular subject. I've tried to make each chapter as self-contained as possible, but of course some topics interact strongly with others, so you might need to read one chapter before you can get the most out of another. I always mention when this is the case at the start of a chapter that has a "prerequisite." Here's a summary of the sections of this book:

- Part I, "Overview," provides a broad examination of the state of multi-OS computing on the x86 platform today—why you might want to run several OSs on a single computer, what OSs are available, and so on. If you already have a good idea of what OSs you want to run and why, you can safely skip this section. If you're dissatisfied with your current OS and are looking for alternatives, though, Part I is a must read.

- Part II, "The Boot Process," describes how an x86 computer boots. This process is critically important in understanding how a single computer can run two or more OSs and in determining how best to configure your system. Different boot loader programs to select between OSs at system startup have very different characteristics, and a poor choice of boot loader can create an inability to install or use certain OS combinations.

■ Part III, "Partitioning and Partition Management," covers the allocation of space to multiple OSs. Most OS combinations can't share disk space except in certain limited ways, or by giving up functionality such as long filenames or the capability to use large partitions. Partitions let multiple OSs coexist, but they're difficult to modify after they're set up. It's therefore important that you configure your partitions correctly when you set up a multi-OS computer.

■ Part IV, "Operating System Installation," covers tools and procedures to follow when installing a new OS. This section doesn't include detailed installation instructions for any specific OSs; instead, it provides an overview of typical steps and tips for how to proceed in such a way as to provide the most functional setup possible. This part concludes with a chapter describing where to go for help in case you need more specific advice. Even if you don't need advice on OS installation, this chapter can be helpful in tracking down help on many other topics, even in a single-OS environment.

■ Part V, "Data Exchange," is devoted to the topic of sharing data between OSs. A multi-OS computer is most useful when you can work on the same documents in more than one OS, either because you happen to be booted into a given OS or because different OSs provide tools that are ideally suited to performing different types of actions on a single data file. This part of the book covers topics that help in achieving this OS-independence goal, including filesystems and common data file formats.

■ Part VI, "Common Configurations and Tools," explores the topic of making your OSs more like one another. You might want to do this if you're forced to use a new OS and want to make it function in a more familiar way than it does by default, or if you need multiple OSs but want to make the OSs seem alike so you're not bothered by annoying differences. Tools I cover in this section include programs that run on multiple OSs, tools to modify an OS's appearance and behavior, and emulators to allow one OS's programs to run within another.

■ Part VII, "Network Access," broadens the scope of the book somewhat by covering the use of an OS in a network of computers. You can get many OSs to work well with others in a network by using protocols that are common to all OSs. You can even use a network to help integrate two OSs on one computer better; for example, you can use file sharing protocols with a separate file server to provide common storage space to two OSs that otherwise would not share a good common filesystem.

■ Part VIII, "Hardware Considerations," covers hardware issues that are unique or particularly important in a multi-OS configuration. Specific subjects include resource requirements of various OSs, obtaining drivers, and locating new hardware when it comes time to upgrade your computer.

What's on the CD

The CD-ROM that accompanies this book includes many tools and utilities to help make your multi-OS experience a pleasant one:

- **A demonstration version of PowerQuest's (http://www.powerquest.com) PartitionMagic software**—This software is a great boon when it comes to partitioning your computer for multiple OSs. The demonstration version includes most of the functionality of the regular retail version.

- **Versions of LaTeX for multiple OSs**—LaTeX is a powerful document layout tool that many people prefer to a conventional word processor.

- **Filesystem drivers for many OSs**—A large number of drivers allow OSs to read each others' filesystems, and this book's CD includes many of these drivers.

- **GNU utilities and tools**—The Free Software Foundation's (http://www.fsf.org) GNU's Not Unix (GNU) project is devoted to developing a freely redistributable version of UNIX. Many GNU tools have been ported to non-UNIX OSs, however, and this book's CD includes many of these ports.

- **GUI utilities for Windows and OS/2**—It's possible to modify the "look and feel" of these OSs by using an assortment of third-party utilities and add-ons, some of which are on this book's CD. (UNIX OSs are almost infinitely variable using tools and programs that usually come with the OS.)

- **XFree86 for OS/2**—The XFree86 (http://www.xfree86.org) GUI environment is common on UNIX systems but is also available for OS/2, and the OS/2 version comes with this book. Commercial X servers are also available for Windows, as described in Chapter 19, "TCP/IP Networking."

- **VNC for Windows, Linux, and OS/2**—The Virtual Network Computing (VNC; http://www.uk.research.att.com/vnc/index.html) tool enables you to use one computer from another computer over a network connection. Versions for Windows, Linux, and OS/2 are included on this book's CD-ROM.

- **VMware for Linux and Windows NT**—This emulator enables you to run any of several other OSs within the host OS. This CD includes a 30-day demo version of the program.

This broad range of tools and utilities can help make your multi-OS experience a pleasant one. There are, of course, many gigabytes of additional multi-OS tools available, and the text to the book includes information on how to locate such tools.

Conventions Used in This Book

This book uses certain conventions to help you get the most out of it, and from your multi-OS computer.

Text Conventions

Various typefaces in this book identify terms and other special objects. These special type-faces include the following:

Type	Meaning
Italic	New terms or phrases when initially defined.
Mono	Information displayed by the computer in a command prompt window, when running in text mode, or that appears in a configuration file. This is also used for filenames, URLs, and information that you type into the computer at a command prompt or when running a program.
Initial Caps	Menus, dialog box names, dialog box elements, and commands are displayed in Headline-Style Capitalization to distinguish them from body text.

Key combinations are represented with a plus sign. For example, if the text calls for you to enter Ctrl+S, you would press the Ctrl key and the S key at the same time. When referring to menu items, each menu label is separated by a comma. For example, if the text refers to Edit, Search, Forward, you would click the Edit menu item, then the Search item from the Edit menu, and then the Forward item from the Search submenu.

Special Elements

Throughout this book, you'll find Tips, Notes, Cautions, Sidebars, and Cross References. These elements provide a variety of information, ranging from warnings you shouldn't miss to ancillary information that will enrich your multi-OS experience but isn't required reading.

 TIP Tips are designed to point out features, annoyances, and tricks of the trade that you might otherwise miss. Tips generally help you use your computer more efficiently by providing you with a quicker or more effective way of doing something than might otherwise be immediately obvious.

N O T E Notes point out items that you should be aware of, though you can skip these if you're in a hurry. Generally, I've added Notes as a way to give you some extra information on a topic without weighing you down.

CAUTION
Pay attention to Cautions! These could save you precious hours in lost work. Don't say I didn't warn you.

Cross References Cross references are designed to point you to other locations in this book that will provide supplemental or supporting information. Cross references appear like this:

▶ To learn more about Linux and BSD distribution Web sites, **see** "Useful Official Contact Information," **p. 264.**

Overview

The Trials and Triumphs of a Multi-OS Computer

In this chapter

Getting Started

Walk down the aisles of any computer superstore and you'll see them. Their boxes gleam. Posters proclaim that they'll solve your problems. You've heard your neighbor's teenage son wax poetic about them. I'm speaking, of course, about operating systems (OSs), and more specifically, alternatives to whatever OS you're running now (probably some variant of Microsoft Windows). The fact that you're reading these words means that you've heard the Siren's song. Fortunately, this Siren isn't as menacing as the ones faced by Odysseus, and this book is designed to steer you clear of a shipwreck, just in case you hear the wrong Siren or plot a dangerous course to meet her.

Throughout this book, you'll find information on specific topics relating to the operation of a multi-OS computer. You'll find information on basic computer functions, tools to set up your system to operate with multiple OSs, utilities to help in the exchange of data between OSs, programs you can use to ease the transition from one OS to another, and information on purchasing hardware that will function with a wide variety of OSs. This first chapter serves as an introduction and preview, providing an overview of what can be accomplished, along with many pointers to areas of this book with more information.

N O T E　This book covers OSs for *Intel-architecture* computers, also known as *x86 computers* or *IBM-compatibles*. This is the most popular type of computer today, with models available from a wide range of manufacturers, ranging from IBM to countless local shops that custom-build computers to your specifications. This book does not cover Macintosh computers or more exotic hardware, such as computers built around the Alpha processor family. It's possible to run multiple OSs on most of these computers, but the details of how to do so aren't the same as they are for x86 PCs. ▪

The Desire and Need for Multiple OSs

I referred earlier to the Siren's call of running multiple OSs. Before proceeding further, it's important to understand something of the multi-OS appeal. When does that Siren's song lure you to something useful, and when does it lead to wasted time and frustration?

You should keep in mind that maintaining a multi-OS environment can be difficult, and it becomes more difficult the more OSs you add. Just two OSs usually aren't too tricky to maintain. Bump it up to three, four, five, or more and the juggling act can become a full-time job. You should be sure that what you get out of adding these additional OSs is worth the effort. You're the only person who can make that determination because every person's needs are unique.

Gaining Access to Additional Software

One good reason to run multiple OSs is to obtain access to software you might not otherwise be able to run. Although a wide variety of software is available for the Windows family, programs are available for other OSs that aren't available for Windows. A plethora of open source programs exist for UNIX and UNIX-like OSs, for example. Many of these have counterparts in the Windows world, and some have even been ported to Windows, but you might have reason to run these programs natively on UNIX, or you might have no choice. This is particularly likely to be true of customized tools with limited distribution, such as scientific or engineering tools developed in-house. Perhaps you need to run a UNIX scientific-simulation program on a desktop computer. Chances are you can get such a program running under Linux, FreeBSD, or a commercial version of UNIX with little fuss. Recompiling the program for Windows might take much more effort.

A variant on this theme is that you might already be running a less-popular OS, such as BeOS, OS/2, or UNIX, and you want to gain access to a few Windows programs. In this situation, you presumably don't want to completely abandon your existing OS—after all, you installed it on your computer for some good reason—but you want to run at least a few of the programs available in the Windows world.

Some key points to consider when you want to add an OS to expand your collection of software include the following:

- Give yourself plenty of disk space. Your new OS might require, say, 200MB of disk space, but the software you add will probably consume several times that space unless you just want one or two specific programs.

- Consider using an emulator to run your additional software. An assortment of emulators exist, the most sophisticated of which is VMware (http://www.vmware.com), which actually runs the target OS under Windows or Linux, as shown in Figure 1.1.

  ▶ To learn more about emulators, **see** "OSs Within OSs: Emulators," **p. 449**.

- Be sure to provide some method for exchanging data between OSs, especially if you want to run a program on the new OS that must read data from programs native to your existing OS or feed data to such programs.

  ▶ To learn more about sharing data between OSs, **see** Part V, "Data Exchange."

Using the Right Tool for the Job

An OS is a tool, and anybody who uses a tool should try to use the best tool available for the job at hand. You *can* pound nails into a wall with a screwdriver, but that's not the most efficient way to get the job done, and you stand a good chance of damaging the screwdriver, the wall, or your hand in making the attempt. Similarly, using the wrong OS for a job can make your life more difficult or produce substandard results for your efforts.

▶ To learn more about the strengths and weaknesses of specific OSs, **see** "Operating Systems for x86 Hardware in 2000," **p. 27**.

FIGURE 1.1
An emulator lets you run programs from one OS under another or even run two OSs simultaneously on one computer.

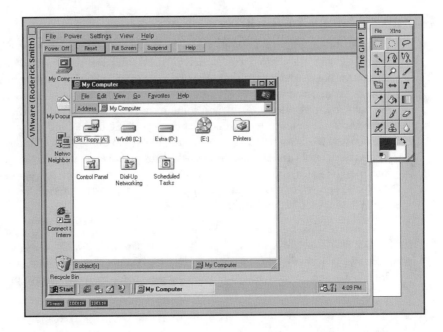

Installing multiple OSs to obtain the best tool is subtly different from installing multiple OSs to obtain additional software. In the first case, tools to perform a task might be available in two OSs, but one OS is inherently better suited to the task than is the other. In the second case, the software simply isn't available in one OS. As an example of the "better tool" case, consider the task of copying your collection of antique 78 rpm records onto modern audio CDs. This task involves three stages:

1. **Digitizing the analog records**—In general, multitasking OSs are less reliable than are single-tasking OSs for recording audio files because programs and even parts of the OS might rob CPU time from the time-critical recording process. Therefore, a single-tasking OS such as DOS is ideally suited to recording the sound files.

2. **Processing the sound files**—Processing the files benefits from good multitasking because this task can be quite time-consuming, and it's useful to be able to run other programs while the computer is churning away removing pops and hiss.

3. **Burning CDs from the resulting audio files**—Burning the CDs is time-critical, but not as much as is audio recording, so multitasking OSs can do better at this task than they do at recording, but only if they multitask well.

Your concerns when installing multiple OSs to get the best software for a given job are similar to those for getting more total software. You might need to investigate your target OS's capabilities more carefully, though, to be sure that you really are getting the tools that are best for your situation.

Transitioning from One OS to Another

Another possible reason to install two or more OSs is that you must move from one OS to another. Perhaps your workplace has a new policy concerning OSs, so you need to change; or maybe you want to use the same OS at home and at work; or perhaps you want to shift from an older to a newer OS. Whatever the cause, such a transition can be painful. As you adjust to a new OS, you'll find yourself yearning for one feature or another of your old one. More important, you might find that you occasionally need some feature of your old OS. You might need to be able to run an application from your old OS in order to access important data files, for example.

▶ To learn more about sharing data between OSs, **see** Part V, "Data Exchange."

If your goal is simply to move from one OS to another as swiftly and painlessly as possible, here are some tips to help you accomplish this goal:

- Put the new OS on a new hard disk, or use dynamic partition resizing software to shrink your old OS as much as you can before installing the new one. Don't overdo it, though—you might find you need to install new software on your old OS, even after your switch is nearly complete, to facilitate data exchange or for some other purpose.

    ▶ To learn more about dynamic partition resizing, **see** "Modifying Partitions After the Fact," **p. 181**.

- Allocate enough disk space for the transition. If your current hard disk is cramped, you really should buy a new one before adding a new OS. You might be tempted to squeeze by on little space, reasoning that you'll soon be rid of the old OS, but this is false economy. Disk requirements increase rapidly under any OS, so you will find a use for new disk space, even after you've reduced your system back to a single-OS configuration.

- Plan for the removal of your current OS. It might take just a few weeks or several months, but eventually you'll want to remove your current OS. If you use a dynamic partition resizer, use one that supports both OSs' native filesystem formats, if possible. Alternatively, plan your partition arrangement so that you can reformat the old OS's drives for use in the new OS with minimal disruption.

Learning About New OSs

Finally, you might want to install several OSs to learn about new or different OSs. Learning in and of itself might not be your goal, though; you might have a more specific goal in mind, such as

- **Determining whether you want to change OSs**—You might have heard great things about a particular OS, and you might be disappointed in the one you're currently using. Instead of taking your neighbor's word for the greatness of the new OS, though, you can evaluate it yourself without destroying your current configuration.

- **Evaluating a market**—Perhaps your company is considering porting a product to a new OS or using that OS as part of your own product. Installing the OS and getting to know it is virtually required, and doing this in a dual-boot environment can give you a good baseline for comparison—you know that any differences between the new OS and the old one really are due to the OS, not to the fact that one machine, for example, has a much faster hard disk than the other.

- **Increasing your job skills**—Knowing multiple OSs isn't likely to hurt you in the job market, particularly if you're in the information technology field. By installing an up-and-coming OS on your home computer, you can learn something about it and use that knowledge at work, or even to find a better job.

- **Playing with the latest and greatest**—Some people just enjoy playing with the latest OSs. It can be a diversion, particularly on those dreary days when you really don't want to go sailing or hike in the woods.

Avoiding Potholes on the Road to Multi-Boot

I've just outlined some of the reasons you might want to install multiple OSs. Even with good reasons to do so, however, many people encounter problems, become frustrated, and either give up or settle for something less than they should. As I mentioned earlier, installing and maintaining multiple OSs can be difficult. If you go about the task properly, you can have several operating systems up and running in a reasonable period of time and have few problems maintaining your multi-OS system. If you go about it the wrong way, though, you'll have nothing but trouble—hardware won't work correctly in some OSs, one or more OSs might be unstable, you might be confused by strange commands and procedures, and so on.

NOTE I cannot explain everything there is to know about every OS in this book. In fact, this book contains relatively little in the way of OS-specific information. When you add an OS, it's generally a good idea to locate a book on that OS. ■

There are some things you can do to help reduce the likelihood of problems as you install, configure, learn, and use new OSs. It's easy to overlook these factors, particularly if you've never installed an OS before, and knowing about them up-front can help keep you from becoming frustrated and disillusioned with your new OS.

Know Your Hardware

Intel PC hardware is extremely varied in capabilities and design. In many ways, it's amazing that today's computers work at all, much less well enough to support half a dozen or more radically different OSs all running on one conglomeration of hardware. Central processing units (CPUs), hard disks, video adapters, keyboards, and more come from different manufacturers. There are often several competing types of each component, and the OS must talk to it all. If you don't know the hardware inside your computer, you're taking a gamble when you install a new OS because your new OS might not understand that hardware. Rule number one when installing a new OS is therefore to check out hardware compatibility.

Why would hardware be incompatible? To understand the answer to that question, it's necessary to understand that hardware manufacturers want to make their hardware both unique and inexpensive. Ideally, the hardware should be unique in some positive way, such as in providing superior performance. This type of uniqueness generally entails a unique design about which the OS must know, however. The OS learns about the hardware's design through a *driver*—a piece of OS software that interfaces between the OS and the hardware. Drivers can be difficult to develop because they're critical pieces of software. If a buggy text editor crashes, the user loses a file. If a buggy driver crashes, the user might lose an entire operating system installation. It's therefore critical that drivers are bug-free and efficient.

To make the hardware inexpensive, however, the manufacturer probably wants to cut costs on developing drivers. That means that the manufacturer likely will not provide drivers for any but the most popular OSs around, and today that means Windows 9*x* and possibly one or two others. OSs therefore often ship with a wide assortment of drivers, but that assortment can't be complete. The rest of this section provides an overview of the most critical hardware components from a driver point of view. This topic is important enough that this book's final three chapters are devoted to hardware in more detail.

The Motherboard, CPU, and RAM   At the core of every modern computer lie three components:

- **The motherboard**—This is generally the largest circuit board in a computer. It contains slots for additional boards, a socket or slot for a CPU, some method of adding memory, and miscellaneous additional components.
- **The CPU**—The CPU performs the computations at the core of every task a computer does. CPU speed is measured in megahertz (MHz), though different models can run at the same speed but perform differently.
- **RAM**—*Random access memory (RAM)* is used to store programs and data. The more RAM you have, the better. Today, 32MB is a small amount of RAM. How much RAM you need depends on the requirements of the most memory-hungry OS you intend to run.

Fortunately, there are few OS-specific incompatibilities with any of these components, unless you're digging an old 286 CPU out of a closet, in which case most modern OSs won't run on it. (Most modern OSs require at least a 386.) Motherboards include circuitry for handling hard disks and, sometimes, video, sound, or other devices that require special drivers. Standard *enhanced integrated drive electronics (EIDE)* hard disk interfaces can be used with generic drivers, but sometimes you'll do better with a driver for a specific class of motherboard.

No special drivers are needed for either RAM or CPU. This book is about OSs for Intel x86-class CPUs, however, meaning CPUs in the family that started with the 8086 and 8088 and continues on to the Pentium III. Other companies, including AMD and VIA (Cyrix was purchased by VIA), make compatible CPUs under other names, such as K6, MII, and Athlon.

Mass Storage Devices   As I mentioned, EIDE controllers can be used with standard drivers that come with all OSs. Some hard disks aren't EIDE, though—they're *SCSI (small computer system interface)*. EIDE and SCSI hard disks aren't interchangeable, and SCSI host adapters require drivers in the OS. SCSI host adapters can also control CD-ROM drives, scanners, tape backup units, and other hardware. For the most part, all these devices use the same SCSI host adapter drivers, although some of these devices (like scanners) might require additional drivers.

Most CD-ROM drives today plug into the motherboard's EIDE port. As with EIDE hard drives, drivers for EIDE CD-ROM drives are common, so you shouldn't have to concern yourself with them. Some CD-ROM drives are SCSI units. Most OSs come with the drivers necessary to use these drives, though you also need a driver for the specific SCSI host adapter.

You can also find *CD-recordable (CD-R)* burners, tape drives, and other mass storage devices. Most of these attach to either EIDE or SCSI interfaces and use their drivers. These devices might require specialized software to function properly, but often not drivers per se. If in doubt, check on driver availability.

▶ To learn more about how to locate drivers, **see** "Finding Drivers," **p. 555**.

Sight and Sound for Today's Multimedia   The areas of visual and audio output are two of the most troublesome for the multi-OS computer. This is because the marketplace supports a vast array of video and sound cards, and this array is constantly changing. It's therefore difficult for OS producers to keep up with the marketplace.

In general, if you're building a computer or buying a component for a multi-OS computer, it's best to stick with a product that has been available for several months. This action increases the likelihood that you'll be able to find drivers for several OSs. If you want to install a new OS on an existing computer, do not assume that you'll get acceptable sound or, especially, a good video display from your new OS. If you're running Windows 9*x*, you can find out what you have by using the Windows Control Panel. From the Control Panel, select the System icon. In the resulting System Properties dialog box, click the Device Manager tab. You can then expand the list of devices in any of several categories by clicking the plus sign (+) next to the category, as shown in Figure 1.2.

FIGURE 1.2
The Windows 9x
System Properties dia-
log box provides infor-
mation about the
hardware and drivers
installed in a com-
puter.

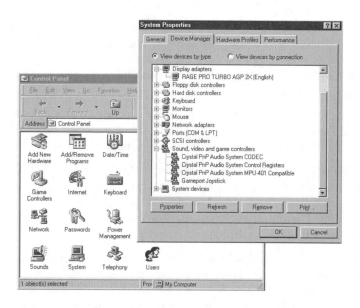

Unfortunately, this information is sometimes not as clear as you might like. For example, the system depicted in Figure 1.2 uses an ATI Xpert 98 video card, which Windows identifies as a Rage Pro Turbo AGP. To use this board under XFree86 (the windowing system used by most UNIX-like OSs), however, you must use the ATI Mach 64 X server. There's no contradiction here; it's just that in this case Windows displays the name of a specific product, whereas the XFree86 configuration requires that you use the name of the *chipset* on the product—that is, the chips that give the product most or all of its electronic personality. Windows actually misidentified this board, but because the actual product and the one Windows identifies it as are similar, no harm comes of this misidentification. Such misidentification is quite common, particularly when you use an off-brand component or products that are marketed under multiple names, as are ATI's boards.

▶ To learn more about how to locate drivers for your hardware, **see** "Finding Drivers," **p. 555.**

Modems and Printers   Modems and printers can be tricky in a multi-OS environment, and for similar reasons: Both device categories are plagued by Windows-only models. These devices require special Windows drivers to function even minimally. It's rare to find non-Windows drivers for such devices, though it's not absolutely unheard-of. In general, you want a laser printer that supports Hewlett Packard's printer control language (PCL) or Adobe's PostScript. Inkjet printers are more of a mixed bag, but Epson and higher-end Hewlett Packard models tend to work well on most OSs. Among modems, your best bet is an external model because most Windows-only models are internals.

Miscellaneous Devices   The more exotic the hardware, the harder you'll find it to obtain drivers. Devices like video cameras and scientific data acquisition boards tend to ship with drivers for only one or two OSs, and might have absolutely no support outside those OSs from any source. If you're using anything even remotely unusual, therefore, you should check into the driver situation carefully.

Fortunately, keyboards are almost universally supported, as are mice and other pointing devices. The exception is universal serial bus (USB) devices, which currently have weak support under most OSs aside from Windows 9*x*, although this support is improving.

Conventional analog monitors also pose few problems across OSs. You might need to be cautious if you have one of the new digital liquid crystal display (LCD) monitors. These pose problems not so much because of the monitor but because of their video cards, which must be supported like any other video card. Note that analog LCD monitors pose no special problems because they work with conventional video cards.

Modern motherboards include serial ports for modems and certain types of mice and parallel ports for printers. All OSs support these ports with standard drivers. Sometimes you can connect unusual devices to these ports, such as scanners to the parallel port. These devices often require special drivers and so might or might not be supported in a given OS.

Know What to Expect of a New OS

One problem that many new users of any OS encounter is unrealistic expectations. Contrary to what you might think from listening to the hype, no OS will solve all your computing woes. If you're trying an OS because you expect it will help you in some way, try to be as precise as possible in your thinking about how that OS will help you. Then research that aspect of the OS. If you expect a new OS to be easier to use than your old one, locate Usenet news postings that compare the two OSs on ease of use, or read Web pages devoted to each OS and compare ease of use features—but be wary of potentially exaggerated advertising claims.

 TIP   You can learn a great deal about an OS from the Deja.com Web site (`http://www.deja.com`). This site contains an archive of Usenet news postings, searchable by keywords. Type `linux` and `windows` and `user` and `interface` into its search box to find postings comparing the user interfaces of these two OSs, for example. Be aware that you might produce a lot of "false alarms"— postings that match the keywords but in a context that's not useful to you. You can also miss relevant postings if you fail to include appropriate keywords. Finally, when researching a comparison of two OSs, you're likely to run across a large number of advocacy postings, which tend to lack objectivity and sometimes even courtesy. Despite these perils, Deja is an extraordinarily useful research tool.

The more carefully you research a potential new OS's features with respect to your own needs, the less likely you are to be disappointed by that OS. You should also be aware of the OS's general strengths and weaknesses. If you don't think to ask about it, you might be surprised to discover that your favorite application isn't available for your new OS—but you might find an alternative that's just as good. Of course, you can't research every aspect of an OS before using it, but you should investigate the basics. You might uncover problems (or benefits) in a few minutes using the Internet that would take you hours of effort to find on your own system.

Give Yourself Adequate Time

Installing a new operating system is a much more complex operation than installing a typical application program. In most cases, you must repartition your hard disk, install the OS, and configure it for your hardware. Depending on the OS, the tools you have at your disposal, and your experience, these steps can take anywhere from several minutes to several hours—or more if you encounter hardware glitches.

After your new OS is installed, you might need to install programs to use with it. Such installations might take longer for each application than it would take to install similar software on your old OS, simply because you're unfamiliar with the new OS's installation procedures.

You might also need to customize the OS for your needs. For example, you might need to set up networking features, either to integrate the OS into a local network or for a PPP dial-up connection to the Internet. These steps might also take longer than they would in your first OS because of unfamiliarity with the new one. In addition, if you require support from your networking department or *Internet service provider (ISP)*, it might not be forthcoming unless the new OS is a version of Windows or the installation is part of an approved corporate shift in OS support.

Overall, I recommend setting aside 5–50 hours for each new OS installation you try, just for basic installation and configuration. Of course, you need not devote this time all at once; an hour a day for a week will cover the low end of the scale, for example. You might also get lucky, if you're installing a small OS or need to perform few customizations, and get it done in just a couple of hours. On the other hand, you might find that you can't install a new OS on your computer because of hardware conflicts, insufficient disk space, or some other reason.

Expect a Learning Curve

After it's installed, your new OS will consume more time. Even if you're just installing an upgrade to an existing OS, such as Windows 2000 as an upgrade from Windows NT 4.0 or Windows 98, your new OS contains new and changed features, and you must set aside adequate time to learn those new features. This time can overlap with the time required to install and configure an OS, of course. For example, you might install your OS in, say, three hours, but put off configuring it to establish a PPP link with your ISP. In the meantime, you might learn about the OS's basic features, the available applications, and so on, only afterward returning to the configuration issue of establishing a PPP link.

Remember when you try a new OS that many features you take for granted in another OS might not apply to a new one. This is particularly true when shifting OS paradigms in a radical way, such as when shifting from Windows to BeOS or UNIX. As an example, in Windows you access hard disks, CD-ROMs, and floppies using drive letters, as in C: or E:. By contrast, UNIX doesn't use drive letters; instead, in UNIX you mount a partition or other disk device in the existing file directory hierarchy, which is anchored at the root filesystem, referred to with a slash (/). For example, the CD-ROM drive that you access in Windows as E: might be referred to as /mnt/cdrom in a UNIX-like OS. You must also generally issue an explicit mount command in most UNIX-like OSs before you can access a removable-media device. (Some UNIX-like OSs support an automount feature to obviate this need, however.)

Precisely how much time you need to get up to speed in a new OS varies considerably, depending on your familiarity with similar OSs, how different the new one is compared to your old OS, and how you go about the task.

Assemble OS-Specific Documentation

One way you can cut down on the difficulty of the learning curve is to assemble documentation specific to your new OS. You might want to begin, and to at least skim some of this documentation, before you install the new OS. That way, you'll be familiar with at least some of the terminology used by the new OS when you install it, and you'll be better able to make informed decisions concerning installation options and configuration options soon after that.

Some good sources of information include

- **Books**—I highly recommend that you purchase at least one book on your new OS before you begin using that OS. A book with a good index and clear table of contents can help you find answers to common beginner's questions more quickly than can any other method, with the possible exception of querying a more experienced co-worker in the office next to yours.

- **Official documentation**—Some OSs come with extensive manuals, sometimes even printed ones. Other OSs come with only online documentation.

- **Usenet newsgroups**—If you have an Internet connection, you can read Usenet newsgroups relating to many OSs. If you're unfamiliar with Usenet news, you can use the Netscape Communicator package to access them. (Netscape Navigator doesn't possess the necessary feature, however.) Many other newsreaders are also available. Most OS-related newsgroups fall into the comp.os.* hierarchy, but some appear in other locations, as well.

- **FAQs**—The acronym *FAQ* stands for *frequently asked questions*, and it can refer either to a specific question posted to a newsgroup or to a document that answers these questions. You can find FAQ lists on OS producers' Web sites and at assorted other locations on the Internet. One particularly good source for locating FAQs is `ftp://rtfm.mit.edu/pub/usenet-by-hierarchy`, which contains numerous FAQs organized by Usenet newsgroup.

▶ To learn more about sources of information for a new OS, **see** "Finding Help," **p. 263**.

After you have documentation in hand, you'll be much better prepared to face the challenges of installing and using a new OS. I've seen many frustrated Usenet news postings from individuals who've jumped into a new OS installation without doing the necessary preliminary research. Save yourself the aggravation and do the research first.

Nessus: The Eight-OS Computer

You might find it helpful to see an example of a multi-OS computer. In this section, therefore, I describe a computer I've configured to use eight OSs. Some of these OSs are closely related to each other (SuSE Linux and Debian Linux are the two most closely related), but others are unique. The configuration of this computer, which I call Nessus on my local network, demonstrates many of the features and techniques described throughout the rest of the book.

The Hardware

Nessus contains some old and some new hardware. In most respects, it's nowhere near a top-of-the-line computer—but that just serves to demonstrate the fact that you don't need top-of-the-line hardware to run multiple OSs on a single computer. Nessus includes the following components:

- Generic ATX-style desktop computer case
- FIC PA-2013 Socket 7 motherboard
- Cyrix M-II 333 CPU (266MHz)
- 64MB PC100 SDRAM memory
- ATI Xpert 98 AGP video adapter
- Acer AW37 Pro ISA sound card
- Linksys LNE100TX 10/100Mbps PCI Ethernet card
- Western Digital 6.4GB EIDE hard disk
- Maxtor 10GB EIDE hard disk
- Compaq 32X EIDE CD-ROM drive
- Northgate OmniKey 101 keyboard
- Logitech Trackman Marble trackball

This computer is connected to a network with two other machines, one of which functions as a print server (among other things), so this computer can access both a Hewlett Packard LaserJet 4000 laser printer and an Epson Stylus Color 400 inkjet printer.

Most of these components are either fairly generic, and so pose no problems in any OS, or are based on widely supported chipsets. For example, the ATI video board uses ATI's Mach 64 chipset, which is common and has at least reasonable support in all the OSs I use. The Linksys Ethernet adapter uses a common PNIC chipset that emulates the popular DEC Tulip Ethernet chipset—again, well supported in all the OSs I use.

▶ To learn more about locating drivers or selecting hardware, **see** Part VIII, "Hardware Considerations."

N O T E Not all the hardware works equally well in all the OSs. For example, the CD-ROM drive is finicky in FreeBSD, although another EIDE CD-ROM drive works fine. ■

The OS Players

Nessus runs eight OSs and could easily run more. The following eight OSs are installed on Nessus:

- Caldera DR-DOS 7.03
- Microsoft Windows 98
- Microsoft Windows NT 4.0
- IBM OS/2 Warp 4.0
- BeOS 4.5
- FreeBSD 3.2
- SuSE Linux 6.2
- Debian GNU/Linux 2.1

Running so many OSs on a single computer can be difficult at times. For example, Nessus has only about 16GB of hard disk space, so with eight OSs, that leaves about 2GB per OS, on average. In the case of Nessus, I stretch this space in two ways. First, I share disk space between OSs whenever possible. Second, one of the other computers on the network functions as a file server, so Nessus can turn to the file server for additional disk space. If I needed a standalone PC to run eight OSs, 16GB would be a borderline amount of disk space.

Disk Partitioning

There are two basic ways to install two OSs on the same computer:

- **In a shared partition**—Both OSs reside on a single partition of the hard disk. This approach has the advantage of providing each OS with full and complete access to the other's files. It's also generally easy to install the second OS because there's no need to change your computer's existing partitioning scheme. Some OSs don't reside well with others on a single partition, however, either because one OS tends to trample over the other's files or because each requires its own special filesystem.

■ **In separate partitions**—Giving each OS its own partition can provide added security because it's less likely that one OS will damage the other's files. This approach is generally more difficult to set up, however, especially if you're adding an OS to a computer that's already configured with another OS.

What do you do when you have eight OSs, though? Depending on the specific OSs in question, either approach can work, but most likely both will be required. This is certainly true of Nessus.

A Tour of the Partitions on Nessus   Figure 1.3 depicts the partitioning scheme used on Nessus.

FIGURE 1.3
Nessus's partitioning scheme is complex and mostly well optimized.

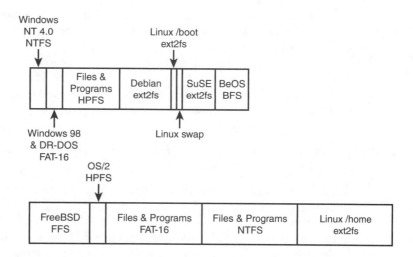

Some key points of this configuration include

■ **Shared space**—One of the middle partitions on the 10GB drive is formatted for FAT-16 and is devoted to files and programs. It serves as a shared space for all the OSs because all the OSs can read from and write to FAT-16 partitions. Similarly, the Linux /home partition on the 10GB drive is shared across both Linux installations, as are the Linux /boot and swap partitions on the 6.4GB drive.

■ **Shared partition boots**—Windows 98 and DR-DOS 7.03 both boot from the second physical partition on the 6.4GB drive. The Linux kernels for both SuSE and Debian are stored in the Linux /boot partition, so in some sense these OSs also share a boot partition—but all the other Linux system files reside on separate partitions on the 6.4GB hard drive.

■ **Microsoft OSs at the start of the first drive**—DOS and Windows NT, in particular, often have difficulty starting when they reside on a partition that's later than the first 2GB of a hard disk.

■ **OSs split across drives**—Splitting OSs across two or more physical hard disks generally makes for faster hard disk access times, so the partitions that are commonly
accessed in an OS are split in this configuration. For example, OS/2 boots from the
10GB drive, but its programs are stored on the 6.4GB drive. Linux system files and
swap space go on the 6.4GB drive, while data files are on the 10GB drive. Windows NT
boots from the 6.4GB drive but has a partition on the 10GB drive for additional data
and programs.

▶ To learn more about partitioning a disk for multiple OSs, **see** Part III, "Partitioning and
Partition Management."

Nessus has a very good partition layout, given the constraints of two hard disks and eight
OSs. There are, of course, compromises, particularly with respect to specific access patterns.
For example, if I want to access the Linux /home partition when running FreeBSD, the hard
disk heads must traverse most of the space between the FreeBSD and /home partitions,
which reside at opposite ends of the 10GB hard disk. If I needed to perform such accesses
frequently, I might want to place those partitions closer together; but doing so might worsen
some other type of performance. In sum, tradeoffs are involved. Nessus does a good job of
balancing those tradeoffs for the way I use the computer. Somebody else might justifiably
choose a different configuration, however.

Partition Types   One important distinction to understand when partitioning a hard disk
involves the three different types of partitions:

■ **Primary partitions**—The designers of the original PC disk partitioning scheme didn't
anticipate the explosion of OSs we've seen today or the need to create multiple partitions for even a single OS. They therefore provided a means for creating only four partitions on a hard disk. Today, these are known as *primary* partitions. In some OSs
today, only one of these partitions can be visible at a time, but most OSs can see several
primary partitions at once.

■ **Extended partitions**—A two-tiered scheme was devised to add partitions beyond the
original four allowed. The first tier involved the allocation of one primary partition to
serve as a placeholder for additional partitions. This special primary partition is known
as an *extended* partition. Unlike an ordinary primary partition, an extended partition
isn't formatted with a specific filesystem. Instead, it contains a few additional pointers
and data structures to define additional partitions. There are two basic types of
extended partition—the original and a new one defined by Microsoft late in Windows
95's lifetime to support hard disks larger than 1024 cylinders.

▶ To learn more about the 1024-cylinder limit, **see** "EIDE and SCSI Hard Disk Handling,"
p. 75.

■ **Logical partitions**—The partitions defined within an extended partition are known as
logical partitions. There effectively is no limit on the number of logical partitions a disk
can contain, and all OSs allow simultaneous access to multiple logical partitions.

Unfortunately, some OSs can't boot from logical partitions, and the BIOS doesn't support direct booting from logical partitions, so even OSs that can boot from them require a boot loader that can redirect the boot process appropriately.

▶ To learn more about booting from logical partitions, **see** "The Job of the Boot Loader," **p. 86**.

In general, I refer to primary and logical partitions in this book. The presence of an extended partition is implied by the presence of a logical partition. Because of this partitioning scheme, logical partitions are normally contiguous; you don't see a run of logical partitions, then a primary partition, and then more logical partitions. Such a configuration would imply two extended partitions, which is wasteful. In fact, I've never encountered a computer configured in this way.

Nessus contains a mix of primary and logical partitions. On the 6.4GB hard disk, the first two partitions (for Windows NT and Windows 98/DOS) are primary partitions. The rest are logical. On the 10GB hard disk, the first two partitions (for FreeBSD and OS/2) are primaries, and the rest are logical. Most OSs' disk partitioning programs allow the creation of a disk with no primary partitions, but some require at least one primary partition.

N O T E Some OSs use their own custom analogs of extended partitions. For example, FreeBSD uses a single primary partition and carves it up into what are effectively its own variety of logical partitions. The FreeBSD partition in Figure 1.3 actually contains two subpartitions: a swap partition and one partition for the entire FreeBSD system. ■

Boot Management

Boot management on a system with eight OSs requires a great deal of sophistication. Nessus therefore uses V Communications's (http://www.v-com.com) System Commander Deluxe as a primary *boot loader*. A boot loader is a small utility that can redirect the boot process to other OSs. System Commander is particularly helpful on Nessus because this software can both redirect the boot process to separate partitions and change which OS boots from a FAT partition. This second characteristic is vitally important when booting Windows 98 or DR-DOS because these OSs reside on a single partition. In addition to System Commander, several secondary boot loaders exist on Nessus:

■ **Linux's LILO**—The *Linux loader (LILO)* is necessary to boot Linux. It resides on the Linux /boot partition. Because both Debian and SuSE boot from this partition, LILO also handles switching between these two versions of Linux. System Commander provides only a single Linux option, and only after that point is the selection of Debian or SuSE made.

■ **Windows NT's OS Loader**—Nessus is configured to boot only Windows NT from the NT partition; however, Windows NT's boot loader could be configured to boot additional OSs.

■ **BeOS's boot loader**—BeOS has its own boot loader, which can boot multiple OSs. On Nessus, it's configured to boot directly into BeOS, much as Windows NT's OS Loader is configured to boot directly into Windows NT.

■ **Single-OS loaders**—The remaining OSs use single-OS boot loaders that can boot only one OS. In the case of DR-DOS and Windows 98, System Commander juggles the boot files so that each OS boots correctly, as if it were the only OS on the partition.

▶ To learn more about boot loaders, **see** "Boot Loaders Simple and Complex," **p. 85**.

Data Sharing Arrangements

With so many OSs, it's quite desirable to share data between them. Two methods of data sharing are available:

■ **Direct access**—If one OS can use a driver for another OS's native filesystem, that driver can be used to read and, sometimes, write data in the second OS's format. On Nessus, Windows NT supports drivers for OS/2's HPFS; OS/2 and BeOS support Linux ext2fs partitions; and Linux supports everything but BeOS's BFS. All these OSs also support the FAT filesystem used by DOS and Windows 98.

■ **Common space**—The FAT-16 partition on the 10GB drive is readable by all the OSs on Nessus. This fact allows this partition to be used as a shared space. If I want to transfer a file from Windows NT to BeOS, I place it in the common space and reboot to BeOS. Similarly for a transfer from FreeBSD to OS/2 or any other pair that doesn't share a more direct link.

I recommend setting aside at least one FAT-16 partition for file sharing between most OS pairs. In some cases you might be able to use some other partition type for this purpose, but FAT-16 is a lowest common denominator—because it's supported by so many OSs, it's a convenient method of data transfer.

Summary

Configuring a computer to use multiple OSs provides unusual opportunities and challenges. You can expand the range of what you can do with your computer, learn about new OSs, or ease a transition from one OS to another. In availing yourself of these advantages, though, you must ensure that you can use your hardware (or at least be sure that unsupported hardware isn't critical to basic computer functions), design a partitioning system, and get your systems to coexist on one computer.

It's possible to place quite a few OSs on a single computer, but the more OSs you install, the more compromises you're likely to face. My own computer, Nessus, is reasonably well configured. Nonetheless, the fact that it runs so many OSs with so few problems is rather amazing when you think about the complexity of each OS and the uniqueness of the hardware involved (not just in Nessus, but in any computer). ●

CHAPTER 2

Operating Systems for x86 Hardware in 2000

Your OS, Please...

When you call a technical support line for an Internet service provider (ISP) or a manufacturer of a hardware component or another computer-related product, one of the first questions you'll be asked is what OS you use. Many firms don't ask the question in such an open-ended way, though. "Do you use Windows 95 or Windows 98?" is more typical. Such is the prevalence of these two operating systems that other OSs, even once-popular ones such as DOS, don't even register as existing as far as many firms are concerned. These two OSs represent only a fraction of the OS choices available, although they do represent a huge proportion of the OS market share.

The very fact that you're reading this book, however, means that you might want to look beyond the most common OSs. Perhaps you're vaguely dissatisfied with Windows and want to know what else is available. Maybe you have specific needs that aren't met by Windows. Perhaps you're curious about an OS about which a friend or colleague is raving. Whatever the case, this chapter gives a rundown of the alternatives, including their strengths and weaknesses.

N O T E This book focuses on a handful of OSs, including DOS, the many variants of Windows, OS/2, BeOS, Linux, and FreeBSD. These are the OSs you're most likely to want to install. However, some pretty obscure OSs are available. Many of these are UNIX variants, but some live in their own private universes. If you're interested in such an OS, many techniques described in this book will still be helpful to you, but you'll need to work out the details on your own. With any luck, the OS's documentation includes information to help you bridge the gap between what this book discusses and what the OS requires. ■

DOS

Microsoft's Disk Operating System (DOS) is generally thought of as the original operating system for Intel-class computers. Unlike the other OSs described in this book, DOS runs on anything, from a lowly original IBM PC with an 8088 CPU to the latest Intel Pentium III or AMD Athlon system. (Most more advanced OSs require at least a 386 to run.) In its long history, DOS has spawned quite a few versions, variants marketed by both Microsoft and IBM, and outright clones. Many of these products are still available—and can be used for productive work—today.

Varieties of DOS

When IBM released its *personal computer* (*PC;* a term that's now often used as a synonym for Intel-based computers), it needed an operating system. Rumors and urban legends abound concerning IBM's selection of an OS from then-tiny Microsoft, but whatever the reason, IBM's choice has had a profound influence on the computer industry, both in terms of the capabilities of PCs felt even today and in the influence of Microsoft on the computer world. This latter point is largely the result of one aspect of the licensing terms used for the original version of DOS: Microsoft retained the right to sell the software independently of IBM. The result was a fork in the DOS product—that is, one product became two. In particular, IBM called its version PC-DOS (after its computer, the IBM PC), while Microsoft called its version MS-DOS (after its company name).

Part

I

Ch

2

For years, the two versions were virtually identical, but eventually differences began to appear, mostly in terms of utilities that were added to the original products, such as disk compression programs. Still, PC-DOS and MS-DOS are very similar OSs that bear a common heritage. Although Microsoft is no longer selling a current OS that it calls DOS, IBM is, under the name PC-DOS 2000. You can find more about PC-DOS 2000 at http://www-4.ibm.com/software/os/dos/index.html.

At the time of the PC's genesis, a company known as Digital Research played a prominent role in the microcomputer industry with its *Control Program for Microcomputers (CP/M)* OS. CP/M was used on a wide variety of systems. As the IBM PC and its clones gained prominence, however, Digital Research found that CP/M for the PC wasn't appealing because software was written for DOS. Digital Research therefore modified CP/M to make it more DOS-compatible and renamed it *DR-DOS*. This software competed with PC-DOS and MS-DOS for quite some time. Digital Research was eventually gobbled up by Novell, which renamed DR-DOS to Novell DOS. Novell quickly sold the product to Caldera, a company better known for its Linux distribution. Caldera renamed the product OpenDOS, but has since returned it to its original name of DR-DOS. Caldera still makes this product available, distributed by its Lineo subsidiary. You can find more information at http://www.lineo.com/products/drdos.html.

N O T E DR-DOS is generally quite compatible with MS-DOS and PC-DOS, although a few programs don't run properly under DR-DOS. ▒

Finally, an effort has emerged to create an open source clone of DOS, known as FreeDOS. This project is hosted at http://www.freedos.org, and it has produced a fairly stable DOS clone, although as of this writing it is still officially in beta-test stage and so has more compatibility problems than the other major DOS versions. As an open source project, it's unclear how soon FreeDOS might catch up to the commercial players.

Windows 3.1: A DOS Extension

Microsoft's Windows was originally not an OS at all, but an application (albeit a very elaborate one) that ran atop DOS. Windows versions prior to 3.0 achieved only limited success in the marketplace, but with version 3.0, Windows took off. This success continued into version 3.1 and the minor update known as Windows 3.11.

continues

continued

Windows 3.x could run atop any version of DOS—PC-DOS, MS-DOS, or DR-DOS (although some versions of Windows failed to run on some versions of DR-DOS, but that problem was rectified by updated versions of DR-DOS). Windows added the graphical user interface (GUI) environment that was missing from DOS and which most users today take for granted. It also added a primitive form of multitasking known as cooperative multitasking. In this setup, each application is responsible for relinquishing control of the computer to allow other programs to function. This contrasts with the preemptive multitasking used by most other OSs, including later versions of Windows, OS/2, BeOS, and all UNIX variants. In preemptive multitasking, the OS can switch CPU time away from one program. The advantage of preemptive multitasking is that it produces smoother operation when more than one program is running than does cooperative multitasking. The drawback is that it makes the OS itself more complex.

It's possible to run Windows 3.x under OSs other than DOS. Specifically, OS/2 2.0 and later use Windows 3.0 or 3.1 run in a DOS box—an emulation of a DOS computer—to run Windows programs. There have also been reports of similar configurations working under Linux's DOSEMU DOS emulator.

Because Windows 3.11 and earlier are not true operating systems, I don't discuss them in any detail in this book. If you want to configure a system that runs both Windows 3.x and some other OS, configure the system as you would for DOS and your second OS. You can then install Windows under DOS and use the system normally. One caveat: If you want Windows 95 or later to be another OS, it might see the Windows 3.x installation and overwrite it, depending on how you install Windows 95 or later. You should therefore be sure to back up your Windows 3.x files before installing Windows 95 or later. For best safety, install DOS and Windows 3.x on one partition and other versions of Windows on another partition.

Table 2.1 summarizes the features that ship with different versions of DOS. Be aware that if you have an earlier version of any given product, it might lack some features that are available in the latest versions. Also, some features can be added to a given DOS version after the fact; for example, there are add-on TCP/IP networking tools for the DOS versions that don't come with this support "out of the box."

Table 2.1 Varieties of DOS

Feature	MS-DOS	PC-DOS	DR-DOS	FreeDOS
Version	6.22	2000	7.03	Beta-3
Available	No	Yes	Yes	Yes
Multitasking	No	No	Yes	No
FAT-32 Support	No	No	No	No
TCP/IP Networking	No	No	Yes	No
Disk Compression	Yes	Yes	Yes	No

Feature	MS-DOS	PC-DOS	DR-DOS	FreeDOS
Virus Scanner	Yes	Yes	No	No
Minimum CPU	8088	8088	8088	8088
Minimum RAM	640KB	512KB	640KB	640KB
Distribution	Commercial	Commercial	Commercial (Free for personal use)	Open Source

Note: Version numbers are not comparable across products.

In general, DR-DOS is the most full-featured of these DOS versions, whereas FreeDOS is the least. You might find specific features of one or another appealing, but in many applications, any of these can be used successfully.

All these versions of DOS are 16-bit systems. Depending on the context, *16-bit* can mean several things. When applied to a PC operating system, it refers to the number of bits used in memory addresses. A 16-bit number allows 2^{16}, or 65536, different memory addresses. This is the source of the "64KB limit" on memory segments in DOS. DOS can access more than 64KB of RAM, but only by using relatively crude memory management tricks. By contrast, a 32-bit OS permits 2^{32}, or 4GB, of memory to be accessed directly (most such OSs impose lower limits for other reasons). The 16-bit nature of DOS is therefore a serious limitation with today's processors, though it was a necessary one with the original 8088-based IBM PC.

In addition to the versions of DOS described here, various more-advanced OSs provide DOS support. Specifically, Windows 95 and 98 are both built on DOS; they contain 32-bit versions of DOS at their cores, and you can even run these systems in DOS mode (without their GUIs) for a high degree of DOS compatibility. For most purposes, a DOS command prompt window is sufficient for these OSs. Both Windows NT (including Windows 2000) and OS/2 contain DOS compatibility, although neither system can run DOS in quite the same low-level manner that Windows 95 and 98 allow. Linux supports the DOSEMU emulator program, which actually emulates a low-level x86 environment; you must provide the DOS software itself (many DOSEMU packages come complete with FreeDOS, though).

Best Uses for DOS

Many people today consider DOS passé. After all, why use an OS that originated in the 1980s as a single-tasking, single-user OS without a GUI, built-in networking, filenames longer than 11 characters, or other features we take for granted today? DOS has several uses even today:

- **As an embedded OS**—Devices such as cellular telephones, computerized gas pumps, automatic teller machines, and palmtop organizers all require an OS. In some cases, the devices are simple enough that the OS is even more primitive than DOS, but today's devices often require a DOS-like level of sophistication. This makes DOS itself an appealing choice, and in fact both Caldera and IBM court this market niche for their versions of DOS. DOS is a proven OS for which a large number of development tools exist, and many programmers are familiar with DOS, so companies using DOS as an embedded OS can call on a wide existing pool of tools and knowledge to help build their products.

- **As a real-time OS**—Certain applications call for precise timing requirements. For example, many scientific experiments call for sampling dozens of continuous data streams thousands of times a second. Multitasking OSs often have difficulty guaranteeing such precision timing, making data collection impossible or at least requiring more sophisticated programming to get around the multitasking limitations. Similar comments apply to many industrial environments, say for the control of automated assembly lines with precision timing requirements. In such environments, a single-tasking version of DOS is an ideal solution. In many cases Windows 95 or 98 run in raw DOS mode works equally well, but if you never use the GUI environment, why install it?

- **As a low-level hardware OS**—Many utilities for manipulating a computer's hardware at a low level are still written for DOS. Examples include utilities to install a new *basic input/output system (BIOS)* on a motherboard or adapter card and utilities to probe or otherwise test specific hardware components. Especially if you don't run Windows, keeping DOS around for such utilities can be a wise move.

- **As a games system**—Most games today are written for Windows or for dedicated game consoles, but there's a considerable set of existing DOS games. Many of these do run under Windows 95 or 98, but some work best under plain old DOS. If you're an aficionado of such older games, therefore, you might want to maintain a DOS configuration on your computer.

- **As an OS for older computers**—You might have an older computer that has served you well for years and that continues to be useful. If you don't want to replace it with a newer system, there's no need to do so; you can simply keep DOS on the system and continue to use it as you always have. If you find that you occasionally need some new program that requires a more sophisticated OS, however, you can install that other OS for the software you now require and keep DOS around. Your older computer might run slowly with the new OS, which can be tolerable for one or two seldom-used programs, but when you boot back into DOS, your system will regain its original speed.

When to Ditch DOS

Because DOS is so small, it's not difficult to maintain DOS along with some other OS. Therefore, if you're currently using DOS, you should give serious consideration to configuring your computer to keep it along with whatever additional OS or OSs you want to run. There are cases, however, when you might want to completely eliminate DOS from your system:

- **The unused DOS**—If you install new OSs and find that you never use DOS, you can wipe it out. Precisely how you do this depends on how you've installed your multiple OSs. You probably won't save a lot of disk space, though, so I recommend bothering only if you're desperate for a few extra megabytes of disk space or if you're performing other software or disk upgrades, such as transferring all your data to a new hard disk.

- **The interfering DOS**—If you're running a multi-OS configuration and find that DOS is somehow interfering with software for another OS, you might want to eliminate DOS. Such interference is extremely rare, though, and is likely to be application-specific (such as a program that by default looks in the c:\DOS directory for files before looking elsewhere).

- **The too-complex system**—If you find that your system is collecting OSs the way the undersides of furniture collect dust bunnies, you might want to simplify matters by eliminating less-useful OSs, which are likely to include DOS.

In general, a system on which Windows 95 or 98 is installed doesn't need a separate installation of DOS because these versions of Windows provide a non-GUI boot mode that is essentially Microsoft's DOS 7. If you don't have one of these OSs, though, and if you need to run DOS programs, keeping a DOS partition can be a useful investment.

 TIP Because DOS is so tiny, it can boot a complete system from a single floppy disk. In many cases, you can use a DOS boot floppy with whatever DOS software you require, instead of maintaining DOS on the hard disk. This approach is particularly useful if you have only one or two DOS programs for an otherwise non-DOS system. For example, you can keep a DOS partition management program on a DOS boot floppy and use it even on a system that contains only Linux and OS/2.

Windows 95 and 98

Windows 95 and Windows 98 are two similar OSs—so similar that they're often referred to collectively as *Windows 9x*. Windows 98 is essentially an update to Windows 95 that modifies the user interface and adds new drivers and utilities, including a closer integration of Internet tools into the OS and integrated support for USB devices. The basic features and best uses for these OSs are therefore largely identical. If you have a choice, you should probably run Windows 98 because it's more up-to-date.

The DOS Heritage of Windows

As I've already mentioned, Windows 9x is built on DOS. As described in the sidebar earlier in the chapter, previous versions of Windows were not technically operating systems at all, but were instead sophisticated extensions to DOS. Windows 95 began to integrate DOS and Windows more closely and bundled them into a single package. Advances of Windows 95 over DOS with Windows 3.11 include

Part

I

Ch

2

- **32-bit support**—Windows 95 was the first popular OS from Microsoft to do away with the 16-bit limitations of DOS, at least for native programs. Windows 95 can still run 16-bit DOS and Windows 3.x programs, but native Windows 95 programs are 32-bit, which means they are much easier to write and can be faster for some types of operations. This 32-bit support does mean that Windows 9x requires at least a 386 CPU.

- **Preemptive multitasking**—When running 32-bit Windows programs and DOS programs, Windows 95 can multitask the programs preemptively, as opposed to the cooperative multitasking performed by Windows 3.11 and earlier. When running older 16-bit Windows 3.x programs, Windows 95's multitasking switches to a hybrid cooperative/preemptive approach.

- **Long filenames**—Windows 95 introduced the VFAT filesystem extensions, which enable users to store long filenames on the *file allocation table (FAT)* filesystem used by DOS. A Windows 95 update later added FAT-32, which extended the maximum size of FAT partitions and added a few more enhancements.

- **Integrated networking**—Windows 95, like the earlier Windows for Workgroups variant of Windows 3.1, integrates networking features into the OS. Windows 98 expands on this trend by providing more protocols. With either system, you can easily connect a workstation to your company's local area network (LAN) or initiate a dial-up, point-to-point protocol (PPP) connection with an ISP.

- **Closer GUI integration**—In the DOS/Windows combination system, the GUI (Windows) is entirely separate from the OS (DOS). In Windows 95, Microsoft merged the two, so that by default, the computer boots directly into the Windows GUI environment. This tends to hide the command-line nature of DOS, which many users find intimidating.

- **Improved GUI**—Windows 3.11's GUI was crude by comparison to other environments of its day, such as those on the Macintosh or OS/2. Windows 95 improved the GUI substantially, making the system easier to use. Figure 2.1 shows a Windows 98 system, highlighting some of the system's key GUI features.

Despite these improvements, Windows 9x remains largely a GUI environment atop a DOS core. This fact is particularly important in the handling of old 16-bit Windows programs, which run in Windows in such a way that they disrupt some of the multitasking improvements. (By contrast, OSs such as Windows NT, Windows 2000, and OS/2 isolate 16-bit programs and run them in a special mode that allows the OS to retain its 32-bit and multitasking advantages.)

Uses for Windows

The Windows 9x line has been extremely successful, in part because it is Microsoft's approved successor to the equally successful DOS and Windows 3.x series, and in part because it is highly compatible with these older systems. Many users don't feel the need to use Windows 9x, though. Should you? Windows 9x does have its places, including

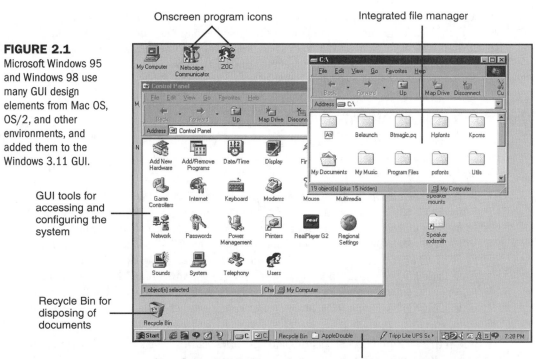

FIGURE 2.1
Microsoft Windows 95 and Windows 98 use many GUI design elements from Mac OS, OS/2, and other environments, and added them to the Windows 3.11 GUI.

Onscreen program icons

Integrated file manager

GUI tools for accessing and configuring the system

Recycle Bin for disposing of documents

Status bar shows running programs and launches new programs

- ■ **As a single-user desktop OS**—Because Windows OSs are so popular, uncounted thousands of desktop productivity applications are available for the Windows family of OSs. At the moment, most of these programs have been written for Windows 9*x* in particular, though many work equally well under the Windows NT family. If you want to do word processing, maintain your financial records, or surf the Web through a dial-up connection, Windows 9*x* can do the job with minimal fuss. In my opinion, however, Windows 9*x* isn't the best choice for this role, at least not with modern hardware. If you require Windows compatibility, Windows NT or 2000 provides greater stability. If you don't need to run specific Windows programs, you might want to investigate OS/2, BeOS, and Linux as alternatives, in addition to Windows NT.

- ■ **As a games platform**—Most games today are written with Windows 9*x* in mind. Many of these games also run on Windows NT, and some run on OS/2 or DOS. A few have been ported to (or are written natively for) OS/2, BeOS, or Linux. Still, if you want to play computer games on a PC today (a steadily growing industry), Windows 9*x* is the single best OS choice available.

- ■ **As a DOS compatibility platform**—Run in DOS mode without its GUI, Windows 9*x* can run most DOS programs as well as DOS itself can. You can therefore use old DOS programs without maintaining a separate DOS installation. You might want to consider keeping separate DOS and Windows NT or 2000 installations, however, rather than compromise with a single Windows 9*x* installation.

In general, Windows 9x is a good enough OS for most computer users. The fact that you're reading this book, though, indicates that it's not good enough for you—at least not in all situations. You might want to keep Windows in addition to some other OS to maintain flexibility or as a fallback while you make the transition to another OS. The success of Windows 9x is due in part to the wide selection of software available for it, and that's no small matter.

When to Consider Alternatives

Windows 95 and 98 are very good for many desktop applications, but they fall short in many situations. Some of these are becoming increasingly common, but others are relatively exotic. In any event, you might want to look to other OSs for

- **Multiuser configurations**—Different people have different tastes when it comes to their OSs and environments. If your home PC is used by several people, each might prefer a different arrangement of desktop icons, wallpaper, and so on. Although you can use add-on utilities to provide customizations for Windows 9x depending on the user, it wasn't designed with this in mind. Windows NT and various flavors of UNIX are designed to provide flexibility in regard to user customization. These OSs also provide security controls to keep users from modifying each others' (or the OS's) files, though Windows NT's default installation doesn't configure these controls in a very secure manner.
- **Security**—Both internal security and network security are lax on Windows 9x, though by default Windows lacks many of the network tools that can provide crackers with access to the system. If you want to connect a system to the Internet and provide services, though, other OSs provide more extensive out-of-the-box security controls.
- **Stability**—Particularly when running a wide range of program types, Windows 9x tends to be unstable. It is common for Windows users to reboot their computers at least once a day because of system crashes. Windows NT, OS/2, and most UNIX variants (including Linux) are more stable than Windows 9x, at least on average. (Specific configurations and poor drivers can undermine any OS's stability, so there are exceptions to this rule.)
- **High performance**—For the best possible computing performance, Windows 9x falls behind. Specifically, OSs such as Windows NT and certain versions of UNIX provide substantially better support for multiprocessor systems and for multitasking several applications.

Windows NT and Windows 2000

Microsoft's Windows NT line began with Windows NT 3.1, which was really a 1.0-level release. As I write this, the current version is 4.0. Microsoft has announced that its next version of Windows NT will not be called Windows NT 4.1 or 5.0, but Windows 2000. This version is now in late beta testing, so it should be available by the time you read these words.

Throughout this book, I use *Windows NT* to refer to both Windows NT 4.0 and Windows 2000. In most cases, my comments apply to earlier versions of Windows NT, as well.

N O T E When Windows NT and Windows 2000 behave differently in relation to multi-OS computers, I've noted this. ■

Microsoft's New Technology

Whatever the name or version number, Windows NT, unlike Windows 95 and 98, represents a substantial break from DOS. In fact, the *NT* part of *Windows NT* means *New Technology.* These new technologies include

- **A new 32-bit multitasking kernel**—An OS *kernel* is the core set of routines for handling low-level hardware, memory accesses, and so on. Microsoft created a new kernel for Windows NT. This kernel isn't as compatible with the existing base of 16-bit Windows and, especially, DOS software as is the Windows 9*x* kernel, but the Windows NT kernel is better suited to perform preemptive multitasking and to work on non-Intel platforms. This new kernel requires new device drivers, which is why some hardware works on Windows 9*x* but not on Windows NT.

- **NTFS for improved disk access**—*NTFS* means *NT Filesystem*, and it's Windows NT's preferred way to arrange data on a disk. Neither DOS nor Windows 9*x* normally understands NTFS, and NTFS support in most other OSs is read-only or unreliable, so NTFS is effectively a Windows NT–only method of storing data. It is faster and more reliable than FAT, though, and it allows partitions larger than 2GB in size, which wasn't true of FAT until the introduction of FAT-32 late in Windows 95's lifetime.

    ▶ To learn more about NTFS access from non-NT OSs, **see** "Foreign NTFS and NTFS 5.0 Support," **p. 343**.

- **Support for multiple users**—Although Windows NT isn't a multiuser OS in the sense that UNIX is, it does include support for multiuser configurations. Each user can store information on preferred icon locations, desktop backgrounds, and so on to create a customized login session.

- **Security improvements**—With a multiuser configuration, it becomes desirable to provide some means to limit users' access to each others' files. Windows NT does this by implementing a feature known as *Access Control Lists (ACLs)* in NTFS. With ACLs, you can make a file private, so that only you can access it. Just as important, ACLs can prevent most users from modifying (and thus damaging) system files. This feature can be particularly important when a computer is to be used by a large number of individuals, some of whom might be fumble-fingered or just plain malicious, as in a college's computer center. Unfortunately, Windows NT's ACLs for system files, as shipped, are fairly permissive, so you must do some work to make your system more secure.

    ▶ To learn more about Windows NT configuration, read Jim Boyce's *Windows NT Workstation 4.0 User Manual* from Que.

Part

I

Ch

2

■ **Server features**—The server edition of Windows NT (which is sold separately from the workstation edition) includes server software to allow a Windows NT computer to be used as a *server* on a LAN or on the Internet. A server is a computer, or the software run on a computer, that responds to requests from remote systems. For example, a Web server sends Web pages to Web browsers; an FTP server delivers files to FTP clients; a mail server receives email from remote sites and then delivers it to individual users or computers; and so on. Even Windows 95 included some server features, in the form of file and printer sharing, but Windows NT's server edition supports more server protocols out of the box, and NT's kernel is better suited to server duty than are the DOS-derived kernels in Windows 9x.

Taken together, these improvements yield an OS that is much more stable than Windows 9x, that is better suited to handling complex multitasking and networking tasks, and that runs the vast majority of 32-bit Windows productivity applications as well as or better than Windows 9x. The cost is a reduced capability to run 16-bit Windows programs and a greatly reduced capability to run DOS software. Although many DOS programs run fine in Windows NT, some programs—particularly games and utilities that access low-level hardware directly—do not.

Windows NT 4.0 to Windows 2000

Although the name Windows 2000 suggests a break from the Windows NT line, Microsoft's OS for the year 2000 is more evolutionary than revolutionary compared to its elders in the NT product line. Nonetheless, Windows 2000 includes improvements in many areas. These include

■ **User interface**—Windows 2000 incorporates changes in user interfaces, including changes to the Start menu, the File Open and Save dialog boxes, customizable menus, and a My Network Places icon to simplify access to certain types of networking features.

■ **Hardware support**—Windows 2000 includes support for more hardware than does Windows NT 4.0. This fact is particularly important for notebook owners, for whom Windows 2000 includes new power management features. Windows 2000 also adds support for USB devices.

■ **Filesystems**—Windows 2000 is the first of the Windows NT line to include support for the FAT-32 filesystem used in late versions of Windows 95 and Windows 98. Windows 2000 also includes extensions to NTFS known as NTFS 5, which adds features that help speed file searches and that support encryption.

■ **Enhanced multimedia**—Windows 2000 supports new multimedia and graphics features, including DirectX 6.0 and OpenGL 1.2.

■ **Improved servers**—The Server edition of Windows 2000 includes a slew of enhancements to its services, such as integration of DHCP and DNS and support for remote administration.

■ **Enhanced reliability and ease of administration**—Microsoft aims to make Windows 2000 more reliable than Windows NT 4.0, and to make it easier to manage. You can perform many system administration tasks in Windows 2000 using a single tool, whereas previous versions of Windows NT used separate tools for these tasks.

The cost of these improvements comes in the form of heavier resource requirements. Specifically, Windows NT 4.0's official requirements are a 486/25 or higher CPU with 12MB RAM (16MB recommended) and 110MB of disk space. By contrast, Windows 2000 officially requires a Pentium 166 or higher CPU with 64MB RAM (128MB recommended) and 850MB of disk space.

When to Use NT Rather than 95 or 98

Part
I

Ch
2

In general, I recommend that you run Windows NT rather than Windows 9x for typical productivity tasks, such as word processing, database management, email, and so on. These types of applications generally run as well under Windows NT as under Windows 9x, and you gain the benefits of Windows NT's increased stability and other features. Many consumers, however, find Windows NT somewhat less user friendly than Windows 9x, and because Windows 9x handles more games and hardware components than does Windows NT, the public at large hasn't made the switch.

If you need high performance, Windows NT is the best suited of Microsoft's OSs to meeting this need. High-performance computing includes computationally intensive tasks, such as scientific simulations that can use a multiprocessor computer, disk-intensive applications such as database access, and network-intensive uses such as serving Web pages. These are the tasks for which UNIX or UNIX-like OSs such as Linux have traditionally been chosen, however, so if you're not tied to the Windows platform, you might want to evaluate both Windows NT and UNIX for these tasks.

Limitations of NT

Despite its strengths, Windows NT does have its weaknesses. Some of these are only important relative to Windows 9x, but others are limitations compared to non-Microsoft OSs, as well. These problems include

- **Imperfect 16-bit support**—As I've already mentioned, not all 16-bit DOS and Windows programs run properly under Windows NT. Even some 32-bit Windows programs might not run under Windows NT, particularly if the software requires low-level access to the hardware.

- **NTFS incompatibility**—NTFS is generally a strength of Windows NT, but it can make certain tasks more difficult. For example, you can't access an NTFS partition from a floppy boot, so if your system ever malfunctions badly enough to prevent the system from booting, you might have a hard time recovering your data. You aren't required to use NTFS, though, so if you're concerned about this, you can use Windows NT from a FAT partition—but you'll then give up NTFS's many strengths. On the whole, I favor using NTFS and keeping good backups of your data.

- **Reduced hardware support**—Because Windows NT is far from the dominant OS, not all manufacturers write Windows NT drivers for their hardware. Most major components do have Windows NT support, but some devices—particularly exotic hardware such as some scientific data acquisition boards or DVD-ROM drives—might not.

> **N O T E** Windows 2000 includes substantial improvements over Windows NT 4.0 in the realm of hardware compatibility. For example, there are DVD players for Windows 2000, as well as support in the OS for USB devices. ■

- **Limited multiuser support**—Although Windows NT supports multiple user configurations, it's not designed to allow several people to use it at the same time, as UNIX can do.

- **Increased administrative costs**—In the computer world, the more features and services an OS offers, the more difficult that OS is to maintain. Because Windows NT does more than does Windows 9x, NT is more difficult to maintain. Compared to UNIX, Windows NT is easier for a new administrator to maintain, but most experienced administrators prefer UNIX because it provides easier access to configuration details that Windows NT hides from administrators.

- **Older user interface**—Microsoft has traditionally provided user interface enhancements first in Windows 9x and then in Windows NT. For example, Windows 95 was the first version of Windows to provide an integrated desktop environment similar to the one in Mac OS or OS/2. Only later did Windows NT receive this advancement. Today, this difference is fairly small, though, because the changes from Windows 95 to Windows 98 are themselves relatively minor. Windows 2000 even includes a small number of enhancements over Windows 98. Figure 2.2 shows a Windows NT 4.0 desktop, which is quite similar to the Windows 98 desktop shown in Figure 2.1.

Windows NT serves as a cross between DOS and UNIX, taking some of the advantages and disadvantages from both worlds. In everyday operation, Windows NT is more like DOS-derived versions of Windows than it is like UNIX, but Microsoft has positioned Windows NT to compete with UNIX in certain markets, such as that for Internet servers. If you're familiar with Windows and want to run such a server, Windows NT will certainly require less in the way of learning than would UNIX or Linux; depending on your specific needs, however, a UNIX variant (or something else entirely, such as OS/2 or BeOS) might serve you better.

OS/2

Like many other OSs, OS/2 has led a varied past. Originally a joint IBM/Microsoft project, OS/2 is now available only from IBM. OS/2 has a reputation as the OS that would not die—despite frequent proclamations of its imminent demise by its detractors, OS/2 has continued to be available, and it has a dedicated user base. Of the other OSs discussed in this chapter, OS/2 is most like Windows NT in capabilities, though many of the details differ.

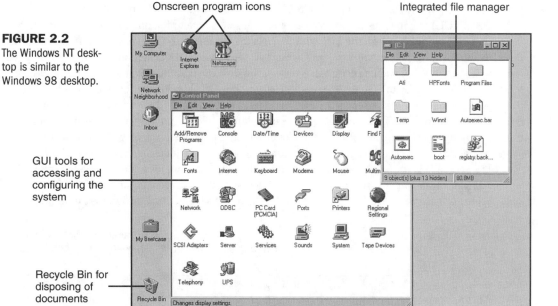

Onscreen program icons

Integrated file manager

FIGURE 2.2
The Windows NT desk-
top is similar to the
Windows 98 desktop.

GUI tools for
accessing and
configuring the
system

Recycle Bin for
disposing of
documents

Status bar shows running programs and launches new programs

The Second OS for the PC

When IBM introduced its *Personal System 2 (PS/2)* computer line, it wanted a new OS to go
with it. These computers used the then-new Intel 386 CPU, and DOS simply did not (and still
does not) take advantage of many of the 386's capabilities. IBM and Microsoft therefore
embarked on a project to develop the second PC operating system, hence the name *OS/2*.

The 1.*x* releases of OS/2 still used a 16-bit memory model, despite the 386's 32-bit capabilities. OS/2 was supposed to be DOS-compatible, but that compatibility was limited at best, so
most people ignored the new OS/2 in favor of the tried-and-true DOS and its substantial stable of applications. IBM and Microsoft parted ways with OS/2 2.0—IBM to develop OS/2 and
Microsoft to market Windows atop DOS and to develop Windows NT (which was once going
to be called *OS/2 NT*). Since version 2.0, OS/2 has used a 32-bit memory model (though
some of its device drivers remain 16-bit), and its DOS and 16-bit Windows compatibility are
far better than in its 1.*x* incarnations.

Like Windows 9*x*, OS/2 maintains a text-based core OS with a GUI layer atop that core. OS/2's GUI is known as the *Presentation Manager (PM)*, and its function is very much like that of Windows, though the look and feel is slightly different. One very important PM application is the *WorkPlace Shell (WPS)*, which provides the GUI desktop environment. Many features of the WPS, such as program icons on the desktop and multi-window file browsers, should be familiar to Windows 9*x* and NT users, but OS/2 had these features long before Windows. (Macintosh users will rightly chime in that many of these features existed in Mac OS long before OS/2 existed.) The WPS is still unparalleled in many of its features, such as its highly *object-oriented* design—each icon (*object*) can be customized with its own special settings and can even be linked to computer programs to extend the capabilities of the WPS. I've seen a WPS-based fax and answering machine application, for example, that's remarkably complete and simple to use but that's small and sits unobtrusively behind a WPS icon. Figure 2.3 shows an OS/2 desktop with the WPS and several OS/2 programs running.

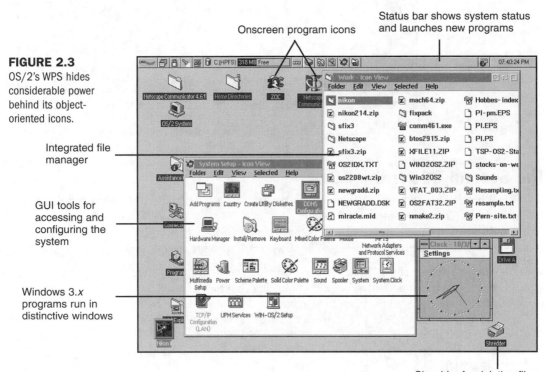

FIGURE 2.3
OS/2's WPS hides considerable power behind its object-oriented icons.

Onscreen program icons

Status bar shows system status and launches new programs

Integrated file manager

GUI tools for accessing and configuring the system

Windows 3.*x* programs run in distinctive windows

Shredder for deleting files

The Three Faces of OS/2

OS/2 is a close cousin to DOS and Windows, but it has also developed a software base of its own. The merging of these two worlds provides enough software to satisfy many OS/2 users. OS/2 has benefited from a third world, too: that of open source software. With the development of libraries designed to ease the porting of UNIX software to OS/2, many of these tools have become available to OS/2 users. This section investigates these three faces of OS/2.

OS/2 as an Evolution from DOS and Windows   As I've said, IBM envisioned OS/2 as a replacement for DOS. To make the transition easier, OS/2 1.*x* included DOS emulation, which was improved with version 2.0. OS/2's own *application program interface (API)*—the rules a programmer uses to communicate with the OS—is similar to that of DOS. OS/2 1.0 also used the FAT filesystem, and to this day FAT is the filesystem that's built in to the OS/2 kernel (though OS/2 also supports an improved *High-Performance Filesystem,* or *HPFS*).

OS/2's PM premiered in the OS/2 1.*x* days, when Microsoft was still working on the project and was also developing the predecessors to Windows. It should therefore come as no surprise that PM and Windows bear many similarities, both in look and feel and in the underlying APIs. These similarities are not enough to allow a Windows program to run natively under OS/2, although with version 4.0, IBM did make available API extensions to aid developers wanting to recompile Windows programs for OS/2.

Because of the dominant position of Windows in the marketplace, IBM has given OS/2 the capability to run 16-bit Windows programs. OS/2 does this by running a copy of Windows inside an OS/2 DOS session. Depending on the version of OS/2 in use, this copy of Windows is either a genuine copy of Microsoft Windows 3.1 or 3.11 or a version recompiled by IBM, known as Win-OS/2. Either way, the Windows program can run side-by-side with OS/2 programs and is even multitasked by OS/2's preemptive multitasking features. Ironically, OS/2 can run many 16-bit Windows programs more smoothly and safely than can Windows 95 or 98 because OS/2 isolates the program from the rest of the system, thus protecting both the OS and other programs from the misbehavior of buggy programs. OS/2 does not, however, have the capability to run most 32-bit Windows programs, which today are the norm in the Windows world.

OS/2's DOS emulation is excellent. OS/2 provides fine control on a program-by-program basis over the features of the emulation. For example, you can provide one program with more memory than another and then run both simultaneously. OS/2 also emulates many aspects of the low-level hardware, so that even many programs that access this hardware can do so (or think they're doing so).

Overall, then, OS/2 is second only to DOS itself as a means of running DOS programs—and OS/2 has the advantage of multitasking those programs in a GUI environment.

OS/2 as a Single-User GNU Platform   The *Free Software Foundation (FSF)* was started with the goal of promoting the availability of free software. (Many people today refer to this software as *open source* software, though the FSF itself still prefers the term *free software*.) To this end, it began a project with the recursive acronym *GNU (GNU's Not UNIX)* to develop a free clone of UNIX. Today several OSs are at least partly derived from the FSF's efforts, but OS/2 has also benefited from the FSF and the GNU project: Many of the GNU tools, utilities, and applications have been ported to OS/2. Two particularly important ports are the GNU C Compiler (GCC) and the XFree86 windowing system (though the latter is not actually an FSF or GNU project). These two tools allow many others to be ported relatively easily, so a person who wants to run UNIX-like tools in a single-user OS can do so by using OS/2. As the supply of commercial software for OS/2 has slowly faded in recent years, the slack has been taken up by open source software, which helps keep OS/2 a viable choice in the OS arena.

Why run GNU software under OS/2 when you can run it under Linux, FreeBSD, or some other UNIX-like OS, though? One reason is that running it under OS/2 provides simultaneous access to DOS, Windows, and native OS/2 software. For all their other strengths, UNIX OSs aren't very good at emulating Windows, and none emulates OS/2. Another reason is inertia; an OS/2 user might simply not want to invest the time and effort in installing and learning a new OS, particularly when many of the tools from that OS are available in OS/2. If you're considering adding OS/2 to your system for its capability to run GNU tools, this argument is less compelling. However, OS/2 is still more similar to DOS and Windows than it is to UNIX in terms of its system administration, so if you're a current DOS or Windows user, you'll probably find OS/2 an easier system to learn.

OS/2 as an Independent Platform   To paraphrase Mark Twain, the reports of OS/2's death are greatly exaggerated. Native OS/2 programs, although not spilling over the aisles of most computer stores, are available. Lotus SmartSuite is perhaps the best known of the major OS/2 productivity applications, but there are others—telecommunications tools such as PM/Fax and Zap-O-Comm (ZOC); backup software such as NovaBack; CD recordable (CD-R) software such as RSJ CD Writer; games such as Avarice; and so on. OS/2's GUI environment is the equal of Windows in most respects, and for applications that take advantage of the WPS, it can be superior.

N O T E   If you want to know what OS/2 software is available, check
`http://www.indelible-blue.com`, `ftp://hobbes.nmsu.edu/pub/os2`, or
`ftp://ftp.cdrom.com/pub/os2`. The first is a mail-order retailer that got its start selling OS/2 software, and the latter two are the most popular OS/2 FTP sites. ▧

In sum, if you want to use OS/2 as a productivity platform, you can—the software is available. This is particularly true if you're willing to use GNU software or older DOS or Windows titles. Even with OS/2's popularity on the decline, it might be worth investigating for the curious or those who are dissatisfied with Windows but unwilling to make the leap to a more radically different OS such as BeOS or UNIX.

Limitations of OS/2

OS/2's benefits are real, at least for some people. Like all OSs, though, OS/2 is not without its warts. These include

- **A narrowing niche marketing strategy by IBM**—Since the release of OS/2 4.0 (prior to the release of Windows 98), OS/2 has not been updated, though a 5.0 server release is in the works. As I write this, many OS/2 users are disappointed that IBM apparently plans no client release of OS/2 5.0, which is likely to further restrict the availability of commercial desktop applications for OS/2.

- **Aging configuration tools**—OS/2 versions from 2.0 through 4.0 have been roughly comparable to a DOS/Windows 3.*x* system in terms of the sophistication of the administrative tools. OS/2 relies on a massive textual CONFIG.SYS file and a handful of binary .INI files for configuration, and tools for performing actions such as adding fonts are crude compared to those in Windows.

- **Limited Windows compatibility**—Although OS/2 does a fine job running 16-bit Windows programs, its capability to run 32-bit Windows programs is severely limited, at least in versions through 4.0.

- **Limited driver availability**—Like Windows NT but more so, OS/2 is seen as a niche operating system by hardware manufacturers, so drivers aren't available for all products. As new hardware arrives on the scene and OS/2's market share slips (assuming current trends continue), this problem is likely to get worse for OS/2 in the future.

- **Single-user design**—Like Windows 9*x*, OS/2 was designed as a strictly single-user OS. It's possible to use add-on tools to provide custom WPS setups for different individuals, but UNIX-style multiuser operation is just beyond OS/2's grasp.

Overall, OS/2's limitations make it unappealing for most potential new users. Existing OS/2 users continue to get good use out of the OS, though, and if you're in that category, you'll be happy to know that it's possible to run OS/2 on the same system with several other OSs—in fact, OS/2 is one of the most flexible options for peaceful coexistence on a single computer.

BeOS

BeOS is the youngest major OS for Intel PCs. Although it was begun in 1991, the same year Linux began life, BeOS was originally developed on the now-defunct AT&T Hobbit processor and was ported to Motorola's PowerPC and finally to Intel x86 (and clone) CPUs. Linux, by contrast, began life on an Intel 386 CPU. BeOS was also developed from scratch as an entirely new OS, whereas Linux was a re-implementation of UNIX, and in fact took many existing software components from the GNU project.

In many ways, BeOS is the most unique OS commonly available for the PC. The others I discuss in this chapter are all derived from or influenced by either the DOS or UNIX molds. BeOS does have some UNIX influences, but it is its own OS. It does not run DOS, Windows, or UNIX programs, though it's often possible to recompile UNIX command-line programs for BeOS without too much difficulty.

BeOS's Macintosh History

BeOS traces its roots back to Apple. This is not to say that BeOS is derived from Mac OS; it is not. Instead, BeOS is tied to Apple and the Macintosh platform in two ways:

- Many of Be's employees had worked at Apple, or at companies that wrote Macintosh software, prior to working at Be. This includes Be's president and many of the developers who designed BeOS.

- BeOS ran on Macintosh PowerPC hardware before it ran on Intel CPUs. In fact, at one time it seemed possible that Apple would purchase Be in order to use it as the core of its next-generation OS. That possibility evaporated, however, when Apple acquired NeXT Computer and embarked on a project to use a UNIX core for what is now known as Mac OS X.

Eventually, Be ported its OS to the Intel platform. In early 2000, BeOS runs on both Intel and PowerPC computers, including pre-G3 Macintoshes. BeOS does not run on G3 Macintoshes, however, because Apple has not released the necessary low-level programming information. Given this fact, it seems likely that BeOS's home will remain primarily with Intel hardware.

Despite BeOS's Apple and Macintosh ties, BeOS does not closely resemble Mac OS, nor can it run Mac OS programs. Actual Macintosh influences on BeOS are relatively minor, such as the fact that BeOS can use networked AppleTalk printers (though as of version 4.5 it can't use AppleTalk file shares). On the surface, BeOS bears some resemblance to certain versions of UNIX. For example, BeOS ships with a command prompt that uses bash, a common UNIX *shell* (a tool for entering text-based commands). The BeOS user interface bears a passing resemblance to some UNIX interfaces (see Figure 2.4). As I've mentioned, it's also possible to port many other UNIX (or, more precisely, POSIX) programs to BeOS with relative ease, so many other UNIX tools are available for BeOS. In this respect, BeOS resembles OS/2, in that it benefits from open source development efforts. More such programs have been ported to OS/2 than to BeOS, though.

BeOS as a Multimedia Platform

BeOS's *raison d'être* is to abandon the weight of previous generations of OSs, with the more specific goal of achieving the levels of performance required for handling future generations of multimedia displays. One of the problems that plagues all OSs after they reach a certain age is that they must maintain compatibility with old software and modes of operation, even when the need to do so hinders the performance of the improved OS. DOS compatibility is a case in point. DOS is fundamentally a 16-bit, single-tasking OS, designed for the Intel 8086 and 8088 CPUs with their 1MB memory limit, in days when a 10MB hard disk was considered huge. Windows 3.*x* is a 16-bit extension to DOS that provides support for more memory and a GUI. Modern software, by contrast, requires 32-bit memory modes, usually consumes well over 1MB of memory per program, and ships on CD-ROMs capable of storing 650MB of data.

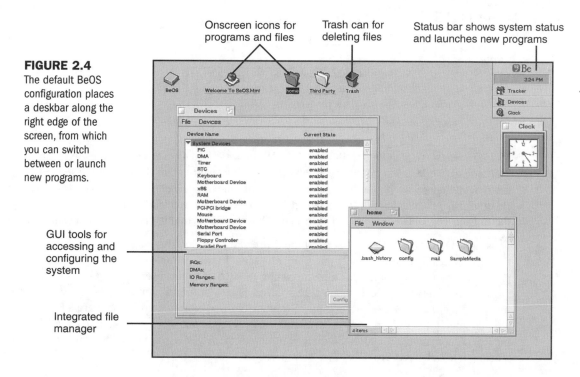

Onscreen icons for programs and files

Trash can for deleting files

Status bar shows system status and launches new programs

FIGURE 2.4
The default BeOS configuration places a deskbar along the right edge of the screen, from which you can switch between or launch new programs.

GUI tools for accessing and configuring the system

Integrated file manager

The need to provide support for the older DOS programs has led to design compromises in the OSs that provide this support. This is particularly true in Windows 9x, but to a lesser extent it's also true of Windows NT and OS/2. Windows 9x uses a hybrid cooperative/preemptive multitasking arrangement, for example, largely to satisfy the needs of older 16-bit Windows software. Windows NT and OS/2 provide superior fully preemptive multitasking, but at the cost of reduced compatibility. By providing no compatibility with past OSs, BeOS's designers hope to produce a technically superior OS to suit the needs of the 21st century.

One key aspect of BeOS's design is that it is massively *multithreaded*. A conventional computer program is written as an essentially linear set of operations. Programs can branch and loop, but they perform only one operation at once. A multithreaded program, by contrast, can perform two operations simultaneously. Figure 2.5 illustrates this contrast with the example of a program that computes the result of the mathematical expression $(2 \times 4) + (8 \times 3)$. Multithreading is essentially a form of multitasking, but where multitasking allows two or more separate programs to run concurrently, multithreading allows for multitasking within a single program.

FIGURE 2.5
Multithreading allows a program to break a task down into chunks that can be worked on concurrently.

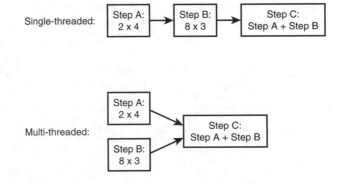

Multithreading is not unique to BeOS; OS/2, Windows NT, and many versions of UNIX can multithread. BeOS relies on this technique to a much greater extent than any of these OSs, though, and uses it to get the best performance possible out of multi-CPU hardware. In fact, Be originally produced both the BeOS software and a special multi-CPU computer known as the BeBox. The BeBox has been discontinued, but the BeOS multithreading design remains.

You might be wondering just what good multithreading can do. After all, within one application, you typically need to do only one thing at a time. In the example of the multiplication problem presented in Figure 2.5, multithreading the two operations presents no speed gain, at least not on a single-CPU computer. This caveat is part of the answer. A multi-CPU computer can more efficiently solve complex problems if they're broken down into parallel chunks than if the problems are presented linearly. A "complex problem" could be a mathematical computation, or it could be the generation or display of a graphics image, the downloading of a Web page, or some other common task.

Even with a single-CPU computer, though, multithreading can come in handy. For example, suppose you want to print a file from a word processor. If the word processor supports a multithreaded design, it can start a thread to do the printing and allow you to continue editing the file. A single-threaded word processor would require you to sit and wait while the file prints, or at least while the word processor formats the document and sends it to the OS's printer queue for printing.

The idea behind the BeOS design is to use multithreading, support libraries, and a clean break from the need to support old standards to produce an OS that's fast and optimized for multimedia performance. BeOS's designers reason that the future of computing lies in intensive multimedia applications, such as the display of films downloaded from the Internet via digital subscriber line (DSL) or cable modems, or interactive games with video quality to rival that seen on television. Such applications require massive speed, in terms of both hardware and software. If an OS can't multitask well enough to download at multi-megabits per second speeds, perform decompression operations on the downloaded data, and display it in a window, the OS won't live up to the expectations of a multimedia-enabled computing environment. BeOS aims to be ready for such an environment.

Of course, BeOS can also perform today's typical computing tasks such as word processing, Web surfing, and checkbook balancing. BeOS's multithreaded design doesn't get in the way of such applications, and can even help, although not as much as the design helps intensive multimedia applications. The fresh design of BeOS means that it contains fewer bizarre design elements that are relics of the past, so the user (it is hoped) might be less frustrated by BeOS than by other OSs.

Limitations of BeOS

For all its hype and promise, BeOS is not without its drawbacks. Many of these relate to its newness. Others are flip sides to its strengths. Specifically

- **Limited application support**—Because it's so new and doesn't have the sort of massive installed base enjoyed by Microsoft OSs, BeOS has comparatively few applications available. BeOS does ship with several basic productivity applications, such as a Web browser, a text editor, and so on. For additional applications, check the BeOS Web site, http://www.beos.com, which has links to the latest programs available.

- **Small user base**—In some sense, this is a limitation of all the non-Windows OSs these days, but BeOS's user base is particularly small. This limitation is important mainly in your ability to find support from other BeOS users. For example, at the time of this writing, there is no BeOS newsgroup in the Usenet comp.os.* newsgroup hierarchy. By contrast, there are several OS/2, Linux, and FreeBSD newsgroups (the FreeBSD newsgroups are in the comp.unix.* hierarchy). The small BeOS user base also presents a chicken-and-egg dilemma as far as application development goes; with few users, software houses aren't motivated to write BeOS programs, and without programs, users aren't motivated to use BeOS. Whether BeOS will be able to grow enough to break this cycle remains to be seen.

- **Lack of backward compatibility**—Although breaking the chains of old OS designs allows BeOS to perform better than other OSs in many ways, it also exacerbates the problem with lack of software. You cannot run DOS, Windows, or Mac OS programs on BeOS. The one partial exception to this rule is that, because of BeOS's partial POSIX compliance, it's often possible to port UNIX software to BeOS with relatively little fuss. Doing so requires that you have access to the source code, however, and you must compile the source code yourself or locate a precompiled version on the Internet.

- **Very limited hardware support**—More so than for Windows NT or OS/2, hardware manufacturers are unmotivated to write BeOS drivers for their products. This need not be a serious problem for a new computer if you purchase your hardware with BeOS in mind, and if you don't need to use any exotic devices. If you're thinking of installing BeOS on an existing computer, though, you should carefully check the hardware compatibility lists maintained on Be's Web site, http://www.beos.com, and compare what's listed there against what's in your computer.

- **Single-user design**—BeOS is slated to become a multiuser system in R5 or R6 (it's at R4.5 at the time of this writing), but until then, it's as single-user as Windows 9x.

Overall, BeOS's limitations prevent its use as a complete replacement for Windows as a desktop productivity OS, at least for most people. It's entirely possible that BeOS's popularity will rise, though, and you might want to install it on your system alongside other OSs to learn its capabilities first hand and to use it when its inherent strengths overcome its weaknesses. Because the OS is young and rapidly changing, you would do well to check Be's Web site for the latest information.

Linux

Mention Linux today in any computer circle and you'll get a reaction. That reaction might be deep scorn or glowing praise, but Linux is *the* hot topic in the computer world at the turn of the millennium. Why? The reasons for Linux's current status are complex, but they include

- **Politics**—Linux is an open source OS developed largely using the GNU *General Public License (GPL)*, which ensures the continued free availability of the source code. This fact elates some people and antagonizes others, for reasons unrelated to the OS's technical merits.

- **Inexpensive UNIX compatibility**—Linux and the BSD OSs (discussed in the next major section) are both available at low cost and perform most of the tasks for which much more expensive UNIX computers have been employed in the past. In 1991, when Linux was just getting started, commercial versions of UNIX cost hundreds or thousands of dollars—well out of the reach of many individuals, and even corporations who might otherwise have deployed UNIX as a desktop OS. Thanks to Linux and the BSD variants, UNIX-like OSs are now available at reasonable cost.

- **OS disenchantment**—Users of other OSs have become increasingly disenchanted with their former OSs. Microsoft users might be put off by Microsoft's business tactics or by the increasing bloat of Microsoft OSs; OS/2 users increasingly feel abandoned by IBM, which seems to neglect OS/2, or at best market it to a narrow niche. Linux provides variety and a sense of user control that's unparalleled in commercial OSs, which is just what many of these disenchanted users want.

- **Robustness and flexibility**—Linux has earned a reputation as an extremely robust computer platform that can perform a wide variety of tasks with ease. Part of this reputation derives from Linux's use of well-tested GNU tools for many of its most important utilities, but some of it is attributable to the Linux kernel itself.

These causes interact with each other; for example, one reason for disenchantment with other OSs might be perceived instability, for which Linux's perceived robustness is a good cure. Whatever the cause, though, Linux is the darling of the computing world, at least for today. It's well worth trying, but only if you're already at least somewhat familiar with UNIX or if you're willing to invest some time in learning it.

A Free Reimplementation of UNIX

Linux began life in 1991 as a project by a then-student named Linus Torvalds in Helsinki. Linus wanted to run UNIX on his new 386 computer but found the commercial offerings too expensive. The only UNIX-like system he could afford, Minix, was too limiting for his taste, so he began a project to reimplement UNIX from the ground up. Neither Linus himself nor any of the programmers who began to contribute to the project thought that the OS would grow to anything like what it is today; they just thought it would be a fun hack and that they might get something personally useful out of it. Today, there's a growing industry built around Linux. One long-standing Linux-based company, Red Hat, saw its stock price jump to more than eight times its starting value when it first went public in mid-1999.

Components of a Linux System Technically speaking, Linux itself is only the kernel of the OS. The kernel handles memory management, hard disk access, and so on. Linux has benefited from the previous (and subsequent) development of many open source tools for UNIX—programs like the Emacs text editor, the bash command shell, and the TeX document production language. Many of these tools were developed under the auspices of the FSF's GNU project, so some people refer to complete Linux distributions as *GNU/Linux*. (I use *Linux* for simplicity's sake and because it's the more common name.)

Most of the tools that give Linux its look and feel were developed with UNIX in general in mind, and most of these tools are available for and sometimes even ship with other UNIX variants. Linux followed this path in part because the tools were available and in part because programmers have traditionally favored UNIX environments for programming, and so naturally wanted to emulate that environment in their new OS.

> **N O T E** Apple is following a different path with its next-generation OS, Mac OS X. It is starting with a UNIX-like core but adding tools derived from earlier incarnations of Mac OS to provide a system with a Macintosh-style look and feel but the underpinnings of UNIX. It will be interesting to see how this experiment fares, both on its merits as an OS and in the marketplace. There are no plans to make Mac OS X available on Intel hardware, however; you must buy a Macintosh to use it.

UNIX, and hence Linux, is primarily a text-based OS. A series of programs known as *the X Window System*, or *X* for short, provides a GUI front-end to UNIX, much as Windows 3.*x* provides a GUI front-end to DOS. X has traditionally been both much more powerful than Windows and much less user-friendly. In the past few years, Linux programmers have embarked on projects to tame the X environment. One of these projects is known as the *K Desktop Environment (KDE)* and is depicted in Figure 2.6. Another is known as the *GNU Network Object Model Environment (GNOME)*. Both of these projects seek to produce an easy-to-use environment similar to that of Windows, OS/2, or Mac OS, but tailored to the needs of Linux (or other versions of UNIX).

Onscreen icons for
programs and files

Integrated file manager

Taskbar displays
currently running
programs

FIGURE 2.6
KDE is only one of several desktop environments available for Linux.

GUI tools for
accessing and
configuring the
system

Trash can for
deleting files

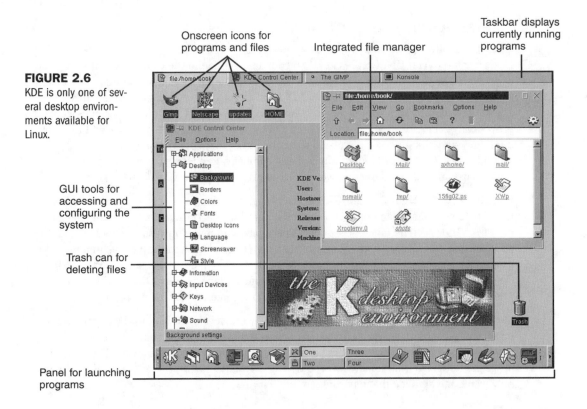

Panel for launching
programs

N O T E In Linux and other UNIX-like OSs, there exists a hierarchy of user interface elements, ranging from X at the lowest level to the desktop environment at the top. In between fall the programming toolkit (which displays information inside windows and over which the user has no control) and the window manager (which displays borders around windows and handles everything not inside a window). For the most part, you can mix and match these components. New Linux users often confuse one component with another. ■

Linux Distributions One of the most important points to understand about Linux is that it comes in several different *distributions*, or collections of the Linux kernel with specific additional components. Depending on the components chosen, two distributions can perform quite differently, and in fact be very different. For example, Distribution A might use the Sendmail mail server, the libc5 library collection, and the KDE GUI environment, whereas Distribution B might use the Postfix mail program, the glibc2 libraries, and the GNOME GUI environment. Some of the more common Linux distributions today include

■ **Red Hat**—Probably the most popular Linux distribution, Red Hat is known for its novice-friendly installation system and *Red Hat Package Manager (RPM)* program distribution file format (which is used by many other distributions, as well). See http://www.redhat.com for more information.

■ **Mandrake**—Mandrake is an offshoot of Red Hat, so it uses a nearly identical installer and set of utilities. Mandrake's programs have been optimized for Pentium-class CPUs, however, compared to Red Hat's 386 optimizations. Check `http://www.mandrake.org` for more information.

■ **SuSE**—This German distribution is extremely popular in Europe and has a substantial following on other continents, as well. It uses RPM but different system configuration tools than Red Hat or Mandrake. See `http://www.suse.com` for more information.

■ **Debian**—Debian is favored by those who want the most "ideologically pure" form of Linux because it's the only major distribution that's maintained by volunteers rather than by a for-profit company. It uses its own package format and is sparse on user-friendly configuration tools. See `http://www.debian.org` for more information.

■ **Corel**—The company famous for its DRAW program and WordPerfect suite makes a Linux distribution based on Debian. Corel Linux 1.0 is one of the easiest versions of Linux to install and configure, although version 1.0 is still a bit rough in some areas. More information is available on the Web at `http://linux.corel.com/`.

■ **OpenLinux**—Caldera Systems' OpenLinux is another RPM-based distribution with its own set of configuration utilities. Caldera has traditionally targeted its distribution toward businesses, as opposed to most of the others, which aim more broadly. See `http://www.calderasystems.com` for more information.

■ **Slackware**—This is one of the oldest distributions still around. As such, it's favored by many Linux old-timers. It is, however, weak on configuration amenities for newcomers, and it uses no package management system comparable to RPM or Debian's package manager, so it is more difficult to maintain. For more information, see `http://www.slackware.com`.

Additional Linux distributions are available, many of which fill specialized niches. For example, there are distributions to fit on just one or two floppies, distributions designed to squeeze the last bit of performance out of hardware, and distributions to run on Macintoshes or other non-Intel hardware.

If you're a newcomer to Linux and want the easiest experience, I recommend you start with Corel Linux or one of the RPM-based distributions that includes GUI configuration tools, such as Red Hat, Mandrake, SuSE, or Caldera. These will be the easiest to install and maintain. If you want to be forced to learn UNIX-style system administration without the help of a proprietary GUI tool, Debian is the best choice, though Slackware has merit as well.

Linux as a Server and on the Desktop

In the early days, Linux wasn't suitable for most real-world tasks; the OS was too crude. At that time, the developers used Linux as a development platform with which to improve Linux itself and on which to develop their own pet UNIX projects. It was during this period that Linux developed a reputation as a "hacker's playground." This did eventually change, however, largely by stealth.

N O T E The term *hacker* is ambiguous at best. Its original meaning is a person who enjoys programming and learning about computers and who uses programming skills to produce
new and interesting programs. More recently, the media have used the term to refer to computer van-
dals and other miscreants—people who break into others' computers, sometimes to steal or destroy
data. I try to avoid using the term, but where necessary, I use it in the first sense. For the second, I
use the term *cracker*, which in the context of computers, refers less ambiguously to a person who
engages in antisocial behavior such as breaking into computers. ■

One of the first serious niches Linux found outside the development community was in the
network server arena. Because UNIX systems functioned as the core of the Internet several
years ago, a great deal of UNIX server software became quickly available for Linux as Linux's
core features matured enough to run these servers. Thus, Linux began running mail servers,
Web servers, and other network services. Concurrent with the development of Linux, additional server programs appeared that allowed Linux to take on office server tasks such as file
and printer sharing in Windows networks.

▶ To learn more about using Linux as a server in an office environment, read my book *Linux:
Networking for Your Office*, from Sams Publishing.

Servers are largely invisible to the average person, although their absence would be immediately felt. When you browse the Web, you generally don't know whether the server runs
Linux, Windows NT, Solaris, or something else. What you notice is the *client* software—your
Web browser. Similar comments apply to other types of network access. Because the server
OS isn't readily apparent to network users, Linux enthusiasts were able to slip Linux into
organizations' network structures unnoticed to meet tight budget requirements, expand services with minimal fuss, or replace a buggy server. Eventually, Linux gained legitimacy in this
role.

Linux as a desktop OS—one that's used by end users for day-to-day tasks such as word processing—is a relatively new phenomenon. For Linux to gain legitimacy in this role, it needed
applications, which had been lacking or weak in Linux's early days. Today, though, there are
an increasing number of desktop applications for Linux, such as Corel's WordPerfect word
processor, the GIMP image editor, and so on. The field of productivity programs is still not as
diverse as it is on Windows, though. Furthermore, Linux's basic user interface is not as polished as that of Windows. It's also variable, because different programs often use different
GUI *toolkits*—libraries that handle the details of menus, buttons, and similar user interface
elements inside Windows. In Windows, OS/2, and BeOS, the OS itself provides the equivalent of an X GUI toolkit, so programs are more uniform in their user interfaces than is the
case in Linux. The X toolkits are converging, however, on more uniform appearance and
behavior, so this unsettling situation is becoming less unsettling as time goes on.

▶ To learn more about WordPerfect for Linux, read my book *Special Edition Using Corel
WordPerfect 8 for Linux*, from Que.

To sum up, Linux strengths include

- A robust, time-tested set of tools derived from UNIX for basic OS services
- Stable multitasking and multiuser capabilities
- Excellent networking capabilities, including a plethora of server programs
- System administration tools that allow for fine-tuning a configuration in ways that advanced users find helpful
- Source code availability for Linux itself and for most basic Linux tools

These strengths endear Linux to programmers and computer enthusiasts. They are, however, less important to the average home user, who probably just wants to write letters, run an occasional game, and surf the Web.

When Not to Join the Bandwagon

Linux is becoming increasingly popular. Judging by Usenet news postings, many individuals hear that Linux is the next great thing in computers and decide to try it out on that basis alone. Unfortunately, this often leads to frustration, because despite Linux's strengths, it's very different from the DOS and Windows systems with which most users are familiar. Learning to use a Linux system effectively takes years. Because of the configuration tools included with some distributions, administering a Linux system is becoming easier, but it's still not as easy as administering a Windows 9x system, at least for a beginner.

Linux's weakest points include

- **A steep learning curve**—A newcomer to Linux will probably feel lost and unable to accomplish much, especially if starting with a user-unfriendly distribution such as Debian. I strongly advise new Linux users to purchase a book on Linux to help learn the system.

  ▶ A general-purpose Linux title you might want to consider is Tackett and Burnett's *Special Edition Using Linux*, from Que.

- **Weak user interface**—Many aspects of Linux's user interface are still crude in comparison to Windows. This limitation is more true of some programs than of others.

- **Increased potential for network security problems**—Because most Linux distributions ship with many network servers enabled, a casual user might unknowingly leave a system open to network attack. These servers can be disabled by editing files such as /etc/inetd.conf, but inexperienced users don't know to do this. After it is configured properly, though, Linux is no less secure than other OSs.

- **Limited number of end-user applications**—Major productivity tools such as word processors are now fairly common on Linux, but more specialized tools are harder to come by. Games and educational programs are particularly rare, although not entirely nonexistent. Porting of commercial games and multimedia hardware drivers useful for game support is picking up as I write this, however.

■ **Some gaps in hardware compatibility**—Linux has accumulated an impressive array of hardware drivers, but some products are still beyond its ken.

Overall, Linux is a good choice if you're already familiar with UNIX and want a UNIX-like OS at home, on your desktop, or to function as a server. It's also a good choice if you want to learn about UNIX. Increasingly, it can be a good choice for office productivity applications. You should avoid it if you're mainly just curious (unless you're willing to spend many hours learning the system) or if you need an OS that will run lots of commercial games or educational programs.

The BSD Variants

The history of UNIX goes back roughly 30 years, to 1969, when researchers at AT&T developed a new OS. Although crude by today's standards, the first versions of AT&T UNIX quickly gathered a following because it was portable across many of the mainframe and minicomputer systems available at the time and because it provided the tools the computer programmers of the day needed. At that time, AT&T was forbidden from marketing computer software, so UNIX wasn't a commercial endeavor; it was more of an academic project, and many of the early UNIX adopters were universities. One of these was the University of California at Berkeley.

Berkeley students and faculty began working on improving the early UNIX, and over time what emerged became known as the *Berkeley Standard Distribution (BSD)*. Many commercial UNIX vendors adopted Berkeley's modifications. Today, several free BSD variants are available, such as FreeBSD (http://www.freebsd.org), OpenBSD (http://www.openbsd.org), and NetBSD (http://www.netbsd.org). This section applies to FreeBSD most strongly because it's the most widely available and popular of the BSD variants, but much of this information applies to the others, as well.

A Free Evolution of UNIX

You might have heard the philosophical question concerning the Greek explorer Odysseus' ship. As posed in the question, Odysseus wandered the Mediterranean sea over the course of several years, and over those years replaced every plank, rope, sail, and other component of his ship. Was the ship at the end of the voyage the same ship as the one at the beginning? The same question might be asked of BSD with respect to the original AT&T UNIX, because that's how BSD came to its current state—as a piecemeal replacement of every component of the original UNIX.

N O T E Today, BSD can refer to either one of the freely available BSD OSs or to a commercial OS that follows the BSD model. In this section, I use the term in the former sense. Later in this chapter, in the section "Commercial Versions of UNIX," I sometimes use it in the latter sense, but I try to make it clear by context the sense in which I use the term. ■

Some of the original BSD replacements were intended as improvements over AT&T tools, but eventually another goal emerged: creating a free UNIX. With the breakup of the AT&T telephone monopoly in the U.S., AT&T was allowed to actively market UNIX and proceeded to do so. Other firms also marketed commercial forms of UNIX, under license from AT&T. Eventually AT&T sold UNIX, but no matter the owner, copyright restrictions remained on the original UNIX code, so distributing that code along with the BSD improvements proved to be difficult. Eventually, the BSD developers succeeded in their goal and produced a work that was unencumbered by AT&T's original copyrights.

To an end user, the difference between this approach and the Linux approach of rebuilding everything from the ground up isn't very substantial; both Linux and BSD can be configured to work in much the same way. As part of UNIX history, though, vendors who licensed UNIX from AT&T had to decide whether to incorporate BSD's improvements. Thus emerged a basic dichotomy between *BSD UNIX* (here referring to a particular set of protocols and tools used in Berkeley's improvements) and *System V* or *SysV* UNIX (AT&T's own release). The modern free BSD variants cling closely to the BSD model, not surprisingly, whereas Linux distributions borrow from both—but to varying degrees—so one Linux distribution might closely resemble BSD whereas another might be more similar to SysV.

One further difference between Linux and BSD is in licensing. The Linux kernel is distributed under the GPL, which "locks in" free redistribution; you cannot legally take GPL code, modify it, and distribute it under another license. The modern BSD variants, by contrast, are distributed under their own license, which does permit a third party to distribute a modified version of the code under another license. For most end users, this difference is in and of itself unimportant, but the GPL seems to promote faster software development. Related to this fact is the culture surrounding the software development; Linux is far more open, which enables people to more easily write and contribute drivers or other add-on components.

N O T E This discussion of differences between Linux and the BSD variants refers to the respective OSs' kernels. The OSs share many important non-kernel components, such as the XFree86 X server. ▮

BSD as a Server and on the Desktop

The BSD variants have found a niche that's similar to that of Linux, as a reliable network server. In fact, there's very little reason to favor one OS over the other in this role, unless the hardware you're using is unsupported in one OS. Otherwise, you should pick whichever OS is more familiar to you. If you're new to UNIX in general, you'll probably find more support for Linux in Usenet newsgroups, but you might know people who are more familiar with BSD.

As a desktop OS, the BSD variants aren't quite as capable as Linux, simply because they receive less attention from the commercial software vendors. There is no version of WordPerfect for any of the free BSD variants, for example. On the other hand, these OSs have the capacity to run Linux programs, so you can run the Linux versions of WordPerfect or other productivity applications under BSD.

Because the development projects to bring a more user-friendly face to Linux are open source, and because programming is nearly identical for Linux and for BSD, these projects have benefited the BSD variants as well as Linux. (In fact, some developers for these projects work on BSD or other versions of UNIX, so these projects aren't strictly Linux-based.) Figure 2.6, which shows KDE running on Linux, could as easily be an image of a FreeBSD system running KDE. Unless the computer happens to be displaying some system-specific information, there's no way to know whether you're looking at a Linux or BSD system from a static screen shot.

When to Use Other Versions of UNIX

BSD isn't for everybody, of course, or even for everybody who wants to run a UNIX-like OS. As a first pass, I'll say that by and large, the same negatives that apply to Linux also apply to the BSD variants, so if you are, for example, a current Windows user who's looking for broader horizons, you can expect a learning curve with BSD that's similar to what you'd experience with Linux. If you want or need to use a UNIX-like OS, you should look to something other than a BSD when

- **You need compatibility with a specific UNIX vendor**—For example, if you need to program an application for Solaris, there's nothing better to use than Solaris. Linux or BSD can serve as a stand-in, but an imperfect one, even if you have access to Solaris at another location.

- **Your hardware isn't supported**—Although BSD's hardware support is respectable, it isn't as broad as that of Linux. Most commercial versions of UNIX don't do any better than BSD on average, but you might find some particular component that has support in a specific commercial product but not in BSD.

- **You need the greatest online support**—Because of Linux's grass-roots popularity among technical users, Usenet newsgroups abound with Linux technical support. Online BSD support exists, of course, but it's not quite as copious as it is for Linux.

On the whole, BSD is a fine OS for learning about UNIX and for using UNIX applications. If you want to learn UNIX, BSD and Linux are both excellent choices. If you already know UNIX, you probably already have some idea of which UNIX or UNIX-like system you would prefer to use.

Commercial Versions of UNIX

The hype in the UNIX world these days goes to Linux, and to a lesser extent the free BSD variants, particularly FreeBSD. The UNIX world is much larger than these OSs, though. In fact, technically speaking, neither Linux nor the free BSD variants is a version of UNIX because UNIX is a trademarked term that can be applied only to products that have passed a suite of tests. These tests are expensive, and most Linux and BSD users aren't particularly concerned with the label, so neither class of system has been tested.

Several commercial UNIX vendors exist, however, most of whom have acquired the right to call their products UNIX. You might want to install one of these OSs for any of a number of reasons, though most do not for casual experimentation because of the expense involved.

Part
I
Ch
2

The Forking of the UNIX Heritage

As I mentioned earlier, commercial UNIX vendors have had to choose between Berkeley and SysV forms of UNIX for years, although more recently the two tracks have merged back together to a large extent. In part this merging is because System V Release 4 (SVR4) has taken the best features of both systems and rolled them into one, and most UNIX vendors have followed the SVR4 lead. More recently, SVR5 has emerged as a standard in the UNIX field. One other current UNIX variant class was specified by the Open Software Foundation (OSF) and is known as *OSF/1*, but this form of UNIX isn't as popular as is SVR4/5.

Some of the commercial UNIX offerings for Intel-architecture machines include

- **Sun's Solaris**—This SVR4 OS is distinguished by being available at cost for personal use, though it's still a for-profit OS if your intended use is commercial. It's therefore a reasonable alternative to Linux or a BSD for personal use. See `http://www.sun.com/solaris/` for more information.

- **SCO UnixWare and Open Server**—These two OSs from the Santa Cruz Organization (SCO) are based on SVR5 and SVR4, respectively. Like Solaris, you can obtain these OSs at low cost for personal use, but commercial-use licenses cost hundreds of dollars.

- **NeXT's NeXTStep**—This OS began life on proprietary Motorola hardware but eventually became available on Intel-based machines. NeXTStep is an unusual UNIX in that it doesn't use X for its GUI. The OS is pretty rare these days—it is no longer available since Apple purchased NeXT. I nonetheless mention it because it's an unusual UNIX variant that achieved some popularity among hobbyists.

In addition to these versions of UNIX, there are many more that run on non-Intel hardware, as well as many now-defunct versions of UNIX for PCs, such as Coherent and XENIX. You cannot run non-Intel systems on an Intel-class PC, but you can often use software written for such systems, assuming the source code is available. The different versions of UNIX (including Linux and the BSD family) are highly compatible on the level of source code, so it's possible to write a program on one system and compile it with few or no problems on another, even when the hardware is radically different. Note that the various UNIX classifications such as SVR4 and OSF/1 are cross-platform, so from the programming and user interface points of view, two versions of UNIX that run on dissimilar hardware might appear to the user to be more alike than two versions of UNIX that run on identical hardware.

OSs for Servers and High-Performance Computing

Many commercial versions of UNIX have a reputation for use in high-performance computing environments, performing tasks such as scientific simulations, animation for films and television, and so on. Commercial versions of UNIX also occupy the same network server niche in which Linux and the free BSD variants reside, and for many of the same reasons—high-quality server software is available, and these OSs have a reputation for stability. In general, the reputation of commercial versions of UNIX has been earned on non-Intel hardware. For example, Sun makes hardware designed specifically for its Solaris OS, in addition to selling a version of Solaris that runs on common PC hardware. Silicon Graphics, Incorporated (SGI) builds high-performance workstations that are especially popular for doing animation and other high-end graphics work, but SGI's IRIX OS isn't available for Intel-based computers.

Still, if you own PC hardware and want to run a commercial UNIX, you can. This can be very helpful in certain situations, such as the following:

- **Common environment**—If you're already familiar with a particular flavor of UNIX, and if it's available for Intel PCs, buying a version of that OS for your PC can make you productive immediately. Similar comments apply if you need to expand an existing network using PC hardware—you can add Solaris nodes, as an example, by converting Windows machines using the Intel version of Solaris rather than by purchasing new Sun workstations.

- **Support**—The larger Linux vendors are now starting to offer support contracts, and third parties such as local Linux or BSD consultants can often offer a support "safety net." Some companies, though, prefer to work with an established name, and the commercial versions of UNIX can offer this.

- **Commercial software availability**—Some of the more exotic commercial UNIX software is not available for the free UNIX-like OSs but is for Intel-based commercial UNIX systems. If you need to run such software, you need the appropriate commercial UNIX system.

- **Advanced OS features**—Commercial versions of UNIX sometimes have somewhat more advanced features than do their free competitors. For example, many commercial versions of UNIX sport journaling filesystems, which handle error recovery more swiftly and surely after a power failure than do conventional filesystems.

N O T E SGI has announced that it is releasing its XFS journaling filesystem as open source,
though at the time of this writing, details are sketchy; XFS might or might not find its way
as a standard component into the Linux or BSD kernels. Other journaling filesystem projects are also
underway for Linux, such as ext3fs and Reiserfs. ▨

- **Education and training**—You might want to invest in learning a specific commercial UNIX for career advancement purposes. Don't think that all commercial versions of UNIX are alike, however, or that the free UNIX clones are any more different from any given commercial UNIX than another commercial UNIX. If you want to learn UNIX in general, a commercial UNIX need not be a bad choice, but neither is Linux or FreeBSD.

Do You Need a Commercial UNIX?

Commercial versions of UNIX have their place. For the most part, if you need a commercial UNIX, you already know that you need it. If you're trying to decide what UNIX or UNIX-like OS to install, there's a good chance you won't find one any better or worse than another. The following are some of the definite drawbacks to commercial UNIX variants:

- **Cost**—Although Solaris and the SCO products are available at very low cost to individuals for private use, commercial use can be expensive, particularly if the intent is to deploy these OSs on many computers.

- **No source code availability**—The lack of source code means that you're at the company's mercy for bug fixes. With Linux or a BSD, programmers worldwide have the ability to fix bugs. This tends to reduce the time necessary for problems to be resolved. Of course, you can change the code yourself—assuming you know how!

- **Incomplete hardware support**—Details differ from one distribution to another, but in general, commercial versions of UNIX lack the sort of wide hardware support that Linux enjoys, much less the level of support boasted by Windows 9x.

Overall, I would have to recommend that you try a commercial UNIX if you have a specific purpose in mind for the OS, and if your preliminary investigation of specific OS features leads you to believe that the commercial product fills those needs better than other products. If you simply want to learn UNIX generally or experiment with a new OS, I favor Linux or a BSD because of their low cost and active online communities of like-minded individuals.

Throughout the rest of this book, I might occasionally refer to commercial versions of UNIX, but I focus more closely on Linux and FreeBSD as potential OSs to install on your system. If in doubt, you should consult your commercial UNIX's documentation to determine how it fits into a multi-OS environment.

Summary

The array of available choices in operating systems for Intel-based hardware is quite wide. Microsoft enjoys a commanding lead in this area, but Microsoft's OSs are not the only available choices—not by a long shot. The options for OSs can be summarized as falling into three categories:

- **Microsoft-inspired OSs**—These range from DOS through Windows NT and OS/2. All share certain features, such as the use of drive letters (A:, C:, and so on) to address different disk devices. Most of these OSs are from Microsoft, though some are clones and one (OS/2) was developed jointly by Microsoft and IBM but is now available only through IBM.

- **BeOS**—BeOS is unique, so it earns a category of its own. Its uniqueness is both a strength and a weakness. You might consider it for serious use today only if interoperability with other systems isn't extremely important. You might want to consider learning about it today, however, with an eye toward using it more extensively in the future.

- **Versions of UNIX**—Whether derived from AT&T's original UNIX code or not, all UNIX-like systems share common features, such as a tree-like hierarchy for partition structures and a multitasking, multiuser design. UNIX is inherently well-suited to function as a server OS and is increasingly becoming well-suited for use on the desktop as well.

OS-watchers, pundits, and advocates will speculate and pontificate concerning the futures of all these OSs. One of the great advantages of the typical Intel-based PC is that you can run several OSs on it, thus hedging your bets for the future while simultaneously getting the best of each OS in the here and now. ●

PART II

The Boot Process

The x86 BIOS: Its Limits and Capabilities

In this chapter

BIOS History and Design Theory

To configure a computer to handle several OSs, you must be able to coax each one into boot-ing. This can sometimes be a challenging task because the original IBM PC was not designed with today's complex configurations in mind, and we're still living with the legacy of the IBM PC's design. In particular, the PC's *basic input/output system (BIOS)* possesses several limita-tions that are important for understanding how OSs boot. In a single-OS system, you gener-ally need not be terribly concerned with these matters because the OS can generally handle things reasonably well. When you install several OSs, though, you must be aware of how the BIOS gets the OS booted because two OSs can interact with the BIOS in different ways, thus wreaking havoc on one another's configurations.

In this chapter, I present some information on the structure of the BIOS for Intel x86-based computers, with a focus on those features that interact with OSs and the boot process. In Chapter 4, "Boot Loaders: Simple and Complex," I continue the examination of the boot process with a look at what happens when the OS takes over the boot process and how you can get several OSs to boot from a single hard disk.

To understand how the BIOS works, it's important to understand its history. Many of the limi-tations that give us grief today were useful features in the days of the 8088-based IBM PC. System designers continue to use suboptimal BIOS features because a huge mass of software exists that relies on these old features. Removing or even updating these features would break a great deal of important software, so change has been slow and awkward at best.

16- and 32-Bit Code

At the core of every computer lies a chip called the *central processing unit (CPU)*. The CPU does most of the important computational work of a computer—adding, dividing, determining which part of a program to run next, and so on. The CPU is nothing, however, without mem-ory—*random-access memory (RAM)* especially, but also other types of memory, such as *read-only memory (ROM)*. When a CPU accesses its memory, it specifies the memory address in the form of a number, which is similar to a street address, as in Figure 3.1. Unlike street addresses, though, computer memory addresses are fixed in length, as if there were a law that said no street address could have more than some number of digits. The number of dig-its in a memory address varies from one CPU to another and is expressed in terms of *binary digits (bits)*, meaning the number of digits in the address when it's expressed in binary (base 2) form. Each memory address can store a number that's a fixed number of bits in size—eight bits (one byte) on most desktop computers, meaning it can store a value ranging from 0 to 255.

The original IBM personal computer (PC), based on the Intel 8088 CPU, used a peculiar memory-addressing scheme. Fundamentally, it was a 16-bit design, meaning that the CPU could address only 2^{16}, or 65536, memory locations. This is the origin of the so-called 64KB limit on DOS memory structures, with which you're probably familiar if you've ever used DOS.

FIGURE 3.1
Each memory address can store precisely one number between 0 and 255.

...	address: 24 content: 234	address: 25 content: 16	address: 26 content: 98	...

The IBM PC, though, could have up to 640KB of RAM, plus more memory for ROM (in which the BIOS resides) and other features. How was this accomplished? By using a special 4-byte segment address in addition to the basic 16-byte address. The combination of these two addresses resulted in an effective memory address range of 2^{20} bytes, or 1MB. Because of this strange arrangement, programs required extra code to use the segment address. Even 1MB was rather limiting, however, so future CPUs raised the limit. The Intel 80286 (or 286 for short) used a more complex scheme that allowed for access to more memory, but it still used separate main and segment addresses. The 386 CPU introduced a true 32-bit address scheme to the Intel line, meaning that a program could directly and easily address 2^{32} bytes, or 4GB, of RAM, which is more than enough even for most needs today. (Both Intel and other manufacturers have designed or are planning 64-bit CPUs, though, for future needs.) The trouble with the 386's 32-bit mode is that it required new programs and new operating systems—or at least special extensions to DOS. CPUs from the 386 through to modern x86 CPUs such as the Intel Pentium III and AMD Athlon can therefore continue to use the old 16-bit memory address modes. Without this capability, modern computers wouldn't be able to run DOS or even Windows 9x.

The BIOS works into this picture in that it was originally designed around the old 16-bit memory address schemes, and changing the BIOS to use 32-bit addressing has proved to be an extremely challenging task. In fact, rather than even try, most Intel-based PCs include a 16-bit BIOS and let the OS use 32-bit code after it's booted. This means that even the most advanced OSs for Intel PCs must include at least a minimal amount of 16-bit code to handle the switch from the 16-bit BIOS to the 32-bit OS. This fact has little consequence to you as an end user, but it's of vital importance to those who design OS boot loader code and OS-selection utilities.

▶ To learn more about different OS boot loaders, **see** "Common Boot Loaders," **p. 98**.

The BIOS as Driver for DOS

One of the original functions of the BIOS was as an interface between the OS (DOS, in those days) and the PC's low-level hardware. The idea was simple: Future versions of the PC might use different low-level hardware than that in the original PC, so if the OS called BIOS routines to access hardware, the OS would not need to be rewritten for every minor hardware variant in existence. Because most non-DOS OSs are 32-bit, though, they can't use the BIOS in this way—or, to be more precise, they can, but only at the cost of serious performance degradation. Instead, modern OSs use *drivers*—special low-level programs that access hardware on behalf of the OS. Fortunately, most hardware components for which the BIOS was written use fairly standardized designs, so few specialized drivers are required to get an OS functioning at least minimally. As time has gone on, though, more and more new devices have been invented, such as CD-ROM drives, *small computer system interface (SCSI)* host adapters, scanners, and so on. Each of these items requires a special driver, often even in DOS.

The end result is that one of the BIOS's original functions is of little importance with most modern OSs. This does not mean that you can do away with the BIOS, however, because it serves other vital functions.

Modern Uses of the BIOS

With a few exceptions, such as OS/2's optional BIOS hard disk driver and Windows 9x's capability to use old DOS access methods, modern OSs don't use the BIOS as a driver for hardware. These systems rely on the BIOS for other functions, however. Mostly these functions relate to handling the boot process before the OS gains control, after which point the BIOS might as well not exist. Occasionally these BIOS functions influence the further operation of the OS, however, and these functions can influence OSs in different ways.

The POST   One of the modern functions of the BIOS is the *power-on self-test (POST)*. As its name implies, the POST performs basic tests of the system's functionality when you turn on a computer. Among other things, the POST determines how much memory you have installed, runs a limited test of the memory, and checks for the presence and basic function of other components, such as the keyboard. If the POST determines that hardware is defective, the BIOS stops the boot process and signals an error in some way, such as by beeping. The POST error codes vary from one BIOS to another.

▶ To learn more about POST error codes, read Scott Mueller's *Upgrading and Repairing PCs, 11th Edition*, from Que.

Boot Handler   Perhaps the most vital BIOS function is as a means of booting an OS. When a computer starts, the CPU is designed to look in particular memory locations for code to execute. In an Intel-based PC, these memory locations contain BIOS code that performs various functions, including the POST. After the POST is complete, the BIOS looks for a hard disk, floppy disk, or some other bootable medium (such as a network boot server). If it finds such a medium, the BIOS passes control to that device. The key point here is that without the BIOS, the PC could not boot.

▶ To learn more about how the BIOS passes control to the code on the hard disk, **see** "The Handoff to the OS," **p. 82**.

The method the BIOS uses to pass control to the OS is standardized and fixed in the BIOS. This fact, along with standards for hard disk layout, plays an important role in determining how different OSs can load themselves, and in the design of tools to help you choose one OS or another at boot time. In particular, these two factors determine the methods that can be used to *partition* a disk, or break it up into segments so that different OSs can coexist peacefully. Non-Intel PCs use different disk partitioning methods than do Intel PCs, so you might not be able to move a disk from one architecture to another and retrieve data from the disk, even if the target OS contains appropriate drivers for the original computer's filesystems.

NOTE Some OSs, such as Linux, include support for foreign hardware's disk partitioning schemes. Such support enables you to remove a hard disk from, say, a Macintosh, and retrieve data from that disk on a Linux computer. Even if you were to install Linux on that disk, however, you wouldn't be able to boot from it using the standard BIOS boot routines because the BIOS wouldn't find intelligible boot code on the disk. ■

Option Setter   One final modern function of the BIOS is as a means of setting assorted hardware options. PC hardware has become quite complex, and depending on the way you configure your system, you might want or need to adjust various aspects of how that hardware works. In some cases, you might need to do this configuration so that it's in effect at the time the OS loads, so the only option is to do it using the BIOS.

The particular BIOS tool that's used is called the *complementary metal oxide semiconductor (CMOS) setup* utility because it's used to store options in a special type of non-volatile memory known as CMOS RAM. The computer accesses its CMOS RAM to set various options, such as

- **Hard disk geometry**—How the system interprets hard disk addressing schemes.

  ▶ To learn more about hard disk geometry, **see** "Understanding CHS Geometry Limits," **p. 76**.

- **Performance features**—Settings related to the speed of memory access, transfer modes for various peripherals, and so on.

- **On-board peripherals**—Whether to enable or disable hardware such as serial ports, and how to configure these devices.

- **Security**—Password protection to prevent unauthorized access to the system.

- **PnP configuration**—Settings that control how the BIOS enables *plug-and-play (PnP)* plug-in cards.

- **APM support**—Settings that control the activation and timing of *advanced power management (APM)* features.

- **System clock**—The date and time, as recorded by the computer.

NOTE Some BIOS options might not be present on some systems, particularly older ones. For example, many 486 and older computers lacked PnP and APM features. ■

The details of how you set these BIOS options varies substantially from one system to another. In general, you press a particular key or keys, such as Del or F2, during the boot process to enter the CMOS setup utility. Most computers include an onscreen message at the appropriate time in the bootup process for you to press this key to enter the setup utility.

Part
II

Ch
3

Figure 3.2 shows a typical BIOS setup screen, but each computer's BIOS is unique, so yours might look slightly or substantially different. Most CMOS setup utilities consist of several screens, one for each class of settings. The screens in Figure 3.2 are called Main, Advanced, Security, Power, and Boot, with an additional item called Exit to leave the utility (these are the labels on the second line).

▶ To learn more about different brands of BIOS, **see** "What BIOS Do You Have?," **p. 71**.

FIGURE 3.2
Most CMOS setup utilities use simple keyboard commands, and many list available options at the bottom of the screen.

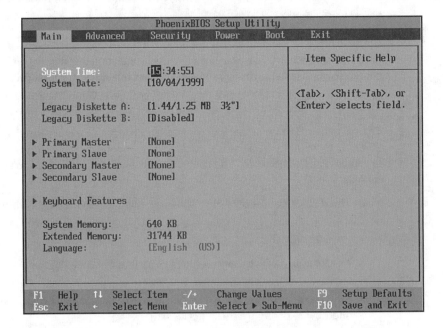

You might want to familiarize yourself with the CMOS setup options on your computer. Because each computer is unique, I can't provide detailed instructions on what you need to do to modify your settings for any given OS. Your computer or motherboard probably has a manual that describes the BIOS options. If you don't have a manual or find it unhelpful, the Web site http://www.ping.be/bios/ might have the information you seek. Fortunately, most OSs work well with the same settings that suit other OSs.

CAUTION

Although you should familiarize yourself with your CMOS settings, I recommend you be cautious about changing them. It's often possible to configure your CMOS in such a way that your computer won't boot any OS. If you find yourself in this situation and can't remember what you changed, try to find a CMOS setup utility option to restore default settings. (Figure 3.2 reveals that F9 will accomplish this task for the CMOS setup utility depicted in that figure.) This option will usually make your system bootable once more.

If you find that an OS has difficulties locating hardware or memory, you might want to try adjusting CMOS settings. The following are some options you might want to investigate:

- **Memory holes**—BIOSs sometimes place a "hole" in memory at 16MB or 64MB. Some OSs (especially OS/2) sometimes misinterpret this hole as the end of memory, so they don't use all the RAM in the computer. Disabling this hole can recover this lost RAM.

- **PnP settings**—When using a PnP-aware OS, it's generally best to let the OS configure PnP devices. Sometimes you might want to make the BIOS do the configuration, though. BIOSs provide varying options for how they assign system resources to PnP devices. You'll have to experiment if you have problems with resource conflicts in a new OS. Be sure to test existing OSs after making changes, too!

- **APM settings**—Some OSs have problems dealing with APM features, so you might need to disable these in the BIOS.

- **Hard disk geometry**—You might need to adjust your hard disk geometry settings to get all your OSs to coexist on one drive. I discuss this feature in more detail later in this chapter.

What BIOS Do You Have?

Up to this point, I've referred to *the BIOS*, as if there were only one BIOS used, albeit with modifications, in all computers. In fact, there are several. Common BIOSs in use today include the following:

- **AMI BIOS**—American Megatrends, Inc. (AMI; http://www.ami.com) produces a popular BIOS that's used on its own and many other companies' motherboards.

- **Phoenix BIOS**—The Phoenix BIOS is another popular one. It closely resembles the AMI BIOS in its layout and options. For more information, see http://www.phoenix.com.

- **Award BIOS**—Phoenix purchased Award, so Award BIOSs are being shipped only on systems that were designed prior to the merger. Many existing Award BIOSs exist, however. The Award BIOS was somewhat different in its overall layout than the AMI and Phoenix BIOSs, but comparable in features. As I write this, the Award Web site still exists at http://www.award.com.

- **MR BIOS**—Microid Research (http://www.mrbios.com) sells after-market BIOS upgrades, mostly for older computer systems. These upgrades can be a useful way to add modern BIOS features to an older computer.

Each of these BIOSs can be considered more of a BIOS family than a single product. Each BIOS must be fine-tuned for each type of computer. For example, a BIOS for an Intel Pentium III motherboard must be different from an AMD Athlon motherboard's BIOS. Even within a CPU family, BIOSs differ because of differences in the motherboard *chipsets*—the collection of circuitry that mediates between the CPU and the memory, add-in cards, and on-board

Part
II

Ch
3

devices. These two factors (multiple BIOS suppliers and unique modifications for each motherboard design) result in a huge range of BIOS features, some of which might interact with some OSs but not others.

Add-On Card BIOSs

Up until now, I've described the BIOS on the computer's motherboard. Certain types of cards you add to your computer have their own BIOSs, however. These BIOSs interact with the motherboard BIOS, sometimes extending the motherboard BIOS's capabilities. In some cases, add-on cards have their own configuration screens that you as a user can access. Other times, the card BIOSs have no options you can set; they simply do their job and stay out of your way. Nonetheless, you should know something about these BIOSs because they are sometimes important in a multi-OS configuration.

N O T E In general, the BIOSs I describe in this section reside on the add-on cards themselves. Occasionally, however, they can be integrated into the motherboard's BIOS. Such integration is particularly common when the hardware itself is integrated into the motherboard. For example, some motherboards include SCSI host adapters or video circuitry, in which case the respective components' BIOSs also reside on the motherboard. You can still access the BIOSs separately, however, when they have their own setup utilities. ■

Video BIOSs

The variety of available video display hardware for Intel PCs is astounding. Because of the range of options, there's a definite need for video BIOSs to control the display of information. On most computers, your only hint of the presence of the video BIOS comes when you first turn on the computer—a line or two of text flashes by, usually for only a second or so. This text identifies the make and model of video adapter, and possibly the BIOS version number. This information is occasionally helpful in diagnosing problems with video hardware, but video BIOSs seldom provide user-configurable options akin to those for the motherboard BIOS.

 TIP Modern video boards sometimes have the capability to use an *interrupt request (IRQ)* line, which is a way for hardware to request service from the OS. The number of IRQs in a modern PC is quite limited, and many OSs don't use the video IRQ. You might therefore want to disable this feature if you think it's not being used. You can often do so in the motherboard's BIOS. If you disable the video IRQ and then experience problems or poor performance, particularly in 3D games, you should reenable the video IRQ.

Boot BIOSs for SCSI and Networking

Standard BIOSs support booting a PC from a floppy disk or an *integrated device electronics (IDE)* or *enhanced IDE (EIDE)* hard disk. These disk types are controlled in the same way as many older drive types, so they can all use the same basic BIOS support to operate. If you want to boot from a SCSI hard disk or run a diskless workstation and boot from a network, though, you must have an appropriate SCSI host adapter or network card with a boot BIOS. This BIOS extends the PC's standard BIOS so that the PC can use the add-on device in place of the standard device for booting the computer. In most cases, you must also provide a driver for each OS to use the new device because the OS won't use the BIOS to access the drive after the OS is running the computer.

For both SCSI host adapters and network cards, the least expensive models often lack boot BIOSs. These cards are perfectly good for using non-boot SCSI devices and for networking a computer that boots from a hard disk, respectively, so if you have such a card, the lack of a boot BIOS might not be sufficient cause to ditch the card.

 TIP Some midrange SCSI host adapters, particularly those based on some SCSI chips from Symbios, lack their own BIOSs, but BIOSs are available and can be installed in the motherboard's BIOS. In fact, some motherboards ship with this Symbios SCSI BIOS support. If you have such a motherboard, you can boot even from a BIOS-less Symbios-based SCSI host adapter. The Symbios BIOS won't do you any good with BIOS-less host adapters based on other manufacturers' chipsets, however, because the Symbios BIOS is specific to Symbios products.

Watch your computer screen carefully as it boots. Many boot BIOSs for SCSI host adapters include setup utilities you can use to configure the hardware. When present, the SCSI BIOS displays a prompt informing you of a key sequence to press to access the utility. You can use these utilities to alter the SCSI termination, adjust the order in which the SCSI BIOS attempts to boot from devices, and so on.

Normally, a PC attempts to boot first from an EIDE drive and only then from a SCSI disk or network device. Therefore, if you have both SCSI and EIDE disks but want to boot from the SCSI disk, you might have difficulties. Most BIOSs produced since 1997, though, include an option to change the boot order so that SCSI hard disks can be tried first. Such computers can also often boot from CD-ROM drives, LS-120 disks, and so on. You control these features from the motherboard BIOS's CMOS setup utility, not from the SCSI host adapter's BIOS. If you select such an option, be aware that you might need to make adjustments in your OS to tell it what the boot drive is. In OS/2, for example, you must ensure that your SCSI host adapter's driver appears before the IBM1S506.ADD IDE/EIDE driver in OS/2's CONFIG.SYS file.

TIP With many more advanced OSs, you can boot from a SCSI device even if the motherboard's BIOS doesn't support this feature. You do so by telling the motherboard BIOS that you have no EIDE devices, even when you do. The BIOS will then fail to detect the EIDE drives and will boot from the SCSI drive. The drawback to this is that, if your OS relies on the BIOS to handle disk accesses, the EIDE drives will be unavailable. If your OS includes its own EIDE drivers, however, you'll regain access to the EIDE drives as soon as the OS has booted.

Additional BIOSs

Devices such as sound cards and modems often contain their own BIOSs, or at least BIOS-like features. In general, you don't access these BIOSs the way you do the motherboard or some SCSI BIOSs; you simply let them do their thing and otherwise ignore them.

Some boards include nonvolatile or volatile RAM in which they store information on configuration options to be used across boots. Occasionally this information can become corrupted or settings from one OS can interfere with the operation of another. You might therefore need to boot one OS to configure a board's options before booting another OS. For example, combination sound card/modems built around many of IBM's Mwave chips have drivers only in DOS, Windows, and OS/2. They can be made to work as 8-bit SoundBlaster-compatible sound cards, however, by booting DOS and enabling the board's SoundBlaster-compatible mode and then booting the target OS. It's generally necessary to do a soft reboot (by using Ctrl+Alt+Del) rather than a hard reboot (by using the reset button on the computer's case) when using DOS to initialize hardware for another OS.

 TIP Even if you don't want to keep a DOS partition, keeping a DOS boot floppy can be extremely useful for running DOS utilities to diagnose problems with hardware or to fiddle with the BIOSs of some devices.

BIOS Updates

All modern PCs include *flash BIOSs*. These are BIOSs that can be overwritten by the user. They reside on *electrically erasable programmable ROMs (EEPROMs)*, which can be reprogrammed while residing in the motherboard. This can be a great feature because you can upgrade your BIOS to eliminate bugs or add features. Typically, the BIOS update utilities are DOS programs, so you need a DOS partition or a DOS boot floppy (the latter is generally safer).

CAUTION

BIOS updates are extremely useful but also potentially quite dangerous. If you select the wrong BIOS file or if something goes wrong during the flash process, your computer will be rendered unbootable. The only way to correct this problem is to replace the BIOS chip in the motherboard. As a safety precaution, I recommend keeping a backup of your existing BIOS file on a floppy disk (most flash utilities provide an option to create such a backup). That way, if your upgrade goes badly, you can take your computer and the floppy to a local computer dealer to have a fresh BIOS chip flashed and installed. Better yet, if you can obtain a spare preprogrammed BIOS chip, you'll have it on hand if anything goes wrong. Some motherboards include an unflashable BIOS in addition to the flash BIOS, so you can recover from such a disaster more easily.

You can check your motherboard manufacturer's Web site for information on updating your BIOS. Similar updates are often available for video cards, SCSI host adapters, and other devices that contain BIOSs. Because of the dangers involved in updating a BIOS, I recommend doing so only if you're having problems that you believe might be solved by a BIOS update. Many BIOS updates are issued only to fix problems experienced by a few people or to add features that you might not need. There's no sense in risking making your system unusable for an "improvement" that won't help you.

CAUTION

Be sure to use a BIOS update file only for the motherboard make and model that you're using. Some manufacturers release motherboards that are very different but that have model numbers that differ by only one character. Using the wrong BIOS file can produce an unbootable system. If you're a more advanced user, you might think that using a BIOS file for a board that uses the same chipset as yours will work. This might indeed be true, but it might also produce an unbootable system because of different customizations used by each manufacturer.

EIDE and SCSI Hard Disk Handling

EIDE and SCSI hard disks are very similar in some ways but quite different in others. As I've already mentioned, the BIOS handles the two differently; the motherboard BIOS can control EIDE disks by itself but requires help from a SCSI host adapter's BIOS to handle SCSI disks.

No matter the disk type, though, there are certain characteristics of hard disks that you should understand if you're to configure your system for multiple OSs. These characteristics relate to a hard disk's *geometry*—the numbers with which the BIOS or OS accesses the data on the disk.

Understanding CHS Geometry Limits

The basic design of hard disks hasn't changed much since the early 1980s, although today's models are orders of magnitude higher in capacity and faster than those from two decades ago. The basic design of a hard disk is illustrated in Figure 3.3. Data are stored on magnetic coatings that cover one or more circular disk platters. To read or write data, the disk platters spin at high velocity (5400 to 10,000 rpm in typical drives today) and the read/write heads read the data off the disks. When a head remains stationary, it reads data from a ring-shaped portion of a platter. Because the platters are stacked on top one another, these ring-shaped areas themselves form a virtual cylinder.

FIGURE 3.3
Data on a hard disk can be addressed by cylinder (distance from the center), head (which platter and side), and sector (position within a cylinder).

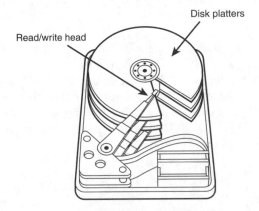

Hard disks read and write data in discrete units of information, typically 512 bytes. Each such unit is known as a *sector*. On older drives, there were a fixed number of sectors per cylinder. Thus, it was natural to describe the layout of a hard disk in terms of three numbers: The cylinder (sometimes referred to as the *track*), the head, and the sector within a cylinder. This triplet of numbers is often referred to as the *CHS address*, as in cylinder 45, head 2, sector 11. On the simple hard drives of the early 1980s, using CHS addressing meant that the hard drives could use simple electronics; they did not need to decode some other addressing scheme into those three numbers. Both the PC's BIOS and assorted hard disk structures therefore express locations of data on a disk in terms of CHS addresses.

The CHS system is convenient for some very old drives, but most drives today, and even in the early 1990s, used a variable number of sectors per cylinder. This design allows more data to fit onto a disk because all other things being equal, more sectors can fit on outside cylinders than inside ones. Thus, IDE and EIDE hard drives actually lie to the computer about their geometries—they make up geometries that allow for the correct data capacity and then quietly translate between their true capacities and what they tell the BIOS. Still, you can pretend that what an IDE drive reports to the BIOS is correct because the limits I'm about to discuss reside mostly in the BIOS, or at least in the communication between the hard disk and the computer.

Unfortunately, the PC's designers, in a day when 10MB hard disks were huge, didn't plan for hard disks as large as we have today. These programmers allocated 10 bits for the cylinder number (mirroring the size of a register in an early PC hard disk controller), 8 bits for the head number, and 6 bits for the sector number. There were two further limitations, though: First, early IDE drives themselves had limits (16, 4, and 8 bits, respectively), which effectively limited the head field to 4 bits. Second, although the sector number is 6 bits, it is numbered starting from 1 rather than 0, so one sector number is effectively lost (it's not lost from the disk itself; there's simply one fewer sector available per cylinder in the numbering scheme). Thus, there was an effective limit of 1024 (2^{10}) cylinders, 16 (2^4) heads, and 63 (2^6–1) sectors per cylinder. Multiply those values together, multiply the result by 512 bytes per sector, and convert to megabytes and you find that the limit on IDE hard drive size is 504MB.

NOTE In general, a megabyte in computer circles is 2^{20} or 1,048,576 bytes. Hard drive manufacturers, however, tend to define a megabyte as 1,000,000 bytes, thus slightly inflating the apparent size of a disk for advertising purposes. (Similar differences exist for definitions of a kilobyte and a gigabyte.) I use the former definition exclusively throughout this book, but you should be aware of the difference. If you buy a hard disk that's advertised as being an 18.2GB unit, don't be surprised to see your disk partitioning software report it as 17.0GB. The disk manufacturer hasn't made a mistake, nor is this a difference between "formatted" and "unformatted" capacities, as some people seem to think; it's merely an artifact of differing definitions of what constitutes a kilobyte, a megabyte, or a gigabyte. Because of this difference, the 504MB limit is sometimes referred to as the 528MB limit. Some people mistakenly regularize the value as 512MB, which is inaccurate by any measure.

SCSI hard disks work somewhat differently. Rather than use a CHS value, SCSI has always used a single linear address space. To interface with a PC's BIOS, though, SCSI host adapters translate the SCSI linear addressing mode into CHS values. Details differ from one SCSI host adapter to another, but most use five bits for the number of heads, and some begin numbering sectors from 0, leading to a 1GB capacity limit. Most adapters today provide options to raise these limits further, as described shortly.

Getting Around the 1024-Cylinder Limit

By 1994, hard drives exceeding 504MB, or even 1GB, were becoming not only desirable, but common. Drives of higher capacity typically reported themselves as having the maximum number of heads and sectors and more than 1024 cylinders. Thus, this problem came to be referred to as the *1024-cylinder limit*, and it's still with us today.

The question in 1994 was one of circumventing this limit. Some of the methods I describe later in this chapter were useful in raising the limit, but by 1997 drives exceeding even these raised limits started to become common. Although many modern OSs aren't bothered by the 1024-cylinder limit, and can in fact handle much larger hard disks, portions of the modern BIOS boot code are still plagued by this limit, and this fact has important consequences for OS installation, as discussed in this and the next few chapters.

Ignorance Is Bliss   One method of getting around the 1024-cylinder limit is to ignore it. This is a perfectly workable solution for OSs that don't rely on the BIOS for disk access. OS/2 and Linux, for example, even in 1994, could access all of a 1GB or larger disk; these OSs simply use more than 10 bits to represent the number of cylinders on a disk, thus allowing direct access to the disk's full capacity. There are several problems with this solution, however:

- To boot an OS, the BIOS must be able to read certain OS files, so those files must fall below the 1024-cylinder limit. Ensuring that this will be the case can be a nuisance.

- If you're running a dual-boot system, some OSs might be able to ignore the 1024-cylinder limit and some might not. Those that can't ignore it might become confused by a disk partitioned by the more capable OS or might become confused by the contents of a partition that spans the limits. For this reason, OS/2 won't format a partition that falls even partly past the 1024-cylinder limit for the file allocation table (FAT) filesystem used by DOS, although OS/2 will use its own high-performance filesystem (HPFS) on such partitions.

- Even two OSs that can each handle over–1024-cylinder drives might have subtle incompatibilities in how they encode partitioning or other data, so they might have problems coexisting on such a system.

Using CHS Geometry Translation   One method of handling over–1024-cylinder drives was what came to be known as *CHS geometry translation* or various truncations of that term. Recall that the reason for using only four bits for the head number was that this was a limitation of IDE drives themselves. Internal to the BIOS, an eight-bit field could be used for the head number. CHS geometry translation typically works by taking excess cylinders and turning them into heads. For example, if a drive reports that it has 2000 cylinders and 16 heads, the BIOS can translate this to 1000 cylinders and 32 heads. The total drive capacity remains the same, the BIOS and most software can handle this system, and the total capacity limit is raised to 7.875GB, depending on how vigorously the software translates geometries.

CHS geometry translation was first done using special software BIOS extensions that were stored in the hard disks' boot sectors. Such software programs were frequently designed for DOS and didn't work well with OS/2, Linux, or other OSs. These OSs eventually learned to spot these programs and adjust their own handling of the drive to fit in. Therefore, if you have an old system that uses such software, you can probably continue to use it, even if you're planning to install a new OS. You might want to check the documentation for your new OS to be sure it's safe, though.

Eventually, CHS geometry translation came to be a standard feature in PC BIOSs, so no additional software was required. Similarly, many EIDE add-on controller cards include BIOS extensions that replace or augment the motherboard BIOS's hard disk routines to provide such support. As with software BIOS extensions, though, each OS must be able to play along with this solution. If an OS queries the hard disk directly about its capacity and uses the values returned by the disk itself rather than by the BIOS, the OS will use incorrect values as far as other OSs are concerned.

> **CAUTION**
>
> It's vitally important that all OSs agree on a single CHS geometry for each drive. If two OSs don't agree, they'll write conflicting data in the partition table and can corrupt data structures all over the disk. The end result can be absolutely disastrous. Fortunately, problems like this are rare and are mostly related to old OSs, such as OS/2 2.1, that don't understand modern CHS translation schemes.

Note that CHS geometry translation is a solution applied to IDE and EIDE drives only. Because SCSI drives don't communicate to their host adapters using CHS values, there's little sense in applying such schemes to them. Instead, SCSI host adapters modified their methods of creating CHS values for attached hard drives, as described in the next section.

Using LBA Mode in EIDE and SCSI Drives   *LBA* stands for *linear block addressing* or *logical block addressing*, depending on whom you ask. By either name, it refers to a system of hard disk access whereby a single sector number is used instead of a triplet of numbers. The sector number used in EIDE LBA mode is a 28-bit number (from IDE's 16-bit cylinder, 4-bit head number, and 8-bit sector number added together). Therefore, LBA mode supports hard drives of up to 128GB (2^{28} sectors $\times$ 512 bytes) in capacity.

SCSI hard drives have always used LBA mode internally and in talking to their host adapters; the SCSI host adapters have been the ones to translate LBA mode into CHS mode. Eventually, EIDE drives began to emulate SCSI drives in this respect. This method of addressing requires that the drive electronics support the change (as is true of most EIDE drives but not the older IDE drives), and it requires support in the BIOS. As with CHS geometry translation, LBA mode results in the capacity to handle hard disks of up to approximately 8GB in size when using old CHS addressing methods (which are still constrained by the BIOS's cylinder, head, and sector number limits), but software that can directly handle LBA mode can use disks of up to 128GB.

In general, LBA mode uses disk space a little more efficiently than does CHS geometry translation because less disk space is lost to rounding errors. Depending on the hardware in use, LBA mode can be slightly faster than CHS geometry translation, as well. Most modern OSs can use LBA mode directly (bypassing the BIOS), but some software, particularly low-level disk utilities, still uses CHS mode.

Part

II

Ch

3

CAUTION

The plethora of CHS mapping schemes makes it dangerous to move a hard disk from one computer to another. If the original computer used CHS geometry translation and the destination uses LBA mode, the destination computer could easily misinterpret the drive's layout and damage its data. Even if both computers claim to use the same translation scheme, differences in the algorithms used to implement these methods could wreak havoc. For similar reasons, you should never change the translation scheme used on a disk unless you've first deleted all the partitions (thus wiping out all the disk's data). When you've wiped the disk clean and changed the geometry mapping scheme, boot a DOS floppy that contains the DOS FDISK utility and type FDISK /MBR. This undocumented command rewrites low-level disk information to conform to the new disk geometry settings. (DR-DOS's FDISK includes equivalent functionality as a menu item from inside the FDISK utility.) These comments apply to both EIDE and SCSI hard disks.

In recent years, there have been some efforts to get around the 1024-cylinder limit more completely by using LBA mode directly, even in programs that work through the BIOS. That is, instead of using CHS addressing from within programs, use the LBA addressing. This system is known as *extended INT13* addressing (INT13 is the name of the BIOS call that's used for CHS disk addressing). The older non-extended INT13 addressing is still used in booting OSs, however, as well as by many older utilities.

The 1024-Cylinder Limit Is Alive and Well   Today's hard disks are commonly in excess of 1024 cylinders again, even when CHS geometry translation or LBA mode translations are used, so we must deal with the 1024-cylinder limits all over again. You must ensure that all your bootable partitions fall below the 1024-cylinder limit. To determine what this limit is, start your BIOS setup utility and locate the information on your hard disk. (You must use your SCSI adapter's setup utility if you're booting from a SCSI disk.) Multiply the number of sectors by the number of heads and then divide by 2. That's the location of the 1024-cylinder limit in megabytes.

Fortunately, most OSs today can cope with hard drives with more than 1024 cylinders, or can use extended INT13 addressing. The list of such OSs includes Windows 98. If you have DOS on your system, you should ensure that its partitions fall entirely below the 1024-cylinder limit, just as do your bootable partitions. Microsoft has introduced new partition types for partitions that fall partly or wholly above the 1024th cylinder, but not all OSs understand these partition types, so if you use them, you might not be able to access these partitions from all your OSs.

▶ To learn more about partition types, **see** "Partition Types," **p. 119**.

Common BIOS Disk Utilities

BIOSs (both motherboard BIOSs and those on SCSI host adapters) often contain utilities to help you perform routine and non-routine maintenance on hard disks. Some of the more common utilities include

■ **Disk detection and configuration**—You can usually tell the BIOS to auto-detect hard disks, either once or at every boot. Many BIOSs then enable you to specify a CHS translation scheme. Figure 3.4 illustrates one BIOS's hard disk detection and translation options. For SCSI disks, you might have an option to support disks larger than 1GB. If enabled, such an option usually moves the 1024-cylinder limit to approximately 8GB, though on some host adapters the limit is only pushed up to 2GB or some other value. Very old SCSI host adapters use physical switches or jumpers to set these options, rather than a BIOS configuration utility.

FIGURE 3.4
BIOSs enable you to adjust hard disk options by using menus or following onscreen prompts.

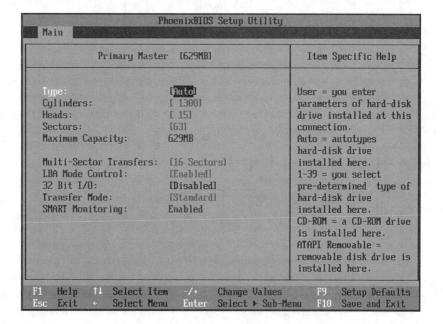

Data transfer methods—Modern hard disks often let you transfer data in large chunks, as in the Multi-Sector Transfers and 32 Bit I/O options shown in Figure 3.4. Options such as this often speed up transfers. Other options might relate to *direct memory access (DMA)* mode transfers, which allow the disk controller to send data directly to memory rather than going through the CPU; and the level of the *AT attachment (ATA)* commands used (the higher the level, the better). For the most part, a BIOS will set itself up for optimal transfer performance for any given drive. These settings can often be overridden by OS drivers.

■ **Disk formatting utility**—Some BIOSs, particularly for SCSI disks, include an option to perform a low-level format on the hard disk. This format rewrites the information the disk uses to locate individual sectors and often erases every sector on the disk. You should therefore use such an option only when you want to completely erase a disk.

Part
II

Ch
3

The main reason to do a low-level format is if the disk has developed a few bad sectors; the formatting process will map these sectors out, so that they're no longer used by the drive. A low-level format can take several minutes, or even hours, to complete, so don't do it unless you have some time to spare.

CAUTION

If a drive develops a few bad sectors, this might be a sign that it's developing serious problems. Rather than cover over the problem by doing a low-level format, you might want to replace the drive.

Sometimes utilities such as these come as a separate utility program rather than as BIOS routines. This is particularly true of disk format utilities. Such utility programs generally run from DOS, so you might want to ensure that you have a working DOS boot floppy in case you need to run the utility program in the future. You can create a DOS boot floppy from a DOS installation by typing FORMAT /S A: or SYS A: on an already formatted disk.

The Handoff to the OS

Perhaps the most important aspect of what the BIOS does is to transfer control of the computer to programs stored on some other medium. These programs are simple *boot loader* programs—programs that boot one or more OSs. Boot loaders can exist on several different media:

- **Floppy disk**—When you boot from a floppy disk, the BIOS loads the boot loader from the first sector of the floppy disk. This sector is often referred to as the *boot sector*.

- **Hard disk**—A hard disk's boot sector is referred to as the *master boot record (MBR)*. It contains information beyond that normally stored in a floppy disk's boot sector, such as information on how the disk is partitioned.

- **Network boot server**—If a computer is configured as a diskless workstation, it can retrieve its boot files from a network server.

- **CD-ROM**—Bootable CD-ROMs have become common in recent years. Typically, these contain a disk image that's identical to a boot floppy, complete with boot sector, along with special CD-ROM structures. This combination is known as an *El Torito* boot CD-ROM.

- **High-capacity removable media**—LS-120 disks, Zip disks, and so on can be made bootable, following either the floppy disk model of a boot sector or the hard disk model of using an MBR.

In all cases, the BIOS must support the specific boot medium. In the mid-1990s, most BIOSs supported only floppy disk and hard disk boots, and SCSI hard disks required support from a SCSI host adapter's boot BIOS. Today, support for bootable CD-ROMs and at least some varieties of removable media is common, as is an ability to switch which device to try first. Network boots and boots from SCSI devices still require boot BIOSs on the respective adapter cards. In the case of SCSI CD-ROM drives, the SCSI host adapter must support booting from El Torito CD-ROM media. Some SCSI host adapters support booting from removable media devices such as Zip drives by using an option to treat removable devices as if they were fixed (non-removable) disks.

In any event, the BIOS loads the first sector (512 bytes) of the disk and uses that as a loader program. By today's standards, 512 bytes is very little space, so boot loader programs are necessarily quite simple. Some boot loaders rely on additional code stored elsewhere on the hard disk to function properly. All of them rely on additional programs to set boot options. These external programs can be as simple as DOS's FDISK, which can rewrite a bare-bones MBR, or as complex as dedicated third-party boot loader utilities such as System Commander.

▶ To learn more about various boot loaders, **see** "Common Boot Loaders," **p. 98**.

Part

II

Ch

3

After the BIOS has loaded the boot loader code, the BIOS runs that code. What happens then varies depending on the boot loader, but ultimately, an OS is loaded into memory and takes over control of the computer. Depending on the OS, the BIOS might then play no further role in the operation of the computer.

N O T E   Boot loader programs aren't the only ones to use the boot sector or MBR. Some varieties of virus also hijack this portion of the disk. These viruses are known as *boot sector viruses*, and they work by taking over the computer before the OS has a chance to load. The virus must then load the OS and hide evidence of what it's done. Viruses of this type often spread themselves on floppy disks because the boot sector can be executed even on non-boot floppies, especially if the disk is left in the computer accidentally. Most boot sector viruses are written for DOS or Windows 9x, and when they infect a computer that runs another OS, they might fail to boot the OS or can be wiped out by the OS during the OS's boot process. ▪

Summary

The BIOS for Intel x86-based computers is steeped in history and is the software component that, on most systems, bears the strongest relics from the modern PC's past as a 16-bit computer designed in the early 1980s. Nonetheless, the BIOS is an extremely important piece of software because it controls an assortment of hardware options and because it handles the beginnings of the boot process.

A variety of BIOSs exist for modern computers. Each motherboard comes with its own BIOS, and several companies produce BIOSs that are licensed by motherboard manufacturers. In addition to the main motherboard BIOS, most computers have one or more BIOSs on plug-in cards such as video adapters, SCSI adapters, and network cards. Each of these BIOSs extends the capabilities of the motherboard's BIOS.

After they're booted, most modern OSs more or less ignore all BIOSs, instead using their own drivers to access the hardware directly. A few OSs, however, such as DOS, continue to rely on the BIOS for access to at least some hardware components. ●

CHAPTER 4

Boot Loaders: Simple and Complex

The Post-BIOS Boot Process

Chapter 3, "The x86 BIOS: Its Limits and Capabilities," presented information on the x86 PC's basic input/output system (BIOS), which controls the early stages of the boot process and provides ongoing services to 16-bit OSs such as DOS. This chapter investigates the boot process in more detail, particularly as it's handled in a multi-OS environment.

When you have only one OS installed on a computer, the boot process is fairly straightforward because you don't need to direct the computer to perform one action or another. When you install two or more OSs, however, you must provide some means of selecting between them. This isn't a trivial proposition because it means the computer must present information on the screen, accept input, and act on that input, all without having an OS present. Fortunately, most OSs come with tools to perform these tasks, and additional third-party tools are available to cover more complex situations. Even when you use these tools, however, you need to understand the boot process so that you can configure your system effectively.

After the BIOS has finished its power-on self-test, it loads the boot sector from a boot device such as a floppy or hard disk (the hard disk's boot sector is also known as the master boot record or MBR). The boot sector is the first sector on a disk, and as such, it's only 512 bytes in length—quite small as programs go, particularly when you consider that the boot sector must also contain non-program information such as the size and geometry of the disk. It shouldn't be surprising, then, that the boot sector generally contains just enough code to load and run additional, slightly larger software, which in turn loads the OS itself. This section examines this process, with a focus on its implications and applications in a multi-OS environment.

▶ To learn more about the POST, **see** "The POST," **p. 68**.

The Job of the Boot Loader

In a DOS environment booting from a hard disk, the boot process proceeds as follows:

1. The BIOS loads the MBR and executes the code it contains.
2. The MBR code loads the boot sector for the partition on which DOS resides and runs the code it contains. This boot sector is separate from the MBR but is similar to a floppy disk's boot sector.
3. The boot partition's boot sector loads and runs critical DOS files.
4. After DOS is in control, it uses the DOS CONFIG.SYS file to control further boot options in order to load drivers and otherwise configure the system.
5. Ultimately, you get a DOS prompt, or if DOS is so configured, Windows 3.x or some other environment might load and run.

This sequence of events is illustrated in Figure 4.1. More or less the same sequence of events occurs when you boot some other OS that resides by itself on the computer. Specifically, the BIOS, the MBR, and the boot sector all execute code before the OS itself runs. When you boot from a floppy, the sequence is similar, except that there is no MBR, and a floppy cannot contain multiple partitions; the BIOS directly executes the floppy's boot sector.

FIGURE 4.1
Booting DOS on a single-OS computer involves transferring control from one small program to another until DOS finally gains control.

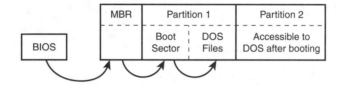

Now, suppose you want to install two or more OSs on the computer and select which to run at boot time. How would you go about doing this? The fact that so many pieces of code are executed prior to the OS itself gives you several options:

- **Custom BIOS**—In principle, you could create a new BIOS that loads multiple OSs directly. In practice, this isn't a reasonable solution because the BIOS is so specialized for specific motherboards and because the BIOS is difficult to program. This solution is therefore not used on Intel-compatible PCs.

- **Custom MBR**—The first piece of code executed by the computer during the boot process is in the MBR. If you replace this code with a version that gives you a choice of what OS to run, you've accomplished your task. Figure 4.2 illustrates this solution with an example of a system that dual boots DOS and OS/2.

FIGURE 4.2
Modifying the MBR code enables you to select which OS to boot; the unbooted OS's partition is never accessed.

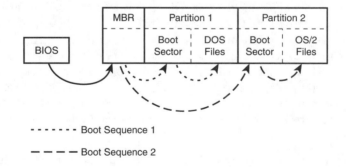

N O T E Figure 4.2 and subsequent figures show multiple OSs installed on multiple partitions because this is generally the most useful configuration. It's sometimes possible to install two or more OSs on a single partition, however. ▪

■ **Custom boot sector**—Just as you can replace the MBR code with a version that supports multiple OSs, you can replace the boot sector of a partition with similar OS-selection code. Figure 4.3 illustrates this layout.

FIGURE 4.3
A customized boot sector can redirect the boot process to any desired partition.

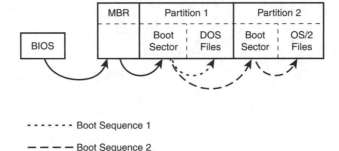

- - - - - - Boot Sequence 1

— — — — Boot Sequence 2

■ **Chained OS booting**—A final option is to use one OS to boot another, as illustrated in Figure 4.4. In this setup, one OS is allowed to partly or completely boot itself, whereupon it presents a menu that enables you to boot a second OS.

FIGURE 4.4
If one OS is allowed to completely or partly boot, it can redirect the boot process using utilities written for the first OS.

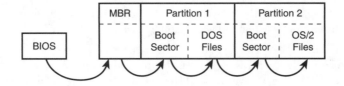

In all these designs, the software that redirects the boot process from one OS to another is known as a *boot loader*. All OSs come with a boot loader of one sort or another. Most work very much like one or more of the designs illustrated in Figures 4.1 through 4.4, but others use some variant, such as bypassing a partition's boot sector or selecting from two or more OSs that reside on a single partition. It's also possible to chain one boot loader after another. In such a multitiered boot process, you might need to make multiple decisions, as in selecting from UNIX or DOS variants, and then for each, selecting the specific OS you want to run (Linux or FreeBSD for UNIX variants, for example, and PC DOS 2000 or Windows 98 for DOS variants).

It's important to realize that even a "normal" MBR can boot something other than the first partition. You could set the MBR to boot the second partition, for example, which could then contain a boot loader that can redirect the boot process to the first partition. A stock MBR can only boot directly to a primary partition, however—one of the four that's most directly supported by the disk partitioning scheme of Intel PCs. Some MBR-resident boot loaders can redirect the boot process to logical partitions, though, which greatly expands your boot options.

▶ To learn more about partition types, **see** "Partition Types," **p. 119**.

Partition Hiding

One additional function of the boot loader is often quite important: partition hiding. Sometimes an OS becomes confused if it sees another OS's partitions. Actually, two related issues are involved here:

- **The active partition**—One of the primary partitions on the disk is normally marked as *active*, meaning that it's the boot partition or that it's the partition seen by the OS in control of the computer. If the wrong partition is marked as active, some OSs become confused.

- **Visible partitions**—Partitions contain codes that help OSs identify them. For example, a Windows 9*x* FAT-32 partition uses a different code than does a BeOS BFS partition. Occasionally a partition should be marked as invisible, however. For example, both OS/2's HPFS and Windows NT's NTFS use the same partition code, which can sometimes confuse one or the other OS. It's therefore helpful to be able to hide those partitions which belong to the OS that's not running.

Different boot loaders handle partition hiding in different ways. For example, Linux's LILO includes sophisticated but difficult-to-configure partition hiding options, whereas IBM's Boot Manager automatically hides all but one primary partition on a disk without user intervention. I provide more details for various specific boot loaders later in this chapter.

The 1024-Cylinder Limit Revisited

Chapter 3 introduced the concept of the 1024-cylinder limit as it relates to the BIOS. In brief, the BIOS is limited in how much hard disk space it can address. BIOSs from the mid-1990s and earlier cannot typically read past 504MB on an IDE hard disk. Today's computers have limits of closer to 8GB because they make more efficient use of the data structures relating to cylinder/head/sector (CHS) addressing.

▶ To learn more about the 1024-cylinder limit, **see** "EIDE and SCSI Hard Disk Handling," **p. 75**.

From the preceding discussion, you might think that the 1024-cylinder limit is of little consequence in booting an OS; after all, the BIOS passes control to boot loaders early in the process. If an MBR boot loader has control of the system, the 1024-cylinder limit should no longer be a concern. Unfortunately, the situation isn't that simple. Specifically, although the BIOS does relinquish control of the computer early in the process, boot loaders and even early disk accesses by many operating systems continue to rely on the BIOS. The problem is that boot loaders are so small that they cannot contain their own disk drivers. For this reason, boot loaders use the BIOS's INT13 calls for disk access until the OS is fully loaded and running its own drivers. The raw INT13 calls are tied to CHS addressing, so they can't load any OS that resides beyond the 1024-cylinder limit. In theory, a boot loader could use a newer BIOS's extended INT13 calls to use logical block addressing mode access to avoid the 1024-cylinder limit, but this would require support at each subsequent step, including the OS's boot sector code and early disk accesses by the OS. Although this support might become common one day, today it's safest to assume that it does not exist.

▶ To learn more about LBA Mode, **see** "Using LBA Mode in EIDE and SCSI Drives," **p. 79**.

N O T E One boot loader that isn't restricted by the BIOS 1024-cylinder limit is the nuni loader, available at

`ftp://metalab.unc.edu/pub/Linux/system/boot/loaders/`

This boot loader is restricted to booting Linux, however, so really it's useful only on a Linux-only system or when you can use it as a secondary loader on a partition that itself falls under the 1024-cylinder limit—in which case it's probably not necessary. ■

When you boot an OS, certain files must fall below the 1024-cylinder limit. Specifically, the files that the OS loads before loading its own disk drivers must be so located. Other OS files can fall above that limit, assuming the OS does not rely on the BIOS for disk accesses. In theory, then, an OS's boot partition can straddle the 1024-cylinder limit, as shown in Figure 4.5. Precisely what files must fall below the 1024-cylinder limit vary from one OS to another. For Linux, the only required file is the Linux kernel. For Windows or OS/2, an assortment of drivers and configuration files must all reside below this line.

FIGURE 4.5
Partition 2 might still be bootable if sufficient OS/2 files fall below the 1024th cylinder.

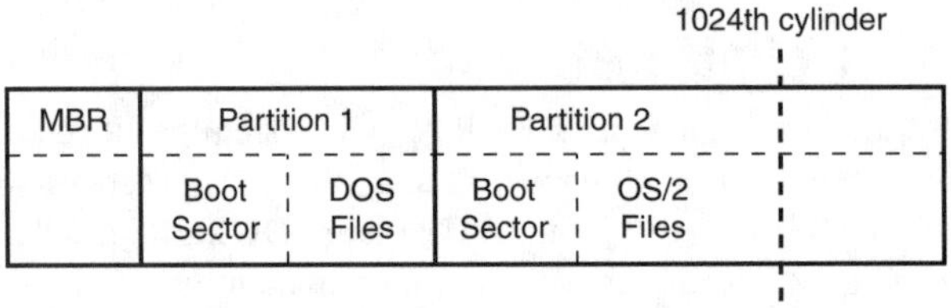

Different OSs and boot loaders use different rules to determine whether to even attempt to boot a partition that straddles the 1024th cylinder. The *Linux loader (LILO)* program used by Linux, for example, will enable you to boot a Linux system in this way as long as the kernel resides below the 1024th cylinder. OS/2's Boot Manager, by contrast, won't even make the effort. Each of these decisions is reasonable, given the design of the boot loaders and OSs in question.

- When LILO configures itself for Linux, it records the raw location of the Linux kernel, so it will no longer work if the kernel moves, whether the kernel moves to a location above or below the 1024th cylinder. If the user subsequently reinstalls a LILO boot loader, the utility locates the new kernel position and makes a new determination of whether it's suitable.

- OS/2 relies on several files to boot. By design, Boot Manager can't know about these files or ensure that they don't move. If Boot Manager allowed selection of a partition that straddles the 1024th cylinder, it might work initially, but the user could update a driver file and find that the system suddenly fails to boot.

N O T E It's possible to trick Boot Manager by creating a partition that falls below the 1024th cylinder, making it bootable, and then expanding the partition's size with a utility such as PowerQuest's PartitionMagic. I don't recommend doing so, however, because a driver update can then result in an unbootable system. ▪

In general, it's safest to keep all your bootable partitions entirely below the 1024-cylinder limit. If necessary, you can create two partitions for an OS to do so, using one that resides below this point to boot and the other for program and data storage.

Multi-Disk Arrangements

Microsoft OSs support booting only from the first physical disk. If you have two or more hard disks, though, you might want to boot from a second or later disk. Many OSs, including OS/2, Linux, and BeOS, support booting from disks other than the first, although you need the help of a boot loader program to configure your system in this way—a single-OS MBR can't redirect the boot process to the second or later disk. Your BIOS must also support booting from a second or later disk, as well. Most BIOSs support booting from a second IDE or EIDE disk, and many support booting from a third or fourth drive, as well. Most SCSI host adapters with boot BIOSs support booting from any of the first four physical disks. Most BIOSs support direct access to only four disks, so booting from a fifth or later disk is generally not possible.

N O T E These capabilities and restrictions refer to physical disks, not partitions. ▪

If you install an OS on a second or subsequent disk, the same rules apply to it that apply to the same OS when run from the first physical disk. For example, if an OS requires a primary partition to boot, it has the same requirement on the second disk as it does on the first. Similarly, the 1024-cylinder limit applies to both physical disks. The 1024-cylinder point might fall at a different location, expressed in megabytes, on each disk present in a computer, however. For example, 1024 cylinders might equate to 8GB on one disk but to 2GB on another.

Part

II

Ch

4

Single-OS Boot Loaders

Figure 4.1 illustrates a single-OS boot process. You can think of both the MBR and Partition 1's boot sector as containing single-OS boot loaders. These boot loaders, unlike the ones I describe in the rest of this chapter, are hard-coded to boot a single OS. By default, most versions of DOS and Windows 9x ship with and install single-OS boot loaders. OS/2 can also be configured in this way. Many other OSs, including Windows NT, Linux, and BeOS, ship with boot loaders that are more capable but that can be configured to behave as if they were single-OS boot loaders.

Most OSs rely on a unique boot sector. For example, Linux's boot sector won't boot DOS, and DOS's boot sector won't boot Linux. For this reason, many OSs overwrite their partitions' boot sectors when they install. If you use a multi-OS boot loader that's located in a partition's boot sector, you might need to reinstall that boot loader after you install a new OS.

Some OSs, including those from Microsoft, also overwrite the MBR at installation time. The standard Microsoft MBR is a single-OS boot loader, even for Windows NT. (NT's multi-OS boot loader resides in the boot sector.) This means that you must reinstall your MBR-based boot loader after installing a Microsoft OS. Most other OSs are more careful to preserve the MBR when they install, or at least give you an option to leave the MBR untouched.

As I mentioned before, a standard single-OS MBR can be configured to boot any one of four primary partitions. This task is usually accomplished by using an OS's FDISK utility. Most FDISK programs refer to the partition that the MBR will boot as the *active* partition, but some might use another term, such as *bootable*. In general, you should have only one active partition per hard disk.

▶ To learn more about DOS, Windows, and OS/2 FDISK programs, **see** "Tools for Disk Partitioning," **p. 133**.

Some OSs, such as OS/2 and some varieties of DOS, can see only one primary partition per physical disk. In the case of primary partitions on the second and subsequent disks, OS/2 sees the active partition, but this designation might not indicate that the partition is actually bootable. (OS/2 and DOS can both see several logical partitions per disk, so you can use logical partitions if you need several partitions.)

Designs for Multi-OS Boot Loaders

You've probably realized by now that there's considerable variety in boot loaders, and that their capabilities vary substantially and interact with the OSs being booted. In this section I describe the basic types of boot loaders, including their strengths and weaknesses. Most boot loaders fall into one of these categories, though some might contain aspects of two or more, and a few can actually be used in any of several categories, depending on how the product is configured.

Floppy-Based Boot Loaders

Figure 4.1 depicts the boot process proceeding from the BIOS to the MBR on a hard disk. Depending on a computer's configuration, though, the boot process can proceed from the BIOS to a floppy disk or to some other medium. In fact, one common configuration has the computer check the floppy disk first, and only if that fails does the system check the hard disk. This arrangement enables you to boot a floppy-based OS quickly and easily, without altering your hard disk configuration or even your BIOS settings. Such a configuration also provides an opportunity for you to use a floppy-based boot loader.

Instead of placing a boot loader on the hard disk, the boot loader can be placed on a floppy. If the boot loader is small, as they usually are, this approach can result in quick booting of the system. Linux's LILO can be installed on a floppy disk in this way. One variant of this approach is to install a small OS, such as DOS, on the floppy and then use a utility program to boot another OS. You can boot Linux in this way by placing the Linux kernel on the floppy disk and using the DOS LOADLIN.EXE program to boot Linux.

Why would you want to use a floppy-based boot loader? For most people most of the time, the technique offers few or no advantages, but there are a few circumstances in which it might be useful:

- **Testing a new boot loader**—If a boot loader allows configuration in this way, it can be tested without modifying your hard disk's contents. Similarly, you can change and test an existing boot loader's operation in this way.

- **As a "key" to entry**—If you want to keep one OS off-limits to some people, you can configure a main boot loader to ignore that OS and then use a boot loader floppy to enable that access. This approach doesn't constitute serious security because it's easy to install a new boot loader, but it might be enough to keep young children from accidentally booting the wrong OS, for example.

- **Testing a new Linux kernel**—Using a DOS boot floppy and LOADLIN.EXE to boot a Linux kernel can be a good way to test a new kernel without modifying your disk structures. If the kernel doesn't work correctly, just remove the floppy and reboot.

- **As a means to run DOS**—You can think of this method as one way to run DOS. You need not have a DOS partition on a computer to run DOS utilities—just boot from a DOS floppy.

Part

II

Ch

4

MBR-Based Boot Loaders

The MBR is a popular location for boot loaders, although many store additional files elsewhere on the hard disk. The MBR is popular because it's the first point at which the boot process can be intercepted in a normal hard disk boot. Taking over the boot process at the MBR means that there are fewer unknowns. For example, if a boot loader works in a partition's boot record, it doesn't necessarily know what's happened at earlier stages of the boot process. If a virus exists in the MBR, the boot sector-based boot loader could behave erratically. Also, the MBR's structure is well defined and does not change across OSs, so MBR-based boot loaders can often work on systems no matter what OSs are installed. Boot sector boot loaders, by contrast, depend on the structure of a given OS's normal boot sector and, if installed in the wrong location, can damage a partition. For example, the Linux LILO boot loader can render a DOS or Windows partition unbootable if installed in that partition's boot sector, though LILO can direct the boot process to such partitions when installed elsewhere.

MBR boot loaders do have their limits, though. Their size, for example, requires that they either be extremely limited or rely on files located elsewhere on the disk. By default, Linux's LILO takes the spare approach (and it still relies on one external file); when a system that uses LILO boots, it presents only a LILO boot: prompt. You can, however, configure LILO to present a somewhat less terse prompt, if you like, as described later in this chapter. You must then type the name of the OS you want to boot, or press Tab to see a list of options. Some others, such as PowerQuest's BootMagic, locate files in a FAT partition with which to present menus complete with graphics.

 If you want to restore a computer's MBR to a "generic" state, you can do so by using the DOS/Windows or OS/2 FDISK program. In MS-DOS or PC-DOS, type FDISK /MBR; in OS/2, type FDISK /NEWMBR. Either action causes the FDISK program to generate a boot loader that boots the currently active partition. (DR-DOS's FDISK program has this functionality, too, but it's a menu item within the FDISK program.) This trick can sometimes be useful even if you're not running any of these OSs. For example, Windows NT boot problems can sometimes be corrected by rewriting the MBR using DOS's FDISK.

Boot Sector–Based Boot Loaders

Boot loaders that reside in boot sectors are very much like MBR-based boot loaders in their advantages and disadvantages. Like MBR-based boot loaders, boot sector boot loaders must either be quite small or must position support files outside the boot sector.

Important differences between MBR boot loaders and boot sector boot loaders include the following:

- Boot sector boot loaders are less susceptible to destruction when an OS installation replaces the MBR. In such a situation, the new OS often ends up booting by default, but changing the active partition to the one hosting the boot loader restores normal boot loader operation.

  ▶ To learn how to set a partition active using various partitioning tools, **see** "Tools for Disk Partitioning," **p. 133**.

  N O T E You might think that a new OS has wiped out a boot sector boot loader because the boot loader is no longer called when you reboot. Chances are it hasn't been, though, unless you've installed the new OS in the same partition that hosts the boot loader. ■

- It's possible to temporarily disable the boot loader and boot an OS directly by changing the active partition. This is unlikely to be useful unless some software is incompatible with the boot loader, and such incompatibility is extremely rare.

- It's possible to switch from one boot sector boot loader to another by changing which partition is active. You might do this if you have two boot loaders, one of which loads OS A well but not OS B, and the other loads OS B but not OS A. A chained boot loader configuration might work better in such a situation, however, as I describe shortly.

Dedicated-Partition Boot Loaders

I am aware of only one dedicated-partition boot loader: IBM's Boot Manager. This boot loader requires its own primary partition in which to function. Its advantages and disadvantages closely resemble those of a boot sector–based boot loader, except that the boot loader itself consumes one primary partition. This can be a serious drawback because the total number of available primary partitions is extremely limited (four per disk, or three if you want to use any logical partitions). Of course, you could use a boot sector–based boot loader as a dedicated-partition boot loader by setting aside a partition just for the boot loader. You might do this if you wanted to use such a boot loader but had no suitable partition. One variant on this idea is to use a boot loader such as System Commander that requires space on a FAT partition on a computer that would otherwise contain no FAT partition, such as a computer that boots between Windows NT using NTFS and Linux using ext2fs.

Booting from a Running OS

Some OSs provide a means to boot from another OS. Typically, the OS that's used as a springboard to the second OS is DOS or Windows 9*x* because these OSs are common and because they allow low-level access to hardware and memory, so they can be shut down by software. The BOOT.EXE program that comes with OS/2 and the LOADLIN.EXE program that comes with Linux are two examples of programs to boot one OS from another.

BOOT.EXE is designed to allow OS/2 and DOS to reside on the same partition. (This program implements a feature known as Dual Boot in the OS/2 documentation.) When run, BOOT.EXE renames critical system files and changes the boot sector so that the specified OS runs on the next boot. The program then shuts down and reboots the computer. For example, if you're running OS/2 and type BOOT /DOS, the program configures the system to boot DOS and then reboots. You boot OS/2 from DOS by typing BOOT /OS2 at a DOS prompt. This utility can be very useful if you need to squeeze OS/2 and DOS or Windows 9*x* onto a single partition, but it's awkward because it provides no means to select the OS you want to run at boot time. If your system had previously been set to run OS/2 and you want to run DOS, you must boot OS/2 before you can run DOS. I generally prefer to install each OS on its own partition, but if you must install two OSs on a single partition, System Commander is generally a superior solution.

▶ To learn more about System Commander, **see** "V Communications's System Commander," **p. 107**.

Part
II

Ch
4

Linux's LOADLIN.EXE, by contrast, is a utility that's designed to directly load and run a Linux kernel from DOS. This can be extremely useful for testing new kernels and for use as an emergency boot method. For example, if you use PartitionMagic to move or resize a Linux boot partition, chances are good that the system will be rendered unbootable. If you have a DOS boot floppy (or a DOS partition) with LOADLIN.EXE and a Linux kernel, however, you can use these tools to boot Linux and restore your usual method of booting.

▶ To learn more about resizing partitions with PartitionMagic, **see** "Using PartitionMagic," **p. 196**.

N O T E When you use LOADLIN.EXE to boot Linux, you are not running Linux under DOS. The Linux kernel takes over the computer completely and removes DOS from memory. There might still be traces of DOS left behind, however. For example, if you used a DOS utility to configure hardware, that configuration will remain unless the Linux kernel explicitly alters it. ▪

  The fact that LOADLIN.EXE leaves changes DOS makes to hardware configurations can be extremely useful. There are a few hardware components that can be used in Linux only after they've been initialized by DOS. For example, sound cards based on IBM's Mwave chipset can be used in Linux as eight-bit SoundBlaster boards after the appropriate DOS initialization software has run. You could create a small DOS partition that runs this software and then runs LOADLIN.EXE to boot to Linux in order to automate this setup process and then list this DOS partition in another boot loader. (In the case of the Mwave adapter, this trick won't work to get the board's modem or 16-bit sound functionality working, unfortunately.)

LOADLIN.EXE can also be used by other OSs. For example, BeOS ships with a copy of LOADLIN.EXE that has been modified to boot a BeOS kernel. LOADLIN.EXE isn't a general-purpose boot loader, though, because it must be modified for each OS.

Chaining Boot Loaders

It's possible to use one boot loader after another one. Typically, you would use a boot sector boot loader after an MBR boot loader, as depicted in Figure 4.6. In this figure, the MBR-based boot loader is used to select between DOS and the secondary boot loader in Partition 2's boot sector, which is used to select between Linux and OS/2.

FIGURE 4.6
Chaining boot loaders enables you to use one boot loader to select OS groups and then pick a specific OS using the second loader.

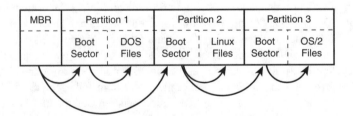

It is possible to chain two boot sector boot loaders in a similar fashion, or to involve a floppy-based boot loader as either the primary or the secondary boot loader. In fact, it's possible—though probably pointless—to configure a loop of boot loaders, where the second loader points back to the first. It's also possible to create a system with three or more boot loaders chained together. (In fact, if one includes single-OS boot loaders, Figure 4.6 depicts one three-stage process to boot OS/2.)

Why bother with two or more boot loaders? In certain specific cases there can be advantages. For example

■ Linux's LILO is very flexible but not pretty to look at. It also requires that the user know the name of the OS to be booted, or at least know to press the Tab key to find the options. You might therefore want to use a more user-friendly boot loader, such as IBM's Boot Manager or PowerQuest's BootMagic, to select between, say, Windows, OS/2, and Linux. LILO enables you to select between several different Linux kernels, however, even when booting a single partition, so it can provide useful options when you get to that point in the boot process.

■ If you install several OSs on a computer but use only one or two with any regularity, you can put those one or two on a primary boot loader, along with a link to a secondary boot loader that provides options for the additional OSs. This can help reduce clutter. Normally the added bother of maintaining the secondary boot loader isn't warranted, but it might be if the computer has multiple users, one or more of whom doesn't want to be bothered with the secondary OSs.

■ If one OS can be used to configure hardware, you can use a chained boot process involving a boot from a running OS, as described earlier, to configure your hardware in preparation for the second OS.

■ If you install OS/2 and DOS on a single FAT partition and use OS/2's BOOT.EXE program to select between OSs, and if you then install a third OS, such as BeOS, you will need a boot loader to select between BeOS and your combined DOS-and-OS/2 partition. As an alternative, however, you might want to consider using V Communications's System Commander to directly select between these three OSs.

In general, you don't need more than one boot loader to select between OSs. Most OSs do require some form of boot loader to boot past that initial selection. With most OSs, this secondary boot loader is a single-OS boot loader that resides in the boot sector, so it's easy to ignore. Linux uses LILO in this situation, and LILO requires more active configuration than do the standard single-OS boot sector boot loaders for most OSs. Most Linux distributions configure LILO automatically on system installation, but you might need to modify the default configuration, and you definitely need to change it when you recompile your kernel. Similarly, Windows NT uses its OS Loader to boot past the primary boot loader, but Windows NT configures OS Loader automatically at installation, so you don't normally need to be concerned with it.

▶ To learn more about LILO configuration and Linux kernel compilation, read *Special Edition Using Linux*, from Que.

Part

II

Ch

4

Many OSs' standard single-OS boot sectors can be damaged in various ways. Most OSs include some means of correcting this problem. In DOS and Windows, that method is to type SYS C:. In OS/2, the SYSINSTX command serves this function. (You might need to look on your OS/2 installation CD to find this program.) These commands rewrite the boot sector and restore certain critical system files. They can be run from a boot floppy, but be sure you boot the same version of the OS you have installed on your hard disk!

In sum, chaining boot loaders is quite common if you consider normal single-OS boot sectors to be boot loaders. Chaining more capable boot loaders is less common or helpful, though some OSs, such as Linux and Windows NT, require that this be done, even if the secondary boot loader is configured in such a way that it loads only one OS.

Common Boot Loaders

Most modern OSs ship with a boot loader that's capable, at the very least, of selecting between DOS or Windows 9x and the OS with which the boot loader comes. Many of these boot loaders are capable of booting a wide variety of additional OSs. In addition, a variety of freeware, shareware, and commercial programs add extra features to the mix, such as fancier selection screens and the capability to select from among several OSs installed in a single partition. Although I can't provide information on all these boot loaders here, this section provides information on some of the more common and capable boot loaders. Table 4.1 summarizes much of this information.

Table 4.1   Boot Loader Features

Feature	Windows NT's OS Loader	IBM's Boot Manager	Linux's LILO	Power-Quest's Boot Magic	V Communication's System Commander
Installation location	Boot sector and FAT or NTFS files	Dedicated partition	Boot sector, MBR, or floppy	Boot sector and FAT files	MBR and FAT files
Selection method	Menu	Menu	User types OS name	Menu	Menu
Configuration method	Edit text file	OS/2 FDISK	Edit text file	GUI tools	Menu-based tools

Feature	Windows NT's OS Loader	IBM's Boot Manager	Linux's LILO	Power-Quest's Boot Magic	V Communi-cation's System Commander
Partition hiding	None	Automatic configuration	Manual configuration (hard but flexible)	Manual configuration (easy but inflexible)	Manual configuration (easy but inflexible)
Boot OSs from logical partitions	Yes	Yes	Yes	Yes	Yes
Boot multiple OSs from single partition	Yes (several Windows versions)	No	Yes (several Linux versions)	No	Yes

Part

II

Ch

4

Windows NT's OS Loader

Windows NT (including Windows 2000) ships with a simple boot loader. This boot loader is an extended boot sector boot loader—its core is the boot sector code, but it loads and runs the C:\NTLDR program, which in turn loads the C:\BOOT.INI file for its configuration information. NTLDR then loads an appropriate boot sector, as specified in BOOT.INI, and executes it.

The end result is that when you boot a Windows NT system, one of the first things you see is a simple text screen that displays the version of the OS Loader and a list of options, such as

```
Windows NT Workstation Version 4.00
Windows NT Workstation Version 4.00 [VGA mode]
```

You use the cursor keys to select which OS you want to boot, and then press the Enter key to do so. In operation, NT's OS Loader is very much like other boot loaders.

Configuring OS Loader is, unfortunately, a bit tedious. If you installed Windows NT over another Microsoft OS, Windows NT will have created entries for whatever other OSs you already have installed. If you want to add OSs that reside on other partitions, you can do so, but you must go through several steps:

1. Open a Windows NT command prompt window.
2. Make the BOOT.INI file visible and writable by typing ATTRIB -H -S -R C:\BOOT.INI in the command prompt window.

3. Edit `C:\BOOT.INI` with a text editor.

4. Add a line for each new OS you want to install. The format for an OS entry line is

   `filename.ext="Menu Item Text" [/switches]`

   `filename.ext` is the name of a file that contains a copy of the boot sector from the partition in question. In most cases, no switches at the end of the line are necessary, though these can be helpful when switching between several versions of DOS or Windows 9x on a single partition.

5. Save the `BOOT.INI` file.

6. Type `ATTRIB +H +S +R C:\BOOT.INI` to restore `BOOT.INI` to its original read-only system file state.

Note that step 4 casually refers to a file that contains a copy of the boot sector for the partition in question. Most OSs make it difficult to obtain such a boot sector. The easiest way I know to do so is to use the `dd` command from a UNIX-like OS. For example, to obtain the boot sector from the first partition of the first EIDE hard disk from Linux, you could type

```
dd if=/dev/hda1 of=bootsect.sct bs=512 count=1
```

This command places a copy of the boot sector in the file `bootsect.sct`, which you can then transfer to your Windows NT partition.

▶ To learn more about transferring files from one OS to another, **see** "Tools for Accessing Foreign Filesystems," **p. 329**.

As an example, consider the following `BOOT.INI` file, which allows the system to boot from Windows NT, FreeBSD, and Linux:

```
[boot loader]
timeout=30
default=multi(0)disk(0)rdisk(0)partition(1)\WINNT
[operating systems]
multi(0)disk(0)rdisk(0)partition(1)\WINNT="Windows NT Workstation Version 4.00"
C:\bsd.sct="FreeBSD"
C:\linux.sct="Linux"
```

The `timeout=` and `default=` entries specify, respectively, the timeout period in seconds and the default selection, as you might imagine. The first entry in the `[operating systems]` section was created by Windows NT on installation. The final two select the two UNIX-like OSs, using copies of their boot sectors stored on the Windows NT drive `C:`.

Unfortunately, Windows NT's OS Loader doesn't handle partition hiding or altering the active partition. Therefore, it's not very useful for selecting between Microsoft OSs on separate partitions. It also doesn't do a good job of booting OS/2 from an HPFS partition. These are serious limitations that restrict the utility of OS Loader in many multi-OS environments.

In most cases, the need to extract a boot sector to a file, and keep that file consistent with the boot sector for another OS, makes NT's OS Loader an awkward boot loader. I therefore recommend you leave it configured as it is at installation, to boot only Windows NT, or possibly to select between Windows NT and other Microsoft OSs that were installed on the system prior to Windows NT. If you want to learn more about this topic, you might want to read http://www.ntfaq.com/ntfaq/misc/directboot.htm, which has more information on configuring OS Loader.

IBM's Boot Manager

IBM distributes a boot loader known as *Boot Manager* with OS/2. Boot Manager also shipped with version 3 of PowerQuest's PartitionMagic partitioning software, but version 4 of PartitionMagic includes its own boot loader, known as BootMagic, which I describe shortly.

Boot Manager is a dedicated-partition boot loader—it requires its own primary partition to function. Boot Manager is configured through OS/2's FDISK or FDISKPM utilities, as shown in Figure 4.7.

N O T E   In the following discussion, I refer to both FDISK and FDISKPM as *FDISK*. ■

FIGURE 4.7
OS/2's FDISKPM utility lets you modify partitions, including Boot Manager.

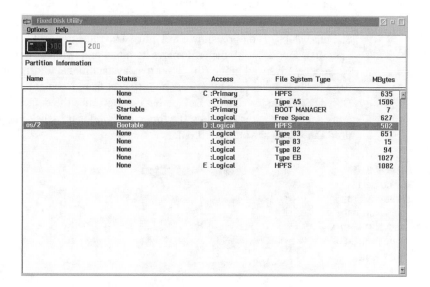

To add and configure Boot Manager, follow these steps:

1. Click an area of free space on the hard disk, preferably at the start or end of the disk. This free space must not be sandwiched between logical partitions, though it can reside between primary partitions.

   ▶ To learn how to create free space if none is available, **see** "Modifying Partitions After the Fact," **p. 181**.

2. Select Options, Install Boot Manager from the FDISK menu.

3. If the free space available exceeds the size required by Boot Manager (one cylinder), FDISK asks whether to locate Boot Manager at the start or end of the available space. Choose whichever is appropriate.

4. Click a partition you want to add to the Boot Manager menu.

5. Select Options, Add to Boot Manager Menu to add the partition to Boot Manager. FDISK responds by displaying the New Name dialog box, in which you enter a name for the OS, as shown in Figure 4.8. Click Set to add the partition.

FIGURE 4.8

Partition names need not resemble the volume labels you specify when you format a partition.

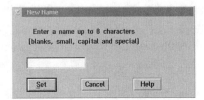

6. Repeat steps 4 and 5 for each OS you want to add to Boot Manager's menu.

7. Select Options, Set Startup Values to set Boot Manager's defaults. FDISK displays the Startup Values dialog box shown in Figure 4.9. You can use this dialog box to determine how long Boot Manager displays its menu and whether to display information in Normal or Advanced mode (the latter displays additional information about the partitions to be booted but is otherwise no different from Normal mode). In addition, the OS you select in the Startup Default list box becomes the default and is booted if you don't select any other OS when the timeout period is up. Click Set when you've configured the values as you want them.

FIGURE 4.9

The Startup Default list box is small, but you can scroll through the items using the arrow buttons on the right of the box.

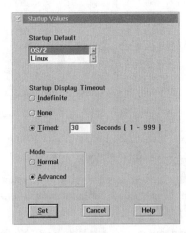

TIP If you want Boot Manager to boot whichever OS you last booted as a default, rather than a fixed OS, do not select Options, Set Startup Values. You won't be able to set the timeout period or change the mode of Boot Manager's display, but it will boot the previously booted OS as a default.

8. Select Options, Exit (F3) to close FDISK and save your changes. FDISK enables you to abandon your changes or save them. If you save your changes, OS/2 forces you to reboot your system immediately.

N O T E If you're using PartitionMagic 3.0 to install Boot Manager, the procedure to install and configure Boot Manager isn't identical to what I've described here, but the principles are the same. Consult the PartitionMagic documentation for details. ▪

Boot Manager is a powerful boot loader capable of booting most OSs. The version that ships with OS/2 4.0 fails to hide non-boot primary partitions when booting a FAT-32 partition, however, which often results in an inability to boot Windows when installed on FAT-32. This might limit Boot Manager's usefulness in such environments. The version of Boot Manager that ships with PartitionMagic, however, handles FAT-32 partitions properly.

Boot Manager's main drawback is that it consumes a primary partition. Given the fact that the PC's partitioning scheme only allows four primary partitions (or three plus an extended partition in which all logical partitions reside), this limit is a major drawback, particularly if you want to install several OSs that must boot from primary partitions.

Linux's LILO

In many respects, Linux's LILO is one of the most flexible boot loaders available. It can install itself on a floppy disk's boot sector, a hard disk's MBR, or a partition's boot sector. This flexibility allows it to easily function as a primary or a secondary boot loader. LILO has flexible support for partition hiding, but by default it doesn't hide any partitions; you must explicitly configure partition hiding yourself.

LILO is controlled through the file /etc/lilo.conf on a Linux computer. A minimal LILO configuration file might look something like this:

```
boot=/dev/hda
map=/boot/map
install=/boot/boot.b
message=/boot/message
prompt
timeout=50
image=/boot/bzImage
        label=linux
        root=/dev/hda2
        read-only
other=/dev/hda3
        label=dos
        table=/dev/hda
```

Part

II

Ch

4

This file enables the user to choose among two options: a Linux partition (identified as `linux` with a root filesystem on `/dev/hda2`) and a DOS partition (identified as `dos` with a `C:` drive on `/dev/hda3`). Important options in this file include

- `boot=`—This line specifies where to install LILO. `/dev/hda` is Linux's way of identifying the first EIDE hard disk; this results in installation in the MBR. LILO could go in the Linux partition's boot sector by specifying `/dev/hda2` instead, or on a floppy by specifying `/dev/fd0`.

> **CAUTION**
>
> If these device identifiers mean nothing to you, read a good book on Linux before you attempt to configure LILO by hand. In some cases, a mistake in partition identification can damage other OSs. A general-purpose Linux title you might want to consider is Tackett and Burnett's *Special Edition Using Linux*, from Que.

> **N O T E**   If you want to use LILO on a system that also runs Windows NT, it's best to place LILO on the Linux boot partition, not on the MBR. Windows NT expects to see a plain MBR boot loader, and doesn't get along well with LILO when it's installed in the MBR. ■

- `map=`—This line specifies the location of the map file, which stores data used by LILO, essentially as an extension to what can be fit in a boot sector. You should not normally need to modify this line.
- `install=`—This line points to a template for a boot sector. You should not normally need to modify this line.
- `message=`—This option specifies a file with additional information to be displayed at boot time. For example, the message file could contain information on the available boot option or a prompt to press the Tab key to see the available options. The message file is an ordinary text file, so you can create it with a text editor.
- `prompt` and `timeout=`—These lines control the boot-time LILO user interface. The first causes LILO to display its boot prompt, and the second causes LILO to boot the default system in the specified time (given in tenths of a second).
- `image=`—This line indicates the start of a specification for a Linux boot option. It points to the Linux kernel to be booted.
- `label=`—This line specifies the boot label to be used for the OS—what the user types to boot the OS.
- `root=`—This line specifies the root filesystem to be used by a Linux boot.
- `read-only`—This line indicates that the filesystem is to be mounted read-only. This is normal (and generally required) for a Linux boot. The kernel later remounts the filesystem in read/write mode.

- `other=`—This line is what you use to indicate booting a non-Linux OS.
- `table=`—This line lists the device on which the partition table for the OS is located. This line can often be omitted.

When you've edited your `/etc/lilo.conf` file to your liking, you must type `lilo` to install the new configuration on the boot device. You should see output listing each partition's label, with an asterisk (*) denoting the default boot partition (the first one listed, unless you use `default=` to change it).

LILO is flexible enough to be used to boot most OSs, but it's difficult to configure and suffers from several additional limitations:

- An error in the `/etc/lilo.conf` file can produce a system that's completely unbootable, and perhaps even damaged. (For example, if you accidentally specify a DOS or Windows partition in the `boot=` line, you'll render that OS unbootable, at least until you repair it by typing `SYS C:` from an appropriate boot floppy.)
- Setting up partition hiding requires specifying several additional rules (see the `user.tex` file in the LILO documentation directory under `/usr/doc` on your Linux installation for details).
- Most other boot loaders present menus that require a user merely to select the desired OS using arrow keys at boot time. LILO, on the other hand, requires that the user type the name of the OS. This isn't a huge problem for people who understand LILO, but it's less obvious to those unfamiliar with the system.

Despite these flaws, LILO is the usual method used to boot a Linux system. Because of its flexibility, it can be configured as a single-OS secondary boot loader, installed on Linux's boot partition. Used in this way, LILO can be transparent in everyday use, although you must still reinstall it whenever you upgrade your Linux kernel. If you don't mind typing the name of the OS you want to boot, LILO can be configured to allow booting several other OSs, too.

PowerQuest's BootMagic

BootMagic is a program that ships with PowerQuest's (`http://www.powerquest.com`) PartitionMagic utility program, and is available separately. BootMagic works by inserting itself into the boot process after the boot sector has done its work. It essentially replaces DOS or Windows boot files, instead loading a boot loader. If the original DOS or Windows system is selected for booting, BootMagic reestablishes the correct files for booting. If the user opts to load another OS, BootMagic passes control to that OS's boot sector.

BootMagic requires a FAT partition in order to operate; you cannot install it if your hard disk contains only non-FAT partitions, such as Linux ext2fs, OS/2 HPFS, and BeOS BFS partitions. It's also most easily configured if you have a working Windows system. Figure 4.10 shows the main BootMagic Configuration window, which lets you add and remove items from the BootMagic menu, as well as configure those items.

FIGURE 4.10
BootMagic's main configuration options are easy to use.

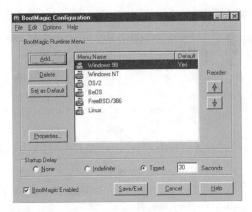

To add an item to BootMagic's menu, click Add. This action produces the BootMagic Add OS dialog box shown in Figure 4.11. If the partition you want to add isn't listed, click the Advanced check button, which expands the list to all available partitions.

FIGURE 4.11
By default, BootMagic lists only those partitions that it identifies as possibly bootable.

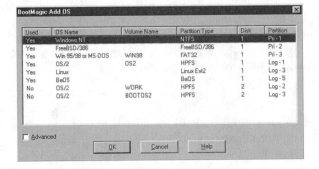

Click one of the partitions, and then click OK. BootMagic responds by displaying the BootMagic Menu Item Properties dialog box shown in Figure 4.12. You can alter the name of the OS and change the icon that appears next to it when you boot. You can also customize which of the system's primary partitions will be visible when you boot this OS by clicking the Visible Partitions tab. You can retrieve the BootMagic Menu Item Properties dialog box by selecting a menu entry and clicking Properties in the main BootMagic Configuration window, should you decide to change something about the setup.

After you've added all your partitions, check that the BootMagic Enabled button in the BootMagic Configuration window is selected, and click Save/Exit. BootMagic sets itself up and, the next time you boot, you're greeted by the BootMagic menu.

Overall, BootMagic is a good boot loader for selecting between OSs stored on separate partitions. Its requirement for a FAT partition can be limiting in a few cases, but not extraordinarily so.

FIGURE 4.12
Each OS can have a lengthy name and a unique icon associated with it.

V Communications's System Commander

BootMagic is essentially the boot loader that comes with an extraordinarily capable partition management program (PartitionMagic, described in more detail in Chapters 6 and 8). V Communications's System Commander, by contrast, is an extraordinarily capable boot loader that, in its Deluxe version, comes with partition management software. System Commander is an MBR-based boot loader that stores additional support files in a primary FAT partition. Compared to the other boot loaders discussed here, System Commander's greatest strength is that it's capable of booting several OSs from a single FAT partition. For example, if you want to run Windows 95, Windows 98, OS/2, and OpenDOS 7.03 all from one partition, System Commander enables this configuration. It does this in a way that's similar to OS/2's Dual Boot mode using BOOT.EXE, by backing up critical system and configuration files and swapping them in and out as necessary. Unlike Dual Boot, however, System Commander gives you the choice of which OS to boot at system startup.

> **N O T E** System Commander comes in several different versions, from the stripped-down Special Windows 98 Edition to the Deluxe version. The Deluxe version is certainly the most capable and expensive, and comes in a red box, compared to the blue and yellow boxes for other versions. Check V Communications's Web site for more information: http://www.v-com.com. I focus on the Deluxe version in this section, though basic operation is the same across the different versions.

Once installed, System Commander is designed to be configured from its own boot menu, shown in Figure 4.13. This frees it from dependence on any OS, except that it must have a FAT partition on which to store its files.

Part

II

Ch

4

FIGURE 4.13
System Commander's
configuration tools are
text-based and detect
many system changes
automatically on boot.

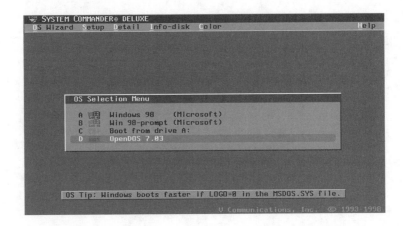

After you've installed System Commander, it attempts to detect the OSs you have installed.
Those it detects it lists in its main boot menu, as shown in Figure 4.13. If you want to change
the list of options, follow these steps:

1. Press Alt+S to enter the Setup Options screen.

2. Type 0 to enter the Selection Order, Add and Removal screen. (This screen looks much
   like Figure 4.13, except that the options along the top of the screen are different.)

3. To remove a selection, highlight it with the arrow keys, and then press Alt+R. System
   Commander asks you to confirm the choice and then removes the option if you confirm
   it.

4. To add a selection, press Alt+A. System Commander provides you with an option to
   choose a partition, a copy of an MBR stored on a disk file, or a floppy disk, as shown in
   Figure 4.14.

FIGURE 4.14
System Commander
provides many options
for a source of boot
information.

NOTE The Special Windows 98 Edition of System Commander supports only two bootable OSs,
and the Personal Edition supports only 12. The regular (yellow box) and Deluxe (red box)
versions both support 100 OSs, or so the ads claim—even *I* haven't attempted to install 100 OSs on
a single computer! ▦

5. Depending on your selection, System Commander presents a screen to select the specific partition, file, or floppy drive. Figure 4.15 shows the selection screen for the partition option. Select the item you want to add to your boot menu and press Alt+T to make it bootable, if necessary. Then press Esc to exit from the selection screen.

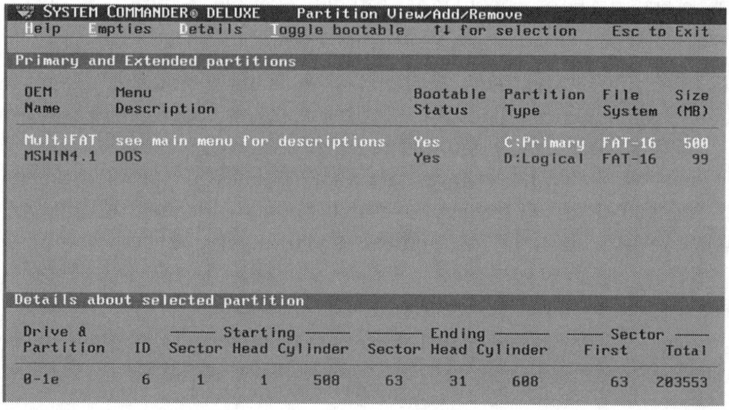

FIGURE 4.15
You can select a partition and mark it bootable even if System Commander didn't initially detect it as bootable.

6. You should now see the new entry has been added to the selection menu.
7. If you like, you can rearrange the selections in the menu by using the Move-to-Bottom and Move-to-Top menu items.

System Commander Deluxe supports many additional features, including security options, partition hiding options, an OS Wizard to help automate the process of installing a new OS, a partition resizer, and even a screen saver for the boot loader. In fact, the program's manual is 163 pages long, so I can't hope to describe it all in just a few pages. Overall, it's the most sophisticated and complete boot loader currently available. Lesser versions of the program support fewer options. All but the Special Windows 98 Edition provide useful features (the Windows 98 Edition's cap of two OSs limits its utility too severely for most situations).

System Commander might not be adequate for all your boot loader needs, despite its boatload of features. As I've mentioned before, Linux and Windows NT are both tightly tied to their own boot loaders. You can certainly use System Commander as your primary boot loader, however, and use these OSs' own boot loaders in a secondary role. Although unlikely, it's possible that you'll find an OS you just can't boot with System Commander, in which case you might need to use something else instead of or in addition to this product. Overall, though, System Commander is a program that can be very helpful after you install more than three or four OSs, and possibly fewer than that if the OSs you install are FAT-based OSs, such as different versions of DOS and Windows 9x.

Part
II

Ch
4

Summary

Boot loaders are what make multi-OS configurations convenient, or even possible. Without multi-OS boot loaders, we would have to use FDISK to change the bootable partition and then reboot. The design of the PC boot process provides several possible locations for "hooks" into the process, where a boot loader can take over and redirect the boot process to suit your desires.

The decision of what hook location is used is important, but it is not the only important factor in determining how a boot loader operates. Most boot loaders are quite limited in one respect or another, so it's important that you understand the features available in your chosen boot loader—or know what features you want, so that you can select an appropriate one for your needs. You shouldn't feel confined to just one boot loader, though; you can chain two or more together to achieve the mix of features you require. ●

PART III

Partitioning and Partition Management

CHAPTER 5

Hard Disk Partition Basics

In this chapter

The Need for Partitions

Most multi-OS configurations necessarily involve at least two *partitions*, or segments of a hard disk. There are several reasons for this, which this chapter explores.

The PC's partitioning scheme has evolved over time, from the simple partitioning needs of the original IBM PC XT running DOS to the needs of today's multi-OS systems with large hard disks. Because of this fact, the PC's partitioning system is a bit convoluted, but it does the job adequately—if you understand it well enough to design an appropriate partitioning setup for your hardware and software.

A partition is a delimited section of a hard disk, analogous to the rooms of a building. Like a building's rooms, partitions can vary in size and tend to be used for different functions. Just as it's difficult to move the walls of a building, it's hard to change the partitions on a disk after you've laid them down, although it's not impossible. Unlike the rooms in most buildings, partitions appear in a strictly one-dimensional logical order—one partition follows another, which follows another, and so on. (Of course, the physical arrangement of partitions on a hard disk can be more complex because of the disk's multiple platters and circular shape, but in discussing partitions it's generally the logical arrangement that's important.)

Partitions serve several very important roles in today's PCs. This is particularly true of multi-OS computers; because of the differing needs of OSs, it's often necessary to create multiple partitions for such systems. Even if multiple partitions aren't strictly required, though, they can be very useful to help protect and organize your data.

Each partition uses a single *filesystem*, which is a method of organizing data on the disk. Filesystems define certain limits for the data on the disk. For example, the filesystem determines the maximum lengths of filenames and what characters filenames can contain; maximum file sizes; and what types of characteristics can be associated with files, such as read-only, ownership, and so on.

N O T E The term *filesystem* can be used in a second sense, too: the structure of directories on a computer. In this sense, *filesystem* refers to what directories go in what other directories, either on a specific system or as part of a convention. For example, UNIX-like OSs have filesystems composed of directories called /var, /usr, /usr/local, /etc, and others. It should usually be clear from context whether a low-level data structure filesystem or a high-level directory structure filesystem is the intended meaning of the term. Where there might be ambiguity, I clarify the matter by being more specific. ■

Breaking Data into Manageable Chunks

One of the most basic functions of partitioning is to break data into chunks of reasonable size. Generally speaking, this segmentation is useful within an operating system, not between OSs. There are several specific ways in which you might want to break data into smaller chunks via partitions.

Partition Size and Disk Consumption Limits   Sometimes it's desirable or even necessary to use several partitions on a single computer, even for a single OS, because of limits on partition size or inefficient disk space use with large partitions. These problems are mostly related to the 16-bit version of the *file allocation table (FAT)* filesystem used in DOS and early releases of Windows 95. Specifically, FAT-16 has a total size limit of 2GB per partition, so to use a larger-than-2GB hard disk with FAT-16, you must break it into partitions. Furthermore, FAT, like all filesystems, allocates space in chunks of discrete size, known as the *allocation block size*, *block size*, or *cluster size*. Unlike most other filesystems, FAT's block size increases as the partition size increases, as summarized in Table 5.1 for FAT-16.

Table 5.1   FAT-16 Block Sizes

Partition Size	Block Size
1–127MB	2KB
128–255MB	4KB
256–511MB	8KB
512–1023MB	16KB
1024–2048MB	32KB

Partitions smaller than 32MB normally use FAT-12, which has its own similar set of block size increments for partitions ranging from 1MB to 32MB. This table presents the block size if you force the use of FAT-16 for a small partition.

N O T E   Windows NT (including Windows 2000) has the capability to create and use FAT-16 partitions of up to 4GB in size, but most other OSs can't use these partitions. I therefore recommend against using such partitions. You're better off using NTFS for partitions of that size with Windows NT. ■

FAT-32, introduced late in Windows 95's life cycle, also shares this characteristic, but its block sizes don't begin to increase until the partition sizes exceed several gigabytes. Table 5.2 summarizes FAT-32 block size increments.

Table 5.2   FAT-32 Block Sizes

Partition Size	Block Size
Under 512MB	Not supported
512MB–8GB	4KB
8GB–16GB	8KB
16GB–32GB	16KB
Over 32GB	32KB

Part

III

Ch

5

On most computers, files vary in size in a more-or-less random fashion; there's no rule that says files typically appear in multiples of the FAT block sizes. Therefore, part of the final allocation block for each file is wasted under any filesystem. On average, the wasted space (sometimes referred to as *slack space*) comes to roughly half the allocation block size per file, as illustrated by Figure 5.1. With FAT-16, this can amount to a substantial amount of disk space when considered across all files on the disk. On most systems, the average file size is somewhere in the 30–50KB range, so an average of 16KB wasted space per file in a 1–2GB partition means you can end up wasting roughly one-third of the hard disk's available space! If you're forced to use FAT-16 for some reason, therefore, breaking it down into small partitions can save a considerable amount of space. Whenever possible, I recommend using partitions of no more than 511MB.

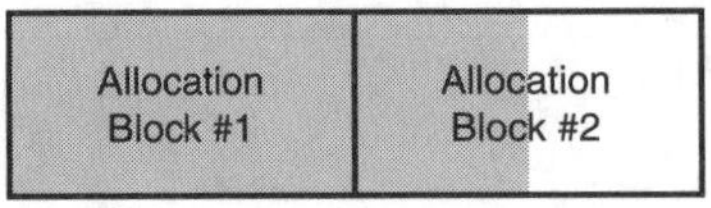

FIGURE 5.1
The average file (shaded area) fills only half of its final allocation block, resulting in wasted disk space.

Other filesystems also suffer from slack space, but not to nearly the same extent. OS/2's HPFS, for example, uses a 512-byte (0.5KB) allocation block size on all files for partitions of any size. Linux's ext2fs block size is variable but is usually set to 1KB. Windows NT's NTFS block size can be set from 0.5KB to 64KB at partition format time, with defaults that increase with partition size.

Isolating Types of Data   It's often helpful to be able to isolate different types of data on different partitions. For example, you might want to put basic OS system files on one partition, program files on another, and data files on a third. This type of arrangement is particularly common on UNIX and UNIX-like OSs, which use *mount points*—each partition is mounted in a single directory structure. Therefore, one partition might be mounted at /home (where some UNIX-like OSs put user files), another at /usr (where certain types of system files reside), and a third at /var (used for many types of temporary system data files, such as printer spools and mail queues). All UNIX-style OSs use a root filesystem, identified by a slash character (/), as a base on which others are built.

You can implement data isolation in this way even on Microsoft-style filesystems, which identify different partitions by partition letters, such as C: and D:. The precise details of how you organize such partitions might differ from UNIX-style to Microsoft-style partition handling, but the basic concept is the same, as are many of the advantages. These include

■ **Easier disaster recovery**—Occasionally, a partition's filesystem will become damaged. If you use a single partition for all your data, this means you might need to restore it all. If you use separate partitions, your task becomes much easier. This is particularly true if the damage doesn't occur on partitions that are critical to booting the OS because you can still boot and use whatever recovery tools are available.

■ **Safer upgrades and reinstalls**—If you decide to upgrade or reinstall your OS, the process can go much more smoothly if your data and programs are isolated from the OS. You might be able to completely wipe all the data from a boot partition and then reinstall the OS, leaving your data files intact on another partition. Unfortunately, application programs often intermingle their files with OS files, especially in Windows, so even if you isolate your applications, you might need to reinstall some of them after an OS reinstall.

■ **Logical organization**—A carefully designed partitioning scheme can impose order on a potentially disorganized installation. Setting aside separate partitions for data files, applications, or other file types can help you keep your system organized and help you find your data files. The same is true of a hierarchical structure of directories, but sometimes a separate partition is just easier to think about, particularly in a Microsoft-style directory structure with drive letters.

■ **System protection**—You can keep a critical partition from filling up by using other partitions for temporary files, data files, and so on. UNIX system administrators often rely on this characteristic to keep a system bootable even if partitions like those holding temporary files or user directories fill up.

■ **Multiple filesystem types**—Even within a single OS, it's sometimes desirable to use two or more different filesystems (in the sense of low-level disk structures). For example, you might want to boot OS/2 or Windows NT from FAT, so that you can easily access the boot partition from a boot floppy, but use HPFS or NTFS for most programs and data files to gain the benefits offered by these more advanced filesystems.

Using multiple partitions in this way does have drawbacks, as well:

■ **More complex configuration**—You must keep the drive letters straight if you use a Microsoft-style OS, or set up more mount points if you use a UNIX-like OS. This usually isn't a big challenge, but it's a minor complexity you might prefer to do without.

■ **Getting the right size**—Judging the correct size for a partition can sometimes be difficult. This is particularly true when you're new to an OS. In fact, it's difficult enough to judge the correct sizes for UNIX-style filesystems that I recommend using as few partitions as possible—generally three: one for root (/), one for /home, and one for swap space.

■ **Shifting drive letters**—If you maintain multiple OSs that use drive letters, those letters can change when you change a partitioning scheme—sometimes even a scheme for some other OS. Occasionally this effect prevents an OS from booting or causes programs to stop functioning.

Overall, creating new partitions to isolate different types of data can be a useful technique when used in moderation. Most OSs can benefit from two to four separate partitions. After you become experienced with an OS, you might want to increase the number of partitions. Many experienced UNIX administrators like to use half a dozen or more partitions.

Part
III

Ch
5

Cross-OS Data Sharing   When two OSs use different filesystems natively and lack the capability to read and write each others' filesystems, it's helpful to use a third filesystem type (generally FAT) to share data between them. Naturally, use of this filesystem type necessitates a separate partition. (In a pinch, you can use a removable media device such as a Zip disk or even a floppy disk, provided your files fit on this medium.) How large you should make a cross-OS file-sharing partition depends on the size of the files you want to place on it. If you exchange only small files, a partition of a few tens or hundreds of megabytes should do. If you want to exchange files that are themselves hundreds of megabytes in size, you'll need a partition of 1GB or larger.

Using a large cross-platform partition can be useful if you want to work on multimedia projects using cross-platform tools. I've used 2GB FAT partitions as audio CD mastering areas, for example. I can record audio files in DOS or Windows 9*x* and then record them to CD-R in Linux.

Isolating OSs from Each Other

One of the most important functions of partitioning is to isolate OSs from one another. If two OSs can read and write the same filesystems, creating partitions might or might not allow much in the way of isolation, depending on the details of how each OS handles partitions. It's more secure than leaving the two OSs on a single partition, however, because you can reduce the accesses by one OS to the other's partitions when each OS boots from a different partition. There are several aspects to this function of partitioning:

- **Isolating boot files**—All other things being equal, it's generally best if each OS boots from its own partition because booting multiple OSs from a single partition often involves juggling critical boot files. A power outage or error during such an operation could make an OS unbootable. Similarly, keeping OSs isolated can reduce the risk of a virus that infects one OS from infecting another similar OS.

- **Protecting filesystems**—Sometimes two OSs treat two filesystems in somewhat different ways. For example, Windows 95 introduced *VFAT*, which is a way to use long filenames on FAT partitions. In fact, VFAT is really just ordinary FAT with a few previously unused data structures taking on meaning, so DOS and OS/2 systems can still read and write VFAT partitions, but without the long filenames. Because DOS and OS/2 ignore the long filenames, though, certain DOS operations, such as moving or copying files, corrupt the long filename information. Furthermore, some DOS and OS/2 utilities can damage all the long filenames on a VFAT partition. It's therefore best to keep DOS and OS/2 from using VFAT partitions whenever possible.

- **Separate configurations**—Sometimes you might want to install two or more versions of a single OS, or even two or more copies of the same version of an OS. You might do this to test the effect of different configuration options, to maintain two configurations that are mutually exclusive in some way, or to keep a minimal boot partition for use in disaster recovery. You might be able to achieve the effect you want with less radical methods than unique boot partitions, but sometimes you really do need separate partitions.

Some OSs, such as those in the UNIX family, give you control over which partitions are routinely mounted. Others, such as those in the lineage from DOS through Windows and OS/2, give less control. With these latter OSs, you might be able to control what's accessible by choosing appropriate filesystem drivers to load at boot time or by using a boot loader's partition hiding features.

▶ To learn more about partition hiding, **see** "The Job of the Boot Loader," **p. 86**.

Improving System Performance

One final reason to use multiple partitions is to improve system performance. If you have a single partition with all your data, you have no control over where the OS places any given piece of data. The result might be that there will be many large head movements as the system tries to locate data across the entire range of the hard disk. If you create multiple partitions, though, you might be able to restrict head movements to some subset of the hard disk, thus improving performance. This sort of isolation is much more likely to be effective in a multi-OS configuration than in a single-OS setup. Figure 5.2 depicts an efficient partitioning of a single hard disk for use by two OSs. Because OS system files are generally accessed frequently, they're located at the center of each OS's likely range of access, counting the shared partition.

FIGURE 5.2
An efficient partition layout clusters together partitions that are likely to be accessed from a single OS and locates the most often-used files near the center of an OS's range.

| OS #1 Data Partition | OS #1 Boot Partition | Shared Partition | OS #2 Boot Partition | OS #2 Data Partition |

Part III Ch 5

▶ To learn more about optimizing partitions for system performance, **see** "Tips for Optimizing System Performance," **p. 163**.

Partition Types

The PC's partitioning scheme provides for three different types of partitions: primary, extended, and logical. I describe each of these in turn in this section. These partition types are different from the partition type codes, which identify the type of filesystem a partition contains.

▶ To learn more about partition type codes, **see** "Filesystem Codes," **p. 130**.

Some OSs use unusual partitioning schemes that extend the number of partition types in one way or another. A handful use entirely different methods of partitioning a hard disk, but these OSs cannot coexist peacefully on a single hard disk. For the most part, these OSs are very old and very rare, so you're not likely to need to use them. One partial exception is FreeBSD, which has an option to use its own partitioning scheme, but it normally uses ordinary primary partitions and applies its own scheme within those partitions.

Primary Partitions

In the early 1980s, hard disks of 10 or 20MB were large, and the number of OSs available for PCs was small. Therefore, the partitioning scheme developed for IBM-compatible computers allowed for a maximum of four different partitions. The idea was that you'd be unlikely to want to install more than two or three OSs, and the idea of using more than one partition per OS seemed pretty silly, as well. Today, of course, matters are different, so the original four-partition scheme has been greatly expanded. The original four-partition limit is still with us, but today these partitions are called *primary* partitions. Information on the locations and sizes of these partitions is stored in the hard disk's *master boot record (MBR)*, which is part of the reason the number of primary partitions is not easily increased; the MBR data structures are simply too well entrenched in too many programs to be easily changed.

▶ To learn more about the MBR, **see** "The Post-BIOS Boot Process," **p. 86**.

Primary partitions are special in part because they're the most "basic" type of partition, but also because the standard MBR boot code only boots OSs that reside on primary partitions. In addition, some OSs (notably FreeBSD and those from Microsoft) must boot from a primary partition; these OSs cannot boot from another partition type. These restrictions make the limit of four primary partitions per hard disk a serious problem in some configurations. If you want to run more than three or four Microsoft OSs, you have no choice but to place two or more OSs on some partitions.

N O T E The OS boot limits don't necessarily apply to the entire OS, only to a few megabytes worth of files, or less in the case of DOS. You can therefore use a single fairly small primary partition to select between multiple Microsoft OSs. The bulk of these OSs can reside on logical partitions or even entirely separate hard disks. ▪

Some OSs' disk partitioning software lets you create only a single primary partition. With other OSs' programs, as well as with most third-party utilities, you can create up to four primary partitions per physical disk.

▶ To learn more about partitioning software, **see** "Tools for Disk Partitioning," **p. 133**.

Extended and Logical Partitions

To get around the four-partition limit, a special type of primary partition was developed. This partition, known as an *extended* partition, serves as a placeholder for additional partitions, which are defined outside the MBR. The partitions contained by the extended partition are known as *logical* partitions. Throughout this book, I refer to primary partitions and logical partitions, but I seldom refer explicitly to extended partitions. This is because extended partitions are themselves rather uninteresting; they serve merely as placeholders for the logical partitions. The MBR entries for extended partitions serve to keep OSs and utilities from allocating disk space for primary partitions where the logical partitions reside. Data structures outside the MBR define the logical partitions themselves. This arrangement is depicted in Figure 5.3. The physical layout of partitions on the disk runs from primary partition 1 through primary partition 3, and then continues with logical partition 1 through logical partition 3.

FIGURE 5.3
The use of extended and logical partitions can increase the total number of partitions available on a hard disk.

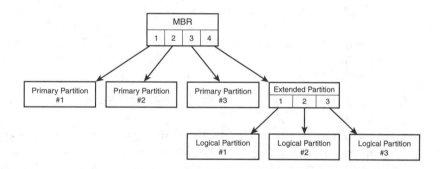

> **N O T E** You might occasionally see references in newsgroup postings to secondary partitions. This isn't a standard term, though. Chances are that either *extended* or *logical* was meant, but without context, there's no way to be certain. ■

Unlike primary partitions, there is no effective limit on the number of logical partitions possible. There are practical limits, however, imposed by factors such as the number of letters in the alphabet for OSs that use drive letters to address partitions.

The extended partition consumes one of the four available primary partitions, so if you use any logical partitions on a hard disk, you can have only three conventional primary partitions. This fact magnifies what can be a serious limitation in configurations where you want to install several Microsoft OSs, or others that consume primary partitions.

Because the extended partition includes size and location information in the MBR, it's not possible to place a primary partition between the logical partitions of a single extended partition. This can be limiting at times when modifying an existing configuration but isn't usually a major problem when creating a new configuration.

TIP Figure 5.3 depicts the extended partition as occupying the final portion of the disk. This need not be the case, however; one or more primary partitions can fall after the extended partition, and hence after all the logical partitions. Most partitioning software wastes most of one cylinder if you attempt to place an extended partition first on the disk, though, so it's generally most efficient to place one primary partition at the start of each physical disk. This procedure can have consequences for drive letter assignment in some OSs, however, which might be undesirable.

For years, all OSs used the same type codes for extended partitions, meaning that all OSs could, at least in theory, access the data within these partitions. As a workaround to the 1024-cylinder problem, however, Microsoft introduced a new type of extended partition. These partitions can't be accessed by OSs that haven't been modified to do so. You should therefore be cautious about activating Microsoft's "large hard drive support" when entering a Microsoft FDISK program if you intend to use non-Microsoft OSs on a large hard disk. Unfortunately, Microsoft OSs might not cope well with the portions of ordinary extended partitions that extend beyond the 1024-cylinder limit (generally around 8GB, but sometimes much less). This means you might have to arrange your partitions to keep all Microsoft OSs below that boundary, or all partitions from OSs that don't understand Microsoft's new large extended partition type off the entire extended partition. (OS/2 is the main OS that lacks support for this partition type.)

▶ To learn more about the 1024-cylinder limit, **see** "Getting Around the 1024-Cylinder Limit," **p. 77**.

A few OSs implement their own schemes to subpartition ordinary primary partitions. The BSD versions of UNIX do this, for example. They use a primary partition that's marked with their own OS code and break it into partitions that function much like logical partitions. Few OSs other than the BSD versions understand the contents of a BSD partition, but this system doesn't interfere with ordinary primary, extended, or logical partitions; the BSD system is normally implemented only within a single primary partition. Linux is one of the few non-BSD OSs that can read the BSD subpartitions or the BSD filesystem.

N O T E The BSD versions refer to partitions as *slices*. This is merely a difference in terminology between the UNIX tradition from which the BSD versions are derived and the tradition in the PC world. ■

N O T E The BSD versions support the use of their partitioning scheme on the entire PC hard disk. Used in this way, the normal PC partitioning scheme is ditched entirely. Such a hard disk can be used only by a BSD OS (or another OS, such as Linux, that can process the BSD partitioning scheme). Because you're interested in a multi-boot computer, you probably don't want to set up your hard disk in this way. When installing a BSD, you should be careful to not select the option to use the BSD partitioning system exclusively. The advantage of using such a scheme is that it's then possible to move the hard disk to a non-Intel computer that runs some variety of UNIX that understands the BSD partitioning scheme and retrieve data from the disk. ■

Some OSs' partitioning programs won't let you create an extended partition until you've already created at least one primary partition. This reflects an arbitrary limitation in the partitioning software, however, not a restriction on the partitioning scheme per se. Still, it might be best to create a primary partition at the start of each disk, both to make the most efficient use of available disk space and to avoid possible problems should some rare utility take exception to the lack of a primary partition.

Software's Varying Approaches to Partition Types

Different OSs and utilities treat the various partition types in assorted ways. Some OSs can access only one primary partition per physical hard disk, for example, whereas others can handle up to four of them. The OSs also vary in how they identify partitions. Understanding how different OSs treat partitions can be vitally important in configuring your system.

Drive Letters in DOS　DOS sets a model for partition management that's used, with variations, by other Microsoft OSs and by OS/2. The first thing to know about DOS is that it uses drive letters to identify disks, both removable and fixed. A: and B: refer to floppy drives. The first hard disk partition is C:, and additional disk partitions get subsequent letters. Devices such as CD-ROM drives, Zip drives, and so on, acquire drive letters after the last hard disk partitions. This lettering scheme means that the drive letters for some devices can change if you add or remove partitions.

DOS itself must normally boot from a primary partition on the first physical disk. The DOS boot partition need not be the first primary partition, but many versions of DOS have problems booting from a partition that comes after a non-DOS partition, so it's generally a good idea to put the DOS partition first on the disk.

N O T E　At least one boot loader, Ranish Boot Manager (http://www.users.intercom.com/~ranish/part/), claims to allow DOS to boot from primary partitions on the second or subsequent physical hard disk. Some BIOSs can also include options to alter the boot order of physical disks to allow booting from a second or later disk. ▪

When booting from a hard disk, drive letters for hard disk partitions are assigned as follows:

1. The boot partition, which is a primary partition on the first physical disk, acquires the drive letter C: (see Figure 5.4).
2. The active primary partitions on subsequent hard drives acquire drive letters. For example, if you have two physical hard disks, each with two primary FAT partitions, the active partition on the second disk is assigned the drive letter D:.
3. Logical partitions on the first physical disk acquire drive letters. For example, if the first physical disk has one logical FAT partition, it acquires the drive letter E:.
4. Logical partitions on subsequent physical disks pick up drive letters. If there are two logical FAT partitions on the second disk, they're assigned the letters F: and G:.

Part
III

Ch
5

FIGURE 5.4
Drive letter assignment in Microsoft-style OSs can produce a complex order of lettering.

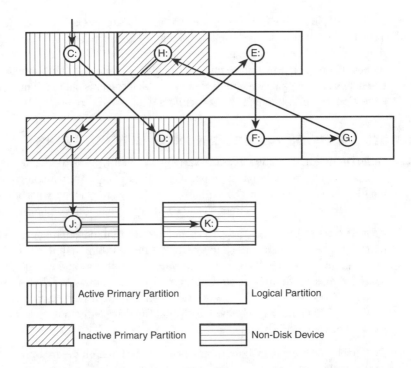

5. In some versions of DOS, previously unmapped primary partitions on all disks are assigned drive letters. Other versions of DOS ignore these partitions. For example, if each physical disk has two primary FAT partitions, the second primaries from the first and second disks will be assigned the letters H: and I:, respectively, if you're using a version of DOS that does this assignment.

6. Other devices, such as CD-ROM drives, Zip disks, and shared network drives, pick up their drive letters in an order determined by the order in which their drivers are loaded. Some of these drivers allow drive letters to be assigned by use of parameters in the driver entries in CONFIG.SYS or AUTOEXEC.BAT.

Aside from step 6, all these rules apply only to partition types that DOS understands—namely FAT-12 and FAT-16. DOS ignores non-FAT partitions, so they're not assigned drive letters. One exception is if you load a DOS driver for some other filesystem, in which case those partitions will be assigned drive letters after all the FAT partitions.

▶ To learn more about DOS drivers for non-FAT filesystems, **see** "Tools for Accessing Foreign Filesystems," **p. 329**.

MS-DOS's FDISK disk partitioning program can create only one primary partition per disk, and it enables you to create logical partitions only after creating at least one primary partition. MS-DOS's FDISK is also quite limited in that it doesn't report the presence of non-FAT logical partitions, so you can't use FDISK to delete other OSs' logical partitions. (Some other DOS versions, such as Caldera's DR-DOS, have partitioning tools that aren't quite so limited in this respect.)

Windows 95/98: DOS Revisited   Windows 95 and 98 are both built around DOS, so the same basic set of rules apply to these OSs as apply to DOS itself with respect to drive letter assignment. These OSs do include some additional support, however:

■ In the OEM Service Release 2 (OSR2) version of Windows 95, which shipped late in the Windows 95 lifetime, Microsoft added support for 32-bit FAT partitions. These partitions are detected and used just like the older FAT-16 and FAT-12 partitions. Windows 98 also includes this FAT-32 support.

■ Also in Windows 95 OSR2, Microsoft added support for the new extended partition type mentioned earlier in this chapter. DOS ignores these partitions, but they're just like other extended partitions as far as Windows is concerned.

■ You can assign drive letters for certain devices, such as CD-ROM drives, by using the Windows System tool in the Control Panel. Click the Device Manager tab, locate the device, and double-click it to get a Properties dialog box for the device. Select the Settings tab, and you can enter a range of drive letters for the device at the bottom of the dialog box (see Figure 5.5).

FIGURE 5.5
You can assign a range of acceptable drive letters for CD-ROMs and some other removable-media devices in Windows 9x.

Part
III

Ch
5

■ Windows 9x supports mapping of shared network drives to arbitrary drive letters. In Windows 98, for example, you can click the Map Drive icon in the toolbar of a Windows browser window to obtain the Map Network Drive dialog box, shown in Figure 5.6. You enter the network identifier for the share you want to mount in the Path field, and select a drive letter in the Drive field.

FIGURE 5.6

Windows 9x's network drive mapping provides more flexible drive letter assignment than does the usual hard disk drive letter assignment.

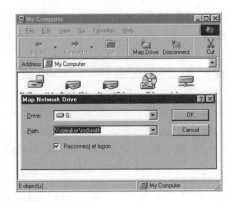

 TIP

For any device for which configurable drive letters are supported, consider assigning high drive letters. For example, if you set the CD-ROM drive letter to Q:, that drive letter likely won't change when you add or remove partitions. Any software that relies on the CD-ROM drive letter being fixed will therefore be unaffected by the change.

Windows NT's Partition Mapping Windows NT (including Windows 2000) is more sophisticated than Windows 9x when it comes to drive letter mapping; Windows NT lets you assign the drive letter associated with most partitions. To do so, you must start the Windows NT Disk Administrator program as the Administrator user. In Windows NT 4.0, Disk Administrator is a standalone program you can launch from the Start menu, but in Windows 2000, it's part of the Computer Management program located in the Administrative Tools folder. Disk Administrator presents a graphical view of the available space on a hard disk, as shown in Figure 5.7 (for Windows NT 4.0) or Figure 5.8 (for Windows 2000). To modify a partition's drive letter, right-click the partition and select Assign Drive Letter (Windows NT 4.0) or Change Drive Letter and Path (Windows 2000) from the pop-up menu. This action produces the Assign Drive Letter dialog box shown in Figure 5.9. You can then assign a drive a new identifying letter.

If you don't assign drive letters explicitly, Windows NT assigns drive letters in much the same way DOS and Windows 9x do, except that Windows NT understands FAT-12, FAT-16, and NTFS partitions and assigns them all in the same sequence. (Windows 2000 also understands FAT-32, but Windows NT 4.0 and earlier don't. Windows NT 3.51 and earlier support HPFS, but this support was removed from Windows NT 4.0 and can only be added back by using drivers from earlier versions of Windows NT.) You might find that FAT partitions receive different drive letters under DOS, Windows 9x, and Windows NT because of the different filesystem support in these OSs.

FIGURE 5.7
Windows NT's Disk Administrator is easier to use and more sophisticated than DOS's FDISK.

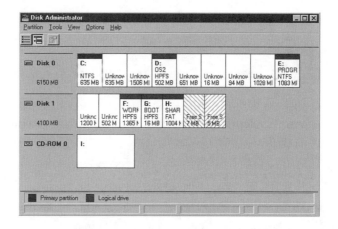

FIGURE 5.8
Windows 2000 combines several administrative tools from earlier versions of Windows NT into one tool.

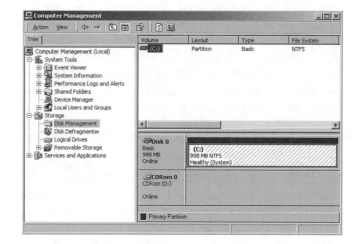

FIGURE 5.9
Click the drive letter selection box to change the drive letter, or select Do Not Assign a Drive Letter to eliminate the drive from those available to Windows NT.

Drive Letters in OS/2   OS/2 behaves very much like DOS when it comes to drive letter assignments. In particular, OS/2 uses the same sequence for assigning drive letters, with the following exceptions:

- **Boot partition**—OS/2 can boot from a logical partition or from a partition on something other than the first physical disk. OS/2 does not necessarily assign its boot partition the drive letter C:, but it does include many references to the boot drive letter in system files. Therefore, if you install OS/2 on anything but a primary partition on the first disk, you run the risk of making OS/2 unbootable if you make changes to your disk partitions that alter the drive letter of the OS/2 boot partition.

- **Multiple primary partitions**—OS/2 doesn't cope well with multiple primary partitions on a single hard disk. For this reason, OS/2's Boot Manager hides anything beyond the active primary partition, as do most other boot loaders that are OS/2-aware.

- **User-specified drive letters**—OS/2 provides no mechanism to override automatic drive letter assignments for removable media such as CD-ROMs.

- **Filesystems**—OS/2 supports FAT-12, FAT-16, and HPFS and assigns drive letters to all three interchangeably. If you use a system with both OS/2 and DOS or Windows, therefore, you might find that in OS/2 the letters assigned to some FAT partitions are higher than they are in DOS or Windows because an HPFS partition appears earlier in the sequence. Some third-party drivers for filesystems such as FAT-32 and ext2fs assign drive letters above those assigned to OS/2's native filesystems, though some of these drivers also support methods to assign drive letters within the usual sequence.

OS/2's FDISK program is one of the easiest to use partitioning programs to come with an OS. It actually comes in two versions: FDISK, which runs in text mode, and FDISKPM, which runs in OS/2's GUI environment. I refer to them both as *FDISK*. OS/2's FDISK doesn't make the presence of extended partitions explicit; instead, it labels each partition as either primary or logical, and FDISK creates extended partitions as necessary for the layout you specify. You can create multiple primary partitions or disks with no primary partitions using OS/2's FDISK.

UNIX Partition Mount Points   UNIX and UNIX-like OSs use a unified directory structure, as described earlier in this chapter. In UNIX, partitions aren't always automatically accessible; they must be mounted first. The OS mounts partitions at boot time according to instructions in the /etc/fstab file. When you install a UNIX-like OS, you might be asked what partitions you want mounted at boot time, and if so, the install routines create an appropriate /etc/fstab file. As the root user, you can also mount additional partitions, and depending on the configuration options in /etc/fstab, you might be able to do the same as an ordinary user.

▶ For more details on unified directory structures, **see** "Isolating Types of Data," **p. 116**.

N O T E DOS-derived OSs use a backslash character (\) to separate directories when specifying a complete pathname. For example, you might refer to the directory \some\directory. UNIX-like OSs, by contrast, use a forward slash (/) for this function, as in /some/directory. This difference can be distracting when changing from one OS to another. ▪

Most UNIX-like OSs don't make much of a distinction between primary and logical partitions, though some do require a primary partition to boot. UNIX-like OSs use a *device file* to provide low-level access to partitions. A device file is a special file that, when used by a program, provides access to a hardware device—a serial port, a keyboard, a hard disk, or a partition, for example. Device files usually exist in a particular directory on the hard disk, such as /dev. The rules governing the naming of device files vary from one OS to another. As one example, in Linux, device files in the /dev/hd*xy* family represent EIDE drives and those in /dev/sd*xy* belong to SCSI drives. In both cases, *x* is a letter from a through d or higher that represents the physical device, and *y* is a numeral representing the partition number. Numerals from 1 through 4 represent primary or extended partitions, whereas numerals of 5 and above represent logical partitions.

Linux ignores primary and logical status and lets you mount whatever partition you want in whatever way you want. Thus, you can mount four primary partitions from a single disk, and you can mount logical partitions before primary partitions. You can't mount a partition before the partition on which it belongs is mounted, though. For example, suppose you have four partitions: the root partition (/), /home, /usr, and /usr/local. You must mount the root partition first, and you must mount /usr/local after /usr. You can mount /home at any time after you mount /, however—before you mount /usr, after /usr but before /usr/local, or after /usr/local. Similar comments apply to other UNIX-like OSs.

UNIX partitioning software varies substantially in capabilities, so it's difficult to make generalizations. Some OSs, such as FreeBSD, can use unusual partitioning schemes, so these OSs' partitioning utilities are required for setting up these partitions. Other OSs, such as Linux, use normal PC partitions, so you can often use other OSs' FDISK programs to create Linux partitions.

▶ To learn more about disk partitioning software, **see** "Tools for Disk Partitioning," **p. 133**.

BeOS Partition Management   BeOS uses a partition mounting system very much like that of UNIX, but with a few modifications:

- ▪ There is no /etc/fstab file to map devices and mount points. Instead, BeOS locates partitions and automatically creates mount points as necessary.

- ▪ To access a device, right-click the desktop and select the device from the Mount option on the resulting pop-up menu. The partition then appears in a directory off the root filesystem.

■ By default, BeOS mounts most partitions in directories named after the partition's label. For example, if you create a DOS partition and call it DRIVEC, when you mount it in BeOS, it will go in the directory /drivec (BeOS converts the name to lowercase). One exception to this rule is the BeOS boot partition, which acquires the name /boot no matter what name the partition has.

BeOS, like most UNIX versions, is largely unconcerned with the distinction between primary and logical partitions. You can boot BeOS from either type of partition, and you can mount partitions of either type in whatever order you like.

Modifying Partition Mapping   Sometimes you want or need to change what partitions are visible to an OS. With a UNIX-like OS, you can do this by modifying the /etc/fstab file. This action won't actually make a partition completely inaccessible, but you can prevent the OS from automatically mounting the partition in this way or add a new partition to the OS.

In Microsoft-style OSs, your options are generally more limited. In Windows NT, you can use Disk Administrator to prevent the OS from mounting a partition, but DOS, Windows 9*x*, and OS/2 all lack similar functionality. For these OSs, your only options are the partition hiding feature of your boot loader and your ability to manipulate available partitions by adding or removing drivers for disk devices if you have a mix of SCSI and EIDE hard disks. Details differ greatly from one boot loader to another, but you can often configure a boot loader to hide a partition from a Microsoft-style OS.

▶ To learn more about partition hiding, **see** "The Job of the Boot Loader," **p. 86**.

> **CAUTION**
>
> Hiding and unhiding partitions can produce effects on assigned partition letters and can sometimes even render an unrelated partition unbootable because of changed drive letters.

Filesystem Codes

So far I've discussed OSs accessing partitions containing filesystems that they understand as if the task of identifying compatible partitions were magic. It's not, of course. Depending on the OS and filesystem type, several common methods of identification are available. These methods interact with the partition hiding techniques as implemented by many boot loaders. Understanding the methods used by OSs to identify the partitions they use can help you manipulate that process, if necessary.

Identifying a Partition's Format

OSs employ three main methods to identify the type of filesystem contained on a partition:

- **Filesystem type codes**—The partition tables in the MBR and extended partition contain special codes that are used to identify a partition's type. A partition type code is a 1-byte value, meaning that it ranges from 0 to 255 (or from 0 to FF when expressed in hexadecimal [base 16], which most partitioning software uses for reporting the type code). Most OSs, including DOS, Windows 9*x*, and OS/2, use the partition type codes as their primary means of partition type identification. For example, the partition types 1, 4, 6, B, C, and E (hexadecimal) belong to various types of FAT partition. If a partition uses some other code, most of these FAT-using OSs ignore it. (OS/2 and Windows NT also see type 7, which they use for HPFS and NTFS partitions, respectively.) If a partition bears one of these codes, the OS attempts to interpret it as that type of filesystem.

- **/etc/fstab entries**—In most UNIX-style OSs, the filesystem type can be specified in the /etc/fstab file. This information overrides partition table filesystem type codes. The drawback to this method is that it relies on the administrator getting the information right—but most OSs perform additional checks and abort a mount if the filesystem specified in /etc/fstab appears to be incorrect, so the risk of damage is minimal. Microsoft-style OSs have no analog to this method of partition identification.

- **Filesystem data structures**—Each filesystem type is unique and therefore bears certain types of data structures that can be used as digital "signatures" to identify a filesystem type. Linux is one OS that relies heavily on these filesystem data structures for filesystem identification. Rather than trust the filesystem type code in the partition table, Linux scans a partition for its signature and uses that information. In the case of a filesystem that's mounted via /etc/fstab with an explicit filesystem specification, this scan is used to double-check the assignment.

Part

III

Ch

5

N O T E   Although UNIX-style OSs, including Linux, often ignore partition type codes in partition tables in favor of /etc/fstab entries, this isn't always true during installation. At that time, no /etc/fstab file yet exists, so the install programs use partition type codes to prevent installation to inappropriate partitions.

It is possible to use two or even all three methods of identification. For example, OS/2 uses the partition type code as an initial filter. Any partition that's of a type OS/2 expects to be able to handle gets passed to each filesystem driver in turn, each of which attempts to match the filesystem data structures against the characteristics it has been programmed to support. If a match occurs, the filesystem is mounted. If not, OS/2 still assigns a drive letter to the partition but reports that the partition is unformatted.

The partition hiding features of boot loaders operate by changing the partition type codes in the partition table. Frequently, boot loaders hide partitions by adding 0x80 to their values—that is, by turning on the most significant bit. Sometimes another value is used for the hidden version of a partition, though. Whatever the precise method, this procedure effectively hides the partition from any OS that scans for the partition type code as an initial filter. OSs that don't use the partition type code in this way are unaffected by such partition hiding, however.

When Codes Collide

Occasionally, two or more partition types use the same partition type code for a partition. This situation can lead to some awkward happenings. The duplicate code use you're most likely to encounter is that between OS/2's HPFS and Windows NT's NTFS, both of which use the partition type code of 7.

Fortunately, neither Windows NT nor OS/2 will attempt to write to a "corrupt" partition, which is how each OS sees the other's type-7 filesystem. These filesystems are therefore fairly safe from true corruption—at least of the automatic sort. Both OSs do, by default, show drive icons for the "corrupt" partitions, and you can easily tell the OS to reformat these partitions. *Doing so will destroy the other OS's filesystem!* In Windows NT, I recommend either using Disk Administrator to hide the OS/2 HPFS partitions or extracting the Windows NT HPFS driver from Windows NT 3.51 or earlier to let Windows NT read HPFS partitions correctly. (For this operation to be legal, you need an unused Windows NT 3.51 license, however.) The only way I know of to hide NTFS partitions from OS/2 is to use the partition hiding features of a boot loader. Unfortunately, these boot loader features often apply only to primary partitions, so you might be stuck if you have any NTFS logical partitions.

Summary

Hard disk partitioning is a fundamental aspect of installing multiple OSs on a single computer. Most computers are delivered from the manufacturer with just a single partition, but you should change this configuration to achieve the best results with a multi-OS setup. To do so, you should understand the differences between primary, extended, and logical partitions, and you might need to know about variants on these used by specific OSs, such as FreeBSD. Each OS has its own unique approach to the interactions between different OS types, and it's important to understand how your OSs treat your partitions, or else you might find that you've installed your OSs in such a way that one or both won't boot reliably. Fortunately, you can often manipulate partition type codes using a boot loader to help achieve consistent booting. Some OSs, such as most UNIX variants, provide fine-grained control over how each partition is to be handled, so you're less likely to encounter serious problems as a result of a changed partition setup when using these OSs.

The next three chapters cover additional disk partitioning topics, and you should read them before embarking on the task of preparing your hard disk for multiple OSs. ●

Tools for Disk Partitioning

Partitioning Mechanics

Chapter 5, "Hard Disk Partition Basics," discussed why you might want or need to create multiple partitions for a multi-OS configuration and described the types of partitions available on x86 PCs. You should definitely read Chapter 5 before proceeding with this one because this chapter assumes a knowledge of these topics. This chapter expands on Chapter 5, describing the mechanics of creating partitions with an assortment of tools that come with various OSs and third-party utilities. You might want to read Chapter 7, "Tips for Optimizing System Performance," before you actually partition your system, however. If you want to install a new OS on a computer that's already running one or more OSs, you might want to modify your existing partition arrangement rather than create a new one from scratch. In that case, Chapter 8, "Modifying Partitions After the Fact," will be of great interest to you.

> **CAUTION**
>
> Do not delete any existing partitions if you intend to use the data on those partitions. If you want to shrink a partition, use an appropriate tool, as described in Chapter 8. Deleting a partition and then re-creating a new one of a different (or even the same) size in its place usually results in the loss of all data on that partition.

MS-DOS's and Windows 9*x*'s *FDISK*

One of the first disk partitioning programs was MS-DOS's Fixed Disk utility (FDISK). This program, which still ships with Windows 9*x*, has changed remarkably little in recent years. MS-DOS's FDISK is a text-mode program with a simple but somewhat awkward user interface. It suffers from limitations in a multi-OS environment but can still be quite useful for creating a basic partition setup.

 TIP MS-DOS's FDISK supports a command-line switch, /MBR, that rewrites the master boot record of a hard disk. This feature can be extremely useful if you want to remove an MBR-based boot loader such as System Commander or Linux's LILO.

▶ To learn more about the MBR, **see** "The Handoff to the OS," **p. 82**.

Creating FAT Partitions

MS-DOS's FDISK is tied tightly to the distinction between primary, extended, and logical partitions. The procedures for creating each partition type are therefore different.

> **N O T E** To learn more about primary, extended, and logical partitions, you should read Chapter 5, particularly the sections titled "Primary Partitions" and "Extended and Logical Partitions." ▪

The following directions assume that you're starting with a completely blank hard disk. You might need to adjust these procedures if that's not the case.

Creating Primary Partitions   To create a primary partition in MS-DOS's FDISK, follow these steps:

1. Run FDISK from the DOS command prompt and select option 1, Create DOS Partition or Logical DOS Drive, from the main screen shown in Figure 6.1.

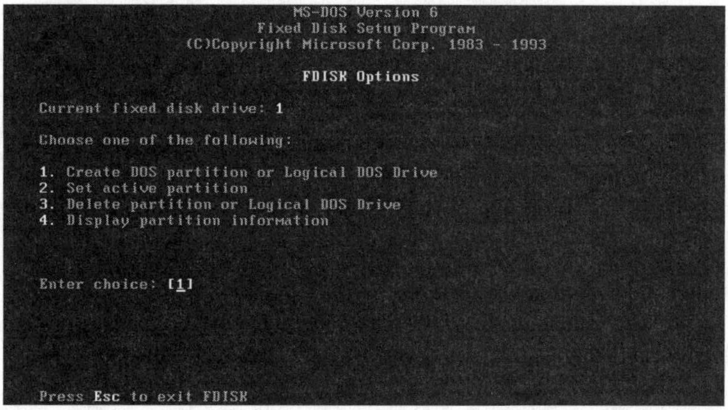

FIGURE 6.1
By today's GUI standards, the main screen of MS-DOS's FDISK is crude, but the program gets the job done.

```
                        MS-DOS Version 6
                     Fixed Disk Setup Program
              (C)Copyright Microsoft Corp. 1983 - 1993

                          FDISK Options

   Current fixed disk drive: 1

   Choose one of the following:

   1. Create DOS partition or Logical DOS Drive
   2. Set active partition
   3. Delete partition or Logical DOS Drive
   4. Display partition information



   Enter choice: [1]





   Press Esc to exit FDISK
```

2. The menu options should now change. One of the new options is titled Create Primary DOS Partition. Select this option.

3. If no other primary partitions on the disk exist, FDISK asks whether you want to devote all available disk space to the primary partition. If you select Y to this prompt, FDISK immediately creates the partition and informs you that it will reboot the computer when you press a key. If you select N, FDISK asks how many megabytes to devote to the primary partition and does not immediately reboot the computer.

4. When you're finished defining partitions, press Esc as many times as necessary to exit FDISK. The program then reboots the computer.

If you intend to boot from the primary partition you've just defined, you might need to make it active. You do this using option 2 (Set Active Partition) from the main FDISK menu (see Figure 6.1). In a multi-OS setup, however, it's possible that your boot loader will automatically adjust which partition is active at boot time, so this step might not be necessary.

Creating Extended and Logical Partitions   To create one or more logical partitions, you must first define a primary partition. After you've done that, follow these steps:

1. From the main FDISK menu (refer to Figure 6.1), select option 1, Create DOS Partition or Logical DOS drive. The menu options now change.

Part
III

Ch
6

2. One of the new options should be Create Extended DOS Partition. Select it. FDISK now displays the current primary partition's information and prompts for the size of the extended partition to be created, as shown in Figure 6.2.

FIGURE 6.2
FDISK interprets partition sizes in megabytes unless the number is followed by a percent sign (%).

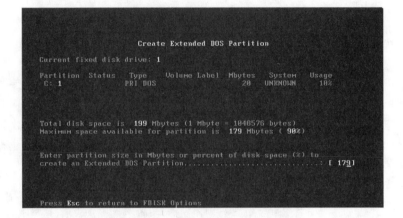

```
                         Create Extended DOS Partition

Current fixed disk drive: 1

Partition  Status   Type     Volume Label  Mbytes   System    Usage
  C: 1              PRI DOS                   20     UNKNOWN    10%




Total disk space is  199 Mbytes (1 Mbyte = 1048576 bytes)
Maximum space available for partition is  179 Mbytes ( 90%)


Enter partition size in Mbytes or percent of disk space (%) to
create an Extended DOS Partition...........................: [ 179]



Press Esc to return to FDISK Options
```

3. Enter the amount of the disk you want to devote to the extended partition. Chances are this will be all of it, even if you intend to define partitions for non-DOS OSs. (You can use an extended partition defined in one OS for another OS's partitions.) The only time you would want to create a smaller extended partition would be if you intend to place non-DOS primary partitions after the extended partition, say to control drive letter assignments while keeping several partitions for one OS close to each other.

▶ To learn more about drive letter assignments, **see** "Drive Letters in DOS," **p. 123**.

TIP If you want to place non-DOS primary partitions before the extended partition, you should define those partitions before using DOS's FDISK to create the DOS logical partitions. In fact, it might be easier to use some other partitioning software to create all your partitions.

4. After you enter the amount of space to be devoted to the extended partition, FDISK displays the new primary partition table, which should have one primary partition (or more if you used another disk partitioning utility to create more) and one extended partition. Press the Esc key to continue.

5. FDISK now prompts you for the size of the first logical partition. Type the value you want and press Enter.

6. If the size you entered was less than the total, step 5 repeats. If you want to stop defining partitions, you can press the Esc key; otherwise, enter a size for the next partition.

7. Press Esc as many times as is necessary to exit from FDISK. The program then reboots the computer.

You can use MS-DOS's FDISK to define partitions to be used by other OSs; however, the partition type codes might not be correct. You might therefore need to use some utility in the second OS to change those type codes. Some OSs change the codes automatically when you format the partition.

▶ To learn more about filesystem codes, **see** "Filesystem Codes," **p. 130**.

Deleting Partitions

You might want to use MS-DOS's FDISK to delete an existing partition, say to make room for a new OS. To do so, follow these steps:

1. From the main FDISK screen (refer to Figure 6.1), select option 3, Delete Partition or Logical DOS Drive. The menu changes to provide four options: Delete Primary DOS Partition, Delete Extended DOS Partition, Delete Logical DOS Drive(s) in the Extended DOS Partition, and Delete Non-DOS Partition.

2. Select the appropriate option. I present instructions that follow the third option, Delete Logical DOS Drive(s) in the Extended DOS Partition, because this is the action you're most likely to take to create space for a new OS.

N O T E You cannot delete non-FAT logical partitions using DOS's FDISK. To do that, you must use another partitioning program. ▪

3. FDISK presents a summary of the logical DOS partitions in the extended partition, as shown in Figure 6.3. Type the letter associated with the partition you want to delete, as in D.

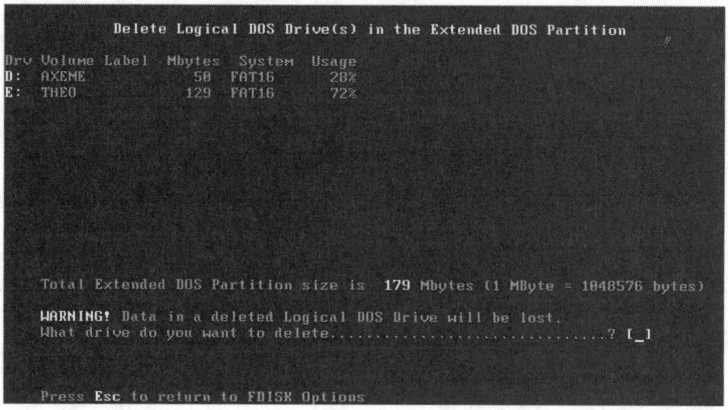

FIGURE 6.3
You identify partitions to FDISK by using their DOS drive letters.

```
              Delete Logical DOS Drive(s) in the Extended DOS Partition

Drv Volume Label  Mbytes  System  Usage
D:  AXEME            50    FAT16    28%
E:  THEO            129    FAT16    72%




          Total Extended DOS Partition size is  179 Mbytes (1 MByte = 1048576 bytes)

          WARNING! Data in a deleted Logical DOS Drive will be lost.
          What drive do you want to delete..............................? [_]

          Press Esc to return to FDISK Options
```

Part
III

Ch
6

4. As a safety precaution, FDISK requires that you enter the label of the partition in question. For example, if you wanted to delete drive D: from Figure 6.3, you would enter AXEME when prompted for the volume label.

5. FDISK then asks for a Y or N response to triple-check that you really want to delete the partition in question.

6. If you want to delete additional partitions, repeat steps 3–5.

7. Press the Esc key several times to exit FDISK. The program then reboots the computer.

Understanding *FDISK*'s Limitations

MS-DOS's FDISK is one of the most limited of the available disk partitioning tools. It's fine for creating multiple partitions for use in DOS alone, and even for use in other OSs that use FAT partitions or that can modify the filesystem type codes. It has several drawbacks, however, including the following:

- **An inability to create more than one primary partition per disk**—FDISK simply won't let you create more than one primary partition, although many versions of DOS can use more than one primary partition.

- **An inability to create an extended partition without a primary partition**— Sometimes you might want to do this to keep drive letter sequences from jumping back and forth across physical drives, but FDISK simply won't create such partitioning schemes.

- **Limited partition placement options**—FDISK always places one partition after another; it gives no options to place a partition at the end of available disk space or to place a gap in a partitioning scheme.

TIP   You might be able to use a "throwaway" partition as a placeholder if you want to leave blank space, so another OS can later add its own partition in that space, for example. Create a partition in the location where you want the blank to be, and then create partitions that fall after this blank. When you're finished, go back and delete the placeholder partition.

- **Limited ability to cope with non-FAT partitions**—MS-DOS's FDISK can't delete non-FAT logical partitions and can even fail to show FAT logical partitions when non-FAT partitions are present in an extended partition.

Although the program has so many problems, MS-DOS's FDISK is fairly safe. That is, the partitions it creates are unlikely to cause problems in other OSs or in other disk utilities. Some disk partitioning software can create partitions that cause problems in certain OSs, which can be a major problem.

Overall, I recommend using DOS's FDISK only to create fairly simple partitioning setups on blank hard disks. It can also be a convenient tool if you want to quickly check or modify a partitioning scheme, particularly in a disaster recovery situation because it can be run from a DOS boot floppy.

Variant *FDISK*s in Other DOS Versions

You might have noticed that I referred to MS-DOS almost exclusively in the preceding discussion. This is because each DOS's FDISK utility is slightly different from the others, though they all follow a similar pattern. Caldera's DR-DOS, for example, includes the capacity to create a partition labeled as FAT-32 and can even create a second primary partition if it's labeled in this way. DR-DOS cannot, however, use or even format a FAT-32 partition. FreeDOS's FDISK is modeled very closely after the MS-DOS utility and includes the same limitations.

The FDISK utility that comes with Windows 9*x* works much as the MS-DOS 6.0 FDISK I used as a model in this section. When you use this version of FDISK, though, you might be asked when you start it whether you want to enable support for large hard disks. If you respond in the affirmative, FDISK can create extended partitions with Microsoft's new extended partition code. These partitions, and therefore all the logical partitions they contain, can't be accessed in older versions of DOS and in some non-Microsoft OSs, such as OS/2 4.0 and earlier. If you use another OS's partitioning utility to create an old-style extended partition that crosses the 1024-cylinder boundary, some OSs might become confused, particularly if you attempt to access a partition that falls partly or completely above that boundary. You must therefore be careful with such large hard disks. You might need to create your partitions carefully, perhaps even using a primary partition on the upper portion of the disk to reduce the effect of this incompatibility.

If you're using a non-Microsoft DOS, most of the information I've presented here applies, although some details might differ.

Windows NT Disk Administrator

Windows NT doesn't ship with a utility called FDISK. Instead, it uses Disk Administrator, which is available to the Administrator user under the Start, Programs, Administrative Tools (Common) menu. Disk Administrator possesses several changes compared to the older FDISK utility:

- **Graphical user interface (GUI)**—Figure 6.4 shows Disk Administrator's main window, which presents a view of all disks' partitions. You can adjust various aspects of the display by selecting items under the Options menu.
- **Delayed changes**—Instead of making changes immediately, they're held until you exit from the utility or select Partition, Commit Changes Now. Holding changes adds some degree of safety to the process.
- **Multiple primary partitions per disk**—You can put several primary partitions on a disk, which is a great boon when designing a partition layout for multiple OSs.
- **Logical partitions without a primary partition**—There's no need to put a primary partition on every disk, which can be useful sometimes when you want to keep all the drive letters in sequence from one physical disk to the next.

FIGURE 6.4
Disk Administrator's GUI interface makes working with the utility much easier than working with DOS's FDISK.

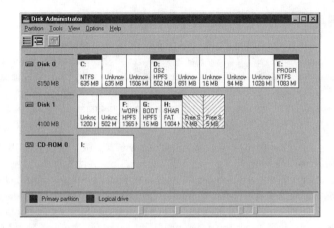

- **Delete partitions for non-Microsoft OSs**—This capability makes Disk Administrator more dangerous, but also more flexible, particularly if you want to eliminate an OS from your system.

- **Drive marking**—When first started, Disk Administrator marks a disk in a unique way. In Windows NT 3.51, these markings were known to interfere with some OSs and utilities, but they are safer in Windows NT 4.0 and Windows 2000.

In Windows 2000, Disk Administrator is called Disk Management and is part of a larger utility known as Computer Management. You run it from the Administrative Tools folder in the Control Panel. Figure 6.5 shows the Windows 2000 Computer Management tool running and open on Disk Management. Other than how you start it, Disk Management works much like Disk Administrator in Windows NT 4.0. Through the rest of this chapter, I refer to both as Disk Administrator.

FIGURE 6.5
Windows 2000's Computer Management incorporates many administrative functions, including those of NT 4.0's Disk Administrator.

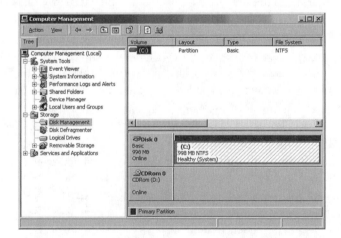

Overall, Disk Administrator is a vast improvement over DOS FDISK. Unfortunately, you cannot use Disk Administrator until you've completely installed Windows NT. (During its installation process, Windows NT gives you access to a stripped-down text-only version of Disk Administrator. You can create and delete partitions with this text-mode utility, but not much else.) Nonetheless, if you already have Windows NT installed and want to prepare your system for a new OS, Disk Administrator might be a better choice than FDISK for the task.

Creating Partitions

To create a partition in Disk Administrator, follow these steps:

1. Select a region marked Free Space, such as one of the two regions at the end of Disk 1 in Figure 6.4.

> **NOTE** Disk 1 contains two regions of free space because the first is at the end of an extended partition and the second lies outside that partition. Notice that the hash marks have different orientations for these two types of free space. You can create logical partitions only in the extended partition free space, whereas you can create primary partitions or (if none already exist) extended partitions in the unpartitioned free space. ▓

2. Select Partition, Create in Windows NT 4.0 to create a primary or logical partition (or Partition, Create Extended to create an extended partition, if applicable). In Windows 2000, select Action, All Tasks, Create Partition to create any partition type.

3. Disk Administrator might or might not present a warning dialog box concerning compatibility with other OSs, depending on whether the partitioning scheme is incompatible with DOS. Disk Administrator then presents a dialog box similar to the Create Primary Partition dialog box shown in Figure 6.6. (In Windows 2000, this dialog box is part of the Create Partition Wizard.)

FIGURE 6.6
Adjust the size of the partition you want to create with the Create Primary Partition dialog box.

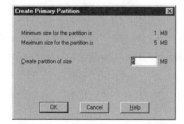

Part

III

Ch

6

4. Enter the size of the partition you want to create and click OK.
5. Repeat steps 1–4 to create additional partitions.

When you're finished creating partitions, select Partition, Exit to quit from Disk Administrator. The program presents a confirmation dialog box asking you if you want to save your changes. If you do, click Yes; if you've made a mistake and want to start again, click No.

Deleting Partitions

Deleting partitions with Disk Administrator is also simpler than deleting them with DOS's FDISK. To delete a partition, follow these steps:

1. Select the partition you want to delete by clicking it.

2. Choose Partition, Delete from Disk Administrator's menu in Windows NT 4.0, or Action, All Tasks, Delete Partition in Windows 2000.

3. Disk Administrator presents a dialog box informing you that deleting the partition will lose the data in that partition. If you're sure you want to delete the partition, click Yes.

4. Repeat steps 1–3 for any additional partitions you want to delete.

Note that there are no special steps to be taken to delete logical partitions, as there are when you use FDISK. This fact alone makes Disk Administrator much easier to use.

Adjusting Partitions' Disk Labels

If a partition is formatted using a filesystem that Windows NT understands, you can adjust its partition label from within Disk Administrator. To do so, click the partition, and then select Tools, Properties (in Windows NT 4.0) or Action, All Tasks, Properties (in Windows 2000), which brings up the Properties dialog box for the drive. You can then enter a new label in the Label field. You can also perform other operations on the partition by selecting other tabs in this dialog box. For example, you can share the drive with other computers on your network by clicking the Sharing tab.

If you want to change the letters assigned to drives, you can do so from Disk Administrator by selecting the partition and then choosing Tools, Assign Drive Letter (in Windows NT 4.0) or Action, All Tasks, Change Drive Letter and Path (in Windows 2000) from the menu. You can then enter a drive letter in the Assign Drive Letter dialog box, as shown in Figure 6.7. (In Windows 2000, you must first choose the drive letter and click Edit in the Change Drive Letter and Paths dialog box.) If you select Do Not Assign a Drive Letter, Windows NT hides the partition, so you can't access it from within Windows NT.

FIGURE 6.7
You can select only unoccupied drive letters in the Assign Drive Letter dialog box.

OS/2's *FDISK*

OS/2's disk partitioning software, like DOS's, is called FDISK. To be precise, there are two versions of OS/2's FDISK—a text-mode version (FDISK.EXE) and a GUI version (FDISKPM.EXE). The two versions of the program function in much the same way, so I refer to them both as FDISK. Figure 6.8 shows the GUI version of OS/2's FDISK.

FIGURE 6.8
The GUI and text-mode versions of OS/2 FDISK look and act much alike, although the former enables you to use the mouse to perform most actions.

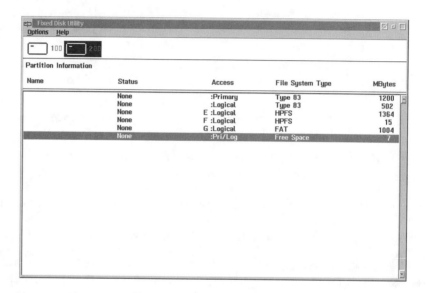

OS/2's FDISK displays all the primary and logical partitions for a disk onscreen, but only in a textual form; there's no graphical representation of the disk's contents, as is present in Windows NT's Disk Administrator or PowerQuest's PartitionMagic. Compared to DOS's FDISK, OS/2's utility provides several enhancements:

- **Improved user interface**—Being able to see all partitions simultaneously and act on them in a fairly direct way is a vast improvement over the menu system in MS-DOS's FDISK.

- **More seamless integration of primary and logical partitions**—OS/2's FDISK doesn't require you to explicitly create or manipulate extended partitions. Instead, OS/2's FDISK automatically creates an extended partition the first time you create a logical partition and expands or contracts the extended partition as necessary when you add or delete logical partitions.

- **Multiple primary partitions**—You can create two or more primary partitions with OS/2's FDISK, although OS/2 itself only enables you to use one primary partition per physical disk.

- **Drives without primary partitions**—You can partition a drive so that it uses only logical partitions. Doing so leaves a one-cylinder gap of unallocated space at the beginning of the disk, however, because OS/2's FDISK won't let you create a logical partition that's not a multiple of one full cylinder in size. (The first cylinder is only partly occupied by the MBR, so the first primary partition normally occupies only part of the first cylinder of the disk.)

- **Delayed changes**—Like Windows NT's Disk Administrator, OS/2's FDISK doesn't make changes immediately, so you can abandon your modifications when you exit from the program.

- **Capability to create and install IBM's Boot Manager boot loader**—Boot Manager lets you select between OSs and is quite flexible, although it requires its own primary partition.

  ▶ To learn more about Boot Manager and other boot loaders, **see** "Common Boot Loaders," **p. 98**.

Like DOS's FDISK, OS/2's FDISK creates partitions in a fairly conservative way, so other OSs are generally quite happy with OS/2-created partitions. One exception to this rule occurs when you use a hard disk that exceeds 1024 cylinders in size. In this case, OS/2 can create partitions that extend past the 1024-cylinder boundary, and some OSs can't handle such partitions. If the partitions are of types that these other OSs can't use, such as OS/2's High Performance Filesystem (HPFS), this usually isn't a problem.

TIP

Like MS-DOS's FDISK, OS/2's FDISK contains a feature to write a fresh MBR to a disk. In OS/2's case, you activate this feature by typing FDISK /NEWMBR at an OS/2 command prompt. You can combine this option with the /DISK:x parameter to rewrite the MBR on a disk other than the first. For example, FDISK /DISK:2 /NEWMBR rewrites the MBR on the second disk.

Creating Partitions

To create a partition with OS/2's FDISK, follow these steps:

1. Click the icon at the top of the window that represents the disk you want to partition. (In the text-mode version, press the Tab key followed by an arrow key, if necessary, to change the active disk, and then press Tab again to return to the partition list.)

2. Select a region of the disk that's marked as Free Space in the File System Type column of the disk.

3. Choose Options, Create Partition. (In the text-mode version, press the Enter key to get the options menu.)

4. FDISK displays the Create a Partition dialog box, shown in Figure 6.9. Enter the information requested—the partition size, whether it's to be a primary or a logical partition, and whether you want it to appear at the start or end of the available disk space.

FIGURE 6.9
Clicking Help provides you with OS/2's help system entries relating to partition management.

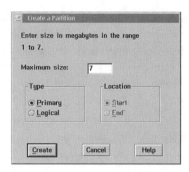

5. Click Create to create the partition.

6. Repeat steps 1–5 for each partition you want to create.

7. If you've created a primary partition that you want to serve as the computer's boot partition, select it and choose Options, Make Startable. This action marks the partition in the same way that DOS's FDISK does when you make a partition active.

When you're finished creating a partition, it appears in the FDISK menu with the drive letter by which you'll be able to access it when you reboot and a File System Type entry of Unformatted.

N O T E   OS/2's FDISK marks all the partitions it creates as having a FAT type. When you format a partition to use OS/2's HPFS, the format procedure changes the filesystem type code appropriately. If you use OS/2's FDISK to create partitions for OSs that use other partition types, you might need to use the target OS's partitioning utility to change the type code appropriately. ▪

▶ To learn more about partition type codes, **see** "Filesystem Codes," **p. 130**.

When you finish defining all your partitions, choose Options, Exit (F3). FDISK informs you that you've made changes and asks whether you want to save the changes or quit without saving. Click Save if you want to keep your new partitions.

Deleting Partitions

The procedure to delete partitions using OS/2's FDISK is similar to the procedure to add partitions. Follow these steps:

1. Select the disk on which you want to operate.

2. Select the partition you want to delete.

3. Choose Options, Delete Partition.

4. FDISK displays a dialog box asking whether you're sure you want to delete the partition. Click Yes.

Part
III

Ch

6

The partition is now gone from the partition listing, replaced by an area marked as Free Space. If you later change your mind about deleting the partition, you can exit from FDISK without saving your changes—just click Quit rather than Save when FDISK prompts you about this on exiting from the program.

Linux's *fdisk*

Compared to Windows NT's and OS/2's disk partitioning programs, Linux's fdisk is not very user friendly. Like the DOS FDISK program, Linux's fdisk is text-mode and menu-based. Key features of this program include

- **Operation on one hard disk at a time**—If you want to partition two or more physical disks, you must do so by starting fdisk two or more times. You specify the disk you want to modify on the command line when you invoke fdisk, as in fdisk /dev/sdb, to access the second SCSI disk.

- **Capability to delete partitions and then re-create them on a second run**—Many partitioning programs write data (albeit only a small amount) to their partitions when the partitions are created. Linux's fdisk doesn't do this, which makes recovery from deleted or altered partitions possible—but only if you know the exact sizes and locations of the partitions you deleted.

- **Flexible partition creation**—Linux's fdisk gives you precise control over the characteristics of the partitions you create, including their partition types, sizes, and locations. This can be good at times, but it's also possible to create partitions with Linux's fdisk that other OSs won't find palatable. For example, you can create an extended partition that spans all available disk space, including the partial cylinder at the start of the disk, but some OSs misbehave when presented with such a partition.

- **Cached changes**—Like most partitioning programs aside from DOS FDISK, Linux's fdisk stores its changes internally until you leave the program, so you can experiment and then abandon the changes.

- **Capability to handle large hard disks**—Linux's fdisk is capable of handling hard disks that contain more than 1024 cylinders, using either standard partition types or Microsoft's newer large-drive partition types. (Support for the latter is relatively recent, so it might be missing from your fdisk executable if it's relatively old.) As described in the section on OS/2's FDISK, using large extended partitions can have negative consequences if all OSs can't understand the system in use.

Linux's fdisk is an extremely flexible tool and is very useful if you want to do something that requires finesse. It's also a great tool for changing partition type codes, which most other disk partitioning software can't do very easily. I recommend against using it to create anything but Linux partitions, however, because of the possibility that the target OS will reject the Linux-created partition.

Creating Partitions

If you do decide to use Linux's `fdisk` to create partitions, follow these steps:

1. Start `fdisk` by typing its name followed by the device file associated with the disk you want to modify, as in `fdisk /dev/sda` to partition the first SCSI drive or `fdisk /dev/hdb` to partition the slave EIDE drive on the primary controller. If the drive is larger than 1024 cylinders, `fdisk` displays a warning that some OSs might have problems with certain types of software.

2. Type p to display a list of current partitions. The resulting output might look something like this:

```
Disk /dev/sda: 255 heads, 63 sectors, 522 cylinders
Units = cylinders of 16065 * 512 bytes

   Device Boot    Start       End      Blocks   Id  System
/dev/sda1             1       153     1228941   83  Linux
/dev/sda2           154       522     2963992+   5  Extended
/dev/sda5           154       217      514048+  83  Linux
/dev/sda6           218       391     1397623+   7  HPFS/NTFS
/dev/sda7           392       393       16033+   7  HPFS/NTFS
/dev/sda8           394       521     1028128+   6  FAT16
```

This output lists the partition identifiers, start and end cylinders, total number of blocks (each block is 1KB), partition ID, and the name of the filesystem associated with the partition ID. This information is useful when adding new partitions.

3. Type n to add a new partition. Depending on what partitions already exist, `fdisk` prompts you to specify whether to add a primary, extended, or logical partition.

NOTE You must create an extended partition before creating a logical partition. ■

4. Enter the partition type you want to create. If you elect to create a primary or extended partition, `fdisk` prompts for a partition number, which must range from 1–4 and be unused by any existing partition. If you create a logical partition, `fdisk` assigns the partition number automatically.

5. You're now asked for a starting cylinder number for the partition. The default value is the first unallocated cylinder.

6. Next, enter the ending cylinder number, or specify the partition's size by preceding the value with a plus sign (+) and trailing it with a K for kilobytes or M for megabytes. For example, you could enter +500M to create a 500MB partition.

7. If you're not creating a Linux filesystem partition, type t to change the partition type code. If your partition is for a Linux filesystem, you can skip ahead to step 10.

▶ To learn more about partition type codes, **see** "Filesystem Codes," **p. 130**.

Part

III

Ch

6

8. Type the number of the partition whose code you want to change.

9. Type the hexadecimal (base 16) code for the partition type. If you don't know this code, type L to see a list of codes known by fdisk. (You can enter other codes, too, but fdisk won't be able to identify the partition's type.) Figure 6.10 displays the results of creating a new partition and changing its type to 0x07 (HPFS/NTFS).

FIGURE 6.10

Linux's fdisk is text based and scrolls information, so you can see your most recent commands by scrolling back in the window.

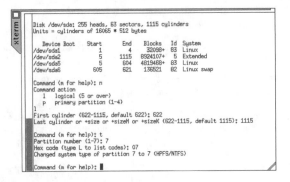

10. Type p again to see the new partition setup and confirm that it's what you wanted.

11. Repeat steps 3–10 for any additional partitions you want to create.

12. If you're certain you want to keep the new partition layout you've created, type w to write the changes to disk and exit. If you want to abandon the changes, type q to quit without saving.

CAUTION

Neither the w nor the q command prompts you again to be sure you're doing what you want, so be sure you want to commit or lose your changes, respectively, before you use these commands.

After you've made changes, it's generally a good idea to reboot Linux, especially if you've made changes to a hard disk that has any mounted partitions. If you've created or altered partitions intended for use in DOS or Windows, you should probably clear the first sector of those partitions. This is because DOS's FORMAT command uses information stored in this sector to determine the size of the partition and could misinterpret random data left in the sector from its previous use, thus causing FORMAT to create a filesystem of the wrong size. You can clear the first sector of the partition by typing dd if=/dev/zero of=/dev/xdyz bs=512 count=1, where *x* is s or h for SCSI or EIDE devices, *y* is the device identifier, and *z* is the partition number. Be very careful entering this command because a mistake could damage another partition. All other things being equal, it's safer to use the target OS to create such partitions than to use Linux. Windows sometimes reacts poorly to Linux-formatted partitions.

▶ To learn more about disk formatting, **see** "Partition Formatting," **p. 157**.

> **CAUTION**
>
> Linux's fdisk enables you to alter partitions that are mounted by Linux itself. This practice is potentially very dangerous. Altering a mounted partition leaves the kernel's information on mounted partitions inaccurate, which can result in substantial data loss. If you want to delete partitions that are normally mounted, I recommend you first unmount the partitions. You might need to boot Linux from an installation or emergency floppy to do so.

Deleting Partitions

Deleting partitions using Linux's fdisk is less involved than is creating them. Follow these steps:

1. Start fdisk by typing its name and the name of the device on which you want to operate, as in fdisk /dev/hda.
2. Type p to display the partition table. Locate the partition you want to delete.
3. Type d to delete a partition. fdisk prompts you for a partition number. Enter it.
4. If you want to delete more partitions, repeat steps 2–3.

> **CAUTION**
>
> Do not skip step 2 when performing a second deletion. Deleting a logical partition renumbers subsequent partitions, so it's easy to delete the wrong partition on the second operation if you don't check the partition numbers again. This is less of a concern if you're deleting primary partitions or if you want to remove all the partitions on the disk.

 TIP   You can remove all logical partitions by deleting their containing extended partition. Doing so obviates the need to delete each logical partition in turn.

5. To finish the operation, type w to write the changes to disk, or type q to quit without saving. As I cautioned earlier, there is no double-check on these operations, so be sure you select the correct one.

Advanced Operations

Linux's fdisk allows for finer-grained control over certain aspects of the partitioning process than do most other partitioning programs. Here are some examples of what you can do with Linux's fdisk:

- **Change extended partition size**—Most disk partitioning programs don't make it easy to change the size of an extended partition, so you cannot convert space from use by primary to logical partitions or vice versa. This task is possible with Linux's fdisk,

Part

III

Ch

6

though it's a bit risky. Basically, you must first write down the precise start and stop positions of all logical partitions; delete the extended partition; create a new extended partition; and re-create the old logical partitions with the exact sizes of the originals. Because Linux's fdisk doesn't touch the data within the partitions, the new configuration's partitions should still work. If you don't reproduce the partitions precisely, however, you'll have a mess on your hands when you reboot. Two safer alternatives are to use OS/2's FDISK or PowerQuest's PartitionMagic, both of which handle this task much more smoothly.

■ **Changing CHS geometry**—You can change the cylinder/head/sector geometry of a disk from the fdisk expert menu. Type x to get to this menu, and then type c, h, and s to change the number of cylinders, heads, and sectors, respectively. This functionality can sometimes be useful if you've moved a disk from one system to another and want to repartition it but are having difficulty getting it to work consistently with the appropriate geometry for the new system. You might also use this feature to temporarily change the CHS geometry to match that used by an older system to recover data from a drive that otherwise can't be read.

▶ To learn more about CHS geometry, **see** "Understanding CHS Geometry Limits," **p. 76**.

> **CAUTION**
>
> Do not attempt to change the CHS geometry of a disk if that disk is currently partitioned and has data you want to keep. Doing so runs a high risk that you'll render the data unreadable.

■ **Miscellaneous functions**—You can display low-level data structures, wipe the partition table clean in one operation, and perform assorted other functions. Type man fdisk at a Linux prompt to learn more about what Linux's fdisk can do.

Linux *fdisk* Variants

There are several variants of and alternatives to Linux's fdisk program. These include the following:

■ cfdisk—cfdisk is a more user-friendly version of fdisk. It presents an interface that vaguely resembles that of OS/2's FDISK. The program lacks some of the finer control offered by the standard fdisk program, however.

■ **Disk Druid**—This is a program used almost exclusively during Red Hat and Mandrake Linux installations. It's much more user friendly than fdisk, but I've seen a few reports of Disk Druid doing strange things to disks. More than most other components, partitioning software must be 100% reliable, so I recommend you avoid using Disk Druid.

Of course, you can also create your Linux partitions with non-Linux tools. If you do so, you might need to use Linux's `fdisk` to change the partition type codes before you can install Linux on your system. (The earlier section on creating partitions included information on changing the partition type codes.)

PartitionMagic

Unlike the other partitioning programs I've described here, PartitionMagic isn't a standard part of any specific OS (although a stripped-down version of it does come with BeOS). Instead, it's a utility you can purchase separately. This program runs under DOS and Windows, but the PartitionMagic CD comes with tools to build working OpenDOS boot floppies from which you can run the DOS version of the program if you want to use the tool on a system that contains neither DOS nor Windows. There are versions of these tools that run from assorted OSs, including Linux and OS/2.

PartitionMagic is the most sophisticated and feature-rich partition management program available. The following are some highlights of its capabilities:

- **GUI partition management**—Even the DOS version of the program, shown in Figure 6.11, provides point-and-click operation of the program, with a graphical display of partitions.

FIGURE 6.11
PartitionMagic lets you manipulate partitions by selecting them and right-clicking to obtain a list of available options.

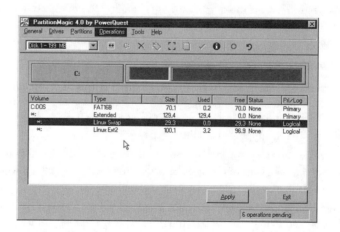

Part
III

Ch

6

TIP The DOS version of PartitionMagic can be controlled by keyboard input alone, but doing so is awkward. The OpenDOS boot floppies you can create from the PartitionMagic CD include a Microsoft Mouse driver that works with a wide variety of mice. If your mouse isn't supported by this driver, you should install the DOS driver for your mouse on whatever DOS boot floppy you use to run the program.

■ **Support for many partition types**—PartitionMagic 4.0 and 5.0 support FAT-12, FAT-16, FAT-32, HPFS, NTFS, ext2fs, and Linux swap partitions, as well as maintenance to (but not creation of) IBM Boot Manager partitions. Earlier versions of the program supported fewer filesystems. This wide range of support makes it easy to create appropriate partitions for many OSs, without using several different partitioning programs to set appropriate partition types, format the partitions, and so on.

> **CAUTION**
>
> You should use PartitionMagic 5.0 to work on the version of NTFS used in Windows 2000 (NTFS 5). Earlier versions of the program are adequate for NTFS as used by Windows NT 4.0 and before, and for creating new NTFS partitions for any version of Windows.

■ **Queued operations**—Like most partitioning programs, PartitionMagic lets you enter a series of operations that you then execute later. This feature enables you to experiment and back out if you decide you don't want to make changes.

■ **Creation of multiple primary partitions**—You can create up to four primary partitions per disk of any type that PartitionMagic supports.

■ **Creation of logical-only disks**—You can create an extended partition and place logical partitions within it without first creating a primary partition.

■ **Filesystem creation**—PartitionMagic can create both partitions and the filesystems that reside on them. Most partitioning programs don't create filesystems, leaving you to do this task with a program such as DOS or Windows' FORMAT or Linux's mkfs.

> ▶ To learn more about creating filesystems, **see** "Partition Formatting," **p. 157**.

■ **Partition resizing and moving**—One great strength of PartitionMagic is its capability to resize and move existing partitions, thus enabling you to make room on a disk for a new OS or eliminate an OS you don't want and reclaim its disk space. This feature works with all supported partition types.

■ **Partition copying**—You can copy a partition from one location to another. This feature is useful if you want to change the order in which two partitions appear, or if you want to move all your data from one drive to another.

■ **Partition conversions**—PartitionMagic enables you to convert between FAT-16 and FAT-32 and to convert FAT-16 to HPFS or (with the help of a Windows NT utility) NTFS. Version 5.0 adds the capability to convert primary partitions to logical and vice versa.

In this section, I describe the use of PartitionMagic for initial disk-partitioning operations. The program is extremely flexible, and I can only begin to cover its basic features here.

> ▶ To learn more about partition resizing, copying, and conversions, **see** "Using PartitionMagic," **p. 196**.

PartitionMagic can be a bit finicky about the partitions it modifies. For example, it's possible in Linux's fdisk to create partitions that appear on the disk in an order that's at odds with their partition numbers. For example, /dev/hda6 might come before /dev/hda5. PartitionMagic doesn't like such configurations and refuses to modify such disks. You can sometimes correct matters by deleting the partitions and re-creating them with Linux's fdisk in the "correct" order—but you must be very careful to re-create the partitions with the exact same sizes and positions that they had before, or your data will be lost.

PartitionMagic ships with a copy of BootMagic, which is a boot loader application used to select between OSs. You don't configure BootMagic from within the PartitionMagic program, however; there's a separate BootMagic configuration program for that function.

▶ To learn more about BootMagic configuration, **see** "PowerQuest's BootMagic," **p. 105**.

Creating Partitions

You can use PartitionMagic to create partitions on a blank disk, to add to an existing set of partitions, or to change partition structures.

> **CAUTION**
>
> PartitionMagic sometimes misidentifies the CHS geometry of a new disk and limits its available size to 2GB. If this happens, use another partitioning program to create a partition (even a temporary "throwaway" partition). PartitionMagic will then use the correct CHS geometry and give you full access to the entire disk.

To create a partition with PartitionMagic, follow these directions:

1. Select the disk you want to partition by choosing it from the list box near the upper left of the PartitionMagic window.

2. Select a portion of the disk that's unallocated. These sections appear gray in the graphical representation of the disk near the top of the window, and their textual representations below that label them as being of type Free Space. You can select the area either in the graphical or textual partition listings.

3. Choose Operations, Create to obtain the Create Partition dialog box, shown in Figure 6.12.

FIGURE 6.12
You can enter assorted information about the partition in the Create Partition dialog box.

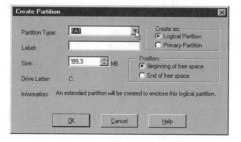

Part

III

Ch

6

TIP Most operations available on a region or partition are listed on a context-sensitive menu you can obtain by right-clicking the area in question. Using this method to access available tools can save some mouse movements.

4. Enter the information for the partition, including its type, label, and size. Depending on what area you select, you might be able to specify that the partition be either primary or logical; PartitionMagic automatically creates, extends, or shrinks an extended partition as required.

TIP If you're creating a partition for an OS whose filesystem PartitionMagic doesn't understand, such as FreeBSD, select a partition type of Unformatted. This causes PartitionMagic to forgo the formatting process, thus saving some time. You can also explicitly create an extended partition if you want to create one of some specific size.

5. Click OK in the Create Partition dialog box to record your options.

6. Repeat steps 1–5 for each additional partition you want to define.

7. Click Apply in the main PartitionMagic window to apply the changes. The program proceeds to do so. Depending on the number and type of operations you selected, this process can take anywhere from a second or so to an hour or more.

CAUTION

If you perform any advanced operations, such as partition resizing, ensure that you don't interrupt the program when it's running, say by powering off the computer. Such an interruption might result in the loss of all data on a partition.

N O T E If you run PartitionMagic from Windows, it might need to reboot your system into Windows 9x's DOS mode to perform some operations. When it does this, you'll see only a text-mode display indicating the completion of each operation in sequence. ▪

TIP Suppose you enter a sequence of changes and then decide to abandon or alter some of them. Rather than delete partitions from the sequence you've entered and create new ones, select General, Discard Changes and start over. PartitionMagic has a tendency to follow every operation blindly, even if an operation is undone in a subsequent step. If PartitionMagic is set to verify its operations (from the dialog box you get when you choose General, Preferences), this tendency can add substantially to the time it takes to complete an operation.

Deleting Partitions

Deleting partitions from PartitionMagic is fairly straightforward:

1. Select the partition you want to delete by clicking it.
2. Choose Operations, Delete to obtain the Delete Partition dialog box shown in Figure 6.13.

FIGURE 6.13
When a partition has no name, you must type NO NAME as the name to confirm a deletion.

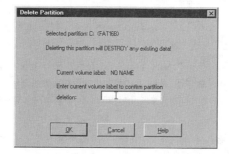

3. Type the name of the partition into the text entry field and click OK to confirm the deletion.
4. Repeat steps 1–3 for any additional partitions you want to delete.
5. Click Apply to apply the changes.

If you want to delete an entire extended partition, you must select the extended partition itself, which appears as a light blue area surrounding the logical partitions in the graphical display; or you can click the line of type Extended in the textual partition display. You cannot delete an extended partition until you've deleted all the logical partitions it contains, though.

Additional Partitioning Software

The utilities I've just described by no means constitute the entire selection of partitioning software available for x86 PCs. Some additional programs include

- **OS software**—Most OSs ship with some partitioning utility. Most of these are custom designed for the OS in question, but some aren't. BeOS, for example, ships with a stripped-down version of PartitionMagic.
- **Partition Commander**—V Communications, the producer of System Commander, also sells a product similar in concept to PartitionMagic. Partition Commander supports fewer filesystems, however, which makes PartitionMagic a better choice for most multi-OS environments. System Commander comes with a stripped-down version of Partition Commander.

Part
III

Ch
6

■ **Ranish Partition Manager**—This program is available on the Internet at http://www.users.intercom.com/~ranish/part/. Like PartitionMagic and Partition Commander, the Ranish Partition Manager aims to not just create and delete partitions, but resize them. It's currently limited to doing so to FAT partitions, however.

■ **FIPS**—The First Nondestructive Interactive Partition Splitting program (FIPS) is quite limited but useful. It's designed to split one primary FAT partition into two primary FAT partitions. The first part contains all the original partition's files. The second part can be deleted or converted to use by another OS. It's therefore a very useful tool for installing a new OS. Because FIPS is open source software, it's distributed with most Linux and FreeBSD distributions.

You might be able to locate additional tools, some designed to perform very specialized tasks. If you need to find a tool to do something specific, try searching the utilities at http://www.winfiles.com or some other online forum or posting a query to an appropriate newsgroup.

▶ To learn more about locating help for your OS problems, **see** "Finding Help," **p. 263**.

Dealing with Large Hard Disks

Large hard disks—those with more than 1024 cylinders—pose unique challenges to partition setups. This is because a variety of solutions sprang up to cope with the so-called 1024-cylinder limit. Therefore, not all OSs cope with large disks in the same way.

▶ To learn more about the 1024-cylinder limit, **see** "Getting Around the 1024-Cylinder Limit," **p. 77**.

Here are some notes on how different OSs deal with the 1024-cylinder limit with respect to partition types:

■ **DOS**—Most DOS versions don't cope well with disks containing more than 1024 cylinders. It's best to keep all FAT-16 partitions below the 1024-cylinder mark. Because DOS ignores non-DOS partitions, you can safely place such partitions above the 1024-cylinder mark.

■ **Windows 9x**—Windows 95 OSR2 added support for new partition types to allow the use of disk space past the 1024-cylinder mark. Of particular interest, if you want to place logical FAT partitions past this point, Windows 9x's FDISK creates a new type of extended partition to do the job. Unfortunately, not all OSs can process this new partition type. OS/2 4.0 is one such OS. Therefore, sharing such an extended partition between OSs can be difficult. One solution is to use a conventional extended partition (created with OS/2's FDISK) and ensure that only non-FAT partitions fall above the 1024-cylinder mark.

■ **Windows NT**—Windows NT (including Windows 2000) is fairly flexible in its handling of partition types and placement of partitions relative to the 1024-cylinder mark.

- **OS/2**—OS/2 4.0 and earlier can understand ordinary extended partitions that extend beyond the 1024-cylinder mark, but OS/2 doesn't understand Microsoft's new large extended partition type. OS/2 also refuses to format a FAT partition of any type that extends beyond the 1024-cylinder mark. OS/2 has no problems with primary HPFS partitions that straddle the 1024-cylinder limit, although OS/2 won't install on such a partition, so if you use one, it must be as a non-boot partition.

- **BeOS**—BeOS has no problems dealing with partitions that extend past the 1024-cylinder limit. This includes both primary partitions and any variety of extended partition.

- **Linux**—Recent versions of Linux understand both old-style extended partitions that exceed the 1024-cylinder mark and Microsoft's new extended partition type. You can therefore place Linux partitions wherever you want them without compatibility concerns. If you're using an older Linux distribution, however, you might need to upgrade your kernel or fdisk version to obtain the support for Microsoft's new extended partition type.

- **UNIX**—Consult your UNIX documentation for information on how it handles the 1024-cylinder limit. Most UNIX versions have no problems with large disks, but some might.

Partition Formatting

With the exception of PartitionMagic and Partition Commander, the tools I've described so far in this chapter create, delete, or otherwise modify partitions, but they don't do much to the contents of those partitions. Before a partition can be used, it must contain an appropriate filesystem. Placing the appropriate filesystem structures on the partition is referred to either as *formatting* or *creating a filesystem*, depending on the OS in use. As I describe shortly, the latter is the more precise term, but the former is quite common, particularly in Microsoft-style OSs.

Low-Level and High-Level Formatting

The problem with the term *format* is that it refers to two different processes:

Part III

Ch 6

- **Low-level formatting**—The low-level format refers to the disk structures that define the positions, size, and other important characteristics of individual sectors on a disk. Used as a verb, the word *format* refers to a process that writes (or rewrites) these data structures. Low-level formatting typically erases not just the filesystem structures but all data structures on the disk, and rebuilds the low-level data structures so that the disk can be used again. Low-level formats typically take a long time to complete because data must be written to every sector on the disk.

- **High-level formatting**—High-level formatting is the type of formatting with which this discussion is concerned. In this process, basic data structures for a filesystem, such as the boot sector, root directory, and so on, are created. After a disk has been high-level formatted, it can be used by an OS to store data. High-level formatting typically takes a short period of time because only a few sectors must be modified. (Some programs do provide an option to verify each sector, however, in which case a high-level format can take roughly as long as a low-level format.)

In DOS, a single program (FORMAT) is used to simultaneously perform both low-level and high-level formats on floppy disks. On hard disks, however, FORMAT performs only a high-level format. There's normally no need to perform low-level formats on hard disks. If you want to perform one, you need a special utility or formatting options in your motherboard or SCSI host adapter's BIOS. Contact your motherboard, EIDE controller, or SCSI host adapter manufacturer if you want to find such a utility.

> **CAUTION**
>
> A low-level format of a hard disk wipes out all partitions on that disk and makes the disk's data irretrievable by any but very sophisticated and expensive data recovery techniques. This is one reason why low-level formats are discouraged.

When to Format a Partition

There are several situations in which you might want to perform a high-level format on a hard disk partition:

- **New partition**—You must always perform a high-level format when you create a new partition. This rule applies to a partition created on a new hard disk. (Some disks might ship with a single partition predefined, however.)

- **Partition conversion**—Suppose you have a partition that had been used by DR-DOS; you find that you no longer need that space in DOS but do need it for programs in BeOS. You can perform a high-level format to convert the partition from DOS's FAT to BeOS's BFS to better use the available space in BeOS.

- **Partition erasure**—If a partition contains no data you need, you can easily erase it all by performing a high-level format. This operation will likely be faster than a file-by-file deletion of the entire partition's contents.

- **Corruption recovery**—Occasionally a partition's data structures become corrupt. Tools like DOS's CHKDSK, Windows' SCANDISK, Linux's e2fsck, or third-party tools such as Symantec's Norton Utilities (http://www.symantec.com), can repair many disk problems, but sometimes not all problems. If you can back up your data, or if you don't mind losing it, you can reformat the partition to regain use of the disk space.

- **Installing a new OS**—You might want to reformat a partition when you install a new OS, even if the OS can install to the same type of filesystem that exists on a partition. Of course, you lose all data when you perform the high-level format, so you should do this only if the partition contains nothing but outdated files.

Tools for Disk Formatting

Because many OSs use their own filesystems, disk formatting tools tend to be specific to each OS. These tools do have certain common characteristics, however. Understanding both the similarities and the differences between disk formatting tools is important when dealing with a multi-OS computer.

GUI Disk Formatting Tools   In an OS with a strong GUI orientation, such as Windows 9*x* or OS/2, it's generally possible to format a partition by selecting a drive icon and then choosing an appropriate menu option. For example, in Windows 98 you can right-click a drive icon and select Format from the pop-up menu. This action produces the Format dialog box shown in Figure 6.14. You can use this dialog box to select various formatting options, such as what type of format you want to perform: Quick writes new data structures, Full checks the disk to be sure it can hold data reliably, and Copy System Files Only makes the partition bootable but doesn't otherwise modify it. In OSs that support multiple filesystems, you can usually specify which filesystem you want when you format a partition. For example, Figure 6.15 shows the dialog box that OS/2 displays when you right-click a drive icon and select Format Disk. This dialog box enables you to select between two filesystems: FAT and HPFS.

FIGURE 6.14
In GUI-oriented OSs, you can enter formatting options in a dialog box when you format a hard disk.

FIGURE 6.15
You might need to choose what filesystem to use when you format a disk.

Textual Disk Formatting Tools   Many OSs—both those that are primarily text-based, such as DOS, and those that have GUI components—also offer text-based commands to format a partition. Examples include

- **DOS and Windows 9x**—The FORMAT command serves the formatting function. You type the command followed by the drive letter you want to format, as in FORMAT D:. In some cases you might need to specify additional parameters. For example, in Caldera's DR-DOS, you must include the /X parameter if you want to format a hard disk.

- **Windows NT**—Like DOS and Windows 9x, Windows NT uses a command called FORMAT to format a partition. Windows NT, however, includes an additional parameter, /FS:fstype, to specify the filesystem (FAT or NTFS). As an example, to format D: for NTFS, you would type FORMAT D: /FS:NTFS.

- **OS/2**—OS/2 also uses a command called FORMAT to format a partition. Like Windows NT's FORMAT, OS/2's command uses a /FS:fstype parameter, but its options are FAT and HPFS, not FAT and NTFS.

- **UNIX**—In UNIX and UNIX-like OSs, the command to perform a high-level format (generally referred to as *creating a filesystem* in UNIX) is usually called mkfs. Details differ greatly from one OS to another, but mkfs generally takes at least two parameters: a filesystem type (preceded by -t) and a device file. For example, in Linux you might use mkfs -t ext2 /dev/hda5 to create a Linux ext2 filesystem on /dev/hda5. Some UNIX versions, including many Linux distributions, can make these commands available under more filesystem-specific names. For example, under Linux you can also type mke2fs /dev/hda5 to create the same ext2 filesystem on /dev/hda5.

Most of these text-mode commands include additional options to set filesystem features such as the volume label. Check the documentation that came with your OS for details.

> **CAUTION**
>
> Most Linux distributions ship with the capability to create FAT partitions via the mkdosfs or mkfs -t msdos commands. In my experience, these partitions are frequently not handled correctly by Windows. I therefore recommend that you create FAT filesystems in DOS, Windows, or OS/2, not in Linux.

Some Additional Comments on Formatting   One important distinction to understand is that, when applied to hard disks partitions, both DOS-style FORMAT and UNIX-style mkfs apply high-level formats. When applied to floppy disks, however, DOS-style FORMAT normally applies both low-level and high-level formats (although there are parameters to change this behavior in some OSs), whereas UNIX-style mkfs applies only a high-level format. If you want to perform a low-level format on a floppy disk in a UNIX-style OS, you must use an additional utility, such as fdformat.

A few partitioning programs—most notably PartitionMagic—create filesystems at the same time they create partitions. This feature can be convenient, but it is also potentially dangerous because, if you create a partition by mistake, this problem can be more difficult to correct.

The capability of PartitionMagic to create partitions for several different OSs in one utility can certainly be a timesaver when you set up your hard disk for several OSs, however.

> **N O T E** If you're partitioning a disk for use by Windows NT 4.0 or earlier, don't bother making your Windows NT boot disk NTFS before installing Windows NT. Instead, format it for FAT. Windows NT 4.0 installs itself to FAT and then converts the FAT partition to NTFS if you opted for an NTFS installation. You can specify an NTFS partition as the Windows NT installation drive, although Windows NT reformats it as FAT first then converts it back to NTFS. Windows 2000 can install itself directly to NTFS, however.

When you create partitions, you also set the partitions' type codes. Some OSs use these codes to determine which partitions to attempt to access. It's therefore important that the type codes match the filesystem contained on the partition. In DOS, Windows, and OS/2, the FORMAT command sets the partition type appropriately when you format a partition. In most UNIX OSs, however, you must manually adjust the type code after running mkfs.

If you want to convert a partition from use by one OS to use by another, you might also need to change the partition type code before reformatting it for the new filesystem to let the new OS see the partition. There are several ways you can accomplish this goal:

- **Use PartitionMagic**—If the destination filesystem is one that PartitionMagic understands, you can use this program to create the new filesystem directly. PartitionMagic changes the type code transparently.

- **Use Linux's fdisk**—Linux's fdisk can change any partition's type code to any other code. Linux's fdisk can therefore be a useful tool in this situation even if neither the source OS nor the destination OS is Linux.

- **Delete and re-create the partition**—If you delete a partition and then create a new one, you change the code. You might need to use the source OS's partitioning program to delete the partition and the destination OS's program to create the new partition.

Summary

Disk partitioning tools are extremely varied, but all manipulate the same data structures. Ideally, all create partitions that are compatible with all OSs, but there are occasional cross-platform glitches in partitioning. It's therefore generally best to use the partitioning tool provided by an OS to create partitions for that OS. Alternatively, you can use a tool that supports multiple OSs to create partitions for several OSs. Table 6.1 summarizes the features of the partitioning tools discussed in this chapter.

Table 6.1 Partitioning Software Features

Feature	DOS and Windows 9x *FDISK*	Windows NT Disk Administrator	OS/2 *FDISK*	Linux *fdisk*	Partition Magic
Creates multiple primary partitions	—	✓	✓	✓	✓
Automatically creates extended partitions	—	—	✓	—	✓
Deletes any OS's partitions	—	✓	✓	✓	✓
Always creates partitions safe for any OS	✓	✓	✓	—	✓
Can change partition type codes	—	—	—	✓	—
Changes filesystem types	—	—	—	—	✓
Resizes, moves, and copies partitions	—	—	—	—	✓
GUI partition display	—	✓	—	—	✓

CHAPTER 7

Tips for Optimizing System Performance

Optimizing Performance

Installing several OSs on a computer so that these OSs all work can be a challenge. Even more challenging is the issue of optimizing these installations so that they perform as well as they can. There are several different types of OS optimization:

■ **Internal optimization**—You can search out and obtain the fastest drivers for your hardware, set OS-specific options to improve performance, and perform routine maintenance to keep your system from becoming bogged down in whatever forms of detritus build up in its files and directories. These topics are beyond the scope of this book; check a book on your specific OS for details on improving system performance through these means.

■ **Hardware optimization**—When you buy, build, or upgrade a system, you're faced with options that affect performance. Do you get the $150 hard disk or the $250 model? The older video card or the more advanced one? For the most part, hardware that's fast in one OS is fast in another, although you must ensure that your hardware is supported in all your OSs. Occasionally a product might work in one OS but provide subpar performance because of weak drivers.

▶ To learn more about obtaining the correct hardware and drivers, **see** Part VIII, "Hardware Considerations."

■ **Optimizing disk allocation**—How you arrange your OSs on a computer can significantly influence how well those OSs perform, especially in disk-intensive tasks. Your initial configuration decisions can also have important consequences if you subsequently decide to add another OS or delete an existing one.

This chapter is concerned largely with the last of these optimization types. As such, this chapter is relatively advanced. You can get a multi-OS configuration up and running without reading this chapter, but you might run into trouble further down the road or be disappointed in your system's disk performance.

I've written this chapter with the assumption that you've read Chapters 5, "Hard Disk Partition Basics," and 6, "Tools for Disk Partitioning." You certainly need to understand these topics to implement any hard disk partitioning scheme.

Minimizing Primary Partition Consumption

The PC's partitioning system limits the user to only four primary partitions. Many OSs, and even some disk utilities such as IBM's Boot Manager, consume a primary partition. These two facts combine to make primary partitions a precious resource, one not to be squandered needlessly. As a general rule, if you can think of two ways to partition your system to achieve a desired result, you should use the method that consumes fewer primary partitions. Other concerns do sometimes intervene, however, so you might need to balance this issue against disk speed, obtaining consistent drive letters across OSs, or some other factor.

OSs That Require Primary Partitions

Many OSs must boot from a primary partition. OSs that are so designed include all versions of DOS, Windows 9x, Windows NT, and FreeBSD. On the face of it, then, it might appear to be impossible to install these four OSs on a single hard disk, at least if any logical partitions are also present. There are several mitigating factors, however:

- **A second hard disk**—FreeBSD requires a primary partition, but that partition need not be on the first physical disk. You can therefore install FreeBSD on a primary partition on the second physical disk or often on subsequent disks, depending on BIOS support. The Microsoft OSs each require a primary partition on the first physical disk, though, so this option is helpful for some OSs but not for all.

- **Boot loader trickery**—The most helpful mitigating factor relates to boot loaders, some of which can swap critical files used by each OS to allow two or more OSs to exist on a single primary partition. V Communications' System Commander is particularly adept at this trick, but Windows NT's own OS Loader can do it, as well. One limitation to this method is that all the OSs must boot from a single filesystem—FAT, in the case of System Commander booting several systems from one partition. This can be a serious limitation if you want to run, say, Windows NT on NTFS rather than on FAT.

- **OSs split across partitions**—When I say that these OSs require a primary partition to boot, I refer only to certain critical files. All these OSs can place the bulk of their files on other partitions, including logical partitions and partitions on second and subsequent disks. For example, you could devote a primary partition of 100MB or so to holding the most basic boot files for several OSs, and place the bulk of the OSs' files on other partitions. (The supplementary partition can reside on the same or a different physical disk than the main boot partition.) In the case of Windows variants, you do this by specifying a drive other than C: as the home of the WINDOWS or WINNT directories. When you do this, you must also use a boot loader that can redirect the boot process to several OSs on a single partition, however; splitting an OS across partitions helps to isolate the OSs' files from each other but doesn't fundamentally alter the primary partition requirements of the OSs.

If you initially create a system layout that places two OSs on separate primary partitions, you might have difficulty combining them into one primary partition should you need to free up a primary partition for some less-compatible OS. If you use System Commander, you should be able to achieve this effect, however, by copying all of one OS's files to the other OS's partition and then using the copied OS's SYS utility (or equivalent) on its new home partition. When you reboot, System Commander should detect the new OS and give you an option of saving the new OS's boot files and booting into it. Whether this operation will succeed in booting the OS in its new home depends largely on the OS in question. DOS and Windows 9x are reasonably robust in this respect, but Windows NT is much more finicky about its boot partition. Of course, you'll also need some way to access both existing boot partitions simultaneously, or use a backup program to do the trick in two steps.

Part

III

Ch

7

TIP   PartitionMagic 5.0 can merge two contiguous FAT partitions into one partition.

CAUTION

If you attempt an operation such as I've just described, be sure you don't overwrite existing files or directories, aside from those backed up by System Commander. (System Commander routinely backs up files such as COMMAND.COM and IO.SYS, which are most critical in booting DOS and related OSs.) For example, if you want to configure two versions of DOS to boot from the same partition, be sure you don't overwrite one DOS's C:\DOS directory with the directory of the same name from the other version of DOS. You might be able to get both versions to cohabit by renaming one C:\DOS directory and making appropriate changes to its CONFIG.SYS and AUTOEXEC.BAT files.

Booting from Logical Partitions

In general, if an OS supports booting from a logical partition, I recommend that you use this option to reduce your use of primary partitions. OS/2, BeOS, and Linux all support booting from logical partitions.

N O T E   The standard boot sequence provided by the BIOS and normal master boot record doesn't support booting from logical partitions. You must therefore use a boot loader such as Linux's LILO, OS/2's Boot Manager, or V Communications' System Commander to boot an OS from a logical partition. Boot Manager itself requires a primary partition, although LILO and System Commander don't. ■

▶ To learn more about boot loaders, **see** Chapter 4, "Boot Loaders: Simple and Complex."

In the case of OS/2, booting from a logical partition (or from a primary partition on a second hard disk, which OS/2 also supports) entails certain risks. Specifically, the OS/2 boot partition's drive letter can change if you alter the partitioning scheme in the future. Because OS/2's boot process is very much tied to the boot partition's drive letter, such a change results in an inability to boot OS/2. Typically, OS/2 complains that it cannot find the file COUNTRY.SYS in such a situation. You might need to readjust your partitioning scheme or boot loader options if you find this happening. Here are some specific suggestions:

■ You might be able to use your boot loader's partition hiding features to hide an extra partition, if the problem is too many partitions.

■ For the brave of heart, you might be able to adjust OS/2's view of the system by permanently altering the partition type codes of partitions that come before the OS/2 partition. This action might permanently remove partitions from view, even from OSs other than OS/2, however, or make partitions visible to OS/2 that should not be. In the latter case, there's the chance that OS/2 will try to write to these partitions, thus damaging them.

- If your new arrangement shifts the OS/2 boot partition's letter down, consider adding one or more small "placeholder" partitions. These add drive letters but are otherwise nearly useless because of their size.

- A variant on the "placeholder" theme is to use such a partition as a location for swap space or temporary files, even across multiple OSs. If you follow this approach, the partitions you create should be large enough for this new function.

Fast and Slow Portions of Hard Disks

All other things being equal, we all prefer faster hard drives to slower ones. Hard disk speed is, however, an often-misunderstood topic, for several reasons. Determining how best to place an OS's partitions can be as much an art as a science because so many variables are involved in how a given OS or person uses the disk, making prediction difficult. I therefore present some general principles and rules of thumb in this section that should help you make appropriate decisions.

Hard Disk Design Consequences

Any discussion of hard disk speed must refer first to the design of hard disks. Hard disks contain many components that interact in ways that are sometimes complex. Fortunately, a few principles suffice to help you place your partitions optimally on the hard disk.

Internal and External Transfer Rates   Although not terribly important in deciding where to place partitions on a hard disk, one factor that's important in understanding hard disk speed in general is the distinction between internal and external transfer rates. Figure 7.1 illustrates the basic design of a hard disk from an electronic point of view. The disk stores data on its platters, and the data are retrieved by the read/write head assembly. From there, the data go to the drive's electronics, which then forward the data over a cable to an interface board or connector on your computer's motherboard.

FIGURE 7.1
The disk platter, drive electronics, and connecting line are all part of the hard disk you buy as a unit; the ribbon cable connects this unit to the rest of your computer.

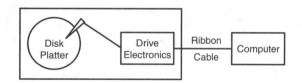

Each of the two lines in Figure 7.1 represents a data transfer, and each transfer has an associated data transfer rate. The transfer rate from the disk platter to the drive electronics is typically referred to as the *internal transfer rate*. The *external transfer rate* is the speed at which the drive electronics can communicate with the computer over the ribbon cable.

Unless you use components of wildly varying age, chances are that the internal transfer rate is substantially lower than the external transfer rate. Typical internal transfer rates at the end of 1999 were in the 10–30MBps (megabytes per second) range, whereas typical external transfer rates are in the 33–80MBps range. Therefore, it's the internal transfer rate that's of most importance in determining the overall speed of the hard drive. Disk manufacturers frequently trumpet their external transfer rates because they sound more impressive, but these values aren't usually very important. You might be able to find the internal transfer rates buried on a technical specifications page on the drive manufacturer's Web site.

External data transfer rates do occasionally play a role, however, because hard disks contain electronic *caches*—portions of memory that temporarily store data retrieved from the disk. Data transferred to or from the disk's cache can achieve rates close to the full external transfer rates. Such transfers help in the drive's overall performance, but not enough to seriously mitigate the importance of the internal transfer rate.

One further complication when you're looking at hard disk specifications is that external transfer rates are typically reported in megabytes per second (MBps) whereas internal rates are sometimes reported in megabits per second (Mbps). This difference is easily overlooked, and if you do overlook it, the internal rates might appear to be much higher than the external rates—the opposite of reality.

Speed Diiferences Across Cylinders   Because the limiting factor in hard disk speed lies in the internal transfer rate, it's important to know what causes that limit. The answer lies in the rotational velocity and data density of the disk platters. In brief, the faster a disk platter spins and the more data it packs into one cylinder, the faster its internal transfer rate. Today's hard disks typically spin at 5,400–10,000 rpm.

Today's hard disks use a variable number of sectors per cylinder. This is done to increase the overall data density of the disk. Each cylinder has a fixed width. Manufacturing techniques allow for a fixed maximum data density on a platter—that is, the amount of data you can fit on a square inch of a disk platter is constant. If outer cylinders contained the same number of sectors as do inner cylinders, however, the outer cylinders would have a much lower data density, meaning that the disk's storage capacity was underused. To compensate, modern designs pack more sectors per cylinder on outer cylinders than on inner ones, as shown in Figure 7.2. (In reality, modern disks use far more cylinders and sectors than are depicted in Figure 7.2, of course, but Figure 7.2's representation is more legible.)

N O T E   The *true* (variable) number of sectors per cylinder bears no resemblance to the values reported by the drive to the computer and used in some OSs for drive access. EIDE hard drives and SCSI host adapters make up appropriate CHS geometries to satisfy BIOS requirements that were invented before the practice of varying the number of sectors per cylinder became commonplace. For system configuration purposes, the fictitious CHS geometries are what's important, but for understanding hard disk speed, the underlying physical reality is important. ■

FIGURE 7.2

Hard disks place more sectors on outer cylinders than on inner ones to fit more data on the disk.

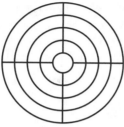
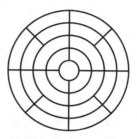

Fixed Sectors/Cylinder
16 Sectors Total

Variable Sectors/Cylinder
24 Sectors Total

How does all this relate to speed? Hard disks' platters spin at a constant rate. Therefore, the number of sectors passing under the read/write heads at any given moment is variable. Because the sectors themselves contain a constant amount of data (typically 512 bytes), the data transfer rate is variable, depending on the cylinder being read or written. Specifically, the outermost cylinders are typically faster—often by a factor of two or more—than the innermost cylinders. On their specification sheets, some manufacturers list both their drives' slowest and their drives' fastest internal transfer rates, some list an average transfer rate, and others present only their fastest transfer rates.

Disk Spin and Data Transfer Rate Designs

The comments concerning hard disk spin and data transfer rates in the main text of this chapter apply to modern hard disks. Older hard disks and standard PC floppies use a constant number of sectors per cylinder (typically referred to as a *track* for floppies), so they have a constant transfer rate. Older Macintosh floppies (the 400KB and 800KB varieties) use a variable number of sectors per track, and depending on the hardware used to read them, might exhibit differing transfer rates in much the same way as modern hard disks. These older Mac floppies can't be read on standard PC hardware, however. (Newer Macintosh 1.44MB floppies can be, provided your OS has Macintosh *hierarchical filesystem* [*HFS*] support.)

CD-ROM drives use a single spiral track, with constant linear sector size, meaning that the number of sectors in a 360° rotation is variable. Older CD-ROM drives spun at a variable rate to maintain a constant data transfer rate, a design known as *constant linear velocity* or *CLV*. This design was necessary for the original music recording function of CDs. Modern drives often use a *constant angular velocity (CAV)* design, much as do hard disks, or a design that varies the spin rate, but not by as much as does a CLV design (partial CAV). CAV and partial CAV CD-ROM designs result in variable transfer rates from the CD-ROM drive. Most manufacturers advertise their devices' fastest transfer rates; a supposed 40x CD-ROM drive can achieve those speeds on its fastest regions, but only 25x on its slower areas. Fortunately, all this is transparent to both the OS and the software that uses the CD-ROM drive, except insofar as the speed influences the performance of the software.

On most hard disks, the outermost cylinders map to the earliest part of the disk, so the first partitions on the disk are the fastest, in terms of raw disk input/output performance. This difference isn't as great as the raw internal transfer rate numbers would indicate, however, because several other factors, such as disk head movements, conspire to reduce transfer rates from both inner and outer cylinders. Nonetheless, the difference is real, and if you want to squeeze the most performance from your configuration, you can use this knowledge in deciding where to place partitions.

Locating Important Partitions Optimally

As you might guess, all other things being equal, you should place partitions on which you want to get the best disk performance earlier than those on which disk performance is less important. Precisely what constitutes a partition that contains data you want to access quickly varies substantially from one installation to another. For example, one person might want to favor OS/2 partitions over Windows partitions for speed, but another person might make the opposite decision. Nonetheless, here are some guidelines:

- **Swap space is important**—Swap space is disk space that an OS uses to store data that normally resides in memory when the OS runs out of memory. UNIX-like OSs typically devote an entire partition to swap space, so you can easily locate the swap partition for optimal performance. Other OSs create a swap file that resides on an ordinary partition, which you would then want to locate optimally to optimize swap performance.

- **Frequently accessed programs are important**—If you regularly run particular programs, try to place those on fast partitions.

- **Frequently accessed large data files are important**—Like major applications, large data files can benefit from placement on a fast partition.

- **Small data files are less important**—The overhead to access a file makes the raw transfer rate from a disk containing many small files less important.

- **Infrequently accessed files and programs are less important**—If you seldom access a file or program, don't waste your fastest disk space storing that file or program.

Unless you create several partitions for each OS, you might be unable to make very fine distinctions along these lines on the order of specific files; but you can certainly locate partitions for specific OSs according to these criteria. If you use one OS 90% of the time and two others each only 5% of the time, chances are you should devote the fastest portions of your hard disks to that first OS. If your usage patterns change, you might want to consider changing your partitioning setup—but in most cases, the trouble isn't worth it unless you're upgrading to a bigger hard disk or need to repartition for some other reason.

Locating Partitions Relative to One Another

A factor that sometimes comes into conflict with the desirability of placing often-accessed partitions in the fastest part of the disk is the desirability of placing partitions that contain files that are often accessed simultaneously adjacent to one another. One of the biggest factors in disk speed is the speed with which the disk heads can move from one cylinder to another on the hard disk. Suppose you want to create two partitions that are both likely to be accessed when performing certain tasks, such as data files and applications partitions for an OS. If you place those partitions at opposite ends of a hard disk, the result is that the disk head will move back and forth over almost the entire length of the hard disk quite frequently, as the OS calls for accesses to files on both partitions. By contrast, if you place those two partitions adjacent to one another, the resulting head movements are shorter. Hard disks can perform shorter head movements in less time than they can large head movements, so closer partition placement results in better disk performance.

In practice, this generally means that it's best to place all the partitions for a given OS close to each other on the disk. For example, if you install OS/2 and BeOS on one disk, chances are you won't be accessing the BeOS partition from OS/2 or vice versa, so if you isolate their partitions in this way, you will greatly reduce the average head seek times.

One corollary of this principle is that a partition that's shared between two OSs should reside between them. For example, if you use a FAT partition for data exchange between your OS/2 and BeOS partitions, that FAT partition should go in the middle of the drive, where it's on the fringes of both OSs' hard disk "territories."

For similar reasons, you should try to place the most heavily accessed and time-sensitive partitions in the middle of an OS's hard disk region. At most, heads seek only half their range to reach a centrally located partition, and the average seek is less than half. When an OS's hard disk territory is restricted, the result can be very short seeks indeed. The desirability of central location of the most-used partition frequently means that partitions containing critical OS files or swap space should reside in these favored locations.

Of course, in practice you're seldom able to produce a perfect partitioning scheme. For example,

- You can have three OSs with a partition that's shared between all three. This shared partition can't be located equidistant between all three OSs' partitions—at least, not if you have only one hard disk.

- You might have cause to create one big partition and two small ones, with one of the small partitions requiring pride of place. Such an arrangement will produce, at best, an off-center location for this important partition.

- You might find the need to create partitions at odd locations because of the 1024-cylinder limit or the need to boot multiple OSs from primary partitions.

- System changes as you add and delete partitions can often create opportunities to easily create partitions at one location but not another, so you can end up with some quite strange partition layouts.

You must prioritize these matters yourself. You might prefer to sacrifice disk performance in an OS that's unimportant to you rather than go to the bother of radically altering an existing disk layout or compromising the performance of an OS that you use more frequently.

Part

III

Ch

7

Splitting OSs Across Multiple Hard Disks

The preceding discussion has focused on hard disk layout across a single hard disk. Modern PCs often have multiple hard disks, however, and you can use such an arrangement to gain some extra speed. The basic principles involved are the same as when arranging partitions for a single-disk system, but with the extra factor that each disk's transfer speed and head movement timing are independent.

Minimizing Head Movements Through Independent Heads

As I discussed earlier, excessive head movements can greatly reduce the speed of your hard disk system. Suppose for the sake of argument that you're using your system in such a way that it issues the following series of disk commands:

```
Read file program on Partition 1
Read file data on Partition 2
Write file program2 on Partition 1
Write file data2 on Partition 2
Read file program on Partition 1
Write file data3 on Partition 2
```

These commands cause back-and-forth head movements. Depending on assorted details, disk caches—both in hardware and software—and advanced disk controller functions can reduce the impact of such back-and-forth accesses; but accesses with certain timing and file size characteristics will always be slowed by such back-and-forth accesses.

Now suppose that, instead of two partitions on one hard disk, Partition 1 and Partition 2 are partitions on two separate disks. Head movements to perform the sequence become much shorter, so overall disk performance improves. For this reason, you should always try to split all your important OSs across all your hard disks. It might seem aesthetically appealing to put Windows NT on one disk and FreeBSD on another, but you'll get better performance if you split the OSs half-and-half. On the other hand, you might prefer to keep your OSs contained to just one partition each to simplify your configurations.

Within each disk, you should follow the rules I outlined earlier concerning partition placement. You're less likely to have large groupings of partitions for each OS when you split them across disks, but you might have some groupings nonetheless.

You might have purchased a new hard disk to provide room for a new OS. If so, you might find it awkward to follow this advice in its fullest because you might have a mass of data on an existing single-partition OS installation on your main hard disk. You can still follow this advice in a more limited manner, however. Start by shrinking your existing OS's partition with a utility such as PartitionMagic, Partition Commander, or FIPS. You can then use the space you've cleared up for some small but frequently used partition for the new OS, such as a swap partition or possibly even a boot partition. You can then devote some space on the new drive to the old OS and use it for data files or new programs.

▶ To learn more about using PartitionMagic to resize an existing partition, **see** "Using PartitionMagic," **p. 196**.

Consequences of Dissimilar Disk Speeds

All this assumes that the two hard drives are roughly comparable in speed. If you've acquired your hard drives over some period of time, however, this might not be a valid assumption. For example, a 340MB hard drive from 1993 isn't even remotely comparable to a modern 20GB unit. You could probably get better performance with a 340MB partition on the slow end of the 20GB unit than you would by using the 340MB drive, even considering head seeks. Add to that the fact that the 340MB drive takes up as much space in your computer case as the 20GB unit and chews up one available EIDE or SCSI assignment, and adding such an outmoded drive quickly turns into a losing proposition. With the costs of hard disks constantly dropping, there's seldom much reason to keep a vastly outdated drive around. There might be some exceptions, however; for example, you might be desperate to have a second drive for, say, a primary partition from which to boot an OS such as FreeBSD, that requires a primary but not necessarily one on the first physical disk.

The situation is less clear-cut when it comes to drives that are only a year or so apart in age. When comparing a typical 20GB unit to a typical 10GB drive, it's often worthwhile to keep the 10GB unit around. You should consider its speed difference in planning your partitioning, though. If at all possible, put the less time-critical files on that drive. Your overall system speed can still increase, although your access times to those specific files might suffer.

In the end, judging the consequences of different hard disk partitioning arrangements in a multi-OS configuration that uses two or more hard disks of varying age can be quite difficult. I recommend that you not agonize over these decisions; just take your best guess, using the information presented here as a rough guide.

EIDE and SCSI Speed Differences

You might want to consider one further aspect in designing a layout for a multi-OS system: the difference between EIDE and SCSI hardware. There are several low-level differences between EIDE and SCSI protocols. One of the most important differences between these relates to the handling of multiple simultaneous input/output requests.

EIDE systems contain a maximum of two devices per chain—in other words, you can put only two devices on an EIDE cable, in addition to the EIDE controller itself. (EIDE chains are also called *channels*.) Modern motherboards include two (or occasionally more) EIDE interfaces, for a maximum of four devices. EIDE only supports transfers to or from one device per chain at any given time. Thus, if you put two EIDE hard disks on one chain, and if the system makes a transfer request of one of those devices, the computer can't access the other hard disk while the first is sending its data. This limitation can cause problems in high-performance applications such as file servers because it results in reduced overall performance. If you have two hard disks and want to overcome this problem, you can place the two drives on separate EIDE chains. In this situation, the computer can transfer files to and from both drives simultaneously.

Most EIDE systems include an EIDE CD-ROM drive, however, and some EIDE hardware limits transfer speeds to the slower of two device interfaces, at least in terms of the external data transfer rate. For example, if you've got an old 16MBps (external transfer rate) CD-ROM drive and a new hard drive capable of 20MBps internal and 66MBps external transfer rate, you might get only 16MBps out of it if it's connected to the same chain as the CD-ROM drive. If you're in this situation, you can end up sacrificing hard disk speed on one drive if you split your drives across both chains.

SCSI, by contrast, allows up to 7 or 15 devices, depending on the SCSI variant in use, not counting the SCSI host adapter. SCSI was designed with simultaneous access to multiple devices in mind, so while a transfer occurs involving one drive, the computer can conduct a transfer with a second drive. Depending on the capacity of the SCSI bus in use and the speeds of the devices, you might be able to access two or more hard disks at full speed simultaneously. Thus, SCSI is a superior system when it comes to multi-disk configurations. Unfortunately, SCSI also costs more than EIDE, both in terms of hard disk prices and because you will need an extra SCSI host adapter card for most computers (a few motherboards include SCSI support, but these boards are rare).

As a practical matter for disk partitioning decisions, the difference between SCSI and EIDE doesn't have major consequences. The same principles that make a multi-disk configuration beneficial apply to both drive types, except that SCSI provides an added benefit to multitasking OSs, especially when running several disk-intensive tasks at once on multiple hard drives.

A Sample Configuration

All this discussion of optimal partition placement calls for an example. I present a hypothetical two-disk layout in Figure 7.3. The sizes of these disks are unimportant as long as they're large enough to hold the software in question. This figure depicts a system with three OSs: Windows 98, OS/2 4.0, and Linux (any version). With the exception of the Windows 98 and Linux boot partitions, all the partitions are logical partitions.

Here are some key points about this layout:

- Windows 98 must boot from a primary partition on the first drive, so it appears in the first position on that drive. If for some reason you wanted to put Windows later on the drive, you could put the OS/2 boot partition on a primary partition before the Windows 98 boot partition; or you might be able to put the Windows 98 boot partition at the end of the disk.

- Linux can boot from a logical partition, but it's given a primary partition in Figure 7.3 to make best use of disk space. (Using only logical partitions would result in a small gap of unusable disk space at the start of the drive.)

FIGURE 7.3
Each OS is split across the two disks to optimize system performance.

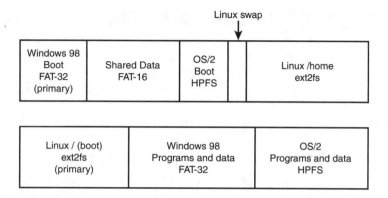

- OS/2 won't be able to see the Windows 98 boot partition because OS/2 can't read FAT-32 without third-party drivers. This means that, to OS/2, C: is the shared FAT-16 partition and OS/2 itself boots from D:. You might prefer to put OS/2 on a primary partition (before the FAT-16 partition or at the end of the drive, if the drive has fewer than 1024 cylinders), making it C:. In either case, the OS/2 programs and data partition is E:. If Windows 98 were installed on a FAT-16 partition, OS/2's drive letters would all be increased by one because OS/2 can read FAT-16. The exception: If OS/2 is on a primary partition, it won't see the Windows partition, even if it were FAT-16.

  ▶ To learn more about drive letter assignments, **see** "Software's Varying Approaches to Partition Types," **p. 123**.

- To Windows 98, the Windows boot partition is C:, the shared data partition is D:, and the Windows programs and data partition on the second drive is E:. Note that the shared data partition receives different drive letters under OS/2 and Windows.

- The Linux swap space resides between the Linux /home partition and the shared data space (presumably used by Linux at least occasionally), which places it near the center of Linux's likely range of head movements for that drive. The OS/2 boot partition falls between the Linux swap and shared data partitions, though, which is a compromise. Moving the OS/2 boot partition out of the way might help Linux performance slightly but would hinder Windows 98 or OS/2 performance.

As you can see, it's possible to create a three-OS system on two disks with very few compromises in performance. The main compromise in Figure 7.3's scenario relates to the placement of the shared FAT-16 partition. When you add more OSs, the likelihood of a need for compromise increases substantially. Depending on which OSs are important to you and how you use those OSs, Figure 7.3's arrangement might not be optimal from the point of view of getting the best speed by location on the disk.

Part
III

Ch
7

Splitting Files Across Partitions

When you're designing your disk layout, you might be tempted to minimize the number of partitions each OS uses. For example, you might think you could get by with a single partition for each OS, at least on a single-disk computer. There are advantages to splitting up a single OS into multiple partitions, however, even on a single-disk computer. Of course, you can also go too far in this direction and produce an unmanageable mess. The key is in moderation. As a general rule of thumb, 2–4 partitions work well with most OSs.

Reliability Advantages of Multiple Partitions

One oft-cited reason for splitting an OS's files across multiple partitions is reliability. Modern hard disk hardware is pretty reliable, on the whole, but disk problems are still common because power failures, OS bugs, and other factors conspire to damage files and even entire partitions every once in a while. If you split an OS's files across multiple partitions, you can make recovery easier. For example

- **Non-boot partition problem**—If a disk failure occurs on a non-boot partition, you can boot with your full OS and use its file recovery tools to recover your data. Most OSs do provide emergency means of recovering data from a damaged partition, but these methods are sometimes awkward and time-consuming, so a boot into the full OS makes life much easier.

- **Boot partition problem**—If a disk failure occurs on the boot partition, you might be able to restore that partition from a backup or even reinstall the OS without having to reinstall your applications or recover your data files. Recovering in this way can be a great time saver.

- **Disk space overflow control**—OSs sometimes react badly if they run out of disk space for certain critical operations. By placing an OS on multiple partitions, you can ensure that some types of runaway disk use won't affect other processes. For example, UNIX system administrators often place directories that are prone to producing overflows on separate partitions. This practice can keep runaway /tmp use, for example, from affecting the system's capability to deliver mail.

- **Disaster recovery**—If the worst happens and you're forced to recover a partition from a tape backup, recovering part of your system is faster than recovering all of it. You might also benefit by having multiple partitions because, if your backups aren't up to date, you won't lose the changes you've made recently in the undamaged partitions.

These advantages apply to most OSs, but some more so to certain OSs than others. For example, Windows programs have a tendency to place configuration files in the Windows directory structure itself, so you might need to reinstall at least some applications after a fresh reinstall of Windows, even if you use a separate applications partition. Files for UNIX programs frequently scatter themselves about several directory structures, so a poor choice of partitions can do little good in this respect for UNIX, too, though some choices (like a separate partition for /usr/local) generally work well.

Flexibility Advantages of Multiple Partitions

Just as disaster recovery and reliability can be augmented by having multiple partitions, you might find that your system is more flexible when you've configured it in this way. Some ways in which this can be true include the following:

- **Multiple boot partitions**—You might want to create two or more boot partitions for one OS. One reason for doing so is to create multiple incompatible configurations. Another is to create a stripped-down partition for disaster recovery or system maintenance purposes.

- **Data organization**—You can separate data according to whatever criteria you like, or whatever is convenient for your OS.

- **Backup ease**—It's sometimes easier to be able to back up a system if the data are split into partitions. For example, if you've got a 4GB Travan tape drive, keeping your partitions under 4GB in size can make it easier to fit your data onto tapes. (Factoring in compression, you might be able to exceed the tape's nominal capacity, but be sure you don't compute "double compression"—that is, don't assume you can compress 12GB of data into 8GB and then fit that into a 4GB Travan cartridge's advertised 8GB compressed capacity.)

Minimizing Head Movements by Isolating Data

As I described earlier in this chapter, you can use careful placement of different OSs' partitions to reduce head movements and improve the performance of all OSs. Similar techniques can be applied within a single OS. Suppose that you've got a hard disk configured as a single partition. You have no control in this situation over where the OS places critical files, and in fact you might end up with some truly awful results, such as a programming language's files at one end of the drive and your own program files at the other end. By creating several partitions, you can exert some control over these matters by restricting where certain types of files go.

Ideally, you create a partition for each common type of operation. For example, you could create a programming partition that contains both your programming languages and language files. This action ensures that when you compile a program, the disk head won't move around too much.

The monkey wrench that's thrown into this theory is that your system might need to access OS files, and in a situation like this, those files exist on another partition, thus increasing head movements, at least if the OS partition exists on the same disk as the special-purpose partition. In practice, it's difficult to do more than minimal tweaking along these lines. You might be able to place critical OS files near the center of the OS's disk range, but more than this is usually inadvisable.

Part III

Ch 7

The Dangers of Too Many Disk Partitions

There are certainly advantages to creating many partitions, even for one OS. These advantages are offset by limitations and even dangers, however. These include

- **Disk space allocation uncertainty**—You might not know how much space to allocate to different partitions, particularly when you're new to an OS. If you guess wrong, you might find yourself running out of space on one partition and having too much on another. Unless you have dynamic partition resizing software such as PartitionMagic, adjusting your partitioning scheme is a tedious process at best. Even with a dynamic resizer, the process takes some time and involves some risk of data loss.

- **Drive letter explosion**—Under Microsoft-style OSs, which refer to hard disk partitions by drive letter, using many partitions can result in a confusing array of drive letter options. Did you put the recipe file on partition T: or S:? You might need to check both if you don't remember.

- **Increased head movements**—I claimed earlier that you can often decrease head movements by partitioning. This is true, but in some cases you might end up increasing head movements instead. For example, if you have a 10GB hard disk but only 5GB of data, chances are a single-partition arrangement will place most of that data contiguously. If you partition the disk, though, the data can be more spread out, considered globally, as shown in Figure 7.4.

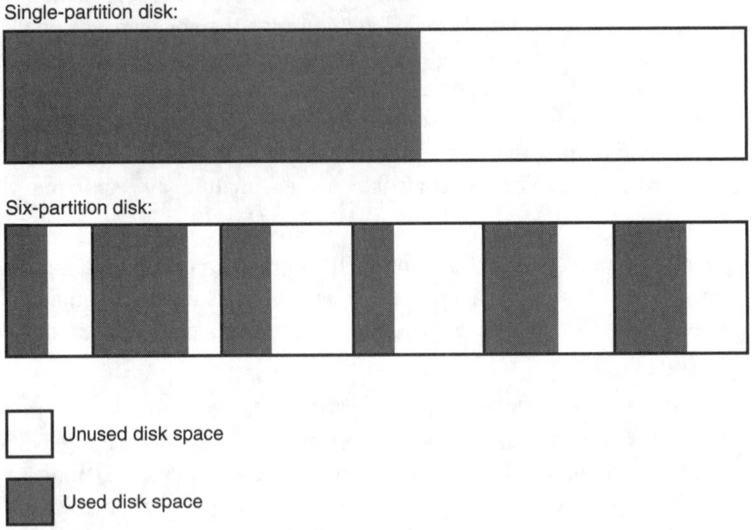

FIGURE 7.4
In the single-partition disk (top), the used portion of the disk space can be compact, reducing head movements; but in a multi-partition arrangement (bottom), the overall pattern of data placement must necessarily remain more spread out.

Single-partition disk:

Six-partition disk:

☐ Unused disk space

■ Used disk space

■ **Increased maintenance**—It takes more time to maintain several partitions. With most OSs, you should occasionally perform routine checks such as CHKDSK in DOS, Windows, or OS/2; or fsck in UNIX-like OSs. Similarly, some filesystems *fragment* easily, or split a single file across a region of the disk. Disk *defraggers* are programs that reverse this process. Running such utilities on multiple partitions is often more tedious than doing so on a single partition, although the total time to perform the operations might not be much greater.

Overall, the need for multiple partitions in a single OS is limited. Personally, I tend to favor two partitions: one for the OS itself and one for programs and data. Some people prefer just one partition for Microsoft-style OSs, others prefer more than I do. UNIX-style filesystem structure is such that an easy split between the OS and programs isn't possible, but it's often easier to split user files from other files in UNIX. Dedicated UNIX servers can often benefit from more partitions, but for an average user who's just trying it out for the first time, a split of / (the root partition), /home (or wherever user files go), and a swap partition does nicely. In fact, Figure 7.3 isn't a bad starting point on which to base a multi-OS configuration, if you have two hard disks. If you have only one disk, try adding the OS-specific partitions from disk 2 near these OSs' disk 1 partitions.

Summary

In designing a partition layout for a multi-OS system, it helps to know something about hard disk technology. The optimum layout strategy depends to a large extent on two disk speed characteristics: the internal data transfer rate (especially how that rate varies over the disk's cylinders) and the fact that head seeks cost time (more time for longer seeks). The second characteristic is the more important in deciding how you should lay out your OSs' partitions. The principles I've outlined in this chapter all derive from these two facts.

In general, you should try to keep partitions that you're likely to access frequently from the same OS together. For any given OS, keep the most frequently accessed partition in the center of that OS's range on the disk, if that OS has more than two partitions (including any shared partitions, if applicable). Place your most important OS on the fastest part of the hard disk—generally the earliest portions.

Various facts of life, such as the 1024-cylinder limit, OS needs for primary partitions, the limited number of primary partitions, and simple geometrical constraints on placing related items in an essentially one-dimensional space might impose themselves to produce a less-than-optimal configuration. Nonetheless, producing a good partition layout is worth some consideration. ●

Part
III

Ch
7

Modifying Partitions After the Fact

In this chapter

Modifying Partitions

Most people who run more than one OS occasionally need to modify their partition arrangements on a working computer. There are several possible reasons for doing so:

- **Adding an OS**—When you add an OS, you must often allocate space for the new OS by giving it partitions. This action entails modifying your current configuration.

- **Deleting an OS**—When you remove an OS you no longer need, its partitions become fair game for use by other OSs.

- **Shifting disk space requirements**—You might find that you use one OS for most tasks and another for a few. You might therefore want to convert disk space from use by one OS to another.

- **Fine-tuning configurations**—You might have a working configuration that's suboptimal in some way. For example, you might find that you need to add a partition for transferring data between two OSs, or you might want to provide more disk space for one partition at the expense of another, even when both partitions are used by the same OS.

- **Adding a hard disk**—When you add (or replace) a hard disk, you must integrate the new disk's space into your existing configuration. In some cases, you might want to move existing data onto the new drive, which in turn necessitates modifying the old disk's partitions if you keep that disk.

This chapter is devoted to issues surrounding hard disk reconfiguration, including methods of doing it and its consequences. This task can be tedious and is subject to the possibility of serious drive corruption, so it's important that you understand the nature of the changes before you embark on making them.

I wrote this chapter with the assumption that you understand the basics of hard disk partitioning. If necessary, you should read Chapter 5, "Hard Disk Partition Basics," before proceeding. You might also find Chapter 7, "Tips for Optimizing System Performance," to be informative.

Consequences of Drive Repartitioning

Your goal in repartitioning a hard disk is typically to make for a better disk layout in any of several ways, as I've just described. Your changes have very specific consequences for how you access your partitions, however, and you must understand and consider these consequences before planning your changes. In some cases, you might find that it's necessary to adopt a less-than-optimal disk arrangement to avoid catastrophic (or at least very annoying) consequences in the way you access your drives.

▶ To learn more about creating an optimized partition layout, **see** "Tips for Optimizing System Performance," **p. 163**.

> **N O T E** The terms *disk* and *drive* are often used interchangeably to refer to both physical hard disks and their partitions. Where there might be confusion on this matter, I use terms such as *physical disk* and *partition* to make my meaning explicit. ■

Drive Letter Changes

In Microsoft-style OSs (DOS, Windows, and OS/2), disk devices (floppies, CD-ROMs, disk partitions, and so on) are identified by drive letters—A: for the first floppy disk, B: for the second floppy disk, C: for the first hard disk partition, and so on. When you add or delete partitions, these drive letters can change. Sometimes the changes are unimportant to the operation of the computer, but in extreme cases they can cause the OS to become unbootable. It's therefore important that you understand the nature of these drive letter changes when you plan an alteration to your partitioning scheme.

Basic Drive Lettering Rules OSs follow specific rules in assigning drive letters to partitions. In brief, OSs search for partitions in a specific sequence and assign drive letters according to the order in which they're found. This sequence is as follows:

1. The active primary partition on the first physical disk.

2. The active primary partition on second and subsequent physical disks.

3. Logical partitions on the first physical disk. If more than one logical partition is present, the drive letters are assigned in sequence, first to last, according to position on the disk.

4. Logical partitions on the second and subsequent physical disks.

5. Unmapped primary partitions on all physical disks, in sequence from first disk to last disk. (Not all OSs perform this step; some ignore anything but the active primary partitions.)

6. Devices for which appropriate drivers exist, such as CD-ROM drives, Zip drives, and so on.

These rules all apply to partitions bearing type codes the OS recognizes. For example, DOS understands assorted FAT partition types but not OS/2's HPFS partitions. OS/2, by contrast, understands both FAT and HPFS partitions. Therefore, on the same system, DOS might give a partition the letter D:, but on OS/2, D: might be occupied by an HPFS partition, and the DOS D: drive would be known as E:. This scenario is illustrated by Figure 8.1. It's sometimes possible to avoid such inconsistent drive letter assignments by reordering partitions. For example, if Figure 8.1's logical FAT partition were placed before the logical HPFS partition, both OSs would see the logical FAT partition as D:.

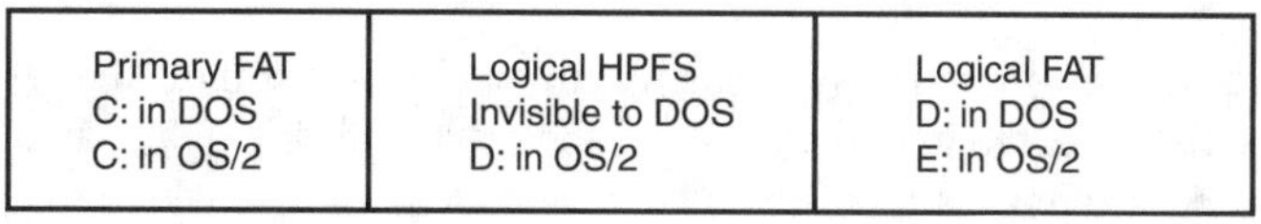

FIGURE 8.1

Drive letters can be assigned differently in different OSs because of varying filesystem support.

Primary FAT	Logical HPFS	Logical FAT
C: in DOS	Invisible to DOS	D: in DOS
C: in OS/2	D: in OS/2	E: in OS/2

The preceding rules can be modified in assorted ways:

- Windows NT has the capability to alter its drive letter assignments by using its partitioning software, Disk Administrator. This feature makes Windows NT the most flexible Microsoft-style OS in this respect, and you can use this capability to keep drive letters synchronized between Windows NT and any other Microsoft-style OS.

> **N O T E** In Windows 2000 (originally named NT 5.0 during its development phase), this utility is renamed Disk Management, which is part of the Computer Management tool. ■

> ▶ To learn more about changing Windows NT's drive letter assignments, **see** "Windows NT's Partition Mapping," **p. 126**.

- In Windows 9*x*, you can adjust drive letter assignments for CD-ROMs and similar devices that require special drivers.

> ▶ To learn more about changing Windows 9x's drive letter assignments for removable-media devices, **see** "Windows 95/98: DOS Revisited," **p. 125**.

- In DOS, Windows 9*x*, and OS/2, programs that allow access to non-native filesystems often allow these filesystems' drive letters to be assigned after the usual sequence. This fact can be useful in keeping existing drive letters stable when you add a driver for something like the Linux ext2 filesystem.

> ▶ To learn more about accessing non-native filesystems, **see** "Tools for Accessing Foreign Filesystems," **p. 329**.

- In OS/2, drive letter assignment proceeds as described earlier for steps 1–4 separately for each disk device driver. Thus, if you mix SCSI and EIDE devices, and if you use primary partitions on both, the primary partition on the second device won't be given a letter until after the logical partitions on the first device. Which device is first and second depends on the order of the device driver entries in OS/2's CONFIG.SYS file.

> **CAUTION**
>
> OS/2 changes its drive letter assignment method partway through the boot process. Initially, it uses drive letters assigned according to the partitions visible to the BIOS. After loading its device drivers, it uses assignments based on what those drivers see. If the OS/2 boot drive letter changes as a result of this shift—for example, because you've listed a SCSI driver before an EIDE driver, which is the opposite of the results of the normal BIOS actions—then OS/2 might fail to boot. It's therefore important that the order of drivers in OS/2's CONFIG.SYS produces results consistent with what the BIOS produces, at least for the boot partition.

If you're not using Windows NT, any partition changes you make that adjust partitions of a type visible to the OS in question affect the drive lettering of all partitions subsequent to that change. For example, suppose you have a single hard disk with a C: primary partition and a

D: logical partition, both formatted for FAT. If you add a new hard disk with a primary FAT partition, that new disk's primary FAT partition becomes D:, shifting the old D: to E:. A similar shift occurs if you shrink C: or D: and add a new partition between them. Even in Windows NT, you might see these letter changes the first time you boot after altering the partitions. You can use Disk Administrator/Disk Management to change the drive letter assignments on subsequent boots of Windows NT.

Boot and Program Requirements Most Microsoft-style OSs install on and boot from the active primary partition on the first physical disk. This partition necessarily becomes drive C: according to the letter assignment rules described earlier. Some caveats and exceptions can have important consequences, however:

- **OS/2**—OS/2 isn't restricted to booting from drive C:. This fact leads to a greater flexibility, which can be a good thing; but it also means you must pay careful attention to the OS/2 boot partition when you plan any partition changes. If your changes alter the OS/2 boot partition's drive letter, OS/2 fails to boot, typically complaining that it can't find the file COUNTRY.SYS. Because the OS/2 drive letter information is contained in many files, including some binary files, changing an existing OS/2 installation to boot using the new drive letter is not practical; you must either reinstall OS/2 or alter your partitioning system or boot loader to restore the original drive letter.

- **Split boots**—Even DOS and Windows 9x can be installed across two or more partitions. A few key files can reside on C:, whereas the contents of the DOS or WINDOWS directories can go elsewhere. As with OS/2, changing the identity of the partition containing this directory can have disastrous consequences on your ability to boot the OS. You might be able to recover your ability to boot DOS in such a situation by altering the DOS CONFIG.SYS and AUTOEXEC.BAT files; but Windows hard-codes the locations of many files within the WINDOWS directory in its Registry, which is much harder to alter.

CAUTION

Don't try to edit the Windows Registry file by hand. It's a very complex binary file, and a mistake can prove disastrous. Instead, plan your partition changes carefully so that you don't need to edit the Registry file.

In addition, any OS can use applications on something other than the boot partition, and these applications can hard-code the path, including drive letter, in a configuration file. If you change the drive letter, you might therefore need to change the applications' configuration files. In many cases, applications let you change these paths from within a setup tool, as shown in Figure 8.2. Other times you might need to edit a text file or even reinstall the software.

All told, drive letter changes are a major nuisance when making partition changes. If possible, you should make your changes in such a way that your existing partitions are unaffected and new partitions are added to the end of the drive letter sequence. This ideal isn't always attainable, however, or it might conflict with other priorities, such as those for obtaining the best possible hard disk performance.

FIGURE 8.2
Applications often provide a means to adjust where they look for critical files.

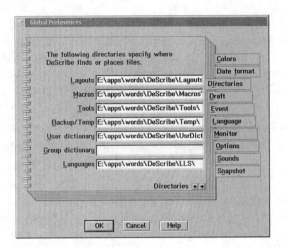

 TIP

When you first configure your DOS or Windows system, or when you reconfigure it to change your partitions, you can specify drive letters for devices such as CD-ROM drives, network drives, and some other devices. Set these devices to use drive letters from late in the alphabet, well beyond the current range for your hard disks. For example, if you have hard disks that range from C: through E:, you might assign drive letters starting with P: for these devices. This way, their drive letters won't change when you next alter your hard disk layout, saving you from having to reconfigure programs that use these devices to use new drive letters.

Partition Hiding   One method you can use to reduce the magnitude of drive letter changes is *partition hiding*. This technique relies on the presence of partition type codes in the partition table to identify the filesystem used on a partition.

▶ To learn more about partition hiding, **see** "The Job of the Boot Loader," **p. 86**.

▶ To learn more about partition type codes, **see** "Identifying a Partition's Format," **p. 131**.

Each filesystem has associated with it one or more codes, and OSs can use these codes to determine what partitions to attempt to access. There are two types of partition hiding:

■ **Permanent hiding**—You can set a partition's type code to something that some OSs recognize but others won't. This method is at the core of the officially correct handling of partition type codes. For example, Linux ext2fs partitions normally take on a type code of 0x83, which isn't recognized by DOS, Windows, or OS/2. Therefore, you can add a Linux ext2fs partition in the middle of a run of FAT partitions and your DOS, Windows, and OS/2 drive letters remain unchanged.

You might be able to use this technique in a more devious way, however, even when using only Microsoft-style OSs. For example, suppose you want to add a FAT partition that's to be visible only to Windows NT but not to DOS or Windows 98. You can assign that partition a type code of 0x07, which is used by HPFS and NTFS, thus hiding the partition from DOS and Windows 98. Windows NT can still see the partition, however, and mounts it as FAT despite the fact that it's labeled as an HPFS/NTFS partition. In the case of some third-party filesystem drivers, OS/2 works the same way, although not for FAT-16 partitions. Linux's `fdisk` is one of the best tools available for setting partition types to arbitrary values. Most other partitioning software can't change partition type codes.

> **CAUTION**
>
> Although providing inaccurate information about a partition in its type code is possibly convenient, it is potentially dangerous. An OS or disk utility might become confused by this misinformation and damage the data in a partition. This technique isn't even guaranteed to work correctly; an OS might try to interpret the partition's data according to the partition type code and then give up when it can't, and fail to try to interpret the data according to the filesystem the partition actually contains.

- **Dynamic hiding**—Most boot loaders have at least rudimentary dynamic partition hiding capabilities; they can hide partitions according to rules at boot time. Most boot loaders restrict partition hiding to primary partitions, however, and sometimes to primary partitions on the first physical disk. Linux's LILO is the most flexible—but also the most difficult to configure—boot loader in these respects. V Communications' System Commander is easier to use but somewhat less flexible (it can't hide logical partitions).

Partition hiding is most useful for hiding primary boot partitions from one another. For example, suppose you have an NTFS Windows NT boot partition. You can hide that partition from an OS/2 boot to keep OS/2 from becoming confused or assigning an unwanted drive letter to the Windows NT partition. (NTFS and OS/2's HPFS both use the same partition type code.)

UNIX Device Identifier Changes

UNIX doesn't use drive letters; it uses a single directory tree with a root entry (/). You access all files relative to this root entry—both directories in the same partition and additional partitions that are *mounted* on directories (that is, placed into the root directory tree). For example, the root partition might contain the directories /usr, /home, /var, /tmp, and /opt. Of these, /home and /usr might be separate partitions—or they might not be. Details differ from one system to another.

> **N O T E** In this chapter, I use *UNIX* to refer to both "genuine" UNIX variants and UNIX-like OSs such as Linux.

Partition changes in UNIX therefore don't create the shifting of drive letters found in Microsoft-style OSs. Instead, the underlying device identifiers change. These identifiers are the *device files*, typically located in the /dev directory, that the OS uses to access the partitions. You don't need to deal with these as a user, but you do as a system administrator. Specifically, you must alter your /etc/fstab file to accommodate the changes. Here's an excerpt from an /etc/fstab file from a Linux computer:

```
/dev/sda8    /         ext2    defaults                     1 1
/dev/sda1    /boot     ext2    defaults                     1 2
/dev/sda6    /home     ext2    defaults                     1 3
/dev/sda2    /win98    vfat    umask=0,uid=500,nonumtail    0 0
/dev/sda5    /os2      hpfs    noauto,user,defaults         0 0
```

Each line is composed of several fields, separated by one or more spaces or tabs:

- **Device**—The first column is the device file associated with a partition. This is the component that you might need to change when repartitioning a drive. The details of which different devices correspond to which partition vary substantially from one UNIX OS to another.

- **Mount point**—The second column lists the location in the directory tree at which the device will be mounted.

- **Filesystem**—The filesystem to be used to access the partition. As with the devices, the filesystems supported by different UNIX versions vary substantially.

- **Options**—Filesystem options, which vary from one OS to another and even from one filesystem to another within an OS.

- **Dump**—A value of 1 indicates that the filesystem is to be processed by the dump utility for system backup purposes; a 0 indicates a partition to be ignored by dump.

- **Check order**—The final column lists the order in which the system is to check the filesystems at reboot time. A 0 indicates no check is to be performed.

The key item for handling a repartitioning is the device file. Details differ greatly from one OS to another, so you should check your OS's documentation about how the OS assigns device files to partitions. After you determine how the partitions change, you should make appropriate changes to the /etc/fstab file. When you reboot, those changes take effect.

 TIP

If possible, make your changes to /etc/fstab before you repartition. In many cases, this practice makes the changes completely transparent from UNIX, aside from the effort to change /etc/fstab and any differences you might see in available disk space. Sometimes you might need to make additional changes, however, such as copying data to new partitions.

N O T E It's sometimes possible to test your /etc/fstab changes without rebooting. Type mount -a to get the OS to reread the /etc/fstab file and then access the changed partitions. This is safe and effective, however, only if your /etc/fstab changes don't involve repartitioning or if your partition changes don't affect any currently mounted partitions (for example, when converting a partition from use by one OS to another, as described shortly). ■

> **CAUTION**
>
> If you change your partitions in such a way that the devices associated with critical UNIX partitions change, you won't be able to boot the OS until you alter /etc/fstab appropriately. You also won't be able to boot if you make incorrect changes to /etc/fstab. For these reasons, it's vital that you have a working emergency boot floppy for your UNIX system before you attempt to repartition your disk.

Converting a Partition from One OS to Another

One of the simplest methods of modifying a partition layout is to convert a partition from use by one OS to use by another. For example, suppose you have a system with five partitions, three used by Windows and two by Linux. If you want to convert space from Windows to Linux, you might be able to do so by converting one of the Windows partitions in its entirety to Linux use. If practical, this approach can simplify your life greatly because it means you need not back up data to an external device or deal with partitioning software.

> **CAUTION**
>
> It's always a good idea to back up your entire system before installing a new OS, particularly one with which you're not already familiar. Some OSs can wipe out entire hard disks during installation if you select the wrong option. Even a simple partition conversion for an existing OS poses risks because you might accidentally reformat the wrong partition.

 TIP If you want to convert space to be used by UNIX, a whole-partition conversion can be nearly transparent. You must find a suitable mount point for the new space—some portion of your disk structure that uses a reasonable fraction of the new space. For example, if you know that /usr/local contains 500MB of data, if the partition you want to convert is 1GB, and if 50% utilization of this new space is reasonable, mounting this partition as /usr/local might be a good choice.

Clearing Away Old Data

The first step in converting a partition is to move any vital data off the partition you want to convert. You should use whatever tools are available to you in the partition's current host OS to accomplish this task. Here are some tips to help you accomplish this goal:

- If the partition contains data files, there should be no trouble in using whatever means your OS provides to move files. For example, you can use a drag-and-drop operation in a file manager, or type cp -rp ./* /new-directory in UNIX to copy the files to a new location.

■ If you're running Windows and the partition contains Windows programs, you might want to use a utility to move applications from one location to another. PowerQuest's PartitionMagic includes such a utility, called MagicMover (see Figure 8.3). Utilities such as MagicMover adjust programs' Registry entries and, often, programs' own configuration files to ensure that the programs function correctly in their new locations.

FIGURE 8.3
MagicMover helps you move Windows applications from one partition to another while keeping them working in their new locations.

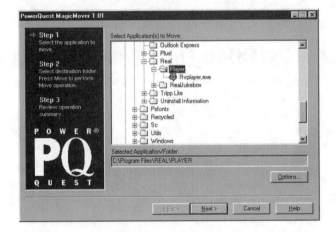

■ If you're moving data off a UNIX partition, you might want to use the following command to ensure you correctly copy permissions and ownership information:

```
tar -cplf - . | (cd /new-directory ; tar -xvplf -)
```

This command copies the current directory's contents to /new-directory.

■ UNIX systems use a fairly rigid file hierarchy, so it's probably not a good idea to dump data from a partition at some random location. When you've moved the data and unmounted the original partition, you should delete the mount point and rename the new directory to use the same name as the former mount point. Some directories are critical for a running UNIX system, so you might need to boot down into single-user mode (using the init command or something similar) or use a boot floppy to accomplish this task.

Recovering the Partition's Space

After the partition's data have been moved to new locations, you can use the partition for some other purpose. You can take either of two approaches to this task:

■ Reuse the existing partition.

■ Delete the existing partition and create one or more new partitions in its place.

N O T E Depending on the OSs in question and the tools at your disposal, you might find it helpful to delete one partition and create a single new partition. There will then be no change
in partition size, but deleting and re-creating the partition has the effect of altering the partition's
type code, which might be required to use the partition in the new OS. ■

One variant on the second option is to clear away two or more contiguous partitions and create one or more new partitions in their place. This variant can be particularly helpful if you
want to merge several small partitions into one large one.

Reusing an Existing Partition The simplest method of converting a partition is to reuse the
partition more or less as it exists. To do so, follow these steps:

1. If the old and new OSs use different filesystems, use a tool that supports changing
    filesystem type codes to make an appropriate change. Linux's fdisk is particularly help-
    ful for this task, even if neither OS is itself Linux. In some cases, the act of reformatting
    the partition does the job. In other cases, you might not be able to accomplish this task
    using tools for any of your OSs, so you might need to delete and re-create the partition
    instead.

2. Reformat the partition. In most Windows-style OSs, you do this with a program called
    FORMAT or using a GUI formatting tool. In UNIX-style OSs, you generally use a tool
    called mkfs or some variant of that. You should perform this step from the OS in which
    you intend to use the partition.

In some cases, you might be able to reuse a partition without reformatting it. For example, if
you want to convert a partition from use by DOS to use by OS/2, you can leave the partition
as FAT and delete all the files on the partition. Even in this case, though, chances are you
should reformat the partition to remove the old files and ensure that the filesystem is clean.
Also, it's rare that two OSs work equally well with the same filesystems. In the case of conversion from DOS to OS/2, OS/2 works better with its HPFS in most situations, so I recommend
reformatting the partition for HPFS.

Creating a New Partition and Reformatting It You might not find it convenient to change
the type of an existing partition, or you might have cause to create a different number of partitions than you've cleared. In these situations, you must delete the old partitions and create
new ones in the resulting free space. In general, I recommend that you use the old OS's partitioning software to delete the partitions and the new OS's software to create new ones. You
might need to adjust this strategy, however, if it would render your system temporarily
unbootable in the new OS.

Moving Data to Its New Home

Moving data to the freshly converted partition works much like moving data off the partition
had, except you must use a different OS's tools. One additional tip for UNIX OSs: You can
mount the new partition in some temporary location and use the tar command I mentioned

earlier to copy files to this partition. For example, to copy /usr/local's contents to a new partition, follow this procedure:

1. Temporarily mount the new partition at some convenient location, such as /mnt or /mnt/temp. You can either use an existing mount point or create a new one. (In the remaining steps, I assume you use /mnt; make changes as necessary.)

2. Change to /usr/local and type

   ```
   tar -clpf - . | (cd /mnt ; tar -xvlpf -)
   ```

3. Unmount the temporarily mounted partition with umount /mnt (there's no typo; *umount* really *is* missing the first *n*).

4. Rename /usr/local to some other name, using a command like mv /usr/local /usr/local-backup.

5. Edit /etc/fstab to reflect the presence of the new partition at /usr/local.

6. Mount the new partition manually. (On some systems, typing mount -a accomplishes the task of mounting all the filesystems listed in /etc/fstab, so it does the trick.)

7. Check that the contents of /usr/local are in order. Try running some programs that rely on that directory's contents, for example.

8. When you're satisfied with the contents of the new partition, delete the backup directory created in step 4.

You can put off step 8 for a while, if you like, to be sure the procedure went according to plan. If the partition you want to move is critical for normal system operation, you might need to drop into single-user mode or use a boot floppy to accomplish this procedure.

Backing Up, Repartitioning, and Restoring

Often, the need to repartition a hard disk results in a need to back up data, wipe out partitions, create new partitions, and restore the backed-up data. For example, suppose you have a hard disk that's partitioned as one large primary BFS (BeOS filesystem) partition and you want to reconfigure your computer to run both BeOS and FreeBSD, without adding a new hard disk. At the time of this writing, no utility exists that can shrink an existing BeOS partition, and because a single partition occupies the entire hard disk, you have no choice but to delete that partition and create two (or more) partitions in its place. When you've done this, you must re-create the BeOS installation, and in most cases the easiest way to do this is to restore data from a backup. (If you'd just recently installed BeOS, you might prefer to install the OS again, of course.)

The backup/repartition/restore dance is a familiar one to people who've run multi-OS configurations in the past. Fortunately, tools exist that make it unnecessary in many cases. Most dramatically, PowerQuest's PartitionMagic can dynamically resize many OSs' partitions.

Other utilities exist that can do the same for FAT partitions and one or two others. You should check on the feasibility of using such a utility before you engage in a complete backup/repartition/restore operation.

▶ To learn more about PartitionMagic and similar programs, **see** "Using PartitionMagic," **p. 196**.

The Need for Reliable Backup

Engaging in a backup/repartition/restore operation requires that you have *reliable* backup hardware and software. As much as is possible, you should test both the hardware and the software before engaging in a repartitioning operation.

> **CAUTION**
>
> Backup isn't a luxury to be reserved for system alterations. If you lack adequate backup facilities, you will lose data, sooner or later. If you don't have some means of backing up your OSs, I strongly suggest you obtain appropriate hardware as soon as possible. Especially in a multi-OS environment, you do not want to have to restore all your OSs and applications because of a hard disk failure, a malicious cracker, a bug, or an accident on your part.

Backup Hardware Options   Many different types of hardware can be used for backup. Some options include

- **Spare hard disks**—Particularly if you need to disrupt only part of your partitioning system, a spare hard disk, or unused space on a partition you don't intend to alter, can serve as an excellent short-term backup medium. For example, if you have two disks, both configured with a single partition, and if your OS can read and write both partitions, you might be able to back up one disk on the other, repartition, and restore to the repartitioned disk. The advantage of a hard disk for an operation like this is that it is both fast and reliable. The disadvantage is that there's a very good chance you won't have enough space to perform the operation. Also, using a hard disk for regular backup purposes isn't so optimal because incidents such as power surges are likely to affect the backup drive as well as the original.

- **Tape drives**—Magnetic tape is the traditional computer backup storage medium. Tapes themselves tend to be inexpensive (anywhere from $2 to $50 for a single tape, depending on variety and size) and high in capacity (typically 4–20GB or more for modern devices). Backup software for tapes is also often designed with emergency restores in mind, and if you need to repartition your boot disk, you will have what is effectively an emergency restore on your hands, albeit an intentional one. Tapes aren't as reliable as disks, however, so it's often wise to create two backups if you know you'll be wiping out your hard disk's data. In general, SCSI and EIDE tape drives are more reliable than those that interface through a parallel or floppy port.

■ **Removable disks**—Removable disks that are essentially ordinary hard disks in special enclosures have the same advantages and disadvantages as ordinary hard disks for a repartitioning operation. Disks such as Iomega Zip disks tend to be slower and smaller in capacity—often small enough to make their use in a repartitioning operation suboptimal, especially given the high cost per megabyte of the media.

■ **CD-R drives**—CD-recordable (CD-R) technology enables you to store 650MB on a single disc. Although 650MB is probably not enough to store an entire modern OS, particularly including all its programs and data files, you can use several discs to get everything. Swapping discs is awkward, but at least the discs themselves are inexpensive. A recent variant on CD-R is DVD-RAM, which stores much more data on similar media. As I write this, DVD-RAM drives and media are expensive, but prices are likely to drop, and availability increase, over the next year or two.

Overall, I favor using magnetic tape. If you have the free space on another drive, using a hard disk can be a viable option, but the free space is often not available. Of the remaining two options, CD-R (or DVD-RAM, if you can afford it) is probably the more flexible. Of course, for the purposes of doing a single repartitioning, you might not have much choice—you use whatever you have available. If you want to buy hardware for general-purpose backup use, though, I recommend a SCSI or EIDE tape drive.

▶ To learn more about magnetic tape backups, **see** "Cross-Platform Backup Needs," **p. 548**.

Backup Software Options   What software you use for backup purposes highly depends on the OS you use. I can't begin to cover all the possibilities, but I can provide a few pointers and some general advice on what to look for:

■ **Special OS and filesystem features backup**—Your backup software should back up whatever special features your OS and its filesystems support. For example, older DOS backup software can back up a Windows 9x FAT-16 partition, but that software won't back up the long filenames used by Windows. After restoring the OS, the result is an unbootable system. Similarly, DOS software won't back up OS/2 Extended Attributes (EAs).

■ **OS-specific software**—As a general rule, it's best to back up each OS using its own backup software, not software designed for another OS. There are exceptions, however. For example, most Windows 9x backup software requires convoluted procedures to do a complete restore. I've had better luck using OS/2 and Linux backup software to back up and restore Windows 9x partitions. (To use OS/2 to back up Windows 9x, though, you need special VFAT or FAT-32 drivers.)

▶ To learn more about VFAT and FAT-32 drivers for OS/2, **see** "OS/2's Handling of FAT," **p. 336**.

■ **Emergency restores**—Whatever software you use should be able to completely restore a bootable OS on a fresh hard disk. Essentially, this is the function that's required if you want to repartition the boot disk. This feature typically requires that you create a boot floppy for the OS in question and install a stripped-down restore program on that floppy or an auxiliary floppy. Some OSs, such as Windows NT, are not easily restored in this way, so you might have no choice but to do a minimal OS installation to recover the rest of your data.

■ **Test the software**—As much as possible, you should test the backup and restore procedure before proceeding with a repartitioning operation (or trusting your regular backups with the software and hardware of your choice). Ideally, you can perform a backup, swap out the hard disk for a spare, restore the backup, and test the results. If this isn't possible, try backing up a test directory filled with unimportant files, delete that directory, and restore the directory using the emergency boot floppy.

Just as with hardware, it's important that the software you select be reliable. It's difficult to test for the reliability of backup software except in actual operation. Sometimes a program fails to restore data correctly. Occasionally such a failure is severe and unnoticed until you try to use the data. More often, the software reports an error, or the error is small, such as an altered date stamp on a file. In sum, backups are something like open-heart surgery—when they work, they can be system savers; but you shouldn't put your system in the hands of such software unnecessarily because backup software is often fickle. Using backup software as part of a repartitioning operation is often a necessary risk, unfortunately. The best practice is to make frequent backups and, whenever possible, test that your recovery procedures still work. If you need to select backup hardware and software, try to find information on alternatives using online or magazine reviews to obtain the most reliable system possible.

Tools to Use for Repartitioning

After you've backed up the partition or partitions you want to modify, it's time to pull out the partitioning software and do the job. I describe these tools in Chapter 6, so I won't go into detail here except to highlight a few critical features and suggestions:

■ As a general rule, you should use the partitioning software for the target OS to create its own partitions. There are exceptions to this rule, though. PartitionMagic is an excellent tool for creating partitions for just about any OS, for example. DOS's and OS/2's FDISK utilities can both create partitions that are inoffensive to other OSs, although you might need to use another tool to change the partition type codes appropriately. (Linux's fdisk is useful for doing this.)

■ DOS's and Windows' FDISK utility isn't able to remove most non-FAT logical partitions. Most other partitioning programs can accomplish this task, however.

■ OSs released earlier than 1997 have a hard time understanding the new type of extended partition Microsoft created for hard disks with more than 1024 cylinders. Examples include OS/2 4.0 and earlier, most versions of DOS, and earlier versions of Linux. Windows might not work correctly with logical partitions that extend past cylinder 1024 when those partitions are in a conventional extended partition, however. You might need to plan your partitions carefully to get around these limitations.

▶ To learn more about tools for creating and deleting partitions, **see** "Tools for Disk Partitioning," **p. 133**.

Restoring Data

When it comes time to restore data to your new partitions, you should follow the instructions that came with your backup software. This software's instructions might not have considered the needs of a multi-OS configuration, however. Here are some tips that can help keep you from running into problems because of this omission:

- **Partition identification**—When you format a partition and restore data, you might need to be especially cautious about the drive letters or UNIX device identifiers you use because these might have changed during the partition modification process.

- **Boot loaders**—You might need to restore (or install from scratch) a boot loader for your existing OS or your new multi-OS configuration. The DOS FDISK /MBR and OS/2 FDISK /NEWMBR commands are quite helpful in this respect. In another way, so are the DOS SYS C: and OS/2 SYSINSTX C: commands. In a UNIX environment, you might need a boot floppy to boot the system and run a configuration command, such as lilo in Linux.

  ▶ To learn more about boot loaders, **see** "Boot Loaders: Simple and Complex," **p. 85**.

- **Changed OS configurations**—If your repartitioning has changed the OS's view of the hard disk, you might need to adjust configuration files. For example, you might need to change drive letter identifications in CONFIG.SYS or AUTOEXEC.BAT in DOS, Windows, or OS/2; and you might need to adjust /etc/fstab in a UNIX OS. In extreme cases, you might need to make these adjustments from a boot floppy before you can boot from the hard disk.

Using PartitionMagic

One of the most convenient methods of repartitioning a hard disk is to use a dynamic partition resizer such as PowerQuest's PartitionMagic (http://www.powerquest.com). PartitionMagic can do much more than most other partitioning programs. In addition to creating and deleting partitions, it can format a partition for any of several filesystems; change a partition's size; move a partition; copy a partition, either on a single disk or to another physical disk; and convert a partition from one filesystem to another (not all conversions are possible, though). This section describes some of PartitionMagic's more advanced features.

▶ To learn more about using PartitionMagic for basic partition creation and deletion operations, **see** "PartitionMagic," **p. 151**.

N O T E The CD that accompanies this book includes Que's edition of PartitionMagic. This version works only in DOS mode but includes most of the functionality described in this chapter. ■

CAUTION

Also, if you use Windows 2000, please note that the version of PartitionMagic included on the CD accompanying this book is incompatible with Windows 2000's NTFS 5. An upcoming release of PartitionMagic is expected to be compatible with Windows 2000. Check http://www.powerquest.com for details.

Alternatives to PartitionMagic

I focus on PartitionMagic because it is the most flexible of a group of dynamic partition resizers. In particular, PartitionMagic supports far more filesystem types than its competitors, most of which are limited to manipulating FAT partitions. Although a capability to handle FAT partitions can be very useful if you want to install a new OS on a computer that currently runs DOS or Windows, FAT support alone is often inadequate when you've installed two or more OSs and want to perform further manipulations.

Nonetheless, PartitionMagic is only one of a class of programs. Some alternative titles include

- **FIPS**—The First Interactive Nondestructive Partition Splitting (FIPS) program is a relatively simple product. It can be used to split a single primary FAT partition into two partitions. It cannot increase the size of a partition, and it works only on FAT partitions. Its greatest merit is that it's free, distributed under the terms of the GNU (GNU's Not UNIX) General Public License (GPL). FIPS is therefore commonly distributed with Linux and FreeBSD, but it can be used when you're preparing a system for installation of other OSs, too.

- **ext2resize**—Like FIPS, ext2resize is a single-filesystem utility, but it works on Linux ext2 filesystems. The program can both increase and decrease the filesystem's size but not move a filesystem. ext2resize works on the filesystem only; to do any good, you must use Linux's fdisk to change the size of the partition in which the filesystem resides. This fact makes data-threatening human error a very real possibility when using ext2resize, so I advise extreme caution in its use. Like FIPS, ext2resize is distributed under the GPL. It's starting to be included with some Linux distributions, and you can look for it on Linux sites such as http://rufus.w3.org/linux/RPM/ and ftp://sunsite.unc.edu.

- **Partition Commander**—This program, by V Communications (http://www.v-com.com), is similar in basic concept to PartitionMagic; it lets you shrink, expand, move, create, delete, and otherwise manipulate partitions. Partition Commander is, however, limited to performing these operations on FAT partitions. V Communications' System Commander boot loader comes with a limited version of Partition Commander.

- **Ranish Partition Manager**—This program is comparable to Partition Commander in its basic functionality. Unlike Partition Commander, though, Ranish Partition Manager is shareware distributed on the Web, at http://www.users.intercom.com/~ranish/part/. Its user interface isn't as sophisticated as those in Partition Commander and PartitionMagic.

If you want to use one or more of these utilities instead of PartitionMagic, you certainly can; they are all helpful in configuring a system for multi-OS use. In this chapter, however, I present instructions that are specific to PartitionMagic because it is the most flexible of these programs and because the Que edition of this program is included with this book. Partition Commander and Ranish Partition Manager are similar in principle to PartitionMagic. FIPS and ext2resize, however, are command-line programs that are somewhat different in operation. Be sure you've read and understood their instructions before you attempt to use these utilities.

PartitionMagic 5.0 comes with both Windows 9*x* and DOS executables. (The version on this book's CD is the DOS executable based on version 4.0 and is incompatible with Windows 2000's implementation of NTFS.) If you're not currently running Windows 9*x*, you can create a boot floppy, using tools for OS/2 or Linux (or other UNIX versions) on the retail PartitionMagic CD, to run the DOS version of the program. Both versions have the same core functionality, although there are a few differences. In particular, the DOS version lacks some of the more sophisticated features of the Windows version. Figure 8.4 shows the Windows version of PartitionMagic (the DOS version appears in Figure 6.11; it is similar to the Windows version).

NOTE The version of PartitionMagic depicted in the upcoming figures is the retail 5.0 version, not the Que edition included on the CD. ■

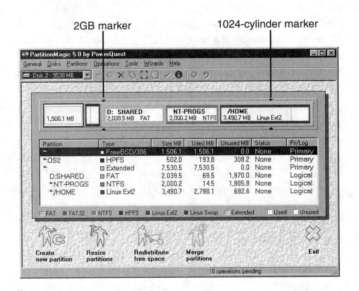

FIGURE 8.4
PartitionMagic provides a GUI environment in both the Windows version (shown here) and in its DOS incarnation.

PartitionMagic 4.0 and 5.0 can handle FAT (12-, 16-, and 32-bit varieties, including VFAT long filenames and OS/2 EAs), OS/2's HPFS, Windows NT's NTFS, and Linux's ext2fs and swap partitions. This is a wide range of filesystems and is enough for many multi-OS configurations. It doesn't cover all possibilities, however; for example, PartitionMagic 5.0 and earlier can't manipulate BeOS's BFS or the filesystems used by any UNIX-like OS aside from Linux. If you need support for such a filesystem, you should check PowerQuest's Web site (http://www.powerquest.com); it's possible that a more recent version of PartitionMagic might handle your needs. It's also possible that some other program might be available to suit your needs by the time you read this, so check with other disk utility manufacturers and with sites that have information on the OS whose filesystem you need to resize.

NOTE PartitionMagic 5.0 adds no new filesystems to 4.0's repertoire, but 4.0 added support for Linux's ext2fs. Version 5.0 adds the capability to merge two FAT partitions into one, to convert from NTFS to FAT, to convert between primary and logical partition types, and to view and edit a set of queued operations. Version 5.0 also includes, in its Windows version only, 2GB and 1024-cylinder markers, as shown in Figure 8.4, along with information on partition names and sizes in the GUI partition display, again as displayed in Figure 8.4. ■

The Need for Reliable Backup Revisited

Earlier in this chapter, I provided information on backup tools to be used in performing a backup/repartition/restore operation. Sadly, I must recommend that you read that section and make adequate backups of your system before you use PartitionMagic or any dynamic partition resizer. The reason is that dynamic partition resizing is an inherently dangerous task; a bug in the software, corrupt data on the partition, hardware failure, or a power outage could result in a complete loss of all the data on a partition. Such catastrophes, although rare, do occasionally occur, so you should take precautions to save your data should you be unlucky.

▶ To learn more about backup hardware and software, **see** "The Need for Reliable Backup," **p. 193** and "Cross-Platform Backup Needs," **p. 548**.

If you must (or at least should) back up your partitions before using a partition resizer, what good does the resizer do? After all, creating the backups is half the work, so by the time that's done, it might seem that the work saved by the partition resizer is slim. There are several mitigating factors, however:

■ As I noted in the section on backups, it's often desirable to create two backups before wiping data from the hard disk because when you wipe and restore a partition, you must have one good backup. Essentially, one backup no longer is a backup—it's the "original" data. Because tape, in particular, is less reliable than a static hard disk partition, it's important that you have a backup of the tape from which you intend to restore your system. When using a dynamic partition resizer, this argument no longer applies; the resizing process, although dangerous, should leave your data intact. The backup tape really is a backup.

■ You should make regular backups of your system. Therefore, if you plan to do your partition resizing just after a regularly scheduled backup, you really don't lose any time to the backup process. Of course, the same might be said of the first backup of a dual backup when using a backup/repartition/restore procedure.

■ The partition resizing process is often less tedious than is an emergency data restore from tape or some other medium. You therefore save some time by using the partition resizer.

■ PartitionMagic, in particular, can perform operations on partitions belonging to several OSs. This can be much more convenient than booting several OSs and juggling several tapes to restore the data from these varied OSs.

Checking Your Data's Integrity

One of the first steps you should perform when manipulating partitions is to ensure that the partitions' filesystems are intact. You can do this either using the OS's utilities—such as CHKDSK in DOS, Windows, or OS/2—or using PartitionMagic itself. In fact, PartitionMagic automatically performs a minimal partition integrity check when it performs any major operation. I do recommend you use the OS's own utilities before running PartitionMagic, however; this practice adds another level of protection against disaster.

To perform a partition integrity check from within PartitionMagic itself, select the partition and choose Operations, Check. The program produces the Check Partition Results dialog box shown in Figure 8.5. If any errors are reported, you should run appropriate disk utilities to fix them before proceeding.

FIGURE 8.5
The Check Partition Results dialog box displays any problems with the partition's data structures.

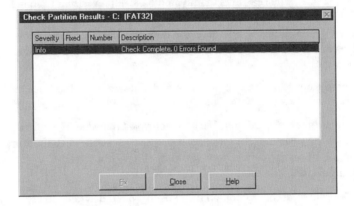

> **N O T E** PartitionMagic won't check any partition with an unsupported filesystem, such as FreeBSD partitions, or the partition from which PartitionMagic has been launched. ■

Moving and Resizing Partitions

To move or resize a partition, follow these steps:

1. Select the partition you want to adjust.

2. Choose Operations, Resize/Move to open the Resize/Move Partition dialog box shown in Figure 8.6. Note that this dialog box depicts the disk space that's used by files, free space within the partition, and unpartitioned space graphically, so you can judge how much space is available for adjustment. In version 5.0, it includes 2GB or 1024-cylinder markers, if they happen to fall within the possible range of sizes for the partition.

> **N O T E** The depiction of used disk space is not an accurate representation of file placement on the disk. If necessary, PartitionMagic moves files to resize or move a partition. Some other utilities, such as FIPS, require that you defragment the partition before resizing it. ■

3. Adjust the size and position of the partition within whatever free space exists on either side of it. You can do so by clicking and dragging the resize tabs on either end of the partition's representation, by dragging the partition body to move it, or by adjusting the values in the spin boxes below the graphical representation of the partition.

4. Click OK to accept your changes.

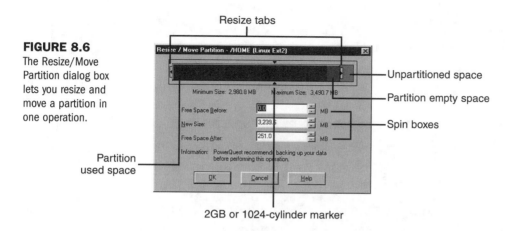

FIGURE 8.6
The Resize/Move Partition dialog box lets you resize and move a partition in one operation.

Resize tabs

Resize / Move Partition - /HOME (Linux Ext2)

Minimum Size: 2,980.8 MB   Maximum Size: 3,490.7 MB

Free Space Before: 0.0 MB
New Size: 3,239.6 MB
Free Space After: 251.0 MB

Information: PowerQuest recommends backing up your data before performing this operation.

OK   Cancel   Help

Unpartitioned space
Partition empty space
Spin boxes

Partition used space

2GB or 1024-cylinder marker

5. Repeat steps 1–4 for each partition you want to resize or move.

6. Choose General, Apply Changes (Ctrl+A) to have PartitionMagic apply the changes. These operations can take a while, during which time PartitionMagic displays the Batch Progress dialog box shown in Figure 8.7. Each operation (such as Resizing Partition in Figure 8.7) consists of several subtasks (such as Checking Inodes, Blocks, and Sizes). Because PartitionMagic lets you chain together several operations, there's also a progress bar for the entire process.

FIGURE 8.7
The Batch Progress dialog box displays the progress of a PartitionMagic operation.

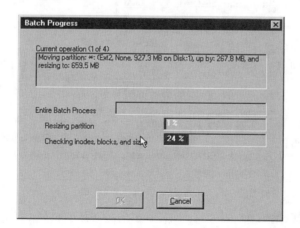

Batch Progress

Current operation (1 of 4)
Moving partition: *: (Ext2, None, 927.3 MB on Disk:1), up by: 267.8 MB, and resizing to: 659.5 MB

Entire Batch Process
Resizing partition   1 %
Checking inodes, blocks, and sizes   24 %

OK   Cancel

NOTE If you use the Windows version of PartitionMagic, it might need to reboot your computer and perform certain operations in DOS mode. If so, you won't see the Batch Progress dialog box, and the reboot will unceremoniously close any programs you have running. It's therefore wise to close any other programs before running PartitionMagic. ▪

Copying a Partition

To copy a partition, follow these steps:

1. Select the partition you want to copy.

2. Choose Operations, Copy to get the Copy Partition dialog box shown in Figure 8.8.

FIGURE 8.8
You can use the Disk selector to choose to which physical disk you want to copy a partition.

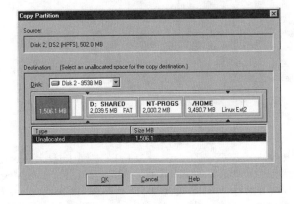

3. Select the free space in which you want to place the copy. If only one region of free space is available that's large enough to hold the partition you've selected, that region will be selected automatically.

4. Click OK.

5. Repeat steps 1–4 for any additional partitions you want to copy.

6. Choose General, Apply Changes (Ctrl+A) to have PartitionMagic do its work. The copy operation can take a while, during which time PartitionMagic displays the Batch Progress dialog box previously shown in Figure 8.7.

You can combine copy and resize operations by performing one after another. If you want to copy a partition into a space that's smaller than the original, you must perform the resize operation and then the copy operation. You might then need to perform a second resize operation to increase the size of the copied partition to fill the desired space.

Converting Partitions

PartitionMagic supports several conversions between filesystem types. Specifically, it can convert back and forth between FAT-16 and FAT-32, convert from NTFS to FAT-16 or FAT-32, and convert from FAT-16 to either HPFS or NTFS, although the latter requires the use of a utility included with Windows NT. PartitionMagic cannot convert from HPFS to anything else, nor can it convert either way between ext2fs and anything else.

To convert a partition, select it and choose the appropriate menu item from the Operations, Convert menu. PartitionMagic displays a dialog box with information about the consequences of the conversion, such as the need for OS/2 to access HPFS partitions. You must choose General, Apply Changes (Ctrl+A) to enact the change, just as with partition resizes and other operations.

In addition to these major changes, you can perform more minor modifications using operations available on the Operations, Advanced menu. Specifically

- **Bad Sector Retest**—Checks the partition for bad sectors and marks any bad sectors found as such.

- **Hide Partition**—Hides a partition from all OSs that use partition type codes.

- **Resize Root**—Changes the number of file entries available in the root of a FAT partition. This option can be particularly useful if you need to store many long filenames on the root of a VFAT partition. It has no effect on the number of files you can store inside folders, however.

- **Set Active**—Marks the partition as the bootable partition.

- **Resize Clusters**—This option enables you to change the allocation block size for a FAT partition. If you select a smaller size, PartitionMagic might resize the partition downward. You can't adjust the allocation block size beyond the limits normally allowed by FAT for a partition of a given size.

    ▶ To learn more about allocation block sizes, **see** "Partition Size and Disk Consumption Limits," **p. 115**.

 TIP Some partition resizers don't adjust the allocation block size when you shrink a partition. Therefore, if you've used another partition resizer in the past, you might want to see whether you can adjust the allocation block size without shrinking your partitions using PartitionMagic.

Not all these advanced operations are available for all partitions. Some, such as Resize Clusters, are meaningful only for particular filesystems. Others, such as Set Active, work only on primary partitions.

Using the Wizards

PartitionMagic 4.0's and 5.0's Windows versions include several *wizards*—features designed to help automate common functions, making decisions for you according to rules determined by the PowerQuest programmers. (These wizards do not come with the version of PartitionMagic included on this book's CD.) The following wizards are included:

- **Create New Partition**—Helps you to create a new partition, resizing and moving existing partitions as necessary to accomplish the task.

- **Redistribute Free Space**—Adjusts partition sizes so that a reasonable amount of free space exists in each partition.

- **Prepare for New Operating System**—Resizes partitions and creates new ones to help you install a new OS. (This wizard comes with the 4.0 version of PartitionMagic but has been dropped from the 5.0 version.)

- **Analyze and Recommend**—Examines your partition layout and recommends changes to help improve performance. (This wizard is also present in PartitionMagic 4.0 but absent in 5.0.)

- **Reclaim Wasted Space**—With some filesystem types (particularly FAT-16), it's often possible to increase the amount of disk space available by reducing the size of a partition. PartitionMagic can examine your disks and determine whether this situation might exist; if so, it suggests a new set of partition sizes to maximize your available disk space. (This wizard is another casualty of the jump from version 4.0 to 5.0.)

- **Merge Partitions**—Helps you merge two FAT partitions into a single partition. (This wizard is present in version 5.0 but not in the older 4.0.)

The wizards are available from the Wizards menu item and from the icons below the partition layout map (refer to Figure 8.4). Their use is fairly straightforward; select the appropriate wizard and it asks you a series of questions, such as what OS you intend to install and to what hard disk. Its end result is a recommended set of changes, which you can command PartitionMagic to perform by clicking Finish from the wizard's final dialog box. Figure 8.9 shows the final dialog box from a run of the Prepare for New Operating System wizard.

FIGURE 8.9
The wizards provide a diagram of proposed changes for your approval.

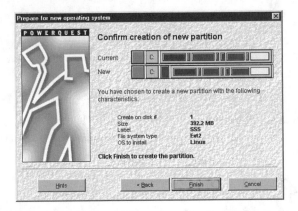

In general, I recommend against using a wizard on any but fairly simple systems. The information contained in this book enables you to design a partition layout that's far better than what a PartitionMagic wizard can produce. For example, the layout in Figure 8.9 uses a primary partition unnecessarily for a new Linux installation and places that partition some distance on the disk from existing Linux partitions, including the swap partition. Wizards also sometimes design wholly inappropriate configurations, such as partitions that are larger than the disk on which they reside. Of course, you can use a wizard to see what PartitionMagic recommends, and if it's acceptable, use it. If you find the results deficient, you can design your own by hand.

Cleanup After the Change

Your task isn't finished when PartitionMagic has done its resizing, moving, and other operations. Depending on what you did and what OSs you're running, you might need to perform additional adjustments, either with PartitionMagic or with other tools. For example

- You might need to set a new partition to be active. You can do this in PartitionMagic by selecting the partition and choosing Operations, Advanced, Set Active. You should need to do this only if you deleted the former boot partition or if you've created a partition for a new OS that you want to be active—for example, if you plan to install Linux on a primary partition and place LILO on that partition as your system's boot loader.

- You might need to rewrite the hard disk's *master boot record (MBR)*. You can do this using DOS by typing FDISK /MBR or from OS/2 by typing FDISK /NEWMBR. You should need to do this only if you intend to remove a boot loader, such as LILO or System Commander, that resides in the MBR.

  ▶ To learn more about the hard disk's master boot record, **see** "The Post-BIOS Boot Process," **p. 86**.

- If you've moved or resized your Linux boot partition, there's a good chance that you must reinstall LILO. You need a Linux boot floppy to perform this task, so it's wise to prepare one before using PartitionMagic to modify a Linux boot partition.

- The same rules for partition letter assignments and device identifiers that apply to any other means of repartitioning apply to the use of PartitionMagic. You might therefore need to adjust applications' drive letter assumptions or the /etc/fstab file in a UNIX system.

If you understand how your OSs use hard disk partitions, you shouldn't have difficulty with these post-partitioning cleanup operations. They can be troubling if you're a novice to such operations, however. If you run into problems, I suggest you read Chapters 3–5, and perhaps 6 and 7 as well. These should provide you with the information you need to get up and running again.

Coping with Troubled Partition Tables

PartitionMagic is unusually sensitive to the layout of partitions on a computer. The result is that it might refuse to operate on certain hard disks that work perfectly well. One of the more common trouble spots is in a partition table that has been laid out with logical partition codes out of sequence relative to their positions on the hard disk. This problem is easy to see if you use Linux's fdisk program, and in fact it's easy to create such a disk layout using Linux's fdisk. Here's an example that demonstrates the problem:

```
   Device Boot    Start      End     Blocks   Id  System
/dev/sda1             1        4      32098+  83  Linux
/dev/sda2             5     1115    8924107+   5  Extended
/dev/sda5           605      621     136521  82  Linux swap
/dev/sda6             5      604    4819468+  83  Linux
/dev/sda7           622     1115    3968023+  83  Linux
```

As you can see, /dev/sda5 begins after /dev/sda6. This partition layout works in most OSs, but PartitionMagic doesn't like it and refuses to modify it. In fact, PartitionMagic reports that the entire disk suffers from a problem, so you can't do anything with this disk from PartitionMagic.

N O T E   PartitionMagic objects to logical partitions that are out of sequence. Primary partitions that are out of sequence pose no problems. ▪

In this particular case, the solution is to use Linux's fdisk to re-create the partitions so that their partition numbers match their order on the disk. To do so, follow these steps:

1. Start Linux's fdisk program.

2. Write down the start and end cylinders for each logical partition. Double- and triple-check these values because a mistake will render the affected partitions truly useless. Similarly, it's wise to record the value from the Blocks column of the fdisk display.

3. Delete all the logical partitions.

4. Create new logical partitions in the order in which they appear on the disk. For example, you would create the partition from cylinders 5–604 in the preceding example first (to become /dev/sda5), then the partition from 605–621.

5. Check the partition start and end cylinders and the number of blocks against the values you recorded in step 2. If any value doesn't match, *stop!* Abort the operation by typing q to quit without saving the changes. *Only if all values, including the number of blocks, are what you expect should you proceed.*

6. Save your changes by typing w.

If all goes well, PartitionMagic will then be able to modify the afflicted partitions. You might need to modify your /etc/fstab file or drive letter handling because these features can change after you alter the logical partition layout in this way.

CAUTION

Altering the partition table in this way is *extremely dangerous!* You should take extreme measures to ensure that you create new partitions that are identical in size and location to the ones with which you began. Also, many disk partitioning utilities alter data on partitions when creating the partitions, so they cannot be used in this way. Linux's fdisk is safe in this respect.

Other problems PartitionMagic finds with partition tables might not be so easy to correct. PartitionMagic might refuse to modify a partition or might insist on leaving a gap between partitions. There is no easy way around such problems, unfortunately. To avoid them, I recommend that you use PartitionMagic to create all your partitions, if you intend to use the program at all. This practice should guarantee that PartitionMagic is able to handle the partitions. If you want to create a partition for a filesystem that PartitionMagic doesn't understand, such as FreeBSD's FFS, you can still use PartitionMagic to create the partition; just change the partition's type (using a tool such as Linux's `fdisk`) before you install the OS.

Summary

Repartitioning an existing hard disk setup is one of the most tedious and dangerous operations that's commonly required in creating and maintaining a multi-OS configuration. This chapter provides an overview of three methods for performing this task:

- Converting a partition from use by one OS to use by another
- Backing up data, repartitioning, and restoring data
- Using a dynamic partition resizer—PartitionMagic, in particular

Whatever method you use, repartitioning a hard disk has consequences on drive letter assignment in Microsoft-style OSs, and on device identifiers for hard disk partitions in UNIX OSs. If you plan your partition changes carefully, you can often avoid painful consequences of your changes. You can often even configure your system so that the changes are transparent after you've made them. ●

Operating System Installation

The OS Installation Checklist

Why This OS?

The preceding chapters have presented a wide range of information on the computer boot process, hard disk partition layout, and related information. Now it's time to begin the process of installing your new OS. This process should actually begin with an evaluation of your OS needs, before you do anything to your hard disk in preparation for installing an OS. Installation continues with checking your hardware for compatibility and preparing your system for the installation. I've touched on many of these topics in previous chapters, but this chapter provides a more detailed look at them.

The first question you should ask yourself is why you want to install a given OS. In general, you install a new OS because the one you're currently running is deficient in some way that the new OS is not. There are some other reasons for installing an OS, however, and in some cases you gain nothing by examining this question in detail. For example, you might be under orders from your boss to install a new OS. Sometimes, though, you might find that a less radical solution than a multi-OS configuration will do what you want, so you should examine your reasons for installing an OS and look for alternatives—both alternatives to installing a new OS and alternative OSs.

It might seem odd that I take a conservative approach to OS installation in this section. After all, this *is* a book on multi-OS configurations, so if you've bought this book you're presumably already pretty serious about installing a new OS. Unfortunately, installing a new OS can easily consume many hours of your time, and I'd be doing you a disservice to recommend that you undertake such a task at the drop of a hat. Better to spend a few minutes investigating alternatives than several hours discovering that your new OS is no better than the old one.

What Faults Do You See in Your Current OS?

One of the most common reasons for installing multiple OSs is that the first OS doesn't meet your needs, or at least not all of them. It's often easy to become dissatisfied with an OS and decide that the best way to proceed is to scrap the whole thing, or at least try an alternative in a multi-boot configuration. Certainly I've felt urges to wipe hard drives in frustration, or even throw a computer out a window. Don't act in haste, though.

Here are some common OS problems and alternatives to creating a multi-OS configuration:

- **Unreliability**—OSs certainly vary in their reliability, but factors other than the OS can often cause unreliable operation. Two common problems are faulty memory chips and buggy drivers. If any OS crashes more than once a day, you might want to look into upgrading the drivers for your video card, sound card, and other devices. If possible, check your RAM for problems, either by having a technician test the RAM or by swapping it with the RAM from another computer. More rarely, defects in other hardware can cause unreliable operation. Even non-obvious components such as the computer's power supply can cause unreliable operation.

Finally, it's possible that upgrading or reinstalling the OS itself will improve its reliability. Microsoft Windows, in particular, has a tendency to accumulate defects that eventually force a reinstall. Removing all traces of an old installation and starting from scratch (often called a "clean install") is the best way to proceed if you think your OS has become corrupt, but installing over an existing setup can sometimes do the trick and is likely to be less disruptive.

■ **Buggy software**—You might feel trapped by buggy software on your current platform. Unlike unreliable OS operation, buggy applications don't cause system crashes, but they do cause the applications themselves to crash or do strange things. In many cases, though, buggy software doesn't require a change in OS, just a change in the application. Of course, if you're using applications for which no alternatives are available on your current platform but for which alternatives do exist on another OS, an OS change can help you open opportunities to find better programs.

Part

IV

Ch

9

■ **Software selection**—Particularly if you're using a relatively exotic OS such as BeOS, you might be frustrated by the available selection of software. The plethora of programs available for Windows, in particular, can be enticing. Often, however, you can find more choices than you might at first expect, even for a less-popular OS. Don't restrict your software searches to the aisles of your local computer store. Check the Web page for the producer of the OS; these pages often contain links to third-party developers whose products might be hard to find. There are also often Web pages maintained by user groups or even simply individuals with useful links to rare software products. Many OSs benefit from ports of open source software, as well. (Check the Free Software Foundation's Web page at `http://www.fsf.org` or Freshmeat, `http://www.freshmeat.net`, for links to many of these.) If you have no idea where else to look for software, try a Web search on `http://www.deja.com` or a search engine such as `http://www.yahoo.com` or `http://www.excite.com`. You might be surprised at how much you turn up.

■ **Familiarity**—If you're used to one OS and have just bought a computer on which another OS is preinstalled, you might want to install your old OS on the new machine. This is certainly a reasonable thing to do, provided the old OS is compatible with the new computer. You might be able to find ways to make the new computer's OS behave more like the OS with which you're familiar, though. If you're not particularly concerned with the availability of specific programs, this might be a simpler solution than installing two OSs on the computer.

▶ To learn more about making one OS work like another, **see** Chapter 17, "Modifying GUI Look and Feel."

■ **Ease of use**—You might be dissatisfied with the ease of use of your current OS. Perhaps its user interface is inconsistent or strange; or maybe it blocks you from doing the things you want to do because it tries to be *too* friendly. Either way, you might be able to find tools to help improve matters. Keep in mind, too, that switching to a new OS imposes its own learning curve unless you're already familiar with that OS. For the most part, OSs are easy to use not because they are innately "intuitive" but because we're already familiar with their tools.

■ **Inadequate features**—You might feel you need to install a new OS because your current OS lacks certain features that you require. For example, if you need to write programs that use 32-bit addressing, you might feel the need to switch away from DOS and its 16-bit memory model. In some cases, though, you can extend an OS's capabilities by using appropriate add-on utilities. Many DOS programming tools include 32-bit extensions, for example. As with GUI tools and available application programs, you must search for the specific tools that might help you overcome a specific OS's limitations.

If you feel vaguely dissatisfied with your current OS, the preceding list can help you identify the cause of your dissatisfaction with greater precision. If not, think harder about what you find unappealing about your current OS. If you don't identify the problems with your current OS, chances are good that the next OS you try won't meet your needs, either.

Does the New OS Meet Your Unmet Needs?

After you've identified the faults in your current OS, you can evaluate your potential new OS with respect to those features. Keep in mind that your new OS will likely be deficient in some area that's a strength of your old one. In a multi-OS configuration, this fact need not be a problem because you can switch back and forth between the OSs to use the one that's best for any given task. Rebooting does take time, however, and it closes all open applications and files, so rebooting frequently isn't practical.

In a multi-OS configuration, therefore, it's best if more than one OS is suitable for performing many of your day-to-day computing tasks. When this is the case, you might not be forced to reboot to perform some minor task. For example, Table 9.1 shows hypothetical ratings of two OSs for several different tasks (higher numbers represent better features for the task in question). As you can see, both OSs can be used for game playing, Web browsing, and word processing, but each OS has its own niche as well. Therefore, if you first boot OS 1 to record an audio file, you can continue to use it for Web browsing, although OS 2 does have a slight edge in that area. If audio recording were OS 1's only strong point, you'd be forced to reboot to browse the Web.

Table 9.1   Hypothetical Applicability of Two OSs to Assorted Tasks

Task	OS 1	OS 2
Audio recording	10	3
Financial analysis	2	9
Game playing	6	6
Web browsing	8	9
Word processing	9	8

Of course, one task might be important enough, or the capabilities of one OS might be far enough in advance of other alternatives, that installing the OS for that task alone might be worthwhile. In the end, you must decide for yourself whether maintaining a separate OS is worth the effort for whatever purpose you have planned for it.

What Features Do You Like in the New OS?

Take a critical look at the features of your potential new OS. Remember that whoever put the CD in the box wants to sell that box to you. Don't assume that a feature in one OS is comparable to a feature in another OS. For example, both Windows 9x and OS/2 support preemptive multitasking and long filenames.

▶ To learn more about preemptive multitasking, **see** "Windows 3.1: A DOS Extension," **p. 29**.

These OSs accomplish these tasks, however, in quite different ways and with varying degrees of success. OS/2, for example, implements true preemptive multitasking for both 32- and 16-bit programs. Windows 9x, however, uses a mixed method of multitasking 16-bit Windows programs, so you don't gain the full benefits of preemptive multitasking when you run 16-bit Windows programs. In terms of long filenames, Windows 9x implements these using the VFAT filesystem, which is an extension to the standard FAT filesystem used by DOS. OS/2 implements long filenames using a completely different filesystem, HPFS, which means that you don't get the benefit of long filenames on FAT partitions, but if you go all the way for HPFS, you get better disk performance. Of greatest importance for a person considering running both Windows 9x and OS/2, neither OS can read the other's long filenames without third-party drivers. Such drivers exist but don't always provide a completely seamless experience for the user.

▶ To learn more about reading one OS's filesystem from another, **see** Chapter 13, "Tools for Accessing Foreign Filesystems."

N O T E OS/2 supports a limited type of long filename on FAT partitions using Extended Attributes (EAs) that can be read by the WorkPlace Shell (WPS), OS/2's desktop environment. These EA-based long filenames can't be read in most application programs, however. ▪

The point of this discussion is that you must look a bit further than a one-line description of a feature for any feature that's important to you. Don't assume that a new OS will do the things your old one does. If you have experience with a feature on one OS, don't assume that the equivalent feature works the same way on another OS. If you're uncertain about the implementation of a feature, research it on the OS producer's Web site or post a question to an appropriate Usenet newsgroup.

▶ To learn more about Usenet newsgroups for many OSs, **see** "Reading Usenet Newsgroups," **p. 282**.

Other Reasons for Installing an OS

Aside from disappointment with your current OS, you might have other reasons for installing a new one. Many of these reasons are outlined in Chapter 1, "The Trials and Triumphs of a Multi-OS Computer." They include curiosity and a change to a new OS imposed from outside. Whatever the cause, you should be sure that the costs are worth the effort. This is particularly true if you're merely curious. Installing and learning a new OS requires a substantial investment of time and effort, and many people who attempt such an installation out of idle curiosity become frustrated and disillusioned. If you want to avoid this fate, you should be sure that your curiosity is sufficient to sustain several hours worth of effort before you can begin to use the new OS for anything useful. It's best if you have some idea of ways in which the new OS can improve on your current configuration, or if you have experience with a similar OS.

▶ To learn more about deciding to use more than one OS, **see** "The Desire and Need for Multiple OSs," **p. 10**.

If the OS change is being imposed on you from outside, you might not have much choice in the matter. You should still evaluate the costs and benefits, however. If the costs are too high, you might be able to alter the decision by presenting a cogent argument against the change.

Alternatives to a Full-Blown OS Installation

In many cases, you can save yourself considerable time and effort by relying on some method of using an OS that doesn't require a complete OS installation. These methods are extremely helpful if you need the alternative only occasionally or for one or two programs. They can't always be used, however, and even when they can be, they can impose requirements on your system's configuration similar to what would be required for a full-blown installation.

An OS on a Removable Medium   One method that's particularly helpful for running DOS is to place it on a floppy disk. DOS is small enough that a basic installation and a respectable assortment of utilities or programs can fit on a single floppy. In fact, many DOS versions even provide an option to install directly to a floppy rather than to the hard disk.

If you have a FAT-12 or FAT-16 partition on your hard disk, DOS installed on floppy can access that partition and run programs from it. Therefore, a DOS boot floppy can be used to run programs from a hard disk. If you have enough DOS programs that they must go on a hard disk, though, why bother with a floppy boot? Reasons include the following:

■ **Primary partition preservation**—Booting DOS from a floppy disk can help preserve the available stock of primary partitions, which are limited to four per hard disk. This factor is particularly important if you want to run several versions of DOS, such as MS-DOS 6.22, PC-DOS 2000, and FreeDOS all on one computer. Some boot loaders, such as V Communications' System Commander, can also help preserve primary partitions, but of course creating a boot floppy is much less expensive than buying System Commander.

- **Multiple configurations**—You can easily create several floppies with varying system configurations, thus enabling you to boot with different `CONFIG.SYS` and `AUTOEXEC.BAT` files merely by changing the floppy disk. You can, however, achieve similar effects by using conditional statements inside these files or by using System Commander to swap these configuration files with backups.

- **Virus protection**—If you always boot from a write-protected floppy, you make it harder for a virus to infect your system. For this benefit to be real, however, you must keep your boot floppies write protected at all times.

- **Infrequent booting**—If you seldom use DOS, placing it on a boot floppy can be simpler and require less maintenance than keeping a boot partition for the OS.

In addition to DOS, some other OSs can reside partly or completely on removable media. A minimal Linux installation can fit on a single Zip disk, for example. Depending on your hardware, you might need an accompanying boot floppy to boot such a system. Such a configuration can be helpful if you have occasional need for Linux, but not enough need to justify placing it on the main hard disk. You might also be able to create a single Linux removable disk installation for use on several computers, provided that these machines' hardware is uniform enough. You could use such a system for certain types of emergency maintenance, for backup using Linux backup tools, or to take your Linux system with you from one location to another.

Iomega (`http://www.iomega.com`) and Symantec (`http://www.symantec.com`) together provide a utility to let you create a minimal Windows 9*x* installation on a combination of a boot floppy and a Zip disk. You must have Windows 9*x* installed on your computer to create this special rescue disk combination, however, so it's not very useful as an alternative to a normal hard disk boot. It is, however, potentially very helpful for emergency recovery purposes.

If you place an entire OS on one removable medium, chances are you must face the challenge of fitting everything into a space that's much more limited than is typical for the OS. You likely won't have space for large packages such as the Emacs editor or WordPerfect on a 100MB Zip disk, for example, although you can fit a GUI environment and many utilities and tools on such a disk, if you're careful to install only the minimum tools necessary.

When you use a removable medium for OS boot purposes, remember that you won't have access to data on the hard disk unless the OS on the removable disk has appropriate drivers. For example, you can't access BeOS BFS partitions from a DOS boot floppy. This fact can occasionally be limiting, particularly if you need to use files larger than can fit onto a floppy disk. You might want to configure your removable-medium boot disk to include foreign filesystem support, or place a native filesystem on the hard disk, even if it's not normally used by the hard disk's OSs, for data transfer purposes.

▶ To learn more about filesystem drivers, **see** Chapter 13, "Tools for Accessing Foreign Filesystems."

Emulators   Emulators provide a means of running one OS's programs in another OS. Emulators come in three basic forms:

- **OS API emulators**—An OS's application programming interface (API) is a set of tools an OS provides to programs to enable the programs to perform useful tasks. Some emulators attempt to provide one OS's API set on another OS, thus enabling individual programs to run. An example is the WINE (which stands for *Windows emulator* or *WINE is not an emulator*, depending on your fancy) program for x86-based UNIX versions, including Linux. In some sense, X servers running under non-UNIX OSs are OS API emulators, although technically speaking, X isn't a UNIX-only environment, so such configurations don't qualify as emulators. An X configuration also requires that the programs be recompiled for the host OS; it doesn't enable you to run, say, Linux executables on OS/2.

- **Machine environment emulators**—These emulators configure the CPU to enable it to run one OS within another. The 80386 and later CPUs in the x86 line include features to facilitate such operation. These features are used by OS/2's DOS box and Linux's DOSEMU programs to provide the capability to run DOS and (in OS/2) Windows 3.1. Because the emulator runs an actual version of the OS in question, programs for that OS run and use the OS in the emulator.

- **CPU emulators**—The most radical form of emulation creates a simulated computer in which an OS and its programs can run. This approach is more extreme than machine environment emulation because a CPU emulator uses one CPU to run programs designed for another CPU. On x86 CPUs, emulators exist for a variety of computers—mostly old eight-bit machines such as the Commodore 64 and Apple II series. The Executor emulator, available from ARDI (http://www.ardi.com) emulates a 680x0-based Macintosh. Some other computers, such as PowerPC-based Macs, have emulators for x86-based computers, enabling these systems to run PC operating systems. A CPU emulator can emulate the target OS using API emulation or it can run the target OS itself, much as a machine environment emulator does. Figure 9.1 shows a Linux system running ARDI.

Emulators are particularly interesting if you need access to only one or two programs or if you want to have simultaneous access to these programs while you work with other programs. In some cases, such as VMware (http://www.vmware.com), setting up an emulator can be as involved as setting up a multi-boot computer. The advantage is the simultaneous access to both OSs' programs. Emulators suffer from two main drawbacks:

- **Imperfect emulation**—Emulators often run programs imperfectly, and sometimes not at all.

- **Speed**—Some emulators, particularly CPU emulators, don't run programs as quickly as they can run on machines of otherwise similar power. In the case of CPU emulators for older systems, the improved speed of modern computers more than makes up for the speed lost to the emulation itself, however; there's plenty of speed to spare in a 400MHz Pentium III for emulation of a 2MHz 6502 CPU, for example.

  ▶ To learn more about emulators, **see** Chapter 18, "OSs Within OSs: Emulators."

FIGURE 9.1
Emulators can present a window in which the OS runs and displays its own windows, as does ARDI in this figure; or they might directly display windows belonging to the emulated OS.

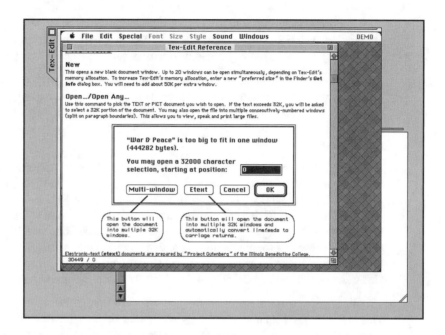

How Great a Leap Is It to the New OS?

One final point to consider before you decide to take the plunge is to examine how divergent your new OS is from your old one or from whatever other OSs you know reasonably well. As described in Chapter 2, "Operating Systems for x86 Hardware in 2000," three main classes of OSs are available for x86 hardware today:

- **Microsoft-style OSs**—These include DOS, Windows, and OS/2. These OSs are characterized by the use of drive letters, a small-computer heritage, excellent legacy support for older DOS programs, single-user operation, and (except for DOS) a single GUI integrated into the OS. Except for MS-DOS competitors, Microsoft has had a hand in developing all these OSs, although IBM is currently the only source for OS/2.

- **BeOS**—BeOS gets its own category simply because it doesn't fit either of the other two. It has been developed from the ground up, but it shares many surface features with UNIX-style OSs.

- **UNIX OSs**—Whether or not they bear the official UNIX stamp, OSs such as Linux, FreeBSD, and Solaris cluster in much the way the Microsoft-style OSs cluster, and in practice perhaps even more tightly. These OSs are multiuser and multitasking. They use an integrated directory tree for all partitions, and they generally use the X Window System GUI environment, which is highly customizable.

In addition to these OSs, a few very exotic OSs don't fit very well in this grand scheme, such as Plan 9 (http://plan9.bell-labs.com/plan9/). In fact, BeOS might be considered one of these "oddball" OSs; I list it in the preceding categorization because it's quite popular, as such OSs go. Non-x86 OSs, such as Mac OS and VMS, also exist, but I don't consider them in this classification system simply because this book is concerned only with OSs for x86 hardware.

In general, moving between OSs within a category has the advantage that many of the features with which you're familiar are present and work in much the way you anticipate. When you switch between categories, though, the number of changes increases dramatically, so such a shift can be more disconcerting, particularly if you have experience with just one or two OSs in a single category.

The presence of powerful GUI environments can help ease the transition from one OS to another, particularly if you pick an environment on your new OS that resembles the environment on your original OS. The K Desktop Environment (KDE) and GNU Network Object Model Environment (GNOME) projects have modeled themselves after the Windows 9x GUI in many ways, for example, which can help ease the transition to a UNIX OS if you're used to Windows. These environments don't change the underlying nature of the host UNIX OS, however, which in some ways creates problems—you might be lulled into thinking that the UNIX system is more like Windows than it really is and therefore make invalid assumptions that lead to trouble.

This discussion should not be taken as advice that you avoid making the transition from the Microsoft-style to the UNIX-style OSs, or vice versa. The transition can certainly be made, and plenty of people are familiar with and productive in both environments. You should simply be prepared for a steeper learning curve when you install an OS from a different OS group than the one with which you're currently familiar.

Checking Hardware Compatibility

After you've determined that an OS is at least likely to suit your needs, you should check that you have appropriate hardware for running that OS. Most modern OSs support a wide range of hardware, but none—not even Windows 9x—supports all the hardware that's available today. In general, hardware support is best for Windows 9x and worst for the more exotic OSs such as Plan 9 and the rarer varieties of UNIX. Of the OSs I concentrate on in this book, BeOS has the most limited hardware support. Windows NT, OS/2, Linux, and FreeBSD have intermediate levels of support—good enough to handle most or all hardware found in most modern computers, although support for the latest and less common hardware might not be present. There are exceptions to these rules for certain specific devices, however; some hardware might work better in an OS such as Linux or FreeBSD than in a more popular OS such as Windows 9x.

Verifying Your Hardware—The Theory

In theory, you should be able to verify that your hardware is supported by checking various sources. First, though, you must know what hardware you have. In most cases, you need to know what chipset a plug-in device uses. You can usually determine this by reading manufacturer codes from the largest chip on a device. (Some manufacturers cover this chip with a sticker, which you can peel away. Others silkscreen their own names on the chip, which makes it harder to identify the chipset.)

▶ To learn more about identifying your hardware and locating drivers, **see** Chapter 22, "Finding Drivers."

When you've identified your hardware, you can check a few sources to try to determine whether your chosen new OS is compatible:

- **The OS distributor**—You can find official Web pages for most OSs that list the supported hardware by device manufacturer or by chipset. If a device is listed here, it's the surest sign that it's supported. If a device isn't listed, though, don't give up. There are other sources for drivers for many devices.

- **The hardware manufacturer**—Hardware companies often distribute drivers for a variety of OSs, or at least have links on their Web sites to sources for such drivers.

- **Compatible hardware manufacturers**—You might be able to find an appropriate driver distributed by the manufacturer of a compatible device. For example, if you have a generic Ethernet adapter that uses a PNIC chipset, you could check the Linksys or Netgear Web sites because these companies also produce PNIC-based Ethernet boards. Such drivers aren't guaranteed to work, but they might.

- **Third parties**—Occasionally, a third party develops a driver, either as freeware or shareware. This practice is particularly common for open-source OSs such as Linux. Tracking down these drivers can be tricky, though. A Web search on Yahoo (http://www.yahoo.com), Excite (http://www.excite.com), or some other search engine might produce useful results. File archive sites such as http://www.freshmeat.net or ftp://ftp-os2.nmsu.edu can also be helpful in locating third-party drivers.

Unfortunately, hardware compatibility can be something of a mysterious art—90% science, 10% voodoo. For example, you might find that your Ethernet board works fine in one computer with a given OS, but when you put that same adapter into another computer that's configured identically except for the motherboard, the Ethernet adapter no longer works. You might also find that an EIDE CD-ROM drive works in all your OSs, but another model EIDE CD-ROM drive works in all those OSs except for one.

Checking Your Hardware Before OS Installation

How do you avoid a hair-pulling session in which you try to get a device to work, but fail? A little planning can help you avoid such situations, or at least know that you might have problems. If you know that a specific device is likely to cause problems, you can research a solution, or even be prepared to replace the hardware with something else. Here are some tips to help you at least see the land mines that lurk in the realm of PC hardware compatibility:

- **Do a Deja News search**—Check the newsgroup archives at `http://www.deja.com` for recent postings concerning your hardware and chosen OS. For example, if you plan to install FreeBSD and have a computer with a Matrox Millennium G400 video card and Crystal Semiconductor (CS) 4237 audio card, you could do searches on `freebsd and matrox and millennium and g400` for the first, and `freebsd and (cs4237 or 4237 or (crystal and semiconductor))`. Do one such search per major device in your system. With any luck, your searches will turn up useful compatibility information.

- **Read the documentation**—Especially if you plan to install drivers from hardware manufacturers or third parties, read the documentation before you do so. Occasionally the documentation lists incompatibilities or special procedures you must follow to get the device working. Remember that hardware often comes with both printed and electronic documentation. Check both sources.

- **Post to a newsgroup**—Particularly if you don't turn up anything useful on a given device, try posting about it to an appropriate Usenet newsgroup. Be sure to provide the manufacturer, model number, and (if you know it) the chipset used by the device. You might consider posting your entire configuration for advice on what might require special attention—but do so only after you've done preliminary research, and indicate you've done this research. Potential newsgroup responders are more likely to help you if you provide evidence that you're not simply trying to get others to do your research for you.

In practice, some devices are far more likely to cause problems than others. Motherboards, CPUs, RAM, hard disks, floppy drives, modern CD-ROM drives, keyboards, mice, and monitors are all well supported in all OSs. Items that are particularly likely to require attention are video and sound cards, scanners, video cameras, and universal serial bus (USB) devices (including USB mice and keyboards). SCSI host adapters, Ethernet adapters, and certain older devices such as add-on serial ports are generally well supported, but with some glaring exceptions. Some particularly exotic devices, such as TV capture boards, are unlikely to have support in any but a handful of OSs.

▶ To learn more about hardware that's more and less likely to pose problems, **see** "Know Your Hardware," **p. 14**.

Doing a Test Installation

In some cases, you might prefer to test your hardware empirically by doing a quick test installation. The goal here isn't to create your desired end-result configuration but to see whether the OS works on the hardware. If you run into problems with specific devices, you can concentrate your research on those devices and not waste time researching others.

Ideally, you should perform a test installation using a spare hard disk that contains no vital information. Unplug your normal hard disk and install the spare disk, and then run your new OS's installation routine. If you don't have a spare hard disk, you can still do a test installation to the partition you intend to later hold the final installation.

Doing a test installation has advantages over and above those of checking your hardware. Specifically, it familiarizes you with the installation procedure and with the basic OS configuration. Particularly if you use a spare hard disk, it might alert you to dangers of installation—for example, you might spot that the installer likes to wipe out existing partitions, which you presumably want to avoid when you reinstall your normal hard disk and install the new OS on it.

In general, a quick test installation in lieu of hardware research is best practiced when the OS is likely to support most or all of your hardware and when you have a spare hard disk on which to perform this test. If you plan to buy or build a new computer on which to run multiple OSs, you should definitely not rely solely on this approach because chances are good you'll end up returning some components, or the entire computer, because of compatibility problems.

Cleaning Up Existing OSs

After you've determined that your hardware is likely to work at least well enough to install the new OS, it's time to clean up your existing configuration. You might be puzzled by this advice, particularly if you plan to install an OS on a new partition, separated from your existing OS. There are reasons to tidy up your existing configuration first, though, such as the following:

- **Reclaiming disk space**—If you repartition your disk, it's helpful to first clear away old files so that you can better judge how much space to devote to each OS. Computers often accumulate megabytes of clutter in the form of temporary files that have lived past their usefulness, disused programs, ancient data files, and so on.

- **Better utility operation**—Partition-splitting programs might require that you defragment the hard disk before you proceed, or they might work more efficiently if you do so.

- **Driver installation**—If you must install new hardware to get a new OS running, you might want to test it in your old OS first, so you can be confident that the hardware works.

- **Anticipating changes**—When you change your partitioning scheme, your existing configuration might change, and you might need to alter configuration files to keep your existing OS running smoothly.

Cleaning Out Unused Files and Programs

Unnecessary files often accumulate on computers. These files come from a variety of sources:

- **Temporary files**—Many programs create temporary files to help them in their work, and you can do the same. Sometimes these files end up going undeleted. They're often stored in directories called tmp, TEMP, or something similar, so you can search for such directories. Deleting everything in a temporary directory might not be prudent, but chances are most files can be safely removed. If your OS includes a trash can or recycle bin, remember to empty it, as well—If you don't, the files end up staying on the disk, just in a temporary storage location.

- **Backup files**—Many programs create backups of files the programs alter. On Microsoft-style OSs, these files often have extensions of .BAK, and on UNIX-style OSs, they usually end in a tilde (~) or begin with a pound sign (#). You might or might not want to delete the files, but using your current OS's file search facilities should at least give you some idea of how many of these files exist and how much disk space they consume.

- **Old data files**—Letters to your city council member from 1992, scanned photos or graphics you no longer need, and other detritus build up on hard disks over time. Occasionally cleaning such files away saves disk space and makes your directories less cluttered, saving time when you go looking for something you do need.

 TIP When you organize an OS's directory structure, it's often helpful to keep program data files separate from the program files. If the data files are isolated in a single directory tree, it becomes easier to "prune" that tree of old and unwanted files.

- **Old program files**—Hard disks often accumulate program files, particularly if you frequently try freeware or shareware programs you download from the Internet or buy collections of such programs on CD. If you never use a program, you might as well delete it.

- **Recovered files**—When you run a disk-checking utility such as CHKDSK, SCANDISK, or fsck, the result is often one or more *recovered files*—data that the utility found in some broken data structure. These files are often difficult to identify, and 99% of the time they're never used again. You might want to delete them or back them up to floppies rather than have them clutter your hard disk. On Microsoft-style OSs, such files typically appear in the root directory of a partition and have .CHK extensions. On UNIX-style systems, they usually appear in special directories, one per partition, called lost+found.

N O T E Recovered files might or might not contain important data. Sometimes they're important programs or data files that have been "lost" by the computer. Other times they're random sectors from the hard disk that consist of old files' contents. If you examine a recovered file, you might be able to identify important data files, but chances are program files won't be easily identified. If a program seems to have vanished or misbehaves after a disk check, the program or one of its support files might have wound up as a recovered file. ■

Depending on how old your system is, how you've used it, and how diligent you are, you can substantially shrink the amount of disk space consumed by cleaning out old files. You can search for such files manually, or you can use a utility such as SafeClean Deluxe (http://www.ministars.com/safeclean/index.htm) for Windows to help you track down at least some types of such files. Figure 9.2 shows SafeClean's report of candidate files for deletion or other action (referred to as *cleaning* in the program).

FIGURE 9.2
Utility programs can often help you track down unnecessary files.

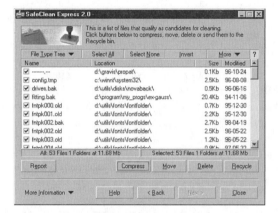

Some OSs, such as many distributions of Linux, include a central database of installed programs. This feature can be used to help you determine what files belong to what packages and to locate and delete unnecessary programs. Figure 9.3 shows the gnorpm program in operation on a Red Hat Linux system, displaying a directory of installed programs.

FIGURE 9.3
The Linux gnorpm tool lets you browse installed programs, find out what each program does, and add or delete programs.

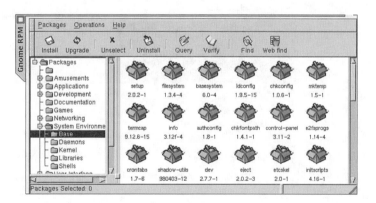

N O T E The central package databases maintained by many Linux distributions contain information only on files added with that distribution's package utilities, such as RPM or Debian packages. If you install a program by compiling it yourself or by untarring it from a *tarball* (a file with an extension of .tgz or .tar.gz), it won't appear in the central database. In general, you should place such program files in the /usr/local directory tree to help isolate them and make them easier to find if you want to do so. ■

Defragmenting Your Hard Disk

As you add and delete files from your hard disk, available space becomes scattered across the disk, a kilobyte here, a kilobyte there. When you create a new file, then, it's possible that it will end up residing in several areas of free space scattered about the hard disk. Some filesystems (especially FAT and NTFS) are particularly prone to such fragmentation. For this reason, tools to defragment (or *defrag* for short) hard disks are common, especially for DOS and Windows. Other filesystems, such as HPFS and ext2fs, are more resistant to fragmentation. Such filesystems can and do become fragmented, but not as quickly or as severely as does FAT. Defragging utilities for these filesystems are often available, but they aren't as popular as defraggers for FAT.

It's sometimes necessary to defrag a hard disk before running low-level partition manipulation tools such as FIPS, which splits a single FAT partition into two parts. In the case of FIPS, this requirement is caused by the utility's incapability to move files or file fragments from one area of the disk to another. When a disk is highly fragmented, it's very likely to have files scattered about most of its area; but defragging also has the effect of compacting the data into a small region of the hard disk, as illustrated by Figure 9.4. You can therefore create a greater reduction in the size of a FAT partition using FIPS after defragging.

FIGURE 9.4
Files and file fragments are scattered over a disk before defragging (top), but defragging compacts the files into a small area (bottom), leaving a large unused space.

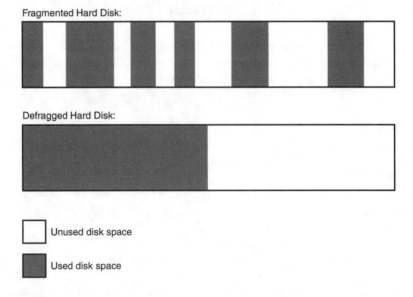

Fragmented Hard Disk:

Defragged Hard Disk:

☐ Unused disk space

■ Used disk space

 TIP Some disk utilities create files that defraggers won't move. If your defragger shows a used sector that can't be moved, find out what the file is and what program uses it. (Most defraggers identify the file when you click such a fragment.) You might need to temporarily disable that program and delete the file if you need to defrag the hard disk to use FIPS. In most cases, the program will re-create the file when you restart it. In other cases, you might need to make a backup of the file and restore it after you've resized the partition. Consult the documentation for the program that created the file for more information.

N O T E Defragging doesn't always compact data, particularly when you defrag a non-FAT partition. Some defragging methods only combine sections of files that have been split, without moving files to occupy a contiguous space on the hard disk. ▪

If you use a more sophisticated partitioning tool such as PartitionMagic, or if you don't need to repartition a hard disk, defragging won't gain you any great advantage with respect to your multi-OS configuration. Defragging can still increase the performance of the OS that uses the defragged partition, however, and so can be a desirable procedure to undertake.

Preparing Your Hardware

If you need to replace hardware to use your new OS, I recommend you install and test it under your old OS before you attempt to install the new OS. This practice is particularly helpful when your old OS is one that's officially supported by the hardware manufacturer but the new OS isn't. This way, if you have problems with the hardware, you'll have fewer questions as to the cause of the problem; you can track down the problem under the OS with which you're familiar, and if you contact the manufacturer for help, you can say that you're using an OS that's officially supported. Of course, in a multi-OS configuration, you can also debug under the OS with which you're more familiar, but you might be more likely to assume that a problem is caused by the new OS rather than by the hardware.

In some cases you might need to make changes to hardware configurations to use a new OS. Unfortunately, such situations tend to be very idiosyncratic to the hardware in question, and it can be difficult to determine when you might need to make such changes. Examples include changing BIOS parameters for memory holes or disk access methods; setting jumpers on cards or other devices; or changing the way you connect peripherals such as printers. In general, unless you've heard of specific tips for your hardware or you have problems with a device, you shouldn't concern yourself with such reconfiguration. If you do have problems, try searching for help.

▶ To learn more about getting help for your OS problems, **see** Chapter 11, "Finding Help."

One step that can be extremely helpful is to record the hardware settings for all your devices, along with information on what those devices are. This way, you'll have this information at hand during the installation process. Most OSs can detect most hardware most of the time, but with a string of *most*s like that, it's not uncommon to encounter a problem detecting a device. In such situations, it's often helpful to tell the OS where to look for hardware. In computer hardware terms, *where to look* usually means the interrupt request (IRQ) line, and possibly also the I/O port and direct memory access (DMA) line. How you determine this information depends on your current OS. Many OSs provide a tool to display such information. For example, Windows 9*x* provides this information under the System Properties item in the Control Panel. Click the Device Manager tab and you can view information on all your devices using the System Properties dialog box, as shown in Figure 9.5. If you select the Computer item and then click Properties, Windows displays the Computer Properties dialog box shown in Figure 9.6. This dialog box can be particularly helpful for recording device information because it displays information by resource used, not by device, thus enabling you to quickly locate unused resources.

FIGURE 9.5

The System Properties dialog box shows all the devices installed in a Windows 9x computer.

FIGURE 9.6

You can locate which devices use specific resources, and what resources are free, using the Computer Properties dialog box.

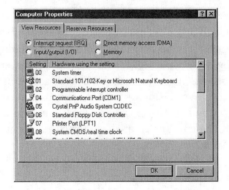

In Linux, this information can be obtained from pseudofiles in the /proc directory structure, and particularly from the /proc/interrupts, /proc/ioports, and /proc/dma files. Various GUI utilities, including the popular KDE, have utilities to present this information similar to the Windows System Properties Control Panel object. In Linux, however, a resource might not show up as used until after its driver has been loaded, so it's easy to miss information on components.

Unfortunately, knowing the resources used by one OS doesn't always help you in another because different OSs can assign Plug-and-Play (PnP) devices' resources in different ways. In some cases you might even run into a situation in which one OS can't assign appropriate resources to all devices because its assignment algorithms lead it into a conflict. If this happens, you might be able to work around the problem by adjusting BIOS PnP parameters or by using whatever overrides your OS provides to assign parameters modeled after those of the working OS.

> **CAUTION**
>
> Windows 9x has a tendency to attempt to redetect hardware if you change BIOS PnP settings or if you move a card from one slot to another. Sometimes it fails in this attempt, leaving you with a crippled or unbootable system. I therefore recommend you attempt such measures only as a last resort if you have Windows 9x installed and working, and only after you back up the working configuration, so that you can restore it if you make changes that prevent Windows from booting.

Anticipating Drive Identifier Changes

If you have a Microsoft-style OS installed, your hard disk partition letters might change after you install the new OS. You should be especially cautious if your OS/2 boot partition resides on anything but c: because OS/2 won't boot if its drive letter changes.

▶ To learn more about drive letter changes, **see** "Drive Letter Changes," **p. 183**.

The best course of action is to design a new installation so that drive letters don't change, or at least so that they change only temporarily. For example, you might use PartitionMagic or some other tool to create a partition that will be used by FreeBSD. That partition might temporarily disrupt your partition lettering system, but after you install FreeBSD, the partition will vanish from your DOS, Windows, or OS/2 system's view, so it won't have any lasting effect on drive letters. On the other hand, if you want to create a shared FAT partition, it's best to create it beyond the last of your existing partitions so its drive letter disrupts only CD-ROM and other removable media.

If you must repartition your disk so that drive letters change, you might need to take any of several actions:

- **Alter configuration file settings**—Files such as CONFIG.SYS, AUTOEXEC.BAT, and the Windows Registry contain information on drive identifiers in paths and for specific programs. You might or might not need to alter these files. The Registry can be particularly tricky to alter because it's a binary file that requires the use of a special editor (the Registry Editor, REGEDIT.EXE). Errors in editing the Registry file can be disastrous, so I recommend you not attempt it unless you know what you plan to change.

- **Alter shortcuts**—If you have shortcuts to files or programs on a drive whose letter changes, you might need to alter them. To do so in Windows, right-click the icon and choose Properties from the resulting pop-up menu. This action produces the Properties dialog box shown in Figure 9.7. Alter the drive letters in the Target and (if it's used) Start In fields. OS/2's program objects can be altered in a similar manner.

FIGURE 9.7
Many programs can adjust to a new location if you merely alter the shortcuts that launch them.

 TIP If you right-click the Start button in the lower-left corner of the Windows display and choose Open from the resulting menu, Windows produces a file browser in which you can edit the shortcuts that appear on the Start menu.

■ **Reinstall programs**—Some programs contain so many references to their drive letters in the Registry or obscure configuration files that you might have little choice but to reinstall the programs. In some cases you can reinstall the programs directly over their old installations and, if you're lucky, your configuration files will remain unchanged, aside from the drive letter changes. Sometimes you can avoid reinstalling programs by using the Registry Editor, but I recommend attempting this action only if you're familiar with the Registry Editor because a mistake can produce an unbootable system.

Some of these changes you can do before installing a new OS. Changes to CONFIG.SYS and AUTOEXEC.BAT are particularly well suited to preinstallation alteration. You might want to put off others, however, such as shortcut alterations and software reinstallation, until after you've made the changes that affect your drive letters. If you're uncertain of what changes an OS installation will bring, wait until it's complete to make any changes in the first OS.

Preparing Disk Space

After you've trimmed any fat from your existing OS, you'll be in a much better position to judge how much space to devote to your old OS and your new one. You can use space requirements as specified by the OS's producer, combined with those for any major applications you want to install, as a starting point in estimating how much space you need. Keep in mind, however, that these space requirements are often extremely optimistic. For a more realistic assessment, consider how much space you use in your current OS, compared to how much space that OS claims it needs. If your current OS claims to need 200MB but it actually consumes 2GB (including applications and data files), a similar tenfold-size adjustment might be in order for a new OS, too. On the other hand, you might need to install fewer or more new programs, thus reducing or increasing the disparity between claimed and actual disk space requirements.

▶ To learn more about disk space requirements for various OSs, **see** "Disk Space Required for Conventional Installations," **p. 530**.

The mechanics of creating and preparing partitions, not to mention installing the new OS, varies a lot depending on the tools you use and the OS you install. Previous chapters have covered these matters in great detail, so I provide only a brief overview in this chapter. OS installation procedures are very specific to each OS, so I don't present much detail here, but I give some additional information in Chapter 10.

▶ To learn more about hard disk partitioning, **see** Part III, "Partitioning and Partition Management."

▶ To learn more about installing specific OSs, **see** Chapter 10, "Installing Specific Operating Systems."

Part
IV

Ch
9

Creating New Partitions

Several different approaches are possible for allocating disk space to a new OS:

▪ **Install a new hard disk**—If you install a new hard disk, you can use all its space for the new OS. This approach has the advantages of simplicity and safety, but it's generally not as efficient as mixing OSs across two or more hard disks. Some OSs, such as those from Microsoft, require at least some boot files on a primary partition on the first physical disk, so this approach might not be completely adequate if you're installing a new Microsoft OS.

▪ **Share a partition**—It's sometimes possible to install two or more OSs on a single partition. This approach often works with multiple Microsoft-style OSs if you use a boot loader such as Windows NT's OS Loader, OS/2's Dual Boot, or V Communications' System Commander. A few Linux distributions can also install in a FAT partition alongside DOS, although this type of configuration is definitely suboptimal for Linux.

   ▶ To learn more about boot loaders, **see** Chapter 4, "Boot Loaders: Simple and Complex."

▪ **Convert partitions**—You can convert a partition for use by one OS to use by another. If you already have several partitions but don't need all of them in your current OS, this approach can be fairly straightforward and poses few risks. It will, however, result in changed drive letter assignments if you currently use a Microsoft-style OS.

   ▶ To learn more about partition conversion, **see** "Converting a Partition from One OS to Another," **p. 189**.

▪ **Backup/repartition/restore**—You can back up your existing system, repartition the hard drive, and restore the data. This approach is the most flexible available but also the most tedious. You must have reliable backup hardware to perform such an operation.

▶ To learn more about backup/repartition/restore operations, **see** "Backing Up, Repartitioning, and Restoring," **p. 192**.

■ **Dynamic partition resizing**—You can use a tool such as PowerQuest's PartitionMagic (`http://www.powerquest.com`) to dynamically resize your existing partitions. This approach can be quite convenient, but it poses a small risk of damage to your existing data. For this reason, I recommend you back up the data on any partition you modify with such a tool.

▶ To learn more about dynamic partition resizing, **see** "Using PartitionMagic," **p. 196**.

As a general rule of thumb, you should probably use the tools provided by an OS when creating that OS's partitions. This practice helps ensure that you don't create a partition that confuses the new OS. One exception to this rule is if you use PartitionMagic because that tool is fussier about partition layouts than most other tools and OSs. PartitionMagic creates partitions to which other OSs don't object.

CAUTION

Some OSs have installation options that cause the installer to completely destroy existing OSs by wiping out those OSs' partitions. You should always pay careful attention to the onscreen prompts and explanations, particularly those surrounding "express" or "quick" setup procedures. If a prompt provides the merest hint that an option might eliminate other OSs' partitions, don't use that option unless and until you've found documentation to the effect that it won't cause harm.

Formatting New Partitions

Most OSs provide some means of formatting one or more partitions during system installation. If you use PartitionMagic to create partitions, and if you intend to install an OS that uses a filesystem that PartitionMagic supports, you can use PartitionMagic to do the formatting before you install the OS.

▶ To learn more about partition formatting, **see** "Partition Formatting," **p. 157**.

During installation, most OSs will install only to partitions that are marked as being appropriate for the OS in question. For example, Windows NT won't install to anything but a FAT or NTFS partition, OS/2 won't install to anything but a FAT or HPFS partition, and most Linux distributions won't install to anything but a Linux partition.

> **CAUTION**
>
> Windows NT 4.0 can install to an existing NTFS partition, but only by first reformatting it for FAT and then converting it to NTFS after the installation is complete. Therefore, you should not attempt to install Windows NT 4.0 to an existing NTFS partition if that partition contains data you intend to keep. Windows 2000 can install to an NTFS partition without wiping out existing data on that partition, however.

Part

IV

Ch

9

You have three ways to control which partitions an OS might try to claim as its own:

- **Create the partition appropriately**—If you use a tool that lets you assign appropriate partition type codes when you create the partition, use that capability. PartitionMagic does this automatically when you tell it to format a partition for a specific filesystem type. Most OS-specific tools create partitions of a type appropriate to the OS by default.

  ▶ To learn more about filesystem codes, **see** "Filesystem Codes," **p. 130**.

- **Change the code**—Some tools, such as Linux's `fdisk`, let you change the type codes for a partition. You can use such a tool to change the code on an existing partition. Typically, the OS installer identifies the partition as belonging to itself and gives you an option to format the partition.

- **Delete and re-create the partition**—If all else fails, you can use the installer's partitioning tool to delete and re-create a partition. For example, you could use OS/2's `FDISK` during OS/2 installation to eliminate an unused BeOS partition and create a new one that OS/2 would then be capable of using.

Occasionally, you might need to format supplementary partitions after OS installation. For example, if you install the OS to one partition but set aside another for data files, the installer might not automatically format the data files partition. You should be able to perform this task after you've installed the OS, however.

OS Installation Order

If you want to install several OSs in close succession (for example, if you've just bought a new computer and want to run half a dozen OSs on it), you must decide in what order to install those OSs. You can generally install OSs in any order you like, although some choices are more likely to cause problems than others because some OSs are more likely to disrupt other OSs' configurations than are other OSs. As a general rule, I recommend installing OSs in this order:

1. **DOS**—DOS tends to wipe out other OS installations if you're not careful. It's therefore often best to install it first, so that it can't do any damage.

2. **Windows 9x**—Windows 9x is somewhat less likely to wipe out other OSs than is DOS. One exception is that Windows 9x might wipe out an existing DOS installation, under the assumption that you're upgrading. You might therefore want to install Windows 9x first, but the difficulty here is that some versions of MS-DOS refuse to install on a system that already contains Windows 9x. If possible, installing Windows and DOS to separate partitions can reduce the likelihood of problems.

3. **Windows NT**—Windows NT can sometimes wipe out other OSs, but in general it behaves itself during installation. If you install it to a FAT partition on which DOS or Windows 9x already exists, Windows NT's OS Loader adds those OSs to its menu, so installing Windows NT later is generally desirable.

4. **Linux**—Most Linux distributions are very flexible and well behaved during installation, but a few include quick setup options that wipe out all other OSs, so be cautious. (Red Hat's workstation and server express options are particularly notorious in this respect.)

5. **BeOS**—In general, BeOS is quite good about not disrupting other OSs' installations, nor is it disturbed by existing OS installations, so BeOS is a good candidate for installation late in the process.

6. **OS/2**—If you select the expert installation, OS/2 is very flexible in where it installs, and it isn't likely to disrupt other OSs. If you install OS/2 along with another OS that uses partitions of a type that OS/2 doesn't understand, those partitions should either appear after the OS/2 boot partition, or the other OS should be installed first to prevent OS/2 from assigning a drive letter to the other OS's partitions. This drive letter would disappear after installing the other OS, thus preventing OS/2 from booting.

You can safely deviate from this order if you have a specific need to do so, but you might need to take extra precautions. For example, suppose you want to install OS/2 before Linux—for example, you want to use OS/2 to download a Linux distribution. You must ensure that OS/2 doesn't assign drive letters to the Linux partitions, or that the subsequent removal of these drive letters won't disrupt OS/2's functioning. You can do so by leaving blank space where the Linux partitions will be or by using a Linux installation floppy (even from an old distribution) to run Linux's `fdisk` and change the partition type codes to 0x83 (Linux native) to hide them from OS/2. Alternatively, you can place the Linux partitions after the OS/2 partitions on the hard disk. If you want to install DOS after installing other OSs, it's best to use separate boot partitions for DOS and for the other OSs. If you want to boot several versions of DOS, Windows, or OS/2 from a single FAT partition, System Commander is an excellent tool, and the System Commander manual includes detailed descriptions of several installation scenarios that enable you to deviate from the preceding advice safely.

Installing the New OS

When you install an OS for the first time, you'll be presented with many options, some of which might be unfamiliar to you. A good guide to your OS can be extremely helpful during installation to help explain these options. If you lack such a guide, make your best guesses. If you guess wrong, you can install again later or perhaps correct the error after installing.

N O T E Different Linux distributions have very different installation routines, so if you install SuSE Linux, for example, a manual describing the installation procedure for Mandrake might not do much good. Even variation from one release to another—of any OS, not just Linux—can be great enough to render outdated documentation less than helpful. ▪

Some of the choices you might need to make during installation include the following:

- **PnP setup**—If you're given a choice, letting the OS find and automatically configure PnP devices is generally a good idea. On rare occasions, however, the detection of such devices can cause the system to crash. If you believe you've encountered such a problem, first wait—PnP detection can take several minutes, so there's no point in giving up too soon. If you've waited half an hour or more, restart the installation and try to bypass the PnP detection. You might need to enter an advanced installation option to do this, and you might need to know more about your hardware to succeed in such a configuration.

- **Hardware specification**—You might need to enter information about your hardware. Such configuration requirements are particularly likely for older OSs and for devices that aren't always easily detected, such as printers, modems, and older monitors. Some UNIX-style OSs require you to enter extensive information about your video card and monitor. It's very helpful to have your manuals handy to obtain this information.

- **Device drivers**—You might need to modify your installation boot floppy to provide access to updated device drivers. Generally, the drivers come with instructions detailing how to do this. Such procedures are especially likely to be necessary for SCSI host adapters that are newer than the OS, at least when the hard disk or CD-ROM drive is run from the adapter in question. If you have problems installing in this way, you might be able to get around the problem by swapping out the unsupported component for a supported model and then installing the appropriate drivers and replacing the original board after installing the OS.

- **Package selection**—Most OSs provide you with options relating to what components you want installed. You can generally add or delete components after system installation, so the main caveat relating to this selection is that you not select so much that you overwhelm the available disk space. Most OSs come in compressed files on the installation CD-ROM and can consume more than the 650MB maximum size of a typical CD-ROM when installed on your hard disk. Some OSs come on multiple CD-ROMs, and some are expected to ship on DVD-ROMs in the near future; such OSs can chew up even more disk space when fully installed.

- **Network configuration**—If your computer is connected to a network, the installation procedure might provide a way to configure the computer's network settings during installation. As with many other configuration options, you can generally perform this configuration after installing everything if you prefer, but you might find it more convenient to do so from the start. You should write down important network configuration options from another OS before you begin the installation. Key information includes whether you use dynamic IP addresses (via the dynamic host configuration protocol [DHCP] or some similar protocol) or a static IP address. If you use the latter, you must also know the IP addresses of your own computer, of a gateway computer, and of domain name service (DNS) servers.

Part
IV

Ch
9

■ **UNIX mount points**—If you're installing a UNIX-like system, you must know where you intend to mount specific partitions in the unified UNIX directory tree. You should record the partition identifiers for the partitions you've created and write down their intended locations in the directory tree, so that you can give this information back to the install routine if required.

■ **UNIX services**—Many UNIX systems provide a choice of *services* or *daemons* to be run automatically at system startup. These terms refer to programs that run quietly in the background looking for some task to perform, such as serving Web pages or enabling remote logins. In general, your system will be more secure if you start as few services as possible, but you might need some (such as lpd, the line printer daemon) even for local functionality. On a first installation, you might want to use the default settings. After you know the OS better, you might want to adjust these defaults as appropriate for your system. As with most other selections, you can alter these after installation.

 TIP Take notes during your OS installation. You can then refer to these notes for problem solving or to guide you toward or away from particular options if and when you need to reinstall the OS.

Reinstalling the New OS

It's rare for a first-time installation of an OS to be perfect, or even satisfactory for more than a brief time. Almost inevitably, you'll discover flaws in your original installation. You might have misjudged the amount of space required by the OS, or you might have picked a wholly inappropriate set of default programs. Worse, you might have chosen the wrong drivers or driver options and found that your hardware doesn't work correctly. All too often, it's not obvious to a new user of an OS how to correct these problems after an install is finished. New users therefore often install the OS anew to correct these problems. Experienced users might change settings from within the OS itself, and if you have adequate documentation, you might try this approach. You should be prepared, however, to throw away your first installation. The second time around, you'll find that the install goes much more smoothly than it did the first time, and you'll probably be happier with the results.

Installing a Boot Loader

Any multi-OS computer benefits greatly from a flexible boot loader to guide the selection of which OS to boot when you turn on or reboot the computer. The selection of a boot loader and its installation is a matter that's tightly intertwined with the OSs you want to run. A good choice for one collection of OSs can be awkward or even completely unworkable for another collection of OSs.

▶ To learn more about boot loaders, **see** Chapter 4, "Boot Loaders: Simple and Complex."

Selecting a Boot Loader

Your choice of boot loader determines what OSs you can boot. Chapter 4 discusses the capabilities of many boot loaders in some detail, so I only provide an overview here. You might consider the following principles when making a decision:

- **Expandability**—If you think you might want to add more OSs in the future, it might be worth using a boot loader that will enable such expansion. For different reasons, Windows NT's OS Loader and IBM's Boot Manager are weak in this area, whereas V Communications' System Commander is unusually strong.

- **Configuration ease**—Most boot loaders can be configured through some sort of menu system. Linux's LILO and Windows NT's OS Loader both require you to edit text files. (Some versions of Linux, such as Red Hat and Mandrake, include GUI utilities that turn this task into point-and-click operations.)

- **Ease of use**—Most boot loaders present you with a menu of choices at boot time; you select which OS you want to boot from that list. LILO uses a different approach: You type the name of the OS you want to boot, which might be a bit harder to use, especially for young children.

- **Installation location**—Boot loaders can reside in various locations, the most common being the hard disk's master boot record (MBR) and the boot sector of a partition. The MBR location is earlier in the boot process, while the boot sector location enables you to use a partitioning utility to disable the boot loader to boot directly into an OS that doesn't reside on the boot loader's partition. LILO is unusually flexible in that it can reside in either of these locations or on a floppy disk.

- **Coexisting boot loaders**—In some cases, you might want to configure your system so that two or more boot loaders coexist. For example, if you plan to install Linux and boot from the hard disk, you must use either LILO or the DOS-based LOADLIN utility. If you don't want to use LILO as your main boot loader, you can configure LILO to install on the Linux boot partition, to boot only Linux, and to do so automatically after no or a very brief delay. You can then use another boot loader to boot Linux via LILO by telling the primary boot loader to boot the Linux partition. The main limitation you must be aware of is that you can't install two MBR-based boot loaders on the same computer.

Fortunately, your choice of boot loader need not be permanent. It's possible to change the boot loader used on a system in the future. In some cases, installing a new boot loader overwrites an existing one. In other cases, you might need to uninstall or disable the old boot loader before you install a new one. If you're using an MBR-based boot loader, the DOS FDISK /MBR and OS/2 FDISK /NEWMBR commands can be particularly helpful in wiping out an MBR-based boot loader.

When to Install the Boot Loader

If you use a boot loader that comes with an OS, you typically install the boot loader as part of the OS installation process. With OS/2, for example, you can install Boot Manager during the disk partitioning process; and with Linux, you install LILO after setting up the system. If you use a third-party boot loader, it's generally a good idea to install the boot loader before you install a new OS, but after you create the new OS's partitions. This practice enables you to switch OSs between any reboots during the install process, should the need arise. You might need to assign boot loader entries to empty partitions that will eventually contain an OS. Most boot loaders take such assignments in stride, although of course if you try to boot such a partition before installing an OS on it, the computer hangs.

N O T E OS/2's FDISK sometimes refuses to add a partition to Boot Manager unless that partition has been previously formatted in OS/2. This can be a major problem. If you intend to use Boot Manager, therefore, it's often best to create the partitions using OS/2's FDISK, format them using OS/2, add them to Boot Manager, and then reformat the partitions for their target OSs. ▓

Some OSs (especially those from Microsoft) tend to rewrite the MBR and set the active partition to the one on which they install, thus wiping out existing boot loaders or redirecting the boot process around them. If you install a Microsoft OS, therefore, you might need to reinstall a boot loader after installing the OS. If your boot loader resides on a primary partition's boot sector rather than the MBR, you can use the DOS or Windows FDISK utility to set the boot loader's partition to be active; the boot loader will then begin to work again.

 TIP If you use Linux's LILO, placing it on a primary partition devoted to Linux enables you to reactivate LILO after you install or reinstall a Microsoft OS, without first booting Linux. This capability can be very helpful at times because it obviates the need for a Linux boot floppy after installing a Microsoft OS.

System Commander has the capability to detect new OSs, both those residing on their own partitions and new additions to the bootable FAT partition. When the software detects a new OS, it prompts you and, if you approve, adds the new OS to the boot menu. If you want to install two or more OSs on a single FAT partition using System Commander, you should definitely install System Commander before the second OS. If you don't, chances are you'll wipe out the first OS's boot files when you install the second OS. (Exceptions to this rule include OS/2 and Windows NT, both of which have ways to coexist on a FAT partition with DOS or Windows 9x. Even with these OSs, though, System Commander should be installed first if you intend to install it at all.)

Summary

You should plan your OS installation carefully to avoid unpleasant surprises and frustration. Part of this planning goes back to the issue of choosing an OS in the first place. An ill-conceived choice of a new OS can result in frustration as the OS fails to meet your expectations. Doing some basic research on OSs and comparing that research to your needs can save you time, effort, and money.

After you've settled on an OS, you should check that your hardware is compatible with that OS and, if necessary, replace hardware so that you can use the new OS. It's generally wise to replace hardware before installing a new OS, so that you can thoroughly test the new hardware to be sure it works correctly. This practice can help you isolate problems if you encounter them after installing the new OS.

Preparation continues with cleaning out the old OS to maximize the amount of disk space available for your installation. As a side benefit, you can improve the performance of your old OS. Installing a boot loader and the OS itself are tasks that vary greatly depending on the products you select. ●

Installing Specific Operating Systems

Preparing for More Than One OS

A great deal of advice and information on OS installation applies to all OSs or to a large number of them. Most of this book is devoted to such general-purpose information, albeit with frequent comments and examples relating to specific OSs. This chapter is different, though, because it focuses on the requirements of specific OSs, particularly with respect to overall system configuration and installation. I can't present a complete guide to installing each OS, but I can and do provide tips that should help you get an OS working in conjunction with others.

DOS and Windows 9x

As the original OS for x86 hardware, DOS is in many ways the most primitive when it comes to working beside other OSs. Based on DOS, Windows 9x has inherited many of DOS's ways with respect to peaceful coexistence with other OSs. Windows 9x has expanded on DOS's repertoire, however, when it comes to hard disk size and filesystem support.

Partition Requirements

Both DOS and Windows 9x must boot from a primary partition on the first physical disk or from a floppy disk. Assuming you boot from a hard disk, the boot partition becomes known as drive C:. Both OSs can access additional partitions, whether they are primary or logical, on both the first hard disk and on subsequent disks, provided those partitions belong to the set of recognized partition types shown in Table 10.1. In fact, although the most basic components of DOS and Windows 9x must boot from C:, it is possible to install the bulk of both OSs (the parts that reside in the WINDOWS or DOS directories) on other partitions.

Table 10.1   Partition Types Recognized by DOS and Windows 9x

Type Code	Filesystem	DOS/ Windows 95	Windows 95 OSR2/ Windows 98
0x01	FAT-12	Y	Y
0x04	FAT-16 < 32MB	Y	Y
0x05	Extended Partition	Y	Y
0x06	FAT-16 > 32MB	Y	Y
0x0b	FAT-32	N	Y
0x0c	FAT-32 LBA	N	Y
0x0e	FAT-16 LBA	N	Y
0x0f	LBA Extended Partition	N	Y

The LBA partition types are sometimes referred to using an X, as in FAT-32X. The structure of these filesystems is the same as in their non-LBA counterparts; the only difference is that they can reside partly or wholly above the 1024-cylinder limit.

N O T E If you boot from a DOS floppy, drive C: might or might not be a primary partition on the first physical disk, depending on whether any such partition is of a type that DOS recognizes. If you don't want to install DOS on your hard disk, you can use a DOS boot floppy occasionally and access a shared FAT partition as drive C:, even if that partition is a logical partition or resides on something other than the first physical disk. ■

In many cases you won't see the partition type codes shown in Table 10.1 because most partitioning programs hide these details from you. Linux's fdisk is one exception to this rule. Some partitioning programs, such as PartitionMagic, show information on the filesystem in use on a partition.

When it was first introduced, Windows 95 supported the same partition types as DOS, except that Windows 95 could store long filenames on these partitions using its VFAT variant of the FAT filesystem. When presented with a VFAT partition, DOS can read the files but reports truncated filenames in place of the long filenames, as in LONGFI~1.TXT instead of LongFilename.txt. There are no changes to the partition type codes to indicate a VFAT partition as opposed to an ordinary FAT partition with no long filenames. With the OEM Service Release 2 (OSR2) version of Windows 95, Microsoft introduced FAT-32 and the special LBA codes for partitions that extend beyond the 1024-cylinder limit. Because FAT-32 is normally used only in Windows 9x (and now in Windows 2000, which also supports long filenames on FAT partitions), FAT-32 partitions almost invariably contain VFAT-style long filenames.

N O T E FAT-32 support in Windows 95 OSR2 and Windows 98 is built into the DOS component of Windows. These OSs can therefore read FAT-32 even when booted into DOS mode. When so booted, however, you can still read only short filenames, even on FAT-32 partitions. ■

The 1024-Cylinder Limit

The OS boot process relies on the BIOS and assorted boot loader programs to access a few low-level OS files, such as the DOS IO.SYS file. Because of limitations in the BIOS, these files must reside below the 1024th cylinder of the hard disk.

▶ To learn more about the 1024-cylinder limit, **see** "EIDE and SCSI Hard Disk Handling," **p. 75**.

Both DOS and Windows 9x suffer from the 1024-cylinder limit for boot purposes; a few critical OS files must reside below that limit for the OS to boot. DOS also suffers from the 1024-cylinder limit even after it is booted; it cannot see any file located beyond the 1024-cylinder limit. In fact, it is wise to ensure that DOS can't see any partition that resides even partly over the 1024-cylinder limit. Other OSs, such as Linux, can create FAT-16 partitions that straddle this limit and that bear partition type codes that DOS recognizes. You should avoid creating such partitions. Instead, make sure that FAT-12 (type 0x01) and FAT-16 (type 0x04 and 0x06) partitions reside entirely below the 1024-cylinder limit or give them type codes that DOS doesn't recognize, such as 0x0e (refer to Table 10.1).

DOS's FDISK disk partitioning software might also have problems coping with hard disks that exceed 1024 cylinders in size. You might therefore need to use another OS's partitioning software or a third-party utility, such as PowerQuest's PartitionMagic or V Communications' Partition Commander, to create partitions on a hard disk with more than 1024 cylinders.

In theory, it is possible to boot Windows from a partition that straddles the 1024-cylinder limit. The trick is to place the critical files below that limit. The problem is that, even if the critical files fall below the 1024th cylinder at the time you install the OS, the files might move because of a disk defragmentation operation, file updates, or some other reason. Thus, I strongly recommend that you keep your boot partition entirely below the 1024-cylinder limit.

After they are booted, Windows 95 OSR2 and Windows 98 can handle partitions that fall above the 1024-cylinder limit. These OSs use special partition types, listed in Table 10.1, to identify such partitions. Throughout this chapter, I refer to such partitions as *LBA partitions*.

N O T E If you install Windows 95 OSR2 or Windows 98 on an older computer that lacks the extended INT13 BIOS routines, you can use partitions that exceed the 1024-cylinder limit only from a regular full boot of the OS. When you boot into safe mode or use a text-only boot, such partitions will be inaccessible. ▨

▶ For more information on extended INT13 BIOS routines, **see** "Using LBA Mode in EIDE and SCSI Drives," **p. 79**.

In addition to the 1024-cylinder limit, DOS is beset with a more severe boot limitation: a 2016MB limit. The DOS boot code allocates a 16-bit number for a value that represents the quotient of the absolute sector number and sectors per track. Because the latter value is usually 63 on modern hard disks, the result is a limit of 4,128,768 (63×2^{16}) on the number of sectors, hence a limit of 2016MB (which is often rounded to 2GB in discussions of the limit). Thus, any DOS bootable partition must reside in the first 2016MB of a hard disk, even when the 1024-cylinder limit works out to much higher values. Windows 9*x* doesn't suffer from this same limit. This 2GB limit also doesn't apply to partitions accessed from DOS after DOS has booted.

Another 2GB limit afflicts DOS and versions of Windows 95 predating OSR2: the limit on the size of FAT-16 partitions. These partitions can't exceed 2GB (2048MB) in capacity because of limits on the size of the file allocation table (FAT; the disk structure after which DOS's filesystem is named). If you use one of these OSs, your partitions must remain smaller than 2GB, although you can create several such partitions—up to four on an 8GB hard disk, for example. If possible, a better solution is to upgrade to Windows 95 OSR2 or Windows 98 and convert the FAT-16 partitions to FAT-32, which can be much larger than FAT-16 partitions.

▶ To learn more about using PartitionMagic to convert from FAT-16 to FAT-32, **see** "Converting Partitions," **p. 202**.

Protecting Other OSs

Some varieties of DOS and Windows tend to eliminate other OSs during installation. The best defense against such an occurrence is to install DOS or Windows first, followed by other OSs. If this procedure is impossible, you should back up your existing OS before installing DOS or Windows. You should also keep a sharp eye out for any prompt during installation that might hint at the elimination of competing OSs. Whenever you're given a choice, select a customized installation because these options are more likely to give you control over what procedures the OS uses during installation. DOS and Windows are less likely to damage OSs that reside on their own filesystems (such as Linux on ext2fs or OS/2 on HPFS) than those that reside on FAT partitions (such as OS/2 on FAT).

Some versions of DOS refuse to install in a partition that already contains a more recent version of DOS or Windows. In most cases, it is easier to install DOS and Windows on separate partitions. Such installations typically proceed more smoothly. If you must install DOS onto a partition that already contains Windows, you need a tool such as V Communications' System Commander to manage the boot process. Consult the System Commander documentation for details of how to configure such a system.

Part

IV

Ch

10

If you install an OS such as Linux that uses a non-FAT filesystem, but fail to change the partition type codes for the non-FAT partitions, DOS or Windows will attempt to read those partitions. You'll see drive letters, but if you try to read the contents of the drive, you'll get an error message, often accompanied by an offer to format the partition. *Do not format such a partition!* Instead, use a tool such as Linux's fdisk to change the partition type to something appropriate. This action should remove the partitions from view by Windows. You might see a similar problem if unpartitioned space is left on your hard disk. In this case, too, I recommend you not format the alleged partition.

Tweaking Hardware After Installation

Windows 95 was the first OS to offer major plug-and-play (PnP) features on PC hardware. The goal was to have the OS detect and, whenever possible, configure all hardware automatically. In many cases, Windows does remarkably well with PnP features, but there are caveats:

- **Legacy hardware**—Older components, and particularly older ISA boards, can't be configured by software. These products require configuration via jumpers or switches on the board. Unless you're ripping components out of old broken computers for use in another system, chances are any such products you have are already configured in a way that works, but it is possible that Windows will try to assign a resource used by a legacy component to some other device. Detection of these legacy devices can also be tricky, and occasionally fails.

- **Component juggling**—Windows sometimes tries to redetect hardware if you move a card from one slot to another. It does the same if you replace one board with another.

In both cases, redetection usually proceeds smoothly, but occasionally fails. Recovering from such a failure can be tedious and sometimes necessitates reinstalling Windows. You might want to try removing a device's drivers before moving the device. Although this procedure isn't guaranteed to prevent problems, it might help.

■ **New hardware**—Windows ships with a collection of drivers suitable for handling most of the hardware available at the time the OS was released. Unfortunately, newer hardware might not be supported. You should have drivers available and ready on floppy or CD when you install Windows. If possible, you should read the documentation that came with the product to find out how to install Windows.

■ **Version numbers**—With each release of Windows 9x, Microsoft has improved the PnP support, at least on average. (Some components work better with Windows 95 than with Windows 98, but such situations are rare.)

Even hardware that's supported by Windows on initial installation might work better if you install updated drivers from the hardware manufacturer's Web site. Such drivers fix bugs and add features over the drivers that ship with Windows. On rare occasions, new drivers can fix problems that make it difficult or impossible to use Windows. You should therefore collect such drivers before you install Windows.

DOS's driver requirements are minimal compared to those of Windows because DOS relies on the BIOS for its most fundamental driver operations. For additional functionality, including such modern-day necessities as CD-ROM handling, you must acquire drivers from the device manufacturer.

Windows NT and Windows 2000

Microsoft's Windows NT family uses a substantially different design than do DOS and Windows 9x. Therefore, Windows NT uses different drivers and has different disk requirements than does Windows 9x. Nonetheless, there are certain similarities between the requirements and capabilities of Windows NT and Microsoft's other OSs.

N O T E Microsoft released Windows 2000 in early 2000. Despite the lack of *NT* in the product name, Windows 2000 is actually part of the NT family (it was at one time referred to as *Windows NT 5.0*, but Microsoft changed the name before release). I use *Windows NT* to refer to both products that bear this name and to Windows 2000. When Windows 2000 behaves differently from earlier versions of Windows NT, I mention this fact. ■

Partition Requirements

Like DOS and Windows 9x, Windows NT must boot from a primary partition on the first hard disk. As with Windows 9x and DOS, it is possible to install the bulk of Windows NT (the portion that resides in the WINNT directory) to something other than the C: partition. You need only specify the appropriate location when you install Windows NT.

Windows NT through version 4.0 understands the same filesystem types as DOS, as shown in Table 10.1, as well as NTFS partitions (type code 0x07). Windows NT 3.51 and earlier can read HPFS partitions, but Microsoft removed this capability from Windows NT 4.0 and Windows 2000. Windows NT 4.0 and earlier do not, unfortunately, understand any of the FAT-32 partition types used by Windows 95 OSR2 and Windows 98. Windows NT 4.0 does, however, understand the LBA extended partition type, so you can place FAT-16 partitions inside such a partition and share them between Windows NT and Windows 9x.

 TIP

The NTFS partition code of 0x07 is also used by OS/2's HPFS. If your version of Windows NT doesn't include HPFS support, Windows NT assigns a drive letter to any HPFS partitions present on the disk but reports that those partitions are incorrectly formatted. If you format such a partition, you lose whatever data it contains. I recommend using Disk Administrator (Disk Management in Windows 2000) to remove such partitions from view to reduce the possibility you might accidentally reformat them.

▶ To learn more about Disk Administrator/Disk Management, **see** "Windows NT Disk Administrator," **p. 139**.

Windows NT is also perfectly happy to deal with ordinary extended partitions (type code 0x05) that extend beyond the 1024-cylinder boundary. Which type you should use depends on which other OSs require access to the logical partitions within the extended partition. For Windows 9x, use the LBA extended partition type. For OS/2 4.0 and earlier, and for old versions of Linux, use the ordinary extended partition type. Likewise, use the ordinary extended partition type for OSs such as DOS that can't read beyond the 1024-cylinder limit, but only if the shared partitions themselves fall below the 1024-cylinder limit. Most modern OSs can use both partition types, so as a general rule I recommend using the LBA extended partition type for compatibility with Windows 9x.

With Windows 2000, Microsoft has added support for the FAT-32 filesystems to Windows NT. This fact can be quite a boon to those who want to use a system with both Windows 2000 and Windows 9x. NTFS is still a superior filesystem for Windows NT use, however, because it supports Microsoft's security model and more advanced filesystem features, such as journaling, which speed recovery in the event of a crash or power failure.

Through version 3.51, Microsoft included support for OS/2's HPFS with Windows NT. It was even possible to install Windows NT on an HPFS partition. Unfortunately, HPFS support disappeared with Windows NT 4.0, although if you have a disused Windows NT 3.51 license, you can add that support back to Windows NT 4.0 by copying the appropriate Windows NT 3.51 drivers into your more recent installation. Windows NT 3.51's HPFS drivers are incompatible with Windows 2000.

▶ To learn more about adding HPFS support to Windows NT 4.0, **see** "Windows NT HPFS Drivers," **p. 347**.

Part

IV

Ch

10

The 1024-Cylinder Limit

Like all x86 OSs, Windows NT is subject to the 1024-cylinder limit, so you must ensure that the boot partition falls below this value. In theory, you can boot from a partition that straddles the limit, but for the same reasons I described with reference to DOS and Windows 9x, I recommend against such a configuration. If necessary, create a small C: partition that falls below the 1024-cylinder limit and supplement that partition with a larger partition to hold the WINNT directory in which most Windows files reside. This supplemental partition can exist beyond the 1024-cylinder limit, on a logical partition, on a second or later hard disk, or some combination of these.

The preceding suggestions, although good for a working installation of Windows NT with appropriate Service Packs installed, don't fully apply to a fresh installation of Windows NT 4.0 on a large EIDE hard disk. This is because Windows NT 4.0 includes a bug in the ATAPI.SYS driver file that prevents the OS from handling large hard disks correctly. To work around the problem, follow these steps:

1. Download the file ATAPI.EXE from Microsoft at ftp://ftp.microsoft.com/bussys/winnt/winnt-unsup-ed/fixes/nt40/atapi/ATAPI.EXE.

2. Run the ATAPI.EXE program in DOS or Windows. The result is a file called ATAPI.SYS.

3. Copy ATAPI.SYS to a floppy disk.

4. Start the Windows NT 4.0 installation process.

5. If the installer asks about detecting mass storage devices, type S to skip auto-detection.

6. When the installer lists available devices (see Figure 10.1), type S, insert the floppy that contains ATAPI.SYS, and press the Enter key twice.

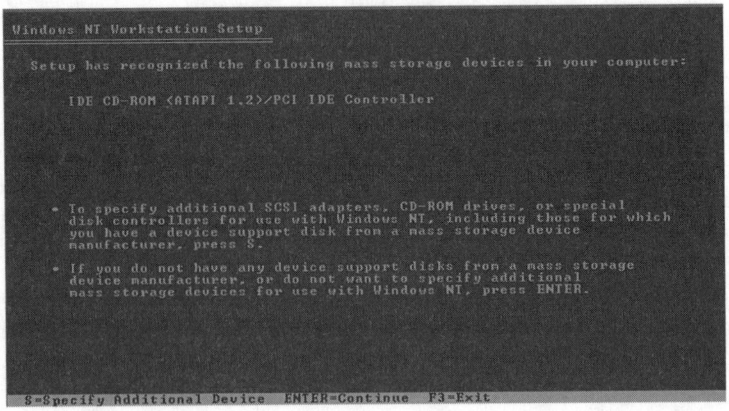

FIGURE 10.1
Windows NT enables you to easily add third-party drivers to its installation routine.

7. The installer should list the Service Pack 4 EIDE driver as a device. Press Enter to accept this driver.

8. If you have other disk devices (SCSI hard disks, for example), you can add their drivers in a similar manner.

9. Installation now proceeds normally. The installer later asks for the disk that contains `ATAPI.SYS`, however, so you should keep it handy.

When you follow these instructions, you should be able to install Windows NT 4.0 on a computer with a hard disk larger than 8GB.

Unfortunately, Windows NT through version 4.0 suffers from the same 2016MB limit that applies to DOS. This fact is usually more restrictive than the 1024-cylinder limit. As a result, it is often necessary to place the Windows NT boot partition first on the disk, or at least earlier than some other OSs' boot partitions. This limit applies to both FAT and NTFS partitions.

Windows 2000 is not so limited as earlier versions of Windows NT, fortunately. It has no problems installing to large hard disks, for example. It does, however, still suffer from the same 1024-cylinder limit as any other OS, so your boot partition must reside below the 1024-cylinder limit.

Part
IV

Ch
10

Adding Drivers to the Install Procedure

In most cases, you can add drivers for hardware that's not supported by Windows NT out of the box after you install Windows NT itself. Devices such as sound cards, video capture cards, and scanners, for example, are not critical to system installation. Follow the driver installation instructions to install these drivers after you install Windows NT proper.

A few devices do require special drivers during installation. Prime among these are SCSI host adapters, when either your CD-ROM drive or your boot disk is a SCSI device. Fortunately, most SCSI host adapters are supported directly by Windows NT, so you don't need to take any special measures with them. If you use a particularly new or exotic SCSI host adapter, however, you might need to add drivers for it during system setup. The device manufacturer should include instructions to help you install appropriate drivers. Those instructions probably resemble those I presented earlier for using a new EIDE driver for hard disks larger than 8GB. The basic idea is that you must insert the appropriate driver at the hard disk detection phase of the OS installation process.

FAT and NTFS

Windows NT 4.0 and later understands two hard disk filesystems natively: FAT and NTFS. Up through Windows NT 4.0, the OS could use only FAT-12 and FAT-16; but with Windows 2000, Microsoft added support for FAT-32. Windows 2000 also introduces changes to NTFS that are generally referred to as *NTFS 5.0*. Most people need not be concerned with these NTFS changes, although you do need at least FixPack 4 to read NTFS 5.0 partitions with Windows NT 4.0.

On the whole, NTFS is a superior filesystem to FAT; NTFS supports Windows NT security features, it is more robust than FAT, and it recovers more quickly after a power failure or system crash. Windows NT 4.0 and earlier, however, cannot install directly to an NTFS partition. Instead, when you tell the installer to install to NTFS, it formats the target partition to FAT, installs, and then converts the partition from FAT to NTFS. This procedure means that you cannot install to an existing NTFS partition without wiping out its contents. Fortunately, Windows 2000 remedies this situation and enables you to directly install to NTFS.

NTFS does have limitations and problems compared to FAT, however. Prime among these is the fact that most OSs don't contain reliable NTFS support. NTFS drivers for non-NT OSs do exist, but they are often read-only or unreliable, or they cost money. Because of these limitations, you might want to consider installing Windows NT on a FAT partition. This procedure enables you to more easily access your Windows NT boot partition from another OS, or even from a floppy boot, should the need arise. On the other hand, installing Windows NT on FAT means that you won't get the security benefits of Windows NT's Access Control Lists. If you do install Windows NT to FAT, I recommend using a separate NTFS partition for Windows NT programs and data files to gain the benefits of ACLs and NTFS's speed and reliability improvements over FAT.

▶ To learn more about NTFS, **see** "Windows NT's NTFS," **p. 312**.

▶ To learn more about Access Control Lists, **see** "Microsoft's New Technology," **p. 37**.

OS/2

IBM's OS/2 is both similar to and different from Microsoft's OSs. OS/2 uses drive letters and assigns them in much the same way as do the Microsoft OSs. OS/2 can also use FAT natively. OS/2 doesn't support VFAT long filenames, however, nor does it support FAT-32. Instead, OS/2 uses its own filesystem, HPFS, to enable long filename support and various other benefits. Its boot requirements are different from those of Microsoft's OSs, as well.

Partition Requirements

OS/2 4.0 recognizes the same partition types as does DOS, as shown in Table 10.1. In addition, OS/2 recognizes HPFS partitions, which bear a type code of 0x07. You can install OS/2 directly to any of these partition types, although the FAT-12 and FAT-16 <32MB partition types are too small for a full-blown OS/2 installation.

N O T E When Microsoft released Windows NT, it reused the 0x07 HPFS partition type code for NTFS. This fact means that OS/2 sees NTFS partitions as corrupt HPFS partitions. Fortunately, OS/2 doesn't try to format or repair these partitions unless you give an explicit command to do so. You should be cautious, however, on a system that contains both HPFS and NTFS partitions. You might be able to use a boot loader to hide NTFS partitions from OS/2; or if your version of Windows NT supports HPFS, you can use HPFS instead of NTFS to gain cross-OS access to both OSs' partitions.

▶ To learn more about boot loader partition hiding, **see** "The Job of the Boot Loader," **p. 86**.

▶ To learn more about HPFS support in Windows NT, **see** "Foreign HPFS and HPFS 5.0 Support," **p. 343**.

OS/2 versions 4.0 and earlier don't understand either FAT-32 partitions or Microsoft's LBA extended partition type. You can add drivers to make OS/2 recognize FAT-32, but the LBA extended partition type is more troublesome. Instead of a special partition type for LBA partitions, OS/2 can use a standard extended partition that extends past the 1024th cylinder. The main problem with this approach comes when a computer contains both OS/2 and Windows 9x OSs; Windows 9x can't read data from logical partitions past the 1024th cylinder except when they're enclosed in LBA extended partitions. You might need to decide which OS to favor when you decide whether to use standard or LBA extended partitions.

 TIP V Communications' System Commander automatically relabels extended partitions as normal (type 0x07) or LBA (type 0x0f) according to the OS it boots. You can therefore place partitions for both Windows 9x and OS/2 in an extended partition and let System Commander change the partition type at boot time.

Unlike Microsoft's OSs, OS/2 doesn't need to boot from a primary partition or from a partition on the first physical hard disk. This fact provides both great flexibility and great potential for disruption. The flexibility part is fairly clear-cut—you can install OS/2 in more places than you can DOS or any version of Windows. The potential for disruption occurs mainly when you change your system's configuration because the boot drive letter can change if you put OS/2 on anything but a primary partition on the first physical disk (drive c:). If OS/2's drive letter changes, the OS becomes unbootable. I therefore recommend putting OS/2 on a partition with the earliest drive letter that's practical.

OS/2 can't see more than one primary partition per physical disk. This fact means that if you want OS/2 to be capable of accessing files belonging to DOS or Windows on a partition other than the OS/2 boot partition, OS/2 must be installed either on a primary partition on the second or subsequent drive or on a logical partition. In either case, OS/2's boot partition becomes D: or higher. One exception to this rule is if you install Windows on a FAT-32 partition and use a third-party OS/2 FAT-32 driver, in which case you can configure the FAT-32 driver to read a primary FAT-32 partition on the same drive as a primary OS/2 boot partition.

▶ To learn more about FAT-32 support in OS/2, **see** "Using Third-Party FAT-32 Drivers," **p. 338**.

Part IV

Ch 10

As a general rule, I recommend creating a separate OS/2 boot partition of 500MB or so, along with one or two additional partitions for OS/2 applications and data files. This arrangement helps isolate OS/2 from its programs and data, enabling you to reinstall OS/2 by reformatting the boot partition and doing a fresh install. Except for sharing files with DOS, Windows, or some other OS, there's little reason to use FAT partitions in OS/2; HPFS is faster (by 10–200%, depending on operations), more efficient, and supports long filenames better than does FAT.

The 1024-Cylinder Limit

OS/2 is no more immune to the 1024-cylinder limit than is any other OS. As with Microsoft's OSs, it is theoretically possible to boot OS/2 from a partition that straddles the limit, but this procedure isn't recommended. In fact, OS/2 won't install to such a partition, although you can create one using PowerQuest's PartitionMagic (http://www.powerquest.com) by resizing or moving an existing OS/2 boot partition.

Bugs in OS/2 4.0's installation routine prevent it from installing to hard disks larger than approximately 4GB in size. You can obtain an updated installation floppy disk image from ftp://ftp.pc.ibm.com/pub/pcbbs/mobiles/warp4iu1.exe. (The character before the .exe is a numeral 1, not a lowercase L.) This file is a self-extracting archive that, when run from DOS, Windows, or OS/2, creates a floppy disk to replace the OS/2 installation Diskette 1.

OS/2 imposes the 1024-cylinder limit on all FAT partitions; the OS refuses to format a partition that falls even partly above the 1024-cylinder limit for FAT. To use disk space above the 1024-cylinder limit with OS/2, you must normally format the partition using HPFS. You can also use any of several third-party filesystem drivers to use filesystems such as FAT-32 or ext2fs from OS/2, even above the 1024th cylinder.

▶ To learn more about using foreign filesystems in OS/2, **see** Chapter 13, "Tools for Accessing Foreign Filesystems."

Adding Drivers to the Install Procedure

As with many other OSs, you can safely put off dealing with many driver issues until after OS/2 installation. If you plan to install OS/2 to a hard disk or from a CD-ROM drive that's driven by a SCSI host adapter that OS/2 doesn't recognize out of the box, however, you must modify your installation floppies. You should consult the documentation that came with the driver for details; however, the procedure is generally something like this:

1. Make backup copies of the installation floppies. Using the DOS, Windows, or OS/2 DISKCOPY command works. The following steps instruct you to modify the installation floppies; make these changes to your backup copies.

N O T E   The OS/2 Installation Diskette must be copied using DISKCOPY or some other whole-disk copy program because it is a bootable floppy. Doing a file-by-file copy (for example, by using COPY in DOS, Windows, or OS/2) produces an unbootable floppy, which won't be useful. ∎

2. Copy the .ADD driver file to the disk that contains other .ADD files. On OS/2 4.0, this disk is called Diskette 1. In many cases, there's not sufficient room on the target disk to hold the new driver. If this is the case, you must remove an extraneous driver file or two. I recommend removing one or more of SONY31A.ADD, MITFX001.ADD, IBM2SCSI.ADD, or AHA152X.ADD. The first two of these files are for very old proprietary CD-ROM drives, the third is for SCSI host adapters for old IBM PS/2 computers, and the last is for a common but old ISA Adaptec SCSI host adapter. Of course, you shouldn't remove these drivers if your system contains the hardware in question, but removing even one will probably clear enough room for your new driver file.

3. Locate the CONFIG.SYS file on one of the installation floppies and edit it. On OS/2 4.0, this file is on Diskette 1. Comment out the lines corresponding to the driver files you deleted in step 2. Do this by adding REM and a space to the start of the line; for example, change BASEDEV=MITFX001.ADD to REM BASEDEV=MITFX001.ADD.

4. Add a line for the new driver file similar to the lines you comment out. For example, if your driver file is called SYM8XX.ADD, add a line that reads BASEDEV=SYM8XX.ADD. This line can usually go just about anywhere. If OS/2 seems to hang when you install it, though, you might want to try moving this line to some other location; although rare, sometimes drivers need to load in a particular order or they cause system hangs.

Part

IV

Ch

10

NOTE   OS/2 assigns drive letters for multiple hard disks on the basis of the order in which their drivers load. The standard driver for EIDE hard disks is called IBM1S506.ADD. Unless you've configured your BIOS so that the system boots SCSI devices before EIDE devices, you should place all SCSI host adapter drivers after the IBM1S506.ADD line in CONFIG.SYS. If after doing part of the installation the system reboots and fails with a message to the effect that it can't find COUNTRY.SYS, try editing the CONFIG.SYS file on the hard disk so that your SCSI host adapter driver falls after IBM1S506.ADD (or before it, if your BIOS is configured to boot from the SCSI hard disk).

5. At the start of the CONFIG.SYS file, add a line reading SET COPYFROMFLOPPY=1. This line tells OS/2 to copy its driver files from the floppy disk rather than from the installation CD. Without this line, you'll lose the new driver midway through the installation, and you'll have to make equivalent changes to the CONFIG.SYS file on your hard disk, and copy the .ADD file to the hard disk manually.

6. Begin the installation procedure using your modified installation disks. The process should proceed normally. There is a possibility that the installer will complain about the lack of the .ADD files you removed. If so, ignore the complaint.

The OS/2 installation floppies are formatted with FAT, so you can modify them with any OS that can read and write FAT floppies—OS/2, DOS, Windows, Linux, BeOS, or even a Macintosh. Some OSs might display stray codes at the beginnings or ends of lines. Leave them alone, and be sure to duplicate them when you add the lines for the new driver and the SET COPYFROMFLOPPY line.

▶ To learn more about different end-of-line codings in various OSs, **see** "Raw ASCII," **p. 359**.

FAT, HPFS, and JFS

OS/2 can install itself directly to either FAT or HPFS partitions, with or without first formatting the partition. Therefore, you can upgrade or replace an existing OS/2 installation, even on an HPFS partition, without damaging other data on the partition. If your computer has Windows NT installed, however, you should be careful not to select an NTFS partition for installation because OS/2 doesn't understand NTFS, although it does assign drive letters to these partitions. Similarly, you should be careful not to format any partition (FAT, HPFS, or NTFS) that you don't want to erase.

Through version 4.0, OS/2 recognizes only FAT-12 and non-LBA FAT-16 FAT variants; OS/2 can't handle FAT-32 partitions without third-party drivers. You can use this fact to hide partitions to be used by Windows 9x and Windows 2000 from OS/2; simply make those partitions FAT-32, and OS/2 won't be capable of using them.

▶ To learn more about FAT-32 drivers for OS/2, **see** "Using Third-Party FAT-32 Drivers," **p. 338**.

Late server editions of OS/2 4.0 introduced a journaling filesystem (JFS), which had previously been used on IBM's UNIX OS, AIX. JFS greatly reduces OS startup time after a power failure or system crash, and so can be quite useful if you have very large hard disks.

If you have a partition in FAT format that you want to use only in OS/2, you can use PartitionMagic (http://www.powerquest.com) to convert the partition from FAT to HPFS. As of version 5.0, PartitionMagic can convert from NTFS to FAT, so you can do a two-stage conversion from NTFS to HPFS, if you so desire. PartitionMagic cannot convert from HPFS to any other filesystem, however; the only way to perform such a conversion is to back up, reformat, and restore.

BeOS

BeOS uses a fairly straightforward installation process, but it is hobbled by weak hardware support. When you install BeOS, it is particularly important that you check that your hardware is supported by the OS. The vast majority of BeOS drivers come with the OS itself; it is unlikely you'll find BeOS drivers from the hardware manufacturer. Before you scrap some piece of hardware, though, check http://www.be.com/software/beware for a driver.

Partition Requirements

Unlike the Microsoft-style OSs I've discussed thus far in this chapter, BeOS cannot be installed on any variety of FAT partition. Instead, you must install BeOS on a partition of type 0xeb, which is used to identify BFS partitions. BFS is an advanced journaling filesystem with almost no support outside BeOS; therefore, BFS partitions are invisible to Microsoft-style OSs.

You can install BeOS on either primary or logical partitions; the OS isn't fussy about that detail. BeOS comes with a boot loader that can be used to boot both BeOS and other OSs; or you can use a boot loader from another OS or a separate boot loader product such as System Commander. You can also install BeOS on a second or subsequent hard disk, provided the disk can be read by your BIOS.

Although you can't install BeOS on FAT partitions, you can access these partitions from within BeOS. To do so, right-click the desktop and select the partition you want to use from the Mount submenu. You can set BeOS to mount non-BeOS native partitions by default by choosing Mount, Settings from the pop-up menu. This action produces the Disk Mount Settings dialog box, shown in Figure 10.2. Select All Disks in the Disk Mounting During Boot section of the dialog box to have BeOS automatically mount all your FAT partitions at boot time. BeOS 4.5 recognizes all FAT partition types (12-, 16-, and 32-bit) and recognizes VFAT-style long filenames. BeOS doesn't currently recognize other PC filesystem types without extra drivers. Third-party drivers are available to enable BeOS to read Linux ext2 partitions and Windows NT NTFS partitions, however.

FIGURE 10.2
BeOS enables you to control what types of partitions to mount at boot time, but not which specific partitions.

▶ To learn more about ext2fs drivers for BeOS, **see** "BeOS ext2fs Drivers," **p. 353**.

▶ To learn more about NTFS drivers for BeOS, **see** "BeOS NTFS Drivers," **p. 345**.

In addition to PC filesystems, BeOS understands the Macintosh's HFS. This support isn't normally important for hard disk use, but it can be handy when accessing floppies or other removable media.

The 1024-Cylinder Limit

Like other OSs, BeOS is limited to booting from the first 1024 cylinders of a hard disk. It doesn't suffer from any further restrictions, though, as do many other OSs. Between this fact and the fact that BFS can't be resized by partition resizers such as PartitionMagic, a BeOS partition is a good candidate to reside out of the way at the end of a hard disk (if the disk is smaller than 8GB).

Linux

Linux is one of the most flexible OSs available in terms of installation location, supported filesystems, and other important installation criteria. Discussing Linux installation generally, however, can be difficult because every Linux distribution supports a somewhat different set of features. For example, most of the major distributions, such as Red Hat, Debian, and SuSE, insist on installing only to Linux ext2fs partitions; however, a few distributions can install to FAT partitions using a special FAT variant known as UMSDOS. UMSDOS isn't as fast as ext2fs, however, and it brings with it many other FAT problems, so I recommend creating separate partitions for Linux use, even if you're using a distribution that supports UMSDOS installation. Even Linux distributions that don't support UMSDOS installation do support reading FAT partitions after installation, so you can still access FAT partitions from these distributions.

Partition Requirements

The partition type 0x83 is used by Linux for partitions it uses for filesystems, and the partition type 0x82 applies to Linux swap partitions. Linux also supports all the partition types identified in Table 10.1, along with many others. Many Linux distributions treat the partition type codes differently during installation as opposed to after installation, however. During installation, many distributions use the partition type codes to ensure that you don't accidentally damage or destroy a partition belonging to another OS. The install routines do this by giving you the option of reformatting and installing to only those partitions with 0x83 type codes. In some cases, you can tell the installer to give you access to other partition types after you've installed Linux, and some enable you to use FAT or other partition types as the source for installation files. After you've installed Linux, however, the OS ignores the partition type codes, although the Linux fdisk utility enables you to modify the codes for the benefit of other OSs, as well as for your own edification when viewing a partition table with fdisk in the future.

Linux install routines often search for partitions of type 0x82 and give you the option of using these partitions as *swap space*—disk space devoted to temporary storage of items in memory, should you load enough programs or data files to overrun your memory. (Many Microsoft-style OSs use disk files on their boot partitions for this purpose.) It is therefore important that you correctly mark swap space with the 0x82 type code to let the installer initialize the partition as swap and use it in that way.

Linux is quite capable of booting from both primary and logical partitions, so you needn't devote a separate primary partition for use by Linux. Linux can also access all primary partitions on a hard disk, unlike OS/2 and some older versions of DOS. Older versions of Linux might be incapable of identifying LBA extended partitions, but newer versions of the OS have no problems with these partitions or with ordinary extended partitions larger than 1024 cylinders. Linux's fdisk requires independent support for LBA extended partitions, so you might need to upgrade your version of `fdisk` independently of your Linux kernel if you're using an older version of Linux and need to use LBA extended partitions.

Linux is capable of booting from any hard disk the BIOS can read, which generally means any of the first four hard disks, although a few BIOSs can only boot from the first two disks.

The 1024-Cylinder Limit

The Linux kernel file (generally called `vmlinuz`, `zImage`, `bzImage`, or some variant of one of these) must reside below the 1024th cylinder in order for Linux to boot. All other Linux files can exist on partitions that lie wholly or completely above the 1024-cylinder mark. Depending on your distribution, the kernel file might reside in the root (`/`) or `/boot` directory.

TIP If you're having difficulty placing the Linux root partition below the 1024th cylinder, try creating a small (5–20MB) partition below that point, and tell the install routines to mount that partition as `/boot`. Even if your distribution places the kernel in the root partition by default, you can change that decision after you've installed the OS, although you'll need to boot from a boot floppy the first time you boot Linux (most distributions give you the option to create such a floppy during the installation process). Because the `/boot` directory is accessed so seldom after bootup, you can place it well apart from other Linux partitions without being concerned with performance degradation, as might happen when separating more frequently used partitions.

Like Windows 9*x* and BeOS, Linux doesn't suffer from any limitations on boot partition location aside from the 1024-cylinder limit, so you can put the Linux boot partition past those for other OSs, such as Windows NT. On the other hand, the capability to create a small `/boot` partition means that it is often desirable to put such a partition early on the disk, particularly when you use large hard disks that contain more space beyond the 1024-cylinder line than before it.

Kernel and Driver Versions

Several different version numbers apply to Linux installations:

- **Kernel**—The Linux kernel bears a version number that applies to the kernel file and its associated drivers as a whole. For example, at the time of this writing, kernel version 2.2.13 is the current stable release. Linux kernel version numbers bear three parts, as in *x.y.z*. Two kernels with the same *x* and *y* components are largely the same, differing only in bug fixes and possibly minor driver improvements or additions. In Linux development, the *y* component signals whether the kernel is a *stable* or *development* kernel. A stable kernel bears an even number and should be used for most serious applications. A development kernel is used by Linux programmers to add features, such as new drivers, major kernel architecture changes, and so on.

  Development kernels are often unstable, so they shouldn't be used for serious work unless you're in desperate need of some feature. At any given time, one stable and one developmental kernel family are current; for example, 2.2.x and 2.3.x. Both acquire additions, but the development kernel accumulates more changes in any given period of time. Eventually, the development kernel matures and becomes the next stable version. Late in the 2.3.x series, the kernel will be relabeled 2.4.0, at which point work will begin on the 2.5.x series and further changes to 2.4.x will be restricted to bug fixes and minor additions.

■ **Distribution**—A Linux distribution collects a kernel and a large number of support programs and adds an installation routine. Many Linux distributions exist at any one time. Popular distributions at the time of this writing include Red Hat 6.1, Mandrake 6.1, Debian 2.1, Corel 1.0, SuSE 6.3, and Caldera 2.3. As you can see, the distributions' version numbers bear little resemblance to one another. They're also unrelated to the Linux kernel version.

NOTE Occasionally a person mistakenly refers to "Linux 6.1" or something similar, apparently confusing the kernel version with the distribution version, or perhaps simply omitting the distribution name. At the end of the twentieth century, there is no such thing as Linux 6.1, and there likely won't be for several years. If you post a Usenet message for help, be sure to identify your Linux distribution, including its version number, and the Linux kernel version you're using. This information will help potential respondents with your query. ■

■ **Drivers**—Within the kernel, individual drivers follow their own development pace. For example, my main Linux computer is currently running Linux 2.2.12; but that kernel includes drivers such as the Tulip Ethernet board driver version 0.91; the Initio SCSI adapter driver version 1.03g; and the VIA MVP-3 EIDE driver version 0.01. Actually, one of these (the Tulip driver) isn't a part of the standard 2.2.12 kernel; I replaced an older file with a newer one to get my Ethernet board working. Chances are you won't need to update any drivers to install Linux on your system.

■ **Software packages**—Programs ranging from command prompt shells to word processors have their own version numbers. Some of these programs come as part of Linux, so it is easy to overlook the fact that they have development cycles that aren't tied to Linux at all. In general, if a program comes with a distribution, the version that's on the CD was current at the time the CD's contents were finalized. In some cases, though, you might want to track down updated packages to get better features or fix bugs.

I've just painted a picture of an OS based on a messy conglomeration of software that's not particularly coordinated across elements, or even within the major component of the kernel. This picture is accurate. It also applies to other OSs, except that it is a little less obvious and perhaps a bit less chaotic in the way the software grows. For example, the kernels of OSs such as Windows NT and BeOS consist of a conglomeration of files to handle the same basic tasks that the Linux kernel handles. These files need updating for a variety of reasons and can be updated at different intervals, resulting in different version numbers for the different files. You as an end user don't see this simply because those systems are closed. Linux, on the other hand, is an open OS, so you can see the differing pace of development more clearly by browsing the version numbers in the different files.

One of Linux's flaws compared to many other OSs is that it is very difficult to add drivers to the installation routines. Some distributions are taking steps that might lead to solutions similar to those used by Windows NT, in which you insert a floppy disk with the necessary files at some point; for the most part, however, you must look for updated installation floppies or change to a distribution with better install-time hardware support. If you already have a Linux system running and want to create a custom installation floppy to install Linux on another computer, you might be able to do so if you're comfortable with Linux kernel compilation and assorted other tasks. The Web site http://www.rodsbooks.com/rhjol/ contains a brief description of the steps needed to create a custom boot disk for Red Hat Linux.

Some hardware manufacturers, such as Initio (http://www.initio.com), create custom boot disks for at least one or two Linux distributions to aid in installation until their drivers are integrated into the Linux kernel proper. As with other OSs, you can often put off installing unusual drivers until after the OS is installed. You don't need support for your sound card, for example, when installing Linux.

LILO Configuration

One critical component of Linux installation comes with the configuration of LILO, Linux's boot loader. Most Linux distributions provide LILO configuration options at some point in the installation process, as shown in Figure 10.3. These simplified options typically enable you to configure the system to boot Linux or one or two other OSs, such as DOS or Windows 9x. You can often add other OSs to the mix if necessary, but the install-time LILO configuration utilities typically don't enable you to use LILO's full power. If you need to set up a trickier configuration, such as one that involves partition hiding or special boot menus, you must do so by editing /etc/lilo.conf after performing a basic Linux installation.

FIGURE 10.3
The Linux Mandrake 6.1 install-time LILO configuration screen enables you to set basic LILO options but doesn't give access to LILO's more advanced features.

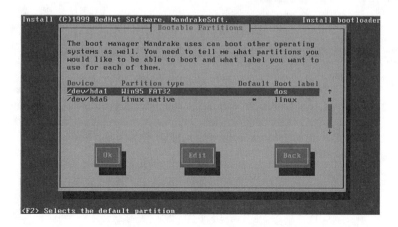

One critical aspect of LILO configuration, no matter how you install it, is to decide where to install it. The usual locations are on the hard disk's master boot record (MBR) and on the Linux boot partition's boot sector. The first choice is most appropriate when you want to use LILO as the first or only boot loader for the computer, especially if the Linux boot partition is a logical partition. If you want to use another boot loader as the primary boot loader, though, you should place LILO on the Linux boot partition's boot sector. In this configuration, you normally include only one LILO option, to boot Linux.

CAUTION

Some Linux distributions, such as Corel Linux 1.0, don't give you the option of where to place LILO. In the case of Corel Linux, the installer puts it on the MBR, thus wiping out any existing MBR-based boot loader. You can usually recover from such a happening by editing Linux's `/etc/lilo.conf` file, reinstalling LILO, and then reinstalling your original boot loader.

After you install Linux, you can modify the LILO configuration by editing the `/etc/lilo.conf` file. When you've edited this file, be sure to run `lilo` to activate your changes.

▶ To learn more about LILO, including details of the `/etc/lilo.conf` file, **see** "Linux's LILO," **p. 103**. The man pages for `lilo` and `lilo.conf` provide more advanced information on LILO.

FreeBSD

On the whole, FreeBSD installation works much like installation of any other OS. It does use an unusual partitioning scheme, however, in which a primary partition is split into subpartitions. In practice, this split partition works much like an extended partition, but the subpartitions created in this way aren't readable by most other OSs.

Partition Requirements

Like Microsoft's OSs, FreeBSD requires a primary partition in which to install. This partition bears the type code 0xa5. Unlike Microsoft's OSs, FreeBSD's primary partition can reside on a second or subsequent hard disk. FreeBSD's partitioning program sometimes refers to PC-style partitions as *slices*.

During OS installation, FreeBSD splits its primary partition into subpartitions, which you assign to mount points. As with Linux, you can also set aside one or more subpartitions to serve as swap space. In sum, then, you perform two partitioning operations when you install FreeBSD: one to create the standard PC partitions and one to carve up the FreeBSD partition into its own parts.

▶ To learn more about mount points, **see** "Isolating Types of Data," **p. 116**.

N O T E When FreeBSD subpartitions its primary partition, the OS really applies a full-fledged partitioning scheme that's used on non-PC UNIX platforms. This scheme can be applied to a hard disk instead of the standard PC partitioning scheme, but then the disk can't be used by most other PC operating systems, such as Windows or OS/2. Applying the BSD partitioning scheme within a primary partition enables FreeBSD to partition a disk in a standard UNIX manner while maintaining compatibility with other PC OSs. ■

Preventing Problems for Linux

Linux is one of the few non-BSD OSs that can parse the FreeBSD partition table. If you intend to use both Linux and FreeBSD on a single computer, and if you want Linux to have access to FreeBSD files, you can do so by including appropriate support in your Linux kernel. Linux then treats the FreeBSD partition table much as it does the logical partitions inside an extended partition. The potential for problems arises because Linux assigns device identifiers to logical partitions beginning with partition number 5 (as in /dev/hda5), but whether the first logical partition identifier is a true logical partition or a FreeBSD partition depends on whether the extended partition or the FreeBSD partition has the lower number.

Figure 10.4 illustrates a case in which a hard disk contains both a FreeBSD partition and an ordinary extended partition. If the FreeBSD partition has a lower number than the extended partition, the first logical partition (/dev/hda5) is assigned to a FreeBSD partition.

In a partition layout such as that shown in Figure 10.4, adding or removing FreeBSD partition table support from Linux changes the identifiers for extended partitions. If the kernel is recompiled without that support, Linux assigns /dev/hda5 to the first logical partition in the extended partition, as shown in the lower portion of Figure 10.4, because Linux can't read the contents of /dev/hda2. To avoid potential problems because of this, I recommend ensuring that the extended partition have a partition number lower than that of the FreeBSD partition. If /dev/hda2 were the extended partition and /dev/hda3 were the FreeBSD partition, removing support for the BSD partition table wouldn't change the identifiers for the logical partitions.

Note that the partition number has nothing to do with the location of the partition on the disk; the extended partition can have a lower number than the FreeBSD partition but reside later on the disk. You can use Linux's fdisk program to check partition numbers and, if necessary, repartition the disk to ensure that partition numbers fall in the order you want.

Because few non-BSD utilities understand the contents of a FreeBSD partition, I recommend placing these partitions at the beginnings or ends of disks. That way, you're less likely to encounter problems if you use a partition resizing utility such as PowerQuest's PartitionMagic. If you place a FreeBSD partition mid-disk, you won't be able to move it with PartitionMagic if you want to consolidate space on both sides of the FreeBSD partition.

The 1024-Cylinder Limit

FreeBSD suffers from the usual boot-time 1024-cylinder limit. As with Linux, the restriction applies to the location of the FreeBSD kernel file, which in FreeBSD's case is /kernel. It is generally safest to ensure that the entire root (/) partition resides below the 1024-cylinder limit. FreeBSD doesn't suffer from the 2GB limit of DOS and Windows NT or any similar problems.

FIGURE 10.4

Adding or removing BSD partition table support from Linux can change the numbering of logical partitions if the extended partition has a higher number than the BSD partition.

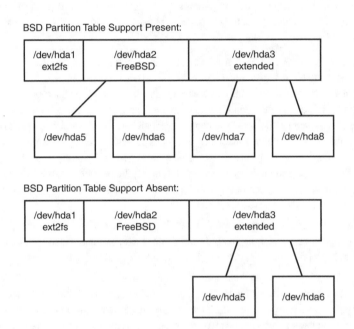

After it is booted, FreeBSD can access partitions that fall beyond the 1024-cylinder limit. You can use this feature both to access parts of a primary FreeBSD partition that straddles the 1024-cylinder limit and to access non-BSD partitions that reside beyond the limit.

Summary

Every OS has unique needs when it comes to installation—OSs vary on whether they can install to logical partitions, the exact nature of how the 1024-cylinder limit applies, the partition types and filesystems they support, and whether and how you can add drivers to their installation routines. There are often subtleties to these installation variables that can cause grief if you attempt an OS installation without proper preparation. This chapter has therefore presented information relevant to installing several common OSs, with the aim of reducing these problems to manageable proportions. ●

Finding Help

When Things Don't Go as Planned...

One of the most frustrating aspects of installing a new OS occurs when you run into problems. Perhaps the OS crashes during installation. Maybe it refuses to recognize the new driver you're trying to install. Whatever the problem, you need help when it occurs. Knowing where to turn for that help can mean the difference between a productive and enjoyable relationship with a new OS and a box on a shelf that gathers dust. This chapter therefore presents information on finding help for your new OS. In some cases, I provide specific information—Web sites, telephone numbers, and so on—that you can use to collect the information you need to get up and running, or to work around some less critical but annoying glitch. In other cases, I provide suggestions for how to go about looking for information more generally, to help you locate new sources of information.

A few years ago, technical support for computers was provided primarily by telephone and by bulletin board systems (BBSs) operated by the companies providing support. Today, the Internet has grown to displace BBSs and rivals or often exceeds voice telephone calls for support. Many of my suggestions therefore assume that you have a working Internet connection. You can use your primary working OS to connect to the Internet to find help for an ailing OS, even if the malfunctioning OS doesn't work well enough to make the connection. If you need to download new files for the ailing OS, it helps to have a shared partition in which to place the files. If necessary, you can use a second computer to make the Internet connection to gain help for the first computer.

▶ To learn more about using a shared partition to transfer files from one OS to another, **see** "Cross-OS Data Sharing," **p. 118**.

The OS Publisher

One obvious source of help when you run into problems is the publisher of the OS you're using. After all, the OS publisher wrote the OS and so presumably knows it fairly well. The problem is that the OS publisher is a bureaucracy, so that expertise might not be directly accessible to you as an end user. Instead, you're likely to find yourself shunted into a queue of customers asking questions of people who access a database of problems and solutions. If this database is well designed, the technical support desk for the OS publisher might be a good source of help. If not, or if your problem is simply esoteric, you might have no luck with the OS publisher. One further potential problem with this approach is that OS publishers often charge money for technical support, so if you run into many problems, you can end up paying substantial sums of money for this support. Even "free" support can cost money if it involves a toll call, particularly if you must spend much time on hold waiting to speak to somebody.

Useful Official Contact Information

To contact an OS publisher, you must first have contact information. You're probably most interested in either telephone-based support or Web pages maintained by the vendor with helpful information, even a searchable database of problems and solutions. There are other potential contact methods, however, including fax, email, and old-fashioned physical mail.

N O T E Most of the contact information in the following pages relates to a company's operations in the United States. If you live elsewhere and want to obtain telephone support, you might want to check your documentation or the company's main Web site for a local office. Web sites, of course, can be used from anywhere, provided you have an Internet connection. ▨

Microsoft

Postal address:

Microsoft Corporation
One Microsoft Way
Redmond, WA 98052-6393

Telephone number:
800-936-5700 (pay per incident)

Telephone number:
425-635-7000 (Windows 95)

Telephone number:
425-635-7222 (Windows 98)

Main Web site URL:

`http://www.microsoft.com`

Technical support URL:

`http://www.microsoft.com/support`

Technical support email:

`WRHELP@microsoft.com`

Microsoft offers a variety of support options, ranging from free access to common information on their Web site to corporate support contracts. Currently, the emphasis for end users is on $35 per incident support calls.

IBM

Postal address:

IBM Corporation
Attn: OS/2 Technical Support Team
Internal Zip 2901
11400 Burnett Road
Austin, TX 78758-3493

Telephone number:
800-237-5511

Fax number:
800-426-8602 or 512-823-6273

Main Web site URL:

`http://www.ibm.com`

Technical support URL:

`http://www.ibm.com/software/support`

Technical support email:

`tcinput@austin.ibm.com`

IBM's technical support features articles on Web pages and paid telephone support, much as does Microsoft's. The structure of IBM's Web site is quite dense, leading to a strong possibility of being led down unproductive paths in search of information.

Be, Inc.

Postal address: Be, Inc.
                                             800 El Camino Real, Suite 400
                                             Menlo Park, CA 94025

Telephone number: 972-389-3740

Fax number: 650-462-4129

Main Web site URL:

`http://www.be.com`

Technical support URL:

`http://www.be.com/support/custsupportform.html`

or

`http://www.be.com/support`

Technical support email:

`custsupport@be.com`

Be, as a much smaller company than Microsoft or IBM, has much less extensive Web pages. In some sense this is a drawback because there's less information available, but at the same time, it can be an advantage because it is easier to locate the information you need—provided that it is available.

Linux Vendors   Because of Linux's distribution model, there is no single source for "official" technical support. You might want to check the Web site `http://www.linux.com`, though, which contains a great deal of useful Linux information and links to other Linux-related sites. Beyond this site, each distribution has its own technical support system.

In general, when you purchase a cut-rate Linux CD without a manual, you aren't entitled to support from the company or organization that produced the distribution. When you buy the same distribution in a box with a manual and a higher price tag, however, you often get at least limited support. If your support doesn't exist, has expired, or doesn't meet your needs, you should consult the various Internet-based help resources, or you might be able to purchase support by the incident or by the hour from the Linux vendor.

▶ To learn more about getting help on the Internet, **see** "The Internet," **p. 279**.

Caldera

Postal address: Caldera Systems, Inc.
                                             240 West Center St.
                                             Orem, UT 84057

Telephone number: 888-465-4689

Fax number: 801-765-1313

Main Web site URL:

`http://www.calderasystems.com`

Technical support URL:

`http://www.calderasystems.com/support/programs/`

Technical support email:

`linux@calderasystems.com`

Caldera offers 90 days or five incidents (whichever comes first) of email-based technical support with purchases of Caldera OpenLinux. This support can be expanded with enhanced support options paid for on a per-incident or annual contract basis.

Caldera's main Web site focuses on its Linux products. If you want information on Caldera's DR-DOS product, check its Lineo subsidiary's Web pages at `http://www.lineo.com/products/drdos.html`.

Corel

Postal address: Corel Corporation
                                             1600 Carling Ave.
                                             Ottawa, Ontario K1Z 8R7
                                             Canada

Telephone number: 613-274-0500 (877-662-6735 with a
                                             service contract)

Main Web site URL:

`http://linux.corel.com`

Technical support URL:

`http://linux.corel.com/products/linux_os/techsupport/support.htm`

Technical support email:

`feedback-linux@corel.com`

Corel's is the newest Linux distribution. Based on Debian but adding a user-friendly GUI-based installation routine, Corel is aiming its Linux distribution at new and desktop Linux users. Purchasers of a Corel Linux boxed set receive 30 days of installation support, and you can buy additional support on a per-incident basis, if required. Corel also maintains a set of FAQs and a free newsgroup on their news server.

Debian

Postal address:

Software in the Public
Interest, Inc.
P.O. Box 1326
Boston, MA 02117

Telephone number:

877-433-2426 (VA Linux support)

Main Web site URL:

`http://www.debian.org`

Technical support URL:

`http://www.debian.org/support`

Technical support email (mailing list subscription information):

`http://www.debian.org/MailingLists/subscribe`

Debian GNU/Linux is unusual in that it is not produced by a corporation that provides printed documentation, support, and so on. Debian is developed by a geographically diverse set of individuals and made available on FTP sites for others to distribute on CDs that might or might not be distributed with extra documentation and support. VA Linux, Silicon Graphics, and O'Reilly have banded together to produce a Debian "boxed set" comparable to what you can find for most other distributions, however. You can obtain paid support for Debian GNU/Linux from consultants (`http://www.debian.org/consultants/`) who offer paid Debian support, or from VA Linux, which offers $34.95 per-incident support.

Mandrake

Postal address:

MandrakeSoft
329 W. Altadena Dr.
Altadena, CA 91001

Main Web site URL:

`http://www.linux-mandrake.com/en/`

Technical support URL:

`http://www.linux-mandrake.com/en/ffreesup.php3`

Technical support email:

`bugs@linux-mandrake.com`

Purchasers of official boxed sets of Linux Mandrake are entitled to 100 days of email technical support. Bynari International (`http://www.bynari.com/`) offers extended support contracts on Linux Mandrake.

> **N O T E** Macmillan Software sells a boxed version of Linux Mandrake that's different from the one sold by MandrakeSoft. You can obtain information on support for Macmillan's version from `http://mcpsupport.linuxcare.com/`.

Red Hat

Postal address:

Red Hat Software, Inc.
P. O. Box 13588
Research Triangle Park, NC 27709

Telephone number: 800-454-5502 or 919-547-0012

Fax number: 919-547-0024

Main Web site URL:

`http://www.redhat.com`

Technical support URL:

`http://www.redhat.com/support`

Technical support email (mailing list information):

`http://www.redhat.com/community/list_subscribe.html`

Red Hat offers a variety of packages of their Linux distribution that differ in the level of support offered. In addition, you can purchase per-incident or annual support packages.

Slackware

Postal address:

Walnut Creek CD-ROM
4041 Pike Lane, Suite F
Concord, CA 94520-1207

Telephone number: 925-603-1234

Fax number: 925-674-0821

Main Web site URL:

`http://www.slackware.com`

Technical support URL:

`http://www.cdrom.com/techsupp/index.phtml`

Technical support email:

`support@cdrom.com`

Slackware is officially distributed through Walnut Creek CD-ROM, which also distributes an assortment of other products, including FreeBSD. Telephone technical support is limited to the hours of 9 a.m. to 5 p.m., Pacific time, Monday through Friday, and is limited to installation support for those who've bought official boxed sets of the distribution. For more involved questions, Walnut Creek recommends you contact a Linux consultant.

SuSE

Postal address:	SuSE, Inc. 580 Second Street Suite 210 Oakland, CA 94607
Technical support telephone number:	888-875-4689 or 510-628-3380
Technical support fax number:	510-628-3381

Main Web site URL:

`http://www.suse.com`

or

`http://www.suse.de`

Technical support URL:

`http://www.suse.com/Support/index.html`

Technical support email:

`isupport@suse.com`

SuSE, unlike most of the popular Linux distributions, originates in Germany, but the company does maintain a presence in the United States. SuSE offers 60 days of installation support on official packages of its product, and in addition the company maintains a database of problems and solutions on its Web site (the English-language version of this database is referred to as "a work in progress," however).

BSD Organizations The different versions of BSD differ among themselves more than do the mainstream distributions of Linux. In general, the BSD distributions are less commercialized than are the Linux distributions, so on average there's less available in the way of formal technical support from the developing organization. Development of the BSDs is geographically diverse; they tend to have little in the way of centralized physical infrastructure.

FreeBSD

Postal address:	Walnut Creek CD-ROM 4041 Pike Lane, Suite F Concord, CA 94520-1207
Telephone number:	925-603-1234
Fax number:	925-674-0821

Main Web site URL:

`http://www.freebsd.org`

Technical support URL:

`http://www.freebsd.org/support.html`

or

`http://www.cdrom.com/techsupp/index.phtml`

Technical support email (mailing list information):

`http://www.freebsd.org/support.html#mailing-list`

Walnut Creek is a major distributor of FreeBSD CDs and related materials, and offers technical support for FreeBSD under the same terms as its technical support for its Slackware Linux CDs.

NetBSD

Postal address: The NetBSD Project
                                                   76 Lippard Ave
                                                   San Francisco, CA 94131-2947

Main Web site URL:

`http://www.netbsd.org`

Technical support URL:

`http://www.netbsd.org/Documentation/index.html`

Technical support email (mailing list information):

`http://www.netbsd.org/MailingLists/index.html`

If you obtain a NetBSD CD-ROM from a vendor, that vendor might or might not provide support. If not, your principal support options are online—mailing lists, newsgroups, and Web sites. The main NetBSD site does have a page devoted to NetBSD consultants (`http://www.netbsd.org/gallery/consultants.html`), however, which might provide some leads if you need one-on-one technical support.

OpenBSD

Postal address: OpenBSD
                                                   812 23rd Ave SE
                                                   Calgary, Alberta T2G 1N4
                                                   Canada

Main Web site URL:

`http://www.openbsd.org`

Technical support URL:

`http://www.openbsd.org/support.html`

Technical support email (mailing list information):

`http://www.openbsd.org/mail.html`

OpenBSD's legal headquarters are in Canada, which allows OpenBSD to internationally distribute its software with stronger encryption technology than is possible in US-based products. The technical support site for OpenBSD includes a list of consultants who can provide paid support for the OS. Other than that and whatever support you might get from a third party distributing an OpenBSD CD, your main sources of support for OpenBSD are on the Internet—mailing lists, newsgroups, and Web sites.

DOS Support   Each of the commercial DOS vendors—Microsoft, IBM, and Caldera—has an entry earlier, although Microsoft is no longer actively promoting its version of DOS. (Caldera's contact information is listed in the Linux section.) There's little in the way of official support for FreeDOS, but you can check the FreeDOS Web site at `http://www.freedos.org` for leads.

Knowing What Information to Have at Hand

Whenever you contact an OS vendor for support, you should have certain types of information available, such as

- **Serial number**—You might need a serial number, registration number, customer number, or some other identification to prove you're entitled to whatever support the vendor offers.

- **Payment information**—If you're calling for paid support, you should have a credit card number, purchase order number, or paid support certificate number on hand.

- **OS version**—Have the precise version number of the OS available, including information on any updates you've installed. You can often obtain all this information in a single location, such as the Windows 98 System Properties dialog box shown in Figure 11.1.

- **Software information**—If your problem seems related to one application more than others, have information on that application handy. You might want to contact the troublesome application's vendor before the OS vendor, however, because problems that occur only in one application are usually related to that application, not to the OS.

- **Hardware information**—You might need to know what sort of hardware you're running. It is helpful to have the original hardware manuals and any configuration notes you took during OS installation.

- **A clear problem description**—Be sure you can clearly describe your problem. If you send a query via email or a Web-based problem report form, include as much detail as possible. If you call a telephone number for support, the technician to whom you speak can ask for information as necessary, but even then it is useful to be able to present the problem clearly at the beginning of the conversation.

FIGURE 11.1

Many OSs provide a dialog box with the OS version number, often along with additional information on your hardware or the system's configuration.

It is helpful to have notes on the problem when you call for help. If you write down the steps you took in an attempt to fix a problem, not only can you think more clearly about the problem before making the call, but you'll also have that information at hand to pass on to a technician.

Part
IV

Ch

11

OS Help Files

Most OSs come with some sort of electronic help files and utilities. These files and utilities vary substantially in nature, scope, and usefulness. The most sophisticated built-in help systems include search engines, indexes, and other helpful features. The most primitive consist of little more than a collection of ASCII files.

The following are examples of built-in help files:

- **README files**—Many OSs place one or more files in some prominent location on the computer's hard disk with the intent that you read them. These files often bear names like README or README.TXT. In Microsoft-style OSs, they often appear in the c: directory after installation is complete. These files' names suggest what you should do with them. You can read these files with your favorite text editor, or you might be able to view them with a utility like less or more.

- **Windows Help**—From the Start menu in Windows 9x or NT, choose Help to use the Windows Help browser, as shown in Figure 11.2. In this browser, you can use the Contents and Index tabs in the left pane to search through subjects much as you would in a printed book; or you can use the Search tab to search for key words or phrases in all the available help files. Many applications and Windows dialog boxes contain help functions that bring up the Windows Help browser, often preset for files that are appropriate to the task or application you were attempting to use when you called the help system.

FIGURE 11.2
The Windows Help browser lets you peruse a substantial collection of online help files.

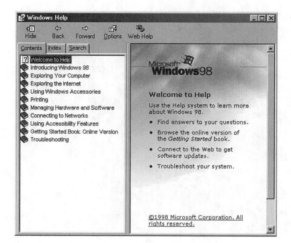

■ **OS/2 Help**—OS/2 provides a wide variety of help utilities, most of them accessible from the OS/2 Warp item on the taskbar, under the Assistance Center item. In addition, you can type HELP followed by the name of a command in a command prompt window, as in HELP DIR, to see a hypertext help system on that command, as shown in Figure 11.3.

FIGURE 11.3
OS/2's Command Reference help browser provides help not only for OS/2 itself, but for many OS/2 programs.

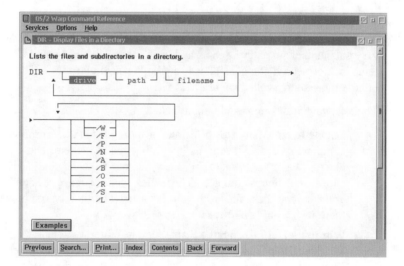

■ **Linux HOWTOs**—Most Linux distributions install a collection of documentation known as the Linux HOWTOs. These files provide information on a wide range of Linux topics, geared towards solving specific problems, such as how to compile a Linux kernel (the *Kernel HOWTO*) or how to perform assorted tasks with a serial port (the *Serial HOWTO*). These documents come in a variety of formats and are often located in the /usr/doc/HOWTO or /usr/doc/howto directory trees. Depending on the formats you've installed, you can print these to a PostScript printer, read them in an editor, or use a Web browser to view them.

- **UNIX man pages**—UNIX systems (including Linux and FreeBSD) include documentation on specific commands in the form of *man pages*, so called because they're accessed via the man command (short for *manual*). To read a man page, type man followed by the name of the command, such as man ls. Man pages have a reputation for being difficult to understand, but they can provide a wealth of information. Many systems also include a utility called xman that can display man pages in an X window with scroll bars and other niceties, as shown in Figure 11.4.

FIGURE 11.4
A UNIX xman window lets you browse man pages in a GUI environment.

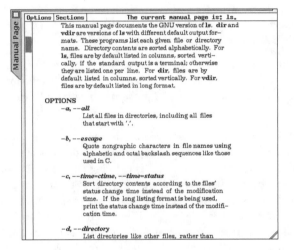

In addition to electronic help files, don't forget the printed manual. Although printed documentation that ships with OSs has become scantier and scantier over the past decade or so, many OSs do still ship with helpful printed manuals. Particularly if you have a problem with basic system installation or are having trouble figuring out how to perform routine tasks, the printed documentation can be a good place to begin looking for help.

Independent Publications

The OS's publisher doesn't have a monopoly on printed matter relating to your OS, although for some of the more exotic OSs, your choices might be a bit slim. For most OSs, though, you can find a great deal of help from third-party documentation. For all but the most casual use, taking advantage of at least some of these sources of information is a good idea. Particularly for the more popular OSs, the selection is wide enough that you shouldn't have much trouble finding material to suit your exact needs.

Part IV
Ch 11

Your Friendly Local Book Store and Library

One excellent starting point for help on most OSs is in books. Buying a book is a particularly good idea if you've purchased a CD-only version of an open source OS like Linux or FreeBSD because you can use the printed documentation even when any documentation on the CD itself is inaccessible—because of problems accessing the CD-ROM drive or during installation, for example. On the other hand, books can be one of the more expensive sources of support.

In general, you'll find the widest selection of books at large book stores and in those that specialize in technical subjects. If you live in a high-tech major metropolitan area, you might even be able to find book stores that carry only computer books. If you can't afford yet another book, or if you're unsure whether you want to keep an OS, check your local library. Although a library isn't likely to have books that are as recent as those in a book store, many libraries have respectable collections of computer titles.

The number of titles relating to all the OSs available is staggering, and every person's needs are unique, so a complete recitation of titles and recommendations for which to read would overflow this volume's capacity. Instead, I present you with my advice for how to shop for a computer book:

Begin with a bookstore with a wide selection. The bookstore must be a walk-in bookstore rather than an online retailer because what you need to do is locate any titles on your desired topic and thumb through them. If you're experiencing any specific problem or have any specific questions, use the indexes and tables of contents to try to locate answers to your current questions in those books. If you've recently solved a problem with the OS, try to find an answer to that problem, too. Read a randomly selected page or two from each book you're considering to judge whether the general level and style suit your level of understanding and needs. Check and compare the tables of contents of the books to see which has more complete coverage and coverage of the topics that are most important to you. Check the copyright dates and, if specified, the versions of the software covered.

All other things being equal, newer books are better—but don't dismiss an older title out of hand. Sometimes an older title is sufficiently superior to its newer competitors that the older title is still better. This is particularly true if the product you're researching is itself fairly old, like just about any version of DOS. Bonus CD-ROMs can sometimes contain useful utilities, and many books on Linux include Linux installation CDs. Because of the nature of the publishing industry, though, these CDs are likely to be a few months out of date by the time you see the book on the store shelves. This isn't necessarily a major problem, particularly if you don't need the latest versions of every program; but if you do want the latest software, downloading it from the Internet might be better than getting it off of a CD bound into a book.

If you live in a remote area or if your OS is obscure enough that even large bookstores don't have a good selection, try online bookstores, such as http://www.amazon.com, http://www.bn.com, and http://www.borders.com. You won't be able to examine the books before buying, but you can at least read the online descriptions, possibly including customer reviews. Keep in mind, though, that two people can rate the same book very differently, and online reviewers are sometimes far from objective, so don't attach too much weight to just one or two reviews. You might want to check an online retailer before setting foot in a conventional bookstore because you can search for titles to find what's available—online bookstores often have wider selections than do their conventional competitors. You might also want to go to a Usenet newsgroup to seek out others' recommendations on good books to buy. If you do so, be sure to include some information on who you are and what you want to get out of the book—it wouldn't do to accumulate positive recommendations for a highly technical tome if you're a rank beginner, for example.

▶ To learn more about Usenet news, **see** "Reading Usenet Newsgroups," **p. 282**.

One specific point bears mentioning for users of UNIX and UNIX-like OSs: Books on one OS might be useful for another, but all other things being equal, you're better off with a book that's specific to your version of UNIX. For example, if you have a book on UNIX in general, you can glean useful information on using a Linux system from that book. Assuming the books are equally well written and cover similar topics, though, you'd do better with a book written for Linux. Even individual Linux distributions can vary in important ways, particularly with respect to installation and system administration using GUI administration tools. On the other hand, if you want to buy a book on specific tools or applications, those often apply across platforms. If you're interested in Emacs, for example, there's little to be gained from a book on Emacs running on Linux as opposed to Emacs running on Solaris, and in fact most such books don't specify the exact platform.

Computer Magazines for Assorted OSs

Another source of information is computer magazines. Books are very useful for learning basic and not-so-basic OS functions, but the lag time between an author writing words and your reading them is measured in months or even years for books. Magazines, on the other hand, provide a much faster turnaround time from the author to the reader and so are more useful for keeping up to date with occurrences relevant to one OS or another. There is overlap between books and magazines in terms of content, but for the most part, these two forms of publication complement each other. Magazines are best used as a means of ongoing education about an OS or topic, rather than as a reference or tutorial. If you subscribe to a magazine, you can learn a great deal over the course of a year, but it is hard to say just what you'll learn in that time.

I recommend you find a bookstore or newsstand with a good collection of computer magazines and browse, much as you would for books. Instead of looking for solutions to specific problems, though, you should look for a magazine that's written to your general level of expertise and that covers topics of interest to you in the specific issue that's on the newsstand.

Most computer magazines today focus largely on Windows, with an occasional foray into some other OS's realm. You can find printed magazines that deal with alternative OSs, though. If you're not sure where to begin looking, start at the Web site for your OS's

Part
IV
Ch
11

publisher or with a major site associated with your OS. You might be able to find a magazine dedicated to your OS. To obtain such a magazine, though, you might need to subscribe rather than pick it up at a newsstand or bookstore.

E-zines: Online Computer Magazines

The publication delay for books is measured in months, and that for magazines is measured in weeks. Unfortunately, in the computer industry, even weeks can be an eternity, particularly when dealing with critical issues such as Internet security and viruses. Thus has developed the business of *e-zines*—electronic magazines. An e-zine provides content that's similar to that of print magazines, focusing on news, reviews, and commentary, but with timelier distribution via the Web. Many print magazines now have much or all of their content available online. Some, such as *Byte*, have converted entirely to online format. Most e-zines are free for the reader, but a few might require registration or even payment to read their contents.

Here are a few e-zines that are worthy of note:

- http://www.byte.com—This e-zine features news, reviews, and commentary on a wide range of platforms.

- http://www.pcworld.com—This site is a spinoff of a print magazine that's still available in paper form. The *PC World* site focuses more narrowly on Windows than does *Byte*'s site.

- http://www.zdnet.com/pcmag/—Another print magazine spinoff (from *PC Magazine*), much like *PC World*'s site.

- http://home.cnet.com—The CNET site is a general-purpose computing site focusing on reviews, downloads, and auctions. It has no companion print publication.

- http://www.os2ezine.com—This site isn't closely connected to any print magazine, and it is specific to OS/2, which at the time of this writing lacks a dedicated print magazine.

- http://www.linuxjournal.com—*Linux Journal* is the oldest of the existing print magazines devoted to Linux, and its associated Web site contains the text from articles published in the print magazine, along with a few extra articles each month.

- http://www.linuxfocus.org—This e-zine is unusual in that it is available in several languages simultaneously, translated by volunteers. As you might guess from the URL, the publication focuses on Linux.

- http://www.samag.com—This site is the online adjunct to *SysAdmin* magazine, which is devoted to UNIX systems generally, and to a lesser extent Windows NT.

It is becoming increasingly difficult to differentiate between online magazines and other forms of online content. Most of the sites I list here as e-zines have or had print versions, but a few have been Web-based from the start. Some of the smaller e-zines are decidedly amateur in nature, and it can be hard to determine just how reliable information in such e-zines is.

The Internet

The Internet is an increasingly fertile source of support for computer-related issues. Four main sources of support information are available on the Internet: Web pages, Usenet newsgroups, Internet relay chat, and mailing lists. Each provides unique advantages and drawbacks, but all can be helpful in learning to use a new OS or in solving specific problems. As a testament to the utility of the Internet as a support channel, consider the fact that the Linux online community garnered the 1997 InfoWorld Best Technical Support award (`http://www.infoworld.com/cgi-bin/displayTC.pl?/97poy.supp.htm`).

Using Web Sites for Online Help

The *World Wide Web* (*WWW* or *Web* for short) can be an extremely useful tool for locating information about just about anything, but especially computers and related subjects, such as OSs. Throughout this book, I present Web *uniform resource locators (URLs)* for finding further information on topics—URLs are the Internet addresses that are preceded by `http://` or occasionally `ftp://` or some other code. You type the URL into your Web browser to go to the relevant site, or you can use an FTP client to access the `ftp://` URLs.

The preceding section included information on e-zines, which are magazines distributed via the Web. Web-based help is not limited to e-zines, however; countless sites are devoted to providing information that's of interest in setting up a multi-OS computer. Most of these sites are devoted to just one OS or product, but taken together, they are an invaluable source of information.

**Part
IV**

**Ch
11**

Getting Started with the Web   To use the Web, you need a Web browser, such as Netscape Navigator, shown in Figure 11.5, or Microsoft Internet Explorer. Most OSs today ship with a Web browser, or you can obtain one from any of several other sources. Web browsers request and then interpret a variety of document formats, prime among these being the *hypertext markup language (HTML)*, which enables information to be read on a wide variety of display devices, complete with links to other documents, as shown in Figure 11.5.

I assume you have a Web browser for at least one OS on your computer, and an Internet connection. If you want to try another Web browser or need one for a specific OS, you might want to consider the following:

- **Netscape Navigator and Communicator**—Netscape (`http://www.netscape.com`) is one of the most popular Web browsers available. Its basic version, Navigator, provides only Web-browsing features. Communicator adds email, a Usenet newsreader, and Web page design features. Netscape is available on a variety of platforms, including all versions of Windows, OS/2, and several UNIX variants, including Linux and FreeBSD.

- **Mozilla**—Mozilla is the name given to the open source version of Netscape Navigator. As such, it is very similar to Netscape. Unless you plan to develop the software or want to run it on a particularly exotic OS for which no Netscape version is available, you're probably better off with Netscape. Mozilla is hosted at `http://www.mozilla.org`.

FIGURE 11.5
Netscape Navigator is
a typical Web browser.

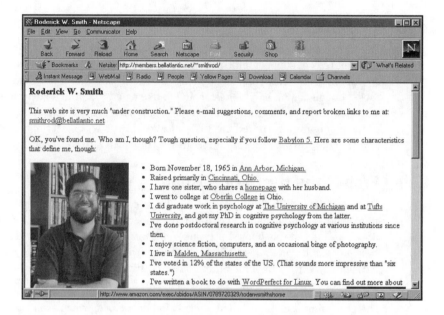

- **Microsoft Internet Explorer**—Internet Explorer (`http://www.microsoft.com/windows/ie/`) is Microsoft's Web browser. It and Netscape Navigator collectively control the vast majority of the Web browser market. On Intel-architecture computers, Internet Explorer is available only for Windows; if you use a non-Microsoft OS, you must look elsewhere.

- **Opera**—The Opera Web browser (`http://www.opera.com`) is a lightweight browser that's nonetheless reasonably complete. It is available for Windows, with versions under development for OS/2, BeOS, UNIX, and other OSs. At the time of writing, the BeOS version was available in beta test form, and an alpha test version of Opera for Linux was available.

- **NCSA Mosaic**—Mosaic (`http://www.ncsa.uiuc.edu/SDG/Software/Mosaic/NCSAMosaicHome.html`) is the Web browser that started the Web. It is no longer being developed, but can still be useful as a bare-bones browser. It is available for Windows and most UNIX OSs.

- **IBM Web Explorer**—This Web browser ships with OS/2. It is limited compared to the likes of Netscape and can't handle many newer HTML features, but can still be very useful as a basic browser.

- **Be NetPositive**—NetPositive (`http://www.be.com/software/beware/network/netpositive.html`) is BeOS's default Web browser. It does a good job of handling modern Web pages, although it is not as full featured as Netscape or Internet Explorer.

- **Lynx**—The Lynx Web browser (`http://lynx.browser.org/`) is a text-mode browser that's available for UNIX-style OSs and for Windows 9x and NT. Because it operates in text mode, it doesn't require you to run a GUI environment. A stripped-down port to DOS is available from `http://www.fdisk.com/doslynx/bobcat.htm`.

- **Arachne**—This browser (`http://home.arachne.cz`) is a graphical browser that runs in non-graphical environments—namely DOS or a Linux text-mode login.

The preceding list represents a mere sampling of the Web browsers available today; a little digging turns up dozens more. Most Web pages work on most browsers, but some pages are heavily optimized for one browser or another (generally Internet Explorer or Netscape). These pages that are closely tied to one or two browsers might pose problems for others, which means you might not have access to a page at all if you use certain OSs. For information on producing Web pages that aren't so encumbered, check the Viewable With Any Browser Web page, `http://www.anybrowser.org/campaign/`.

A Rundown of Helpful Web Sites   To find helpful information on the Web, you must first know where to begin looking. After you've found an appropriate jumping-off point, you can often use it and its links to locate a great deal of information. If you have no other clue, you can begin your Web research using a search engine or general-purpose portal site, such as `http://www.excite.com`, `http://www.yahoo.com`, or `http://www.metacrawler.com/index.html`. Many other sites offer useful information and links, however, particularly when you're looking for information on specific topics. Sites that are particularly likely to be of interest for you in working through problems with an OS installation include the following:

- **OS publisher Web sites**—As described earlier in this chapter, OS publishers maintain Web sites, which contain both useful information and links to outside sites with additional information. Check the entry earlier in this chapter for your OS publisher for a URL.

- `http://www.winfiles.com`—This site is a very good source for downloadable freeware and shareware programs for Windows systems.

- `http://www.metrics.com/WinFAQ/index.html`—*Frequently Asked Questions (FAQs)* about all varieties of Windows, and their answers.

- `http://www.ntfaq.com`—Information about Windows NT.

- `http://www.warpcast.com`—A site dedicated to news relating to OS/2.

- `http://www.os2ss.com`—The OS/2 SuperSite, devoted to news, discussions, and downloadable files for OS/2.

- `http://www.benews.com`—A site on current events in the BeOS community.

- `http://www.bebits.com`—A file-download portal, containing links to useful BeOS programs.

- `http://www.linuxdoc.org`—A site dedicated to Linux documentation, including the Linux HOWTOs and other Linux Documentation Project (LDP) files.

- `http://www.linux.org`—A general-purpose Linux site featuring links to dozens of more specific Linux sites.

- `http://www.linux.com`—Another general-purpose Linux site with information and additional links.

- `http://www.linuxhelp.org`—Yet another source of Linux information and links to other Linux sites.

- `http://www.slashdot.org`—A site dedicated to news, current events, and discussion of computing technology, with an emphasis on Linux and other open source projects.

- `http://www.freshmeat.net`—Information on software updates for open source programs.

- `http://www.gnu.org`—The home of the *GNU's Not UNIX (GNU)* project, which has produced a wide variety of open source software for UNIX-like systems. Much of this software has been ported to other platforms, as well.

- `http://www.xfree86.org`—The home of the XFree86 Project, which developed the windowing system used by Linux, the BSDs, and some other UNIX-like OSs.

When you start from one of these sites, you should have little trouble locating information on the OS you're researching. If you want to solve a specific problem, however, you might not have much luck, particularly on sites that focus on current events rather than those that deal with tutorial information. In these cases, a Web search engine might provide a quicker route to a solution because there are countless sites dedicated to specific topics; those sites might not be indexed from the major sites. Web search engines often turn up these sites, however.

Reading Usenet Newsgroups

To a person unfamiliar with it, the phrase *Usenet news* probably conjures notions of reporters, organized summaries of events, and so on. Such images couldn't be farther from the truth. Usenet news is, in fact, a chaotic and haphazard forum for the exchange of ideas, more closely resembling an open field with thousands of soapboxes than the staid world of professional journalism. Despite the chaotic nature of Usenet news, the newsgroups can provide a wealth of information to anybody searching for help on configuring or using any operating system. The trick is in finding appropriate posts and in separating the good advice from the bad.

Usenet Organization   To use Usenet news most effectively, you should understand its organization, which is hierarchical. In order to focus discussions, Usenet news is broken into a large number of forums, each of which has a name, such as `comp.os.linux.hardware` or `rec.photo.darkroom`. The period-delimited portions of these names indicate increasing specificity of topic. For example, the `comp` high-level hierarchy is devoted to computer topics, whereas `rec` is devoted to recreational subjects. Within the `comp` hierarchy you find groups and hierarchies devoted to OSs (`os`), networking (`networks`), computer languages (`lang`), and so on. Thus, one way to find an appropriate newsgroup is to search for something bearing a name that you find logical, given this organization. For help on a topic relating to a specific OS, searching in the `comp.os` hierarchy often produces a match.

Unfortunately, the organization of Usenet newsgroups, although hierarchical, sometimes defies expectations. For example, you might expect to find discussion groups for specific Linux distributions listed under the `comp.os.linux` hierarchy, but this isn't the case. There are, however, groups devoted to certain distributions, such as a `linux.redhat` hierarchy and a `linux.debian` hierarchy. (In these cases, `linux` is at the top level of the hierarchy; there is no leading `comp.os` in these newsgroup names.) Therefore, you might need to search for a keyword in the list of available newsgroups—you can search for *linux* or *beos* to find groups on these OSs.

One fact that's particularly important to understand about Usenet news is that it is decentralized. Typically, you read Usenet news from a repository of articles maintained by your Internet service provider (ISP). This news server feeds articles to you as you request them. (Some newsreaders also support an *offline* mode, in which you grab a number of news articles and read them at a later time, generally after disconnecting from your ISP.) Your ISP's news server also communicates with one or more outside news servers, which in turn communicate with others, and so on. The protocols governing news article transmission result in propagation of articles across this loosely organized network of machines, but this propagation can take anywhere from seconds to hours or even longer for your article to become visible at any randomly selected location. In some cases you might see a response to an article before you see the original post. In other cases an article might not reach a particular news server at all, and in fact such missing messages are a serious problem with some ISPs.

Different news servers maintain different numbers of newsgroups. For example, my current ISP maintains approximately 40,000 newsgroups, whereas my previous ISP maintained only 30,000, and others carry fewer still. Some of these newsgroups are obsolete or have been abandoned and so carry no traffic, so an absolute number of newsgroups isn't necessarily the most meaningful statistic.

Article retention time is another variable that's of interest to Usenet news users. Some news servers maintain posts for only a day or two before purging them; others keep posts for a week or longer. Many ISPs vary the retention period with the newsgroup, purging more frequently in groups that generate a great deal of traffic or large posts.

If you begin reading Usenet news and find your ISP's news service to be inadequate, you can contract with a third-party news service. Instead of reading news from your regular ISP's server, you can read it from this third-party server. Companies providing such services include News Guy (`http://www.newsguy.com`), Supernews (`http://www.supernews.com`), and Giga-news (`http://www.giganews.com`). You pay separately for such a third-party news account, however, so you might find it more economical to change ISPs to one that has a better news server. In fact, some ISPs contract with a third-party news service provider; instead of maintaining their own news server, they direct news traffic from their customers to the outside provider.

Some organizations maintain their own public news servers that aren't linked to Usenet as a whole. For example, Corel maintains a news server at `cnews.corel.com`. This server maintains newsgroups devoted to various Corel products, but not the usual assortment of Usenet newsgroups. You can point your news reader to such specialized news servers if the topics covered by these servers interest you. Most newsreaders provide some mechanism to read news from multiple servers, so you don't need to sacrifice your ability to read news from your ISP's news server when you use a specialized server.

Using a Newsreader   The traditional means of reading news (and posting your own articles) is via a *newsreader*. This is software that retrieves article descriptions and articles from a news server, enables you to scan and read those articles, and enables you to post a reply or an original message to the newsgroup or to email a reply to a posting. The following list provides examples of newsreader software for each listed OS:

- **Windows**—Forte Agent and Free Agent (`http://www.forteinc.com/`), Netscape Communicator (`http://www.netscape.com`), Outlook Express (included with Windows; `http://www.microsoft.com`)

- **OS/2**—EmTec News (part of EmTec Network Suite; `http://www.emtec.com`), Netscape Communicator (`http://www.netscape.com`), IBM NR/2 (comes with OS/2)

- **BeOS**—BeInformed (`http://beinformed.neog.com/`), NewsBe (`http://www.vargol.freeserve.co.uk/newsbe/`), trn (`http://home.beoscentral.com/chrish/Be/software/networking.shtml`)

- **UNIX (including Linux and the BSDs)**—knews (`http://www.matematik.su.se/~kjj/knews.html`), Netscape Communicator (`http://www.netscape.com`), tin (`http://www.tin.org`)

The preceding list represents only a handful of the possible choices. Check an appropriate file archive site to locate additional newsreaders for an OS. You might also want to check the Good Net-Keeping Seal of Approval (GNKSA) Web page, `http://www.xs4all.nl/%7Ejs/gnksa/`, which lists various Web browsers and rates them on assorted criteria for friendliness to both humans and news servers. (Not all the newsreaders I've listed here attain high GNKSA ratings; some of them are simply quite popular despite failing the GNKSA tests.)

The details of newsreader operation vary substantially from one program to another, but all must provide some way to subscribe to specific newsgroups, browse the contents of those newsgroups, read messages, and post messages. Figure 11.6 shows the OS/2 EmTec Newsreader, which contains controls and features that are as typical as can be expected in a field that's quite variable.

To read Usenet news, follow these steps:

1. Launch the newsreader.

2. Configure the newsreader for your system. On a typical home dialup connection, you must specify the name of your ISP's news server, such as `news.bigisp.net`. You might also need to provide the name of a mail server, your email address, and other details. On UNIX systems, this information is sometimes collected from system configuration files rather than entered in the newsreader itself.

3. Subscribe to one or more newsgroups. Typically, newsreaders include some mechanism to let you view a list of available newsgroups, from which you can select those to which you want to subscribe. On subsequent uses, you'll automatically see those groups to which you've subscribed, but not other groups. You can add or delete newsgroups as you wish, of course. In Figure 11.6, the newsgroup subscriptions window shows the subscribed newsgroups, but not all available newsgroups.

Newsgroup subscriptions window   Newsgroup article listing window

FIGURE 11.6
EmTec News provides separate windows for each function, but some newsreaders collapse all functions into one window, or use a text-mode display that prevents a windowing user interface.

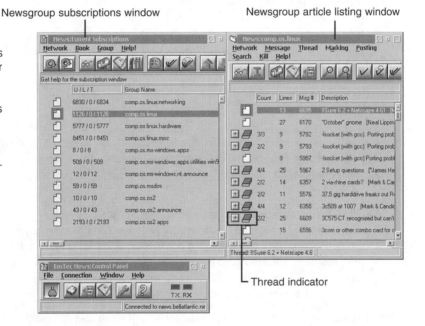

Thread indicator

NOTE   The first time you start your newsreader or access a new news server, you'll probably experience a delay as the newsreader downloads the list of available newsgroups for a site. This file can approach or, on some sites, exceed 1MB in size, so it can take some time to download it. Similarly, the first time you enter a newsgroup you might experience a delay as the newsreader scans the group for existing messages. On subsequent launches of the newsreader or entries to a group, the newsreader need only download new groups or message headers, so the delay is greatly reduced. ▪

4. Select a newsgroup to browse its contents. With most newsreaders, you do this by clicking or double-clicking the group name, or by using the arrow keys to select the group and then pressing the spacebar or Enter. The result might be a change in the display to reveal news articles rather than group names or a new window such as Figure 11.6's newsgroup article listing window.

5. Scan through the displayed articles for titles that sound interesting. You typically read the article by using a method much like that you use to select a newsgroup. Most newsreaders make some attempt to group together related articles. There's typically some indication of this grouping, which is known as a *thread* in Usenet parlance. Figure 11.6 shows the thread indicator used by EmTec News.

6. In most newsreaders, you can search for articles that bear specific titles or that originate from specific individuals. Look for a menu option called *search* or *find* and explore its features.

7. If you want to post an article, you can do so. Most newsreaders offer a variety of posting options, including the capability to post a reply to the newsgroup, send email to the author of an existing post, or post a new article.

> **CAUTION**
>
> Some newsreaders, such as Netscape, post articles in HTML, which is considered bad form on most newsgroups. You should disable HTML posting if it is an option on your newsreader. In Netscape, you can do so from the Formatting section of the Mail & Newsgroups area of the Preferences dialog box (choose Edit, Preferences to display this dialog box).

8. When you're finished reading a newsgroup, most newsreaders enable you to finish in one of two ways: You can exit from the group, leaving the unread articles visible next time you enter it; or you can use a *catch-up* or *mark all articles read* feature to hide all the present articles the next time you enter the group. This latter option can greatly reduce the amount of time it takes you to catch up on postings because it results in your seeing only new articles the next time you enter the newsgroup.

When you post to a newsgroup, it is helpful to keep some ideas in mind to maximize the results you might get from your posting:

■ **Check the FAQ**—Most newsgroups maintain a FAQ list, which can generally be obtained from `ftp://rtfm.mit.edu` under the newsgroup name in the `/pub/usenet-by-group` directory. You might also want to do a search on Deja News before posting a question, to see if your question has been asked recently.

> ▶ To learn more about Deja News, **see** "Using Deja News," **p. 288**.

■ **Select appropriate newsgroups**—Post a query to as few newsgroups as possible. If you cross-post to too many newsgroups, your message might even be automatically deleted! In general, you should post to no more than two or three newsgroups, and usually only to one.

■ **Use a clear subject heading**—Summarize your question, problem, or statement in as few words as possible, but provide sufficient detail to help a reader decide whether to read the entire post.

■ **Report your problem clearly and completely, but not redundantly**—It might be a difficult task to decide just how much information is relevant. In general, it is best to err on the side of too much information.

- **Quote an original message**—If you reply to a posting, quote relevant portions to provide context to readers. Most newsreaders automatically quote the entire message by including it in a reply, preceding each line with a character like a colon (:) or greater than sign (>). You should trim the quoted material to that which is most relevant to your reply. Quoting provides the context that's necessary for interpreting your reply, particularly when the original message is unavailable to the reader. In most newsgroups, the accepted practice is to place the quoted material before the reply, and if necessary, to include several quote-reply blocks to make it clear to which statement any given reply belongs.

- **Provide an email address**—Some people intentionally corrupt the email addresses they include in posts, in order to avoid *spam*—unwanted commercial email. This practice is somewhat controversial, but common. If you follow this practice, make an exception for a post asking for help, or include your real email address in the text of your post. Some people prefer to respond by email, particularly to common questions or to those that seem unusually obscure, and hiding your true email address can cut you off from such responses.

CAUTION

Spammers—those people who send spam—routinely monitor newsgroups in order to gather new email addresses. The more you post to Usenet newsgroups, the more spam you're likely to get. This fact might be the biggest drawback to asking for help on Usenet newsgroups.

Before posting to any newsgroup, it is wise to familiarize yourself with newsgroup etiquette (often called *netiquette*). You can do so by reading the postings to some newsgroups that are devoted to helping new Usenet users: news.answers, news.newusers, and news.newusers.questions.

After posting, wait a while, then check back in the newsgroup, and check your email account for replies. It is not uncommon to receive a reply to a query within a few hours of making the original post, although there are no guarantees. You might garner a dozen helpful replies within a day, or none at all. If your post didn't evoke any replies, reconsider your subject heading, your phrasing, and the groups to which you posted your question. Make adjustments, and try again.

 TIP It is easy to overlook a reply to your posting, particularly in a high-volume newsgroup. You can use your newsreader's search feature to locate the thread you began with your posting by searching for the subject you used. In most newsreaders, the replies appear associated with the original posting in some way, although some newsreaders enable you to display posts in a non-threaded manner. If you're using such a system, search again to locate any replies. You might be tempted to request an emailed reply to avoid this problem. Such requests are sometimes interpreted as a sign of laziness, however, so tread lightly if you do so.

> **CAUTION**
>
> When you receive a reply, or when you read newsgroup postings generally, remember that anybody with Internet access can post. A great deal of information posted on Usenet is flat-out incorrect, or at least of questionable utility. A surprising amount is helpful, however, and if a thread garners more than a couple of replies, chances are somebody will point out the problems in a post that contains incorrect information.

Using Deja News   In addition to using a conventional news server with your own news client software, a number of Web sites exist that let you read news via your Web browser, even if your browser doesn't have an integrated newsreader. One of the most popular of these sites is Deja News (`http://www.deja.com`). This site is distinguished by a relatively long retention period and an easy-to-use search engine that enables you to scan not just the subject headers, but the entire text of posts. For example, suppose you want to find information on using Linux with Initio SCSI host adapters. You could type `linux and initio and scsi` in the search box to locate all the recent postings that contain all three keywords. Deja News returns the list, which when I performed this search included 41 postings (Figure 11.7 shows the first few).

FIGURE 11.7
The Deja News search results provide a mix of helpful and not-so-helpful news postings.

In many cases, a Deja News search produces more junk than useful replies because the keywords you specify appear in posts that aren't of interest to you. Sometimes you might not get all the replies that are relevant because a poster used a synonym or even a misspelling instead of a word in your search string. You can often improve your results by broadening or narrowing your search criteria. Separating words with and tells Deja News to return only posts that contain both words, whereas or indicates that either word is acceptable. You can group collections of words using parentheses in order to apply these operators to other groupings. For example, suppose you want to find postings comparing the Mandrake and Red Hat Linux distributions. Given that people might or might not put a space between the words *Red* and *Hat*, a query like the following should do fairly well:

```
linux and mandrake and (redhat or (red and hat))
```

When I tried this, however, I got 1,119 matching posts, which might be a bit much. You can further refine the search by including a word or words to indicate what sort of comparison interests you, such as ease of installation. Adding and installation to the preceding query reduces it to 135 messages.

In my opinion, Deja News is one of the most helpful of the Internet-based computer information resources. Given the huge amount of information that's posted on most topics—and particularly computer-related topics—every day, it is not difficult to find answers to many questions within a minute or two by using Deja News. Of course, the same caveat concerning misinformation applies to Deja News as applies to Usenet news in general. Deja News doesn't trim the flawed responses from its database, so you can retrieve misleading information as well as brilliant analyses. If you go in with a critical eye and are cautious about applying information gained from Deja News in potentially dangerous ways, you shouldn't have too many difficulties because of these problems.

Using IRC to Get Help

Internet relay chat (IRC) can be used to obtain help, with many of the same caveats as apply to Usenet newsgroups. As a first approximation, you can think of IRC as a real-time news system. When you connect to an IRC server, you can participate in any of the many IRC *channels*, which are discussion areas in which individuals exchange messages. An IRC channel is much like a room in which individuals can chat with one another. Anything one person types in IRC is visible to all the other people using that same channel. Unlike Usenet news, IRC propagation is rapid; other participants are likely to see your messages within moments of your sending them. Therefore, if you can find an appropriate IRC channel, you can engage in real-time OS debugging. A helpful individual could give you instructions to get around a problem, you can try those instructions, report the results and get new instructions, if the first didn't work, within a minute or so.

As with Usenet news, you need an IRC client to begin using IRC. Some popular IRC clients include:

- **mIRC**—mIRC is one of the most popular Windows IRC clients. You can learn more or download it from http://www.mirc.com.
- **GammaTech IRC**—This product is a shareware IRC client for OS/2. You can learn more at http://www.gt-online.com.
- **Felix**—This is a GUI IRC client for BeOS. Its main Web page is located at http://www2.powerteam.net/~xavier/.

Part
IV

Ch
11

- **ircII**—The ircII client is a popular text-mode client on UNIX and UNIX-like OSs. It comes with most UNIX-like OSs, and has been ported to a variety of other OSs.

- **xIrc**—This is an X-based IRC client for UNIX and UNIX-like OSs. You can learn more at http://www.croftj.net/~xirc/.

After you've installed an IRC client, you need to connect to an IRC server. The *relay* portion of *Internet relay chat* refers to the fact that many IRC servers link together, relaying messages back and forth. You can therefore connect to an IRC server that's close to you and chat with somebody connected to a different IRC server. There are several such independent IRC networks. You can learn more about these networks, including the addresses of sites on these networks, at http://www.irchelp.org/irchelp/networks/.

After you've connected to a server, you can enter commands in your IRC client. IRC commands begin with a slash character (/), and can take arguments, as in /join #linuxhelp to join the #linuxhelp channel. You might want to join an IRC help channel the first time you use IRC. Many networks include at least one such channel, often called #irchelp. A few particularly useful IRC commands include:

- /—A slash (/) followed by a space indicates text that you want to send. For example, if you type / Can somebody help me install BeOS?, anybody reading the channel will see your plea for help installing BeOS. Remember to include the space, though, or the first word of your query will be interpreted as a command.

- /list—Lists available channels. Using /list alone is a bad idea on most networks. Instead, use it with a wildcard to find channels of interest, as in /list *solaris* to find channels dedicated to the Solaris OS.

- /join—Joins a new channel. Channels typically begin with the pound character (#).

- /help—Displays help text, usually a list of available commands.

- /bye or /exit—Exits from IRC.

IRC channels aren't organized in the hierarchical way that Usenet newsgroups are, so finding an appropriate channel can be a hit-or-miss proposition. If you don't have luck on one network, try another.

Subscribing to Internet Mailing Lists

The final Internet support resource is that of *mailing lists*. A mailing list is a discussion group that's usually handled on a subscription basis and delivered via email. To subscribe, you typically either fill out a form on a Web page or send email to a special account. Thereafter, you should see messages appear in your email account, and you should be able to post messages to the mailing list.

TIP One of the first messages you receive when you subscribe to a mailing list generally contains information on how to cancel the subscription. *Keep this message!* If you tire of the mailing list or change ISPs, having that message can save you time and effort in tracking down the information on the Web.

Some mailing lists produce very little traffic—perhaps one message every few days. Others generate hundreds of messages a day. The more voluminous mailing lists often offer a *digest* form, in which all the messages posted to the list are held and then sent at some interval, such as once a day.

Because of their closed nature, mailing lists often cater to more advanced and esoteric topics than do Usenet newsgroups. Mailing lists also have less of a tendency to degenerate into *flame wars*—uncontrolled name-calling and similar childishness. (Many of the `comp.os.*.advocacy` newsgroups contain little but flame wars.)

One of the difficulties with mailing lists is in locating them. Here are some ideas for where to start:

- **OS vendor contact information**—Debian GNU/Linux and the BSDs rely on mailing lists for many support functions. You can find information on joining mailing lists on these OSs' Web pages. Similar information exists on other OS vendors' Web pages, as well, even when the OS publisher provides other means of support.

  ▶ To learn more about mailing list Web pages for Debian GNU/Linux and the BSDs, **see** "Useful Official Contact Information," **p. 264**.

- **Locate a Web page on the topic**—Web pages devoted to particular topics sometimes contain information on joining a mailing list for that topic. This is particularly true of the home Web pages for specific products. Therefore, if you want to learn more about a particular program, consult that program's documentation for its home page and check there for information on mailing lists. You might also try doing a search at a Web search engine, including terms like *mailing list* along with the topic at hand.

  ▶ To learn more about Web search engines, **see** "A Rundown of Helpful Web Sites," **p. 281**.

- **Check a FAQ**—You can find FAQs on many topics at `ftp://rtfm.mit.edu/pub/usenet-by-group`. These FAQs often provide pointers to relevant mailing lists.

- **Query an appropriate newsgroup**—Try checking on Deja News (`http://www.deja.com`) and, if that fails, post a query to an appropriate newsgroup asking if there are mailing lists on a topic.

Mailing lists are most useful as a means of education and support for specific products—mailing lists are more specific, on average, than are individual newsgroups. Newsgroups tend to cover broad classes of products, such as *applications* or *games*. Mailing lists are more likely to cover a specific application or game. There are, of course, exceptions to this rule, but in general, mailing lists are a good means of support when you need to delve into a narrow area in some depth, as compared to newsgroups, which provide a much broader range of support.

Mailing list etiquette is much like the netiquette I described earlier for newsgroup postings, and the same rules apply when it comes to phrasing a subject heading, deciding what information to include in a post, and so on.

▶ To learn more about netiquette, **see** "Using a Newsreader," **p. 284**.

Local User Groups

Heading out of the electronic area once again, it is possible to attain support in another way: from one-on-one interactions with individual human beings. If you have a friend, relative, or co-worker who is knowledgeable about the subject at hand, you can often rely on that person's expertise to help you over rough spots in your installation. Even if you don't have such a resource, though, you can frequently find one-on-one help in the form of a *user group*. This is a group of individuals who share an interest in a topic. User groups are typically geographically restricted to one metropolitan area, or sometimes in some other way, such as to a college campus. The groups often maintain Web pages and usually meet regularly—once a month is a typical schedule.

User groups can be very helpful for learning about a new OS, and occasionally for obtaining help on specific problems. The time between regular meetings, however, means that user groups are usually inadequate when it comes to fixing a specific problem immediately. You might, however, be able to avail yourself of group members' expertise much as you would your relative's, friend's, or co-worker's, if you regularly attend meetings and become friendly with other members. Don't abuse such opportunities, though. Only the most dedicated (or sleepless) advocate of an OS will cheerfully accept a phone call at 3 a.m. asking for help!

User groups often focus on a specific OS, or occasionally on specific programs or types of uses for an OS. Occasionally a user group has broader focus, but such groups are rare. Also, user groups are less prominent now than they were a few years ago, and some of the larger groups, such as the Boston Computer Society, have broken up.

Locating a User Group

As with mailing lists, one of the troubles with user groups is in locating them. Here are some ideas of where to start:

- **Ask at computer stores**—The employees of local computer stores are often familiar with user groups in the area.

- **Ask friends and co-workers**—You might know somebody who knows of a user group. If your office employs somebody for computer-related duties, that person is the most likely to know about local user groups.

- **Check the telephone directory**—Unless the group has offices, you're unlikely to find them in the telephone book, but you might just luck out if you're in a large metropolitan area.

- **Check local computer publications**—Many areas support small monthly computer newspapers. These papers often include notices or ads relating to user groups.

- **Do a Web search**—Check a Web search engine for local user groups. When I entered `boston and linux and user and group` at `http://www.excite.com`, the second result I found was the Boston Linux & UNIX User Group (`http://www.blu.org`). You might have similar success with your search.

- **Ask on Usenet news**—You can post to an appropriate newsgroup (after first checking Deja News, `http://www.deja.com`) asking about user groups. In addition, announcement newsgroups for many OSs often carry user group meeting notices. You can't normally post a message to such a newsgroup, but if you subscribe and watch it for a while, you might see a relevant post cross your path.

User Group Regular Meetings

User groups generally meet once a month, although some might meet more or less frequently than this. Some groups—particularly the larger ones—have both general meetings and meetings devoted to specific topics.

User group meetings frequently feature presentations by members or by outside individuals, such as executives or programmers from companies that develop software of interest to user group members. These presentations can be a good way to learn about a topic, and you can sometimes get a glimpse of prerelease software. You can also ask questions of others in the group, and just plain chat and socialize.

Most user groups allow you to attend meetings free of charge, and some charge no fees whatsoever. Others offer paid memberships in the group that afford you certain benefits, such as access to closed Web sites or members-only events.

User Group Special Events

In addition to regular meetings, user groups sometimes host or participate in special events. These can include public demonstrations (often hosted in conjunction with a computer retailer), training sessions for new users, auctions or flea markets, and so on. One type of event that might be of particular interest to you if you have yet to install your OS is a so-called *install fest*, at which users bring in their computers to obtain help installing a new OS on it. Install fests are particularly common among Linux user groups—but even there, you can only expect to see a handful of install fests per year in any given area.

Another type of event in which user groups often participate is *computer shows*. A typical computer show consists of a large number of computer dealers gathering their wares under one roof (often at a hotel or convention center). You can often purchase computer equipment at very low prices at computer shows. User groups also often participate in, and occasionally even organize, such shows. The groups might present informative sessions, recruit new members, and generally make their presence felt at such events.

If you can find a Web page for a user group in your area, that page should contain a calendar of events—both regular meetings and special events. The group's Web page also probably has a map and directions to the meetings and events.

Summary

Obtaining support for your new OS can seem to be a daunting task. Fortunately, most OSs sport a variety of support mechanisms, ranging from formal support from the publisher to informal support on newsgroups and mailing lists, and from local user groups. You face two contradictory challenges in obtaining support, especially support from informal channels: First, you must locate appropriate support venues; and second, you must separate the good suggestions from the bad. Fortunately, a bit of common sense, caution, and watching for corrections to bad advice can go a long way in identifying the support that's worthy of attention. ●

Data Exchange

Filesystems for Assorted OSs

Understanding Filesystems

Consider the following task: You possess a gigantic roll of paper onto which you want to glue copies of all your important documents—your will, your car loan paperwork, your child's kindergarten drawings, and so on. Add in your less important and temporary documents, such as grocery shopping lists, directions to the dentist's office, and so on. Aside from being physically unwieldy, this method of data storage presents certain problems of efficiency. Even assuming you can paste over old documents, there's the question of locating whatever you need when you need it. On a truly long roll, you might search for hours or days before finding what you want. You might try to allocate space by subject, but what happens if you don't give enough space to some category? Then there's the issue of multi-page documents, which might require a run of space longer than any available, if you use this system for a sufficiently long time.

The preceding situation is closely analogous to that faced by OS designers when they confront a hard disk, or even a floppy disk. To solve the problems of this scenario, OS designers have developed several *filesystems*—methods of storing data on a hard disk. A simple filesystem for the paper roll analogy might place a few pages at the beginning of the roll listing the titles and locations of every other document on the roll. Disk filesystems tend to be more complicated than this, but the basic analogy is sound.

From your point of view as a person who wants to use two or more OSs, one major concern is that different OSs favor different filesystems. Sometimes an OS rejects older filesystem designs because the older designs lack features or performance characteristics the new OS requires. Other times, the new OS rejects an older filesystem for legal or even ideological reasons. Whatever the case, though, the number of filesystems available for x86 PCs today is large. It is helpful to know something about the characteristics of these filesystems before you decide which ones you want to use.

▶ To learn more about accessing a filesystem for one OS from another, **see** Chapter 13, "Tools for Accessing Foreign Filesystems."

The fundamental goal of a filesystem sounds simple to a human: to associate data stored on a disk with a filename that's easy for a human to use. For example, you might want to link the filename `letter.txt` to a particular region of the hard disk. If you make changes to `letter.txt`, you want to either overwrite those same regions or, if necessary, change the association to a new part of the disk. In addition to this basic goal, filesystems support many other features, such as storing the date and time the file was created, last modified, or last accessed; recording who may access a file, including whether a given user has the right to modify it; creating a hierarchical structure of files; and so on. The precise set of features required by an OS, and thus by its filesystems, varies, which is one reason so many filesystems are available today.

Features Supported by Assorted Filesystems

Some of the features supported by filesystems include the following:

- **Hierarchical file structure**—No doubt you're already familiar with the hierarchical structure of file storage, in which most files reside inside *subdirectories* or *folders* (the two terms are synonymous in this context). This hierarchical structure helps you to locate your files by separating them into categories and by isolating your files from those used by the OS and its applications. A hierarchical organization also speeds file access because the OS doesn't need to sort through all the tens or hundreds of thousands of file entries on a disk to find one file, just the tens or hundreds in particular directories. Most filesystems use ordinary file entries as subdirectories. The subdirectory files' contents, however, are structured and interpreted as directories. This structure is roughly analogous to placing only chapter titles at the start of a book, and placing chapter subheadings on the first page of each chapter.

  ▶ To learn more about directory structures, **see** "Key Filesystem Data Structures," **p. 303**.

- **Filenames**—Each filesystem has its own rules for file naming. For example, the original specification for DOS's FAT filesystem allowed only 11 characters for filenames, which were split into an eight-character base and a three-character extension. Only uppercase letters, numbers, and some punctuation characters were allowed in DOS filenames. Most other filesystems allow for much longer filenames than does DOS, along with mixed case in the filenames. Microsoft-style OSs use *case-retentive* filename handling, in which case is stored on the filesystem but isn't important. For example, if a file called `letter.txt` exists, you can load it as `letter.txt`, `Letter.TXT`, or any other variant that differs only in case. UNIX-style OSs, by contrast, use *case-sensitive* filesystems, in which `letter.txt` and `Letter.TXT` refer to different files.

- **Dates**—All common filesystems support the recording of file creation dates and times. Many also support storing information on the date the file was last modified or the date it was last accessed. Precisely how a filesystem stores the date information varies from one filesystem to another, of course. For example, Microsoft-style OSs and filesystems use the local time, but UNIX-style OSs use Greenwich Mean Time (GMT) and translate that to local time. This last factor can sometimes result in distortions to files' timestamps when accessing foreign filesystem types.

- **Versioning**—Some filesystems support the storage of a version code with the file to aid in the maintenance of multiple versions of a file. This feature is extremely rare on filesystems used on x86 computers, however; the only filesystem I discuss in this chapter to support this feature is ISO-9660, which is used on CD-ROMs (major PC OSs ignore this feature on ISO-9660 filesystems).

■ **File type**—Filesystems often provide one or more codes to indicate the type of a file. At a minimum, this feature is used to distinguish directories from ordinary files. UNIX-style OSs make heavy use of this feature for certain special files, such as *device files*, that provide access to low-level hardware devices, and *links*, which redirect access to another file.

■ **Access control**—Most filesystems provide, at a minimum, some method of telling the OS whether a file can be modified or not. Additional methods of access control include *hiding* the file (making it invisible to casual searches), *ownership* information (providing privileged access to the file to one user), *permissions* information (specifying which of several classes of users can access a file in specific ways), and *access control lists* (*ACLs*; a fine-grained method of providing file access to specific users). Many OSs rely heavily on specific access control methods provided by a filesystem. For example, UNIX-style OSs use a specific type of permission information for implementing their security arrangements and to determine whether a file is a program file or a data file.

■ **Disk quotas**—Sometimes it is desirable to limit the amount of space that any given user's files can consume on a hard disk. This feature is known as a *disk quota*, and some filesystems include features to help support it. Of course, a filesystem and its driving OS must first support the concept of separate users for disk quotas to make much sense.

■ **Encryption**—If you're particularly concerned about security, you might want your filesystem to support encryption. In a normal filesystem, if the hard disk is removed from the computer, it can be read in another computer, thus bypassing any security features of the OS. If an encrypted filesystem is used, though, the new computer won't be capable of parsing the hard disk's contents.

■ **Compression**—Compression was a popular feature a few years ago, when demand for storage space grew faster than available space on popular models of hard disks. If you're short on disk space and lack the funds to upgrade, you might want to look into a compressed variant of your filesystem. Compression can make a filesystem harder to read from alternative OSs, however, and it slows access to your files.

N O T E   You can often add utilities to enable encryption or compression even on filesystems that don't explicitly support these features. In fact, some OSs, such as DOS and Windows, might come with such utilities. Filesystems with built-in support for these features simply implement them in a more consistent and efficient manner. ■

■ **Ancillary information**—Some filesystems support the storage of certain data types in special areas associated with the base file. Information such as file icons and type codes can be stored in this way. OS/2 and BeOS, for example, both make heavy use of this feature, OS/2 with *Extended Attributes* (*EAs*), and BeOS with attributes.

■ **Data streams**—Some filesystems support storing what is effectively multiple files under a single name. Windows NT's NTFS supports this feature, but the popular OS that does the most with it is Mac OS, which calls the concept *forks*. Because Mac OS isn't an x86 OS, however, this fact isn't of great importance on the PC, unless you use a PC as a server for Macintoshes on a network or you need to access files on a Macintosh disk using a PC.

- **Allocation block size**—Like the pages of a book, the basic unit of data storage on a hard disk is large enough to contain a non-negligible amount of data. Directly indexing every byte of data would be impractical, so filesystems break the hard disk into chunks that are larger than a byte. This size can vary from 512 bytes (0.5KB) to 64KB, depending on the filesystem and the size of the partition. The allocation block size is often referred to as the *cluster size* and sometimes as the *block size*, although the latter term is also used for the minimum amount of data that can be transferred to or from the hard disk hardware. Typically, the allocation block size is a power-of-two multiple of the hardware block size.

- **Partition size limits**—Filesystems have maximum size limits. Except for the older FAT variants, these limits are all well beyond the size of modern hard disks. The less well-endowed of modern filesystems may begin running into problems because of these limits within a decade or so, however. The most capable filesystems are likely to remain adequate in this respect well into the twenty-first century.

- **File size limits**—Filesystems and OSs both impose maximum limits on the size of files they can support. These limits are of most interest to people who work with extraordinarily large files, such as huge databases or video recordings.

Table 12.1 summarizes the preceding list of filesystem features and indicates where each of the major filesystems I discuss in this chapter falls with respect to these features.

Table 12.1   Filesystems and Major Filesystem Features

Feature	FAT	NTFS	HPFS	BFS	ext2fs	FFS	ISO-9660
Read/write access	Y	Y	Y	Y	Y	Y	N
Hierarchical file structure	Y	Y	Y	Y	Y	Y	Y (limited to 8 levels)
Filename length limit	8.3 plain; 128 VFAT	255	254	254	256	255	8.3 for Level 1; 32 for Level 2; more with extensions
Filename case sensitivity	Insensitive or retentive	Retentive	Retentive	Sensitive	Sensitive	Sensitive	Insensitive

continues

Table 12.1 Continued

Feature	FAT	NTFS	HPFS	BFS	ext2fs	FFS	ISO-9660
Date recording	File creation	File creation & modification	File creation & modification	File creation & modification	File creation, modification, & access	File creation, modification, & access	File creation
Version codes	N	N	N	N	N	N	Y
Type codes	Directory, system	Directory, system	Directory, system	Directory	Directory, device, link, and so on	Directory, device, link, and so on	Directory; others with extensions
Access control	Write protection	ACLs	ACLs (in OS/2 server)	UNIX-style permissions	UNIX-style ; permissions ACLs (unused in Linux)	UNIX-style permissions	None except with extensions
Disk quotas	N	Y (in NTFS 5.0)	N	N	Y	Y	N
Encryption	N	Y (in NTFS 5.0)	N	N	N	N	N
Compression	N	Y	N	N	Y (hooks present, but unimple-mented)	N	N
Ancillary information	N	Y	Y	Y	N	N	N
Data streams	N	Y	N	N	N	N	N
Allocation block size	2KB–32KB	1KB–4KB	0.5KB	1KB–8KB	1KB–4KB	4KB and up	2KB
Maximum disk size	128MB (FAT-12); 2GB (FAT-16); 2048GB (FAT-32)	2^{70} bytes	2^{41} bytes (2048GB)	2^{61} bytes	2^{42} bytes (4096GB)	2^{41} bytes (2048GB)	650MB (typical CD-ROM size)
Journaling	N	Y	N	Y	N	N	N

Some features can be added by special utilities but aren't supported by filesystem data structures. For example, many OSs and third-party utilities support compression and ancillary information on FAT. Features can also be supported by the filesystem, but not by the hosting OS; for example, Linux's ext2fs has hooks for features such as ACLs and compression, but the OS doesn't support these features.

OSs and filesystems tend to be designed around one another. For example, if you were designing a new OS and wanted to support certain unique security features, you would probably want to place support for those features in the filesystem. Similarly, you might design the filesystem to optimize performance for the types of operations you expected to occur in your OS. If you expected users to create large numbers of tiny files, for example, you might design a filesystem with small allocation block size to minimize slack space; but if you expected most files to be large, you might favor a larger allocation block size to reduce the overhead for storing and searching through disk allocation information.

▶ To learn more about the concept of slack size, **see** "Partition Size and Disk Consumption Limits," **p. 115**.

Key Filesystem Data Structures

OS developers have invented many different methods of keeping track of information on hard disks. Certain data structure types are common to all these methods, whereas other data structures are unique to just a few filesystems. Even when two filesystems use similar methods, though, the structures might be called different things and might store data in incompatible ways. For example, suppose you wanted to create a table of contents for a book. You might use a data format something like this:

Chapter 1 5

Alternatively, you might do something like this:

Chapter 1 (5)

A human has no trouble with either convention, but the equivalent in terms of filesystem data structures would render the two filesystems completely incompatible. Of course, filesystems can vary in more significant ways, as well. I briefly describe a number of common filesystem data structures in the following pages, but not all filesystems contain all these data structures. These data structures are collectively referred to as the filesystem's *metadata* because they're data that enable you to access the data in which you're really interested—your files and programs.

Boot Block   The *boot block*, which is also known as the *superblock*, is the first block of a partition. It often contains special code that helps the OS boot, hence its name. In addition, the boot block contains information on the size of the filesystem, the locations of key data structures, and so on. Some filesystems effectively extend the boot block into several subsequent sectors, to increase the size and complexity of the boot sector code.

Bitmaps   Bitmaps are a common type of data structure in filesystems. A bitmap records, as a 1 or 0, the status of some larger data structure, such as an allocation block, as shown in Figure 12.1. For example, a *free space bitmap* might mark occupied allocation blocks as 1 and free blocks as 0. Similarly, an *inode bitmap* can record the availability of inodes in an inode table. (I discuss inodes shortly.) Using a bitmap allows the OS to determine where it can place data without searching through the entire disk to find free space. A bitmap can also

Part
V

Ch
12

ease the task of deleting data because it is necessary to change only the bitmap, not the data storage space itself.

FIGURE 12.1
Bitmaps are often used in filesystems to indicate whether an allocation block or other data structure is in use.

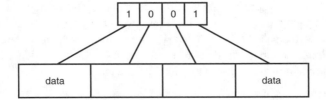

N O T E Most filesystems don't remove data from the disk when you delete a file, they just clear the file's entries in appropriate bitmaps or other data structures. Special utilities are required to overwrite a file's contents with random data if you want to be sure the data aren't recoverable. For the truly security-conscious, even this step isn't enough because residual traces of the old data might exist and can be recovered, albeit with the exertion of considerable effort. For this reason, national security agencies routinely crush old hard disks that have contained sensitive data. ■

The locations of bitmaps in a filesystem can substantially affect the filesystem's performance characteristics. Many modern filesystems place bitmaps throughout the disk to keep the bitmaps close to the data they represent. This proximity can improve disk performance.

FAT The *file allocation table (FAT)* is a data structure used in the filesystem of the same name. Its function is much like that of a free space bitmap, but the FAT uses a *linked list* internal data structure to indicate which allocation blocks are associated with each other. In a linked list, one item points to another, which in turn points to a third, and so on until the list ends. List items can appear out of sequence and can be interspersed with one another. These characteristics make a linked list an obvious choice for representing file allocation on a hard disk. The FAT filesystem's directory entry contains a pointer to the first allocation block of a file; the FAT takes over from there. Figure 12.2 represents a linked list data structure.

FIGURE 12.2
A linked list can be used to indicate both free space and file location.

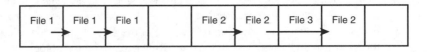

Whereas a free space bitmap uses one bit to represent each allocation block, the FAT uses several bits—12, 16, or 32, to be precise, depending on the FAT variant in use. The size of these pointers, in conjunction with the allocation block size, determines the maximum size of the hard disk, as shown in Table 12.2 for FAT-16 and in Table 12.3 for FAT-32.

Table 12.2   FAT-16 Allocation Block Sizes

Partition Size	Allocation Block Size
1–127MB	2KB
128–255MB	4KB
256–511MB	8KB
512–1023MB	16KB
1024–2048MB	32KB

Partitions smaller than 32MB normally use FAT-12, which has its own similar set of block size increments for partitions ranging from 1MB to 32MB. This table presents the block size if you force the use of FAT-16 for a small partition.

Table 12.3   FAT-32 Allocation Block Sizes

Partition Size	Allocation Block Size
Under 512MB	Not supported
512MB–8GB	4KB
8–16GB	8KB
16–32GB	16KB
Over 32GB	32KB

The FAT filesystem places the FAT at the beginning of the disk, which can reduce disk performance because the disk head might need to swing back and forth frequently between the FAT and data files.

Directories   Some portion of the disk must be set aside to store filenames in *directories*. Directory entries often contain additional information, such as pointers to inodes, file timestamps, or file attributes. Several different methods have been used to store directory entries. Two of the most common are

- **Lists**—The FAT filesystem and many UNIX filesystems use unsorted lists for their directory entries. Lists are easy to maintain but add substantially to file search time. For example, suppose you have a directory with 2000 files, and each directory entry consumes 32 bytes. To determine with certainty that a file exists or does not exist, it is necessary to search through a 62.5KB list of files. Compared to many filesystem operations, this process is time-consuming.

- **Trees**—A *tree* is a type of data structure that can help in the search for information. For example, Figure 12.3 shows a binary tree representation. The *root* of the tree (not to be confused with the root of a filesystem directory structure) is at the top of the diagram. Each *node* (directory entry) in this tree has two *branches*, one of which points to an entry that's less than the original (that is, it comes earlier in an alphabetical listing),

Part

V

Ch

12

and the other of which is greater than the original. Thus, you can search for an entry by following appropriate branches, greatly reducing the amount of data you must examine. For example, suppose you want to find the file protocols using the tree in Figure 12.3. You begin at the root, with mailcap, but protocols falls after mailcap alphabetically, so you follow the "greater than" link (to the right). Comparing protocols to smb.conf, you find that you must go to the left, which leads you to the correct file. Several tree variants exist that can help reduce search time by keeping the tree balanced, to prevent long sequences coming off of one branch and little or nothing deriving from another, as in fact happens in Figure 12.3. Trees are more difficult to explain than lists, and they're more difficult to maintain, but they can dramatically reduce the time it takes to locate a file.

FIGURE 12.3
A sorted binary tree allows for quick search for data, which can be a great boon to a filesystem.

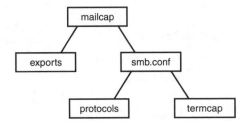

A filesystem must have a *root directory*, from which all other directories derive. Some filesystems, such as FAT, hard-code the location and size of the root directory. Others, such as NTFS, treat the root directory just like any other, except that there must be a special pointer to the root directory in some known location for the filesystem to be capable of accessing any files on the disk. Like the location of bitmaps and FATs, the location of directory entries can play a significant role on disk performance. OS/2's HPFS, for example, attempts to place all directories near the center of a partition because statistically speaking, moving the head to the center of the disk takes the least amount of time.

Inodes The *inode* is a concept that's common in UNIX-style OSs that has spread to others, although not always under the same name. HPFS uses the term *fnode*, for example, and NTFS uses the term *file record*, but the basic concept is the same. FAT doesn't use inodes *per se*; the equivalent data are spread across the directory entries and the FAT.

An inode contains the most critical information on file location and identity, including the position of data on the disk, file modification times, file permissions, and file ownership. OS/2 allows small EAs (extended attributes) to be stored in its fnodes, with additional space being allocated for larger EAs. File allocation information can be stored either in terms of lists of allocation blocks associated with the file or in *extents*, which come as a pair of numbers: a starting allocation block and a number of contiguous blocks. In either case, the inode might not have enough space to completely describe the file's allocation. When the inode is insufficient, the filesystem enables the OS to allocate one or more allocation blocks as a supplement to the inode, to complete the description. Figure 12.4 illustrates the relationship between various types of data structures in an inode-based filesystem.

FIGURE 12.4
An inode mediates
between the user-
accessible filename in
a directory and the file
data.

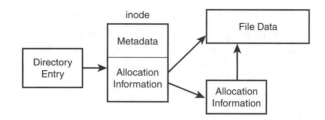

Most filesystems that use inodes attempt to keep them close to the data to which they refer. For example, Linux's ext2fs breaks the disk into several *bands*, each of which has its own free space bitmap, inode bitmap, and inode table, among other things. Whenever possible, a file is linked to an inode in the same band.

Filesystem Speed and Robustness

Many variables characterize different filesystems. Two of the most important are speed and robustness. In the preceding discussion of filesystem data structures, I've indicated the importance of locating data structures close to the files with which they're associated, and most modern filesystems attempt to do just this. There's more to issues of speed and robustness than data location, however.

One important issue is that of *caching*. Most modern OSs support the caching of data while reading from or writing to a filesystem. When caching disk reads, the OS reads more data than requested, on the assumption that more will eventually be requested. It is also possible to cache critical data structures, such as free space bitmaps or FATs. Write caches are more important in considering the tradeoff between speed and robustness, though. In a write cache, the OS puts off writing data to the disk on the assumption that more data going to the same part of the disk is likely to be forthcoming. By combining two or more file writes, the OS can improve overall disk performance. The cost comes in reliability, though; in the event of a system crash or power outage, heavy write-caching can prove disastrous. Some filesystems, such as the UNIX Fast Filesystem (FFS), carefully arrange the order in which cached data are written to disk to reduce this reliability problem. Others use journaling (described shortly) to reduce system startup time after a system crash.

To some extent, the cache policies, and therefore a place on this speed/robustness tradeoff curve, can be determined by the OS independent of the filesystem in use. The filesystem designer, however, probably had a particular cache policy in mind when designing the filesystem. A heavily cached filesystem should have more in the way of redundancy, disaster-proof data structures, and recovery tools than a filesystem that's not as heavily cached.

Journaling Filesystems

One of the problems associated with filesystems in general, and particularly those on which write caching is performed, is the issue of recovery after a system crash or power outage. In normal operation, the OS sets a special flag in the filesystem to indicate that it is in use. When you shut down the computer or unmount the filesystem, the OS removes that flag. When the OS tries to mount the filesystem, therefore, the presence of that in-use flag is a signal that the system crashed or otherwise failed and the data on the partition might not be valid. Unfortunately, the computer has no way of knowing what, if any, data might be corrupt. The system therefore undergoes a fairly lengthy process of examining all the major data structures on the disk—the FAT, the bitmaps, the disk directories, the inodes, and so on—in an effort to locate and, if necessary, repair any inconsistencies. As hard disks have increased in size, this filesystem check time has increased, despite increases in disk speed. It can take quite a few minutes or even hours to check a filesystem on the largest disks available today after a system crash. This fact is a major concern to those who use such systems, particularly in critical environments such as servers.

In an effort to overcome this problem, a new filesystem feature has been developed: *journaling*. The idea is that, rather that write data willy-nilly to the hard disk, the computer keeps on disk a record (the *journal*) of changes that are in the write cache but pending. Keeping the journal requires relatively little disk access, so it has a minimal impact on system performance. Whenever the OS flushes its write cache to disk, it does so by following the operations as recorded in the journal, and it gives priority to these operations so that they proceed quickly. After the system completes a set of journaled changes, it ensures that the filesystem is in a valid state—there are no directory entries that point to nonexistent data, no bitmaps that indicate space that's used when it is not, and so on.

Because the system writes data to most of the disk (outside of the journal file) in bursts, most of the time the disk is clean and should require no checking if the system crashes. On bootup after a crash, the computer checks the journal file and clears the pending operations (which are now lost, just as they would be in any system that uses write caching). In the rare event that a crash should occur during a write operation, the OS uses the journal to undo the operations that had completed. It does this to ensure that the disk is in a valid state—a disk operation might be composed of several steps that create an invalid configuration and then a valid one, so the system doesn't want to risk leaving the filesystem in an invalid state.

The end result is that a journaling filesystem makes recovery after a system crash, power outage, or other problems much faster than it can be with a conventional filesystem. Both Windows NT's NTFS and BeOS's BFS are journaling filesystems, but none of the other filesystems I discuss in this chapter fill that description. Work is underway, however, on two filesystems for Linux that will be journaling: ext3fs and ReiserFS. Silicon Graphics has announced that it plans to release its journaling XFS as open source, so it might be usable by Linux or the BSDs, depending on the exact licensing terms Silicon Graphics selects. IBM also has a journaling filesystem (JFS), which it ships with its AIX UNIX OS and the server edition of OS/2 4.0.

FAT and Its Variants

FAT is one of the oldest filesystems in common use today. Poked, prodded, tweaked, and mutated over the years, FAT endures in part because Microsoft simply offers nothing better on its Windows 9*x* OSs and partly because of its huge installed base. FAT is used not just on hard disks, but on floppies and other removable media (CD-ROMs are one major exception).

From Floppies to Hard Disks: FAT's Long Tenure

FAT traces its heritage back to 1981, with critical concepts dating back even earlier. At that time, hard disks were luxurious extravagances, at least for personal computers. Floppy disks with well under 1MB capacity were considered huge in the small computer industry. For that medium, FAT is a reasonable filesystem. The FAT data structure itself is, for a floppy disk, small enough to cache entirely in RAM. Because the FAT incorporates features of both free block bitmaps and inodes of other filesystems, this capability to cache the FAT in RAM gives FAT a performance edge—for early 1980s technology. Given today's large hard disks, though, the FAT design leads to performance degradation when compared to newer filesystems.

With each stage in the evolution from 180KB floppy disks to 18GB hard disks, it has been easier to stretch or adapt FAT than to devise an entirely new filesystem, at least for the DOS and Windows 9*x* OSs. The FAT went from using 12-bit to 16-bit and then 32-bit pointers to increase the capability of the filesystem to handle larger and larger disks. With Windows 95, Microsoft introduced a modification to enable the filesystem to handle long filenames, by hijacking multiple filename entries for use by a single file. Microsoft and IBM introduced a way to store HPFS-style EAs on FAT by placing them in a special file (called EA DATA.SF—a filename that, because of its embedded space, would normally not be permitted on FAT). Even Linux programmers jumped on the FAT modifications bandwagon, producing UMS-DOS, a FAT variant that can store UNIX-style permissions, ownership, and other data. I examine a few of these variants in the following pages.

Classic FAT

The two most common FAT variants prior to 1995 were FAT-12 and FAT-16, the versions with 12- and 16-bit pointers in the FAT data structure. FAT-12 is most commonly used on floppies, but it can be used on hard disks. On hard disks, FAT-12's capacity is limited to 128MB because of the 32KB maximum allocation block size limit ($2^{12} \times 32KB = 128MB$). The adjustment of FAT to use 16-bit pointers raises this limit to 2GB.

> **NOTE** Windows NT can use 64KB allocation blocks with FAT-16, raising its maximum FAT partition size to 4GB. These partitions can't be read by most other OSs, however, so I recommend using NTFS instead of FAT for any partition over 2GB. For performance reasons, NTFS is a better choice for most partitions of less than 2GB, as well, when using Windows NT. ▓

As implemented in DOS, FAT suffers from extreme limits on file naming: Filenames are eight characters long, followed by an optional three-character extension (the so-called *8.3 filename limit*). Plain FAT filenames can contain uppercase letters, numbers, and certain punctuation marks, but not lowercase letters, periods (aside from the one separating the base filename from its extension), spaces, or certain other punctuation marks. The only filesystem in

Part
V

Ch
12

common use that's more restrictive than FAT is ISO-9660 Level 1. These restrictions represent a major advantage to OS/2 1.2 and above over DOS and Windows 3.11 and below because OS/2 supports HPFS and its much less intrusive file-naming limits.

VFAT

In fact, the file-naming limits of FAT were such a problem that Microsoft introduced a means of overcoming them while retaining backward compatibility. This system is known as VFAT, and Microsoft introduced it with Windows 95. FAT and VFAT are identical in their major data structures, and in fact the same disk can always be read using either system. The only difference between the two is that VFAT uses multiple filename entries to record long, mixed-case filenames. VFAT accomplishes this task by using flags in the extra entries to force DOS, OS/2, and other OSs that aren't VFAT-enabled to ignore the long filename entries. The result is a filesystem that contains two filenames: an 8.3 filename and a long filename. You can see both names when you use the DIR command from a Windows DOS prompt. This command might produce output something like this:

```
Directory for A:/

SPAM-F~1 TXT    105696 11-08-1999   19:46   spam-FAQ-19990815.txt
YACL-E~1 TXT      4172 11-08-1999   19:46   yacl-egcs.txt
WIN2K    TXT      1601 11-08-1999   19:46   win2k.txt
         3 files              111 469 bytes
                           1 345 024 bytes free
```

You can see the long filename to the right and the 8.3 filename to the left. In Windows, you can use either filename to access a file, although in most 32-bit programs you see only the long filename and in 16-bit programs you see only the 8.3 filename.

> **CAUTION**
>
> Disk utilities intended for a VFAT-unaware OS can sometimes damage the long filenames on a VFAT disk. Windows 9x relies on these filenames to boot, so I recommend you never run CHKDSK, a disk defragger, or any other disk utility from DOS, OS/2, or any other VFAT-unaware OS on a VFAT partition. Even deleting a file that has an associated VFAT long filename using a VFAT-unaware OS can have negative consequences because that OS won't remove the VFAT long filename. No real harm is done by this, except that one or more directory entries are wasted until you use Windows 9x's SCANDISK utility to correct the problem.

N O T E The term *VFAT partition* seems to suggest that the partition is fundamentally different from an ordinary DOS FAT partition. Aside from the presence of long filename information, though, this isn't true. A more precise description would be *FAT partition containing VFAT-style long filenames*, but this phrase is extremely awkward, so I use *VFAT partition* in its place. ◼

TIP Because VFAT uses several filename entries for each long filename, you should refrain from using long filenames in a partition's root directory. The root directory normally contains enough space for 512 entries, but that number can go down substantially if you use VFAT long filenames. Subdirectories can be expanded as necessary, so similar logic doesn't apply to subdirectories. This restriction also applies only to VFAT on FAT-16 partitions; FAT-32 partitions use an expandable root directory structure.

FAT-32

With the 2GB limit of FAT-16 (including its VFAT variant) looming, Microsoft introduced an increase in the FAT pointer size with OEM Service Release 2 (OSR2) of Windows 95. This change gave FAT a new lease on life, radically increasing its maximum disk size. Because all FAT-32 partitions are used with Windows 9*x* (or, now, Windows 2000), they are almost invariably used with VFAT long filenames. It is possible to store nothing but 8.3-compliant filenames on a FAT-32 partition, however.

> **N O T E** Linux supplies two different ways to mount a FAT partition: You can use the `msdos` filesystem code for 8.3 filenames or the `vfat` filesystem code for long filenames. You can use either filesystem with 12-, 16-, and 32-bit FAT variants, so from Linux you can easily enforce 8.3 filenames on a FAT-32 partition, should you be so inclined. You could do much the same by booting Windows 9x only into its DOS-mode shell, which doesn't support long filenames. ■

Some people confuse VFAT and FAT-32. They are different, but compatible, variants of FAT. VFAT should be thought of more as a way to do something new with an existing disk or partition (namely, store long filenames on it), whereas FAT-32 is a new filesystem type (albeit one that's closely related to older FAT versions).

Is It Time to Retire FAT?

FAT is nearly two decades old, which is pretty ancient as computer standards go. It uses many archaic and performance-robbing features, such as the FAT data structure after which the filesystem is named and the simple list structure used for its directories. As a general rule, I advise against the use of FAT, at least on hard disks where performance is a concern. You have little choice in the matter when you use Windows 9*x*, but for most other OSs, you do have a choice, and those choices are generally superior. There are, however, some situations in which FAT is still a good filesystem:

■ **Floppies**—FAT was designed with floppy disks in mind, and it still performs reasonably well at this task, even on 1.44MB floppies. More important than performance, though, is the widespread support for FAT. You can write a FAT floppy with OS/2 and read it on another computer with Linux; or write with BeOS and read with Windows NT. FAT does lack filesystem characteristics used by some OSs, such as ownership as implemented in UNIX-like OSs, but for data exchange between systems, this fact usually isn't a debilitating problem.

Part
V

Ch
12

■ **Higher-capacity removable media**—When you use a Zip disk or similar high-capacity removable media, FAT can be a reasonable choice. Part of the reason for this is FAT's widespread support, just as this factor is important for floppies. In addition, some OSs have weak support for their own higher-performance filesystems on high-capacity removable media. OS/2, for example, supports HPFS on removable media, but not as smoothly as it supports FAT on the same media. Other OSs, such as Linux, have no such limitations, however, and so their native filesystems might be better choices for removable disks.

■ **A data exchange partition**—FAT is the lowest common denominator for data exchange between OSs. For example, there effectively is no other filesystem that can be used to exchange data both ways between FreeBSD and BeOS. In some cases you might be able to exchange data in one direction using built-in support, but not in the other direction; or your OSs might be capable of reading, but not writing, each others' partitions. For example, at the time of this writing, read-only drivers existed to enable BeOS to read Linux's ext2fs, and for Linux to read BeOS's BFS; but neither allowed write access to the others' filesystem.

■ **Legacy installations**—You might have installed an OS using FAT for reasons that seemed good at the time but that no longer apply. It might be better to leave such installations alone than to try to convert them to a better filesystem. In some cases, however, you can use PowerQuest's PartitionMagic (http://www.powerquest.com) to convert from FAT to HPFS or NTFS, or from FAT-16 to FAT-32. Windows NT also includes a utility to convert from FAT to NTFS.

▶ To learn more about converting filesystem types, **see** "Converting Partitions," **p. 202**.

■ **Minimal FAT boot partition**—Because FAT is so easy to access, including from a DOS boot floppy, you might want to use a small FAT boot partition in conjunction with larger partitions of a more sophisticated filesystem. This approach can be particularly helpful for Windows NT because boot floppy support for NTFS is rare.

Chances are we'll continue to see FAT in use for several years in the future, although probably in a diminishing capacity as more sophisticated filesystems become more popular with the spread of OSs such as Windows 2000, Linux, and perhaps others.

Windows NT's NTFS

The New Technology Filesystem (NTFS) is Microsoft's favored advanced filesystem. Aside from FAT, NTFS is the only hard disk filesystem natively supported by Windows NT since version 4.0, although earlier versions of Windows NT supported HPFS in addition to FAT and NTFS. Windows 2000 adds several features to its NTFS support, requiring on-disk changes to the filesystem.

▶ To learn how to enable HPFS support in Windows NT 4.0, **see** "Foreign HPFS Support," **p. 346**.

CAUTION

If you want to run a computer that contains both Windows 2000 and Windows NT 4.0, you must install Service Pack 4 or later for the latter OS, to enable Windows NT 4.0 to cope with the changes to NTFS imposed by Windows 2000. These modifications are referred to as *NTFS 5.0*. Even after installing Service Pack 4 or later, Windows NT won't be capable of performing low-level disk maintenance on an NTFS 5.0 partition; you'll need to boot into Windows 2000 to perform disk checks and the like.

NTFS is unusual in that all its filesystem metadata are themselves files. For example, one file represents the boot block, another represents the journal, and so on. Because these metadata reside in files, it is theoretically easy to expand them dynamically, although in practice you still need a utility such as PartitionMagic to do so. Windows 2000 includes some utilities that can help dynamically modify NTFS partitions.

NTFS's features include the following:

- Filenames up to 255 characters in length
- Case-retentive long filenames
- Storage of 8.3 filenames matched to long filenames
- Directories stored in a sorted tree structure
- Allocation block size adjustable at format time, but defaults increase with disk size (see Table 12.4)
- Maximum partition size of 2^{70} bytes (that's a 22-digit number when spelled out in decimal)
- Maximum file size of 2^{64} bytes
- Storage of EAs
- Support of ACLs for security
- File compression
- File encryption (in NTFS 5.0)
- Multiple data streams
- Journaling

Table 12.4   Allocation Block Sizes for NTFS Partitions

Partition Size	Allocation Block Size
1–511MB	0.5KB
512–1023MB	1KB
1024–2047MB	2KB
2048–4095MB	4KB

Part V

Ch 12

continues

Table 12.4   Continued

Partition Size	Allocation Block Size
4096–8191MB	8KB
8192–16383MB	16KB
16384–32767MB	32KB
32768MB and up	64KB

NTFS's Strengths and Weaknesses

NTFS is well-suited to duty in a server environment. Its journaling, ACLs, and support for truly huge partitions are features that are very helpful in such an environment. NTFS is more reliable than FAT, the only other serious choice for filesystem in most Windows NT installations.

On the other hand, many of NTFS's features are overkill for smaller configurations. It's unlikely that hard disks will even approach the capacity of which NTFS is capable for quite a while, for example. NTFS's support for EAs and multiple data streams has as yet gone largely unused, and individual users might not use NTFS's ACLs very extensively. (This last point is largely a matter of the default configuration of an NT system, however, which is lax on security.) None of these are reasons not to use NTFS, but they do mitigate its advantages, leaving room for the major disadvantage to play a role—namely, the inaccessibility of NTFS from OSs other than Windows NT. Read-only NTFS drivers exist for a variety of OSs, including Linux, OS/2, and BeOS. Read/write NTFS support is rarer, and most of the implementations are currently unreliable. You can purchase third-party read/write NTFS drivers for DOS and Windows 9x, however, which use Windows NT's own drivers in a special environment. Another drawback to NTFS is that it is more susceptible to fragmentation than are many other filesystems, although it's not as bad as FAT in this respect.

▶ To learn more about NTFS drivers for non-NT OSs, **see** "Foreign NTFS and NTFS 5.0 Support," **p. 343**.

When to Use NTFS

On the whole, NTFS's strengths outweigh its weaknesses, in my opinion. You should certainly use NTFS for Windows NT–only files and programs, if you have enough of them to justify creating a separate partition; the same is true if you need Windows NT's security or other special features. The main times when you should not use NTFS are when you need to access data from another OS. Because it is often desirable to access an OS's boot partition from another OS for emergency recovery purposes, this can at least potentially include the boot partition.

> **TIP** You can mix and match NTFS and FAT. For example, you can boot Windows NT from a FAT partition but place your programs and data on NTFS partitions. You can also place the `WINNT` directory (in which Windows NT stores most of its files) on an NTFS partition, even when the most basic boot files reside on a FAT `C:` partition. Another option is to create a minimal Windows NT installation on a FAT primary partition, and put a full Windows NT installation on a separate NTFS primary partition. You can then use the FAT-based installation to repair damage to your main NTFS-based installation, if necessary.

OS/2's HPFS

OS/2's High Performance Filesystem (HPFS) was developed for OS/2 1.2 as the successor to FAT. HPFS abandoned the FAT concept for a more UNIX-like approach using inodes (called *fnodes* in HPFS), free space bitmaps, and so on. The filesystem also incorporates native support for OS/2 EAs. It was designed to be fault-tolerant and to work well with large hard disks (at least, large by the standards of the mid 1980s). It organizes data in 8MB bands, each of which contains a free space bitmap for that band and additional metadata. Because of this organization, the allocation block size for HPFS remains constant no matter what the partition size. The allocation block size is normally set to 0.5KB.

HPFS's features include the following:

- Filenames up to 254 characters in length
- Case-retentive long filenames
- Directories stored in a sorted tree structure
- Constant allocation block size of 0.5KB
- Maximum partition size of 2^{41} bytes (2048GB)
- Maximum file size of 7.5GB (OS/2 contains other limits that reduce the maximum file size to 2GB)
- Storage of up to 64KB of EAs with each file
- Support of ACLs for security (in OS/2 server versions)
- Highly resistant to fragmentation

Two different HPFS filesystem drivers are available for OS/2. Client versions of the OS ship with 16-bit drivers written largely in assembly language, whereas server versions ship with 32-bit drivers written largely in C. Which version works best varies a lot from one system to another, but the 32-bit version has an edge on modern computers simply because it supports larger caches. The 32-bit server version also supports ACLs, whereas the 16-bit client version does not.

HPFS's Strengths and Weaknesses

HPFS's advantages over FAT are substantial, and include the following features:

- Faster performance, especially on large hard disks
- Less wasted disk space, especially on large hard disks
- Support for larger hard disks
- Support for long filenames
- More reliable operation

Overall, these advantages are enough to recommend HPFS for serious use of OS/2. The filesystem does have the following drawbacks, however:

- Increased memory requirements for the HPFS cache
- Long filenames are invisible to DOS and Windows programs
- Few third-party HPFS disk recovery utilities
- Weak support for HPFS in non-OS/2 OSs

▶ To learn how to use HPFS in other OSs, **see** "Foreign HPFS Support," **p. 346**.

This final drawback is the most serious in most modern multi-OS configurations. HPFS read/write drivers exist for Linux (in the 2.3.x kernels and later), Windows NT (using drivers included in Windows NT 3.51 and earlier), and DOS. Also, OS/2 boot floppies support HPFS, so you can perform emergency maintenance on HPFS more easily than you can on NTFS. Some of these drivers might be difficult to obtain or use, however; for example, you need a license to Windows NT 3.51 or earlier to use HPFS from Windows NT.

When to Use HPFS

My recommendation is to use HPFS whenever possible in an OS/2 installation. In particular, you should probably use it for the OS/2 boot partition and for OS/2-only applications and data. Doing so will give you HPFS's advantages in contexts where its major disadvantage (lack of non-OS/2 support) is minor. Most of HPFS's other drawbacks are easily overcome or are balanced by HPFS advantages. For example, the paucity of third-party disk utilities for HPFS is balanced by HPFS's increased robustness; and it's easy enough to give 8.3-compliant filenames to files and directories you need to use with DOS and Windows programs, although this strategy does mitigate one of HPFS's strengths—its support of long filenames.

BeOS's BFS

Be's original conception for a filesystem was one that included a large number of database features. This concept, though, proved to be too awkward in practice, and so Be developed the Be Filesystem (BFS), which retains some database-style features but for the most part is a fairly conventional filesystem. BFS borrows some features from UNIX filesystems, such as UNIX-style permissions. It shares other features with NTFS and HPFS, such as its support for EAs (known as *attributes* in BeOS).

BFS's features include the following:

- Filenames up to 254 characters in length
- Case-sensitive long filenames
- Directories stored in a sorted tree structure
- Allocation block size of between 1KB and 8KB, configurable at format time
- Maximum partition size of 2^{61} bytes (that's a 19-digit number when spelled out in decimal)
- Maximum file size of approximately 2^{44} bytes
- Storage of special attributes
- Use of attributes to support database-like functionality
- Support of UNIX-style permissions for security (not used by BeOS 4.5 and earlier)
- Highly resistant to fragmentation
- Journaling

BFS splits the partition into several *allocation groups*. These are sections of the disk that are used to improve performance and reduce fragmentation; BeOS tries to place all files from a single directory in one allocation group, for example, and when two processes open separate files, they're opened in separate allocation groups to reduce the possibility of fragmentation. In these respects allocation groups resemble HPFS's bands, but allocation groups are purely logical structures; they don't contain separate free space bitmaps or other unique data structures.

Like HPFS's EAs, BFS's attributes can often be stored entirely in a BFS inode. When the inode isn't large enough, BFS creates a structure that's essentially a directory without a name in which to store the extra attributes.

BFS's Strengths and Weaknesses

BFS is an impressive filesystem in many respects. Its strengths include

- Large maximum partition and file sizes
- Journaling
- Fast performance

BFS isn't without its limitations, though, such as the following:

- Weak or nonexistent support in most OSs
- Unsupported by PartitionMagic

Part
V

Ch
12

Unlike Windows NT and OS/2, there's no easy standard of comparison for BFS. That is, you can install Windows NT or OS/2 on a FAT partition or on their more-advanced filesystems; this isn't true for BeOS. Of course, if you really want to, you can use a FAT partition for data storage using BeOS, but the comparison isn't as useful as it is for Windows NT and OS/2. Therefore, these BFS strengths and weaknesses are based on a broader comparison of BFS to other advanced filesystems, such as NTFS, HPFS, and ext2fs, on a relatively abstract level.

When to Use BFS

You must use BFS when you use BeOS. BeOS relies on BFS features, such as its attributes, to implement certain key OS features. This fact makes the selection of BFS an easy choice. What might be somewhat more complex is the decision of when not to use BFS.

In a multi-OS configuration, you might need to maintain one or more shared partitions. Ideally, you should place all your shared files in shared partitions. For example, if you want to use BeOS to work on multimedia files, but also need access to these files from Windows, you can place the files in a FAT partition. Unfortunately, FAT's performance isn't up to the standards of BFS, which can degrade your ability to work with the files in BeOS. If this happens, you'll need to decide whether to work with the files using the performance-robbing FAT or copy the files to a BFS partition. You can, of course, copy files back and forth between BFS and FAT partitions as the need arises; but keep in mind that you can't access BFS from Windows, so you must copy the files back to FAT before you reboot to Windows.

Read-only BFS drivers exist for Linux, as do read-only ext2fs drivers for BeOS, so if you want to exchange data between these two OSs, you might be able to do so without resorting to a FAT partition.

▶ To learn more about accessing non-native filesystems, **see** Chapter 13, "Tools for Accessing Foreign Filesystems."

Linux's ext2fs

Linux has gone through a string of native filesystems, starting with the Minix filesystem it borrowed from the older Minix UNIX clone OS, and then moving on to the Extended Filesystem (extfs) and the Xia Filesystem (xiafs), and finally settling on the Second Extended Filesystem (ext2fs). The internal design of ext2fs is heavily influenced by that of the UNIX FFS and resembles OS/2's HPFS. Like these filesystems, ext2fs uses a free block bitmap to indicate what space is free, and inodes to provide useful file information. Unlike HPFS, ext2fs uses an unsorted list for its directory structures. Like HPFS, ext2fs uses separate bands, each of which contains its own free space bitmap and inode bitmap. Major ext2fs features include the following:

- Filenames up to 256 characters in length
- Case-sensitive long filenames

- Directories stored in linked lists
- Allocation block size of between 1KB and 4KB, configurable at format time
- Maximum partition size of 2^{42} bytes (4096GB)
- Maximum file size of 2GB
- Support for UNIX-style permissions for security
- Support for ACLs (Linux doesn't use ACLs, but ext2fs reserves space for them)
- Highly resistant to fragmentation

ext2fs's Strengths and Weaknesses

Linux's ext2fs is optimized for speed. Linux's implementation of the filesystem relies heavily on its cache, and in operation it contains few features to ensure consistency of the filesystem in the event of a failure. In particular, ext2fs lacks a journal. This means that a Linux system that suffers from a power loss or system crash must endure a lengthy filesystem check process on the next bootup. Depending on your point of view, these heavy speed optimizations at the expense of a long disk check after a crash might be a positive or a negative feature.

Some of ext2fs's best features include

- Fast performance
- Redundant copies of the boot block maintained in each band
- Moderately widespread support outside Linux

The ext2 filesystem does have its downsides, too:

- Lengthy disk consistency check (via `e2fsck`)
- Low partition and file size limits compared to filesystems available in other server OSs

When to Use ext2fs

Linux doesn't require the use of ext2fs, but it is the best filesystem for use in Linux, at least as of the 2.2.x kernel series. If you want to buck the crowd, you could use xiafs, although most Linux distributions don't explicitly support it during installation. A few distributions do support installation to a UMSDOS filesystem, which is FAT with tacked-on support for UNIX-style permissions, ownership, and other necessary features. Whenever possible, I recommend against using UMSDOS, however, because it is slower than ext2fs and drags along too many of FAT's drawbacks. This is particularly true when using UMSDOS on a FAT-16 partition.

Source code availability and the enthusiasm of Linux programmers who also use other OSs has led to an interesting phenomenon: The Linux ext2 filesystem is one of the most widely supported filesystems in existence, aside from FAT and CD-ROM filesystems. Drivers for ext2fs exist for DOS, Windows 9*x*, Windows NT, OS/2, BeOS, FreeBSD, and others. For most of these OSs, the ext2fs support is read-only, but there are exceptions to this rule. OS/2 and FreeBSD, in particular, support read/write ext2fs access, although FreeBSD can only access primary ext2fs partitions, not logical partitions. (You need a third-party driver for OS/2's ext2fs access.) You might therefore want to use ext2fs as a shared data partition type for certain OS combinations. In fact, the OS/2 ext2fs drivers include instructions for installing the bulk of OS/2 on an ext2fs partition, although there aren't many reasons to make such an attempt.

As I write these words, work is underway on a new Linux filesystem, tentatively called the Third Extended Filesystem (ext3fs). This filesystem is based on ext2fs but incorporates several improvements, including journaling and probably changes to partition and file size limits. At the time of this writing, however, the exact specifications of ext3fs are still open to change. In addition to ext3fs, other filesystems will almost certainly work their way into the Linux kernel. Silicon Graphics' XFS, for example, might one day become popular among Linux users. Another journaling filesystem, known as ReiserFS, is also under development and might compete with ext3fs and XFS for popularity on Linux in the next few years.

UNIX's FFS

Back in the days when UNIX was a side project of AT&T and students and faculty at the University of California at Berkeley were modifying AT&T's work, one of the projects undertaken was an improvement of the original UNIX's filesystem. The result was known as the Fast Filesystem (FFS), and it and minor variants of it are still in use today. Although the details differ, FFS closely resembles Linux's ext2fs—or perhaps it would be fairer to say that ext2fs resembles FFS because FFS predates ext2fs. For its day, FFS was quite speedy, but ext2fs is faster for most operations, largely because it does less to ensure the consistency of the filesystem in the event of a crash. FFS is in use today in several UNIX and UNIX-like OSs, including the open-source BSDs.

N O T E   Different implementations of UNIX have altered various aspects of FFS, so these implementations aren't quite 100% compatible with one another. Sometimes a new name comes along with these changes, as well. One particularly common variant name is *UFS (UNIX Filesystem)*. Linux refers to FFS as UFS, perhaps to avoid confusion with the Amiga FFS, which is an entirely different filesystem supported by Linux. ■

FFS was designed in a day when physical hard disk geometry was known to the OS, and it takes pains to lay out its data in such a way as to minimize head movements. In today's computers, such actions are unnecessary and sometimes even counterproductive because physical hard disk geometry isn't known to the OS. Modern drives are designed such that head movements can be minimized by minimizing the seek distance in terms of the absolute number of sectors, which is a much simpler task for an OS's filesystem drivers to perform.

▶ To learn more about hard disk geometry, **see** "Understanding CHS Geometry Limits," **p. 76**.

FFS features include the following:

- Filenames up to 255 characters in length
- Case-sensitive long filenames
- Directories stored in linked list
- Allocation block size of 4KB or above, configurable at format time
- Maximum partition size of 2^{41} bytes (2048GB; but specific OS implementations often reduce this to 1024GB)
- Maximum file size of 2^{46} bytes (65536GB)
- Support for UNIX-style permissions for security
- Highly resistant to fragmentation

N O T E FFS is unusual in that its theoretical largest file size is larger than its theoretical largest partition size. Of course, in practice you won't find any files larger than the partitions on which they reside!

Unique FFS Partition Requirements

Because FFS originated on mainframe computers of years past and because these mainframes were typically dedicated to a single UNIX OS, FFS has historically been closely tied to one particular partitioning scheme—one that's not commonly used on PCs. Rather than break with this partitioning system, the BSDs have implemented a partition-within-a-partition strategy. When you install a BSD OS, you create a standard primary PC partition and then create subpartitions within that partition following the UNIX partitioning scheme. The result is very similar to a regular PC extended partition, which contains several logical partitions. Alternatively, you can partition an entire disk using nothing but the UNIX partitioning system, but if you do so, you won't be able to use that disk from most other OSs. This second approach is therefore of limited interest to those wanting to run multiple OSs—you might consider using it if you want to dedicate an entire second hard disk to BSD, but not otherwise.

▶ To learn more about BSD partition requirements, **see** "Partition Requirements," **p. 260**.

FFS's Strengths and Weaknesses

FFS has aged remarkably well, given its origin in the early 1980s—around the same time that FAT appeared. FFS was an early adopter of many modern filesystem features, and in a few ways it is superior to even more recent UNIX filesystems, such as Linux's ext2fs.

From the perspective of a person using a modern x86 PC, FFS's main strengths include the following:

- Near ubiquity among UNIX OSs
- Time-proven and robust design

Part

V

Ch

12

FFS does have its drawbacks, however:

- Ties to unusual partitioning design, at least in the BSDs
- Low partition size limit
- Weak support in non-UNIX OSs
- Unsupported by PartitionMagic
- Lackluster performance by today's standards

For these reasons, many commercial UNIX versions have incorporated proprietary filesystems with more modern designs. IBM's AIX uses JFS and Silicon Graphics uses XFS, for example.

When to Use FFS

FFS is best used on the BSDs and other UNIX-style OSs that don't yet support more modern filesystems. In theory, a BSD user could use Linux's ext2fs instead of FFS, but FFS is far better tested than ext2fs for the BSDs. I have seen very little information on the reliability of ext2fs under any BSD OS, and so I can't recommend its use except in data transfers with Linux.

Similarly, using FFS from OSs that don't use it natively is possible, but at least potentially risky. Linux includes FFS support, for example (Linux calls it *UFS*), but read/write FFS support in Linux 2.2.x is considered experimental and thus shouldn't be trusted. Read-only FFS access should be reasonably safe, however, so you can read your BSD files in Linux using Linux's UFS driver.

In some cases, you must abandon FFS and even UNIX-style filesystems entirely from BSD or other FFS-using OSs. These situations are similar to those in which you must abandon native filesystems for BeOS, Windows NT, OS/2, or Linux—when exchanging data with an OS that doesn't understand FFS. For example, you can use a FAT partition to exchange data between OS/2 and FreeBSD.

CD-ROM and DVD-ROM Filesystems

Hard disks aren't the only media on which filesystems are used. Removable disks, including floppies, magneto-optical disks, and Zip disks, can use the same filesystems as hard disks. In some cases you must take special steps to use a removable disk with certain filesystems; for example, OS/2 provides no easy way to use HPFS on floppies, although the task can be accomplished with some ingenuity or special utilities.

CD-ROM and, now, DVD-ROM (Digital Versatile Disc ROM) media are an exception to this rule. These media possess unique characteristics that make the use of special filesystems desirable. For example, these media are essentially read-only, although CD Recordable (CD-R) and CD Rewritable (CD-RW) technology has changed this fact recently. CD-ROM media also typically possess much higher head seek times than do hard disks. In any event, special filesystems exist for read-only media, and these filesystems deserve comment.

If you own a CD-R or CD-RW drive, you need special software to create CDs. Traditionally, this software requires you to assemble your files in some way and then burn a CD-R that contains all these files. Some software, however, enables you to use a CD-R or CD-RW drive more like an ordinary disk.

Plain ISO-9660: The Lowest Common Denominator

At the core of most CD-ROM filesystems is ISO-9660, named after the specification produced by the International Standards Organization. ISO-9660 is a somewhat more tightly specified version of the earlier High Sierra format, so if you have an old CD-ROM that's marked as being written in High Sierra, you can think of it as ISO-9660.

ISO-9660 comes in several different varieties, known as *levels*:

■ **Level 1**—The original version of the ISO-9660 standard, Level 1 is the most restrictive in terms of filenames. Specifically, Level 1 CD-ROMs are limited to 8.3 filenames similar to those of DOS, but even most punctuation characters permitted by DOS aren't allowed in a Level 1 CD-ROM. The only punctuation characters permitted by Level 1 are the underscore (_) and period (.), and the latter only to separate the filename's base and extension.

■ **Level 2**—Similar to Level 1, but filenames can be up to 32 characters in length. Level 2 CD-ROM filenames are still restricted in terms of acceptable punctuation characters, use only uppercase characters, and can contain only a single period (.).

■ **Level 3**—This third level of ISO-9660 doesn't affect file-naming conventions; it adjusts some of the internal details of how the filesystem operates. Specifically, it adds support for fragmented files. Earlier levels of ISO-9660 assumed that, because ISO-9660 is a read-only filesystem, mastering software could always produce a fragmentation-free disc. Some recent CD-R and CD-RW software, however, works better when files can be fragmented. As an end user, you're unlikely to notice the differences between Level 3 and Level 2 when reading a CD, unless your OS's drivers don't support Level 3.

Part
V
Ch
12

ISO-9660 places several restrictions on the filesystem that seem odd from the point of view of most ordinary filesystems. For example, ISO-9660 limits the depth of nested directories to eight—that is, you cannot have more than eight levels to a directory structure. Some CD-R burning programs enable you to ignore some ISO-9660 restrictions, at the possible expense of problems reading those CD-Rs on some systems. The directory depth and restrictions on punctuation in filenames are two limits that CD-R mastering software often allows you to ignore.

ISO-9660 is supported by all modern OSs, either directly or through commonly available OS drivers. Because the filesystem was designed for read-only use, the standard OS drivers only support reading ISO-9660 filesystems; you cannot create an ISO-9660 filesystem on a partition and then modify it with the standard drivers. If you create a CD-R with an ISO-9660 filesystem by using any of the many CD-R burning packages available, you can use that CD to exchange data between most OSs.

 TIP DOS can't handle filenames longer than the ISO-9660 Level 1 specification permits. Therefore, if you create a CD-R that you want DOS to be capable of reading, be sure to use Level 1 rather than Level 2 or Level 3. CD-R mastering software automatically creates unique 8.3 filenames even when your original files use long filenames. You can use ISO-9660 Level 1 in conjunction with Rock Ridge, Joliet, or the Macintosh's HFS to create a CD whose contents are readable in DOS and that retains long filenames in at least some other OSs. (I describe Rock Ridge and Joliet shortly.)

Rock Ridge Extensions to ISO-9660

Even when ISO-9660 was first introduced, its restrictions on filenames and lack of support for features such as permissions made it woefully inadequate for UNIX OSs. Therefore, UNIX vendors developed an extension to ISO-9660 to support these features. The resulting Rock Ridge extensions add such features as

- Mixed-case long filenames
- UNIX-style file ownership information
- UNIX-style file permissions
- Symbolic links
- Directory trees deeper than eight levels

Because Rock Ridge is an extension to ISO-9660, the basic ISO-9660 structure remains, and Rock Ridge CD-ROMs can be read as ordinary ISO-9660 CD-ROMs in OSs that don't support Rock Ridge extensions. Such OSs, however, won't see the long filenames or other extended features. If the CD contains more than eight levels of directory entries, the extra levels appear in a special directory called RR_MOVED. Rock Ridge CDs often contain a file in each directory called TRANS.TBL that contains both the ISO-9660 8.3 filenames and the matching Rock Ridge filenames for that directory, to make locating files easier on OSs that don't understand Rock Ridge. This file isn't a requirement of the Rock Ridge specification, though; it is simply a customary adjunct to it.

Rock Ridge is supported by most modern UNIX-like OSs, including Linux and FreeBSD. It's also supported by BeOS. The Microsoft-style OSs don't support Rock Ridge, however.

N O T E The capability of an OS to read Rock Ridge is independent of the capability of an OS to create a Rock Ridge CD. It is possible to create a non-Rock Ridge CD from a UNIX OS, and a few software packages exist for Windows that can create Rock Ridge CDs. If you create a Rock Ridge CD from Windows, the CD will retain long filenames when read from a UNIX OS, but because the filesystems understood by Windows lack some of the features implemented in Rock Ridge, you won't be able to control those features unless the mastering software provides some workaround to do so. ■

The Joliet Filesystem

Like Rock Ridge, Joliet is a way to fit long mixed-case filenames, deeply nested directory structures, and other advanced features on a CD-ROM. Microsoft produced Joliet as an adjunct to its Windows 95 OS, and Joliet has spread since then. Most OSs implement it in the same driver that handles ISO-9660.

> **N O T E**   The prerelease code name for Windows 95 was *Chicago*. Joliet is a town outside Chicago, perhaps best known outside the area for its mention in the film *The Blues Brothers*. ▪

Joliet takes a somewhat different approach to its job than does Rock Ridge. Where Rock Ridge extends the ISO-9660 filesystem, much as VFAT and UMSDOS extend ordinary FAT, Joliet implements an entirely new set of filesystem structures. Joliet can coexist on a single CD-ROM along with ISO-9660, however; Joliet uses a pointer in the original ISO-9660 specification to an alternative disc descriptor, allowing Joliet and ISO-9660 filesystems to describe the same set of files. A few commercial CD-ROMs use the two filesystems in a somewhat different way. These CDs provide full access to all files only from Joliet and place only a README file on the ISO-9660 filesystem to inform the user that Joliet is required to access the CD-ROM. Fortunately, most CD-ROMs that use Joliet do provide full access using ISO-9660, albeit without long filenames and other features.

Microsoft's Windows OSs since Windows 95 support Joliet. The default OS/2 4.0 and earlier versions do not support Joliet, but updates available in various FixPacks enable OS/2 to read Joliet filenames. You must add the /W parameter to the CDFS.IFS driver line in the OS/2 CONFIG.SYS file to enable Joliet support with these updates. BeOS and recent versions of Linux also support Joliet, although you can disable this support in Linux by omitting the Joliet option when you compile the kernel, or by using the -o nojoliet mount option.

Because Rock Ridge functions as an extension within the ISO-9660 filesystem description and Joliet functions as an independent filesystem, it is possible to create a CD-ROM that contains both Rock Ridge and Joliet long filenames. Such a creation can be very helpful if you expect the CD to be used from multiple OSs; Windows 9*x*, Windows NT, and OS/2 can read the Joliet portion, whereas UNIX-style OSs can use the Rock Ridge portion. When using X-CD-Roast to create a CD, it is important to note that the Select Image-Type option should be set to Rock-Ridge + Win95/NT, which is X-CD-Roast's way of saying Rock Ridge and Joliet. The ISO-Filesystem Options box shows the specific features that are enabled and disabled by this option.

Like ISO-9660, Joliet has several versions, referred to as *levels*. Level 1 and Level 3 are the most common varieties of Joliet. Unless your filesystem driver supports one level but not another, you're unlikely to see any difference between them as a user.

UDF

The Universal Disk Format (UDF) is a relatively new filesystem that's intended to be used on current and future read-only and rewritable media, including CD-ROMs, DVDs, DVD-ROMs,

Part
V

Ch
12

and recordable and rewritable variants of these technologies. Because it was designed from the ground up with rewritable technology in mind, it provides a more elegant method of providing direct read/write access to these media than some of the clunky methods used by some of the proprietary software that has appeared to date. At the moment, UDF support is still quite limited, however; many OSs don't support it, or support it only to a very limited extent.

NOTE Video DVDs use UDF, so if you insert a video DVD in a DVD-ROM drive on a computer with even minimal UDF support, you can see several files and directories that correspond to the film you view on a video DVD player. The file formats used to store the video information are proprietary, but these formats have been reverse-engineered by a group of Linux programmers, and as I write these words there's a flurry of activity to produce useful programs in Linux and other OSs using this information. Unfortunately, the DVD industry frowns on this activity, to the point of instituting lawsuits against the programmers who distribute unauthorized DVD video decoding programs. By all accounts, court battles over this issue are likely to be quite lengthy. Check http://opendvd.org for information on DVD video playback software derived from the reverse-engineered code. The Web site for the DVD Copy Control Association (the industry organization which brought the lawsuit) is http://www.dvdcca.org.

Miscellaneous Additional Formats

A few additional formats are occasionally used on CD-ROM and similar media. For example, some CD-R software offers the use of a format called *Romeo*, which is an extension of the ISO-9660 format to permit more than 32 characters in the filename. I recommend against using such unusual formats when you burn a CD-R.

One additional format deserves mention, and that's the Macintosh Hierarchical Filesystem (HFS). Macintosh CD-ROMs often use this filesystem, and a few CD-R programs for x86 OSs provide an option to burn CD-Rs that use it, either instead of or in addition to ISO-9660. In fact, a few programs, such as the UNIX mkhybrid program, let you create a CD-R with ISO-9660, Rock Ridge, Joliet, and HFS support, all pointing to the same files on the CD-R. Such a CD-R represents the pinnacle of multiple filesystem support on a single removable medium, at least at the turn of the century. If you find yourself needing the ability to read an HFS CD-ROM on an x86 PC, you must normally seek out extra drivers. BeOS includes HFS support by default, and Linux kernel versions from 2.2.0 and up also include this support, although it might not be compiled in any given kernel binary. A separate HFS driver is available for OS/2, and is included on the CD that accompanies this book. Various commercial programs exist to read HFS disks in DOS and Windows.

Summary

The design of the filesystem used by an OS can greatly help or hinder the OS in performing the tasks for which it is intended. Filesystem speed and reliability, and the types of metadata supported by the filesystem all influence your ability to work in your OS of choice. In some cases, you have choices about what filesystems you can use—Windows NT and OS/2 both enable you to use FAT or a more sophisticated filesystem; and Linux supports several UNIX-like filesystems. In other cases, you might need to use a non-native filesystem for data storage and exchange to work most effectively across multiple OSs. Your choice of which filesystems to use can influence the ease with which you can work across multiple OSs. ●

Part

V

Ch

12

Tools for Accessing Foreign Filesystems

Providing Shared Access to Filesystems

When it comes to exchanging and sharing data between OSs, one of the most fundamental issues is that of providing shared access to a common filesystem. Although I discuss some ways around this issue toward the end of this chapter, the most convenient way to share data is usually by providing two or more OSs with access to a single filesystem—either a filesystem native to one of the OSs or a third filesystem (often FAT) that both can access.

If providing optimal access and file sharing were as simple as using the OSs' native filesystems, this chapter wouldn't be necessary. Many OSs, however, don't ship with all the drivers necessary to access desirable foreign filesystems; or use of those foreign filesystems involves special configuration that you might not ordinarily undertake. I've therefore written this chapter to make you aware of what options you have for multi-OS access to various filesystems and to help guide you through the process of using these filesystems.

Many of the programs I discuss in this chapter are under active development, so there might be changes in some of them by the time you read these words. Many of the drivers I discuss in this chapter are available on the CD that accompanies this book. You might also find the Filesystems HOWTO document at `http://www.penguin.cz/~mhi/fs/Filesystems-HOWTO/Filesystems-HOWTO.html` useful.

> **CAUTION**
>
> Many of the filesystem programs I discuss in this chapter are described by words such as *alpha software*, *beta software*, or *experimental*. When used in reference to filesystem software, such words are synonymous with *extremely dangerous*. A buggy filesystem utility can wipe out not just one or two files, but your entire filesystem, and potentially even several filesystems. In general, experimental read/write software is much more dangerous than experimental read-only software, but even read-only filesystem drivers can be dangerous because a bug in such a driver can often lock up the computer.
>
> I present some information on the general stability of various read/write utilities and drivers, but you might be more or less lucky than the average user, or the software might have improved (or acquired a bug) in a version more recent than the ones to which I have had access, so caution is advisable in all cases.

Table 13.1 summarizes the availability of filesystem support for various OSs. As you can see, there are remarkably few gaps in coverage, although many of the available drivers are read-only, experimental, or lacking in important features.

Table 13.1 Filesystems Supported by Major OSs

File-system	DOS	Windows 9x	Windows NT	OS/2	BeOS	Linux	FreeBSD
FAT-12 & FAT-16	Y	Y	Y	Y	Y	Y	Y
FAT-32	N	Y (Windows 95 OSR2 and above)	Y (Windows 2000 or third-party only)	third-party	Y	Y	Y
VFAT	N	Y	Y	third-party	Y	Y	Y
NTFS	third-party	third-party	Y	third-party (read-only)	third-party (read-only)	Y (experi-mental)	Y
HPFS	third-party	third-party	Y (Windows NT 3.51 and earlier)	Y	N	Y (read-only in 2.2.x; read/write in 2.3.x)	third-party
BFS	N	N	N	N	Y	third-party (read-only)	N
ext2fs	Y (read-only)	Y (read-only driver; read/write utility)	Y (read-only driver; read/write utility)	third-party	third-party (read-only)	Y	Y
FFS	N	N	N	N	N	Y (experi-mental)	Y

Part

V

Ch

13

Methods of Filesystem Access

When you think of filesystem access, you probably think first of the usual methods used in your OS, such as your OS's GUI file browser or normal file manipulation commands such as DIR and COPY. You also probably assume that you can both read and write files on a filesystem, unless it's a locked floppy or a read-only medium such as a CD-ROM. There are alternatives, however, both to the tools used to access a filesystem and to the capability to both read and write a disk.

Using Access Utilities for Quick Access

One method of gaining access to a foreign filesystem is to use a utility dedicated to this task. Such a utility reads the foreign filesystem's data structures and presents a list of available files. Depending on the utility's features, you can then copy files to and from the foreign filesystem, delete files, and so on. Precisely how you perform any of these tasks varies from one program to the next; some are text-mode tools, others are GUI-based, and each has a unique set of capabilities and commands. Figure 13.1 shows the GUI interface of one such utility, Explore2fs, used to access Linux ext2fs partitions from Windows.

FIGURE 13.1
A filesystem access utility might use a GUI interface that resembles that of the native OS's file browser, or it might not.

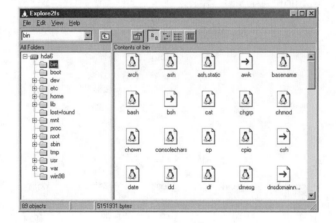

Access utilities enable you to quickly and easily gain entry to a foreign filesystem. They usually don't require the installation of special drivers, so there's little chance that a buggy driver will crash your system. The lack of drivers also means that you need not be saddled with a potentially large number of non-native filesystems that are constantly available; you can start and stop the utility as you see fit. Because these utilities don't rely on the OS's underlying filesystem handling, they can sometimes provide access to features of the filesystem that aren't supported by the OS under which they run. For example, Explore2fs can display and change Linux's ownership and permissions information.

Access utilities do have a big drawback, however: They don't enable direct access to the filesystem from ordinary programs running on the native OS. For example, if you want to use WordPerfect under both Windows and Linux, you can't use Explore2fs to provide the Windows version of WordPerfect with access to your WordPerfect documents stored on a Linux partition. You must first copy the Linux WordPerfect documents to a Windows partition. You can then read and modify the file using WordPerfect for Windows. When you're finished, you must either use Explore2fs to copy the modified file back to the Linux partition or rely on Linux tools to access the copy of the file on the Windows partition. Overall, the lack of direct access makes the use of access utilities rather awkward if your goal is seamless file integration across two or more OSs. They are an excellent choice, though, if you need only infrequent access to a few files or if your goal is to copy files from one location to another.

Access utilities are particularly common for DOS, although they do exist for other platforms, as well. The mtools package for UNIX-style OSs is particularly worthy of mention; it gives access to DOS floppies and other DOS media through a series of DOS-like commands (mcopy, mdir, and so on).

Using Drivers for Integrated Access

If you need frequent access to a foreign filesystem, or if you need to access files on a foreign filesystem directly using specific programs or OS features, you must locate a driver for the filesystem in question. Most modern OSs contain explicit support for filesystem drivers. For example, in OS/2, you add a filesystem driver to the system by creating an appropriate IFS= entry in the OS/2 CONFIG.SYS file. OS/2's kernel includes support for FAT, but all other filesystems, including OS/2's HPFS and CDFS (ISO-9660) filesystems, are implemented through this installable filesystem method. For example, here's the CONFIG.SYS entry for HPFS:

```
IFS=C:\OS2\HPFS.IFS /CACHE:2048 /CRECL:4 /AUTOCHECK:C
```

This entry loads the HPFS.IFS driver file and sets various parameters, such as the cache size and the drives to be checked for invalid shutdown when the system loads. Each driver might have its own parameters, which influence performance and available features. For example, the ext2fs driver for OS/2 provides options to force case-retentive or case-sensitive handling of the ext2 filesystem.

NOTE   OS/2 is a case-retentive filesystem, whereas ext2fs is a case-sensitive filesystem, so some means of reconciling these differences is necessary. ∎

▶ To learn more about ext2 case sensitivity, **see** "Features Supported by Assorted Filesystems," **p. 299**.

Other OSs use other means of adding filesystem drivers. For example, Linux incorporates all filesystem drivers into its kernel, either compiled into the main kernel file itself or loaded as a module, much as you can load drivers for serial ports, networking protocols, and so on as modules.

Part
V

Ch

13

If you obtain a third-party filesystem driver for your OS, you should be sure to read the documentation that comes with it, to be sure you install it correctly. Also, some filesystem drivers are at least potentially buggy, and a buggy filesystem driver is a dangerous filesystem driver.

Read-Only Versus Read/Write Access

Given adequate documentation, a skilled programmer can generally develop a means of reading data from a filesystem without too much difficulty. The task is basically just one of following a series of pointers and data structures to locate data. Of course, there are a lot of details to be worked out, but reading a fixed data structure is simple compared to modifying that structure. Therefore, most third-party filesystem drivers and utilities start out supporting only read access to a filesystem. Adding write access is a much more difficult task than creating a read-only product because there might be undocumented subtleties concerning data placement, and because a bug when writing data is much more serious than a bug when reading data.

Read-only filesystem drivers are somewhat commonplace, particularly for popular filesystems and those for which sample code is widely available. For example, read-only utilities and drivers for Linux's ext2fs exist for all the OSs I cover in any detail in this book. Read/write drivers, however, are rarer, even for widespread filesystems.

The Ubiquity of FAT

FAT is everywhere. Most OSs for x86 computers come with drivers for FAT, and these drivers usually support read/write access with a high degree of reliability. In fact, even non-x86 OSs, such as Mac OS and non-x86 UNIX variants, usually support FAT, if only for the capability to exchange files on floppy disks with users of DOS and its descendants.

It's not enough to leave the subject of FAT with the words "you can use it," however. Although those four words are almost certainly true, there are differences in how various OSs handle FAT. For example, some OSs support FAT-16 but not FAT-32. Others support 8.3 filenames but not VFAT long filenames. Other OSs make assumptions about their filesystems that FAT doesn't meet, so various options exist to work around these problems. This section covers these details, which should help you work around problems when you need to use FAT to share or exchange data, either between OSs on your computer or between your computer and others.

DOS's Handling of FAT

DOS was the original OS that used FAT, so in some sense DOS sets the standard for FAT handling. In today's world, though, DOS's handling of FAT is downright primitive, suffering from limitations that other OSs have long since left behind, such as the following:

- DOS is limited to filenames eight characters in length, followed by an optional period and three-character extension (the so-called *8.3 filename limit*).

- 8.3 filenames are limited to using uppercase characters, numbers, and a variety of punctuation marks. They should not contain spaces or lowercase characters. (Some utilities intentionally create such illegal filenames, though, for a variety of purposes.)
- DOS can use FAT variants with 12- and 16-bit file allocation tables, but not the newer 32-bit FATs. (Windows 9*x* running in DOS mode is an exception to this rule; it can use FAT-32. This capability applies even to a Windows 9*x* DOS-mode boot floppy.)

As a result of these limits, DOS is also limited to a maximum partition size of 2GB. You can use larger hard disks with DOS, but when you do so, you must split the disk into multiple partitions. Even so, DOS can't use any part of a hard disk past about 8GB because DOS uses the BIOS INT13 calls to access the hard disk, and INT13 can't read past the 1024th cylinder, which works out to about 8GB on modern BIOSs.

▶ To learn more about the 1024-cylinder limit, **see** "Getting Around the 1024-Cylinder Limit," **p. 77**.

DOS's support for FAT is closely tied into the OS; there's no need to load any special drivers for FAT.

Windows 9*x*'s Handling of FAT

Windows 9*x* uses a 32-bit version of DOS at its core, so using a FAT filesystem is as natural to Windows 9*x* as swimming is to a fish. With the release of Windows 95, however, Microsoft expanded FAT to include support for long filenames, using the VFAT extensions. Windows 9*x* can access VFAT long filenames in 32-bit Windows programs, which at this point in time means most GUI programs for Windows. 16-bit DOS and Windows programs, however, lack the means to handle long filenames, so those programs continue to use 8.3 filenames. VFAT includes explicit support to enable such access.

N O T E Although 32-bit Windows programs display long filenames in their file operation dialog boxes, you can enter the matching 8.3 filename and access the file in that way. This trick can be useful when you're confronted with an extraordinarily long name that you need to type. You must first find the appropriate 8.3 filename, though. You can often guess it correctly—it's usually the first six characters of the long filename followed by a tilde (~), a number, and then the first three characters of the filename extension. If your guess doesn't work, you can look the short filename up using a DOS prompt and the DIR command. ■

Midway through Windows 95's lifetime, Microsoft introduced an updated version of the OS called Windows 95 *OEM Service Release 2 (OSR2)*. Among other changes, this version introduced FAT-32, which increased the maximum possible size of FAT partitions and reduced the size of allocation blocks for large partitions, thus reducing disk space lost to slack.

▶ To learn more about allocation blocks, **see** "Features Supported by Assorted Filesystems," **p. 299**.

▶ To learn more about the concept of slack space, **see** "Partition Size and Disk Consumption Limits," **p. 115**.

Part

V

Ch

13

Windows 95 OSR2 also introduced several new partition types that are used on hard disks with more than 1024 cylinders (see Table 10.1). These partition types don't affect the FAT filesystem itself, but Windows 9x uses these partition types to mark partitions that straddle the 1024-cylinder boundary, to avoid confusing DOS and other OSs that can't handle more than 1024 cylinders.

Windows NT's Handling of FAT

Windows NT, like other Microsoft OSs, has always included support for FAT. The Windows 9x line has always been Microsoft's leader in terms of support for new FAT features, however. For example, it was only with Windows NT 4.0 that Microsoft introduced VFAT long file-names to Windows NT, and Windows 2000 is the first in the Windows NT line to support FAT-32, several years after its introduction in Windows 95 OSR2.

If you want to access FAT-32 partitions from Windows NT, you have two choices:

- Upgrade to Windows 2000, which includes FAT-32 support.
- Purchase a FAT-32 driver for Windows NT from Winternals, http://www.sysinternals.com/fat32.htm.

Aside from its lagging support for the latest FAT features, though, Windows NT handles FAT in much the same way DOS and Windows 9x do. You will therefore find few or no incompatibilities or problems in exchanging data between these various Microsoft OSs, aside from any you might encounter because of different FAT variants (for example, Windows NT 4.0's incapability to handle FAT-32 or DOS's lack of VFAT long filename support).

One exception to the rule of Windows 9x trailblazing on FAT is in the fact that Windows NT supports a 64KB allocation block size, whereas the maximum allocation block size for DOS and Windows 9x is 32KB. Because of this difference, Windows NT can support FAT-16 partitions up to 4GB in size, whereas most other OSs, including DOS and Windows 9x, support only 2GB FAT-16 partitions. A 64KB allocation block size is pretty huge, unfortunately, and results in an average slack space of 32KB per file, which adds up quickly. Because of the wasted disk space and because of the lack of support for 64KB allocation block sizes in other OSs, I recommend using NTFS, or possibly FAT-32 in Windows 2000, rather than 2–4GB FAT-16 partitions.

OS/2's Handling of FAT

Although OS/2 is radically different from DOS in many respects, it was intended as a replacement for DOS. OS/2 therefore incorporates support for FAT into its kernel, much as does DOS. This support is often limiting in today's world of VFAT and FAT-32, however, and third-party drivers exist to help fill that gap.

Using OS/2's Native FAT-16 Support   OS/2's native support for FAT-12 and FAT-16 is similar to that of DOS. OS/2 supports the filesystem with the same basic limitations as does DOS, including 8.3 filename limits and a maximum partition size of 2GB.

OS/2 relies heavily on Extended Attributes (EAs), however, to implement various OS features, including much of the functionality of OS/2's desktop environment, the WorkPlace Shell (WPS). OS/2's HPFS supports EAs natively, but FAT doesn't contain this functionality. Therefore, OS/2 implements a means of storing EAs on FAT by using a hidden file, called EA DATA.SF. This file contains the EAs for any files that use them. Unused bits in the files' directory entries are used as pointers into the EA DATA.SF file.

> **CAUTION**
>
> Some DOS and Windows disk utilities can damage OS/2 EAs on a FAT partition. This damage occurs when the utility ignores the EA pointer bits in directory entries, thus wiping the pointer out when rewriting a directory. The same thing can happen if you copy a file with an attached EA from DOS, Linux, or some other EA-unaware OS. Fortunately, many DOS and Windows disk utilities include enough support for EAs to keep from destroying their links, but you should still be cautious about using such utilities on any partition that contains vital EAs. The most important of these partitions is the OS/2 boot partition (if it's a FAT partition). You should also be aware of the fact that you might lose EAs if you copy files from most OSs. Likewise, a backup/restore operation from DOS, Linux, or most other OSs loses the OS/2 EAs, which renders OS/2 unbootable, if you perform such an action on the OS/2 boot partition.

OS/2 EAs include a long filename of sorts. This filename is visible from the OS/2 WPS, but not from most other OS/2 programs. The WPS's FAT long filenames are therefore not nearly as well integrated into OS/2 as are VFAT long filenames into Windows 9x and NT.

Using Third-Party VFAT Drivers If you use Windows 9x or some other OS that uses VFAT long filenames, you can use a third-party OS/2 driver to access these partitions. The driver is located at http://www.dsteiner.com/products/software/os2/ifs.htm. This driver is based on the Linux VFAT driver and is distributed under the terms of the GNU General Public License (GPL).

Because FAT support is integrated into the OS/2 kernel, any VFAT driver must find a way to wrest control of VFAT partitions away from the kernel, which is a tricky proposition. For this and other reasons, the OS/2 VFAT driver contains various limitations:

- **No boot support**—You can't boot your computer from a partition that's handled by the VFAT driver.
- **No swap file support**—You can't place the OS/2 swap file on a VFAT partition.
- **No EA support**—The VFAT driver doesn't support OS/2 EAs.
- **No FAT-32 support**—The VFAT driver supports only FAT-12 and FAT-16 partitions, not FAT-32 partitions. Fortunately, there is a separate FAT-32 driver, which I describe shortly.
- **No short filenames**—If a file has a long filename, you can't access it using the associated short filename, as you can in Windows.
- **Not perfectly stable**—The driver can be unreliable at times, particularly when used in read/write mode. On some systems, it might work in read-only mode but crash the computer on startup in read/write mode.

Part **V**

Ch **13**

Despite these limitations, the VFAT driver can be a useful addition to an OS/2 system, particularly if you don't need read/write access or don't mind running risks with your VFAT partition's integrity. You can specify which partitions you want to access as VFAT on the driver's initialization line in CONFIG.SYS, so you need not access all your FAT partitions as VFAT.

Using Third-Party FAT-32 Drivers   Just as a third-party VFAT driver for OS/2 exists, there's a third-party FAT-32 driver. This driver is available from http://www.os2ss.com/information/ kelder/index.html. When installed, it gives you access to any FAT-32 partitions on your hard disk.

The FAT-32 driver's derivation is independent of that of the VFAT driver, but it is distributed as freeware, as is the VFAT driver. On the whole, the FAT-32 driver offers more features and is more robust than the VFAT driver, but it still has its limitations:

- **Requires a partition filter**—Because OS/2 doesn't normally recognize the FAT-32 partition types, the FAT-32 driver requires the use of a partition filter to make these partitions visible to the driver. This filter enables OS/2 to use partitions of types that OS/2 ordinarily can't use. Normally this isn't really a drawback, but it might have the consequence of altering the order in which your drives mount, depending on the options you select. If so, you might find that your system becomes unbootable after you install the filter. Removing the relevant driver lines from CONFIG.SYS will correct the problem, and you can then try again with other options.

- **No boot support**—You can't boot your computer from a partition that's handled by the FAT-32 driver.

- **No swap file support**—You can't place the OS/2 swap file on a FAT-32 partition.

- **No EA support**—The FAT-32 driver doesn't support OS/2 EAs.

- **Long filename tradeoffs**—You can use the FAT-32 driver in either of two modes relating to VFAT-style long filenames. In one mode, the long filenames are used throughout the driver and OS, which means that anything not conforming to 8.3 filename standards is invisible to DOS and Windows programs run from OS/2. (This behavior is the same as that of HPFS partitions.) In the other mode, the driver and OS/2 use the 8.3 filenames internally, which enables DOS and Windows programs to see all the files, but also produces short filenames in OS/2 command prompts and causes a few other minor display problems.

- **Beta software**—Although most people report that the OS/2 FAT-32 driver is quite stable, it is officially beta-level software, which means you might do well to be cautious about trusting it with vital data.

On the whole, if you want to share a FAT partition between Windows and OS/2, and if long filename support is important on this shared partition, using FAT-32 with the OS/2 FAT-32 driver is a better choice than using FAT-16 with the OS/2 VFAT driver, at least if you're running Windows 95 OSR2 or later. If you want the best assurance of stability or if you need support for OS/2 EAs on the FAT partition, however, plain FAT-16 with the OS/2 drivers remains the best option.

TIP If sharing long filenames is important, another option is to use a file archiving format such as zip. Using a zip file compression utility, you can then transfer files with long filenames from an HPFS partition to a VFAT partition or vice-versa, using appropriate archiving tools on both sides to add and extract files from the archives. This solution might be awkward for frequent use, but it's a good solution if you only need to transfer files with long filenames infrequently.

Using FAT in BeOS

BeOS includes read/write support for FAT in the OS. This support includes access to VFAT long filenames and 12-, 16-, and 32-bit FAT variants. Because BeOS has never been limited to 8.3 filenames, BeOS's FAT support doesn't provide access to the 8.3 filenames on FAT partitions when VFAT long filenames exist.

To use a FAT partition, you must first mount it. The default BeOS configuration doesn't mount FAT partitions when the OS first starts, but you can mount them manually by right-clicking on the desktop and selecting the partition you want to mount from the Mount menu, as shown in Figure 13.2. Partitions marked with check marks are already mounted. After you mount a partition, an icon for the partition appears on the desktop, similar to the doswin icon in Figure 13.2. You can then access the partition much as you would a BeOS partition.

FIGURE 13.2
BeOS shows all available partitions, even those it can't identify or mount, such as the INTEL 0xb5 and 0x17 partitions in the list shown here.

If you regularly mount FAT partitions in BeOS, you can modify the BeOS mount defaults. Right-click the desktop and choose Mount, Settings to produce the Disk Mount Settings dialog box shown in Figure 13.3. Click All Disks in the Disk Mounting During Boot area of the dialog box and then click Done. Next time you boot BeOS, it will mount all the FAT partitions on your system.

No matter how you mount FAT partitions, they suffer from certain drawbacks compared to BFS partitions under BeOS. In particular, FAT partitions perform more slowly than BFS partitions, and they lack support for BeOS attributes. This latter characteristic means that you might lose certain types of information associated with files such as stored email messages if you copy them to FAT partitions. For this reason, you cannot boot BeOS from a FAT partition.

Part
V

Ch

13

FIGURE 13.3
BeOS lets you specify whether to mount non-BeOS partitions every time you boot.

Linux's FAT Options

Linux provides a wide range of options related to handling FAT partitions. You configure the availability of Linux filesystem drivers in the kernel configuration scripts before you compile your kernel. Depending on the distribution you use, none, some, or all of these options might be included in your system already, although "none" is an unlikely possibility.

Linux's FAT support is quite robust overall. The main difficulty in using this support is in understanding many of the kernel and mount options. One exception is that the UMSDOS filesystem is not quite as stable as the other variants. These problems are unlikely to cause serious data loss, but you might see strange files or be unable to perform certain operations in Linux when you use UMSDOS.

In addition to the kernel filesystem drivers, you can use the mtools package from Linux to provide access to FAT partitions and floppies. This option can be convenient for performing quick file transfers, especially from floppy disks.

▶ To learn more about the mtools package, **see** "UNIX's FAT Possibilities," **p. 342**.

Specifying Kernel Options   When you compile your kernel, you'll find four options related to FAT filesystems under the Filesystems area. These options are

- **DOS FAT filesystem support**—This kernel option is used as a base for the rest of the options; if this option isn't selected, you won't be able to select any of the others. This option provides the fundamental code necessary to access FAT filesystems, with or without long filename support. It includes support for 12-, 16-, and 32-bit versions of FAT, at least in kernels since late in the 2.0.x series. Earlier kernels lacked FAT-32 support.

- **MSDOS filesystem support**—If you select this option, you'll be able to access FAT partitions and floppies much as DOS does, using 8.3 filenames. Linux includes FAT-32 support, though, so you can access FAT-32 partitions using only 8.3 filenames if you like. One important deviation of Linux's 8.3 filename support from the MS-DOS standard is that Linux converts the filenames to lowercase. The MSDOS filesystem support is required if you're to use the UMSDOS filesystem.

- **UMSDOS filesystem support**—UMSDOS is the name given to Linux's own long file-name extension to FAT. This feature places information on UNIX-style long filenames, ownership, permission, and additional features in a file called `--LINUX-.---`. UMSDOS then uses that information to provide you with an extended view of the FAT filesystem. UMSDOS is useful mainly for installing Linux on a FAT filesystem to coexist with a DOS or Windows installation.

N O T E UMSDOS does not currently use VFAT-style long filenames in any way; its own long file-names are completely independent. ■

- **VFAT filesystem support**—This option provides access to VFAT-style long filenames from within Linux. Other than a change in the filename support, the VFAT and MSDOS options work in the same way.

If you compile all these options into your kernel, you can mount the partitions containing FAT filesystems using any of three filesystem types: `msdos`, `umsdos`, and `vfat`, for MSDOS, UMS-DOS, and VFAT handling, respectively. The first and last of these options use an assortment of additional options, as I describe in the next section, to determine what ownership and permissions a file receives. The UMSDOS option defaults to MSDOS behavior—8.3 filenames, no permissions, and so on. You can enable UNIX-style permissions and long filenames in a directory by using the `umssync` command, which creates the `--LINUX-.---` file for a directory.

Using Mount Options   Linux provides a large number of mount options that modify how Linux treats FAT partitions. You can learn about these options by typing `man  mount` at a command prompt and searching for information on the various FAT filesystems. (Many of the options are listed only in the MSDOS section of the `mount` man page.)

Some of the more useful options include the following:

- `-r` or `-o  ro`—Mount the filesystem read-only. Linux's FAT support is quite stable, so the main use for this option is to protect yourself from user error or bugs in application programs.

- `-o  uid=`*xxx*—Set the user ID for all the files on the partition. For example, `-o  uid=502` sets the user ID to 502 for all files. You can check the contents of the `/etc/passwd` file to determine an appropriate user ID. Locate in that file the user who you want to own the files. The user ID is the third colon-delimited field.

- `-o  gid=`*xxx*—Set the group ID for all the files on the partition. This option works much like the `-o  uid=`*xxx* option. You can find groups and their ID numbers in the `/etc/group` file; the group ID is in the third colon-delimited field of each line.

- `-o  umask=`*xxx*—Set the umask (a bitmapped mask for values that are not present) for the default permissions. For example, if you want to give all users full access to the partition, set a umask of `000`, which denies no permissions. To deny all access to everybody but the owner, use a umask of `077`.

Part

V

Ch

13

■ -o conv=b[inary] | conv=t[ext] | conv=a[uto]—Set conversion options for end-of-line characters. Microsoft-style OSs use different characters at the ends of lines in text files than do UNIX-style OSs, including Linux. This option can attempt to correct the matter by converting between UNIX-style and Microsoft-style end-of-line encodings when you copy a file. Using t forces Linux to convert end-of-line characters in all files, whereas a converts end-of-line characters on all files that don't have known binary file-name extensions. Both of these options are potentially dangerous because they can corrupt binary files. Therefore, the b option is the default; this setting performs no conversions.

You can apply these options to any of the three actual filesystem types, and you can combine multiple -o options by separating them with commas. For example, you could issue the following mount command:

```
mount -t msdos -o uid=502,gid=100,conv=a /dev/hda2 /dosstuff
```

This command mounts the /dev/hda2 partition at /dosstuff using the MSDOS filesystem and gives ownership to the user with ID 502 and group ID 100. You can also include the -o options in your /etc/fstab entry for the partition to apply them automatically when you mount a partition at boot time.

UNIX's FAT Possibilities

Linux isn't the only UNIX-like OS to sport FAT file access features. Details on kernel-level filesystem driver support vary substantially from one UNIX to another, so I can't provide details on all of them here. Consult your OS's documentation for details.

Most UNIX OSs (including Linux) include or can use a common FAT access tool called mtools. The main mtools Web page is at http://mtools.linux.lu/, so you can check there for source code if your version of UNIX doesn't come with the package.

The basic idea behind mtools is to provide a command-line interface to FAT filesystems without the requirement of kernel-level support for FAT. Commands in mtools include mdir, mdel, mformat, mcopy, and so on. These commands are similar to their equivalents in DOS, except that their names all begin with m.

Most mtools installations are configured so that you can easily access the floppy drive by specifying its name as a:, much as you would in DOS. For example, typing mdir a: obtains a directory listing of the disk in the floppy drive. It is possible to create a configuration to access disk partitions using mtools, as well; consult the mtools documentation for details.

At present, mtools supports VFAT long filenames as well as 8.3 filenames; you can access files using either filename. If your computer has an older version of mtools that doesn't support long filenames, you can upgrade the package if you need long filename support.

Because mtools is an ordinary user program, when you copy a file to a UNIX filesystem using this program, the copy acquires whatever permissions any program would grant. Because mtools doesn't mount disks, there's no need to grant permissions to all the files on a FAT disk that's accessed with mtools. You must, however, have at least read access to the low-level disk device, and read/write access if you want to be able to write to the FAT disk. Many UNIX systems are configured with restrictive access to these low-level disk devices, so you might need to change the permissions on the device file or add your ordinary user to a special group with access to the device you want to use.

Foreign NTFS and NTFS 5.0 Support

Foreign support for NTFS is available for a variety of OSs and in many forms, but NTFS support is still not as widespread as is support for FAT. Nonetheless, NTFS is a viable file-sharing option for some OS combinations, particularly if you don't need write access to NTFS from OSs other than Windows NT.

Windows 2000 includes changes to NTFS (known as *NTFS 5.0*) that necessitate alterations to the on-disk storage format of NTFS. Older versions of Windows NT cannot use the modified NTFS without updated drivers. (You must apply Service Pack 4 or above to Windows NT 4.0 to obtain this support.) Some third-party NTFS drivers do not work with NTFS 5.0, although as development of these drivers continues, this situation is likely to change.

DOS Drivers for NTFS

You can obtain read-only NTFS drivers for DOS from http://www.sysinternals.com/ntfs30.htm. The NTFS for DOS package is easy to use—you type NTFSDOS or create an entry in your AUTOEXEC.BAT file and the driver loads into memory, locates all NTFS partitions, and assigns them drive letters. NTFS for DOS correctly skips HPFS partitions, despite the fact that these partitions share a type code with NTFS. You can even use NTFS long filenames—at least at a Windows 98 DOS mode command prompt. Many applications won't be capable of using the long filenames.

A full read/write version of NTFSDOS, called NTFSDOS Professional, is available for $149. This product is actually not very closely related to the read-only version of the program. Instead, NTFSDOS Professional uses the NTFS drivers from Windows NT; the package creates an environment under DOS in which those drivers can run. As such, this package can handle NTFS 5.0 partitions if you give it Windows NT drivers from Windows NT 4.0 Service Pack 4 or above or from Windows 2000.

NTFSDOS isn't without its bugs and flaws. The program's Web page includes a listing of problems, most of them minor. The program doesn't always work with all versions of DOS; for example, NTFSDOS might fail to give anything more than directory listing access when run from DR-DOS. Officially, NTFSDOS requires MS-DOS; no claim is made concerning compatibility with other versions of DOS.

Part

V

Ch

13

Windows 9x Drivers for NTFS

Winternals, the company that produces NTFSDOS, also produces NTFS for Windows 98, which provides NTFS access to Windows 9x systems. Like NTFSDOS, a read-only version is free, and a read/write version costs money ($49 at the time of this writing). Both versions work on the same principle as NTFSDOS Professional—they use Windows NT's own drivers and utilities to access NTFS partitions from within Windows 9x. If you use NTFS 5.0–aware drivers, therefore, this product supports NTFS 5.0 partitions. You can find more information on this product at http://www.sysinternals.com/ntfs98.htm.

Because NTFS for Windows 98 uses files from Windows NT, you must either have Windows NT installed on a FAT partition or copy certain key files from your NTFS boot partition to a FAT partition to use the program. Specifically, you must copy the following files:

```
<WINNT>\SYSTEM32\DRIVERS\NTFS.SYS
<WINNT>\SYSTEM32\NTOSKRNL.EXE
<WINNT>\SYSTEM32\AUTOCHK.EXE
<WINNT>\SYSTEM32\NTDLL.DLL
<WINNT>\SYSTEM32\C_437.NLS
<WINNT>\SYSTEM32\C_1252.NLS
<WINNT>\SYSTEM32\L_INTL.NLS
```

In each case, <WINNT> indicates the Windows NT system directory—usually C:\WINNT. You'll save some time if you copy these files before you try to install NTFS for Windows 98.

After it's installed, you can configure NTFS for Windows 98 by running the NTFS Configure program, which comes with the package, as shown in Figure 13.4. One of the most important aspects of this configuration is the drive letter assignment. If you leave the Drive Letters field blank, your NTFS partitions appear in whatever order their positions on the drive mandate, as if they were FAT partitions. This can potentially cause problems if it forces changes to other partitions' drive letters.

▶ To learn more about drive letter assignments, **see** "Drive Letter Changes," **p. 183**.

FIGURE 13.4
Indicate drive letters for NTFS partitions by entering them one after another without spaces in the Drive Letters field.

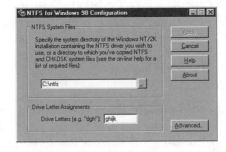

Unlike NTFS for DOS, NTFS for Windows 98 misidentifies HPFS partitions as NTFS partitions because both filesystem types share the same partition code. This misidentification should cause no problems unless you attempt to format an HPFS partition.

OS/2 Drivers for NTFS

Earlier in this chapter, I mentioned the OS/2 VFAT driver, which is based on Linux's VFAT code and is available from http://www.dsteiner.com/products/software/os2/ifs.htm. In truth, this driver is more than a VFAT driver; it also supports NTFS and ext2fs. The NTFS support in this driver is currently read-only, and like its VFAT and ext2fs support, is based on filesystem drivers that originated with Linux.

To use the NTFS support, you must add the -NTFS parameter to the VFAT.IFS line in OS/2's CONFIG.SYS file and, possibly, modify the -VFAT: parameter to include the NTFS drive letters.

This NTFS driver support is very preliminary and has seen very infrequent updates. It doesn't work with NTFS 5.0 partitions. It might or might not work at all on your computer. The author of the program has also made the NTFS driver available separately from the VFAT driver.

BeOS NTFS Drivers

You can obtain BeOS drivers for NTFS from http://www.cs.tamu.edu/people/tkg0143/be/index.html. This driver currently supports only read access and is still quite new as of this writing (version 0.05). Despite its newness, it does support reading NTFS 5.0 partitions. When installed, it enables you to mount NTFS partitions in much the same way you mount BFS or FAT partitions, by right-clicking the desktop and selecting the partition from the Mount menu.

> **CAUTION**
>
> As of this writing, the BeOS NTFS drivers are considered *alpha-level* software, which means they are potentially unstable, which could make your BeOS system crash. Use them at your own risk.

Linux's NTFS Drivers

The Linux kernel comes with read-only NTFS support, which does work with NTFS 5.0 partitions. Since version 2.2.0, the kernel comes with read/write NTFS support, but that support is considered experimental and is widely regarded as highly dangerous. This situation might improve by the time the 2.4.0 kernel is released, but nobody can make any guarantees of this matter.

> **CAUTION**
>
> If you have cause to investigate NTFS read/write support in Linux, I recommend you begin with a Deja News search for the latest information on NTFS stability. If you decide to test the support, try it on a partition that contains no valuable data or that has been completely backed up. *Do not test Linux read/write NTFS support on your Windows NT boot partition!* Of course, it's entirely possible that Linux's NTFS support will become quite stable and robust in the future. Unless you're certain that the support is safe, though, I must strongly advise you to exercise extreme caution in dealing with Linux's read/write NTFS support.

Because NTFS doesn't support UNIX-style security, Linux's NTFS driver provides mount-time options similar to those of the FAT driver to set the owner and permissions on all files on an NTFS partition. Specifically, you can use the `uid=xxx`, `gid=xxx`, and `umask=xxx` options just as you can with FAT partitions. You can use these options even when you mount an NTFS partition read-only, although in that case write access granted via the `umask` option won't do any good.

FreeBSD's NTFS Support

You can obtain a read-only NTFS driver for FreeBSD from `http://ukug.uk.freebsd.org/ ~mark/ntfs_install.html`. The FreeBSD NTFS driver is currently being integrated into the main FreeBSD kernel, so the very latest versions don't require special kernel recompilation. If you're using an older kernel (such as a 2.2.x kernel or an early 3.1 kernel), you must patch your kernel and recompile, however, as described on the preceding Web page.

Foreign HPFS Support

Support for OS/2's HPFS, like Windows NT's NTFS, has cropped up in a variety of OSs, often in read-only form. Most of these drivers are freeware of one variety or another. Most appear to be unique reimplementations with little or no shared code between them.

DOS and Windows 9x HPFS Drivers

Two major HPFS drivers for DOS exist, iHPFS (`http://www.student.nada.kth.se/ ~f96-bet/ihpfs/`) and HPFSa (`ftp://ftp.cdrom.com/.1/os2/mdos/hpfsa102.zip`). The first is a read-only driver distributed under the terms of the GNU GPL, and the second is a read/write shareware driver, although as of early 2000, the package had not been updated since 1995.

iHPFS works under Windows 9x, although only from a DOS prompt window because you can't access HPFS partitions from Windows programs or from the Windows Explorer.

Windows NT HPFS Drivers

Windows NT through version 3.51 included an HPFS driver, so it could work with HPFS partitions natively. If you own a copy of Windows NT 3.51, you can continue to use this driver in Windows NT 4.0 (but not in Windows 2000); the trick is installing it. The easiest method of installing the Windows NT 3.51 driver in Windows NT 4.0 is to install 4.0 as an upgrade over 3.51; this upgrade preserves the 3.51 HPFS driver.

> **CAUTION**
>
> Editing the Windows Registry file is potentially dangerous! Exercise extreme caution if you use the following procedure. The values you enter are case sensitive, so be sure to enter the information exactly as it's presented here.

If you have a Windows 3.51 license but don't want to use the upgrade method, follow these steps:

1. Locate the file PINBALL.SYS on the Windows NT 3.51 boot partition or installation CD-ROM (it should be in the I386 directory on the CD-ROM). Copy this file to the <WINNT>\SYSTEM32\DRIVERS directory on the Windows NT system, where <WINNT> is the system directory (usually C:\WINNT).

2. Run the REGEDIT program and choose Registry, Export Registry File to back up the registry file. Close this registry editor.

3. Run the REGEDT32 program and use the tree view in the left pane to locate HKEY_LOCAL_MACHINE\SYSTEM\ControlSet001\Services. (See Figure 13.5.)

FIGURE 13.5
This figure shows the Registry entries created as described in the text.

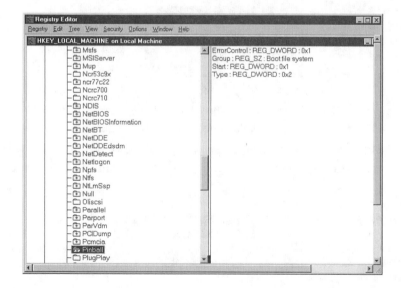

Part V

Ch 13

4. Choose Edit, Add Key. This action produces the Add Key dialog box shown in Figure 13.6.

FIGURE 13.6
Create new Registry keys with the Add Key dialog box.

5. Enter a Key Name of `Pinball` and click OK.

6. Select the new `Pinball` key in the left pane and choose Edit, Add Value to produce the Add Value dialog box shown in Figure 13.7.

FIGURE 13.7
Create Registry key values with the Add Value dialog box.

7. Enter a Value Name of `ErrorControl`, select `REG_DWORD` as the Data Type, and click OK.

8. The Registry Editor now asks you for data using the DWORD Editor dialog box, shown in Figure 13.8.

FIGURE 13.8
Enter data for Registry keys with the DWORD Editor dialog box.

9. Enter a Data value of 1, ensure that the Radix is set to Hex, and click OK.

10. Choose Edit, Add Value to get the Add Value dialog box again (refer to Figure 13.7).

11. Add the Value Name `Group`, select REG_SZ as the Data Type, and click OK.

12. Use the String Editor dialog box, shown in Figure 13.9, to enter a string that reads `Boot file system`.

FIGURE 13.9
Enter a string value to be stored in the Registry with the String Editor dialog box.

13. Choose Edit, Add Value again to get the Add Value dialog box (refer to Figure 13.7).

14. Add the Value Name Start with a Data Type of REG_DWORD, and click OK.

15. Use the DWORD Editor dialog box (refer to Figure 13.8) to enter 1 for the Data value, of Radix Hex, and click OK.

16. Choose Edit, Add Value to get the Add Value dialog box once more (refer to Figure 13.7).

17. Add the value Type of Data Type REG_DWORD and click OK.

18. Enter the value 2 as the Data Value in the DWORD Editor dialog box (refer to Figure 13.8), with a Radix of Hex, and click OK.

19. Check your results with those displayed in Figure 13.5. The entries in the right pane should be the same, including the case of all text. If there are any discrepancies, correct the errors.

20. Close the Registry Editor.

21. Shut down the system and reboot.

When Windows NT starts up again, you should be able to both read from and write to your HPFS partitions. If there are any problems, I recommend restoring your Registry from the backup you created in step 2. When you reboot after doing so, your system should be back to normal, albeit without HPFS access.

CAUTION

This procedure does not work with Windows 2000. In fact, if you follow the preceding instructions with Windows 2000, it won't boot when you restart your computer! Try searching Deja News for information on getting HPFS to work with Windows 2000; with any luck somebody will eventually come up with something that will work.

▶ To learn more about Deja News, **see** "Using Deja News," **p. 288**.

Linux HPFS Drivers

Linux ships with read-only HPFS drivers, which might or might not be compiled by default in any given Linux distribution. If HPFS support is present, you can mount HPFS partitions by using the -t hpfs parameter to the mount command. The Linux HPFS drivers support options similar to those for the Linux FAT drivers for setting ownership and permissions on HPFS partitions. In addition, there is an -o case=lower | asis option that affects how the Linux driver treats mixed-case filenames—by converting them all to lowercase or by leaving them as is. The default is to convert them to lowercase.

If you want read/write support for HPFS in Linux 2.2.x, you must patch your kernel with read/write HPFS support available from http://artax.karlin.mff.cuni.cz/~mikulas/vyplody/hpfs/index-e.cgi. As described in the documentation that comes with the driver, it's necessary to replace the contents of the original Linux kernel HPFS directory with the new files, and to copy two additional files to the `/usr/src/linux/include/linux` directory. You can then recompile your kernel or kernel modules and use the read/write features. This support has been incorporated into the 2.3.24 and later kernels.

Reports on the Internet indicate good success with these drivers, even doing read/write access. Nonetheless, the read/write support is quite new and untested compared to most of Linux's other read/write filesystem drivers, so I advise caution when using the read/write feature. You can continue to mount some partitions read-only by using the `-r` or `-o ro` mount options on some partitions, while using `-w` or `-o rw` on the partitions to which you want to write. You should be especially cautious when using this driver with server versions of OS/2 because the Linux driver doesn't understand the ACLs and a few other HPFS features used by OS/2 server versions. The documentation reports that the driver should force a read-only mount of the partition if it detects these features in use.

The HPFS read/write support takes advantage of HPFS's EA features to store UNIX-style ownership, permissions, and even symbolic link information. This fact makes HPFS at least theoretically suitable for many more functions than are most other non-UNIX filesystems, but there are still limitations. For example, the Linux kernel won't compile from an HPFS partition because of file naming restrictions—specifically, HPFS is a case-retentive filesystem, but the kernel compilation creates a few files that differ only in case, so a case-sensitive filesystem is required. Under OS/2, the Linux-created EAs shouldn't interfere with normal functions, but won't provide any added functionality, either. You can disable the HPFS driver's use of EAs for storing UNIX-style information by using the `-o eas=no` mount parameter.

FreeBSD HPFS Drivers

Beta-level HPFS support for FreeBSD is available from `http://iclub.nsu.ru/~semen/hpfs/hpfs.html`, but as of version 0.4 it's poorly documented, so I can't recommend you try it unless you're experienced with FreeBSD kernel modification. The driver supports both read and write access, but as beta-level software, you should consider the write support quite dangerous.

Linux's BFS Support

Although not part of the standard kernel, a read-only Linux driver for BeOS's BFS is available from `http://hp.vector.co.jp/authors/VA008030/bfs/`. If you want to try it, you should get the most recent version directly from the Web site.

> **CAUTION**
>
> This driver is considered *alpha-level* software, which is about as unstable as you can get. Despite the fact that it's a read-only driver, therefore, I advise extreme caution when using the Linux BFS driver. Although a read-only driver shouldn't damage the partition it accesses, a bug in the code could conceivably lock up the Linux kernel, and thus the computer.

Foreign ext2fs Support

Thanks to Linux's open source nature, the Linux ext2fs drivers have migrated onto several other platforms. Despite the ready availability of authoritative read/write ext2fs source code, however, many of these implementations remain read-only because interfacing the Linux driver code to foreign OSs provides an opportunity for the introduction of serious bugs.

DOS ext2fs Access Tools

Two DOS tools provide read-only access to Linux ext2fs partitions: ext2tools and lread. ext2tools hasn't been modified since 1996, but lread is being maintained. As access tools, these programs don't provide DOS programs with direct access to the ext2fs partition; you must copy files from ext2fs using the tool, and then use the copied file from a FAT partition. lread is available from `ftp://sunsite.unc.edu/pub/linux/utils/dos/`.

Windows 9*x* ext2fs Drivers

Windows 9*x* enjoys a pair of ext2fs access methods. One (fsdext2) is a read-only filesystem driver, and the other (Explore2fs) is a read/write file access utility.

Using the fsdext2 Filesystem Driver   The Linux ext2 filesystem driver, fsdext2, is available from `http://www.yipton.demon.co.uk/`. The driver comes with an installation script. After running that script, reboot your computer. Rebooting loads the driver, but the driver imposes one Linux-like characteristic on your system: You must explicitly mount the Linux partitions. You do this much as you would in Linux, with the mount command (included in the fsdext2 package). Its syntax is mount /dev/*xxx d*, where *xxx* is the Linux-style device identifier for the partition you want to mount, and *d* is the drive letter. For example, mount /dev/hda6 g mounts /dev/hda6 as drive G:.

After you've mounted a Linux partition, that partition works very much like a FAT partition, except that you can't write to it. You can access files directly from programs, including both 16- and 32-bit programs. The driver creates a "fake" 8.3 filename for every file that requires one, so you have full access to all the files on the disk even from DOS programs. You can use regular long filenames, of course, from programs that support long filenames.

The author reports that he isn't further developing the driver, so unless somebody else picks it up, it will remain read-only into the indefinite future.

Using the Explore2fs Utility   The Explore2fs utility, available from `http://uranus.it.swin.edu.au/~jn/linux/Explore2fs.htm`, appears in Figure 13.1. It provides a user interface much like that of the Windows Explorer file manager. Unlike fsdext2, Explore2fs is a read/write utility, although the author labels it a "pre-1.0" release—very close to being 1.0, but not quite there. The utility's Web page indicates that this status isn't likely to change because the author has little time to further develop the program. I therefore advise some caution in using it in read/write mode on any important Linux filesystem.

Part
V

Ch
13

Explore2fs gives you access to features of the ext2 filesystem that Windows itself doesn't support, such as ownership and permissions information. You can therefore use it to perform fine-grained modifications to the filesystem, which can occasionally be helpful in an emergency situation—for example, if your Linux installation won't boot because of incorrect permissions on critical files.

The author's Web page indicates that a design goal of Explore2fs was to create a package that will enable Linux to be installed from a running Windows NT installation, which explains the reasons for many of the package's features. These features also make the program useful for other purposes, however, including day-to-day access to ext2fs from Windows 9x or NT.

Windows NT ext2fs Access

Windows NT drivers for ext2fs are still quite limited. The author of fsdext2 indicates that he's working on a Windows NT ext2fs driver. Check his Web site (http:// www.yipton.demon.co.uk/) for more information on its availability. Another read-only Windows NT ext2fs driver is currently available from http://www.chat.ru/~ashedel. It requires that you install a driver and then edit and run a short script to provide access to your ext2fs partition. The author has a separate read/write version available from the same site.

> **CAUTION**
>
> The existing ext2fs Windows NT driver is currently at version 0.04, which represents very early alpha software. Because of the possibility of a kernel crash due to bugs, I advise extreme caution in using this driver. These comments apply doubly to the read/write version. Of course, this caution might be moderated as later releases appear.

At present, a more reliable method of accessing ext2fs partitions from Windows NT is to use the Explore2fs program, described in the previous section. This program runs under Windows NT as well as under Windows 95—indeed, Windows NT appears to be the developer's primary platform for this program.

OS/2 ext2fs Drivers

One of the earliest ports of ext2fs was to OS/2. This driver is available from http://perso.wanadoo.fr/matthieu.willm/ext2-os2/. Because of its maturity or the persistence of its developer, Matthieu Willm, the OS/2 ext2fs port is unusually complete. It includes ports of the Linux utilities mke2fs, e2fsck, and tune2fs, which are used to format an ext2fs partition, perform a filesystem check, and alter various parameters of an ext2fs partition, respectively. You can therefore use ext2fs from OS/2 even if you don't have Linux installed on your computer.

By default, the OS/2 ext2fs driver runs in read-only mode, but read/write support is available. This support is mostly, but not completely, reliable, so caution is in order when using read/write ext2fs support from OS/2. Like the OS/2 FAT-32 support, the OS/2 ext2fs support requires a special filter to make ext2fs partitions visible to the ext2fs driver. Depending on its parameters, this filter might alter the drive letters assigned to existing FAT and HPFS partitions.

▶ To learn more about partition letter changes, **see** "Drive Letter Changes," **p. 183**.

The ext2fs driver creates files on the ext2fs partition that are owned by root. This fact can be quite annoying when you reboot into Linux, only to find that you must have root privileges to modify or delete these files.

In addition to the separate OS/2 ext2fs drivers, the OS/2 VFAT drivers, described earlier in this chapter, include ext2fs support. If you only want ext2fs support, I recommend using the original ext2fs-only drivers.

BeOS ext2fs Drivers

Third-party read-only ext2fs drivers for BeOS are available from http://www.cs.tamu.edu/people/tkg0143/be/index.html. This filesystem is read-only but is quite stable. When you install it by moving two files into appropriate directories, you gain access to ext2fs partitions in much the same way as you can access BFS or FAT partitions, except of course that you can't write to these partitions. In fact, Figure 13.2 shows several ext2fs partitions among the mount options.

The BeOS ext2fs documentation indicates that the author is working on read/write ext2fs support, but at the time of this writing, that support had not yet been released. When it is, I advise taking a cautious approach, at least initially, for the same reasons I advise caution when using any early read/write support for foreign filesystems.

FreeBSD ext2fs Drivers

FreeBSD includes support for Linux's ext2fs in its kernel. To mount an ext2fs partition, though, you use the mount_ext2fs command rather than the usual mount command. Other than this variation, you can use ext2fs partitions much as you would use native FFS partitions. You might need to recompile your FreeBSD kernel to enable the ext2fs support.

One major restriction on the FreeBSD ext2fs support is that you can't mount logical ext2fs partitions; you can only mount primary ext2fs partitions and unpartitioned devices such as floppy disks.

Because Linux and FreeBSD use the same permissions system, you get full access to ext2fs ownership and permission information when you mount an ext2fs partition in FreeBSD. FreeBSD and Linux might not, however, assign the same user and group ID numbers to various specific users and groups, respectively. For example, FreeBSD might give the user jennie an ID of 1001, whereas Linux might give her the ID 504. This means that jennie won't be able to access her Linux files from FreeBSD, at least not with full ownership permissions. You might want to be careful when you create users and groups on both OSs, therefore,

Part
V

Ch
13

to force the creation of synchronized user IDs. If you've already created user accounts, you can use the Linux command usermod to adjust the Linux accounts' user IDs to match those on the FreeBSD system. Type man usermod from a Linux shell for more information.

Linux's FFS Support

Linux includes support for the FFS of BSD versions of UNIX. Under Linux, this support comes by specifying a type code of ufs. You need kernel support for UFS to use this feature, and you probably also need kernel support for the BSD partition table, or possibly some other OS's partitioning scheme if you intend to place a hard disk from such a system in your computer and read it.

> **CAUTION**
>
> If your BSD partition has a lower partition number than that of your extended partition, the BSD partition numbers will usurp the numbers used by the extended partition, thus pushing those numbers up. You can adjust any partition identifiers that are so affected in /etc/fstab, but you must be aware of and plan for this eventuality. Also, if you make such a change and later boot a kernel that lacks BSD partition table support, the process will reverse, denying you access to any logical partitions via the standard /etc/fstab entries. All in all, it's better to plan your partitioning scheme such that the extended partition has a lower number than the BSD partition.

Because the FFS has mutated into several variant forms, it's often necessary for you to specify the exact variant when you mount the partition. You do this with the -o ufstype=*typecode* parameter to mount. Possible values of *typecode* include the following:

- old—A default value for many older versions of UNIX.
- 44bsd—The version of the filesystem used by the open source BSD variants (FreeBSD, NetBSD, and OpenBSD).
- sun—Sun's version of the filesystem, used in SunOS and Solaris on Sun hardware.
- sunx86—Sun's filesystem as used in Sun's x86 OS versions.
- nextstep—NeXT's version of the filesystem.
- nextstep-cd—NeXT's version of the filesystem, as used on NeXT CD-ROMs.
- openstep—The version of the filesystem used in OpenStep.

Linux's FFS support includes both read-only and read/write access. Read/write access is a separate option in the kernel configuration, so be sure to select it if you want it. Read/write support is limited to the 44bsd, sun, and sunx86 variants of the driver; the others are limited to read-only support, even when you select read/write access in the kernel.

> **CAUTION**
>
> The Linux kernel configuration marks UFS/FFS read/write support as experimental. I therefore recommend that you avoid using read/write support if at all possible. If you do enable read/write support, be sure that your files are backed up, or use the write capability only on partitions that contain no important data.

Just as with FreeBSD accessing ext2fs, Linux accessing FFS gives you access to the usual assortment of UNIX filesystem features, such as ownership and permission information. If you want to give your users access to their files on both OSs, you must ensure that the users' user and group IDs match across both OSs, so pay attention to this detail when you create accounts. You can use the Linux `usermod` command to alter existing Linux accounts to use FreeBSD IDs, if necessary.

Alternatives to Sharing Filesystems

There are ways to share data across OSs without sharing filesystems, and therefore without using common disk filesystem drivers. I briefly describe two such options in this section.

Raw *tar* Files

One time-honored method of transferring data between UNIX OSs is to place a `tar` file directly on a transportable medium, such as a tape or a floppy disk, without using a filesystem. The UNIX `tar` program is a utility that combines several programs into a single file. That file can then be written "raw" to a removable medium, without using a filesystem. In some sense, the `tar` format itself is the filesystem; but `tar` wasn't designed as a filesystem, so you don't access the medium in the same way.

To create a floppy disk that's transportable in this way, you issue a command similar to the following:

```
tar -cvf /dev/fd0 /home/jennie/stuff
```

This command creates a raw `tar` archive from the contents of the `/home/jennie/stuff` directory on the `/dev/fd0` device (the floppy device on Linux and FreeBSD; you might need to use a different device file on other UNIX versions). If you want to omit the complete pathname, you can change to the directory you want to transfer and use `./` rather than the complete path indicator. To extract the file on another computer, you could use a command similar to this one:

```
tar -xvf /dev/fd0
```

You can obtain and use `tar` programs for a variety of non-UNIX OSs, but these programs might not support use on "raw" floppy or tape devices. Consult the documentation for the non-UNIX `tar` program for details.

Part
V

Ch
13

> **N O T E**   You must have write privileges to the device in question to write tar files in this way. Many
> UNIX-like OSs deny such access to any but the `root` user by default, so you might need
> to become root or change the permissions on the floppy or other device file to use `tar` in this
> way. ■

Networking

If you have two or more computers, you can use networking as a means to transfer files not
just between the two computers, but between two OSs on the same computer. For this strategy to work, one computer must be capable of running a *file server* program of some type. A
file server is a program that enables other computers to read and write files on the server
computer. Examples of file server programs include FTP servers, Windows networking,
Samba (an implementation of Windows networking for UNIX versions), and the UNIX
Network Filesystem (NFS).

When you transfer files back and forth between two computers via a network, you need not
use the same server protocol for each transfer, although the server must understand all the
protocols involved. For example, suppose you want to provide access to data files from both
Windows NT and FreeBSD. You can set up a network that uses a computer, such as a Linux
computer, as a server. The Linux computer would run both Samba and NFS, to communicate
with Windows NT and FreeBSD, respectively. Each of those two OSs would then use its
respective client software to access the files on the Linux computer. Effectively, Linux's ext2fs
becomes a shared filesystem between the Windows NT and FreeBSD computers. Note, however, that neither Windows NT nor FreeBSD needs to understand ext2fs for this operation to
work; it's the Windows networking and NFS protocols that the client OSs use in this situation.

▶ To learn more about using a network to share files between OSs, **see** Chapter 20, "File and
Printer Sharing."

Summary

The range of filesystems and filesystem implementations available on x86 hardware today can
make the selection of filesystems for sharing data between OSs a difficult task. Above all else,
you should look for a filesystem that's *stable* in all the OSs that will use it. Because filesystem
drivers run in a privileged state within an OS, a buggy driver can cause the system to crash.
Worse, a buggy read/write filesystem can irrevocably corrupt the data on a partition.

In general, FAT is the safest choice for file sharing between OSs, but it's not always the most
convenient choice. Some OSs lack support for important features such as long filenames
when using FAT, and some OSs lack support for certain FAT variants, such as FAT-32.
Therefore, other filesystems hold a certain appeal in many situations. NTFS, HPFS, BFS,
ext2fs, and FFS are all viable alternatives for file sharing in certain specific situations. There
are also options that don't involve traditional disk-based filesystems, including the use of non-
filesystem data transfers such as `tar` files and the use of networked file transfer methods. ●

CHAPTER 14

Application Data File Formats

Platform-Independent File Formats

Operating systems by themselves are useless. Chances are that most of the time you spend using your computer isn't spent moving files about using the OS's file manager. Instead, you probably spend most of the time at your computer writing with a word processor, creating graphics with graphics programs, or otherwise using applications. The result of using an application is usually a data file of some sort—a text file containing the letter you've written, a binary file containing a graphics image, or what have you. This chapter focuses on these data files.

Some data file formats are easily interchanged between platforms, either because they're entirely non-proprietary or because they use formats that, although technically proprietary, are so common as to be universal. Other file formats, though, are limited to a handful of OSs or even just a single platform. In a multi-OS computer, you're generally best off favoring the most easily exchanged data file format that suits your purposes. In some cases, though, you might have no choice, or you might not know which file formats are the most easily used across multiple platforms. This chapter should provide you with some answers to the question of what file formats are most appropriate for you, or at least provide some pointers in the right direction.

As a general rule, you can determine a file's format by examining its filename *extension*—that portion of the filename that follows the final period (.) in the name. For example, .txt indicates a text file, .jpg indicates a JPEG graphics file, and so on. Unfortunately, not all files are appropriately marked, and occasionally two programs use the same extension for different file types. The filename extension is therefore a helpful guide but shouldn't be taken as 100% reliable.

For a user of a multi-OS computer, the best way to store information is in a file format that is not tied to any one OS or even to a group of OSs. When you use such a platform-independent file format, you can move the file back and forth between any OS and use it equally well in any OS.

For consideration as a platform-independent file format for the purposes of this book, I require a file format to be supported natively on all the major PC OSs, either by OS utilities or by common third-party applications. Furthermore, I require that the format not need any sort of translation, or at least that the translation process be very simple, reliable, and easily reversed. These criteria rule out formats for many specific applications.

N O T E Having a platform-independent file format does you no good if the file is stored on a filesystem or medium that is not usable by all your OSs. Chapter 13, "Tools for Accessing Foreign Filesystems," covers drivers and utilities to help you access one OS's files from another OS. ■

Platform-Independent File Formats for Text

Text processing is one of the most common uses for computers. Fortunately, the basic format for text on PCs (the *American Standard Code for Information Interchange*, or *ASCII*) is more or less identical across platforms. Where trouble emerges is in extensions to ASCII to support features such as fonts, italicized text, and so on.

> **NOTE** Some OSs use codes other than ASCII. IBM mainframes often use the *Extended Binary Coded Decimal Interchange Code (EBCDIC)*, for example. PCs increasingly support *Unicode*, a 16-bit encoding form that supports many alphabets beyond the Roman alphabet used by English and other European languages. (ASCII uses only seven bits, although most PC OSs store characters in eight bits, and therefore include extra symbols.) ▪

Raw ASCII The most basic format for text exchange is in raw ASCII files, also called *text files*, *plain text*, or sundry other variants. Raw ASCII is very good for exchanging textual information that doesn't require special formatting or characters that are outside the range commonly used in English. For the most part, an ASCII file created on one OS poses no problems to another OS. Programs to read, write, and alter ASCII files (*text editors*) are common and come with all OSs.

> **NOTE** Various schemes exist to support languages with more complex encoding needs. Some of these are simple extensions to ASCII, whereas others, such as Unicode, are much more complex. Support for multiple alphabets and even non-alphabetic writing systems exists in most OSs, but exchanging such files presents unique challenges that I can't cover in this book. ▪

There is a fly in the ASCII ointment, unfortunately: *end-of-line (EOL)* characters. A special ASCII code is required to signal the end of a line of text. This code doesn't print on the screen; instead, it causes the next character to print at the start of the next line. Microsoft-style OSs use a two-character code (*CR/LF*, short for *carriage return/line feed*, depicted by the hexadecimal characters 0x0d and 0x0a, one after the other). UNIX-style OSs, on the other hand, use a single character (*LF*, 0x0a). In Microsoft-style OSs, and on devices such as printers that are configured to use this form of EOL encoding, each of the two characters has a different effect. The CR moves the cursor to the beginning of the line, whereas the LF moves the cursor down one line. Therefore, using UNIX-style EOL characters on such devices often produces a "stair-step" effect, something like this:

```
Line 1
      Line 2
            Line 3
```

When you try to use a Microsoft-style file in a UNIX OS, the result is often either the appearance of a strange code at the end of each line (often ^M) or double-spacing where the original file was single-spaced. When displaying a file, the extraneous LF sometimes doesn't display, depending on the program you use to view the file.

Fortunately, several solutions exist to the problem of coping with different EOL characters. These include

- **Automatic handling in editors and word processors**—Many editors and word processors can convert the EOL handling, either automatically or through some command or even a simple search-and-replace operation.

> **CAUTION**
>
> Editors often save files in their platforms' native formats, even when the files use another platform's EOL conventions. Therefore, if you use one OS to edit another's configuration files, you should ensure that the file ends up with the correct EOL type. Incorrect EOL types in configuration files can cause serious problems for some OSs and utilities.

- **Conversion programs**—Programs to convert EOL characters are trivial to write, and so are quite common. UNIX and UNIX-like systems often come with programs called `unix2dos` and `dos2unix` to perform these conversions.
- **Automatic filesystem conversions**—In some OSs, the filesystem drivers can be configured to convert files at access time. This is particularly true of Linux, which includes such options in its FAT, HPFS, and NTFS drivers.

Because the conversion is so simple and, if not applied inappropriately to binary files, flawless and reversible, I consider all forms of ASCII to be similar enough to place ASCII text in the platform-independent format category.

N O T E The Macintosh uses yet another EOL code variant. Like UNIX, Mac OS uses a single character, but the Mac OS's character is CR rather than LF. Therefore, when you read a Macintosh file on DOS or UNIX systems, it is common to see a complete lack of line breaks. The same is true when you read a UNIX ASCII file on a Macintosh. When you read a Microsoft-style file on a Macintosh, though, you often find a stray character (usually a box) at the start of each line. Some editors automatically recognize Macintosh-style EOL encodings, however, and conversion utilities similar to those for converting between UNIX and Microsoft-style encodings exist. Therefore, the Macintosh-style EOL encoding adds to the variability but doesn't pose any fundamentally new problems to text exchange.

Enhanced Text Formats A file format that has become extremely common in the past few years is the *Hypertext Markup Language*, or *HTML*. This is the format used for most text on the Web. The idea behind HTML is that it is plain ASCII, but certain character combinations hold special meaning, and a Web browser normally reformats the text in ways that the user can specify. For example, text enclosed in less-than (<) and greater-than (>) characters is interpreted as a *tag*, which can be used to indicate formatting or the presence of links to other documents. The ampersand character (&) can be used to specify special characters—

both unusual characters such as copyright symbols (©) and those that are otherwise used by HTML, such as the greater-than symbol used in tags. The following HTML example demonstrates these principles:

```
<HTML><HEAD>
<TITLE>Sample Web Page</TITLE>
</HEAD>
<BODY BGCOLOR="#FFFFFF" TEXT="#000000">

<CENTER><H1 ALIGN="CENTER">SAMPLE WEB PAGE</H1></CENTER>

<EM>LAST REVISION: 5/25/2000</EM><BR>
BY: Rod Smith,
<A HREF="mailto:smithrod@bellatlantic.net">smithrod@bellatlantic.net</A>
<HR>

<P>Is the mathematical statement 27 &gt 24 true?</P>

</BODY></HTML>
```

The preceding lines represent a complete (if short) Web page, including an assortment of tags and a use of &gt for the greater-than (>) symbol. Tags such as <EM> provide the capability to emphasize certain types of text (most Web browsers use italics for emphasized text). Other tags enable you to specify fonts and perform other types of formatting.

HTML is, in fact, only one of several enhanced text formats. Two others that are quite popular are TeX and its extension LaTeX, which have long been used on UNIX (and to a lesser extent other platforms) as a means of describing printed pages. The *Extensible Markup Language (XML)* is another that is becoming popular, but it is not yet as popular as HTML. Many others exist, as well. Each of these formats has its strengths. Because they're based on ASCII text and use a few ordinary characters to signal special functions, you can create such files on any platform. In the case of the rarer of these file formats, you can't process them on some platforms, however.

ApplixWare Anywhere Office   Applix (http://www.applix.com) produces a Java-based version of its ApplixWare office suite. Because it is Java based, the software runs on any platform for which Java is available, which is quite a wide range, albeit not quite every OS in existence. The Applix Word component actually uses an enhanced ASCII text format for its documents; I mention this product in a separate section simply because you're likely to interact with the software in a different way than you would with an HTML editor or its ilk.

In addition to the Java-based programs, Applix makes more conventional binary programs available for several UNIX variants, including Linux. These programs can therefore be an excellent basis for exchanging text (and other document types) across platforms, and especially among various UNIX OSs.

Part
V

Ch
14

PDF   Adobe's (http://www.adobe.com) *Portable Document Format (PDF)* is different from most text file formats in that it is designed for the distribution of finished documents, not the exchange of documents that are in the process of being edited. PDF is a compressed document format that incorporates both text and graphics elements. It enables you to create a document with precisely specified formatting and layout, much as if you were creating a printed document; but it also provides for hypertext links between different "pages" of a single document and other features not available on printed documents.

A PDF *viewer* or *reader* is a program that can display PDF files on a computer. Adobe Acrobat Reader is one such program. This program is available for Windows, OS/2, and various UNIX versions; Figure 14.1 shows Acrobat Reader for Linux in operation. An assortment of third-party programs can also read PDF files. For example, BePDF (http://www.frbug.org/pdf/) enables you to read PDF files on BeOS. BePDF is based on the UNIX xpdf program (http://www.foolabs.com/xpdf/). Third-party PDF readers have problems with some PDF files, but they're good enough for many purposes.

FIGURE 14.1
You can read a PDF file, including complex formatting and graphics, on any platform for which a PDF viewer exists.

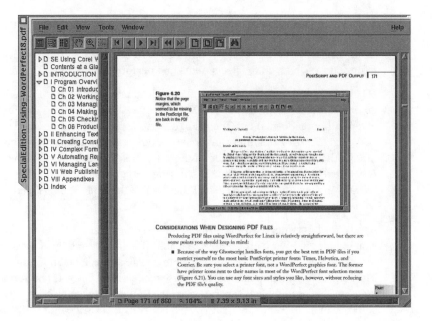

To produce a PDF file, you need a special program. One popular program for producing PDF files is Adobe Acrobat Distiller, which is available for Windows and some UNIX variants. If you're using another platform, you can use Ghostscript (http://www.cs.wisc.edu/~ghost) to convert PostScript into PDF. Used in conjunction with a PostScript printer driver, Ghostscript can do a good job converting basic documents but doesn't provide access to some of the flashier features that PDF enables, such as tables of contents and links.

▶ To learn more about reading and creating PDF files, **see** "Document Exchange: PDF Readers," **p. 409**.

Platform-Independent File Formats for Graphics

Most computer users today expect their machines to provide substantial graphics capabilities. When it comes to editing graphics files, there are two basic classes of file formats:

- **Bitmapped graphics**—The image you see on your computer screen is composed of hundreds of thousands or even millions of tiny dots, known as *pixels* (short for *picture elements*). One way to store graphics is to record the color value of each individual pixel and store that value in a file. For example, a graphic image might consume an area of 10×10 pixels, each of which requires a certain number of bits for the color value (the *color depth*). The larger the image in terms of pixels and the greater the color depth, the more realistic the image appears to be. Bitmapped graphics are very good for recording photographs and scanned images.

- **Vector graphics**—A second way to describe an image is by means of the lines, arcs, and other shapes that compose the image. This type of representation is known as a *vector* or *raster* image. The great advantage of vector graphics is that they *scale* well—that is, you can adjust the size of the image up or down and get results that are as good as your screen or printer allows. If you scale a bitmapped graphic, you lose detail or create an image that looks chunky compared to other images on the same device. Vector graphics, however, don't work well for photos or scanned images.

Bitmapped Graphics Formats   There are a variety of platform-independent file formats for bitmapped graphics. These formats differ in terms of how well they compress their data and in whether any compression system they employ is *lossy* or *lossless*. A lossless data compression scheme results in no loss of data; what goes in is what eventually comes out. A lossy compression scheme, on the other hand, loses some details to achieve greater data compression.

The following are some of the more popular bitmapped graphics formats:

- **TIFF**—The *Tagged Information File Format* is a relatively straightforward file format that is in moderately common use. In its most basic form, TIFF offers no compression, although more advanced variants of TIFF do offer lossless compression. TIFF files usually have a filename extension of .tif. Because TIFF images are often uncompressed, they also often consume more disk space than do other image types.

- **GIF**—CompuServe's *Graphics Interchange Format* became quite popular in the 1980s because of its lossless compression techniques. GIF is more limited than TIFF, however; GIF offers only 256 colors per image (eight bits of color depth). It is also encumbered by patents owned by Unisys, which means that many open-source programs don't support GIF. GIF files typically bear a .gif filename extension.

- **PNG**—The *Portable Network Graphics* or *PNG's Not GIF* format is a relatively recent graphics file format. PNG was created as a direct response to the 1995 announcement that Unisys would charge royalties on GIF format graphics. The format is becoming increasingly popular as a substitute for GIF. You can read more about it at http://www.cdrom.com/pub/png/. PNG files usually have a .png extension.

Part

V

Ch

14

■ **JPEG**—This format's name is derived from the *Joint Photographic Experts Group*, the committee that wrote its specification. Unlike other popular graphics formats, JPEG can—and usually does—employ a lossy compression scheme. This fact allows JPEG images to be much smaller than those of other image formats, but at the cost of a potential degradation in quality. I say *potential* because, at high-quality settings, the degradation might be unnoticeable. Figures 14.2 and 14.3 illustrate the effect of using a low-quality setting. Figure 14.2 uses a high-quality setting but consumes 67KB of disk space; Figure 14.3 uses a low-quality setting but consumes only 7KB of disk space. JPEG files usually have `.jpg` or `.jpeg` filename extensions.

FIGURE 14.2
A high-quality JPEG looks good but consumes a lot of disk space.

In general, JPEG is useful for digitized photographs, whereas a lossless format such as PNG or TIFF is most useful for cartoons, scanned line art, and other images that contain large amounts of the same color. The reason is that JPEG's lossy compression method, when applied to real-world images, is difficult for the human eye to spot—at least not until the compression level is set quite high. JPEG's compression method, however, tends to introduce color variations in wide swaths of identical colors, even at low levels of compression, and such variations tend to stand out.

Most popular graphics programs on most platforms support at least two or three of these formats, and you can find programs to create and edit any of these formats on any but the most obscure OSs.

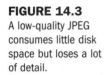

FIGURE 14.3
A low-quality JPEG consumes little disk space but loses a lot of detail.

Vector Graphics Formats   Vector graphics formats tend to be tied into specific applications and aren't as portable across platforms as are bitmapped graphics formats. Therefore, few such formats are truly cross-platform in nature. One of the few that does meet this criterion is *Encapsulated PostScript (EPS)*. As you might guess by the name, EPS is closely related to PostScript, which is a common format for data sent to printers. Many graphics programs can create EPS versions of their data files, and a variety of word processors, layout software, and other utilities can read EPS files. Few of the programs that can read EPS files can display them onscreen as such, however; frequently, you must print the document to a PostScript printer (or through a filter such as Ghostscript) before you can see the results. This fact makes EPS a poor format if your goal is to use a common data file format for editing a graphic on multiple platforms. EPS can be a good choice, however, if you want to create a graphic in one OS and incorporate that finished graphic into a larger document you create on another OS. EPS files typically have .eps filename extensions.

Platform-Independent File Formats for Spreadsheets

Spreadsheet formats are not as standardized as are those for text or graphics. Therefore, there is relatively little in the way of standardized spreadsheet formats. There are a handful of proprietary formats that most spreadsheet programs can read and write, however.

▶ To learn more about exchanging proprietary spreadsheet formats, **see** "Platform-Limited File Formats for Graphics, Spreadsheets, and Databases," **p. 372**.

Part
V

Ch
14

One of the few spreadsheet formats that is relatively cross-platform is the *comma-separated value (CSV)* format. A CSV file is essentially an ASCII file format that uses commas to separate the values of the spreadsheet cells. For example, here is a simple CSV spreadsheet file:

```
23,45,87,49
34,54,91,51
28,50,90,51
```

Because the CSV format is so simple, if you use it to exchange spreadsheet data, you'll likely lose complex spreadsheet features, even if both the source and destination spreadsheet programs support those features. Nonetheless, as a lowest-common-denominator format, a CSV file can be a useful way to ensure that data can be read on multiple platforms. CSV files usually have `.csv` filename extensions.

Some programs support CSV-like formats in which tabs, spaces, or other characters are used in place of commas. Sometimes any non-numeric character is taken as a column separator. You can generally use a text editor's search-and-replace features to convert between CSV format and one of these variant formats if the need arise.

The ApplixWare (`http://www.applix.com`) office suite is available in a Java-based form, as I mentioned earlier. This fact means that you can run this software on a variety of platforms. ApplixWare includes a spreadsheet component, so if you're looking for a cross-platform spreadsheet, Applix's entry to the field is worth considering.

Platform-Independent File Formats for Databases

Like spreadsheets, database programs tend to use their own proprietary file formats. Also like spreadsheets, however, databases can often read and write CSV files. You can therefore use such files to exchange data across platforms.

In some sense, you can consider many other file formats to be databases. For example, email programs store email messages in one or more files, and you use your email program to access the messages by sender, title, date, or some other means. Such formats are often cross-platform in nature, although they aren't database files in the strictest sense.

Platform-Independent File Formats for Archives

In computer terms, an *archive* is a file that contains several additional files. Archives are extremely useful for transferring a large number of files from one location to another. Rather than copy, say, 500 files individually, you can place those files in an archive and transfer only one file. Most archive formats also support storing entire directory structures, so you can transfer several directories in a single file. Finally, you can compress an archive file, either using a compression feature of the archive format itself or using a separate program to compress the archive file. Such compression reduces storage and data transmission costs.

Fortunately, a variety of cross-platform archive formats are available. In practice, only a couple are in common use. The following list covers the most common and a few not-quite-as-common formats:

- **Zip**—The zip file format, denoted by a `.zip` filename extension, is extremely popular and is supported by several different utilities, including PKZIP (`http://www.pkware.com/`), WinZip (`http://www.winzip.com/`), and InfoZip (`http://www.cdrom.com/pub/infozip/`). This file format is extremely popular in the Microsoft, OS/2, and BeOS arenas. It includes both archiving and compression features in one program.

- **tar**—The UNIX tar program is an archiver only. Originally intended to create tape archives (from which function the program's name is derived), tar takes a string of files and merges them into one. Common practice in the UNIX community is to create a *tarball* by compressing a tar file with a separate compression utility such as gzip or compress, which compresses but does not archive files (despite the similarity in names, gzip has nothing to do with zip). Tarballs typically have `.tgz`, `.tar.Z`, or `.tar.gz` filename extensions, whereas uncompressed tar files have `.tar` extensions. Many Windows zip utilities can read tar files and tarballs.

N O T E   One recent trend is to use the bzip2 program rather than gzip to compress tar files. Using bzip2 yields smaller files in most cases, but bzip2 isn't as widely used as gzip, it is slower, and the resulting file format is incompatible with gzip compression. ■

- **RAR**—RAR is infrequently used, probably because zip files and tarballs are more familiar to most users. In many cases, RAR files can be noticeably smaller than corresponding zip files or tarballs. Like zip, RAR is both an archiver and a compresser. You can obtain more information from `http://www.rarsoft.com/`. RAR files typically bear `.rar` extensions.

- **ARJ**—ARJ is another infrequently used but cross-platform archiving and compression scheme. ARJ files typically have `.arj` extensions. Many general-purpose Windows archive utilities support ARJ files.

- **LHA/LZH**—The LHA/LZH format experienced a brief burst of popularity in the 1980s, but has since fallen by the wayside. On most platforms, the extractor program is called LHA, whereas the files bear `.lzh` extensions. This compression format is encumbered by the same patents that plague the GIF graphics file format.

In Windows, many archiving programs support several different file formats, so you can work with (or at least extract files from) any of these formats using a single utility. On most other platforms, you need a separate utility for each archive format.

If you intend to exchange archived files cross-platform, the best choice is usually zip, although if obtaining the smallest possible file size is important, RAR might be preferable. If you want to exchange files between UNIX variants, a tarball is often in order. If you're creating archives for your own personal use, you can use whatever you like. If you try an exotic format, though, you might want to ensure that it supports important filesystem features, such as ownership, UNIX-style permissions, ACLs, or the preservation of system and hidden bits.

TIP Windows and DOS files are often distributed as self-extracting archives. These files have .exe extensions, and you run them as programs. Typically, the extractor places the files in a directory and might then run an install program, which sometimes deletes the temporary files after installing the software. These self-extracting archive files generally use an archiving format such as the ones described earlier, or such as the CAB format that is used on Windows. You can generally use a stand-alone extraction program to pull the files out of a self-extracting archive even if you aren't running Windows or DOS. You might even prefer to use this method if you are running Windows or DOS, because doing so reduces the possibility that a virus in the self-extracting archive code will infect your system.

Platform-Limited File Formats

In addition to the platform-independent file formats I've just described, many file formats exist on a few platforms, but not all of them. These formats are typically tied to one or two applications that have been ported across two or three OSs. The result can be a reasonable degree of cross-platform utility if you happen to have supported OSs. I also include in this category file formats that are widely, if imperfectly, supported by programs other than those that originally used them.

In some cases the line between a platform-independent and a platform-limited file format can be a tricky one to draw. For example, both the zip file archive format and the *Rich Text Format (RTF)* word processor format can be used on just about every platform, but I classify zip as platform-independent and RTF as platform-limited. The reason is that zip archivers are almost universally interoperable, whereas RTF files often pose difficulties when loading into specific word processors.

Platform-Limited File Formats for Text

The platform-limited text file formats are primarily word processor formats. In general, these file formats are ASCII text with embedded non-ASCII characters to support the word processors' unique features. Each word processor uses its own unique format for its files. Most word processors include import/export filters that let you load other programs' file formats and save files in foreign programs' formats. These filters are invariably imperfect, however; they might be unable to translate features that aren't present in the target program, and even when features exist on both programs, the filter might translate incorrectly because of a bug or incompatible means of attaining a given effect. Thus, although you might find support for popular formats on most or all platforms, that support is extremely limited unless the program that originated the format is available on the OS.

AbiWord   AbiWord (`http://www.abisource.com/`) is an open-source word processor that is designed with cross-platform use in mind. Compared to the other word processors I describe here, AbiWord is relatively crude and limited. AbiWord runs on Windows, various UNIX versions (including Linux and FreeBSD), and BeOS, but not on OS/2. The fact that AbiWord runs on BeOS sets it apart from the other cross-platform word processors I describe here. If you want a cross-platform word processor that supports BeOS, your choices at the time of this writing are AbiWord and using a text editor to create TeX, LaTeX, or some other platform-independent text format.

Corel WordPerfect   Corel's (`http://www.corel.com`) WordPerfect is one of the oldest surviving word processors. The program was the dominant one in the late 1980s and early 1990s on DOS, in its 4.*x* and 5.*x* incarnations. Today it is up to version 9.0 on Windows and, soon, Linux (version 8.0 is already available for Linux). Versions from 6.0 through 9.0 all use the same file format, no matter the platform. Versions 5.2 and earlier used different file formats, and each version number used its own format, so even loading a 5.0 file on WordPerfect 4.2 isn't possible.

The following are the OSs on which WordPerfect is available and the maximum version numbers for each platform:

- Windows (9*x* and NT): 9.0 (in WordPerfect Office 2000)
- Windows 3.1: 7.0
- Assorted UNIX versions: 8.0
- Linux: 8.0 (9.0 expected mid-2000)
- OS/2: 5.2 (discontinued)
- DOS: 6.1

If you want a word processor that is available on a wide range of OSs, you can do far worse than WordPerfect. Some of these variants can be difficult to find, however. The OS/2 version is particularly hard to find because it was discontinued. When available, it was quite buggy. (The 5.2a update was better, but still buggy.) Corel makes a limited version of its Linux 8.0 program available for free, but more complete versions of this program, as well as the versions for other platforms, cost money.

▶ To learn more about WordPerfect for Windows, **see** Acklen and Gilgen's *Special Edition Using Corel WordPerfect 9*, from Que. To learn more about WordPerfect for UNIX or Linux, **see** my *Special Edition Using Corel WordPerfect 8 for Linux*, from Que.

WordPerfect documents usually have `.wpd` extensions, but `.wp#`, where # is the major version number (4, 5, 6, and so on) is also sometimes used.

N O T E WordPerfect for the Macintosh uses an entirely different numbering scheme and file format than does WordPerfect for other platforms. If you need to exchange files with WordPerfect for Macintosh users, it is best to use an Intel-based WordPerfect file format (5.2 or 6/7/8/9). ▥

Lotus WordPro Lotus (http://www.lotus.com) produces an office package called SmartSuite that contains the WordPro word processor. This program is available for both Windows and OS/2 platforms. Currently, version 9.5 (also known as the *Millennium Edition*) is the latest version of SmartSuite.

Unlike WordPerfect, WordPro was never popular enough to inspire widespread import/export filters in competing products, although a few do support WordPro's format. Therefore, support for WordPro's file format is effectively limited to the Windows and OS/2 platforms.

▷ To learn more about WordPro, **see** Habraken's *Using Lotus SmartSuite Millennium Edition*, from Que.

Microsoft Word Microsoft's (http://www.microsoft.com) Word program is available both separately and bundled with its Office suite. On x86 PCs, the program is currently available only on Microsoft's Windows OSs, although older versions were available for both DOS and OS/2. The extraordinary popularity of the program ensures that import/export filters for Word are commonplace on all platforms. One program that deserves special mention in this respect is MSWordView (http://www.csn.ul.ie/~caolan/docs/MSWordView.html), which is a stand-alone program to convert Microsoft Word documents to HTML format.

Certain features of Microsoft Word's file format can make it difficult for an import operation to succeed. You can improve matters by disabling Word's fast save feature:

1. Choose Tools, Options to get the Options dialog box shown in Figure 14.4.

FIGURE 14.4
You can adjust details of how Word saves documents, thus improving other word processors' chances of successfully importing files.

2. Click the Save tab.

3. Uncheck the Allow Fast Saves option.

4. Click OK to activate your changes.

One effect of disabling fast saves, in addition to making it easier to import files in other programs, is to reduce the size of the Word files. In addition to disabling fast saves, you should ensure that you don't embed TrueType fonts or use a password on your files. You can change these options from the same Options dialog box and Save tab as you use to disable fast saves (refer to Figure 14.4).

Microsoft has changed the details of Word's file format with each major release through Word 97. (Word 2000 uses a format that is mostly unchanged from Word 97's.) All these formats use `.doc` filename extensions. Unfortunately, Microsoft chose the `.doc` filename extension despite the fact that ASCII documentation files sometimes use the same extension, although this practice has become quite rare in the Windows world as a result of Word's popularity.

▶ To learn more about Microsoft Word, **see** Camarda's *Special Edition Using Microsoft Word 2000*, from Que.

Sun StarWriter   Sun, best known for its SunOS and Solaris UNIX OSs and its Java cross-platform language, also distributes the StarOffice suite (`http://www.sun.com/dot-com/staroffice.html`), which includes a word processor component known as StarWriter. This suite is available for Windows, OS/2, Linux, and Solaris. The package uses the same file formats across all platforms, making it a good choice for cross-platform work on those OSs. Unfortunately, as with Lotus WordPro, import/export filters for StarWriter in other programs are hard to come by, so if you decide to change to another word processor in the future, you might need to keep a copy of StarWriter to read your existing files, or convert all your existing files before you make the switch.

Unlike most of the other office suites, StarWriter is available free from Sun. Sun plans to make the program more network-centric in future versions, apparently with the goal of enabling users to use a small shell program while the program's core runs on a remote server. The current version (5.1a) is a traditional office suite that runs on desktop computers.

N O T E   StarOffice's user interface bears a close resemblance to that of Microsoft Office, so existing Microsoft Office users should have little trouble learning to use StarOffice. Despite this similarity and the presence of Microsoft Office import/export filters, however, the programs are unrelated and use different file formats. ▪

▶ To learn more about StarOffice, **see** Koch and Murray's *Special Edition Using StarOffice* from Que.

Part
V

Ch
14

Rich Text Format   *Rich Text Format (RTF)* is a word processor file format that is native to no word processor but is supported by the vast majority of them. RTF can therefore be useful as a means of exchanging data between word processors, even if the programs don't understand each others' formats. Unfortunately, RTF import/export is as imperfect, on average, as import/export of other formats—you might not achieve better results with RTF than you would with other formats. RTF files generally have `.rtf` extensions.

TIP   If you want to exchange files between word processors, try saving the file in at least three formats: the original word processor's format, the destination word processor's format, and RTF. Chances are the destination program will be capable of reading at least one of these formats. For added security, add any other formats that are supported by both programs. Microsoft Word and Corel WordPerfect are two formats that are commonly supported.

Additional Word Processors   Most OSs claim several native word processors. Most of these have file formats that are usable only on one platform, although these programs can often read and write other word processors' files, with the usual caveats concerning the limitations of such file imports and exports. A few programs are available on multiple platforms, though, in which case you can usually use the same files on several OSs. The now-defunct DeScribe word processor, for example, was available on both Windows and OS/2, so it could be used in a cross-platform manner.

Platform-Limited File Formats for Graphics, Spreadsheets, and Databases

Platform-limited file formats for graphics, spreadsheets, and databases are mostly limited to office suites, such as SmartSuite and StarOffice. These programs often contain modules to support graphics, spreadsheets, and databases, and to the extent that these software packages are cross-platform, so are their file formats.

As with word processing, Microsoft Excel is something of a *de facto* standard, as is the Lotus 1-2-3 spreadsheet. Import/export filters for these formats are therefore common in both spreadsheets and databases, even on platforms that aren't supported by the originating software itself. As with word processor import/export filters, however, spreadsheet import/export filters often fail to handle the subtler points of the spreadsheet and might in fact completely drop important features. You should therefore be cautious when using such a filter, especially because the damage to the file might not be immediately obvious.

Business-oriented databases are often written with a cross-platform networking environment in mind. The idea is to run the core database functionality on a robust server OS such as some form of UNIX, OS/2, or Windows NT, while running client access programs on separate Windows 9x or NT computers. Databases such as IBM's DB2 (`http://www-4.ibm.com/software/data/db2/`) and Oracle (`http://www.oracle.com`) are available for a variety of clients and servers.

Platform-Specific File Formats

Fortunately, truly platform-specific file formats are rare, although in practice, limitations on imports and exports might make platform-limited formats little better than platform-specific formats. For example, the component applications of Microsoft Office are available only on Windows (on x86 hardware; there is a Macintosh version of Office). Because file imports and exports are invariably imperfect, using a non-Microsoft program to create Microsoft Office files is a suboptimal solution at best. Transferring files back and forth through import/export filters several times often adds to the problems on each transfer. Therefore, if your goal is to use two OSs to work with a file in an arbitrary manner, you should stick to platform-independent formats or formats for which native application support is available on both the OSs you want to use. Import/export filters are often useful for one-time conversions—for example, to read a document that a colleague has attached to an email message or to send a document to a colleague when you use an unusual program that your colleague does not have.

Platform-Specific File Formats for Text, Spreadsheets, and Databases

Platform-specific text, spreadsheet, and database file formats are mostly those for the more obscure programs in their categories—programs such as Sundial's ClearLook word processor for OS/2 (http://www.sundialsystems.com) or Greytrout's NeXS spreadsheet for UNIX (http://www.greytrout.com/). Of course, if you want to use such a program, there is nothing wrong with doing so, but if you expect to exchange files with other programs, you won't be able to use the program's native format. It is therefore important that you research the program's import/export filters carefully. Ideally, try to get a demo version that has these filters enabled to see whether they work adequately for you. Failing that, it is possible you'll be able to contact a helpful current user of the program who might be willing to import or export a few files for you to check the results.

Platform-Specific File Formats for Graphics

Most OSs have their own file formats for graphics, if only for desktop icons. There is seldom much call to convert these files from one OS to another, but utilities to do so nonetheless often exist. Check the Web and FTP sites for your OSs to search for such utilities. Searching on words such as *icon*, *bitmap*, and *conversion* or variants might turn up useful utilities.

 TIP

If you want to use an icon from one OS in another and can't find another way to transfer it, consider using a screen capture program to grab all or part of a display that contains the icon you want. Save the file in some convenient cross-platform format, such as PNG. When you boot into the target OS, use its graphics and icon manipulation tools to create an appropriate icon file. Note that many icons include transparent bits, through which you see whatever color or pattern lies below the icon. The transparent bits are usually lost in transfers like this, so you might need to restore them manually.

A few graphics applications exist that use proprietary formats, and these formats are often single-platform in nature. In the case of bitmapped graphics, you can almost always use a platform-independent format to transfer files between such applications and those on other OSs. Vector graphics are often harder to transfer, unfortunately. If you don't need to edit the file after moving it to another OS, EPS can make a suitable intermediary format. For example, if you use the OS/2 PM Draw program to create an image you want to include in a document you're preparing on a UNIX system, you can use EPS as a go-between format. EPS does have the drawback, however, that it often works only when the output device is a PostScript printer. If this isn't an acceptable situation, you might be able to locate some other format that is common to the two applications and use it instead.

Platform-Specific File Formats for Archives

Most common archive file formats cross all platform lines. There is, however, one common archive format that is platform specific: the Windows CAB file. This file format is used by Microsoft for distributing its own software, and many other Windows software houses have adopted the same format, either in plain `.cab` file format or using a self-extracting version in `.exe` files. The use of this file format has the unfortunate consequence of locking users of non-Windows OSs out of access to the archives' contents. Fortunately, this format is used almost exclusively for the distribution of Windows program files, so there is relatively little need for non-Windows users to access these files—a fact that might account for the dearth of non-Windows CAB file access utilities.

On rare occasions, you might want to access a CAB file from a non-Windows OS in order to extract files that were damaged in your main installation, or to gain access to files that you might be able to use in a cross-platform environment, such as font files. In such a case, you should probably either boot to Windows or use an emulator to run a suitable Windows extraction utility.

▶ To learn more about running Windows programs in an emulator, **see** Chapter 18, "OSs Within OSs: Emulators."

Summary

Most applications produce data files, and these files take different formats depending on the application's type, details of the features supported by the program, and the design decisions made by the application's programmers. Some data types are widely supported in most or all OSs, whereas others have limited or no cross-platform support. As a user of a multi-OS computer, you should give serious consideration to the portability of the data file formats for your major applications. Even if you intend to do most of your work in one OS, portability to other OSs might be important if you need to exchange your files with co-workers or if there is a chance you might change your primary OS in the future.

File import/export features and conversion utilities can help ease the pain of using platform-limited file formats, but only to a point. Such utilities are invariably imperfect, and so are best applied to one-time conversions, as when you need to read a document you find on the Web or that has been sent to you by a colleague who uses an OS or software package that is not of your choosing. I recommend against using import/export features to move a document back and forth repeatedly between two or more applications. If you find the need to work on the same document in multiple OSs, instead consider using a cross-platform program or an emulator. ●

Common Configurations and Tools

Cross-Platform Utilities

Making It All Work Together

This chapter and the next are devoted to the topic of using the same (or at least compatible) software natively on two or more OSs. The idea is that using the same tools recompiled for all your OSs can make you more productive by enabling you to share files and use programs with a common user interface across OSs. This common user interface can also reduce the amount of time it takes to learn a new OS if you already use such cross-platform tools on your present OS. Therefore, I recommend using cross-platform tools even when you don't need to do so; choosing the more widely available tool might pay off in the future, if you decide to expand your stable of OSs further or replace an older OS with a newer one.

Many of the cross-platform tools I describe in this chapter are distributed as open source, which means you can pass the programs on to others and modify them as you see fit, provided you possess the necessary programming know-how. It is this very characteristic that has led to these tools' availability on so many platforms; programmers who learn the tools and then develop an interest in a new OS naturally try to port the tools with which they're familiar.

In this chapter, I've classified cross-platform utilities into three categories: GNU utilities, non-GNU open source tools, and standards-based tools. The first two categories include programs that are available on multiple platforms; they're based on the same source code so they behave identically on all platforms, except for changes needed to get the software to run on different OSs. The third category includes tools and features that might be based on unique source code for each platform, but which nonetheless provide a high degree of interoperability. To some extent the placement of a tool in one category or another is a judgment call. For example, alternative implementations of both the major tools I discuss in the non-GNU open source category exist, so those tools could be listed under the standards-based category.

The GNU Utilities

The *Free Software Foundation* (*FSF*; http://www.fsf.org) has long been a leader in the open source community, even well before the term *open source* was coined. (In fact, the FSF's founder, Richard Stallman, doesn't like the term *open source*; he prefers *free software*.) The FSF is best known for a project to develop a complete and freely redistributable UNIX-like OS. This project is known as *GNU*, which is a recursive acronym for *GNU's Not UNIX*, and the OS that is the goal of this project is known as the Hurd (http://www.gnu.org/software/hurd/). Many of the programs developed by the FSF bear the *GNU* label, as do a few that aren't closely associated with the FSF.

The OSs to benefit most from the FSF are the open source UNIX clones, and particularly Linux and Hurd. In fact, typical Linux distributions use so much GNU software that many people refer to the OS as *GNU/Linux* rather than *Linux*. This practice is particularly common in reference to the Debian (http://www.debian.org) distribution. Still, UNIX-like OSs aren't the only ones to benefit from GNU tools. Many of the more popular GNU tools have been ported to all but the most obscure OSs. You can find Emacs, the GNU C Compiler (GCC), and others on Microsoft OSs, OS/2, and BeOS. To the extent that you need such utilities, therefore, you can make your life easier by using the GNU utilities on all your OSs.

How to Get GNU Programs

The Web site `http://www.gnu.org/order/ftp.html` contains information on obtaining GNU software from FTP sites—both the official GNU FTP site and various mirror sites located around the globe. The software on this site comes in source code form, compressed as tarballs. This fact presents a chicken-and-egg dilemma: Without access to certain GNU tools, such as tar, gzip, and GCC, you can't use any other GNU software. Fortunately, precompiled binary forms of most GNU tools are available from other sources. Some that are worth investigating include

- `http://www.cygnus.com`—Cygnus is a company that sells packages that include both GNU tools and extensions to them. Of most importance for this discussion, Cygnus' Cygwin product contains ports of a wide variety of GNU tools to Windows. Although Cygnus sells its packages, you can obtain its ports of the GNU tools free from various sources, including `http://www.cnet.com`.

- `ftp://ftp-os2.cdrom.com/pub/os2/unix`—Many OS/2 FTP sites include ports of GNU utilities, generally in a `unix` directory.

- `http://www.be.com/software/beware/`—The BeOS software clearinghouse. Enter `gnu` into the Search BeWare field to locate GNU software for BeOS.

- **Linux distributions**—Linux distributions invariably ship with a large number of GNU utilities. You can often find updates at the distribution's main Web or FTP site.

- **Other UNIX versions**—Chances are you can find precompiled binaries of all the major GNU tools for your particular UNIX variant on an appropriate Web or FTP site or possibly even with the OS. The BSD versions ship with a large number of GNU tools, although for ideological reasons the BSD maintainers prefer to use tools that have different license terms than the FSF's GNU General Public License (GPL).

The CD-ROM that accompanies this book contains an assortment of GNU tools for Windows, OS/2, and BeOS. Each OS has its own subdirectory under 3rd Party, and a GNU directory under that, when applicable. In the case of Windows, most of the tools are in the `full.exe` file, which contains the entire set of Cygwin tools. The tools for OS/2 and BeOS appear in separate archive files.

Using GNU Shells for Common Command Prompts

In computer parlance, and particularly in the UNIX world, a *shell* is a program that accepts simple commands and that launches other programs. Shells are also known by terms such as *command-line interfaces (CLIs)* and *command prompts*. All PC OSs come with at least one shell, but the shells used by DOS, Windows, and OS/2 use commands that are somewhat different from the commands used by typical UNIX shells. Table 15.1 lists some of the more common shell commands used by both environments.

Table 15.1   Microsoft-Style and UNIX-Style Shell Commands

Command in Windows, OS/2, and DOS	Command in UNIX	Effect
CD	cd	Change to a new directory
COPY	cp	Copy a file
DEL	rm	Delete (remove) a file
DIR /W	ls	List files (compact)
DIR	ls -l	List files (verbose)
FORMAT	fdformat	Low-level formats a floppy disk
FORMAT	mkfs	Create a filesystem
MKDIR	mkdir	Create a directory
MORE	more or less	Display a text file one screen at a time
MOVE	mv	Move a file
RENAME	mv	Rename a file
RMDIR	rmdir	Delete a directory
TYPE	cat	Display a text file

Note: Windows, OS/2, and DOS commands are not case-sensitive, but UNIX commands are case-sensitive.

In DOS, Windows, and OS/2, most of the commands shown in Table 15.1 are built into the shell, but in UNIX systems most of the commands in Table 15.1 are external programs, which are typically located in the /bin directory. Therefore, a port of a UNIX shell to a non-UNIX OS also entails porting assorted additional small programs.

Several UNIX shells are in common use: bash, csh, tcsh, zsh, and others. Each has its own unique set of features, but each also supports a basic set of capabilities, which includes

- **Basic built-in commands**—Commands such as cd are handled by all shells.
- **Capability to run external commands and programs**—All shells can run programs such as ls and mv to perform more complex operations.

- **Pattern matching**—Shells can expand filenames using wildcards such as the familiar asterisk (*) to match any group of characters. UNIX shells contain much more powerful pattern matching capabilities, however, enabling you to match, for example, filenames that contain any number as their final character (`*[0-9]` accomplishes this particular task).

- **Shell scripting**—A *shell script* is a set of commands stored in a text file that the shell can run when you type its name. Shell scripts are similar to DOS and Windows batch (`.BAT`) files and OS/2 REXX (`.CMD`) files, but most UNIX shells sport much more complete scripting languages than the DOS/Windows batch file format supports.

BeOS comes with its own version of the bash shell, so you don't need to install anything special to use bash on BeOS. Most UNIX versions store information on the default shell in the `/etc/passwd` file. The system administrator can change this information by using the `usermod` command, as in `usermod -s /bin/tcsh rodsmith` to change `rodsmith`'s shell to `tcsh`.

If you spend most of your time with your OSs using a GUI environment, obtaining and using a common text-mode shell likely won't help you much. UNIX text-mode shells can be extremely powerful tools, however, in large part because of their scripting capabilities. Harnessing this power across platforms can be quite useful. In addition, if you use command prompts on different OSs, using the same command prompt on all your OSs can be convenient because you'll be less likely to mistakenly type a command for one OS when you're in another.

▶ To learn more about shell scripting, **see** Sriranga Veeraraghavan's *Sams Teach Yourself Shell Programming in 24 Hours*, published by Sams.

Using GNU File Utilities

The GNU project has produced a wide variety of tools that are helpful in working with text and other types of files. These tools include text viewing utilities, search tools, and so on. To the uninitiated, these tools have strange names and seem quite cryptic, but they are very useful, and learning the basics of their use can be helpful when you work in a multi-OS environment.

N O T E Because of time and space constraints, I can only present the barest overview of these utilities in this chapter. Consult the UNIX man pages or the documentation that comes with your OS's version of the programs for more details on how to use these tools, including the options they take to modify their behavior. ■

Using *cat* to Merge Files The `cat` utility, which takes its name from the second syllable of the word *concatenate*, is the method UNIX uses to merge files together. The command takes one or more specified files and sends them both to *standard output*—that is, to the screen. Used in this way, `cat` is similar to the TYPE command in DOS, Windows, or OS/2. You can, however, redirect cat's output to a file by using the redirection operator (>). Used in this way, you can merge two or more files together. For example, the following merges file1.txt and file2.txt into bigfile.txt:

```
cat file1.txt file2.txt > bigfile.txt
```

When you use cat in this way, be sure to remember the redirection operator (>), or else you'll end up seeing the files scroll by on your screen!

cat has various options that let it modify the files as it concatenates them. For example, -b and -n number the lines (-b doesn't number blank lines, -n does) and -s reduces a series of blank lines to one blank line. You can learn more about cat's options in the cat man page on a UNIX system or in its documentation files on a non-UNIX system.

Using *diff* to Find Differences   The diff command compares two files and reports on differences between them. In the case of binary files, the program merely reports whether it finds a difference. In the case of text files, diff describes the differences in detail. (For either file type, if diff doesn't produce any output, it means that the files are identical.) As an example, here is the diff output from files that varied on just one line:

```
$ diff file1 file2
14c14
< vary depending upon the newsgroup.
---
> vary depending on the newsgroup.
```

Lines beginning with the less-than symbol (<) were present in the first file, whereas those that begin with the greater-than symbol (>) are their replacements in the second file. In the preceding example, only one line was changed, and in it only one word changed—*upon* was changed to *on*.

The details of diff's output usually aren't used by a human, except to tell whether files differ at all. Instead, diff's output can be redirected to a file and then used by the patch utility to alter the original file into the new file. The idea is that this procedure can be used to distribute a small file (a *diff file* or *patch file*) to enable people to update source code when changes to the program come out. For example, suppose you've written a 10,000-line program but find a bug that requires changing a dozen lines. Rather than distributing the entire 10,000-line program to every current user, you can distribute a patch file, which would probably be only a couple dozen lines in length.

Even if you're not a programmer, though, diff can be very helpful in finding files that differ from one another. For example, suppose you're having problems with a program, and you suspect that the program file has become corrupt. If you have access to a known "clean" version of the program, you can use diff on the two versions of the program file and any support files until you find the damaged file and then replace only that one file. You might also use diff on text files to quickly locate changes between drafts or to determine which version is more recent.

NOTE You can't normally use diff to find specific changes in text file formats that include non-ASCII characters, such as most word processors' files. diff interprets such files as binary in nature, and only reports that there are differences, not what they are in detail. A few word processor file formats, however, use only ASCII characters, so diff can be used on these files. AppWare is one such program. You can also export two files to RTF format and use diff on the RTF files, although diff might pick up on uninteresting nontextual differences in this case. Some word processors include revision tracking features that can help you locate differences between two versions of a document. ■

Using *find* to Locate Files Most OSs include some sort of file-finding utility, often wrapped inside a GUI shell. For example, Figure 15.1 shows the Find utility in Windows 98, which you can activate by choosing Find, Files or Folders from the Windows Start menu.

FIGURE 15.1
Many OSs include GUI file-finding utilities.

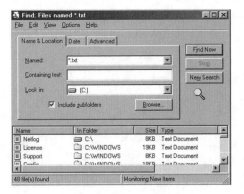

The GNU find program performs much the same function as GUI-based utilities that come with many OSs, but GNU find is more flexible than most. You can search for files by name, date, size, owner, permissions, and so on (some of these options apply only on UNIX-like systems). The basic format of the find command is

```
find [path] [expressions]
```

The *path* is one or more directory names in which you want to search, and the *expressions* are the means used to control the search. Typically, an expression includes a keyword preceded by a dash (-) and followed by the relevant data. The following is an example:

```
find ./ -name "*.txt" -maxdepth 2 -amin -60
```

This command searches for all files that end in .txt (-name "*.txt") that exist in the current directory or one directory level down but no farther (the start location of ./ in conjunction with the -maxdepth 2 expression), and that have been accessed in the last hour (-amin -60).

TIP   UNIX shells expand wildcards prior to passing parameters to programs. Therefore, using wildcards in the -name specification often fails unless you enclose the wildcarded filename in quotes—the quotes override the normal filename expansion rules.

Using *grep* to Locate Text in Files   One of the most useful GNU text utilities is grep. This program with the strange sounding name searches through the contents of files to locate strings that you specify. You can use this tool to locate a file when you don't remember which file contains the information you want. For example, suppose you're confronted with an old directory structure from the days when you used DOS. You want to find a specific file that you know contains information you now want to retrieve. Unfortunately, the 500 filenames in the data directory all resemble BGLTR2AB.TXT, which provides no clue about the files' contents. If you can remember some word or phrase that is likely to appear in the file you want to find but few or no others, you can use grep to search through all the files and return information on those files that contain the searched-for string. For example, suppose your target file was a letter to the BigDish Cable Company. You could use grep in this way:

```
grep BigDish *
```

The result might look something like this:

```
BDCCLTR1.TXT: BigDish Cable Company
BDCCLTR1.TXT: when the BigDish installer arrived.
BDCCLTR2.TXT: BigDish Cable Company
JBLTR12.TXT: experience with the BigDish Cable Company, which did
                strange things to
Binary file BDGT1992.XLS matches
```

These results show that the string *BigDish* appears in four files. The first file contains two instances of the target string, whereas the second and third each contain one. Each of the first three files is an ordinary ASCII text file, and grep quotes the lines that contain the search string, so you can get some idea of the context. Based on that context and the DOS-style filenames, it is safe to say that the first two files are letters to the BigDish Cable Company itself, whereas the third is a letter to somebody else. The fourth file is a binary file. Like diff, grep doesn't attempt to display the context in which the searched-for string appears in a binary file, but grep does report the presence of the string in such files. The filename of the binary file (BDGT1992.XLS) seems to suggest that this is a spreadsheet file containing budget information for 1992. With this information, you should be able to locate the information for which you were looking quite quickly. If you were looking for the BigDish Cable Company's address, for example, either letter should contain it. You might also decide to do some housecleaning—do you really need your household budget spreadsheet from 1992?

grep has quite a few options that you can use to adjust its output. For example, you can use -n to display a line number along with every match or -r to perform a recursive search (that is, to locate every match within an entire directory tree, not just one directory). You should consult the grep documentation for more details.

Some possible uses for `grep` include

- Locating documents, as described earlier
- Finding a configuration file that adjusts some setting or option
- Quickly displaying information from a large text file

Using *less* to View Files   You might sometimes need to quickly display the contents of a file. For example, you might want to read a README file that comes with some software. For years, UNIX users have used a command called `more` to do this, and in fact `more` also comes with many non-UNIX OSs, including DOS, Windows, and OS/2. The `more` command displays a text file one screen at a time. Pressing the spacebar in `more` causes the program to scroll the text to display the next screen's worth of information.

Although `more` is a useful program, it can be improved. For example, `more` can scroll forward in a text file but not backward. In a twist of humor, the improved version of `more` is known as `less`. To use it, type `less` *filename*, where *filename* is the name of the file you want to read. Table 15.2 summarizes some of the commands you can issue when reading a text file with `less`.

Table 15.2   Commands Within *less*

Keystroke	Effect
j, Enter, or down arrow	Scrolls down one line
k or up arrow	Scrolls up one line
spacebar	Scrolls down one screen
Esc+V	Scrolls up one screen
< or g	Go to the start of the file
> or G	Go to the end of the file
*n*g	Go to line number *n* in the file
p*xx*	Go to a point *xx* percent into the file
/*searchtext*	Search forward for *searchtext*
/	Repeat last forward search
?*searchtext*	Search backward for *searchtext*
?	Repeat last backward search
N	Repeat last search, but in opposite direction
=	Display information about the current file
h	Display help screen
q or Q or ZZ	Exit from `less`

`less` is an extremely useful utility for reading documentation files and any other ASCII text files that you might want to read. It is often easier to use `less` than to load the file into an editor, and there is no chance that you'll accidentally alter the text file with less, as might occur with a text editor. Some UNIX-style OSs use less for displaying man pages, so even if you prefer to use an editor for reading ASCII files, it is helpful to learn a bit about less when you use such an OS.

Using *tar* and *gzip* for File Archiving

As mentioned in Chapter 14, "Application Data File Formats," the usual file archiving format on UNIX systems is a *tarball*, formed by archiving files with the tar utility and then compressing these files with gzip or compress. A tarball typically uses a filename extension of .tgz, .tar.gz, or .tar.Z (the older UNIX compress utility uses a .Z extension, whereas the newer GNU gzip utility uses the .gz extension).

▶ To learn more about cross-platform archive file formats, **see** "Platform-Independent File Formats for Archives," **p. 366**.

tar is available in both non-GNU and GNU varieties. Some details differ, but for the most part, the two produce compatible archives and use similar commands. gzip is a GNU product, designed as a replacement for compress, which ships with many commercial UNIX versions. You can use gzip to extract compress .Z archives, but when you use gzip to compress a file, the result is a .gz archive that compress cannot handle. Most open source UNIX variants use gzip exclusively.

All these tools are available on platforms other than UNIX versions, which means you can use them to transfer files across platforms. The following are two strengths to this approach, as opposed to using formats such as the zip format that is popular on Microsoft-style OSs:

- The tar utility was originally designed to back up information to magnetic tapes, and in fact it still makes a serviceable tape backup utility. You can therefore use tar to write directly to magnetic tape, floppy disk, or other media to transport files from one computer to another. If you use a .zip archive, you must place it on a disk with a filesystem, which your target OS might not support.

- It is possible to take a tarball or .tar file created on a UNIX system and use the Windows port of mkisofs or mkhybrid (http://www.ps.ucl.ac.uk/~jcpearso/mkhybrid.html) to create a CD-R with Rock Ridge extensions that preserves the UNIX ownership and permission information. This capability can be useful if you want to create a CD with the contents of an FTP site for use on a UNIX system but must burn the CD on a Windows machine—you can use the ability of many FTP servers to send data in .tar format and then create the CD from the .tar file.

▶ To learn more about Rock Ridge extensions, **see** "Rock Ridge Extensions to ISO-9660," **p. 324**.

Tables 15.3 and 15.4 summarize some of the more useful options of tar. You must use precisely one of the parameters listed in Table 15.3, and you may use any number of the options listed in Table 15.4. You can combine two or more single-character `tar` parameters in a string, as in `tar -cv` to create a `.tar` file with the verbose option enabled. If you need to use more than one option that requires its own parameter, you might need to use the long form of the option; but for just one parameter, you can use the short form, as in `tar -cvf test.tar`. With the GNU version of `tar`, you can omit the leading dash (-) in single-character commands, but some non-GNU versions of tar require this character in all cases.

CAUTION

The options to `tar` are case-sensitive! Some letters do double duty, having a different function in uppercase than in lowercase, so getting the case wrong can produce unexpected results.

Table 15.3   Required *tar* Parameters

Parameter	Meaning
-A or --concatenate or --catenate	Concatenate one .tar file to another .tar archive
-c or --create	Create a .tar archive
-d or --diff	Compare the contents of an archive to files on disk
--delete	Delete files from a .tar archive
-r or --append	Append files to an existing .tar archive
-t or --list	List the contents of a .tar archive
-u or --update	Append files from disk that are newer than their equivalents in an existing .tar archive
-x or --extract	Extract files from a .tar archive

Exactly one of the parameters from this table is required when using tar.

Table 15.4   Optional *tar* Parameters

Parameter	Meaning
-f *filename* or --file *filename*	Use the .tar file *filename*. If you omit this parameter, many systems use the tape backup device by default.
-h or --dereference	Store symbolic links as the files to which they point.
--ignore-failed-read	Keep going even if a file can't be read.
-k or --keep-old-files	Don't overwrite existing files with those from an archive.
-l or --one-file-system	Create an archive only from files on a single filesystem.
-M or --multi-volume	Operate on multi-file .tar archives.

continues

Table 15.4   Continued

Parameter	Meaning
-p or --same-permissions or --preserve-permissions	Preserve all UNIX permissions information.
-P or --absolute-paths	Don't strip the leading / from pathnames.
-T filename or --files-from filename	Obtain list of files from filename.
-v or --verbose	List all files as they're processed.
-W or --verify	Verify files after performing operation.
--exclude file	Exclude file from operation.
-X filename or --exclude-from filename	Exclude files listed in filename from operation.
-Z or --compress or --uncompress	Apply UNIX compress program to archive.
-z or --gzip or --ungzip	Apply GNU gzip program to archive.

On the Windows OSs, you might find it more convenient to use a Windows GUI tool for handling tarballs. Many of the tools that create and manipulate zip archives can also process tarballs, so for casual use, these tools can be very helpful when extracting tarballs.

> **CAUTION**
>
> Don't use any tar utility under Windows to extract files that will ultimately be used in a UNIX-style OS. The Windows tools and filesystems can't handle UNIX-style ownership and permissions, and these features might be critically important to the ultimate use of the files under UNIX. If the contents of the tarball are cross platform (documentation or graphics files, say), there should be no problems. You might also want to extract files from a UNIX tarball to read the package's documentation. Just be sure to extract the files under UNIX and to a UNIX filesystem before you try to use the files.

Developing Software with GNU Compilers and Debuggers

One of the first projects undertaken by the FSF was the development of a C compiler, which came to be known as the *GNU C Compiler* or the *GNU Compiler Collection* (*GCC*; http://www.fsf.org/software/gcc/gcc.html). This compiler has been used as a model for additional compilers, including *GNU Pascal* (http://agnes.dida.physik.uni-essen.de/ ~gnu-pascal/), FORTRAN (now included as part of GCC), and others. Because C and C++ are the languages of choice for so many programmers, I focus on these languages, but you might be able to use other GNU compilers for specific cross-platform purposes.

NOTE I cannot even begin to teach programming in this book. For an introduction to C programming, Stephen Prata's *Waite Group's C Primer Plus, Third Edition*, from Sams, is a good starting point. C was originally defined in Brian W. Kernighan's *The C Programming Language*, from Prentice-Hall. ■

Obtaining GCC for Your OSs   Open-source UNIX variants such as Linux and the BSDs rely on GCC quite heavily. These OSs typically include GCC and associated tools such as gdb (`http://www.fsf.org/software/gdb/gdb.html`), the GNU debugger. For other platforms, you might need to look elsewhere:

- **DOS**—A port of GCC to DOS is available under the name DJGPP (`http://www.delorie.com/djgpp/`). Because GCC was designed for 32-bit or wider systems, this port creates only 32-bit DOS binaries that require DOS extenders (included with the package) to run.

- **Windows**—Cygnus (`http://www.cygnus.com`) has ported GCC to Windows. This port is the bulk of the `full.exe` self-extracting archive file included on this book's companion CD.

- **OS/2**—Eberhard Mattes ported GCC to OS/2 and named the resulting package after himself (EMX). This port of GCC can also be used to create 32-bit DOS executables; in fact, for non-GUI programs, the same executable can run under both DOS and OS/2. EMX is available from `ftp://ftp-os2.nmsu.edu/pub/os2/dev/emx/`, among other OS/2 FTP sites.

- **BeOS**—The Geek Gadgets project (`http://www.ninemoons.com/GG/index.html`) has ported many GNU utilities, including GCC, to BeOS. A binary version of GCC is included with the x86 version of BeOS. (In fact, BeOS was compiled with GCC.)

- **GCC extensions**—Assorted projects have sprung up over the years to extend GCC in various ways. The most influential of these has been EGCS, which was a fork of the GCC development tree to add major new features. EGCS and mainstream GCC are now in the process of merging together again. Many Linux distributions ship with EGCS instead of or in addition to GCC. Another popular GCC extension is PGCC, which provides better Pentium optimizations than does GCC. Information on various GCC extensions can be found at `http://egcs.cygnus.com/extensions.html`.

Many of these ports of GCC and associated tools appear on the CD that accompanies this book, so you can use these tools immediately.

GUI GCC Front Ends   GCC is a command-line compiler. That is, to compile a program, you issue a command such as

```
gcc -o myprog myprog.c
```

This command compiles the source code file `myprog.c` into the executable file `myprog`. (On DOS, Windows, and OS/2 platforms, you would probably call the executable file `myprog.exe`.) Developers of more complex programs, which span several source code files, typically use the `make` utility to ease the program-building process. `make` uses a special file, typically called

`Makefile`, to tell the system which files to compile into the final executable and which files depend on which other files. That way, if you change just one source code file, `make` determines precisely which files need to be recompiled. The next time you run `make`, it recompiles those files that need recompiling, in addition to the files you changed.

Many commercial development environments, particularly for Windows, provide a GUI front end to this process. The front end, often called an *Integrated Development Environment* (*IDE*; not to be confused with the type of hard disk), takes over the functionality of `make` and provides a user-friendly face to the development process. Various IDEs are available that work around GCC; Figure 15.2 shows one of them, Code Crusader.

FIGURE 15.2

An IDE provides a programming-oriented editor, a list of files in a project, and other features helpful to programmers.

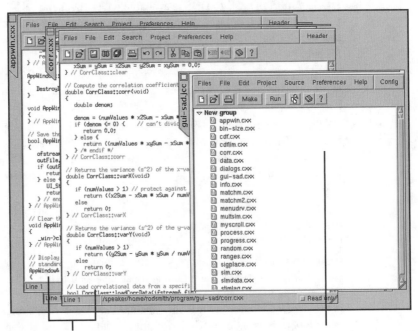

Editor window provides color coding according to the programming language's rules

Project control window provides listing of included source code files

Most of these IDEs are available for UNIX systems. These IDEs include

■ **Metrowerks CodeWarrior GNU Edition for Linux**
(`http://www.metrowerks.com/desktop/linux/`)—Metrowerks, which produces its own Windows and MacOS compilers, has entered the Linux arena. Its initial entry wraps the Metrowerks IDE around GCC. Metrowerks CodeWarrior is commercial software. Another version uses the same IDE along with the Metrowerks C compiler.

■ **Code Crusader** (`http://www.newplanetsoftware.com/jcc/`)—This is an open source IDE for UNIX-like OSs modeled loosely on CodeWarrior.

■ **Cygnus Code Fusion** (`http://www.cygnus.com/codefusion/index.html`)—This is another commercial IDE for Linux, built around GNU tools.

Using Cross-Platform Libraries   One of the keys to GCC's cross-platform utility lies in the UNIX compatibility libraries that each port provides. Every OS provides a set of *Application Programming Interfaces (APIs)*, which are "hooks" provided by the OS for the benefit of programmers. For example, an OS provides APIs for tasks such as opening files, placing text onscreen, and so on. Ports of GCC to non-UNIX environments usually include a set of compatibility libraries that provide UNIX-like APIs within the host OS. The upshot of this fact is that it is easier to port UNIX programs to a new OS using GCC than it is with most other compilers.

N O T E   Although ports of GCC to non-UNIX OSs include UNIX compatibility libraries, they usually also provide full access to the underlying OS's APIs, so you can create OS-specific programs using these compilers. ■

When a program has been compiled with GCC, the program usually relies on a set of libraries—both the compatibility libraries for non-UNIX OSs and a set of C libraries (generally called *libc* on UNIX systems). Therefore, even if you don't program in C yourself, you might find yourself installing these support libraries. In fact, EMX is so popular on OS/2 that even many OS/2-only programs rely on the EMX libraries. In general, when you're faced with two programs that require different versions of a particular library, you should install the more recent version of the library.

The basic cross-platform libraries that come with GCC don't help when it comes to porting GUI applications. Each OS's GUI API is unique and quite complex. If you want to develop a cross-platform GUI program, you have several choices:

■ Isolate the GUI code and write it anew for each platform you want to support. This approach is manageable when the bulk of the program lies in underlying non-GUI tasks, such as scientific or engineering simulations that use a GUI only for accepting input values and displaying output. This approach becomes difficult for more interactive programs such as word processors or graphics packages.

■ Use a GUI emulator package. OS/2 4.0 and above includes a set of libraries that implements a large part of the Windows GUI API, for example, so you can reuse a great deal of Windows code in OS/2. Similarly, you can use an X Window System server on most platforms to recompile UNIX X-based programs on non-UNIX OSs.

  ▶ To learn more about using X, **see** "The X Window System: The Chameleon of GUIs," **p. 439**.

■ Use a cross-platform GUI library as a sort of meta-API. Tools such as TCL/TK (`http://www.neosoft.com/tcl/default.html`), YACL (`http://www.cs.sc.edu/~sridhar/yacl/`), Qt (`http://www.troll.no/`), and Java (`http://www.sun.com/products-n-solutions/software/oe-platforms/java2.html`) can be used to produce cross-platform GUI applications using a common code base.

If you want to engage in cross-platform programming, it is important that you carefully evaluate your needs and available options. A huge number of tools are available, and a poor choice can make your task difficult or impossible. I can't provide anything approaching comprehensive information on the available cross-platform tools in this book. Instead, I advise you to consider your options with reference to the following factors:

- **The nature of your project**—A text-only utility is easy to write, even using different compilers on different OSs. Sometimes a cross-platform text-formatting library, such as curses, can be helpful. For a GUI project, you should look into more sophisticated cross-platform tools.

- **Your language of choice**—A plethora of cross-platform tools exist for common languages such as C. Others, such as Java, are cross-platform by design. If you want to use a more obscure language, you might have a hard time finding cross-platform tools for it.

- **Speed requirements**—Cross-platform GUI libraries often rob your application of speed, but the extent to which this is true varies substantially. Qt, for example, is fairly speedy as such tools go.

- **Access to OS-centric features**—If you want to integrate your application into each OS, plan to spend more time on OS-specific features. For example, you might want your application to integrate well into the OS/2 WorkPlace Shell (WPS) when run on that platform. Such code won't be portable to other OSs. If such integration is important, be sure your chosen cross-platform solution enables you to access the OS-specific features in a convenient way.

- **Future expandability**—Even if you need support for only a couple of OSs now, you might want to add support for others in the future. Therefore, you might want to use tools that support more than your current favored OSs.

Editing Text with GNU Emacs

Along with GCC, perhaps one of the best-known and most-used GNU programs is GNU Emacs. Emacs began life as an editor but has grown to be much more. Today, Emacs includes a LISP language interpreter, email and Usenet news clients, programming tools, and more. Emacs provides so much functionality, in fact, that a standard quip is that Emacs is the OS, and UNIX is just a loader for Emacs! (Substitute whatever OS you run for UNIX, if necessary.)

Depending on the platform and the version of Emacs being run, the program might show a very plain text-mode appearance or a relatively complex GUI screen. Figure 15.3 shows Emacs running on Windows NT in GUI mode.

FIGURE 15.3
Emacs is extremely flexible, although it is not as pretty as other editors.

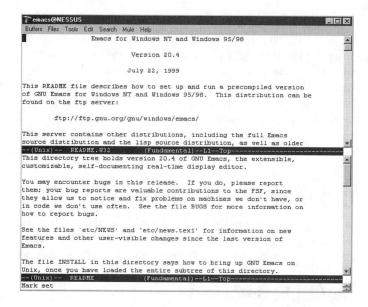

Emacs is an extremely complex and highly configurable text editor. Its default configuration relies heavily on certain *meta* keys—Esc, Alt, and Ctrl, primarily. Emacs commands combine meta keys with ordinary keystrokes, often in pairs. For example, Ctrl+X, Ctrl+F (that is, press Ctrl+X followed by Ctrl+F) is the command to open (find) a file. Some particularly important Emacs commands for newcomers to the program include those listed in Table 15.5. Don't for a moment think that Table 15.5 is a comprehensive list of Emacs commands, though; Emacs has so many commands that attempting to list them all here would be a futile exercise. To learn more about Emacs, I suggest you begin with the tutorial you get by pressing Ctrl+H, t while in Emacs.

Table 15.5   Helpful Emacs Commands

Keystroke	Action
Ctrl+G	Abort operation
Ctrl+H, t	Start a tutorial
Ctrl+H, f	Display an Emacs FAQ
Ctrl+X, Ctrl+C	Exit from Emacs
Ctrl+X, Ctrl+F	Load (find) a file
Ctrl+X, Ctrl+S	Save the current file
Ctrl+X, Ctrl+W	Save the file under a new filename
Ctrl+X, i	Insert a file into the current file
Esc, <	Move to start of file
Esc, >	Move to end of file

Many Emacs variants have emerged over the years. If you use a UNIX system and like GUI-based editors, one that deserves special comment is XEmacs (http://www.xemacs.org), which closely resembles ordinary Emacs but contains better integration into the X GUI environment. A few XEmacs commands differ from their Emacs counterparts, however. On all platforms, many smaller programs have modeled themselves after Emacs to a greater or lesser extent, and some even include *Emacs* in their own names, such as Micro Emacs. In general, these editors copy many of the more common Emacs keystrokes and features but consume less memory and disk space and don't reproduce Emacs' more complex and esoteric features. Two particularly common small Emacs variants are jove and jed.

Non-GNU Open Source Tools

The FSF doesn't control open source development, although it has contributed many of the most basic tools for cross-platform programming and technical computer use. In this section I highlight a couple of the more useful cross-platform non-GNU open source tools.

The XFree86 GUI Environment

XFree86 (http://www.xfree86.org) is an implementation of the X Window System (*X* for short) for x86 computers. X is a windowing environment that is common on UNIX systems and less common on other platforms. Nonetheless, XFree86 is available for OS/2 and BeOS, and commercial X implementations are available for Windows (see http://www.hcl.com/products/nc/exceed/index.html, http://www.starnet.com/, and http://www.microimages.com/freestuf/mix/ for three).

X can be a useful cross-platform tool for several reasons:

- If you want to develop cross-platform applications, one way to accomplish this goal is to code for X rather than the platform-specific APIs. This solution has the drawback of using non-native GUI tools, however, and it requires that the user have X installed on the target platform, which isn't a trivial undertaking.

- If you find X to be a suitable GUI environment, you might be able to use it to the exclusion of the native GUI, thus providing a consistent look and feel across platforms. The problem with this procedure, however, is that native programs don't run under X, so you must switch back to the native GUI to run those programs.

- X is a networking GUI environment, meaning that you can use one computer to display programs that run on another. Therefore, if you have a home network, you can use a less-powerful computer to run programs on a more-powerful computer. As with using X full-time, however, X enables you to run only X programs remotely, not Windows, OS/2, or BeOS programs.

▶ To learn more about remote GUI access to various OSs, **see** "Remote GUI Control," **p. 493**.

Perhaps the most significant use of X is as a merger of these first two points. In particular, the presence of X on platforms such as OS/2 and BeOS means that these OSs can benefit from software development in the UNIX world. These OSs host ports of popular X-based software, such as the LyX word processor (http://www.lyx.org/) and the GNUPlot scientific data–plotting program (http://www.cs.dartmouth.edu/gnuplot_info.html) in large part because the presence of XFree86 on the host OSs makes porting the software much simpler than it otherwise would be. This fact can ease the transition from one OS to another because you can take some of your applications with you—at least, assuming you currently use at least some X-based programs.

Using InfoZip for File Archiving

The InfoZip program (http://www.cdrom.com/pub/infozip/) is a freeware utility for handling the popular zip file format for archives. Zip files are particularly popular in the DOS, Windows, OS/2, and BeOS worlds. The basic InfoZip tools, which go by the names zip and unzip, are text-mode utilities available on a wide variety of platforms. In addition, there is a GUI tool, known as WiZ, available for Windows from the same team that produces InfoZip itself, as shown in Figure 15.4. Assorted GUI front ends to the InfoZip tools are also available for OS/2, such as PM-Zip (a.k.a. ZipMeister; available from most OS/2 FTP sites and on this book's CD).

FIGURE 15.4
WiZ provides a point-and-click interface atop the InfoZip tools.

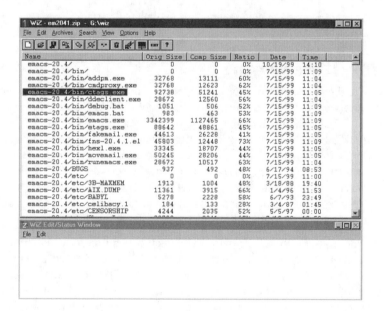

Both zip and unzip take the name of an archive and a list of files to be archived (the file list is optional in the case of unzip). For example, to archive all the files in the current directory, you might issue the following command:

```
zip somedir.zip *
```

The asterisk (*) wildcard character indicates that all the files are to be archived. (Details of how wildcard characters are interpreted varies from one OS to another, though; for example, you might need to use *.* in DOS.)

By default, unzip extracts any subdirectories stored in the archive, but zip doesn't store sub-directories. To store subdirectories using zip, you must include the -r switch, as in

```
zip -r somedir.zip *
```

If you want to see a list of files in an archive without actually extracting those files, you can use the -l switch to the unzip command, which displays the filenames without extracting the files.

Both zip and unzip sport a variety of additional options that affect their functions. If you type the utilities' names without any parameters, they respond with a list of options.

Standards-Based Tools and Protocols

Beyond the freely available software that has been ported to a variety of platforms, there are tools and protocols that are built on standards. In the case of a standards-based tool, the programs available might differ from one OS to another, but they're compatible across platforms because they create common file formats or intercommunicate across a network.

▶ To learn more about file formats used on multiple platforms, **see** Chapter 14, "Application Data File Formats."

Using TCP/IP Networking

One of the most commonly used standard protocols is that used on the Internet: the *Transmission Control Protocol/Internet Protocol (TCP/IP)*. Every modern OS includes support for TCP/IP, and there are even add-on packages to provide TCP/IP support for DOS. TCP/IP by itself is something like a telephone line without a telephone, though. At the top of every TCP/IP system lies a collection of programs, each of which can be classified as a *client* or a *server*. Server programs respond to requests for information, which are issued by clients. For example, when you browse the Web, you use a Web browser such as Netscape Navigator, which is a Web client program. Navigator sends a request for a Web page to a Web server, which responds by sending the Web page, as illustrated in Figure 15.5.

In order to work, this client/server architecture requires strict adherence to the protocols defined by TCP/IP, including the protocols used by specific top-level programs such as HTTP (for Web browsing), FTP (for file transfer), and SMTP (for mail transfer). The actual code used to implement both the lower levels of the TCP/IP stack and the specific clients and servers need not be shared by the machines that are communicating, however. In this way, a BeOS computer can exchange files with a Windows computer, although the two computers use TCP/IP stacks with little or no shared code.

FIGURE 15.5
TCP/IP networking is based on the principles of a client/server architecture.

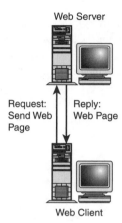

Web Server

Request:
Send Web
Page

Reply:
Web Page

Web Client

TCP/IP is of interest in a multi-OS configuration for two reasons:

- You can use several OSs to access the Internet using a single ISP, and you can exchange documents with remote users no matter what OS you use. For example, you can use email to send a document you created in StarOffice for Linux to a colleague who uses StarOffice for Windows. If you happen to be using OS/2 when your colleague sends back changes to that document, you can read the email in OS/2 and, if you have StarOffice for OS/2, use it to view the changes. The open standards used at every step of the way make it unimportant what OSs you and your colleague use.

- If you have a local area network (LAN), you can use TCP/IP networking protocols to provide a common networking environment across OSs. For example, you can use a *file server*—a computer that stores files for use by other computers—to provide common storage space for several OSs.

The details of how you configure and use TCP/IP networking vary substantially from one OS to another and from one network to another. You should therefore consult an appropriate reference for your OS to learn how to configure networking. After it is configured, you can use protocols such as FTP for file transfers, Telnet for remote logins, and assorted file- and printer-sharing protocols for making disk and printer resources on one computer available on others.

▶ To learn more about using networks, **see** Part VII, "Network Access."

Using TeX and LaTeX for Text Formatting

When you use a typical what-you-see-is-what-you-get (WYSIWYG) word processor, you issue keyboard or mouse commands to control the appearance of your text—you might type Ctrl+I to italicize text, for example. The word processor then displays the text more or less as it will appear on the printed page. (Early word processors often used substitute formatting, such as reverse video instead of italics, because of the lack of GUI environments and limited video display hardware capabilities of the day, but the principle was the same.)

TeX and LaTeX (pronounced *tek* and *lay-tek*, respectively), by contrast, are document-formatting systems that use explicit commands. Instead of typing Ctrl+I or selecting an *italics* menu item and then seeing your words appear in italics on the screen, you type \itshape to begin formatting text in italics. The string \itshape appears in your document as such, and you don't see the italics until you print your document. Because TeX and LaTeX operate on ordinary ASCII text, you can use any text editor you like to create TeX or LaTeX documents—you can use Emacs, vi, edit, or even a word processor such as Microsoft Word or Corel WordPerfect, provided you save the files as plain ASCII.

As an example, consider the following LaTeX file:

```
\documentclass{article}
\begin{document}
\Huge
Today (\today) is the first day of the rest of your life!
\end{document}
```

When this file is processed through an appropriate LaTeX program, it produces an output page similar to that shown in Figure 15.6. The first few lines tell LaTeX what type of document is to be created and how to format it (for example, \Huge specifies a huge font size). The text is processed more or less as shown, but \today is replaced by the current date, and LaTeX splits the text across lines as necessary. Depending on the document type chosen, LaTeX might add features such as the page number shown at the bottom of Figure 15.6. LaTeX is much like the Hypertext Markup Language (HTML) used on Web pages in principle, although not in the details. LaTeX is also generally used to produce documents printed on paper, whereas HTML documents are typically viewed with a Web browser.

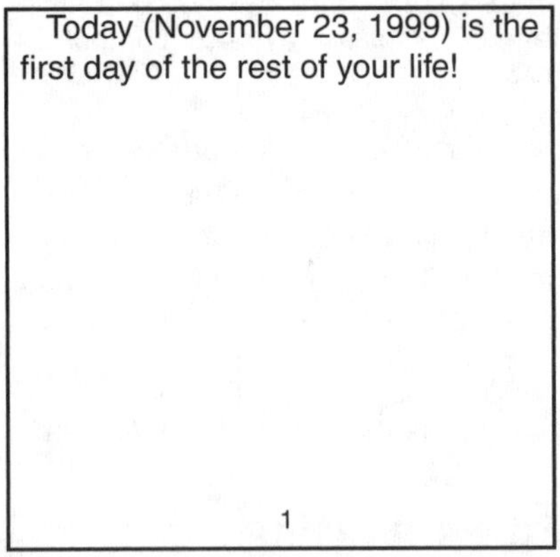

FIGURE 15.6
LaTeX output is high quality, but the file that produces the output isn't WYSIWYG.

> Today (November 23, 1999) is the first day of the rest of your life!
>
> 1

The original TeX is quite basic in its capabilities, so it is almost never used alone. Instead, packages that build on TeX are available. The most popular such package is known as LaTeX. LaTeX adds support for many document-oriented features such as headers and tables of contents. There are several independent implementations of TeX and LaTeX on various platforms, which is why I classify TeX and LaTeX as standards-based tools. This book's companion CD-ROM includes versions for several OSs, but not for UNIX—TeX and LaTeX ship with many UNIX versions, including most Linux distributions and the BSDs.

The idea behind TeX and LaTeX is that you, as a writer, should not have to be overly concerned with the minutiae of formatting. Instead of manually inserting blank lines, using tabs at the beginnings of paragraphs, and so on, you issue commands indicating what type of text you're entering. LaTeX then handles the formatting details, thus ensuring consistency within the document. If you later decide to alter the spacing between paragraphs, you can do so globally, without altering the text on a paragraph-by-paragraph basis. Many modern word processors offer similar functionality through the use of a *styles* feature, but LaTeX was designed from the beginning with this feature in mind, and in practice most word processor users underuse their software's capabilities in this respect.

LaTeX is particularly well-suited to writing large documents, especially those that contain complex formulas and equations. For this reason, LaTeX is popular in certain scientific fields in which publications contain many equations.

As a cross-platform tool, TeX and LaTeX are important as a document exchange format. A LaTeX file is plain ASCII, so it can be easily moved from one OS to another. If you find that you need to work on text documents in multiple OSs, LaTeX can be a good way to accomplish this goal. You might also want to investigate cross-platform word processors, though, particularly if you're more comfortable with the idea of a WYSIWYG word processor than with LaTeX's command-based approach to document creation.

Summary

Utility programs are quite useful in turning a so-so computing environment into a very good computing environment. By enabling you to search for files, edit files, develop programs, transport files, and so on, utilities help to fill in the gaps left by major application programs. In many cases, utilities are necessarily single platform—it makes no sense to run an OS/2 WPS maintenance utility on Windows, for example. In other cases, though, cross-platform utilities can help a multi-OS installation, both by providing cross-platform functionality (as in cross-platform file archiving tools) and by providing a common user interface across OSs, thus reducing the amount of time and effort it takes to learn multiple OSs. Although sometimes cryptic, the common availability of UNIX tools on most modern OSs makes them a good target for your attention. Learning how to use tools such as gzip, grep, and find can go a long way when you need to learn another OS—just install these tools on the new OS and you'll instantly become more productive. ●

Cross-Platform Applications

Applications or Utilities?

Chapter 15, "Cross-Platform Utilities," covered the use of cross-platform utilities to help create a consistent working environment across multiple OSs. Most people, though, don't often use the sorts of utilities discussed in Chapter 15. (Computer programmers and heavy users of LaTeX are exceptions to this rule.) Instead, most people make heavy use of *applications*—tools designed to do day-to-day work. In truth, the distinction between a utility and an application can be a difficult one to draw. Programming tools, Emacs, and LaTeX could all be considered applications as easily as they could be considered utilities, for example, and some of the programs I discuss in this chapter could be considered utilities. As a general rule, a utility is used to accomplish some task that is closely tied to the computer itself, whereas an application is used for broader purposes, such as writing letters or performing bookkeeping.

Fortunately, a variety of tools are available that can help you perform these day-to-day tasks in a multi-OS environment. If you're a typical computer user, you will be particularly interested in the cross-platform office applications, each of which runs on at least two common OSs. I also discuss the creation and reading of Adobe Acrobat files and the use of a variety of Internet applications, all of which can work alike across multiple OSs.

Office Suites

Over the years, one of the most popular uses for desktop computers has been as a general-purpose information tool for office workers. With a computer, you can write memos, letters, and reports; perform both simple and complex numerical analyses; retrieve information stored in databases; create images; and perform other tasks familiar to office workers of this and previous ages. It should therefore come as no surprise that the tools for performing these tasks have come to be bundled into *suites*, which are packages of related programs. In general, office suites include a word processor and a spreadsheet. All include other tools, such as a database or a graphics editor, but the details vary from one suite to another. The individual programs in a suite can generally integrate together fairly well, so that you can, for example, include a spreadsheet or graphics image into a word processor document. Many suites also include some sort of overarching control program that can be used to launch the suite's components, adjust configuration settings, and so on.

You can, of course, collect the components available in a suite from separate sources, and many of these separate components might be available across platforms. AbiWord (http://www.abisource.com), for example, is a word processor that runs on many platforms. At the moment, though, it is only a word processor and is not as sophisticated as many other programs I discuss here.

Some office suites, such as the popular Microsoft Office (http://www.microsoft.com), include all the requisite components I'll discuss here but aren't cross-platform. (At least, this is true for x86 hardware; a Macintosh version of Microsoft Office is available.)

Applixware

Applixware, from Applix (`http://www.applix.com`), is an office suite that was originally designed for UNIX systems. A Java version (Anywhere Office) is now available, which makes it usable in a multi-OS environment. Both the original Applixware and Anywhere Office include the following components:

- **Applix Words**—Word processor
- **Applix Spreadsheets**—Spreadsheet
- **Applix Graphics**—Graphics editor
- **Applix Mail**—Email client
- **Applix Presents**—Presentation program

UNIX versions of the program (including the Linux version) also include Applix Data, for accessing databases, and Applix Builder, which enables you to build custom applications. Data and Builder aren't currently available in the Java version of the program, unfortunately.

Most of the component programs in the Applixware suite aren't the most feature-laden examples of their classes, but they generally hold surprising power—the Applixware user interface appears simpler than one would expect for an application bearing the features the programs actually hold. Figure 16.1 shows Applix Words at work.

Part VI Ch 16

FIGURE 16.1
Component applications of Applixware include the usual features, such as button bars, rulers, and point-and-click formatting.

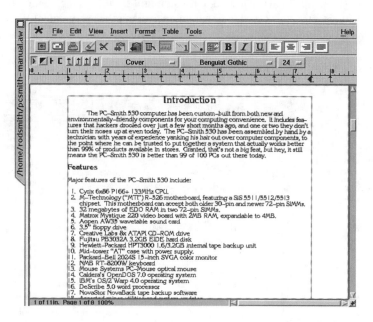

Overall, Applixware is an excellent choice for office productivity applications, particularly when you expect a large part of your work to be done in a UNIX OS for which a native binary version of the program is available. Applixware has an edge as an established program in the UNIX world.

Corel WordPerfect Office

Corel WordPerfect Office suite is, as of early 2000, available only for Windows. One of its most important components, however—the WordPerfect word processor—is available for several UNIX versions, including Linux. The rest of the suite is being ported to Linux and should be released sometime in 2000. Components of Corel's suite include

- **WordPerfect**—Word processor
- **Quattro Pro**—Spreadsheet
- **Presentations**—Presentation program
- **Central**—Personal information management
- **Trellix**—Web publishing

In the Office 2000 package, each of these components is at version 9.0 except for Trellix, which is at version 2.0. The stand-alone version of WordPerfect for UNIX and Linux is at version 8.0. You might still be able to find versions 7.0 and 6.1 of WordPerfect for Windows 3.1 and DOS, respectively, although development has halted for these platforms. WordPerfect 5.2 for OS/2 is much harder to find, but you might be able to locate it on the used market. (WordPerfect 5.2 for OS/2 is much buggier than other versions of WordPerfect, though, and I don't recommend that most people use it.) Versions of WordPerfect from 6.0 through 9.0 all use the same file format, so you can safely exchange documents across platforms and WordPerfect version numbers. Figure 16.2 shows WordPerfect 8.0 for Linux in operation.

FIGURE 16.2
Although the window and menu details differ, the general layout and available options of WordPerfect are the same across OSs.

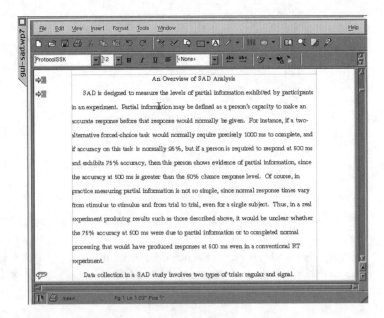

WordPerfect has long been regarded as one of the best tools available for writing long and text-intensive documents such as books, and WordPerfect's strengths in this area haven't diminished with time. The word processor is also unusually comprehensive; for example, it includes a simple graphics program and limited spreadsheet capabilities, even aside from the suite's tools. Although Quattro Pro was never as popular as the spreadsheets against which it competes, it is nonetheless a competent program.

N O T E To learn more about WordPerfect Office for Windows, see Trudi Reisner's *Special Edition Using Corel WordPerfect Office 2000*, published by Que. To learn more about WordPerfect for UNIX or Linux, see my *Special Edition Using Corel WordPerfect 8 for Linux*, also published by Que.

WordPerfect Office's main weakness in a multi-OS environment lies in its limited number of supported OSs. Even with the release of the full suite for Linux sometime in 2000, the suite will be available in its latest incarnation on only two platforms—Windows and Linux. If you use DOS, you can exchange word processing files with older DOS versions of the program, and versions for non-Linux variants of UNIX will continue to be available, but interoperability is limited with OS/2 and nonexistent with BeOS. Nonetheless, if your main interest is in Windows and Linux, WordPerfect Office is a good choice.

Lotus SmartSuite

Lotus produces an office suite package known as SmartSuite (`http://www.lotus.com/home.nsf/welcome/smartsuite`), which is available for both Windows and OS/2, although the OS/2 release lags behind the Windows release in terms of version number. On both platforms, SmartSuite includes the following major components:

- **Word Pro**—Word processor
- **1-2-3**—Spreadsheet
- **Approach**—Database
- **Organizer**—Schedule manager
- **Freelance**—Presentation graphics

Lotus 1-2-3 was one of the most important office applications of the late 1980s; it dominated the DOS spreadsheet market, and even today it is an excellent spreadsheet. Word Pro and the other SmartSuite programs are also good choices.

N O T E To learn more about Lotus SmartSuite, see Joe Habraken's *Using Lotus SmartSuite Millennium Edition*, published by Que. This book focuses on the Windows version of the program.

Compared to some of the other cross-platform options available, SmartSuite is limited primarily in its range of available platforms; the package supports nothing but Windows and OS/2. If spreadsheets are important to you, the historical popularity of Lotus 1-2-3 at least ensures that many other programs accept Lotus 1-2-3 files, so you should be able to import and export these files with minimal fuss. Lotus Word Pro (formerly known as AmiPro) has never been very popular, though, so import/export filters for its files are rare.

Sun StarOffice

Sun distributes a cross-platform office suite known as StarOffice (`http://www.sun.com/dot-com/staroffice.html`). Version 5.1 of this package is available for Windows, OS/2, Linux, and Solaris, and offers an unusually large number of components:

- **Writer**—Word processor
- **Calc**—Spreadsheet
- **Impress**—Presentations
- **Draw**—Vector graphics
- **Image**—Bitmapped graphics
- **Schedule**—Schedule manager
- **Mail**—Email client
- **Base**—Database management
- **Discussion**—Usenet news reader
- **Math**—Equation editor

Sun classifies some of these modules on a finer-grained basis than do other vendors. For example, other word processors include an equation editor similar to StarOffice's Math, but the equation editor is considered just one feature of the word processor component. Nonetheless, StarOffice includes an unusually broad range of components, and the program is available on more platforms than most. These facts make it an appealing choice for many cross-platform users.

The StarOffice user interface is reminiscent of that used by Microsoft Office, so Microsoft Office users should have little trouble picking up the program. (Figure 16.3 shows StarOffice running on OS/2.) As a general rule, the individual components of the suite aren't the most powerful available, and the package has a reputation for requiring a great deal of memory and for being slow to start up, but StarOffice is more than adequate for many purposes.

N O T E To learn more about StarOffice, see Michael Koch's *Special Edition Using StarOffice*, published by Que. This book focuses on the Windows and Linux versions of the program, but most of the information also applies to the OS/2 and Solaris versions. ◼

FIGURE 16.3
StarOffice works much like Microsoft Word; it even emulates the Windows Start button in the lower-left corner of its window.

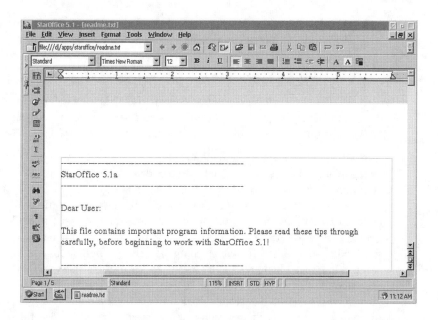

On the whole, StarOffice is one of the most flexible cross-platform office suites in terms of the breadth of its coverage. The package also benefits from the fact that Sun distributes the software free from its Web site (or you can purchase a CD or a CD with documentation). It includes import filters for Microsoft Office and a few other file formats. Unfortunately, few other programs can import StarOffice files, which limits StarOffice's capability to interact with other programs.

Document Exchange: PDF Readers

A handful of file formats are popular for exchanging text and other types of files:

■ **Plain text**—Raw ASCII text is the most universal file format for text in the Roman alphabet. The features of all more advanced formats might seem good, and sometimes they're necessary, but often they're superfluous or can cause more problems than they're worth.

▶ To learn more about ASCII text, **see** "Raw ASCII," **p. 359**.

■ **Word processor formats**—Microsoft Word is a particularly popular document-exchange format, but it is less than ideal from a multi-OS perspective. If you and the person with whom you are exchanging a document share a specific word processor, you can use that program's format with impunity.

■ **HTML**—Hypertext Markup Language (HTML) is the most common file format on the Web, and it is increasingly being used for non-Internet purposes such as program documentation files.

▶ To learn more about Web browsers, **see** "Using Netscape Communicator," **p. 417**.

■ **PDF**—The *Portable Document Format (PDF)* is the file format used by the Adobe Acrobat line of products (http://www.adobe.com). Particularly in the UNIX world, many non-Adobe products can also create and read PDF files.

As a general rule, HTML is a good format for use when the precise layout of information is unimportant. HTML was designed with the idea that the Web browser would dynamically determine features such as line lengths, fonts, and so on to suit the capabilities of the reader's hardware and the preferences of the user. HTML does offer some layout features, but they're fairly simple and there is no guarantee that any given browser will implement those features. Sometimes it is desirable or even necessary to distribute information using a more finely specified format, in which you can control precisely where an image appears relative to the surrounding text, change the font as you see fit, or otherwise control the appearance of the document. For example, if you want to make a printed publication available electronically, these features are often desirable. PDF files are a good solution for such functions. PDF takes a page-oriented approach, in which text appears on virtual "pages" through which the reader can scroll. Fortunately, it is possible to both read and create PDF files on a variety of OSs.

As a multi-OS tool, PDF is useful mainly as a way of reading existing documents or creating new documents for others to read. PDF files aren't intended to be modified in the way that word processor files can be, so PDF isn't useful as a means of working on a document in multiple OSs. You can, however, create one file with the intention that you or others read it in a variety of OSs, or obtain files in PDF format and read them in almost any OS.

Adobe Acrobat Reader

The premiere PDF reader is Adobe Acrobat Reader. This program is available for free download from Adobe's Web site (http://www.adobe.com/products/acrobat/readermain.html) for a variety of platforms, including Windows (both 32-bit and 16-bit versions are available), OS/2, and various UNIX variants (Linux and Solaris are both supported on x86 hardware). Because Adobe created the PDF standard, the Acrobat Reader is widely regarded as the ultimate test of the correct rendering of a PDF file. Therefore, if your OS supports the Acrobat Reader, using it for your PDF viewing needs is generally a good idea. Figure 16.4 shows the OS/2 version of the Acrobat Reader.

Toolbar

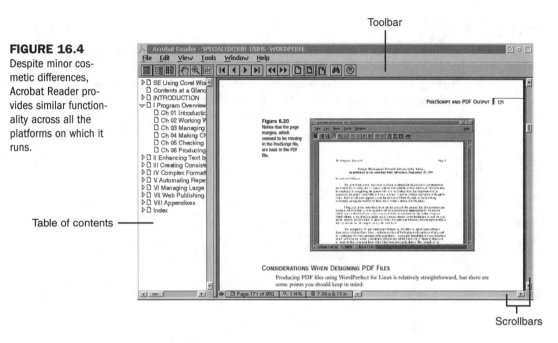

Part

VI

Ch

16

Table of contents ——

Scrollbars

FIGURE 16.4
Despite minor cosmetic differences, Acrobat Reader provides similar functionality across all the platforms on which it runs.

Acrobat Reader enables you to perform several actions on PDF files, including

■ **Paging**—You can scroll through the document using scrollbars and page scrolling icons in the toolbar. You can also use the View, Go to Page (Ctrl+5) feature to jump directly to a numbered page, or use the table of contents (shown in Figure 16.4) to locate a portion of the file.

■ **Zooming**—You can adjust the magnification factor to see an entire page, the width of a page, or some greater or lesser area. Toolbar items and options on the Tools menu control zooming.

■ **Text search**—In some, but not all, versions of Acrobat Reader, you can search for text by using the Tools, Find (Ctrl+F) option.

■ **Read notes**—PDF files can contain *notes*, which are bits of text that supplement ordinary text. The text of a note isn't normally visible, but you can display a note window by double-clicking on a note icon, which typically appears in the left margin.

■ **Printing**—You can print a PDF document to any printer supported by the host OS by choosing the File, Print menu bar item. It is possible for a PDF file to disable printing, however.

Xpdf and BePDF

Adobe Acrobat Reader is available on a variety of platforms, but not on all platforms. Acrobat Reader is also a fairly large application that takes a while to start up and consumes substantial system resources while running. The open-source Xpdf program, shown in Figure 16.5, is much smaller and faster than is Acrobat Reader, but at the cost of some of Acrobat Reader's more advanced features. Xpdf has been ported to BeOS, where it is known as BePDF. At this time, however, BePDF is still an early port, and might not work as reliably as does Xpdf.

FIGURE 16.5

BePDF is much like Xpdf (shown here), but BePDF uses a menu bar rather than icons at the window's bottom for program control.

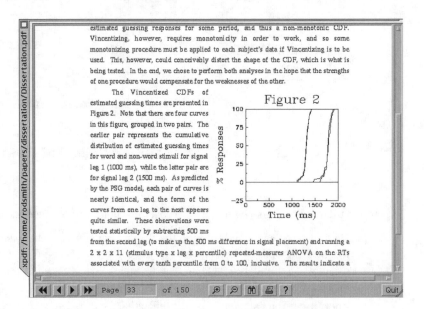

Xpdf and BePDF are capable of handling many PDF reading tasks, particularly when you have control over the PDF creation process. They are limited when compared to Acrobat Reader in several ways, however:

- **Font smoothing**—At screen resolutions, fonts often take on a chunky appearance that can make them difficult to read. Acrobat Reader includes an *anti-aliasing* or *font smoothing* feature that uses shades of gray to create the illusion of a smoother font outline. Many people find that font smoothing helps the legibility of PDF documents, but others dislike the effect. In any event, Xpdf and BePDF lack this feature.

- **Embedded fonts**—These programs don't always handle embedded fonts very well. PDF files can either use a small number of standard fonts or can embed fonts within the PDF file itself. Xpdf and BePDF sometimes substitute default fonts for embedded fonts, which can make for some suboptimal displays.

- **Encryption**—One of the features of the PDF file format is encryption. Commercially distributed PDF files often use encryption to prevent users from extracting text or printing the document. Neither Xpdf nor BePDF supports encryption, so these files can't be read with these programs.

- **Table of contents, links, and notes**—Xpdf and BePDF don't support the table of contents, links, or notes features of PDF files. You can still read files that use these features, but you can't use them from Xpdf or BePDF.

On the whole, Xpdf and BePDF are useful programs for displaying simple PDF files. For more complex files that use encryption or other advanced features, you're better off using Adobe Acrobat Reader instead. If you use a version of UNIX for which no Acrobat Reader binary exists, you can use a Ghostscript-based PDF viewer to get around the lack of encryption in Xpdf, should the need arise.

Ghostscript-Based Viewers

Ghostscript (`http://www.cs.wisc.edu/~ghost/`) is a program that is available on many platforms for interpreting PostScript and PDF files. A bit of history might be helpful in understanding the role of Ghostscript. Adobe developed PostScript in the 1980s as *page description language (PDL)*. PostScript is a computer programming language, much like C, Pascal, or BASIC, but PostScript is optimized for describing and manipulating graphical objects, including text. In the mid-1980s, PostScript began to appear in laser printers, which at that time possessed as much computing power as many desktop computers. Rather than have the computer *rasterize* each image—that is, turn a description of text and shapes from a program into the millions of individual points of light and dark on a sheet of paper—the computer can send a high-level description of the page's contents to the printer, which proceeds to use PostScript to determine which points should be light and which should be dark. This approach reduces the computing load of printing on desktop computers.

Unfortunately, not everybody had PostScript printers, and as the years wore on, computers became more powerful. PostScript files nonetheless began to be exchanged on the Internet, and on UNIX systems, PostScript became the *de facto* printing standard—UNIX programs routinely generate PostScript code as their printing output, working under the assumption that the computer can print to a PostScript printer. Enter Ghostscript.

Rather than place the PostScript interpreter inside the printer, Ghostscript is a program that interprets PostScript in the computer and sends a bitmap image of the result to the printer. In effect, Ghostscript turns a non-PostScript printer into a PostScript printer, without actually modifying the printer. Ghostscript can do more than interpret PostScript for printers, though; it can turn a PostScript file into a bitmap graphics format or display the file on a computer's screen. These capabilities, and their contrast to a conventional PostScript printer arrangement, are illustrated in Figure 16.6.

▶ To learn more about bitmapped graphics file formats, **see** "Bitmapped Graphics Formats," **p. 363**.

FIGURE 16.6
Ghostscript is a PostScript interpreter that resides on the computer and can send its output to both printers and nonprinting files and devices.

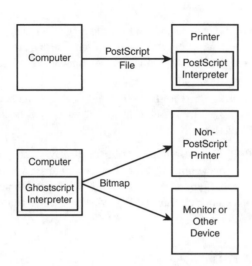

PDF is closely related to PostScript, so after PDF was developed, Ghostscript's developers adapted the program to process PDF files as well as PostScript files. The upshot of this fact, in terms of PDF viewing, is that you can use Ghostscript to view or print PDF files.

In its most basic form, however, Ghostscript is a command-line program with a user interface that is weak for tasks such as PDF viewing. Therefore, several Ghostscript front-end programs have emerged. These programs put a user-friendly GUI face atop Ghostscript, enabling you to use the program much as you'd use Adobe Acrobat Reader or Xpdf. Figure 16.7 shows one such interface, GSview, which is available for Windows and OS/2. (Compare Figure 16.7 to Figure 16.4, which shows the same file in Acrobat Reader.) Others include gv, Ghostview, and KGhostview (all for UNIX-like systems). You can find links to these programs from the Ghostscript Web site.

For the most part, the Ghostscript-based PDF viewers have capabilities and limitations similar to those of Xpdf and BePDF. There are some differences, however:

- **Encryption**—As delivered, Ghostscript lacks the capability to process encrypted PDF files; however, replacing a single file enables this capability. Specifically, you must obtain the pdf_sec.ps file from http://www.ozemail.com.au/~geoffk/pdfencrypt/. The reason for the omission has to do with United States export restrictions on encryption technology.

- **Font smoothing**—Some, but not all, Ghostscript-based PDF viewers provide an option to enable font smoothing.

- **PostScript capacity**—Ghostscript-based PDF viewers can invariably display PostScript files, as well as PDF files.

FIGURE 16.7
GSview and other Ghostscript-based PDF viewers have similar capabilities but dissimilar user interfaces.

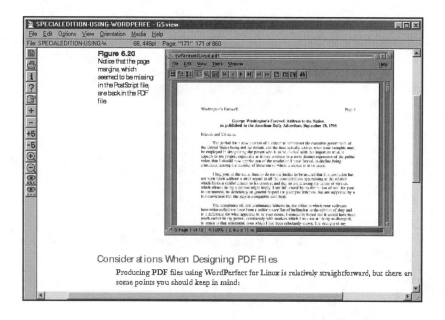

TIP

In general, Xpdf displays PDF files more quickly than do Ghostscript-based viewers. Occasionally one viewer or the other will have problems with a specific PDF file, so if you have both viewers available and experience problems, try the other viewer.

Creating PDF Files from PostScript Using Ghostscript

Ghostscript is an extremely versatile tool for processing both PostScript and PDF files. Not only can Ghostscript display PDF files and print them (which might entail converting PDF to PostScript), but Ghostscript can also convert PostScript into PDF. In effect, the "other device" shown in Figure 16.6 can be a PDF file. Creating a PDF file can be a good way to distribute textual documents that require complex formatting when you don't know the OS that will be used to read the file. You might also want to create PDF files for your own personal use across multiple OSs.

Creating a PostScript File   To create a PDF file using Ghostscript, you must begin by creating a PostScript file. If you're using a UNIX-like OS, you can generally do so by using an application that can print to a PostScript printer, but selecting a *print to file* or *export to PostScript* option. Details differ substantially from one application to another, unfortunately, so you should consult your application's documentation for more details.

In OSs that use integrated printer drivers, such as Windows and OS/2, the driver often includes a print to file feature similar to those available for UNIX applications, as shown in

Figure 16.8. When selected, the driver either sends the PostScript file to a fixed location or asks you for a filename. You might be able to configure the driver to send output to a file by default, which can be useful if you frequently need to create PostScript or PDF files.

FIGURE 16.8
Details differ from one driver to another, but most Windows and OS/2 PostScript drivers include an option to send PostScript output to a file.

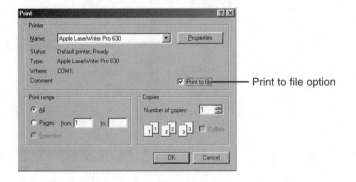

Print to file option

 TIP   You might want to install a PostScript printer driver even if you don't have a PostScript printer to use it to create PDF files. Use a generic PostScript or Apple LaserWriter PostScript series printer driver from the OS publisher.

Converting to PDF   After you've created some PostScript output, you must convert it to PDF format. Modern versions of Ghostscript ship with a script that is designed for doing just this. This script is called `ps2pdf`, and you pass it the name of a PostScript file you want to convert to PDF format:

```
ps2pdf file.ps
```

The resulting file bears the same name, but with a `.pdf` filename extension rather than `.ps`. You can try viewing the PDF file in Acrobat Reader or some other PDF viewer.

Capabilities and Limitations of *ps2pdf*   Ghostscript is definitely a low-end PDF creation utility; it lacks many of the more advanced features of commercial products such as Adobe Acrobat Distiller. For example

- **Fonts**—When your input file uses the standard PostScript fonts (Times, Helvetica, and Courier), the resulting file relies on the PDF viewer to use its own fonts. This process generally works well. In its 5.x versions, however, Ghostscript converts other fonts into bitmaps when creating a PDF file. This process produces chunky fonts in the PDF file. Version 6.0 of Ghostscript might improve on this matter.

- **Advanced features**—It can be difficult or impossible to access advanced PDF features using Ghostscript as the creation program. In particular, encryption, tables of contents, and links are all off-limits.

- **Formatting errors**—Sometimes a PostScript file is simply too complex for Ghostscript to render properly as a PDF file. If you run into this problem, check for a more recent version of Ghostscript. Fortunately, such formatting errors are rare with 5.x versions of Ghostscript, although they were more common in the 4.x series.

As a general rule, Ghostscript is a good way to create PDF files when you need a direct translation of an existing document, when you don't care about links or similar features, and when you're willing to restrict yourself to the basic PostScript font families. If you have more sophisticated requirements, you might need to look elsewhere for PDF-creation software, such as Adobe Acrobat Distiller, which is available for Windows. Another option is the PStill program, `http://www.this.net/~frank/pstill.html`, which works in much the same way as does `ps2pdf`—you create a PostScript file and then run it through the conversion utility. PStill does a better job with fonts than does `ps2pdf`, provided you've installed the relevant fonts in PStill itself; but PStill isn't as good as Ghostscript at handling complex page layouts. The program is shareware and is available for Windows and a variety of UNIX versions.

Part
VI

Ch
16

Internet Applications

The Internet is an extremely useful resource for many purposes. Indeed, this book is littered with *uniform resource locators* (*URLs*)—Internet addresses that typically begin with `http://` or `ftp://` (indicating Web and FTP sites, respectively). You can use the Internet for far more than computer-related research and support, though. The Internet hosts information on biology, physics, business, current events, parenting, movies, and just about anything else you care to learn about. You can even use Internet applications between two or more computers in your own home or business, if you create an *intranet*—a small network within your own walls.

▶ To learn more about using networking in a multi-OS environment, **see** Part VII, "Network Access."

As a user, you spend most of your time accessing the Internet using *client* programs—programs that request information from remote (*server*) computers. The number of types of client programs is vast, and the total number of client programs is even more staggering, so I can't cover them all in this section. I can, however, give an overview of how some of the more common and useful types of programs work.

Using Netscape Communicator

The Netscape Communicator package (`http://www.netscape.com`) is a suite of Internet tools that covers three of the most popular parts of the Internet: The *World Wide Web* (*WWW* or *Web* for short), electronic mail (*email*), and Usenet news. Netscape's products are far from the only ones for handling any of these three parts of the Internet, but considered as a cross-platform tool, Communicator is one of the most widely available. Some of the details I present in this section vary for alternative tools, but the broad outlines should be the same no matter which tool you use.

N O T E Netscape Communicator is distributed free but is technically a commercial product. An open-source version called Mozilla also exists—see `http://www.mozilla.org` for details. Mozilla is currently under development and will be the basis of version 5.0 of Netscape Communicator. ■

Browsing the Web with Navigator   The Netscape Communicator component that is most strongly associated with the Netscape name is Navigator. The Navigator Web browser was the first to popularize the Web. On Microsoft OSs, Microsoft Internet Explorer is also quite popular, but Internet Explorer isn't available for non-Microsoft x86 OSs. On these OSs, there are other alternatives, such as Mosaic (http://www.ncsa.uiuc.edu/SDG/Software/Mosaic/NCSAMosaicHome.html) and Opera (http://www.opera.com/index.html). Mosaic is no longer being developed but remains useful, whereas Opera is in the process of being ported to a variety of platforms.

▶ To see a larger, but still incomplete, list of Web browsers, along with a description of the Web in general, **see** "Getting Started with the Web," **p. 279**.

Figure 16.9 shows the main Netscape Navigator 4.7 window and demonstrates several features common to both Netscape and other Web browsers.

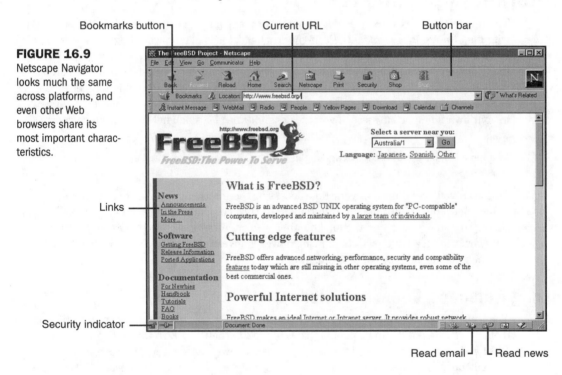

FIGURE 16.9
Netscape Navigator looks much the same across platforms, and even other Web browsers share its most important characteristics.

- **Button bar**—Provides quick access to common Web navigation features.
- **Current URL indicator**—This field displays the URL of the Web page that is currently being displayed. You can also click in the field to edit it—say, to enter a URL you read from this book.
- **Bookmarks**—Most Web browsers maintain a list of *bookmarks*—URLs stored in a simple database for easy retrieval.

■ **Links**—Most Web pages contain *hyperlinks* or *links*, which are references to other online documents. You can move your mouse pointer to a link and click it to display that document.

■ **Security features**—The Web, although primarily a means of delivering information to you, can also function as a two-way communication medium. Unfortunately, the Internet wasn't designed with security in mind, so it is often possible for strangers to snoop on your data transfers. Most modern Web browsers support encryption, which makes it much more difficult to eavesdrop on secure transmissions using current technology— or, rather, eavesdropping is possible, but produces nothing but gibberish. In Netscape Navigator, the security padlock moves to a closed position to indicate that any information you send using the current page will be encrypted.

Reading Mail with Messenger   The Web can be a great resource (or a time-waster, depending on your point of view), but it is rather impersonal, and extremely public. For more one-on-one communication, you should use email.

Netscape includes an email component, known as Messenger. From the main Navigator window, you can start Messenger to create or read your email by clicking the Read Email icon (refer Figure 16.9). The result is the Netscape Messenger window shown in Figure 16.10.

Button bar

FIGURE 16.10
Netscape uses one component for both email and Usenet news reading.

Message list pane

Mail and news folders pane

Message pane

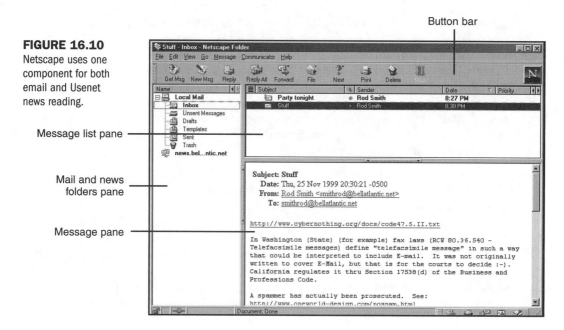

N O T E   Netscape supports several display options for Messenger, so yours might not look quite like the one shown in Figure 16.10. ■

You can retrieve messages in Netscape Messenger by using the Get Msg button in the button bar, and you can read messages by clicking them in the message list pane. (You might need to first select the appropriate mailbox in the mail and news folder pane, though.) In addition, you can save messages, print them, move them to specific mail folders, and so on, using appropriate menu and button bar options.

▶ To learn how to use email to exchange documents, **see** "Exchanging Documents via Email," **p. 483**.

TIP

If you use Netscape Messenger on several OSs, you might be able to share mail files across OSs. When using the Windows or OS/2 versions of the program, you can use the User Profile Manager tool, which should be accessible from the Netscape folder or Start Menu item, to create a new user profile in one or both OSs. The goal is to use a single set of configuration and mail files for both OSs. During the profile-creation process, Netscape asks for the location of the profile. Select a directory that is accessible to both OSs. If you're sharing between OS/2 and Windows, repeat this procedure in both OSs before you customize your settings. In UNIX OSs, Netscape automatically creates profiles in the user's home directory, in the `~/.netscape` directory. You can replace files in this directory with symbolic links to their equivalents on a Windows or OS/2 partition—but be aware that some file-names, such as `bookmark.htm` and `bookmarks.html`, might be different across OSs.

Reading Usenet News with Messenger   When you click the Read News button in the Navigator window (refer to Figure 16.9), Netscape responds by displaying the same Messenger window used by Netscape's mail reader. The difference is that, assuming you entered information for your news server into your user profile when you installed Netscape or configured a profile, Messenger highlights the newsgroup options rather than the email options in the mail and news folders pane.

To read news, you must first subscribe to one or more newsgroups. To do so, you should right-click the name of your news server and select Subscribe to Newsgroups from the pop-up menu. (The first time you connect to a news server, you might have to wait several min-utes for Messenger to download the list of available groups.) The result is the Subscribe to Newsgroups dialog box shown in Figure 16.11. After you select one or more newsgroups, you can click the Subscribe button to subscribe. After you're subscribed to a newsgroup, you can read and post messages to the group, much as if you were exchanging email. The difference is that instead of one person reading your messages, many people will read them. Messenger provides a variety of message posting options, however, so that you can tailor your responses—you can respond by email only, post to the newsgroup, or both.

▶ To learn more about Usenet newsgroups, **see** "Reading Usenet Newsgroups," **p. 282**.

FIGURE 16.11
Select a newsgroup by browsing for it or by clicking the Search tab to search for a keyword in the newsgroup name.

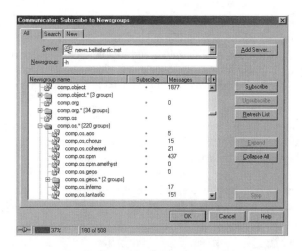

> **CAUTION**
>
> Before posting to Usenet, it is a good idea to change the default Netscape posting format. Netscape defaults to posting messages and sending email in HTML format. This is considered bad form on most Usenet newsgroups, however. You can correct the matter by choosing Edit, Preferences to get the Preferences dialog box and then using the Category pane to select Mail & Newsgroups, Formatting. Change the Message formatting item from Use the HTML Editor to Compose Messages to Use the Plain Text Editor to Compose Messages. This change is also a good idea for exchanging email. If you fail to make this change, expect to receive complaints.

Because of the massive number of postings to most newsgroups, chances are that you won't want to read them all. There are two steps you can take to help manage matters:

- In each newsgroup, choose View, Messages, Threads with Unread or View, Messages, New. This step makes Messenger display only unread messages, so you won't be bothered with those five-day-old postings (unless you haven't read news for five days or more). The details of what is shown depend on the precise option you choose.

- After you've read the messages you want to read in a group, choose Message, Mark, All Read. This option tells Messenger to pretend that you've read all the messages in a newsgroup. In conjunction with the previous step, the result is that you won't see any of those messages the next time you open that newsgroup.

Using FTP Programs

The *File Transfer Protocol (FTP)* is one of the most popular Internet protocols. As its name implies, FTP is used for transferring files from one computer to another. In some sense, email, Web browsing, and even Usenet news accomplish the same goal, but FTP is designed for exchanging generic data files, possibly in an unattended way and using a password for at least minimal security. Web browsers can accomplish this goal and are increasingly being used in this capacity, but FTP is still popular and it is generally easier to transfer a large number of files using an FTP client than it is by using a Web browser. (In fact, Web pages can contain links to files on FTP servers, so you might be using FTP even when you think you're using the Web!)

FTP programs come in a variety of forms. The easiest to use are GUI programs such as the UNIX xmFTP, shown in Figure 16.12. The lowest common denominator, though, is in text-based FTP programs. These typically use similar commands, which I describe in this section. GUI FTP tools simply place a point-and-click interface atop these textual commands, so if you understand the textual interface, you should be able to find the correct button to push or menu item to choose to achieve your desired effect with a GUI program.

FIGURE 16.12
GUI FTP programs provide a friendly face to a protocol designed for text-based use.

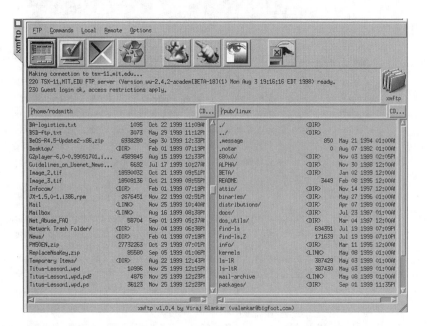

xmftp v1.0.4 by Viraj Alankar (valankar@bigfoot.com)

To begin using a text-based FTP client, type `ftp host.computer.name`, where `host.computer.name` is the computer's name or IP address. You do not type the `ftp://` portion of an FTP site's URL, if you've read it in that form. The result is usually some form of login prompt. For example, when I used FTP to access `tsx-11.mit.edu`, I received the following login prompt in return:

```
Name (tsx-11.mit.edu:rodsmith):
```

The login prompt includes my username on my local computer (`rodsmith`), indicating that this is the default login username. Most of the FTP sites you're likely to access on the

Internet, however, are *anonymous* sites. This means that they take the username anonymous to let anybody in—albeit usually with very limited access to the computer. So, I typed anonymous at the login prompt. I was then confronted with the following text:

```
331 Guest login ok, send your complete e-mail address as password.
Password:
```

The first line is simply an indication that the system accepts anonymous FTP logins and a request that you send your email address as the password. I did so, and a great deal of information scrolled down my screen. I could then access the rest of the system.

Of course, the details of this interaction vary from one FTP site to another. Furthermore, if you need to access a non-anonymous site, you must have an account on that computer to get in. You should issue your normal username and password to access files on such a computer.

Part

VI

Ch

16

> **CAUTION**
>
> Just as credit card information can potentially be lifted from an insecure Web transaction, your username and password can potentially be obtained by computer criminals when you use FTP. There are secure FTP variants and alternatives to FTP for which this problem doesn't exist, but these alternatives aren't as common as regular FTP. I therefore advise caution when sending a username and password for FTP access; don't do so unless you need to, and if possible, change your password via a secure protocol soon afterward. This caution doesn't apply to anonymous FTP access, which doesn't exchange sensitive login information. Miscreants might be able to snoop on any files you transfer via anonymous FTP, but that is not normally an issue because the files are publicly available to anybody.

After you're logged in, you can issue several commands, including

- ■ ascii—Change the transfer mode from binary to ASCII. Use ASCII mode when you transfer plain text files (but not word processor files) to automatically handle end-of-line differences.

  ▶ To learn more about end-of-line characters, **see** "Raw ASCII," **p. 359**.

- ■ binary—Change the transfer mode from ASCII to binary. If in doubt, use binary mode because it ensures your files will transfer without being altered.
- ■ bye—Close open connections and exit from the program.
- ■ cd—Change to a directory on the server. This command doesn't affect the current directory on your local computer, only on the server.
- ■ close—Close the current connection.
- ■ delete *filename*—Delete *filename* from the server. You might not be able to use this command on anonymous FTP connections.
- ■ dir—Show files in the current directory on the server. (The ls command is similar.)
- ■ exit—Close any open connections and quit from the FTP client. (Some clients don't recognize exit and use bye instead.)

- `get` *filename*—Retrieve *filename* from the server. The most basic of FTP clients show little indication that anything is happening during a transfer, but more sophisticated clients show a progress indicator of some type.

- `help`—Display help information on the available FTP commands.

- `lcd`—Change to a directory on your local computer. Subsequent transfers occur to or from the new local directory.

- `ls`—Show files in the current directory on the server. On some combinations of client and server software, `ls` and `dir` are identical; on others, `dir` provides more information than does `ls`.

- `mget` *filenames*—Retrieves multiple files from the server. You can either specify several filenames or use a wildcard such as an asterisk (*) within a filename. Some clients ask you for confirmation of every file transferred.

- `mput` *filenames*—Sends multiple files to the server.

- `open` *remote.machine.name*—Opens a connection to the named computer. If you specify the name of the FTP server when you launch the client, you don't need to issue this command.

- `prompt`—Toggles interactive prompting on or off. With prompting on, you're asked to confirm every transfer when you perform an `mput` or `mget` operation. Turning prompting off enables you to transfer a large number of files much more easily.

- `put` *filename*—Send a single file to the remote system.

- `pwd`—Display the current directory on the FTP server.

- `quit`—Close current connections and exit from the program.

- `reget` *filename*—Transfer *filename* from the server, but if *filename* already exists on the client and is smaller in size than the server's file, assume that a previous transfer was interrupted and resume the transfer where it left off.

- `send` *filename*—Synonymous with `put` *filename*.

- `size` *filename*—Display the size of *filename* on the remote machine.

Armed with these commands, you should be able to transfer files using a basic text-mode FTP client. Note that you can easily transfer files destined for one OS using another, provided of course that you have some way to transfer the file between OSs locally, such as a shared partition.

Using Telnet for Remote Access

Telnet is a word that refers both to an Internet protocol and to a program that implements that protocol. Considered as a protocol, Telnet is a means of sending and receiving text in an interactive manner suitable for remote text-mode logins, as were commonly used in the days before GUIs, and which are still commonly used in many environments. As a program, Telnet is usually the simplest available program on a computer to implement the Telnet protocol. Many OSs claim multiple programs that are capable of handling the Telnet protocol.

Generally speaking, these programs are known as *terminal programs*, and they're often derived from programs used to access mainframe computers remotely via modems. With the popularity of the Internet, though, these programs have been adapted to use TCP/IP networking instead of dial-up modem connections.

On most OSs, using the basic Telnet program is a matter of typing `telnet` *host.computer.name*, where *host.computer.name* is the name or IP address of the computer to which you want to connect. After you're connected, what happens depends on what is running on the remote computer. Typically, you'll see a login prompt followed by a password prompt. After that point, you should be able to use most or all of the text-mode programs available on the remote computer.

▶ To learn more about using Telnet to access one of your computers from another, **see** "Remote Logins," **p. 491**.

CAUTION

Just as with FTP, basic Telnet is an insecure protocol, so your password and other sensitive data can potentially fall into the wrong hands when you use Telnet. Alternative protocols such as SSH can get around this problem, and I recommend you use such protocols whenever possible. In function, SSH works much like Telnet.

Many basic Telnet programs, particularly in the UNIX world, provide a means to control the program locally by typing an escape character, typically Ctrl+], at any time after you launch the program. Telnet then displays a `telnet>` prompt, at which you can issue an assortment of commands such as `close` to close a connection or `open` to start a new one. Type `help` to see a complete list of available Telnet commands, or press the Enter key to resume normal interaction with the host computer.

The basic Telnet program included with Microsoft Windows doesn't include the Ctrl+] functionality; instead, it provides options available through its menu bar, as shown in Figure 16.13.

FIGURE 16.13
You can set options and control the connection of Microsoft's Telnet via its menu bar and dialog boxes.

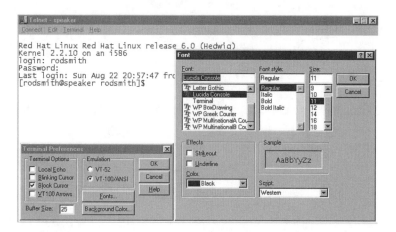

Part
VI

Ch
16

Summary

When you work in a cross-platform environment, the availability of common tools across OSs can be extremely useful. If you use a cross-platform office suite for doing your work, you can do that work in any OS supported by that suite, which can free you up to more easily move from one OS to another or to boot whichever OS is most appropriate for tasks other than working with the office suite. The ability to read or create PDF files in any OS can also be a great boon, particularly with more and more documentation becoming available in PDF format. Finally, Internet applications shared across OSs can enable you to access the Internet equally well in any OS. With careful placement of configuration files, you can even share your local email records across OSs, provided you use a tool such as Netscape Communicator that is available in all your OSs. ●

Modifying GUI Look and Feel

GUI Add-Ons for Windows

Chances are you work with the graphical user interface (GUI) environment of your computer a great deal. Especially in the Windows, OS/2, and BeOS worlds, most major applications are GUI in nature—they use windows with menus to display their information, dialog boxes to interact with the user, and so on. As you use multiple OSs, you begin to see flaws in each OS's GUI environment—major or minor details of operation that you'd like to change. Even if you're laid back about such matters, you might want to make different GUI environments look or act more like one another, simply as a matter of consistency. After all, if you spend some time working with one OS and get used to its conventions, it can be jarring to boot into another and have to adapt your work style to the second OS. Computers should adapt to people, not the other way around. This chapter presents some tools and techniques you can apply to alter each OS's defaults for its user interface, ranging from minor matters such as color schemes to major facelifts that can make one OS look and act very much like another.

The Windows GUI environment is the best known in today's computing world. Chances are you're already familiar with it, and if you're going to adapt an OS's GUI environment, you'll likely make a new OS behave more like the familiar Windows. You might be coming from a non-Windows realm, though, and find that you miss some feature from your original OS. Even if your new OS isn't Windows, you might find some feature of a new OS so indispensable that you want to retrofit it onto Windows. Fortunately, Windows is so popular that a huge number of third-party add-on utilities exist to modify its default GUI behavior. Many of these tools are freeware or inexpensive shareware programs. Look for them on Windows file archives such as http://www.winfiles.com or http://download.cnet.com/downloads/. Many of these files also appear on the CD that accompanies this book, in the GUI-utils directory.

Virtual Desktop Pagers for Windows

A *virtual desktop* is a concept that is simple and whose utility is substantial, but it is also something that you might not realize you're missing until you use virtual desktops on a new OS. The idea is to reduce desktop clutter by maintaining not one, but several virtual screens or desktops. On one desktop, you can run your word processor and spreadsheet, which you're using to prepare a report; on another desktop, you can run a Web browser and email client for Internet connectivity; and on a third, you can run the CD-R burning software you're using to create a new FreeBSD installation CD. The combination of these five programs, if run in a single screen, would be enough to produce quite a clutter. You could, of course, minimize the unused programs, but that can become tedious, especially for programs that open several windows or if you need one screen to simultaneously display two or more programs. The virtual desktop solution enables you to keep all the programs open and running at the same time and to switch between sets of programs by selecting an appropriate desktop in a pager application that is common to all the desktops.

The number of virtual desktop pagers available for Windows is quite large. Most work on both Windows 9x and Windows NT, but you should check that detail before installing any given program. The smallest of these programs imposes only a very small performance penalty, but the more feature-rich can chew up enough RAM to make a noticeable impact on your system's speed. Just a few of the available programs include

- **sDesk**—Semik's Desktop, or *sDesk* for short, is a very basic virtual desktop pager, based loosely on the function of the pager included in the UNIX fvwm environment. One of its best points is that it is open source. You can learn more about it at the sDesk Web site, `http://mujweb.cz/web/tomasek/sdesk/index_en.html`.

- **Desks at Will**—This shareware pager is more complex than is sDesk; Desks at Will includes much more in the way of configuration options, including several methods of switching between desktops and the capability to apply password protection to one or more desktops. You can learn more at the product's Web page, `http://www.idyle.com/daw/index.html`.

- **Control Center**—This shareware product is one of the more advanced virtual desktop pagers available for Windows. In addition to basic virtual desktop management, the program includes system resource monitors, program launch utilities, and more. It is also a component of Stardock's more advanced retail product, Object Desktop for Windows. Read more about Control Center at `http://www.stardock.net/products/odnt/cc.html`.

Part

VI

Ch

17

Figure 17.1 shows Stardock's Control Center in action. In its default configuration, the program chews up a fair amount of desktop space for its pager and other features—the bar along the right of the screen is constantly visible. You can reconfigure the program to hide the Control Center until you move the mouse to an edge or corner of the screen, however. Some other virtual desktop pagers consume much less screen real estate; sDesk, for example, is quite small and unobtrusive. A large control area in a pager does have its advantages, though. Control Center, for example, shows a miniature icon representing each open window in each desktop, so you can locate the program you want to access without checking each desktop.

FIGURE 17.1
Control Center provides information on available disk space, a clock, and other features in addition to its virtual desktop pager function.

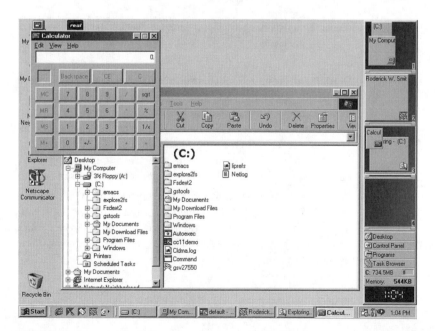

Changing the Appearance and Function of Windows and the Desktop in Windows

You might not like the appearance of your windows or desktop or the actions you can perform with your windows. Numerous utilities are available, including some that come standard with Microsoft Windows, that enable you to alter the way your windows look or act. If you have a specific effect in mind and I don't mention it here, check a Windows shareware file site; there is a good chance that somebody's written something to achieve the effect you want. The following is a sampling of what is possible:

■ **Color adjustments**—You can use the Display Properties dialog box, shown in Figure 17.2 and obtained by opening the Display Control Panel item, to alter the color scheme used for window elements and the desktop. You can also use a bitmapped graphics file as wallpaper, which is displayed "beneath" your desktop icons and programs.

FIGURE 17.2

The Display Properties dialog box lets you alter various aspects of the Windows display, including colors and fonts used in window elements.

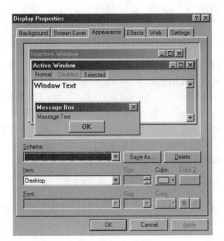

■ **Desktop themes**—Windows ships with a set of *themes*, which are color combinations and icon replacements for the standard Windows desktop. Many themes include animated icons and sound effects. You can find additional themes on Windows file archive sites. Figure 17.3 shows just one of the many themes that are available for Windows. You can select the theme you want to use by using the Desktop Themes icon in the Control Panel. It is also possible to selectively apply changes to some parts of the GUI but not others; for example, you can alter everything but the desktop wallpaper.

■ **Talisman**—This shareware program replaces the Windows desktop with a new system with a look and feel that is highly integrated into the theme you choose. You can choose themes based on a science fiction spaceship control system, an office, and so on. Learn more about it at `http://www.lighttek.com/talisman.htm`. Figure 17.4 shows one of the many Talisman themes.

Modified
wallpaper

Changed fonts
and colors for
window elements

FIGURE 17.3
A theme is a set of
changes to the
Windows GUI that
provide a consistent
look to the standard
icons and window
decorations.

Replacements for
standard icons

FIGURE 17.4
Each Talisman desktop
provides a unique set
of controls.

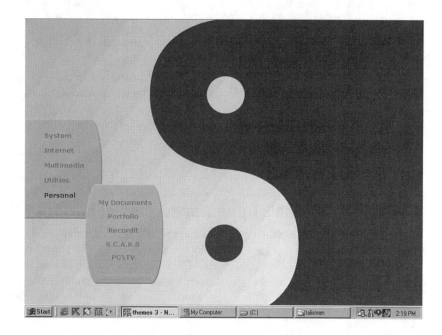

- **WinShade**—If you've used a Macintosh in recent years, you've probably encountered the *collapse window* feature, in which you can click a control to make the contents of the window disappear, leaving only the window's title bar. WinShade (`http://www.bluecarpet.com/winshade/index.html`) adds this feature to Microsoft Windows.

- **Window Blinds**—Stardock's (`http://www.stardock.com`) Window Blinds is a shareware utility that changes the appearance of window borders, menu items, dialog box buttons, and other standard GUI elements. The end result is a GUI environment that can closely resemble another OS or that is unique unto itself. You can even modify the settings to create your own custom window appearance. For example, examine Figure 17.5, which is a window from a Windows 98 computer running Window Blinds and its BePC environment, which resembles the BeOS user interface.

FIGURE 17.5
Window Blinds transforms your window decorations to resemble those of another OS.

- **Object Desktop**—Stardock's commercial desktop management utility includes a variety of tools to customize the appearance and behavior of your windows and desktop. This package includes Control Center, Window Blinds, and more.

> **CAUTION**
>
> Although modifying your desktop and windows with third-party utilities is often useful, it can sometimes lead to problems. In particular, if such a utility is buggy, it can cause your entire computer to become unstable. Small utilities typically impose little in the way of performance penalties, but add several of them together and they can degrade the performance of a low-RAM system. I recommend installing such utilities one at a time. If your system seems stable after using one for a while, you can add another. Be sure you have a way to back out of an installation.

Altering the Mouse's Appearance and Behavior in Windows

The built-in desktop themes of Windows modify several aspects of Windows' appearance, including the mouse. You can modify the mouse separately, however. To do so, open the Mouse item in the Windows Control Panel. In the resulting Mouse Properties dialog box (see Figure 17.6), you can alter the appearance of the mouse pointer, how it responds to button clicks, and how quickly the mouse moves when you push it across your desk.

FIGURE 17.6
You can select from several predefined mouse pointer styles using the Mouse Properties dialog box.

Many mice come with Windows drivers that add to the features of the Mouse Properties dialog box. For example, you might be able to define functions for buttons beyond the two that Windows most directly supports or define how a wheel on a mouse that is so equipped functions. The details of such controls differ from one mouse to another.

 If you have anything but the most generic mouse, you might want to check the mouse manufacturer's Web site every few months to see whether an updated driver is available. Manufacturers sometimes add features to their mouse drivers, and these can be worth obtaining.

N O T E I use the term *mouse* generically to refer to any pointing device. Don't feel excluded if you use a trackball, touch pad, or some other pointing device. (In fact, I use trackballs on my own computers.) ■

By default, Windows (and most other OSs) use a model in which you must click a window to give it *focus*—that is, display the window atop other overlapping windows and send input to it. Some X Window System environments in UNIX, however, use other focus models, in which you need only move the mouse over a window to give it focus, or in which focus can be granted to a window even when it is partly hidden by other windows. You can customize your mouse's behavior by using the XMouse utility, which is part of the free PowerToys utility bundle from Microsoft (http://www.microsoft.com/windows95/downloads/contents/wutoys/w95pwrtoysset/default.asp?RLD=13).

GUI Add-Ons for OS/2

Just as with Windows, it is possible to use OS/2's built-in features and add third-party utilities to modify OS/2's look and feel. OS/2's windowing environment is known as the *Presentation Manager (PM)*. PM handles the display of windows, menus, and so on. The OS/2 desktop environment is built atop the PM and is known as the *WorkPlace Shell (WPS)*. Newcomers to OS/2 sometimes confuse the two or don't realize that there is a distinction between them.

OS/2's GUI add-ons and modifications can be classified in much the same way as can Windows', and with equal fuzziness; sometimes a program performs more than one task or does something that is not easily categorized.

Virtual Desktop Pagers for OS/2

Virtual desktop pagers exist for OS/2 just as they do for Windows. There is nothing OS/2-specific to add to the description of the function of virtual desktop pagers I presented earlier in this chapter. Of course, the specific programs available under OS/2 are different from the programs available in Windows:

■ **PageMage**—This utility is a fairly basic freeware desktop pager for OS/2, shown with its configuration window in Figure 17.7. Like sDesk on Windows, PageMage was inspired by the UNIX fvwm pager. Unfortunately, it has not been updated since 1996, and some of its functions are not entirely intuitive.

FIGURE 17.7
PageMage provides an outline of open windows in alternative desktops.

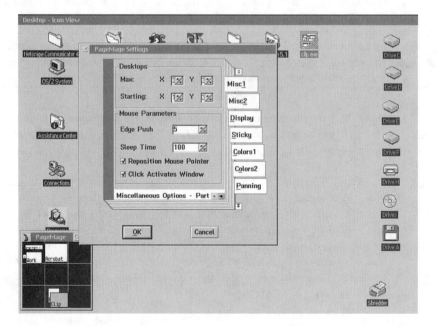

■ **PM Virtual Desktop**—This is another basic freeware desktop pager. It provides only plain buttons in its pager display but is otherwise similar in operation to PageMage. Fortunately, it is a bit easier for novices to use than is PageMage.

■ **Object Desktop**—Stardock's (http://www.stardock.com) commercial desktop utility suite is available for OS/2 as well as for Windows. In fact, the program began life on OS/2 and was only later ported to Windows. Unlike the Windows program, though, you can't download demo versions or purchase the individual components separately for OS/2.

Changing the Appearance and Behavior of OS/2's Windows

Utilities to alter the appearance and behavior of OS/2's windows are common. Some of the more useful of these utilities include

■ **Color schemes**—OS/2 supports the creation and application of a set of window and background changes similar to Windows' themes, but OS/2 refers to them as *schemes*. OS/2's schemes don't change WPS icons or fonts, unlike Windows' themes. You can select from several existing schemes or create new ones using the Scheme Palette shown in Figure 17.8, which you open from the System Setup window. Drag a scheme to a window, or hold the Alt key and drag it to the desktop to apply the scheme to all windows.

N O T E In OS/2, you perform WPS drag operations, including those used to alter schemes, colors, and fonts, using the right mouse button. (If you configure your mouse for left-handed operation, use the left button.) ■

Part
VI

Ch
17

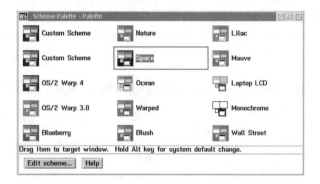

FIGURE 17.8
The Scheme Palette lets you set a color scheme for your OS/2 desktop.

■ **Individual adjustments**—In addition to setting an entire scheme, you can adjust the colors, fonts, and backgrounds individually. You do this by dragging colors and fonts from the Mixed Color Palette, Solid Color Palette, and Font Palette items in the System Setup window, as shown in Figure 17.9, which also shows the PM Virtual Desktop pager.

■ **Theme/2**—This utility converts Windows themes so that they can be used with OS/2's scheme system. The large number of available Windows themes makes this utility worthwhile if you enjoy such things.

FIGURE 17.9
Note the varying title bar fonts and colors (reproduced here as shades of gray).

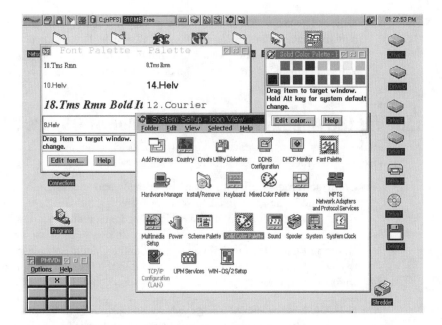

■ **Change Controls**—This shareware utility alters the OS/2 window controls' appearances. Compared to the changes effected by Window Blinds on Windows, the effects of Change Controls are minor.

■ **Object Desktop**—As on Windows, Stardock's Object Desktop provides the capability to alter the appearance of windows in a quite dramatic manner.

Altering the Mouse's Appearance and Behavior in OS/2

OS/2 provides the means to customize the appearance and function of your mouse by using the Mouse dialog box, available by opening the Mouse item in the System Setup window. As with Windows, you can adjust the mouse's speed and other operational details. You can also edit each of several mouse pointers by selecting the appropriate pointer and clicking Edit from the Pointers tab (see Figure 17.10). Several packages are available on OS/2 FTP sites that include sets of modified mouse pointers.

A pair of utilities, FeelX and XFeel, both alter the behavior of the mouse so that it works more like the mouse in some X Window System window managers. Specifically, these tools can adjust the OS/2 mouse so that you can send OS/2's keyboard and mouse input to a window merely by moving the mouse over the window, without clicking it or bringing it to the front of the stack. FeelX also enables you to program the function of the middle mouse button if you have a three-button mouse.

FIGURE 17.10
Adjust your OS/2
mouse pointers using
the Mouse dialog box.

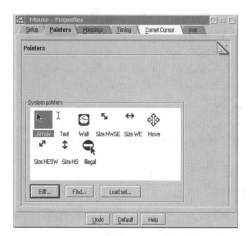

WPS Add-On Utilities

OS/2's WPS is a powerful desktop environment. One of the keys to understanding the WPS is to realize that it is intensely *object oriented*—that is, each icon, file browser window, or other object is a tool that can be customized. Typically, you access an object's features by right-clicking it. It is a fairly simple matter to adjust the menus available when you do so, and many tools exist to modify the default WPS behavior in one way or another. In fact, it is even possible to design entire applications around WPS objects, forgoing the usual program window. With such a program, you right-click the desktop object to obtain a menu with which to control the application. Sadly, few programs take full advantage of the WPS's capabilities. Some that modify it or use it in a limited way include

- **Multiple desktop utilities**—Programs such as Login and Muser create multiple WPS setups. You can use these on a system that is used by more than one person to enable users to customize their desktops. These programs do not, however, provide the sort of multiuser security that is possible with Windows NT or any UNIX system.

- **WPS class extensions**—Utilities such as WPClsExt and WPFldExt change the default behavior of existing WPS features or add functionality, such as displaying extra information about the contents of a directory window or adding new arrangement options to the main desktop menu.

- **Object Desktop**—Stardock's Object Desktop again deserves mention. In addition to adding a virtual desktop pager and modifying the appearance of windows, Object Desktop adds several new object types, some of which integrate quite closely into the WPS. For example, Object Desktop adds the capability to process several archive file formats, such as zip files. The WPS integration means that you can double-click a zip file and view the archive's contents as if it were a folder. You can then add, extract, and delete items by using drag-and-drop operations with other windows and WPS icons.

GUI Add-Ons for BeOS

Compared to Windows or even OS/2, BeOS is a new OS, and its user base is small. Therefore, it hosts relatively few GUI add-on utilities. In fact, many of the GUI customization tools for BeOS are included with the OS itself. These features include

- **Icon customizations**—You can change the icon for individual desktop objects by right-clicking the object and choosing Add-Ons, File Type from the resulting context menu. You can then edit the icon by double-clicking the image in the icon well (see Figure 17.11).

FIGURE 17.11
You can customize icons one at a time using the File Type dialog box.

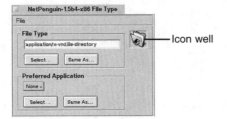

- **Workspaces**—This feature isn't truly a GUI add-on, but BeOS includes a desktop pager. You can switch between desktop screens by typing Alt+F*n*, where *n* is the desktop number. You can also select a visual pager application by choosing Preferences, Workspaces from the Be menu. Unlike most pagers for other OSs, BeOS's pager enables you to set different screen resolutions on your different desktops, so you can run one desktop at high resolution and another at low resolution if you need to do so.

- **Window decor**—Just as Object Desktop lets you change window decorations in Windows or OS/2, BeOS includes a similar (but more limited) capability, but it is hidden. To use this feature, hold down the Ctrl, Shift, and Alt keys on the left side of your keyboard and click the main Be menu. You should see a new menu item titled Window Decor. Subitems on this menu are BeOS, AmigaOS, MacOS 8, and Windows 95/98. Select an item to change the window border appearance to match the OS in question.

- **Font settings**—You can change the fonts used on menus, dialog boxes, and so on by choosing Preferences, Fonts from the Be menu. This action produces the Fonts dialog box shown in Figure 17.12. Change the three font types to whatever you like.

FIGURE 17.12
The plain, bold, and fixed font types are each used in various capacities, such as for window title bars and dialog box text.

BeOS file archive sites, such as http://www.be.com/software/beware, contain utilities that help you customize other aspects of the BeOS GUI. Most of these utilities offer improvements to existing tools, such as new ways to switch between workspaces or add minor new features. As time goes on, though, the number and flexibility of these GUI utilities is likely to increase.

The X Window System: The Chameleon of GUIs

In their effort to make their OSs easy to use, companies such as Microsoft, IBM, and Be have tied various levels of their GUI environments together quite closely, or at least minimized the appearance of different levels from the end user's perspective. Not so with the developers of UNIX GUIs—UNIX GUIs remain clearly stratified into distinct products, which can often be mixed and matched to achieve whatever specific effect a person desires. This flexibility comes at the cost of consistency, however. Even a single desktop can display programs using half a dozen or more distinctly different user interfaces. This fact can be frustrating to many new users, but it is not too distressing when you're used to it. The consistency of UNIX user interfaces has increased in recent years, as well, as developers have begun to focus on a handful of GUI toolkits and as these toolkits have begun to converge in look and feel.

Part

VI

Ch

17

N O T E You as a user determine some aspects of the GUI environment for all your programs, but the programmer specifies other features. This mix of control is what is responsible for both UNIX's end-user customizability and the potential for variable user interfaces on a single desktop. ■

Understanding the X GUI Model

The GUI environment used in most UNIX versions is known as *the X Window System*, or *X* for short. There are competing GUIs, but most of these are quite rare. If you have a NeXT computer or run NeXTStep, you use one such alternative GUI. The rest of this discussion applies only to X.

The layers of the X GUI environment are as follows:

■ **X**—X itself occupies the low end of the X GUI hierarchy. X is a set of protocols for a network-based GUI environment, which means that the computer on which a program runs need not be the same as the computer at which the user sits. This fact makes X extremely powerful in a networked environment—several people can use a single UNIX workstation simultaneously, even using X programs. Each user needs a computer that runs an *X server*, which is the program that handles display and keyboard input. On free UNIX-like OSs such as Linux and FreeBSD, the most common X server is known as *XFree86*, but alternatives do exist. Many commercial UNIX versions come with their own proprietary X servers. In theory, and usually in practice, you can replace one X server with another without disrupting other elements of the X GUI environment. For example, you could replace XFree86 with Xi Graphics' (http://www.xig.com) Accelerated X without modifying your window manager or desktop environment. There are even computers designed to do nothing but function as X servers. These machines are known as *X terminals* and are common in university computer centers and corporations that rely heavily on UNIX.

■ **Window manager**—The *window manager* is the portion of the X GUI environment that displays the border decorations around the window. Besides its aesthetic function, the window manager provides controls to move and size windows and frequently provides program launch, background bitmaps, and virtual desktop paging tools as well. The window manager does not influence anything displayed within the window, however, such as text, buttons, menus, or scrollbars. In most cases, you can change your window manager at will without affecting the functionality of your programs. Some window managers, however, are buggy and interact poorly with some programs.

■ **GUI programming toolkit**—A *GUI programming toolkit* (also known as a *widget set*) is used by a programmer to create a GUI environment under X. This toolkit affects the appearance and operation of all the GUI elements displayed within a window, such as text, buttons, and scrollbars. Unless you modify a program's source code, you have no control over the GUI toolkit used for any given application. Some toolkits provide the user with ways to modify the behavior or appearance of program GUI elements, however.

■ **File manager**—A *file manager* is a tool that you use to work with files and launch programs. A variety of file managers exist for UNIX-like systems, ranging from the simple to the complex. A recent trend has been to integrate file managers with desktop environments.

■ **Desktop environment**—A *desktop environment* is an integrated set of tools, usually centering around a file manager and associated configuration programs. Expressed in UNIX parlance, OS/2's WPS is a desktop environment. Three common desktop environments today are the commercial Common Desktop Environment (CDE), the open-source K Desktop Environment (KDE), and GNU Network Object Model Environment (GNOME).

Aside from the programming toolkit and, occasionally, specific incompatibilities or requirements, you can select each of the components separately. In some sense, X's GUI approach is similar to that of assembling a stereo system from individual components—you can purchase a receiver, tape deck, CD player, and speakers from different vendors. This contrasts with the approach of Windows, OS/2, and BeOS, in which all these components come together in one box, and might in fact be inseparable, much like a one-piece stereo system or boom box.

Selecting a Window Manager

Your choice of window manager determines a great deal about how your GUI environment looks and acts. Figures 17.13 and 17.14 show the same programs run with two window managers, wmx and IceWM, respectively. (Most of the UNIX screen shots in this book use wmx because it is distinctive, thus making it easier to determine which OS is running in a screen shot.) An excellent site that lists many of the available window managers is available at http://www.plig.org/xwinman/. Most of the window managers listed on this site are open source, so they can be used on any UNIX-like OS or any other environment running X.

FIGURE 17.13
wmx is a minimalist window manager that uses unique side-mounted title bars.

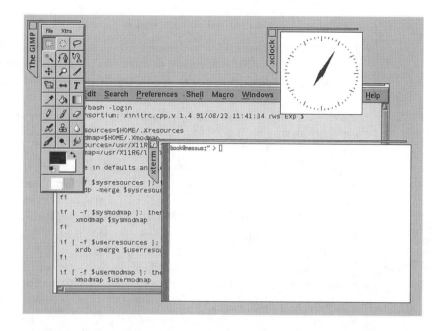

FIGURE 17.14
Several window managers, including IceWM, can emulate the Windows look quite closely.

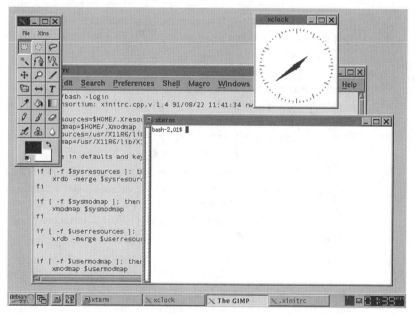

Part
VI

Ch
17

The following are some of the most notable window managers available today:

- **fvwm**—For many years this was the standard window manager on open-source variants of UNIX, but it is fading in popularity as other window managers become available. Find out more at `http://www.fvwm.org/`. Many fvwm variants exist, including fvwm2 and fvwm95.

- **mwm**—The Motif window manager comes with Motif. In many respects, fvwm is modeled after mwm. This is one of the few commercial window managers and is somewhat common on commercial versions of UNIX.

- **IceWM**—IceWM is an increasingly popular window manager. Highly configurable and lightweight but not Spartan, IceWM can be made to resemble several other window managers and OSs, including Mac OS, OS/2 3.0 and 4.0, Windows 3.1, and Windows 9x. The official IceWM Web site is at `http://www.kiss.uni-lj.si/~k4fr0235/icewm/`.

- **Enlightenment**—This window manager is probably the best available when it comes to modifying its appearance. The Enlightenment Web site (`http://www.enlightenment.org/`) includes links to sites with dozens of Enlightenment themes, many of them quite wild. Enlightenment is the default window manager of the GNOME desktop environment (`http://www.gnome.org/`).

- **Window Maker**—Window Maker emulates the NeXT user interface, at least to the extent that a window manager can. It has become popular among many people who want a relatively straightforward window manager with minimal glitz. Its main Web site is at `http://www.windowmaker.org/`. Window Maker is also designed to integrate into GNUStep (`http://www.gnustep.org/`), a project to provide an object-oriented desktop environment modeled after that of the NeXT.

- **wm2 and wmx**—These window managers are similar to each other, but wmx is the more complete—or perhaps it would be fairer to say that wm2 is the more minimalist because both eschew many of the features that are common on even relatively lightweight window managers today. You can learn more at `http://www.all-day-breakfast.com/wmx/`.

- **KWM**—The KDE window manager can't be easily disentangled from the rest of the KDE project, but it deserves mention here nonetheless because of KDE's popularity. You can find more information at `http://www.kde.org/`. Since version 1.1.2, KDE has included a theme manager that enables KWM to emulate other environments, including MacOS and Windows 9x.

Newcomers to UNIX-like OSs often post to Usenet newsgroups asking what the "best" window manager is. There is no such thing. Window manager choice is highly personal, like your preferences in food or clothing style. To some extent these preferences boil down to the aesthetic issues, but they also relate to the memory requirements of the window managers and the features they offer. For example, most of the window managers I've mentioned here provide built-in virtual desktop pagers, but a few, such as wm2, do not. Most window managers provide some means to add programs to a menu of program choices, obtainable through a pop-up desktop menu or a control bar of some sort. How you configure and access these menus varies from one program to another. Therefore, all I can suggest is that you try several window managers until you find one you like.

Fortunately, changing window managers is fairly simple. You must normally create a file in your home directory called `.xinitrc`, `.xsession`, `.profile`, or something similar. (Different distributions use different X startup filenames.) This file is a text file that contains information on programs to start when you launch X or log in using a GUI login procedure. Include the name of your window manager as the last item in this file, and you're finished. Remove that entry, or replace it with the name of your original window manager to return to using it. Some window managers even include a way to close down and launch another window manager without disrupting running programs, so you might be able to switch back and forth within a single login session.

Selecting a File Manager

The file manager you select influences how you perform routine file maintenance and might provide alternative means of launching programs, beyond an xterm window or menus available in your window manager. File managers play an important role in the increasingly popular desktop environments, but there are alternatives beyond these environments, including the following:

- **Midnight Commander**—Midnight Commander, or mc, is a text-based file manager modeled after the once-popular Norton Commander DOS program. As a text-based program, you can run it even when you're not using X, but it also works fine in an xterm window, as shown in Figure 17.15.

FIGURE 17.15
Midnight Commander uses a two-paned view to display your files and directories.

- **XFM**—XFM is a crude file manager by most standards, but it remains useful, particularly on low-memory systems. The program uses two windows, one for file browsing (on the left in Figure 17.16) and the other for launching programs. To add a program to the second window, you must edit a text configuration file.

FIGURE 17.16
XFM uses an older GUI programming toolkit, so it has a decidedly crude appearance.

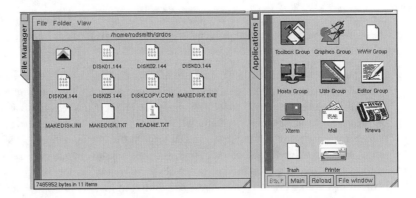

- **DFM**—The Desktop File Manager (DFM) is based loosely on OS/2's WPS but is not nearly as complex. Nonetheless, DFM does support program and file icons placed in directory windows or directly on the desktop, as shown in Figure 17.17.

FIGURE 17.17
DFM can display directories in several formats, and can launch programs via program icons or by association with data files.

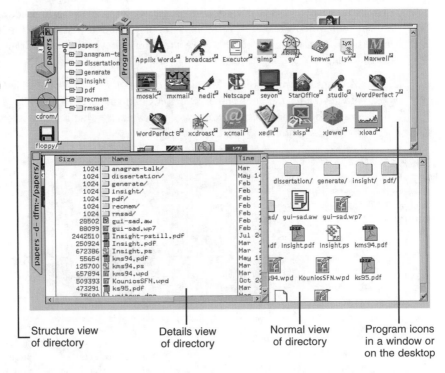

Structure view of directory

Details view of directory

Normal view of directory

Program icons in a window or on the desktop

- **Desktop environment file managers**—The common UNIX desktop environments all contain file managers. These typically resemble the file managers of Windows, OS/2, BeOS, or DFM, although the details differ. I describe these environments in greater detail shortly.

Like window managers, file managers are tools that you select based in large part on your own individual needs and personal preferences. If you're used to a complex GUI environment such as that of Windows or OS/2, you might want to use a desktop environment such as KDE or GNOME along with its file manager. If you want to use a more minimal GUI environment, you can use a simpler file manager such as DFM, XFM, or even Midnight Commander. You can also mix and match these programs as you see fit; there is no reason you can't use Midnight Commander from within GNOME, for example.

Complete Desktop Environments

In the open-source UNIX world, a battle is raging between KDE and GNOME. Each of these environments contends to be the dominant desktop on OSs such as Linux and FreeBSD. KDE has the lead; it is an older project and has developed a substantial following. GNOME has its adherents, though, and is supported by Red Hat and Debian, two of the major Linux distributions. If you're familiar with Windows or OS/2, you should find both KDE and GNOME manageable, although not quite as polished as the environments with which you're familiar.

Both KDE and GNOME include a window manager, a file manager, and a slew of programs to control and configure assorted aspects of the OS, such as keyboard repeat rates and desktop background colors or images. In addition, both packages include several ancillary programs such as text editors and even Web browsers. In most cases, these ancillary programs can be run with or without the main desktop environment, but the desktops come configured to run the ancillary programs from appropriate menus.

UNIX desktop environments vary from those of OSs such as Windows 9x and OS/2 in several important ways:

■ **Each user has a unique configuration**—In general, a system's account editing programs create identical configurations for each user as a starting point. Each user can alter the same starting point into a unique desktop layout, however, much as in Windows NT. In fact, different users on the same system can use entirely different desktop environments—one can use KDE, a second GNOME, and a third a custom configuration built on, for example, Window Maker and DFM.

■ **New programs aren't automatically added to a user's layout**—When you add a program in Windows or OS/2, it is common for the setup program to add an icon or folder to the desktop to let you easily run this new program. Not so in UNIX-like OSs. As a system administrator, you might be able to edit a system-wide configuration file, if all your users use a single environment, to provide access to a new application; or you might need to instruct each user to add appropriate icons or menu entries manually.

■ **Ordinary users have limited access to hardware**—Because UNIX is a multi-user OS, ordinary users aren't given access to most low-level hardware devices. For example, an ordinary user can't install a new sound card driver, although an ordinary user generally can adjust the keyboard repeat rate or the audio card's volume settings. You might therefore need to log in as root to perform some tasks, even from within a desktop environment.

Part
VI

Ch
17

KDE KDE is built around Troll Tech's (http://www.troll.no/) Qt cross-platform development libraries. This simple fact is one of the prime reasons why the competing GNOME project was begun; at one time, Troll Tech used a license for Qt that could easily have derailed the open-source KDE project, should Troll Tech have decided to change the license terms. Since that time, however, Troll Tech has developed a new license that ensures the continued availability of Qt for open-source development, so the sharp ideological furor surrounding the KDE versus GNOME debates has subsided substantially since 1998. The remaining issues relate to the environments' features and supported applications.

Figure 17.18 shows a KDE desktop featuring a file browser and the KDE Control Center. The KDE file browser is modeled after a Web browser, and in fact doubles as one—you merely need to type a URL into the Location field in the window to open a Web browser on a page.

File browser doubles
as a Web browser

FIGURE 17.18
KDE offers a variety of features familiar to users of other OSs.

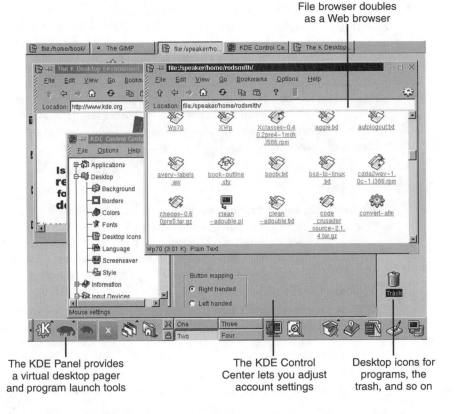

The KDE Panel provides a virtual desktop pager and program launch tools

The KDE Control Center lets you adjust account settings

Desktop icons for programs, the trash, and so on

The details of a KDE desktop layout vary from one installation to another. Figure 17.18 shows the default configuration for a SuSE Linux 6.2 installation (you can see a pair of SuSE logos in the Panel). Most installations include several desktop icons to access commonly used programs and directories, as well as program entries in the Panel, under the KDE *K* logo on the extreme left side of the Panel. The KDE logo menu functions much like the Windows Start menu, in fact.

KDE is tightly tied to its own window manager, KWM. This fact can be limiting if you're not fond of KWM. KDE 1.1.2 and later support a theme feature that lets you modify the look and feel of KWM, KDE applications, and even some non-KDE applications. KDE is associated with a variety of projects designed to build applications that integrate well into KDE. The most notable of these is the KOffice project (`http://koffice.kde.org/`), which is working to produce an office suite (word processor, spreadsheet, and so on). You can use KOffice, and even many of the programs that come bundled with KDE, without running the full KDE package. For example, if you like the KEdit text editor, you can use it from GNOME or any other environment, although you might need to install several KDE support tools and libraries to use KDE programs in non-KDE environments.

GNOME GNOME is built around the GIMP Toolkit (GTK+) widget set, which in turn was originally developed to support the GNU Image Manipulation Program (GIMP) image editor. As you might suspect given the expansion of these names, GTK+ is fully open source, and in fact is favored by the Free Software Foundation. The open-source nature of GTK+ was one of the reasons it was chosen for use in developing GNOME. GTK+ is also becoming an extremely popular GUI toolkit. (GTK+ is being used in the Mozilla project for the next generation of Netscape on UNIX-like OSs, for example.)

Figure 17.19 shows a Linux system running GNOME, along with applications that are the equivalents of those in Figure 17.18's KDE display.

Part
VI

Ch
17

Desktop icons for programs,
the trash, and so on

File browser can display
files in a variety of forms

FIGURE 17.19
GNOME offers func-
tionality and user inter-
face features similar to
those of KDE.

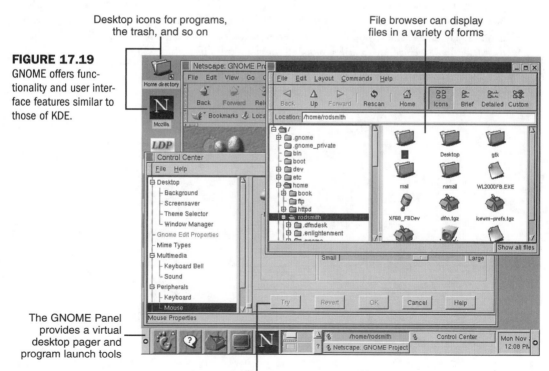

The GNOME Panel
provides a virtual
desktop pager and
program launch tools

The GNOME Control Center lets
you adjust account settings

Unlike KDE, GNOME isn't tied to any one window manager. Instead, GNOME includes features that enable it to integrate well with compliant window managers. Most GNOME systems, on installation, use the Enlightenment window manager, but you can substitute IceWM, Window Maker, or other window managers if you prefer.

Whatever window manager you run, GNOME offers desktop icons and program launch facilities via the GNOME Panel similar to those of KDE (GNOME uses a G-shaped footprint logo for its program launch menu). GNOME also includes a virtual desktop pager, a clock, and similar features.

Summary

One of the challenges in using a multi-OS system is in adapting to the differing user interfaces across OSs. Some details, such as the colors and designs of window borders, are trivial, although you might want to change such features for purely aesthetic reasons. Other details, such as the presence or absence of virtual desktop pagers, are more critical to your experience with an OS. Fortunately, a variety of utilities exist to help you adjust the appearance and behavior of most OSs' desktop environments. In Windows and OS/2, these tools take the form of small utilities or built-in configuration options that modify some small aspect of the user interface. Occasionally, as in Stardock's Object Desktop, these tools are bundled together into a package that can do many things. In UNIX-like OSs, you modify the user interface by swapping out one entire component, such as a window manager, and replacing it with another. The increasingly popular integrated desktop environments for X place a uniform and user-friendly interface on a variety of small tools and utilities, which can help you learn a UNIX-like OS by providing increased internal consistency. ●

OSs Within OSs: Emulators

When to Use an Emulator

Running several OSs on a single computer can be a liberating experience, but it can sometimes be a frustrating one, particularly if there are programs and utilities that you must use under two or more OSs. For example, suppose that you need to create Microsoft Word documents to satisfy your boss, but you also need to use a UNIX-like OS for a programming project. If you have only one computer with more than one OS, the result will be a lot of time spent rebooting the system between OSs—particularly if you need to write up documentation on your UNIX program using Microsoft Word!

▶ To learn about cross-platform data file formats to help free you from single-application limitations, **see** "Platform-Independent File Formats," **p. 358**.

One solution to a dilemma such as this is to use multiple computers. This solution, however, costs in desk space, electricity use, and of course cold hard cash for the equipment itself. Another solution is somewhat less costly, if also somewhat imperfect: *emulators*. An emulator is a program that enables you to run one OS's software in another OS. Emulators can be broken down into three basic classes:

■ **OS API emulators**—An OS's *application programming interface (API)* is the collection of methods that a program can use to request services from an OS, such as opening a file or displaying a new window. An API emulator implements one OS's API in another OS. WINE, discussed later in this chapter, is an example of an API emulator.

■ **Machine environment emulators**—A machine environment emulator goes one step further and sets up a virtual computer using special CPU features. A copy of the emulated OS, sometimes modified slightly, can then run in the virtual environment. The DOS emulators I discuss in this chapter use this method.

■ **CPU emulators**—A CPU emulator is like a machine environment emulator, except that it also emulates the computer's *central processing unit (CPU)*, the core of the computer. The Executor program (http://www.ardi.com) uses this method to enable a PC to emulate a Macintosh, to name just one example.

In most cases, you aren't particularly interested in which of these three categories best describes the emulator; you want to emulate a specific OS, and there is seldom more than one choice to emulate a given OS in another. I describe many of these products in the pages that follow.

Emulating Non-x86 OSs

Although the focus of this chapter is on emulators for common x86 OSs, additional emulators are available. For the most part, these emulators let you run software for older computers, such as Apple II or Atari ST machines. Emulators for game consoles are also available, as are a few emulators for non-x86 computers that are somewhat more modern in design.

One Web site that is particularly helpful if you're interested in emulators for video game systems is http://www.explosionnet.co.uk/emu/. This site contains links, FAQs, and other information about video game emulators.

Executor, written by ARDI (http://www.ardi.com/), is an x86-based emulator of 680x0 Macintoshes. It can be a useful tool for running older Macintosh software under x86 OSs.

The site http://www.champ.force9.co.uk/emu.html has information on a large number of emulators, both for video game systems and for serious computers.

One word of warning: Many of these CPU emulators require ROMs from the systems they emulate—or, rather, image files of those ROMs. To use these emulators legally, you must generally own the computer or video game system you're emulating, and not use that system while using the emulator.

N O T E "When to Run an Emulator, Multi-Boot, or Use Multiple Computers," later in this chapter, includes tips on how to decide whether to run an emulator, run multiple OSs in a more conventional way, or use several computers. ■

DOS Compatibility and Emulators

As one of the oldest and, for a long time, most popular OSs on PCs, DOS has been the target of a great deal in the way of emulation efforts. OS/2, originally intended as a replacement for DOS, included a DOS emulator even in its first version, although OS/2's DOS emulation improved substantially with OS/2 2.0. Microsoft's Windows products support DOS emulation—in fact, Windows 9*x* is built atop a 32-bit version of DOS, so calling Windows 9*x*'s DOS support *emulation* might be a bit of an exaggeration. Even Linux includes DOS emulation.

Most of these DOS emulators use a special operating mode of the x86 CPU. In this mode, the CPU sets up a special environment in which DOS software can execute a subset of the available x86 instructions, without interfering with the control of the host OS over most of the system's hardware. The result of this bit of trickery is that DOS—either an off-the-shelf variety or a version tweaked by the OS producer—believes it has full control over the computer, when in fact is has control only over its *virtual DOS machine (VDM)*.

Support for DOS in Windows 9*x*

There are two ways to run a DOS program within Windows 9*x*:

■ **In a regular Windows boot**—Generally speaking, the DOS program runs in a window, although you can configure Windows to run the program in its own screen, hiding the normal Windows desktop. Running DOS programs within Windows is generally the most convenient method of running these programs, but because Windows controls a great deal of the computer's hardware, some programs can't run properly in this mode.

■ **From a DOS mode boot**—You can boot Windows 9*x* without the GUI, leaving only the core DOS components. This method provides the greatest DOS compatibility, but at the cost of an inability to use any of Windows' more advanced features, including multitasking and its GUI environment.

Part
VI

Ch
18

I present information on both of these methods in upcoming sections. Many games require a DOS-mode boot, but most non-game programs (and even many games) work equally well in either method. It is important to understand something of how Windows 9x handles its DOS duties, and why it does so as it does, however. I therefore begin with a description of the history of the Windows 9x architecture.

An Historical Perspective on Windows 9x and DOS Windows 9x is built atop DOS. In 1995, Microsoft took MS-DOS and Windows 3.1 and merged them into a single product: Windows 95. The resulting OS included DOS at its core but added support for preemptive multitasking, 32-bit Windows programs, and assorted other features that had long been present in other OSs, including Microsoft's own Windows NT.

▶ To learn more about preemptive multitasking, **see** "Windows 3.1: A DOS Extension," **p. 29**.

Why, then, would anybody want to use a product that had been, essentially, patched to support modern features rather than a clean design such as Windows NT, which also supported 32-bit Windows programs? Four reasons existed for the success of Windows 95 over NT:

- **Price**—Windows 95 cost less than Windows NT.
- **System resources**—Windows 95 consumed less RAM, CPU power, and hard disk space than did Windows NT, meaning that Windows 95 could run on less powerful computers.
- **User interface**—Microsoft introduced user interface improvements in Windows 95 that didn't make their way into the NT line until Windows NT 4.0.
- **DOS compatibility**—Windows 95 did a better job of running DOS programs (especially games) than did Windows NT. At the time Windows 95 was introduced, DOS programs were still common. Although Windows NT can multitask older 16-bit Windows programs better than can Windows 9x, Windows 9x can run more 16-bit Windows titles, so to the general consumer, Windows 9x retains an edge in running older Windows programs, as well.

With the exception of user interface differences, these comparisons are still valid today, although the current comparison is of Windows 98 to Windows 2000.

Running DOS Programs in a Window You can run DOS programs within a window on your Windows desktop, as shown in Figure 18.1. To do so, you need only double-click a DOS program icon, much as you would a Windows program icon. You can also create shortcuts and Start menu items to launch DOS programs. Not all DOS programs run well in such windows, however; some use 32-bit memory extenders or directly access the computer's hardware, and such programs frequently present problems when run under Windows.

Assuming your program runs in a window, you can adjust various aspects of its functioning from the program's Properties dialog box (see Figure 18.2), which you obtain by right-clicking on the program file or shortcut and choosing Properties from the resulting pop-up menu.

FIGURE 18.1
When you run a DOS program, such as WordPerfect 5.1, in a window, you retain access to Windows programs.

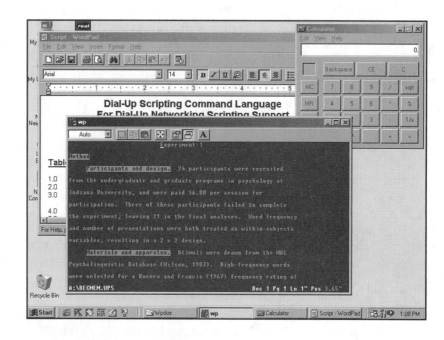

FIGURE 18.2
The Properties dialog box for a DOS program lets you fine-tune the program's environment.

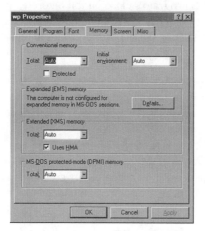

The Properties dialog box has several tabs, each of which has settings controlling related aspects of the DOS environment that Windows creates for the program. These tabs and their settings are

■ **General**—The General tab provides more in the way of information than control. You can learn the file's size, its name, and so on. You can also set filesystem attributes for the program file (read-only, hidden, and archive).

■ **Program**—You can set the working directory and determine whether the program runs in a minimized, maximized, or normal-sized window. In addition, if you click the Advanced button, you can tell Windows whether to let the DOS program detect that it is running under Windows or configure the program to temporarily shut down most of Windows and enter full MS-DOS mode.

■ **Font**—If you configure the program to run in a window (using the Screen tab), you can use the Font tab to specify what font you want the program to use.

■ **Memory**—Over the years, DOS has accumulated a variety of memory management tools to get around the 640KB limit imposed by the original 8088 CPU and design of the IBM PC. You can tell Windows to provide varying degrees of memory under each of three such schemes (EMS, XMS, and DPMI). You can also tell Windows how much of the low 640KB to provide to the program.

■ **Screen**—You can specify various aspects of how the program interacts with the screen using this tab. For example, you can tell Windows to run the DOS program inside an ordinary window (the default) or full-screen (not to be confused with a boot into full DOS mode). You can also select or remove assorted options designed to improve performance or give you access to font settings and so on when you run the program.

■ **Misc**—This tab enables you to set various options that simply don't fit elsewhere. For example, the Warn if Still Active check button causes Windows to display a warning dialog box if you click a DOS program's close button before exiting from the DOS program; and the Idle Sensitivity slider helps you fine-tune the DOS program to interfere least with other running programs. (DOS programs tend to chew up CPU time even when they're doing nothing.)

 TIP You can set these options either from the program file or from a shortcut that points to the program file. If you create multiple shortcuts, you can create a different configuration for each shortcut. For example, one shortcut could launch the program in a window and another could do so full-screen.

This assortment of controls can be useful in fine-tuning your DOS applications to run well in Windows. One application might require XMS memory, whereas another might need EMS memory. You can run both programs without rebooting by creating appropriate settings for each program. Indeed, you can run these programs simultaneously, despite their differing requirements.

Booting Windows into DOS Mode   In some cases, a program simply doesn't work well (if at all) from within the full Windows GUI environment. This situation is particularly common among DOS games, which often require unfettered access to the low-level PC hardware. Because Windows controls such access, it is best to run such games from DOS or from a Windows DOS mode boot.

The easiest way to run programs using DOS mode is to open the program's Properties dialog box, click the Program tab, and click the Advanced button. You can then select the MS-DOS Mode check button, as shown in Figure 18.3. You can specify a unique CONFIG.SYS and

AUTOEXEC.BAT file for each program to set environment variables or drivers needed by only one program. After Windows is configured in this way, it shuts down its GUI and multitasking features when you launch the DOS program. When you exit from the DOS program, Windows reloads its full environment.

FIGURE 18.3
Selecting MS-DOS Mode in the Advanced Program Settings dialog box causes Windows to strip itself down to DOS essentials when you launch the program.

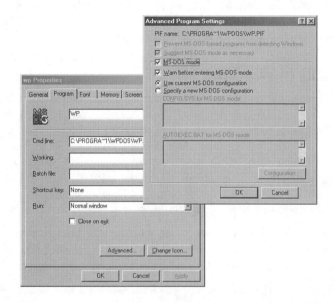

CAUTION

When you launch a program that is configured to run in full MS-DOS mode, Windows closes all other open programs. Therefore, you should be sure to leave the Warn Before Entering MS-DOS Mode check box checked. If you uncheck this box, you could accidentally shut down open programs if you mistakenly launch a program that is configured to run in full DOS mode. Most programs will give you the option to save your files even with Warn Before Entering MS-DOS Mode unchecked, however.

You can also configure your system to launch directly into DOS mode in various ways. When this happens, Windows acts very much like DOS, except that it provides access to FAT-32 partitions (assuming you're using Windows 95 OSR2 or later). The following are some ways to boot directly into DOS mode:

■ **Boot floppy**—If you create an emergency boot floppy, booting from it results in a DOS-mode boot.

■ **Boot loader**—Some boot loaders, such as System Commander, can provide an option to launch Windows into DOS mode or full GUI mode.

▶ To learn more about System Commander, **see** "V Communications's System Commander," **p. 107**.

Part
VI

Ch
18

- AUTOEXEC.BAT—If you call COMMAND.COM in your AUTOEXEC.BAT file, Windows boots into DOS mode. You probably want to wrap such a call around a simple menu system to let you choose DOS or GUI boots.

- **Built-in boot options**—If you press the F8 key as soon as Windows 95 begins to boot, when you see Starting Windows 95 on the screen, Windows responds by presenting a series of boot options. One of these is to boot in DOS mode. In Windows 98, similar functionality is available when you press and hold the Ctrl key during the boot process.

Support for DOS in Windows NT

Windows NT isn't built on DOS and therefore relies on more explicit DOS emulation than does Windows 9x. As a result, Windows NT has no equivalent to the Windows 9x full DOS boot, and Windows NT can't run many DOS programs that rely on full and complete access to the computer's low-level hardware. Nonetheless, Windows NT includes DOS support that is capable of running many DOS programs and especially DOS programs that don't require low-level hardware access. This category includes most DOS business applications but excludes many DOS games. Therefore, Windows NT's DOS support is good for business uses but not as good for a home game player.

You install and configure a DOS program in Windows NT much as you do in Windows 9x. The DOS Properties dialog box, however, includes some variations compared to its Windows 9x counterpart shown in Figure 18.2:

- **Security tab**—You can set security information on a program file or shortcut. You could use this feature to allow some users to access the program while denying access to others.

- **Windows NT PIF Settings**—Instead of the Advanced button on the Program tab, Windows NT provides a Windows NT button, which produces the Windows NT PIF Settings dialog box, shown in Figure 18.4. You can enter the name of AUTOEXEC.BAT and CONFIG.SYS files for the program, but you can't set the program to run in full DOS mode, as you can in Windows 9x.

FIGURE 18.4
You can customize some aspects of a DOS session's environment by specifying unique configuration files.

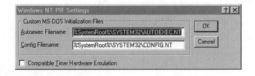

Support for DOS in OS/2

At one time, an advertising slogan for OS/2 was "a better DOS than DOS, a better Windows than Windows." This slogan was based on the fact that OS/2 offers an extremely configurable DOS emulation—you can tell OS/2 to provide specified amounts of memory to DOS programs, provide access to sound card hardware, and so on. If you disable VGA graphics settings, you can even provide DOS programs with more than the usual limit of 640KB of conventional memory. In most respects, OS/2's DOS emulation is more flexible than the DOS support for DOS programs run from within Windows 9x or Windows NT. OS/2 does still suffer from an incapability to run certain DOS programs, however. Like Windows NT, OS/2 uses the x86 CPU's VDM to provide DOS programs with a working environment, so programs that try to perform actions not permitted by the VDM usually crash or fail to run at all.

To configure a DOS program in OS/2, follow these steps:

1. Create a new program object by dragging the New Program icon (in the Programs folder on a new OS/2 installation) to a convenient location. OS/2 displays the Properties dialog box shown in Figure 18.5.

FIGURE 18.5
You can include parameters to pass to a program and specify a default working directory when you create an OS/2 program object.

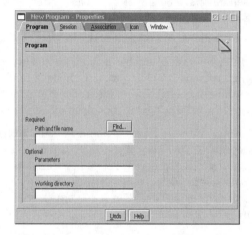

Part

VI

Ch

18

2. Type the complete path to the program in the Path and File Name field, or use the Find button to locate the program file.
3. Switch to the Icon tab and enter a name for the program object in the Title field.
4. Switch to the Session tab. If you selected a DOS program file, the DOS Full Screen and DOS Window radio buttons should be available. Select whichever you want to use.
5. If you want to fine-tune your DOS session for best performance, click the DOS Properties button. In OS/2 4.0, this produces the DOS Settings - Categories dialog box, from which you can select what categories of settings you want to adjust. If you pick All DOS Settings and click OK, OS/2 displays the DOS Settings - All DOS Settings dialog box shown in Figure 18.6. If you select some subset of settings, only those in the category you select will be available.

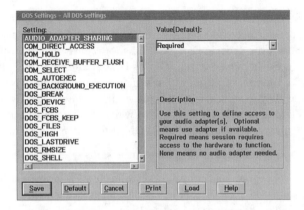

FIGURE 18.6
You can customize the DOS VDM using the DOS Settings dialog box.

6. Scroll through the settings and adjust their values as desired. The Description field shows what effect a given setting has on the DOS environment.

7. Click Save to save your settings, and then close the Properties dialog box.

You can now launch your DOS program by double-clicking its icon in the OS/2 WorkPlace Shell (WPS). A DOS program running in OS/2 works much like a DOS program running in Windows, except that the features accessible from the icon bar in Windows are available from a menu when you single-click the close widget in the upper-left corner of the window.

OS/2's DOS emulation provides you with access to both FAT and HPFS partitions, but you can't see long filenames from DOS. Therefore, if you use long filenames on an HPFS partition, you can't see those files from DOS programs. Note that this restriction applies to directory names as well as filenames—the file D:\LongDirName\SFN.TXT is invisible to DOS programs, despite the fact that the SFN.TXT portion is 8.3-compliant. If you move the file to another directory, DOS programs can see it.

If you share a FAT partition between Windows and OS/2, OS/2's DOS emulation enables you to read files with long VFAT filenames because those files have short 8.3-compliant names. In fact, OS/2 works just like DOS in this respect.

Linux's DOSEMU

Not to be left out of the DOS action, Linux programmers have developed *DOSEMU*, a program that sets up a VDM much like the one used by OS/2. Through much of its development, DOSEMU required that you have an existing license of a commercial DOS to run the program. More recently, however, many Linux distributions have shipped with both DOSEMU and a copy of FreeDOS, so you can often make do without a license to a commercial DOS. If you want to, however, you can run MS-DOS, PC-DOS, or DR-DOS within DOSEMU. In fact, DOSEMU even runs Windows 9*x* in DOS boot mode.

TIP If you have a license to a commercial DOS, it is generally a good idea to use it instead of FreeDOS. This is because FreeDOS is incapable of *redirection*, which is a feature used by DOSEMU to provide access to Linux filesystems from DOSEMU.

DOSEMU is configured through a file that is typically called /etc/dosemu.conf. The syntax used by this file has changed several times over DOSEMU's history, so I suggest you check your documentation to determine how to modify the entries to suit your needs. Typically, though, you set parameters similar to those available under Windows or OS/2, as in

```
$_xms = (1024)
$_ems = (1024)
$_dpmi = (off)
```

These lines set the amounts of XMS, EMS, and DPMI memory available to the DOS session. One particularly important aspect of DOSEMU configuration is the specification of the boot disk. DOSEMU can use several different types of disks:

- **Floppy disks**—You can point DOSEMU to the floppy disk device files (such as /dev/fd0) on your computer.

- **Hard disk partitions**—Just as with floppy disks, you can point DOSEMU at a hard disk partition, such as /dev/hda1.

N O T E DOSEMU can't use a device file if that device is already in use—for example, if you've mounted a partition to access it in Linux. If you need simultaneous access to a device from both DOSEMU and other Linux programs, you must use redirection. ■

- **Disk image files**—An *image file* is a file that contains a filesystem. For example, many DOSEMU installations use a file called hdimage as a stand-in for a hard disk. You can install a complete copy of DOS on hdimage and then boot DOSEMU from it. When a Linux distribution ships with FreeDOS for DOSEMU to use, FreeDOS comes on a ready-made disk image file.

- **Redirected disks**—DOSEMU includes a utility program called LREDIR that enables you to access Linux files from within DOSEMU. You must explicitly mount a Linux directory tree onto a DOS drive letter. For example, you might make /mnt/cdrom available as D:.

Using disk image files is generally the easiest method of disk access, followed by device files. Setting up redirection can be tricky, particularly because this procedure doesn't work with FreeDOS. You must also normally have a non-redirected disk (a disk image or a disk accessed via a device file) available as the boot disk.

Compared to Windows and OS/2, Linux's DOS support is both difficult to configure and inflexible—it is not easy to configure DOSEMU to run different programs with different options. Nonetheless, if you're willing to invest some time in configuring DOSEMU, it can be an excellent way to retain access to a limited collection of DOS programs for which no Linux substitutes exist.

Windows Emulators

In today's computing world, Windows emulation is generally more interesting than is DOS emulation. Although DOS applications continue to hang on in certain categories, most new mainstream programs are written for Windows. Therefore, Windows emulation is an important consideration for many people running multi-OS configurations.

Two broad classes of Windows programs are important in any discussion of Windows emulation:

- **Win16**—16-bit Windows programs use the so-called *Win16 API*, which was popularized by Windows 3.1 and its predecessors. This type of program uses 16-bit memory addresses, which means that programs must break large data structures into 64KB (2^{16} byte) chunks—an annoying proposition from a programmer's point of view, and one that reduces the speed of programs that deal with large data structures.

- **Win32**—32-bit Windows programs use the *Win32 API*. In fact, there are several Win32 variants. Essentially, Win32s (a 32-bit extension for Windows 3.1), Windows 9*x*, and Windows NT sport slightly different Win32 APIs. Fortunately, there is enough overlap that most Win32 programs run on both Windows 9*x* and Windows NT. An emulator attempting to run Win32 programs must navigate its way around this minefield of minor variants in the Win32 APIs, however.

OS/2's Windows Emulators

OS/2 sports two means of running Windows programs, although only one is a complete system. The complete emulator is *Win-OS/2*—Windows 3.1 running on OS/2's DOS emulation. The incomplete system is Odin, which is in the early stages of development. It is designed to enable OS/2 to run Win32 programs. In addition to these two projects, there are efforts underway to use the UNIX WINE program, described later in this chapter.

OS/2's Win-OS/2 Subsystem   Since version 2.0, OS/2 has shipped with some form of Windows emulation. Most versions of OS/2 have included a complete copy of Windows 3.1, recompiled by IBM and renamed *Win-OS/2*. IBM also released versions of OS/2 2.1 and 3.0 that used an existing Windows 3.1 installation for Windows emulation purposes. These versions have come to be known as the *for Windows* versions of OS/2, although this term was only a part of the OS/2 2.1 product's title. I refer to all these methods of running Windows within OS/2 as *Win-OS/2*.

N O T E   Because Win-OS/2 uses a genuine copy of Windows (either as provided by Microsoft or recompiled by IBM), many people don't consider Win-OS/2 to be an emulator. For similar reasons, many people don't consider OS/2's DOS subsystem to be an emulator, either. I refer to both of these as emulators, however, both because doing so simplifies the discussion and because these methods rely on the special VDM feature of the x86 CPU, even if they do use "genuine" OS code for the emulated OS. ■

Whatever the details, Win-OS/2 enables OS/2 to run 16-bit Windows programs. Because Win-OS/2 builds on OS/2's DOS emulation, you can adjust property settings for Win-OS/2 sessions just as you can for DOS sessions. In addition to the DOS settings, there are four additional Win-OS/2 settings you can adjust:

- WIN_RUN_MODE—The options are Standard and Enhanced Compatibility. Despite the name, Enhanced Compatibility is actually detrimental for many programs, so I recommend you stick with Standard unless you experience difficulties.

- WIN_DDE—*Dynamic Data Exchange (DDE)* is a method of sharing data between applications that is supported by both Windows and OS/2. Enabling this option allows data to be shared by DDE between Windows and OS/2 programs.

- WIN_CLIPBOARD—The clipboard is used by cut-and-paste operations for data sharing. Turning on this option enables you to cut and paste data between OS/2 and Windows programs.

- WIN_ATM—OS/2 includes a copy of *Adobe Type Manager (ATM)* for Windows, but it is disabled by default. To enable it you must use this option. ATM enables you to use PostScript Type 1 fonts in Windows programs, in addition to the TrueType fonts that Windows supports natively.

Just as with DOS programs, OS/2 supports running Windows programs in full-screen mode or in a window. In full-screen mode, when you launch or switch to a Windows program, your OS/2 display vanishes and is replaced by a Windows 3.1 display. OS/2 is still running, though, and you can switch back by pressing Ctrl+Esc. For more seamless visual integration, you can run a program in windowed mode, in which the Windows program appears on the WPS desktop aside OS/2 programs, as shown in Figure 18.7.

Part
VI

Ch

18

FIGURE 18.7
When running in windowed mode, a Windows program runs side-by-side with OS/2 programs.

OS/2 program

Windows program

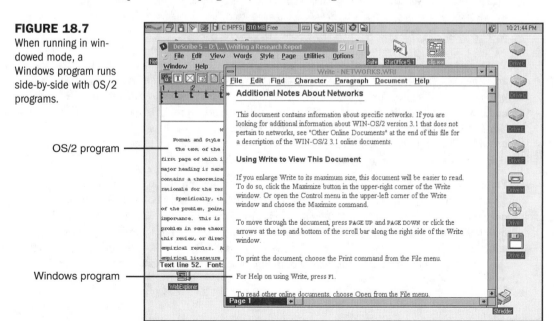

In general, windowed mode is best for productivity programs that you run along with DOS and OS/2 programs, whereas full-screen mode is best for games or other programs that require the best possible video display speed—windowed mode adds overhead that slows down programs' video displays.

One important concept to understand when dealing with Win-OS/2 is that of a *session*. In the context of Win-OS/2 programs, a session is a single DOS VDM running a single instance of Win-OS/2 and one or more Windows programs. When you run two Windows programs on OS/2, you can run them either in the same session or in separate sessions. When you run two Windows programs in a single session, those programs multitask against each other using the Windows 3.1 cooperative multitasking procedures, but the entire Win-OS/2 session multitasks against DOS and OS/2 programs in a preemptive manner. The end result is poorer multitasking between the Windows programs but no adverse effect on DOS or OS/2 programs. When you run two Windows programs in separate sessions, they gain the benefits of OS/2's preemptive multitasking between them, but the cost is increased memory consumption for the additional session.

▶ To learn more about cooperative multitasking, **see** "Windows 3.1: A DOS Extension," **p. 29**.

You can force a program to run in a separate session from other programs by checking the Separate Session check button on the Session tab of the Properties dialog box for the program. OS/2 also opens a separate session for two programs if they have different WIN_RUN_MODE settings. Otherwise, Windows programs all fall into the same session.

TIP   Some programs require certain DOS or Windows settings to operate correctly. For example, you might want to enable ATM for a Windows word processor. If you start a Windows program that uses default settings before you start the one that requires changed settings, you'll lose those settings that you require in the second program. It is therefore best to either start such programs first or set them to run in separate sessions to ensure that they get the settings they require.

Win-OS/2 works well for most Win16 programs, but not for most Win32 programs. There are, however, a few Win32 programs that can run in Win-OS/2. These are known as *Win32s* programs because they use a Windows 3.1 extension of that name. Win32s programs typically come with a copy of Win32s that installs along with the program. OS/2 4.0 can work with versions of Win32s through 1.25, so if you have a program that installs a later version of Win32s, you might need to track down an earlier version to get the program to work under OS/2. (OS/2 3.0 can only use through version 1.15 of Win32s.)

Project Odin, a.k.a. Win32-OS/2   The lack of support for most Win32 programs is a serious shortcoming of Win-OS/2. To overcome this limitation, some efforts have been made to develop a new system, originally known as Win32-OS/2 and now known as Odin. Odin is unusual in that it is not really an emulator; it is more of a translator. Odin takes the executable files for a program and changes their API calls into OS/2 API calls. In some respects this process is similar to the process of compiling a program from source code, except that instead of converting a human-readable file into a machine-readable file, Odin converts from one machine-readable format to another one.

The Odin project stalled in 1998, when it was still known as Win32-OS/2, but a new group has taken it up and renamed it Odin. If you're interested in running Win32 programs on OS/2, you should keep an eye on the Odin Web site, http://en.os2.org/projects/odin/. A few small applications, such as the Windows Solitaire game, already run with Odin, but as of version Alpha 5, no serious applications work with Odin.

WINE in UNIX-Like OSs

WINE is an acronym that stands for either *Windows Emulator* or *WINE Is Not an Emulator*. This bizarre dual meaning derives from the fact that WINE is an OS API emulator, as opposed to a machine environment or CPU emulator. Some people would not apply the term *emulator* to what I call an API emulator because the tool is really a reimplementation of an existing API, not a way to emulate a complete machine environment.

Semantic hair-splitting aside, WINE is a tool for running Windows programs on x86-based versions of UNIX, including Linux and FreeBSD. WINE is currently *alpha* software, which means it is not ready for public consumption. It works well enough, however, to run several programs, including some fairly major ones, with good reliability. Other programs fail miserably, and some likely always will because they need low-level hardware access or other services that simply aren't available on a UNIX platform.

Versions of WINE   WINE isn't yet numbered in the way most computer programs are. Instead, each WINE release is identified by the date on which it was built. You can find precompiled WINE binaries or source code "snapshots" at the main WINE Web site, http://www.winehq.com. Typically, a new snapshot becomes available every 2–4 weeks. If you want to participate in WINE development, you can obtain WINE via *Concurrent Version System (CVS)* distribution, which is a way for a group of people to develop a program without trampling each others' work.

In addition to the date-numbered versions of WINE, WINE can be distinguished by two ways in which it can be used:

- **As an emulator for running Windows programs**—This is the method in which you're probably most interested. In this mode, you use WINE to run a precompiled Windows program. Because most Windows programs come only as precompiled binaries, this is the only way most Windows programs will ever function via WINE.

- **As a GUI programming toolkit**—If you have the source code to a Windows program, you can use WINE to compile that source code into a program that runs natively under the host OS. For example, you can use WINE to produce a native Linux or FreeBSD program. Used in this way, WINE is often referred to as WINElib. Using WINElib to compile a program results in a faster program than you could get by running the original Windows binary under the full WINE emulator. WINElib is also generally more reliable than WINE used to run precompiled Windows binaries.

▶ To learn more about GUI programming toolkits, **see** "Understanding the X GUI Model," **p. 439**.

N O T E Corel (`http://www.corel.com`) is using WINElib to develop its WordPerfect Office 2000 for Linux. WordPerfect 8.0 and earlier for Linux used the commercial Motif GUI toolkit, but Corel decided that using WINElib and sharing the source code base for the Windows and Linux versions of its products would be a better approach than maintaining two sets of source code. WordPerfect Office 2000 for Linux is not currently available, so it remains to be seen how effective Corel and WINElib will be in handling a major application suite. It is certainly a bold move on Corel's part, and the changes they contribute to the WINE project can only improve WINE for all users. ■

Because WINE development is an ongoing process and has been for several years, it is common to find that specific programs start and then stop working over the course of several different WINE releases. The overall trend is positive, but sometimes an upgrade actually breaks important programs, especially from a single user's perspective. If you find a version of WINE that works well for you, therefore, I advise caution in upgrading. You can always return to an older version if necessary—just don't discard the old version's files until you're sure a new version works as well as or better than the old one.

Using WINE to Run Windows Programs   WINE (run as an emulator, not as a library) often requires files from a Windows installation. Specifically, many Windows programs require *dynamic link libraries (DLLs)* that come with Windows and that provide some of Windows' functionality. How well WINE handles a given program might depend on which Windows DLLs you use in conjunction with WINE—those from Windows 3.1, Windows 95, Windows NT, or others. In general, the easiest way to provide WINE with access to Windows files is to mount your Windows partition and edit the `wine.conf` file (which by default goes in the `/usr/local/etc` directory, although some binary versions of WINE might place it elsewhere). The `wine.conf` file is similar in layout to a Windows 3.1 `WIN.INI` file: It consists of several sections, each identified by a bracketed name. Each section contains a series of variable assignments. For example

```
[Drive C]
Path=/win98
Type=hd
Label=WIN98
Filesystem=unix
```

N O T E Individual users can override the contents of the `wine.conf` file by creating a modified version of that file, called `.winerc`, in their home directories. ■

This section identifies the directory that WINE uses as a stand-in for the Windows C: drive. The directory used is /win98, it is a hard disk (Type=hd), it is given a label of WIN98, and it uses a UNIX-style filesystem (using long filenames, most importantly). Of particular interest, aside from the drive identifiers, is the section identified as [wine], in which the Windows and System identifiers are set. WINE looks here for Windows files, so you should point those variables to the C:\WINDOWS and C:\WINDOWS\SYSTEM directories. For example

```
[wine]
Windows=C:\windows
System=C:\windows\system
```

After you have installed WINE and created an appropriate wine.conf file, you can start WINE and run a program by using the following command:

```
wine program.exe
```

The file *program.exe* must reside in a directory that is accessible to WINE programs—that is, it must be in a directory that is given a drive letter in wine.conf or a subdirectory thereof. You can also specify several parameters to wine, including

- -desktop *widthxheight*—WINE normally displays Windows programs directly on your X display. If you use the -desktop option, however, WINE creates an X window for the Windows desktop and places the Windows programs within that desktop window. You specify the dimensions of the desktop window you want to create.

- -managed—WINE normally bypasses your window manager and displays windows with Windows-style borders and control widgets. You can force WINE to use your window manager, however, by including the -managed option.

- -winver *version*—Specifies the version of Windows that WINE emulates. Possible values of *version* include win31, win95, nt351, and nt40. Many programs fail to work with win31, which is the default.

Figure 18.8 shows WINE running the Windows Free Agent newsreader (http://www.forteinc.com/), using the -managed display option. Free Agent is one of the applications that runs reliably enough to be useful under Linux. For information on other programs' status, check the WINE applications database, http://www.winehq.com/Apps/.

The Willows TWIN Project

The Willows TWIN project (http://www.willows.com) is remarkably similar in goals and approach to WINE, with the exception that TWIN supports non-x86 CPUs, whereas WINE works only on x86 computers. Like WINE, TWIN includes both a set of libraries for building native programs using the Windows API and an emulator program that is used to run precompiled Windows programs.

FIGURE 18.8
Font size is a common problem with Windows programs run under WINE, but careful adjustments to the `wine.conf` file can sometimes improve matters.

In general, TWIN is not as far along as is WINE, but it is possible that TWIN runs some specific program that WINE does not. It is also possible that TWIN will eventually catch up to or surpass WINE. For these reasons, you might want to check the current status of TWIN, particularly if you have problems with a specific program under WINE.

ReactOS: A Windows Clone

Although not strictly an emulator, one additional project deserves mention: ReactOS. This project, hosted at `http://www.reactos.com`, aims to produce an OS that is a clone of Windows NT. ReactOS is currently in an extremely early stage of development, though; it really can't be used for any serious work. I only mention it at all because you might want to join as a developer if you enjoy such things. Check the Web page for more information, including a current status report.

VMware

VMware (`http://www.vmware.com`) is an unusually versatile emulator. The emulators I've discussed so far all emulate just one OS or at best a small range of OSs. (In principle, something like DOSEMU or OS/2's DOS subsystem could run non-DOS 16-bit OSs, but in practice this capability is very limited and is seldom if ever used.) VMware, by contrast, can run any of several different OSs. As of version 1.1, VMware can run the following OSs (known as *guest* OSs when run in VMware):

- DOS
- Windows 9*x*
- Windows NT (including Windows 2000)
- FreeBSD
- Linux

VMware must run under an OS, of course, and that host OS is either Linux or Windows NT (including Windows 2000). VMware does not run under Windows 9*x*. It is possible that the list of OSs supported by VMware—both as a guest and as a host—will grow in the future.

N O T E   VMware is a commercial product, but a 30-day demo version is available for download from the VMware Web site. This version is also included on the CD that accompanies this book, in the 3rdParty/Windows/VMWare directory. Both Linux and Windows NT executables are in this directory. ■

Emulating a PC on a PC

The DOS VDM form of emulation used by DOSEMU and OS/2's DOS boxes uses a special feature of the x86 CPU. When this feature is active, the CPU helps the emulator by creating a virtual CPU that supports a subset of the CPU's instructions (similar to those available on a 286 CPU) without interfering with the more advanced instructions of 386 and better CPUs. VMware is a machine environment emulator, just as are most DOS emulators, but instead of using the x86's capacity to create a virtual 286 CPU, VMware uses software trickery to set up a virtual environment based on the CPU you have installed. VMware even enables access to *multimedia extension (MMX)* functions if your CPU is MMX-enabled. Thus, you can run more advanced OSs using VMware than you can with DOSEMU or other VDM-style emulators.

As part of its emulation, VMware includes its own BIOS separate from your computer's BIOS, and it sets up virtual hardware, including a virtual hard disk, CD-ROM drive, serial ports, and so on. VMware maps most of these hardware components to your actual hardware, so that you can use, for example, your CD-ROM drive from within VMware. The hard disk is a major exception to this rule; by default, VMware uses a disk image similar to the one used by DOSEMU, although the two disk image formats are not interchangeable. It is possible to point VMware to an actual IDE hard disk partition instead of the virtual disk file, however.

> **CAUTION**
>
> VMware virtualizes hardware and presents it as something other than what it actually is. For example, you might have a SCSI CD-ROM drive, but VMware virtualizes this drive as an IDE device. If you use a hard-disk partition with VMware, the VMware and actual hardware might not match, so the OS might not work correctly either from VMware or when you boot the OS directly. The VMware Web site (http://www.vmware.com/support/hardwareprofiles.html) includes instructions on configuring Windows 9x and Windows NT to get around this problem.

What Is Needed to Run VMware?

The following is the official list of requirements for running VMware version 1.1 for Linux or 1.0 for Windows NT:

- **CPU**—Intel Pentium or later or a compatible CPU (AMD, Cyrix, or others). A Pentium-II 266 or faster CPU is recommended.
- **Disk space**—6MB required for VMware itself. 500MB or more is recommended for guest OS disk image files or access to the guest OS on an IDE hard disk partition.
- **RAM**—Enough memory to run the host OS. 96MB or more is recommended.
- **Host OS**—The Linux version requires kernel 2.0.32 or higher for basic operation, kernel 2.2.0 or higher for SMP support. The Windows version requires Windows NT 4.0 with service pack 3 or above, or Windows 2000. *VMware does not run on Windows 9x!*
- **Display**—Video adapter capable of 256-color display. For Linux, X is required.
- **Networking**—To use networking, you must have an Ethernet board that is supported by the host OS.

VMware doesn't emulate the CPU. Therefore, CPU-intensive programs tend to run with little in the way of a speed penalty. The user interface is another matter, however. The layers of emulation required for handling the display, hard disk, and other components means that the guest OS seems sluggish when run under VMware as compared to when it is run directly on the same hardware. Furthermore, VMware usually provides less in the way of memory to the guest OS than what is available on the host computer. For example, VMware assigns 32MB to a guest OS by default when the host computer has 64MB of RAM. This fact can further degrade performance, particularly for memory-hungry OSs such as Windows 2000. For best performance, then, you should have a computer with copious memory and a very fast CPU.

Running VMware

Setting up VMware tends to be about as complex as setting up a new computer. In a virtual sense, that is precisely what VMware is, after all. After VMware is configured, running it is fairly simple, however; you start the program and tell it to boot, and that is it.

Creating a Configuration After you install VMware, you must create a configuration for each guest OS you want to run. This configuration includes information such as how VMware's network interacts with your real network and the size of the virtual hard disk.

When you first start VMware, it presents you with three options:

- Run the configuration wizard
- Run the configuration editor
- Open an existing configuration

If this is your first time using the program, you should select the first option, which begins the process of creating a configuration in which you can run an OS. After you read some opening text and click the Next button, VMware asks what your guest OS will be (see Figure 18.9). Select the OS you'll be running and click Next.

FIGURE 18.9
The configuration wizard asks you a series of questions to optimize its performance and set up its disk images.

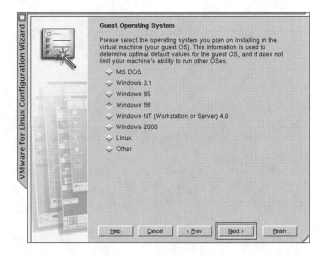

You're next asked to specify a directory in which to store the virtual machine's files. Be sure you specify a directory that resides on a partition with sufficient space to hold the files. VMware creates disk image files that are initially much smaller than they have the potential to be; these files grow as you add files in the VMware guest OS.

The wizard asks you a series of questions about your disks, including whether you want to use a CD-ROM drive and floppy drive and the size of your virtual disk. Similarly, the wizard inquires after your desired networking options. You have three main choices for networking:

- **No networking**—VMware configures itself like a computer with no Ethernet card.
- **Host-only networking**—The VMware guest and host OSs will be capable of communicating with one another over a virtual network, but the guest OS won't be capable of accessing any real network to which the host computer is connected.
- **Bridged networking**—The host OS serves as a network bridge between the guest OS and any network to which the host computer is connected. You can use this option to provide the guest OS with full Internet connectivity.

If you create a configuration and later decide you want to alter it, you can do so by loading that configuration and then choosing Settings, Configuration Editor from the main VMware menu. This action produces the dialog box shown in Figure 18.10. You can use the panel on the left to choose which options you want to alter and then change those settings on the right. When you finish adjusting your settings, choose File, Save from the main VMware menu to save them.

FIGURE 18.10
VMware settings vary
between the Linux
(shown here) and
Windows NT versions of
the program.

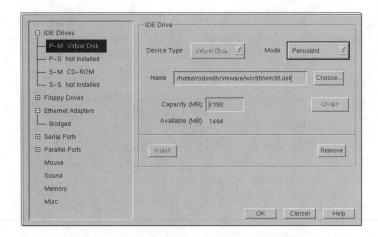

Installing a Guest OS   To install a guest OS, boot VMware's virtual machine and follow the
steps you would ordinarily follow for installing the guest OS. Booting VMware is merely a
matter of clicking the Power On button in the VMware toolbar (see Figure 18.11).

FIGURE 18.11
VMware's main screen
enables you to turn on,
turn off, and reset the
virtual machine, just as
do switches on a real
computer's case.

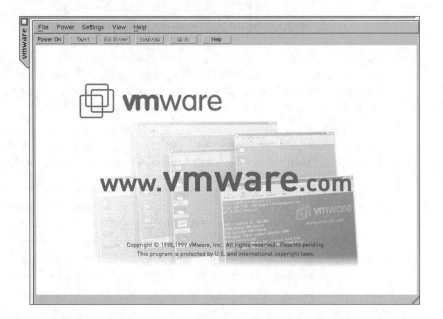

When you power on VMware, it begins to boot, but it might not immediately accept keyboard
or mouse input. To interact with VMware as you would an ordinary computer, you must click
in its window. When you do so, your host OS's mouse pointer disappears and is replaced by

the mouse pointer of the guest OS (if it has one, which in the early stages of booting and installation it will not). To regain control of your mouse and keyboard for your host OS, press Ctrl+Alt+Esc. You can also run VMware in full-screen mode by clicking the Full Screen button in the toolbar. Use Ctrl+Alt+Esc to exit from full-screen mode.

> **TIP**
>
> VMware's graphics are smoother and faster when you run VMware in full-screen mode.

▶ To learn more about OS installation, **see** Part IV, "Operating System Installation."

It is possible to configure VMware to run multiple OSs in either of two ways:

- **Create multiple configurations**—You can then optimize each configuration for each OS, but to access another configuration's files, you must edit the configuration to use another's virtual disk or partition as a second or subsequent IDE hard disk. If you want to run several OSs in VMware, this restriction might be a problem.

- **Run several OSs in one configuration**—You can partition a VMware virtual disk and install several OSs on it, just as you can with a real hard disk. You can then install a boot loader that enables you to select from among your guest OSs. The VMware optimization settings might make all but one OS run a bit more slowly than they otherwise would, however.
  - ▶ To learn more about disk partitioning, **see** Part III, "Partitioning and Partition Management."
  - ▶ To learn more about boot loaders, **see** Chapter 4, "Boot Loaders: Simple and Complex."

After you've installed your guest OS, you might want to install an appropriate VMware tools package for that OS. Three such packages are available, one each for Windows, Linux, and FreeBSD. When you install the VMware tools package, your options for screen resolutions improve, and the guest OS will run more smoothly than it does without the tools package. Note that you install the tools package in the guest OS.

Running a Guest OS   To run an OS, you must first load the appropriate configuration file. You can do so when VMware starts by choosing the Open an Existing Configuration option, or you can switch OSs after shutting down a VMware session by choosing File, Open from the main menu. In either case, you must locate the `.cfg` file corresponding to the OS you want to run. When you've selected an appropriate configuration file, click the Power On button. You'll see VMware's screen go through an ordinary BIOS boot sequence, and your guest OS will boot. Figure 18.12 shows one possible result: Windows 98 running under Linux.

Because your VMware guest OS runs more slowly than it does when you boot it directly, you'll probably prefer to keep the OS running quickly by using less in the way of speed-robbing add-ons. For example, you might want to forgo elaborate themes or exotic desktop replacements in Windows. In Linux or FreeBSD, you might want to use a simple window manager such as IceWM or wmx rather than a complete desktop environment such as KDE or GNOME.

Part

VI

Ch

18

FIGURE 18.12
If configured to do so, a guest OS can access the Internet, as illustrated by Netscape Navigator running in this Windows 98 VMware machine.

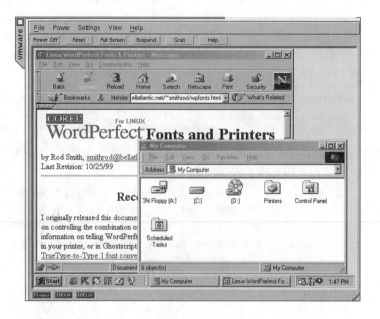

As a general rule, VMware runs its guest OSs quite reliably, albeit with a speed penalty. Overall, in fact, VMware is one of the most reliable emulators available—it far surpasses WINE and TWIN, for example. It is better at running DOS than are VDM-based emulators, although for most programs the difference in speed favors the VDM solutions.

 TIP   You can configure your host and guest OSs to use network file sharing protocols to give the guest OS access to the host OS's files. For example, if you run Windows in VMware under Linux, you can configure Linux with a Samba server and use Windows' built-in file sharing to access your Linux files. Chapter 20, "File and Printer Sharing," covers file sharing protocols.

When to Run an Emulator, Multi-Boot, or Use Multiple Computers

Emulation is one of several possible solutions when you need to run multiple OSs. Each option has certain strengths and weaknesses:

- **VMware**—VMware is a good way to gain access to software designed for one OS when running another. It can also be a great way to test software or configurations before using them in your regular OS installation. Particularly if you're diligent about backing up your VMware virtual disk files, you can quickly recover even from serious software problems when you use VMware. On the other hand, VMware robs your software of speed, and you might not be able to run it at screen resolutions as high as you can run without VMware. Finally, VMware doesn't provide access to exotic hardware—you might be stuck if you need to use, say, a scientific data acquisition board. Only the hardware that is virtualized by VMware is available to the guest OS.

- **Specific OS emulators**—Emulators such as WINE, Win-OS/2, and the DOS modes of most Microsoft-style OSs can be extremely useful when you need to run a few specific programs. These emulators are typically less complete in their virtual environment emulations than is VMware; for example, with the exception of DOSEMU, they provide relatively direct access to the host OS's filesystems. Depending on the emulator in question, emulation quality ranges from very good to very weak. Overall, I recommend using non-VMware emulators to fill a few gaps in software options on a host OS and using VMware when you need to run several programs, programs that are unreliable in other emulators, or programs that interact heavily with the OS in question.

- **Multi-booting a single computer**—This solution provides full speed and access to all your hardware, while keeping hardware costs down. You can use several OSs and boot between them as necessary to accomplish your goals. The main downside to a multi-OS configuration is that it doesn't provide simultaneous access to all your OSs and applications, short of the use of an emulator. Configuring a hard disk for several OSs can also be difficult—but this book should help you get around such problems!

- **Multiple computers**—If you have a large enough budget and enough desk space, running multiple computers can be an effective way to gain simultaneous access to several OSs. Each OS runs at full speed, although if your hardware varies in speed, VMware running on your fastest computer might do as well. Each OS has full access to the hardware on each computer. Problems with this approach include the cost, both in money and desk space, and the difficulty of providing access to the same files from two or more computers. You can set up a network to ease file-sharing tasks, but attaining a cross-platform file-sharing solution can itself be tricky.

Part
VI

Ch
18

N O T E To learn how to use Linux as a file and print server in a small network, see my book *Linux: Networking for Your Office*, from Sams. ▣

Emulators certainly have their place on many computers, but you should weigh the costs when considering such an installation. Fortunately, many emulators are free or come with the OS on which they run, and a time-limited demo version of VMware is available. You can find a copy on the CD-ROM that accompanies this book. You can therefore try an emulator on your system to determine whether it is suitable for you without expending a great deal of money.

Summary

Emulators can be very helpful on a multi-OS computer or even on a single-OS computer on which you want to run an occasional program from another OS. Most emulators that run programs for one x86 OS on another are designed to emulate either DOS or Windows because those are the most popular OSs on x86 hardware. The flexible VMware emulator, however, enables you to run any of several OSs in emulation, and its range of supported guest OSs might grow as the product matures. ●

Network Access

TCP/IP Networking

In this chapter

Using FTP for Cross-Platform Data Exchange

Most of this book focuses on the use of multiple OSs on a single computer. This chapter and the next, however, branch out into the realm of integrating your stable of OSs into a networked environment. The network could be one you maintain at home for convenience or a large network maintained by your employer. In any event, it is often important that you be able to use exotic OSs in a network, and these two chapters should help you attain that goal.

Most OSs today implement a version of *Transmission Control Protocol/Internet Protocol (TCP/IP)* networking. TCP/IP networking enables communications between anything from a tiny and outmoded DOS computer to the largest supercomputers. The open standards at the heart of TCP/IP and related protocols are what permit the Internet to function, and you can put them to work to get a gaggle of computers running disparate OSs to communicate with one another.

The TCP/IP *File Transfer Protocol (FTP)* has long been an effective means of transferring files from one networked computer to another, even when those computers use different OSs. A wide range of FTP packages are available on most platforms, so I can't cover every possible combination here. Instead, I present an overview of what FTP does and a few representative examples.

> **N O T E** In many cases, a file-sharing protocol such as the Network File System (NFS) is more convenient than is FTP for networked file exchange. File-sharing protocols perform the same basic task as does FTP, but file-sharing protocols are typically implemented in the client OS in such a way as to make transfers work just like normal hard-disk accesses. FTP, by contrast, generally uses special client programs that aren't so well integrated. For example, you can't use an FTP server to store files directly from a word processor, but you can do this with a file-sharing protocol. ■

> ▶ To learn more about file-sharing protocols, **see** Chapter 20, "File and Printer Sharing."

The Two Sides of FTP: Client and Server

FTP, like other TCP/IP protocols, labels each of the two computers (or, more precisely, programs) involved in a transfer. The program that places a request is known as the *client*, whereas the program that answers a request is known as a *server*. In the case of FTP software, you control the client program directly—you tell it to which FTP site you want to connect, you use the client to determine which files to download, and so on. The FTP server, by contrast, runs with little or no human supervision. Not all TCP/IP protocols break down this way in terms of human interaction, however; for example, when you use the X Window System in a networked manner, you sit at a computer on which the server runs and use client programs on a remote computer. The identification of programs as clients and servers relates to their interactions with each other; the server program provides services that are requested by the client.

N O T E   You might have heard of a distinction between client/server networking and peer-to-peer networking. In a client/server network, most of the computers run only client software, and a small number of computers run server software. For example, your office might have a centralized FTP server and a dozen workstations that function as clients. In a peer-to-peer network, by contrast, most or all of the computers can function as both clients and servers. Instead of using a centralized FTP server, all the computers can be configured to accept FTP connections from each other. Even in a peer-to-peer network, there is a client and a server for any given network interaction, but the client/server roles can completely reverse from one transaction to another.

As a general rule, peer-to-peer networking can be convenient for small networks, but it becomes more and more awkward as network size increases. With more than half a dozen or so computers, it is almost always beneficial to switch to a client/server network design. ▪

In the case of FTP, the server sends requested files to the client and can accept files from the client. In some sense this is what most networking protocols do: exchange files. Many other protocols also filter and process files in various ways, but in an FTP exchange, the files usually transfer from one computer's hard disk to the other computer's hard disk with little or no additional processing. (FTP does support automatic changes to set end-of-line encodings to match the target OS on text files, however.) This characteristic makes FTP an excellent way to exchange data between two computers.

N O T E   In the UNIX world, the term *daemon* is often used in reference to servers. A daemon is a program that runs in the background and watches for some event, usually a network event. It is therefore very convenient to write a server as a daemon, but in principle you could write a non-daemon server, and a daemon might not be a network server. In most cases, though, daemons are servers and servers are daemons. ▪

Security Implications of Running Servers

When you run a network server on your computer, you make your computer accessible to other people on the network. If your computer is connected to the Internet, even sporadically, this accessibility can become a liability as computer crackers try to gain access to your computer. (Crackers are often referred to in the media as *hackers*, but the term *hacker* more properly refers to people who enjoy writing computer programs and learning about computers in legal and non-destructive ways. A *cracker* is a person who breaks into other people's computers.)

Many UNIX and UNIX-like OSs come configured by default to run many servers, which can be a security problem for two reasons. First, if a cracker obtains or guesses a password for your computer, the cracker can obtain access to your system by using the server's normal functionality. Second, servers sometimes contain bugs, and these bugs occasionally enable a cracker to gain access to your computer even without a normal username and password. Therefore, I recommend shutting down services that you don't use.

It is possible to take much more extensive measures to secure a computer, such as setting up a separate firewall computer to filter access to your main systems. Even if you have just one or two

continues

continued

computers, you can set up firewall software on a single computer. Although not as effective as a stand-alone firewall computer, firewall software for one computer provides substantially greater security than you would have leaving your computer completely exposed.

You can find out much more about network security issues from *Maximum Security, Second Edition* and, if you run a Linux computer, *Maximum Linux Security*, both published by Sams.

Setting Up an FTP Server

If you want to use FTP to exchange files between two computers on your local network, you must configure at least one computer as an FTP server. The details of how to do this vary greatly from one OS to another, and in fact several FTP server programs might be available even on a single OS. In general, though, FTP servers might be configurable through text files or through GUI front ends.

NOTE Not all OSs ship with FTP servers. If yours doesn't include an FTP server, you might need to acquire a third-party server or upgrade your OS to a server edition of the same OS, which typically includes FTP and other network servers not included in the basic version of the OS. ▓

Using Text Files to Configure FTP   One of the most popular FTP servers is the Washington University FTP server, wu.ftpd. This program is available on most UNIX-like OSs, although it is far from the only FTP server available for UNIX. Its configuration is typical of textually configured FTP servers, though, on both UNIX and non-UNIX OSs.

On most UNIX systems, wu.ftpd, like many other daemons, is called from inetd, which is a *super server*—rather than having potentially dozens of daemons constantly running, inetd runs and watches for TCP/IP activity. When inetd sees an incoming FTP request, inetd starts the appropriate FTP daemon and passes the request on to it. This approach reduces the memory load of running several servers, particularly when they're not often used. You can also configure inetd to pass the connection request through a third utility, known as *TCP Wrappers*, to filter connections as a security measure. Not all systems are configured to use inetd by default, however, so you should check your system's documentation or configuration files to be sure.

If inetd is installed, it is controlled through a file called /etc/inetd.conf. To tell inetd to work with wu.ftpd, you must ensure that a line similar to the following is present:

```
ftp     stream  tcp     nowait  root    /usr/sbin/tcpd  wu.ftpd -a
```

This line sets up `inetd` to respond to FTP requests by launching `/usr/sbin/tcpd` as `root`. `tcpd` is the TCP Wrappers program. It in turn launches `wu.ftpd` and passes it the `-a` parameter, which enables use of the `/etc/ftpaccess` configuration file. If you don't use TCP Wrappers, you can eliminate the call to `tcpd` and call `wu.ftpd` directly.

If your `inetd.conf` file originally had no line for FTP access, or if that line had been commented out, you must restart `inetd` after adding the FTP line by issuing a command sequence such as

```
# ps ax | grep inetd
4437  ?  S    0:00 inetd
# kill -SIGHUP 4437
```

The first command finds the process ID of the existing `inetd`, which is displayed at the start of the second line. The third line forces `inetd` to reload its configuration file and so enables the FTP daemon.

At this point, you should be able to use an FTP client to access your UNIX computer's files. You'll need to send a username and password to log in to the FTP server. If you want to configure your FTP server for anonymous access, in which no password is required, you should consult your server software's documentation.

> **CAUTION**
>
> FTP normally sends its login information, including the username and password, in *cleartext*, which means that an unscrupulous individual on an intervening computer can read the username and password. This isn't a problem for a small local network (unless such an unscrupulous individual has access to your network), but it is a concern when you use nonanonymous FTP on the Internet as a whole. I therefore recommend minimizing use of nonanonymous FTP outside local networks whenever possible. Of course, setting up an anonymous FTP server poses potentially still greater security risks.

Part

VII

Ch

19

Using GUI Tools to Configure FTP Some FTP servers can be configured using GUI tools. Such tools come with or are available for Windows 9*x*, Windows NT, OS/2, and BeOS. Many UNIX-like OSs come with GUI tools to help you configure `wu.ftpd` or other FTP daemons. The details of how you configure a GUI FTP server vary from one OS or server to another. As an example, though, consider BeOS 4.5, which comes with an FTP server built in. To use it, follow these steps:

1. From the Be item on the BeOS's Deskbar, choose Preferences, Network to open the network configuration tool and then switch to the Services tab (see Figure 19.1).

2. If it is not already checked, enable the FTP Server check box.

3. Click the Login Info button to enter a username and password for FTP access, as shown in Figure 19.2. Click Done after you've entered this information.

FIGURE 19.1
GUI tools enable you to easily enable or disable FTP services by checking appropriate configuration options.

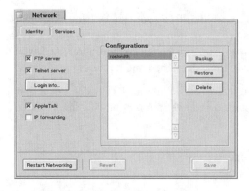

FIGURE 19.2
FTP uses a username and password to control access to your computer.

> **NOTE** BeOS 4.5 limits you to a single login username and password for both FTP and Telnet. Most other systems enable you to maintain multiple accounts. Some OSs use your ordinary login names and passwords for this purpose. BeOS enables you to create multiple configurations, though, and switch between them to enable different login usernames and passwords. ■

4. Click Restart Networking in the Network dialog box. After a few seconds, you should be able to access your BeOS computer via FTP.

Of course, these procedures vary from one OS or FTP server to another, but the basic principles are the same—you must enable the server and enter some sort of information for user authentication (or rely on the OS's underlying user account processing to do so).

Using an FTP Client

Chapter 16, "Cross-Platform Applications," includes a description of using a text-based FTP client program. You can follow those directions if you want to use the sort of basic FTP tool that probably came with your OS. You can also use a GUI FTP client, however, such as xmFTP, shown in Figure 19.3. When using a GUI FTP client, you typically type an FTP site's address or select a site from among several you've recorded in a built-in address book. When connected, most GUI FTP clients present a list of local files in one window or one side of a window (the left pane in Figure 19.3) and a list of remote files in another window or pane (the right pane in Figure 19.3). You transfer a file by clicking the file you want and choosing a transfer menu item or toolbar icon.

FIGURE 19.3
xmFTP is one of many
GUI FTP clients.

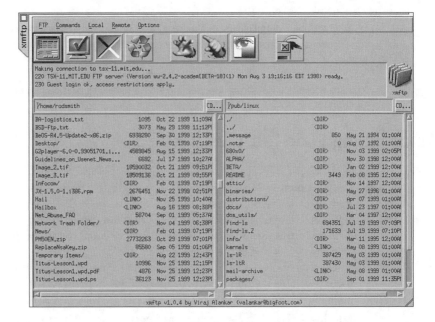

Exchanging Documents via Email

Email can be a convenient method of exchanging documents. These days, just about everybody who uses a computer has an email account, so you can use email to send documents to friends and colleagues around the world. Because the Internet's email protocols are standardized across different OSs, you can exchange email even when you and your correspondent use entirely different OSs.

The fact that the email protocols are standardized does not, however, mean that the documents you exchange will necessarily be readable on a remote computer. When you exchange a document by email, you should make sure that your recipient can read the file.

▶ To learn more about good file types to use for cross-OS data exchange, **see** Chapter 14, "Application Data File Formats."

One final word of warning: Sending large files via email can be a problem for several reasons. One reason is that many people use slow modem connections to the Internet, so a file of more than a few kilobytes can take a while to download. Another reason is that some mail servers refuse delivery of very large files. Therefore, if you want to send somebody a large file, FTP or some other method might be more appropriate than email. Precisely what constitutes a "large file" varies substantially, though. For some systems, it might be as little as 50KB; for others, it might be 10MB or more. I recommend you consult your recipient before sending anything larger than 50KB or so.

Part
VII

Ch
19

N O T E I assume that you're already familiar with an email client program and can use it to perform basic mailing tasks. The range of email client programs available, even for a single OS, is huge. ■

▶ To learn about the Netscape Messenger mail program in particular, **see** "Reading Mail with Messenger," **p. 419**.

Transmitting Plain-Text Messages

If the message you want to send is plain ASCII, you have several choices for how to proceed:

- **Cut-and-paste**—Most OSs include a cut-and-paste feature that enables you to copy text from one application into another. In Windows or OS/2, for example, you can usually select text in one window, press Ctrl+C, position your cursor in the mail program's window, and press Ctrl+V to paste the text into an email you're composing. In UNIX-style OSs, you select text in the origin window using a left mouse button drag operation, position the mouse pointer in the destination window, and press the middle button to paste text. This method is particularly useful for sending a short section of a larger document.

- **File insertion**—Many mail programs enable you to insert a complete ASCII document in a message you compose. Typically, this option is available as an item called Insert File or something similar from one of the mail editor's menu items, or by typing a keyboard sequence such as Ctrl+I. When you use such a feature, the email program places the file you select into the text of your message at the current cursor location. You can then edit the included file, if necessary, and send it. The recipient sees the result as a single ASCII mail message.

- **Attachments**—You can send an ASCII file as an attachment, much as you can send binary files. I describe this option in more detail shortly. Attachments are often harder to read than are plain ASCII messages, however, so I recommend sending ASCII files as attachments only when it is important that the original file be preserved exactly—cut-and-paste and file insertion methods sometimes alter details such as the placement of line breaks, which can be undesirable when transmitting computer source code, configuration files, or system log files, to name just three examples.

Plain text is universally readable, assuming the language you use is based on the Latin alphabet. If you use a language for which ASCII is inadequate, both you and your recipient must have mail clients that can handle your language of choice. Alternatively, you could exchange mail as a word processor document in an attachment, in which case you must have compatible word processors.

Using UUencoding to Send Binary Files

Years ago, it became desirable to send non-ASCII files via email. Unfortunately, the email protocols weren't designed with such operations in mind, so attempts to send binary files tended to damage the files in transit. The solution was to use *UNIX-to-UNIX encoding (UUencoding)* to convert the binary files into text files. UUencoding works by taking a group of three eight-bit bytes and converting that group into four bytes, using only six bits from each of the original bytes in each new byte, as illustrated in Figure 19.4. The resulting four bytes are each then converted into a range of values that are valid ASCII characters. Extra control characters are added to the mix, including a character at the start of each line indicating its length, and begin and end codes. The result of UUencoding a file looks like this:

```
begin 644 stuff.txt
B66]U(')E86QL>2!A<F4@8F]R960L(&%R96XG="!Y;W4_"@``
`
end
```

FIGURE 19.4
UUencoding "unpacks" binary files so that they can be encoded using the more restricted range provided by ASCII.

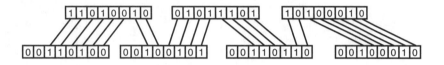

> **N O T E** UUencoding a file increases its size—four bytes are used where there had been only three, and additional bytes are consumed in carriage returns and other control characters. ■

Of course, most UUencoded files are much longer than the small example shown here, but this example illustrates the point. Some email programs include an option to attach a file using UUencoding, but most do not. UUencoding is a bit old-fashioned by today's email standards, so you probably shouldn't use it unless your correspondent doesn't have the capacity to handle the more recent binary attachment options. If you receive a UUencoded file, though, and if your email program doesn't automatically decode it, you should extract the mail message and use a UUdecoder on it. A UUdecoder reverses the process of UUencoding to create a binary file from a UUencoded file. Most UNIX and UNIX-like systems include a program called uudecode to perform this operation, and it or similar utilities are available for other platforms.

> **N O T E** UUencoding originated in the UNIX world and spread to PC OSs such as DOS and Windows. UUencoding was never as popular in the Macintosh world, although Macintosh utilities for handling UUencoded files do exist, and Mac/PC or Mac/UNIX communications often used UUencoding. A protocol similar in principle to UUencoding, known as BinHex, was more popular for Macintosh-to-Macintosh communication. If you receive an email that contains a BinHex file, you might be able to decode it using the hexbin program, which is part of the MacUtils package, which has been ported to a variety of platforms. ■

Part
VII

Ch
19

Attaching Documents to Send Binary Files

Most modern mail programs support a method of sending binary files that results in a more seamless operation than does UUencoding. This method is known as *attaching* a file to an email message. Attaching a file works by a method similar to UUencoding, but the email program includes special codes to help identify the portion of the message that corresponds to the attachment. Email clients that can attach files can also read attachments. Some such clients can start appropriate programs when they recognize the type of the file—for example, an email program might launch a graphics viewer when it recognizes a graphics file attachment. Other file types should be saved directly to disk, and the email program can perform this function, as well. Precisely how you perform such operations varies substantially from one email client to another. Most provide you with some clue that a message contains an attachment, as illustrated by the UNIX XCmail mail reading window shown in Figure 19.5. You can generally click the attachment or select an appropriate menu item to save or view the attachment.

FIGURE 19.5

Many mail readers provide an indication of the presence of attachments and automatically launch appropriate programs when you click the name of an attachment.

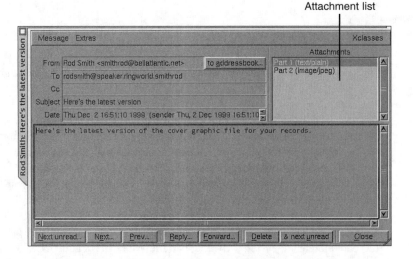

Attachment list

CAUTION

So-called *email viruses* have become a popular pastime among a certain class of ethically challenged individuals. Email viruses take two forms. One is as a message that claims an email virus is on the rampage and that merely reading an infected email will have dire consequences. This warning is almost certainly a hoax, but it consumes network resources because gullible individuals pass the warning on to their friends and colleagues.

The second type of email virus is more serious because it is real, and is spread in an email attachment. The virus typically takes the form of a Microsoft Office macro but occasionally is an executable program or some other type of file. The more insidious of these programs rummages through your own email address book and sends itself off to your friends and colleagues, making it more likely that they'll use the attachment themselves.

If you receive an email message with an attachment that you weren't expecting, you should proceed with caution. Check a Web site that reports email virus outbreaks, such as `http://www.ciac.org`, `http://www.cert.org`, or a commercial virus scanner's Web site. You should be especially wary if you use a popular Windows email client such as Microsoft Outlook or Netscape Messenger, because virus writers often target the capabilities of these packages because of their popularity and near-automatic handling of attachments. This last feature makes it more difficult for you to control what happens to an attachment. You can still read such messages safely, but you should be very cautious about handling suspicious attachments when using such programs.

Using a Web Site for Platform-Independent Communications

Web sites can be a good way to communicate with a wide audience. You can use FTP to retrieve files from around the world or transfer them between your own computers, and you can use email for one-on-one communication, but Web sites let you communicate with anybody interested in whatever you have to say. Web sites can also be useful on local networks as a means of distributing information when people are in or out of the office or for distributing documents that should receive wide dissemination within your organization.

There are two aspects to Web site creation:

- **Web server configuration**—Individuals use Web client software (Web browsers) to retrieve documents from Web servers. Therefore, the first step in using the Web for communication is to configure a Web server. For most people, this step is performed by somebody else, such as an Internet service provider (ISP) or an organization's computer services department.

- **Web page preparation**—You design the content of your Web site much as you'd design a printed document, using a text editor of one sort or another. You should then test your Web page and upload it to the Web server. At that point, your Web page becomes accessible to the world.

Configuring a Web server is beyond the scope of this book. It is also something that is beyond the means of most individuals and even small businesses, because it requires a computer that runs 24 hours a day, seven days a week, with full Internet connectivity at all times—at least, if you want the Web server to be publicly accessible. Web page preparation, however, deserves a few words, particularly with respect to creating a Web page that is friendly to multiple Web browsers and multiple OSs.

Creating a Web Site with a Word Processor or HTML Editor

Most Web sites are Hypertext Markup Language (HTML) documents. It is possible to create HTML documents using nothing but a text editor and an HTML reference, and in fact many people do so (typically, this is known as hand coding). It is also possible to use an editor designed specifically for HTML or an ordinary word processor to create HTML (often called a WYSIWYG—what you see is what you get—editor, although it is important to realize that what *you* see might not correspond exactly to what your *reader* sees, given the nature of the Web). Doing so makes it easier to create a Web page but makes it harder to control precisely what sort of HTML you produce. If the WYSIWYG editor gets it wrong or automatically loads lots of unnecessary HTML features, your page might be handicapped on some platforms. Most WYSIWYG editors do a reasonable job, though.

▶ To learn more about HTML, **see** "Enhanced Text Formats," **p. 360**.

Details of Web page creation vary from one tool to another, but as an example, consider WordPerfect 8 for Linux. You create a new Web page in this program by choosing File, Internet Publisher from a document window's menu. The result is the dialog box shown in Figure 19.6. Choose New Web Document to start a new Web page, or Format as Web Document to convert an existing WordPerfect file to Web page format.

FIGURE 19.6
Modern word processors often offer special Web page formatting modes.

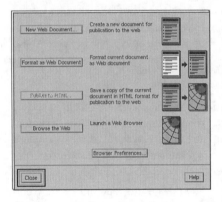

You can then type text much as you would when creating other WordPerfect documents. WordPerfect restricts your formatting choices when you create Web pages, however. For example, you can't create footnotes because HTML makes no provision for footnotes. If you convert an existing document that includes features not supported by HTML, WordPerfect discards those features.

The features that you can use in designing a Web page include

- Italic and bold font variants
- Text color changes
- Font changes
- Monospaced (or fixed-width) text

- Bulleted and numbered lists
- Tables
- Graphics
- Text alignment—left, center, and right

In addition, you can create links to other HTML documents. To do so, highlight a word or phrase that you want to serve as the link and choose Tools, Hyperlink from the WordPerfect menu. This action produces the dialog box shown in Figure 19.7. Enter the URL of the document to which you want to link in the Go To Other Document field, as shown in Figure 19.7. You can create links to anonymous FTP sites by using `ftp://` rather than `http://`, and you can create an email link by using `mailto:`.

FIGURE 19.7
To create a link to a document, enter the URL in the Go To Other Document field.

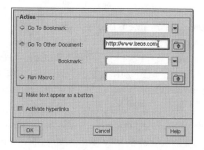

When you're finished creating or editing your Web page, choose File, Internet Publisher again. This time, pick Publish to HTML to save your document as a Web page.

> **CAUTION**
>
> In WordPerfect for Linux, if you select File, Save (Ctrl+S) or File, Save As (F3), the result is a file in WordPerfect format. WordPerfect can load the resultant file, but a Web browser won't be able to do much with it.

The preceding directions apply to WordPerfect, but other WYSIWYG HTML editors use similar features and functionality. Tools that are designed from the start as HTML editors typically provide finer control over HTML than do word processors. In either event, the details might differ, but the basic types of operations you can perform in an HTML editor are the same across tools.

Good Web Site Design Tips

Many Web sites today feature flashy graphics, fonts, colorful backgrounds, and other advanced features. Such sites often look very good—when viewed with the one or two

Part
VII

Ch
19

browsers the site designer used. When viewed with other browsers, the result can be horrific. Here are some tips to help you create a widely accessible Web page:

- **Keep Web pages and graphics small**—Big Web pages take a long time to load, as do big graphics. It is easy to overlook this problem if you test a Web page locally, as most people do.

- **Don't rely on graphics**—Some people use non-graphics browsers (this is particularly true of those with visual disabilities), and some disable graphics loading even in graphics-capable browsers. You can use an ALT tag to add a description of a graphic that displays in such situations.

- **Don't use wide graphics or tables**—People use all sorts of devices to access the Web, and wide HTML elements can cause a great deal of annoyance to people with smaller displays.

- **Use sensible backgrounds**—If you use a background bitmap, make it one that is low in contrast but that is high in contrast compared to your text color. Better yet, don't use a background bitmap at all. If you set a background color, be sure to set a text color, and vice-versa; if you set one but not the other, a person with unusual default color settings might not be able to read your Web page.

- **Avoid the use of frames**—A *frame* is a Web feature that splits the Web browser's view. It is typically used to provide fixed controls while navigating a Web site, but most Web sites that use frames do so unnecessarily, and many older browsers can't handle frames at all. In some cases, you can use a table to control text spacing instead of frames, but even that has its pitfalls because a too-wide table can greatly annoy a person with a narrow display.

- **Specify fonts only if they're vital to your page**—Web pages don't distribute fonts. Therefore, when your Web page specifies a font, it is really a request that the Web browser might not be able to fulfill. If the Web browser doesn't have the font, or if its implementation is different from yours, the results might look pretty bad. This problem is particularly severe if you use an HTML editor on an unusual platform, such as WordPerfect for Linux, because font names might not match across platforms.

- **Include contact information**—Place your email address in at least one link on each page, so that readers can contact you.

Following these guidelines can help you create a Web site that is accessible to all users on all OSs. Using advanced features might make for a distinctive Web site, but although that distinctiveness might be positive on some platforms, it might be quite negative on others. This is because native Web browsers might be unable to process the unusual features you've used in any meaningful way.

Before you put your Web pages up on a Web server, you should test them. I recommend doing this in two ways:

- **Test in multiple browsers**—Try to display your Web page using several browsers, preferably on several platforms. If you see problems, go back and correct the document.

- **Use an HTML checker**—Tools such as Weblint (http://www.weblint.org/) and the W3C HTML Validation Service (http://validator.w3.org/) enable you to check your documents for HTML errors. Most Web browsers are fairly forgiving of minor errors, but some aren't or respond to errors in differing ways. It is therefore a good idea to have a computer check for such errors—after all, you might not notice a missing </P> code, but if it causes problems with just one browser, you'll have reduced your document's audience. This step is particularly important if you hand code your HTML files.

If you're interested in learning more about creating Web documents that are accessible on any Web browser or OS, you might want to check the Campaign for a Non-Browser Specific WWW site at http://www.anybrowser.org/campaign/. This site includes many useful articles and links to help you design a Web site that is both appealing and accessible to all.

Remote Logins

If you run a small network that hosts several OSs, you might find it convenient to use some small feature of one OS when you're physically seated at another. If your remote OS supports network logins, you might be able to satisfy this desire. All UNIX-style OSs can be used in this way, as can BeOS and, to a more limited extent, OS/2. You can even find appropriate third-party login servers for Windows NT.

Logging In to a Multiuser OS

Just as with FTP, remote logins require a special server program. The protocol that is most frequently used for this function is known as *Telnet*. Like FTP, however, Telnet is an inherently insecure protocol; it is possible for an unwanted party to snoop at various points on an Internet link to acquire a username and password for entry to a computer. Therefore, various extensions and alternatives to Telnet have come into use, such as *Secure Shell (SSH)*. SSH uses encryption to send password data in such a way that it is useless to somebody who intercepts the transmission. (See http://www.dreamwvr.com/ssh/ssh-faq.html for more information on SSH.)

Whether you use Telnet or SSH, a network login gives you access to a shell running on the remote computer. You must typically provide a username and password to complete the login process, although some Telnet programs use a script to automate this process. After you've logged in to the remote computer, you can run text-based programs.

▶ To learn more about shells, **see** "Using GNU Shells for Common Command Prompts," **p. 381**.

Part
VII

Ch
19

One limitation of remote logins is that the capabilities of the terminal program you use for access most likely aren't the same as those of the host computer's display. As an extreme example, you can't run graphical video games or GUI programs using a text-based login alone. Even non-graphical programs sometimes require specific characteristics of a text-mode display. For example, consider a text-based editor, such as the jed program shown in Figure 19.8. When you issue commands to move the cursor around in a text file, the editor must have some way to tell the terminal program to make the appropriate response. Even more special commands might be required when you begin to make changes to the file. In the past, UNIX mainframes faced this problem with respect to the assortment of incompatible physical terminals used to access the computer, so UNIX programmers developed libraries to translate programs' display requirements into codes that the terminals understood.

FIGURE 19.8
Complex text-based programs need a way to communicate cursor positioning and attribute changes to terminal programs.

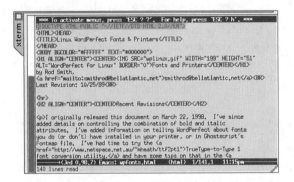

Software terminal programs entered the scene and quickly emulated the codes used by physical terminals, hence the phrase *terminal emulation*. Many terminal programs offer a choice of emulations, and you might find that one emulation works better than another when you use a particular computer or even particular programs. On UNIX systems, you can find what terminal the host OS believes you're using by typing env | grep TERM, and you can adjust the terminal by setting the TERM environment variable, as in export TERM=vt100 when you use bash.

Accessing Alternative OS Resources via Remote Login

The extent to which you can make productive use of an OS using a text-based login varies substantially from one OS to another. UNIX systems were developed in an environment in which most users worked from remote terminals, so you can perform many tasks remotely on UNIX-like OSs. Assuming you have sufficient privileges, you can even reboot a UNIX-like OS from halfway around the world; you need only issue the shutdown command with appropriate parameters.

If the computer you access remotely is itself a multi-OS machine, you might be able to access some of the resources of the computer's other OSs remotely. For example, you can

- **Access disks**—If the OS supports mounting other OSs' partitions, you can use that feature remotely by issuing the same text-mode commands you would use to accomplish the task locally. For example, in Linux, mount /dev/hda2 /mnt/dos mounts the /dev/hda2 partition on /mnt/dos, whether you type the command locally or from a remote login. You can then copy files, move files to the DOS partition, or perform other operations.

- **Use an emulator**—If an emulator runs in text mode, you can run it remotely. For example, the Linux DOSEMU program can be run from a remote login. You can then run DOS programs remotely.

  ▶ To learn more about DOSEMU, **see** "Linux's DOSEMU," **p. 458**.

- **Edit files**—If you use a file format that is common across platforms, you can edit those files remotely even if you don't normally use the OS that supports remote logins for this purpose. For example, you might have developed a Web page using a Windows HTML editor. If you then log in to this computer when it is running FreeBSD, you can use Emacs to edit the HTML file to correct a problem.

  ▶ To learn more about shared file formats, **see** Chapter 14, "Application Data File Formats."

There are limits to what you can accomplish using a remote text-based login, of course. For example, unless you're in the same room, audio utilities are useless. Although you might be able to run the programs, the speakers the computer uses won't do you much good if you're logging in to a computer in Fort Worth when you're in Indianapolis. The feature you're most likely to miss, however, is the capability to run GUI tools. Fortunately, there are ways around this problem.

Remote GUI Control

With the increase in the prevalence and importance of GUI methods of using a computer, it is important that remote login procedures enable GUI access. Two methods are in common use to allow such access:

- The *X Window System* (or *X* for short) was designed from the ground up as a networked GUI. This fact means you can use X programs remotely with very little additional effort—provided you have appropriate software on two computers.

- The *Virtual Network Computing (VNC)* program provides an alternative to X that works across more platforms than does X. It works in a substantially different way than does X, but the user experience can be similar.

Part
VII

Ch
19

X is useful mainly for running programs on UNIX OSs, although you can use a non-UNIX OS as a control station. VNC, by contrast, is available on Linux, UNIX, and Windows, in both client and server versions, so you can use it to control Windows hosts in addition to UNIX-like computers. Assorted OS/2 VNC implementations are under development, although none is yet truly complete.

Using an X Server to Control UNIX-Like OSs

The client/server architecture of X is confusing to many UNIX newcomers. Most people don't have too much difficulty grasping the concept of a server when it applies to a file server, mail server, or the like. X server terminology, though, tends to cause problems because it is just the opposite of what most people expect. To be concrete, suppose that you use a Windows computer to connect to a FreeBSD computer and run X programs on the FreeBSD computer using the Windows computer's display and keyboard. Contrary to most people's expectations, the server runs on the Windows computer. To understand this matter, pretend that you're an application. The Windows computer provides services—display, keyboard, and mouse—to the programs on the FreeBSD machine, just as a file server provides services to applications.

To use an X server, then, you must install the server software on the computer you intend to use to connect to a remote system. If you have two UNIX-like OSs, chances are they both came with X servers, so this task is finished. For OS/2, XFree86 (http://www.xfree86.org) can be used in this capacity and is included on this book's CD. For Windows, a variety of commercial X servers is available, including MI/X (http://www.microimages.com/freestuf/mix/), Exceed (http://www.hcl.com/products/nc/exceed/index.html), and X-Win32 (http://www.starnet.com). The client computer doesn't normally need any special software aside from an appropriate X application and possibly some support utilities such as a window manager or xterm.

To run an X program remotely, using the computer bill to run programs on the computer linus, follow these steps:

1. Start the X server on bill.
2. If bill runs a UNIX-like OS, issue the command xhost +linus to permit linus to use bill's X server. This step isn't necessary with most Windows X servers. It is also unnecessary if you use a UNIX SSH program in step 3.
3. Using a Telnet or SSH program, log in to linus from bill.
4. If you use Telnet, you might need to issue the command export DISPLAY=bill:0, or something similar, to tell linus to use bill's display. This step isn't necessary if you use certain SSH programs in step #3, but it is with others. The digit 0 might need to be changed to something else if you run multiple displays on bill.
5. Use your Telnet or SSH login to launch X programs just as you would from an xterm window at linus's console. The result is X programs displayed on bill's screen but running on linus, as shown in Figure 19.9.

FIGURE 19.9

The xclock, nxterm, and xeyes windows belong to a remote UNIX system, whereas the My Computer window is local to Windows.

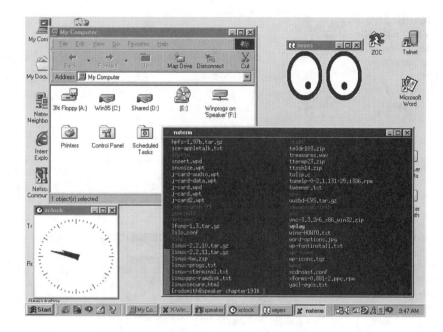

The details of how linus's programs display on bill vary substantially from one OS and X server to another. Figure 19.9 shows X programs running in Windows using normal Windows frames—essentially, Windows provides the window manager for X programs. This is the default approach taken by X-Win32 and by X servers running on UNIX-like OSs. XFree86 running on OS/2, however, provides an entirely separate display, much like a full-screen Win-OS/2 session. You can run both local and remote X programs in this one XFree86 session, though. Other X servers might display X windows inside a single rooted window, which enables you to run programs such as DFM that place icons on the X desktop.

▶ To learn more about window managers, **see** "Understanding the X GUI Model," **p. 439**.

▶ To learn more about DFM, **see** "Selecting a File Manager," **p. 443**.

Another method of using X remotely is to run an *X Display Manager (XDM)* login program on the UNIX computer and configure your X server to log in directly using this system. This approach bypasses the Telnet or SSH login requirement. It sometimes causes problems because of conflicts between window managers and the Windows X server, though. If you want to try it, follow these steps:

1. Ensure that your UNIX computer is running XDM. This is the default for many UNIX systems. If you see a graphical login prompt such as that displayed in Figure 19.10 when you boot the computer, chances are you're running XDM or something like it. If you get a text-mode login prompt when you boot your UNIX computer, you must install and run XDM. This can sometimes be accomplished by changing the runlevel in the /etc/inittab file, but details vary substantially from one OS to another.

FIGURE 19.10

An XDM login prompt uses proportional fonts and sometimes includes a graphical background image.

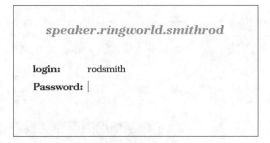

2. Consult your X server's documentation and adjust its operation to use the XDMCP protocol. Figure 19.11 shows X-Win32's configuration window and its XDMCP options. Details differ substantially from one X server to another.

FIGURE 19.11

Windows X servers typically let you configure XDM-based logins using GUI configuration utilities.

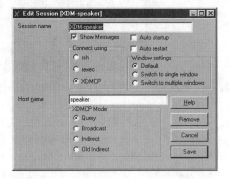

3. Launch your X server and, if necessary, tell it to start an XDM-based login. If all goes well, you should see a login prompt similar to that in Figure 19.10.

Using VNC to Control UNIX or Windows

Like an X server, VNC (http://www.uk.research.att.com/vnc/index.html) enables you to control one computer from another. VNC works on different principles, however. With X, most of the work of displaying information, including font handling, the drawing of shapes from primitive objects, and usually the window manager, is done on the server computer— the one at whose keyboard you type. With VNC, by contrast, the X server runs on the computer whose programs you run. The server performs the font rasterization, window manager handling, and so on, and creates a bitmap image that is transmitted to the computer at which you sit. This computer runs a simple client program that displays the bitmap and returns information on your keypresses and mouse actions. Thus, the terminology of client and server is reversed for VNC as opposed to conventional X servers.

Advantages and Disadvantages of VNC More important than the terminology differences, VNC includes tradeoffs compared to X servers:

- **Wider host choice**—VNC enables you to control Windows computers remotely, as well as UNIX systems. You can't use VNC to allow two people to use a single Windows computer at once, though, at least not in any meaningful way. When used on Windows, the VNC server simply copies what is displayed on the local Windows screen, so two people using one computer via VNC see the same display, and their actions end up "fighting" one another. This problem doesn't apply to VNC on UNIX systems, though, because VNC can run servers for several individuals.

- **Free Windows client**—At the time I write this, all Windows X servers cost money, although the MI/X server is only $25. VNC, on the other hand, is open-source software and is free.

- **Slower performance**—In general, VNC is slower than an X server because VNC transmits more information over the network. You can often improve VNC's performance by reducing the color depth of your display, however.

- **UNIX login inflexibility**—When used on UNIX-like OSs, you can't simply run a single VNC server to handle logins from multiple individuals, as you can with XDM. Instead, each user must log in via Telnet or SSH and run a separate VNC server. The user must then access that server by number—that is, the user specifies, for example, gingko.biloba.com:4 as the VNC host.

Starting a VNC Server on UNIX Follow these steps to start a VNC server on UNIX:

1. Extract the software—You must first extract the VNC software from the tarball in which it is distributed. A command such as tar -xvf vnc-3.3.3_x86_linux_2.0.tgz does the trick, although of course the exact filename differs from one OS to another. This command creates a subdirectory in which the server resides. (This book's companion CD-ROM includes the Linux version of VNC.)

2. Move into the VNC directory and copy the executable files to an appropriate location on your path, such as /usr/local/bin. The executables you must copy are vncviewer, vncserver, vncpasswd, and Xvnc.

3. Start the VNC server by typing vncserver. Be sure to do this using the account you intend to use when you log in remotely. Be sure to record the number of the server session used by VNC. For example, VNC might report that it is running as gingko.biloba.com:1. The server session number is 1, and you'll need that information to log in to this session.

NOTE VNC uses a password to control access. The first time you run the program, it asks for a password, which it stores in an encrypted form in the ~/.vnc directory. You can change the password at a later date by using the vncpasswd program.

Part **VII**

Ch **19**

You might want to change some aspects of how VNC operates, such as the size of the virtual desktop or the color depth. You can do so by editing the `vncserver` program file, which is actually a Perl script that can be edited with an ordinary text editor. Consult the VNC documentation for details.

Using the VNC Client on Windows   Follow these steps to access a remote VNC server from Windows:

1. Use PKZip or some other zip utility to uncompress the VNC files. You should get a folder that contains two subfolders: `viewer` and `winvnc`. (This book's companion CD-ROM includes the Windows version of VNC.)

2. Open the `viewer` folder and run the viewer program in that folder. The result is a dialog box in which you enter the name of the server computer and its display number, as shown in Figure 19.12.

FIGURE 19.12
You can set VNC connection options by clicking the Options button.

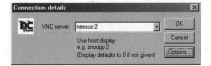

3. Type the host name and display number into the VNC Server field (the VNC server displayed this information when you started it). VNC then asks for a password.

4. Enter the password, and VNC displays its main screen, as shown in Figure 19.13.

FIGURE 19.13
A VNC window presents the host OS's window managers and desktop utilities within the VNC window's borders.

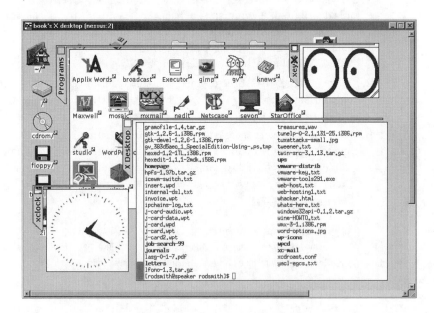

VNC enables you to run most X-based programs as if you were logged in to the server computer directly, or as if you were using a conventional X server. One peculiarity is in mouse handling: VNC uses two mouse pointers, one of which lags behind the other. The faster pointer, which is a small dot, represents the position of the mouse on the client system. The slower pointer shows the position of the mouse on the server system.

VNC is useful and is improving in quality, but it does have its quirks. For example, typing text into the Nedit text editor under VNC doesn't work. If you have problems, check for a more recent version of both the server and client at `http://www.uk.research.att.com/vnc/index.html`.

Accessing Windows from UNIX by Using VNC   Just as you can use a VNC client on Windows to work with UNIX programs, you can place the client on UNIX and the server on a Windows 9x or Windows NT computer to reverse the connection. To do so, follow these steps:

1. Install the VNC server on Windows by running the `Setup.exe` program in the `winvnc` subdirectory that you created when you extracted the VNC files earlier. Follow the prompts in the installer to configure the server.

2. Locate and run the VNC server program. It should be wherever you told the installer to place it. When you run the server for the first time, it displays the Current User Properties dialog box (see Figure 19.14).

FIGURE 19.14
You can set properties such as the password in the Current User Properties dialog box.

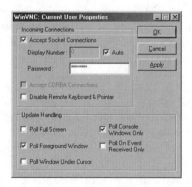

Part
VII

Ch
19

3. Type `vncviewer remotename:0` on your UNIX system. You should use the name of your Windows VNC server computer in place of `remotename`, of course, and you might need to use a number other than `0`—use whatever number the server provided when it started. The program then asks for a password.

4. Enter the password and VNC displays a window, as shown in Figure 19.15. Use this window to control the remote Windows system much as you use a Windows VNC server to control a UNIX session.

FIGURE 19.15
At first glance this looks like a Windows screen, but notice the Linux wmx window manager border at the side.

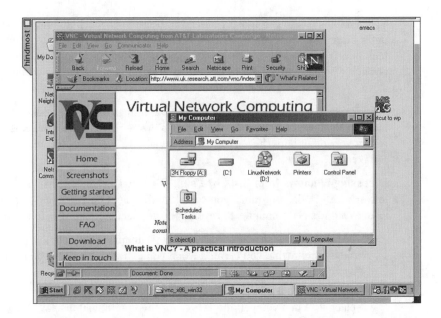

You can also access one Windows computer from another by using VNC; you must follow the instructions for setting up the Windows VNC server along with a Windows VNC client on another computer. Likewise, you can use VNC for remote access to one UNIX computer from another, although in most cases using X's networking capabilities provides a better solution.

Summary

Creating a small or large network can greatly enhance a multi-OS setup. You can run several OSs simultaneously with several computers and a network. The problem with doing so is that spreading your resources across several computers tends to scatter your data and can make it more difficult to integrate your work across applications. TCP/IP networking tools help to overcome these problems, providing you with access to files and even programs on one computer when using another. Tools such as FTP, email, Telnet, and VNC can help knit a network of computers into a unified whole. The next chapter continues with this topic, covering file and print servers in a multi-OS environment. ●

File and Printer Sharing

Understanding File and Printer Sharing Basics

Chapter 19, "TCP/IP Networking," covers an assortment of tools that are useful in integrating computers running different OSs on a network. This chapter continues this discussion with an investigation of an important subset of networking topics: file and printer sharing.

Ordinarily, your computer can access files stored on its local hard disk and on any removable disks you insert in appropriate removable disk drives. Similarly, your computer can print to printers that are directly attached to its parallel, serial, or universal serial bus (USB) ports. When you place a computer on a network, however, it is possible to provide your computer with access to files and printers that reside on the network. From a user's or program's point of view, these networked printers and filesystems look very much like local resources. The advantages of using file and printer sharing can be substantial. Rather than invest in dozens of printers, an office can purchase one or two. Instead of using floppy disks or awkward FTP accesses to share files, users can read files directly from a dedicated file server or from other users' computers. Even in a small home network, file and printer sharing can be a great boon—you can let your children use your laser printer for their school reports without using floppies or worrying about software incompatibilities when you load a file created on one computer onto another, for example.

 TIP Even if you don't have a real network at all, you can use file-sharing protocols between the guest and host OSs when you run the VMware emulator. For example, suppose you run Linux under VMware from Windows NT. You can use file-sharing protocols to provide Linux with access to files on your Windows NT NTFS partitions.

Several major sets of protocols are in common use for file and printer sharing on PCs today:

- **NFS/1pd**—The UNIX *Network Filesystem* and *line printer daemon* provide protocols for file and printer sharing among UNIX computers. There are NFS and 1pd implementations for non-UNIX computers as well, so you can use these protocols from Windows or other OSs if your network is dominated by UNIX systems.

- **SMB/CIFS**—The *Server Message Block* protocol is built into all versions of Windows since Windows 95 and is available for DOS, Windows 3.1, and OS/2. (Samba's client tools, but not the server side, are available for BeOS, as well.) The Samba package provides UNIX systems with the capability to work with these networks. This protocol provides both file and printer sharing. It has been renamed the *Common Internet Filesystem*. I use *SMB/CIFS* to make it clear that these two terms refer to the same protocols.

- **NCP**—The *NetWare Core Protocol* is the file sharing protocol used on NetWare networks. Support for NCP and its underlying protocols, such as IPX and SPX, is available in many OSs.

- **AppleTalk**—AppleTalk is the protocol used by Apple's Macintosh computers. AppleTalk isn't much used by x86 PC OSs, however. I mention it mainly because BeOS uses AppleTalk for network printer support and because you might want to use it for some functions in a mixed PC/Macintosh environment.

This chapter covers the basics of NFS/1pd and SMB/CIFS networking. I don't cover NCP or AppleTalk because these protocols are largely redundant with others or because they're rare on PC networks.

N O T E SMB/CIFS, NCP, and AppleTalk all can use their own networking stacks instead of the more common TCP/IP stack. SMB/CIFS and AppleTalk can both be used over TCP/IP, however, and in fact the Samba package for UNIX works only in this way. Therefore, using Samba to integrate UNIX computers with DOS, Windows, or OS/2 computers necessitates the use of TCP/IP instead NetBEUI, the protocol that otherwise underlies SMB/CIFS. Configuring Windows and OS/2 in this way is automatic if you install both SMB/CIFS and TCP/IP functionality. ▓

TIP You're not restricted to running NFS/1pd or SMB/CIFS exclusively; you can run both protocols together on the same network and even on the same computer. The same is true of NCP and AppleTalk. For example, you can run a file server with two, three, or even all four protocols to serve files to a wide variety of OSs. You can even serve the same files and printers using different protocols.

There are several ways to access a shared filesystem:

- **Mounting**—You can mount a shared filesystem, much as you mount a local filesystem in UNIX-like OSs. When you mount a remote filesystem in Microsoft-style OSs, the remote filesystem acquires a drive letter.

- **Browsing**—Microsoft Windows and OS/2 support access to remote filesystems through a network browser interface. Instead of explicitly mounting a shared filesystem, you access its files by specifying the name of the host computer, as in \\somemachine\filename.txt. You can perform most file operations in this way, but some programs insist on using drive letters and can't use network resources in this way.

- **Utilities**—The Samba package for UNIX-like OSs includes a package with an FTP-like interface for accessing SMB/CIFS shares. You can't use this tool to access files using most programs, however; you can only copy files, delete files, and so on, much as you can with FTP. This is the portion of Samba that is available for BeOS.

Mounting and browsing are the most common methods of access, and in fact the distinction between them can be quite subtle. Browsing in Windows or OS/2 closely resembles mounting in UNIX, at least in terms of the way a file's name is specified, because of the lack of drive letters.

Printer sharing generally requires that you define a printer queue on your local computer and point that queue to a remote printer. After printer sharing is configured, printing to the shared printer works just like printing to a local printer, with a few exceptions such as the lack of bidirectional communication, which disables some printer utilities.

Table 20.1 summarizes the file- and printer-sharing protocols that are most appropriate for various client/server combinations. This table doesn't show all the possible protocol combinations, however; these are merely my suggestions for when you have no compelling reason to

Part
VII

Ch
20

use another protocol. You might want to deviate from Table 20.1's recommendations for any of several reasons, such as greater experience with one protocol over another or a network that is dominated by one type of machine. I don't cover every protocol combination listed in Table 20.1 in this chapter, because some of them are quite obscure on PC-oriented networks. This chapter does cover the most important protocols, however.

Table 20.1 File and Printer Sharing Protocols

Client OS	Server OS: DOS, Windows, or OS/2	BeOS	UNIX-like OSs
DOS, Windows, or OS/2	File sharing: SMB/CIFS Printer sharing: SMB/CIFS	File sharing: None Available Printer sharing: AppleTalk (requires special client OS software)	File sharing: SMB/CIFS (Samba server) Printer sharing: SMB/CIFS (Samba server)
BeOS	File sharing: SMB/CIFS (Samba smbclient on BeOS) Printer sharing: AppleTalk (requires special server OS software)	File Sharing: None available Printer sharing: AppleTalk	File sharing: SMB/CIFS (Samba on client & server) Printer Sharing: AppleTalk (Netatalk on server)
UNIX-like OSs	File sharing: SMB/CIFS (Samba on client) Printer sharing: SMB/CIFS (Samba on client)	File sharing: None available Printer sharing: AppleTalk (Netatalk on client)	File sharing: NFS Printer sharing: `lpd`

The distinction between a *client/server network* and a *peer-to-peer network* is an important one. These terms apply to entire networks, and in some sense they're really ends of a continuum; a network might have some client/server characteristics and some peer-to-peer characteristics. A client/server network makes a sharp distinction between client and server computers. A server computer provides services to the clients on the network. For example, you might have one or two file and print servers that perform nothing but these server tasks. Clients, on the other hand, function only as clients—you cannot access one client's hard disk from another client. In a peer-to-peer network, by contrast to a client/server network, each computer can access every other computer's file and printer resources. There is no separate server computer in a peer-to-peer network; each peer functions as both a client and a server. Figure 20.1 illustrates these differences.

FIGURE 20.1
A client/server network (top) uses a server as a central clearinghouse, whereas a peer-to-peer network (bottom) distributes resources across the network.

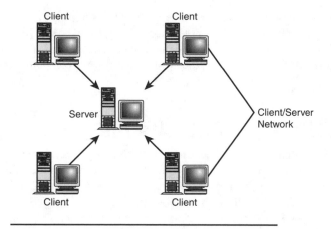

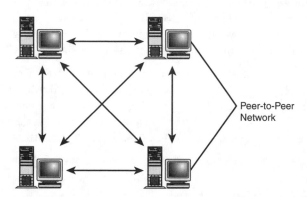

Peer-to-peer networking can be quite convenient on small networks because you don't need to devote a separate computer to function as a server. In an office with only three computers, for example, peer-to-peer networking generally works well. As the number of computers on the network rises, however, peer-to-peer networking becomes awkward because adding, deleting, or re-configuring a single computer can have consequences for many others. Larger networks therefore often follow the client/server model, which enables centralized administration of security and can greatly simplify life for the users of the client computers. The client/server model can also be quite useful in a small network when many of the computers run multi-OS configurations, because it reduces the possibility of problems due to computer reboots or incomplete or incompatible network protocols on one or another OS. In this situation, it is important that the server computer run an OS with very flexible networking capabilities.

NOTE To learn how to use a Linux computer as a file and print server in a mixed-OS network, see my book *Linux: Networking for Your Office*, from Sams. ▪

Part
VII

Ch
20

Whether your network uses a peer-to-peer, client/server, or some hybrid design, the same underlying networking protocols are at use. NFS/1pd and SMB/CIFS are both useful in both types of network, and their configuration on a per-machine basis is the same in both types of network. The difference is in whether you configure your computers to function as clients, servers, or both.

NFS for UNIX-Style File Sharing

If your network consists largely or entirely of UNIX-like OSs, chances are you'll want to use NFS for file sharing. NFS was designed for UNIX systems and therefore includes support for UNIX filesystem features, such as ownership and UNIX-style permissions. This fact makes NFS more suitable for UNIX-to-UNIX file sharing than SMB/CIFS. NFS client software is available for BeOS, as well, but currently no BeOS NFS server is available. You can also use NFS in a mixed environment of UNIX and non-UNIX systems, or even between two or more non-UNIX hosts. In most cases, SMB/CIFS is more appropriate for such situations, particularly when DOS, Windows, or OS/2 computers are involved, because NFS doesn't include support for the filesystem features used by these OSs, but SMB/CIFS does.

The instructions I present in this chapter relate to using NFS between UNIX systems. If you want to use NFS with non-UNIX OSs, you should consult the documentation for your non-UNIX NFS implementation. Intergraph (`http://www.intergraph.com/nfs`) produces an NFS implementation for Windows. A free NFS client for BeOS is available from the Beware Web site (`http://www.be.com/software/beware/network/benfs.html`).

▶ To learn more about filesystems and their features, **see** "Understanding Filesystems," **p. 298**.

Basics of NFS Configuration

Some of the preliminary steps for NFS use are very much OS-specific. For example, in Linux, you might need to ensure that your kernel includes support for NFS as a client and possibly as a server, depending on the NFS server software you use. Most Linux distributions ship with this support enabled, but if you have problems enabling NFS, you might want to double-check this matter, particularly if you've recompiled your Linux kernel.

UNIX-like OSs that support NFS do so through an NFS daemon. This daemon watches for NFS connection requests, verifies that the requests are legitimate, and provides access to the files if the requests are valid. In most cases, the NFS daemon goes by the name nfsd or some variant of that, so you can check to see whether it is running by issuing a command such as

```
ps ax | grep nfsd
```

This might return results such as

```
503 ?        S      0:01 rpc.nfsd
```

▶ To learn more about daemons, **see** "The Two Sides of FTP: Client and Server," **p. 478**.

N O T E It is also possible to run nfsd through inetd, but many systems don't run nfsd in this way in order to improve NFS response times. You can check your /etc/inetd.conf file to see whether it contains a reference to nfsd. ▧

▶ To learn more about inetd, **see** "Using Text Files to Configure FTP," **p. 480**.

If nfsd isn't running, you can probably start it by typing nfsd, rpc.nfsd, or something similar—check your UNIX version's documentation for details. You should put off starting nfsd until you've configured your system to accept connections from the clients to whom you want to grant access, however.

NFS works on a *trusted hosts* security model, which means that NFS accepts connections from certain computers that you specify. If an access request comes from a trusted host, that request is granted, without any further authentication required. The NFS trusted hosts are listed in the /etc/exports file, along with information on the directories to which each host has access. Here is an example of an /etc/exports file:

```
/home nessus(rw) teela(ro,squash_uids=500-501,503)
/mnt nessus(rw) teela(rw)
/opt nessus(ro)
```

This file enables the computers nessus and teela to access the host system. Other computers are denied access to the server. Each line in /etc/exports begins with a directory and is followed by a list of the hosts that have access to that directory. Each hostname can include one or more options in parentheses. The following are some of the more useful options:

- rw—Provides read/write access.
- ro—Provides read-only access.
- root_squash—Treats accesses from the root user on the remote system as if they came from the user nobody. This is a desirable security precaution in most instances and is the default.
- no_root_squash—Disables the root_squash feature. Don't use this option unless you really need it.
- all_squash—Treats all accesses as if they came from the user nobody.
- squash_uids and squash_gids—Specifies a list of users or groups to be squashed.
- map_static=*mapfile*—Sets up a user ID *map file*, as described shortly.

Most NFS daemons support more options; consult your documentation for details. The default values for some options can vary from one NFS implementation to another. For example, some NFS servers provide read/write access by default, whereas others provide read-only access by default. I therefore recommend specifying rw or ro access explicitly in all cases.

Part

VII

Ch

20

Controlling User ID Mapping

One important matter concerning NFS is its handling of usernames. Normally, when you mount an NFS share, the server uses the client system's user ID codes to determine whether a user on the client system has access to the server's files. For example, suppose that the user johnk has a user ID of 523 on two UNIX systems, teela and nessus. If teela exports its /home directory, johnk will be able to access his files on teela from nessus, including the capability to read, write, and execute files just as if he were logged in to teela directly.

N O T E Execute permission makes sense only for scripts and for binaries run on the same OS. You can't run, say, an AIX binary on a Linux computer. ▪

Unfortunately, there is no guarantee that any two randomly selected computers will use the same user ID for the same user, even if that user has accounts on both systems. For example, johnk might have a user ID of 523 on teela but a user ID of 519 on nessus. In this case, when johnk logs in to nessus and tries to access his files on teela via NFS, he might not be able to do so because he'll be trying to access his files with the permissions of whomever has user ID 519 on teela. What is potentially worse is that the user who has user ID 523 on nessus *will* be able to access johnk's files on teela, even if this user doesn't have an account on teela.

On a small network with few users, the easiest way to fix this problem is to ensure that your user IDs match up across systems. This solution requires some forethought, however, and it might be impractical on systems with many users. In such cases, you might need to use a *map file*, which tells the server to convert one user ID to another for a particular mount. Each line in a map file consists of three fields: uid or gid, to specify a user or group ID; the remote ID; and the local ID. These fields might be followed by a comment that begins with a pound sign (#). For example

```
uid 0-99    -    # squash these
uid 519     523  # johnk
uid 509     -    # dianes has no local account; squash access
gid 502     501  # cogsci group
```

You specify a map file in the server's /etc/exports file, using the map_static=*mapfile* option. This fact means that you can use different map files for different clients, and even for different exports for a single client. You might not need to create a map file, however, even if usernames don't match up. For example, if you don't export user files, but only program or configuration files, you don't need to use a map file. You might do this if you export, say, a /usr/local directory to provide access to program files, but not a /home directory for access to users' files.

Accessing Remote Files with NFS

After you've configured an NFS server, it is time to access it from a client computer. You can do so as root by using the `mount` command, as in

```
mount teela:/home /nfs/t-home
```

This command works very much like the `mount` command used to mount local filesystems. The example mounts the `/home` directory located on the host `teela` on the `/nfs/t-home` mount point. Just as with local mount points, you can add entries to your `/etc/fstab` file to mount NFS shares when the computer starts up or to enable ordinary users to mount and unmount NFS shares. For example, an `/etc/fstab` entry to automatically mount `teela:/home` at startup would look like this:

```
teela:/home          /nfs/t-home      nfs      defaults    0 0
```

You can replace `defaults` with whatever specific options you want; consult your OS's documentation for details concerning supported NFS `/etc/fstab` options.

SMB/CIFS for Microsoft-Style File Sharing

SMB/CIFS is a very different system than is NFS in many ways, but the basic goals and functionality in operation are similar. Because SMB/CIFS was designed for file sharing among Microsoft-style OSs, it supports the filesystem features that are common on DOS, Windows, and OS/2, but not the filesystem features used in UNIX-style OSs. Windows and OS/2 come with implementations of SMB/CIFS. The Samba package (`http://www.samba.org/`) is a widely available implementation of SMB/CIFS for UNIX-like OSs, and in fact it ships with many UNIX versions, including most Linux distributions. For DOS, check `ftp://ftp.microsoft.com/bussys/Clients/MSCLIENT` for a two-floppy software package that provides an SMB/CIFS implementation for DOS. The rest of this section focuses on the Windows and Samba implementations of SMB/CIFS.

▶ To learn more about filesystems and their features, **see** "Understanding Filesystems," **p. 298**.

Part
VII

Ch
20

Configuring Windows to Share Files

Windows uses point-and-click configuration for file sharing, just as it does for most other options. To begin using file sharing in Windows, follow these steps:

1. Open the Network icon in the Control Panel window. This action produces the Network dialog box shown in Figure 20.2.

FIGURE 20.2

The Windows 9*x* Network dialog box enables you to add networking protocols and set systemwide networking options.

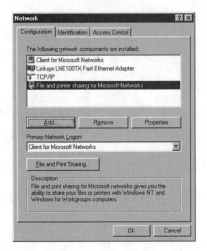

N O T E   Some of the details described in this section vary from one version of Windows to another. For example, the functionality of the Network dialog box shown in Figure 20.2 is located in the Local Area Connection Properties dialog box in Windows 2000. ▪

2. If the File and Printer Sharing for Microsoft Networks item isn't present, click Add to add it; this protocol is listed under the Service selection.

3. Click the File and Print Sharing button and check the types of items you want to share (files and, if you like, printers).

4. Click the Identification tab in the Network dialog box. This tab enables you to enter a name and workgroup for your computer, as well as a description. Be sure that your computer's name is unique and that the workgroup is one that is used on your network. (In Windows 2000, you set these features by opening the System item in the Control Panel and using the Network Identification tab of the System Properties dialog box.)

NOTE A single computer can have different names for SMB/CIFS and TCP/IP networking. For example, a computer can be `GINGKO` on an SMB/CIFS network and `polk.threeroomco.com` on a TCP/IP network. To avoid confusion, though, it is generally best to use the same name on both network types, although the SMB/CIFS name corresponds to the machine name without domain name—such as `polk` in the previous example. ■

5. Click the Access Control tab. You can then set either share-level access control or user-level access control. The former lets you set a separate password on each filesystem or printer you make available on the network, whereas the latter lets you use username/password pairs for complete access to your system. On the whole, share-level access control is generally easiest on Windows 9x. User-level access control works better in Windows NT, including Windows 2000.

6. Click OK in the Network dialog box to dismiss it.

7. Right-click a drive icon in the My Computer window and choose Sharing from the resulting pop-up menu to see the Sharing tab in the Properties dialog box (see Figure 20.3).

FIGURE 20.3
The Properties dialog box enables you to set sharing options for each partition.

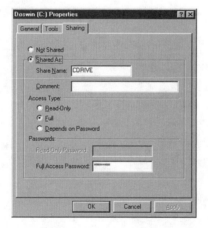

8. To share the partition, click the Shared As radio button. Most of the remaining options in the dialog box should then become active.

9. Enter a name for the shared resource. You'll later use this name to access the partition from another computer. In Windows NT, you must click New Share to enter a new share name.

10. Set the Access Type—You can use Read-Only, Full (read/write), or Depends on Password. Windows NT relies on its internal security model instead of the relatively crude Windows 9x Access Type model.

11. Enter one or both passwords, depending on the access type you selected. Again, Windows NT does things differently: It requires that you enter your ordinary login username and password for access.

12. Click OK to save your access method changes.

13. Repeat steps 7–12 for any additional partitions you want to share.

Configuring a Samba Server in UNIX to Share Files

To participate in SMB/CIFS networking using a UNIX-like OS, you must first install Samba. Samba is included with many modern UNIX-like OSs, so consult your OS's documentation first. If you find nothing there, consult the main Samba Web page, `http://www.samba.org`, to find a binary distribution for your OS, or at least the source code you can compile yourself.

After you've installed Samba, you can configure the server by editing the `smb.conf` file, which generally resides in the `/etc` directory. Alternatively, if you run the *Samba Web Administration Tool (SWAT)* daemon, you can administer your Samba server from a Web browser in any OS, as shown in Figure 20.4. To do so, point the browser at port 901 by including `:901` in the URL, as in `http://samba.server.net:901`. Some versions of UNIX, including many Linux distributions, support Samba configuration through their own system configuration tools, such as Red Hat's `linuxconf`.

FIGURE 20.4
SWAT provides a GUI interface to Samba configuration.

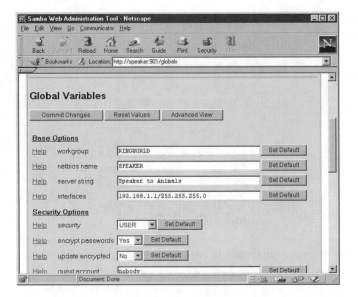

> **CAUTION**
>
> If you use SWAT, be aware that it sends your administrative password over the network unencrypted. This feature isn't a problem if you use SWAT on the computer on which Samba is running, but it can be if you use another computer. I recommend not using SWAT except from computers on your local network and preferably from the computer on which Samba runs. Don't use SWAT from a computer linked to the Samba server by the Internet at large.

Whether you use a GUI configuration tool or configure smb.conf manually, the configuration includes three main parts:

- **Global configuration options**—These options set Samba features such as security options, the SMB/CIFS workgroup name, and so on. In smb.conf, the global options appear in the lines following the [global] line.

- **Shares**—File sharing options. Each share has its own named entry in smb.conf, such as [datafiles], in which you set features such as the path to the share, whether the share is read-only or read/write, and so on. The [homes] share deserves special mention: It resolves to the user's home directory, based on the username used to log in to the Samba server.

- **Printers**—Printer sharing options. Like file sharing, each printer has its own printer entry, such as [epson400]. Printer entries are very much like file-sharing entries, except that printer entries include the print ok = Yes option. More on printer sharing later in this chapter.

Security features in Samba can be confusing to newcomers, largely because SMB/CIFS supports two different security models, and different versions of Windows default to different security models. Both methods require that the client system send a username and password pair. The methods differ in terms of whether or not those items of information are encrypted. In an unencrypted (or *cleartext*) login, the data passes over the network in an unencrypted form. In an encrypted login, the data is encrypted and can't be as easily snooped by an unwelcome individual. When using unencrypted logins, Samba uses the host OS's authentication method, so Samba users' passwords are compared to those used for normal logins—if johnk uses the password pa4erp7 to log in to the Samba server box using Telnet or other methods, johnk must also use pa4erp7 for SMB/CIFS file sharing. With encrypted passwords, though, Samba maintains its own separate password file, /etc/smbpasswd, so a user can have different passwords for SMB/CIFS file sharing as for other operations.

Windows 95 OSR2 and later, as well as Windows NT 4.0 with Service Pack 3 and later, use encrypted passwords by default, so if you want to use a Samba server with a recent version of Windows, your easiest course of action is to set Samba to use encrypted passwords. You can follow these steps to set Samba to use encrypted passwords:

1. Edit smb.conf to include the line encrypt passwords = Yes.
2. Create an /etc/smbpasswd file (if necessary) by using the command cat /etc/passwd | mksmbpasswd.sh > /etc/smbpasswd.
3. Edit the resulting /etc/smbpasswd file to remove accounts that don't need Samba file access.
4. For each user, issue the smbpasswd command to enter a Samba password. For example, if you type smbpasswd johnk, you can enter a Samba password for johnk.

In addition to encryption, Samba supports various security options to determine when a user needs to send a password. The usual option is user, in which a client sends a username and password once for each connection session and is authenticated based on this identity. This is similar to the default SMB/CIFS security model in Windows NT. Another option is share, in which Samba requires separate authentication for each shared directory or printer. share security is modeled after a Windows 9x access method in which only a password is required. Samba, however, requires both a username and a password, so Samba tries the password against all the users authorized to use a resource. The result is that share security is rather awkward in Samba, so unless you have a compelling reason to use it, I recommend sticking with user security, which is the default.

N O T E To learn more about Samba configuration, see Gerald Carter and Richard Sharpe's *Sams Teach Yourself Samba in 24 Hours*. ■

Accessing Remote Shares from Windows

The easiest way to access remote shares from Windows is to use the Network Neighborhood browser. This Windows feature enables you to view the computers on your network and the shared resources on each computer, as shown in Figure 20.5. You can then access files on networked drives by clicking or double-clicking on them. Similarly, you can use a file open dialog box in most applications to directly access networked resources.

FIGURE 20.5

The Network Neighborhood feature lets you browse SMB/CIFS resources much as you can browse local files.

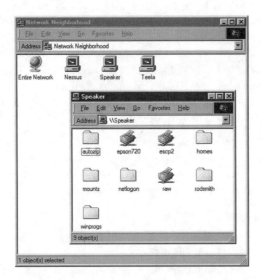

TIP Rather than browsing through a maze of networked computers, you can enter a path to the computer or even the file you want. You do so by entering the path in the Address field of any open file browser window (see Figure 20.5). The form this direct specification takes is

*machinename**sharename**pathname*—for example, \\speaker\drive-d\documents, to open the directory documents on the drive-d share on the computer called speaker.

A few programs, including many older DOS and 16-bit Windows programs, can't handle the network addressing methods used by Windows networking. For these programs, you must first assign a drive letter to a share. To do so, follow these steps:

1. Locate a share in the Network Neighborhood browser. For example, you might use the `rodsmith` share shown in Figure 20.5.

2. Right-click the share you want to use and select the Map Network Drive option in the resulting pop-up menu. This action produces the Map Network Drive dialog box shown in Figure 20.6.

FIGURE 20.6
The Map Network Drive dialog box looks different in different versions of Windows but performs the same function in each.

3. Choose a drive letter from the Drive list box.

 TIP   If you intend to use a share regularly, select a high drive letter. That way, you won't need to change it if you subsequently change your partitioning scheme or add removable-media devices.

▶ To learn more about drive letter changes, **see** "Drive Letter Changes," **p. 183**.

4. If you want to use this drive letter assignment every time you boot your computer, check the Reconnect at Logon check box.

5. Click OK (or Finish in Windows 2000).

You can now access the drive using a drive letter, as in `M:\documents` rather than `\\speaker\rodsmith\documents`. Your DOS programs can also now access the network drive using this same drive letter.

UNIX-Style *lpd* Printer Sharing

Printer sharing is, in many ways, simpler than file sharing, particularly in a multi-OS network. This is true because file sharing necessarily involves an assortment of issues relating to file-naming conventions, permissions, and so on, whereas these issues aren't as important for printer sharing. When sharing a printer, a given user or computer either does or does not have permission to use a printer.

Configuring the Shared Printer

UNIX's *line printer daemon* (`lpd`) is a tool that is used to handle both local and network printing. Configuring `lpd` for local printing actually does most of the work required to configure the system for network printing.

Configuring Local Printing UNIX printing works through printer queues that are defined in the `/etc/printcap` file. The following example shows a `/etc/printcap` entry:

```
lp|color-inkjet:\
        :sd=/var/spool/lpd/lp:\
        :mx#0:\
        :sh:\
        :lp=/dev/lp0:\
        :if=/var/spool/lpd/lp/filter:
```

Each `/etc/printcap` entry is theoretically a single line; the backslash (\) characters at the ends of most lines extend one line across several lines, for ease of reading by humans. Each field in the printer entry is delimited by colons (:). The meanings of each of the fields in the preceding entry are

■ `lp|color-inkjet`—These are the names by which the printer is known—`lp` and `color-inkjet`. `lp` is the traditional name for the default printer. You specify multiple names by separating them with vertical bars (|). You can use multiple names to provide long and short variant names, as in this example, or to maintain an old printer name for historical purposes even after replacing a printer.

■ `sd=/var/spool/lpd/lp`—The `sd` parameter sets the *spool directory*—the directory where files reside while they're waiting to be printed. Many OSs place additional configuration files in this directory, as well.

■ `mx#0`—The maximum file size to be accepted for printing. A `0` indicates no maximum size; `lpd` accepts any file, regardless of size.

TIP Setting a maximum file size can help prevent abuse of a networked printer, particularly if somebody finds a way to submit unauthorized jobs to your printer.

■ `sh`—This option suppresses the printing of job headers—sheets that precede each print job and identify the user who initiated the print job. For a personal computer, the `sh` parameter is useful, but in a large office environment, you might want to remove this option to help identify print jobs.

■ `lp=/dev/lp0`—The printer device file. This example specifies `/dev/lp0`, the parallel port on a Linux computer. Device filenaming conventions vary from one OS to another, so yours might look quite different.

■ `if=/var/spool/lpd/lp/filter`—The *input filter*, a program that processes the print job before sending it to the printer.

Traditionally, UNIX computers have used PostScript printers. As a result, many UNIX programs work under the assumption that they print to PostScript printers. This fact can be a problem if you have a non-PostScript printer, as is true of most x86 PCs. Fortunately, the Ghostscript program (`http://www.cs.wisc.edu/~ghost/`) converts PostScript into a variety of formats that can be understood by most modern inkjet and laser printers. The `if=` entry in `/etc/printcap` can pass a print job through Ghostscript with appropriate options to print it to a non-PostScript printer.

If you want to share a non-PostScript printer with Windows, OS/2, or some other OS that has drivers for the specific model you're using, you might want to configure a "raw" printer queue. In a raw queue, you don't specify an `if=` line, so `lpd` passes the input file directly to the printer. Then, you can use the printer's drivers on the client OS for printing. If you configure a queue that expects PostScript input, on the other hand, you would use a PostScript printer driver on the host OS, even if you print to a non-PostScript printer.

In practice, many UNIX-like OSs come with tools that are designed to help configure your printer. For example, Figure 20.7 shows the Red Hat Linux `printtool` program in operation. If such a tool is available for your OS, it is probably easier to use it than to configure `/etc/printcap` by hand. Nonetheless, it is useful to know something about that file, both because the printer configuration utilities ultimately modify it and because you might need to tweak a configuration by hand in some cases.

FIGURE 20.7
You use `printtool` to set up printer queues in Red Hat Linux. Similar tools exist for many other UNIX-like OSs.

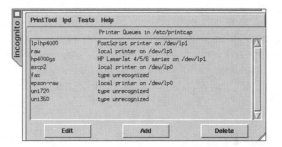

Before attempting to make a printer available on a network, you should check that it works locally. You can usually do this by using the `lpr` command, which prints a file to a printer. For example, `lpr -Php4000 test.ps` prints the file `test.ps` to the printer `hp4000`. Note that there is no space between the `-P` parameter and the printer identifier.

N O T E Depending on how your printer queue is configured, you might be able to print ASCII text files, PostScript files, or an assortment of other file types to any given printer queue. Unrecognized file types might print gibberish or not print at all. ▪

Making a Printer Available on a Network After you've configured your printer locally, making it available for network printing is straightforward: You need only add entries to the `/etc/hosts.lpd` file for each computer you want to be able to print to your local printer. You can specify machines by numeric IP address, by complete machine name, or by the machine name minus the domain name if both client and server share the same domain name. For example, suppose that you want to give several computers access to printers on the UNIX computer `polk.threeroomco.com`. The following `/etc/hosts.lpd` file can accomplish the task:

```
192.168.1.20
tyler.fourroomco.com
fillmore
```

This file enables three computers to access `polk`'s printers. Note that one of these computers (`tyler.fourroomco.com`) isn't in the same Internet domain as `polk`. You could easily specify `fillmore` as `fillmore.threeroomco.com`, if you prefer to be explicit about this matter.

> **CAUTION**
>
> You can provide printer access by entering hostnames in the `/etc/hosts.equiv` file instead of the `/etc/hosts.lpd` file, but doing so is inadvisable. Computers listed in `/etc/hosts.equiv` are given far more than printer access to your computer. Specifically, such computers acquire access through `rlogin` and other so-called *r services*. Unless you're absolutely positive about the security of those hosts, providing such access is inadvisable to the point of foolhardiness. Even if you control the remote hosts, using `/etc/hosts.equiv` simply for printer access is dangerous because a security breach on one computer can then become a breach on others in short order.

After you've configured your system to accept remote print jobs by editing `/etc/hosts.lpd` and restarting the printer daemon, you must do no more on the server end. Your computer accepts jobs destined for any printer listed in `/etc/printcap`—even including other network printers. This last fact can be useful if you want to provide access to, say, an SMB/CIFS printer to UNIX computers; you can use a computer that understands both protocols as a translator.

Accessing the Shared Printer

On the client end, accessing a network printer is a matter of configuring a printer queue in `/etc/printcap` and creating appropriate spool directories, just as you would do for a local printer. The main difference is that, instead of using an `lp=` option in the `/etc/printcap` entry, you use two new entries, `rm=` and `rp=`. The first specifies the name of the computer on which the remote queue exists, and the second specifies the name of the remote queue. The local and remote queues need not bear the same name. For example, a modification of the prior example `/etc/printcap` entry incorporating these changes might look like this:

```
lp|canon-inkjet:\
        :sd=/var/spool/lpd/lp:\
        :mx#0:\
        :sh:\
        :rm=polk.threeroomco.com:\
        :rp=color-inkjet:\
        :if=/var/spool/lpd/lp/filter:
```

GUI printer configuration tools such as `printtool` usually provide some means of entering the relevant information when you indicate you want to configure a remote `lpd`-style printer.

N O T E Because remote printing using `lpd` relies on the trusted host security model, there is no need to store a username or password for remote printer access. If your server refuses print jobs from one client but not another, it is because the server's `/etc/hosts.lpd` file needs updating, or the `lpd` server needs to be restarted to recognize the new configuration. ■

SMB/CIFS for Microsoft-Style Printer Sharing

The SMB/CIFS networking protocols include support for printing as well as for file sharing. In fact, from a networking point of view printer sharing is a subset of file sharing. In printer sharing, the client sends a file (the printer data) to the server, along with an indication of the printer to which that file should be sent. This action is essentially identical to saving a file to a shared directory, except that after the file is received, the server sends it to a printer rather than saving it to disk—and in practice, sending a file to a printer usually involves temporarily saving it to disk in a printer queue directory.

Configuring Windows to Share Printers

To share printers in Windows using SMB/CIFS, you must perform two preliminary steps:

- Install and configure the File and Printer Sharing for Microsoft Networks networking feature, as described earlier in this chapter.

  ▶ To learn more about installing Microsoft's file and printer sharing client software, **see** "Configuring Windows to Share Files," **p. 510**.

- Install and configure a printer driver. Most printers sold today come with drivers on a CD with automated installation tools, and I recommend you use these tools when available. If you're using an older printer or want to use the drivers that come with Windows, you can do so by clicking or double-clicking the Add Printer icon in the Printers folder within the My Computer or Control Panels folder, depending on your version of Windows. Windows then steps you through the printer installation process. Be sure your printer works locally before you make it available for network printing.

After you've installed these two components, you can proceed to configure printer sharing by following these steps:

1. Right-click the icon for the printer you want to share and choose Sharing from the resulting pop-up menu. This action opens the Properties dialog box on the Sharing tab, as shown in Figure 20.8.

2. Click the Shared As radio button.

3. Enter a share name. This is the name by which the printer will be known to other computers.

4. Enter a comment. The comment isn't required, but it can be helpful, particularly in a large network with many printers.

5. Enter a password.

N O T E These instructions assume that you use share-level access control in Windows 9x. If you use user-level access control (the default in Windows NT, including Windows 2000), you won't need to enter a password. ■

6. Click OK to save these changes and activate printer sharing.

Part
VII

Ch
20

FIGURE 20.8
The Sharing tab in the Properties dialog box lets you set the options you need for printer sharing.

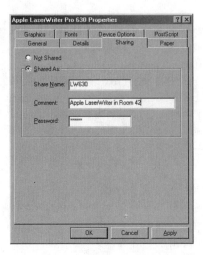

After you've configured printer sharing, you should test it from another computer to be sure that it works correctly. If not, review the previous steps and the steps in "Accessing Remote Printers from Windows," later in this chapter, to be sure you've followed the steps correctly. Also, be sure you enter share names and passwords correctly. Try reentering a password in the share definition if you think the problem might be password related.

Configuring a Samba Server in UNIX to Share Printers

Basic Samba server configuration for printer sharing is identical to Samba server configuration for file sharing. You control printer sharing from the same `smb.conf` file as you do file sharing, and the `[global]` portion of this file applies to both file and printer sharing. For example, if you configure your system to use encrypted passwords, that setting applies to both file and printer sharing.

▶ To learn more about basic Samba configuration, **see** "Configuring a Samba Server in UNIX to Share Files," **p. 512**.

You can configure Samba to share printers in one of two ways: using a default configuration for all printers or defining printers individually.

To create a default configuration, you create a share entry called `[printers]` and provide it with the printer-sharing options you want to use. For example, the following provides basic printer sharing capacity:

```
[printers]
    path = /var/spool/samba
    print ok = Yes
```

N O T E You might need to use the `browsable = Yes` option to make your printers appear in Windows network browsers. This feature isn't strictly necessary to use a printer, but it might be convenient in configuring printing on the client computer. ■

Be sure that the directory specified by the path option exists. Samba stores files there while it spools them to the UNIX printer queue. You can use a single Samba printer path for several printer shares.

When you create a [printers] section, Samba searches through your /etc/printcap entry and creates one printer share for each entry in /etc/printcap. Samba uses the first name for each printer when it creates the printer share. There are several reasons you might not want to create a default printer share, however, such as these:

- **You want to change printer names**—If you want to change some or all of the printer names for Windows users, you can do so by specifying a share using the name you want Windows users to see, and then using the printer = *printername* directive to point Samba at the appropriate local printer queue.

- **You don't want to export all printers**—It is often convenient to create multiple printer queues in UNIX to handle printouts in different ways. For example, you might create three queues, each of which prints at a different resolution. In Windows, you probably use the printer driver's options instead. To hide unnecessary queues, you can omit the [printers] section and create separate queues for each printer you do want to export.

- **You want to use unique options**—You might want to use some advanced Samba option on a subset of the available printers. For example, the user option controls who can access a share. You might use this feature to enable only some users to access a printer.

Just as with file sharing, you can use the SWAT utility to configure printer shares, as shown in Figure 20.9. Because SWAT operates as a Web server, you can configure your Samba server from the local computer or any other networked computer, no matter what OS it runs, but remember that SWAT requires you to send your root password in an unencrypted form, so it is unwise to use SWAT from anything but your local network.

Accessing Remote Printers from Windows

Printing to a shared printer from Windows is similar to printing to a local printer. In most cases, configuring network printing is quite simple, but when you use a UNIX-like OS running Samba for your print server, you might be faced with some additional options regarding printer drivers.

Part

VII

Ch

20

Choosing a Driver   If you use a DOS, Windows, or OS/2 computer to print to a non-PostScript printer shared using Samba on a UNIX-like OS, you have two choices for how to proceed. These choices require coordination between the server's printer queue configuration and the drivers you select on the client OS:

- **Native printing**—You can configure the server to share a "raw" printer queue—one that passes the client's data to the printer unchanged. When you do so, you should configure your client OS to use the printer driver from the printer's manufacturer or a driver for that or a related model printer as shipped with the OS.

- **PostScript printing**—You can configure a UNIX-like OS to convert PostScript into a format that is suitable for most printers. When you export a printer queue that uses a print filter to do this automatically using Ghostscript, you should select a PostScript printer driver on the client OS. In general, drivers for Apple LaserWriters work well for most laser printers, whereas drivers for the QMS Magicolor PostScript printer work well for most color inkjet printers.

FIGURE 20.9

SWAT lets you configure your Samba server via a Web browser directed to port 901 of the server computer.

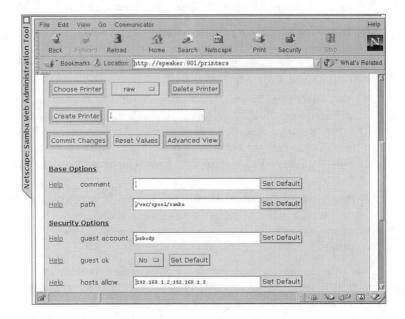

NOTE If you have a printer that supports PostScript natively, these two options are essentially the same. In this case, your printer's native driver is a PostScript driver, and your UNIX server need not use Ghostscript to process PostScript input. ■

As a general rule, native printing produces better results, especially on graphics-heavy printouts, and provides you with access to all your printer's features. Native printing usually consumes more network bandwidth, however. PostScript printing, by contrast, often produces poorer graphics output and imposes a heavier CPU load on the server, but takes less in the way of network bandwidth. PostScript output can also be useful when you want to use a single PostScript driver for all your printers or when you want to print a document that includes an Encapsulated PostScript (EPS) graphics file. For greatest flexibility, you can create two printer queues, one using native printing and the other using PostScript.

If your print server runs DOS, Windows, or OS/2, it is normal to use the native printing solution. You might be able to install Ghostscript (http://www.cs.wisc.edu/~ghost) or a commercial PostScript rasterizer to implement the PostScript printing option even in these OSs, however.

Installing a Driver and Printing To access a shared printer from Windows, you must first install and configure a printer driver on the Windows computer. Most printers come with drivers on CD, or you can install one that comes with Windows itself by double-clicking the Add Printer icon in the Printers folder. Installation details differ, but at some point, the install routine will ask where the printer is located. For example, when installing a Hewlett-Packard 4000 printer, the installer asks you to select a port. The default options include only local ports, but if you click the Browse button, the installer presents the Browse for Printer dialog box shown in Figure 20.10. You can use this dialog box to either enter the printer name directly or select it from the expandable list of network resources.

FIGURE 20.10
Many printer driver installers let you select a printer from a list of network resources.

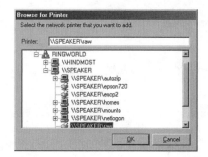

In some cases, a printer driver installer might not provide the option of connecting to a network printer. If you're in this situation, you can usually correct the matter after the fact. To do so, follow these steps after installing the driver:

1. Right-click the printer's icon, choose Properties from the pop-up menu, and click the Details tab (which is called Ports in Windows NT). The result is the Properties dialog box shown in Figure 20.11.

FIGURE 20.11
You can change a printer's port after installing the printer from the Details or Ports tab in the Properties dialog box.

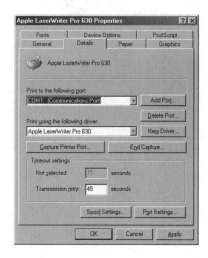

Part
VII

Ch
20

2. You might be able to select the printer directly from the Print to the Following Port list. If so, use this feature.

3. If the printer doesn't appear in the list, click Add Port; Windows responds by displaying the Add Port dialog box shown in Figure 20.12.

FIGURE 20.12

When you add a port, that port becomes available for any printer drivers you subsequently install.

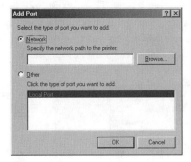

4. Type the printer name, complete with its host computer (as in \\speaker\hp4000) or click Browse to display the Browse for Printer dialog box shown in Figure 20.10. In Windows 2000, you must select the Standard TCP/IP Port option and click New Port. This action brings up a wizard to help you locate the printer.

5. Click OK in both the Add Port dialog box and the Properties dialog box.

Printing to a networked printer works just like printing to a local printer. The most important difference in most cases is that the Print dialog box displays a network path in the Where field, as shown in Figure 20.13. Some printer drivers, however, can use bidirectional communication to retrieve error codes, display ink cartridge capacity, and so on. These features don't work when you access a networked printer, although they might be available on the computer that functions as the server for that printer.

FIGURE 20.13

After you've set up a network printer, select it just as you do a local printer.

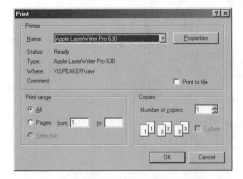

Accessing Remote Printers by Using Samba

Configuring a UNIX-like OS to print to a printer on a DOS, Windows, or OS/2 computer is done in much the same way as configuring the computer to print to a remote `lpd` queue. There are some differences, however:

- You don't use an `rm=` or `rp=` item in `/etc/printcap`.
- Set the `lp=` entry to point to `/dev/null`.
- In the printer queue directory, create a file called `.config` and type the following lines into the file:

  ```
  server=servername
  service=printername
  password=password
  ```

  Use appropriate names for *servername*, *printername*, and *password*, of course.
- On the `if=` line in `/etc/printcap`, list the `smbprint` script that comes with Samba. For example, if `smbprint` is in `/usr/bin`, this line should read `if=/usr/bin/smbprint`.
- Add an `af=` line to create an accounting file. It doesn't matter what this file is as long as it doesn't overwrite an existing file.

Many UNIX-like OSs include printer configuration tools that can help automate this process. For example, if you use Red Hat Linux, its `printtool` enables you to specify a Windows printer just as easily as it lets you specify an `lpd` printer.

> **CAUTION**
>
> The `.config` file you create for SMB/CIFS printing includes the printer's password in an unencrypted form. It is therefore important that this password not be used on any computer for any critical purpose. Of particular importance, if you use Windows NT or a UNIX-like OS with Samba as the print server, you should create a printing-only account that provides no other means of access to the computer. That way, if a cracker breaks into the client and steals the password from the `.config` file, the potential for damage is limited.

After you've created the printer queue (and restarted `lpd`, if necessary), you can print to the remote SMB/CIFS queue just as if it were a local or `lpd` queue. The procedure described earlier omits a filter to choose between sending the results through Ghostscript or sending the data directly to the printer, however, so you might be unable to print PostScript files using this queue. If necessary, you can get around this problem by creating a script that calls your print filter and then sends the result on through `smbprint`. Call this script in place of `smbprint` on the `if=` line of `/etc/printcap`.

Part

VII

Ch

20

Summary

Using file and printer sharing across two or more computers can be a very useful way to integrate your computing resources across OSs. You can use a server computer running a single OS to provide services to one or more additional computers running an assortment of other OSs. For example, you can configure a Linux computer with several file-sharing protocols and use it to access StarOffice files from another computer or computers that boot Linux, Solaris, Windows, and OS/2. You can then work on the same data files in all four OSs and print those files to the same printers. You can also use file and printer sharing to integrate OSs run in the VMware emulator package with resources available in the host Linux or Windows NT system. (VMware can directly access printers, but sharing a filesystem is best left to file-sharing network protocols.) ●

Hardware Considerations

Ensuring Adequate Resources

Resource Considerations

OSs vary in the hardware resources they require. Some, such as DOS, need only a few megabytes of hard disk space and can operate with so little RAM that any new PC you might buy would have enough memory to run the OS. Others, such as Windows 2000, are designed for the high-end systems of early 2000.

In this section, I examine the varying needs of OSs for three main types of resources: disk space, memory, and central processing unit (CPU) speed. Disk space is shared between OSs, so adding new OSs increases your need for disk space; when you boot an OS, however, it takes over the memory and CPU, so adding a new OS doesn't affect your old ones with respect to these resources. Toward the end of this chapter, I also cover a resource that many individuals neglect: backup. Installing an OS is a time-consuming proposition, particularly when you consider the time you invest in customizing your configurations. You can protect that investment by obtaining an adequate backup device and performing regular backups of all your OSs.

Hard Disk Space

With few exceptions, OSs require hard disk space. (The exceptions involve placing the OS on a removable medium, such as a floppy disk, or embedding it in the ROM of a specialized device such as a personal digital assistant [PDA].) Even if your multi-OS configuration uses a single partition, as in an installation of Windows 9*x* and a Linux variant that uses UMSDOS, each OS's files consume space on that partition. It is important before you embark on an OS installation to ensure that you have adequate disk space already or to obtain a new hard drive on which to install a new OS. Fortunately, you can often reduce total disk space requirements by sharing disk space for temporary files and the like.

OS Disk Space Requirements

OS packages typically list the minimum amount of disk space required to install an OS. In practice, of course, an OS typically requires more space than this to accommodate optional OS features, third-party software, and your own data files. Under some circumstances, it is possible to install an OS on less than the officially required disk space, but such installations generally leave you with a stripped-down version of the OS. It is also often necessary to create a full installation before you can create a stripped-down installation.

Disk Space Required for Conventional Installations   Table 21.1 summarizes the disk space requirements of various common OSs, along with their needs for other system resources. As you can see, these requirements vary substantially. You should keep in mind that Table 21.1 shows disk space requirements for the OS only. It is hard to say how much additional space you need in addition to your OSs' requirements because these needs vary depending on how many and what types of programs you use and the sorts of data files you generate. For example, if you use Windows 2000 to write short letters with its built-in WordPad word processor, you won't need much space atop its 850MB minimum. By contrast, if you use a DOS system to collect 64-channel event-related potential "brain wave" recordings in a scientific laboratory, your data files will consume tens of megabytes each, dwarfing DOS's disk space requirements.

Table 21.1 OS Hardware Requirements

Resource	PC-DOS 2000	Windows 98	Windows NT 4.0	Windows 2000	OS/2 4.0	BeOS 4.5	Linux 2.2	FreeBSD 3.3
Minimum Disk Space	6MB	210MB	110MB	850MB	200MB	150MB	Varies; 60MB typical	60MB
Recommended Minimum Disk Space	100MB	500MB	500MB	2GB	500MB	500MB	500MB	500MB
Minimum RAM	512KB	24MB	12MB	64MB	12MB	16MB	Varies; 8MB typical	5MB
Recommended RAM	8MB	32MB	32MB (Microsoft claims 16MB)	128MB	32MB	32MB	32MB	32MB
Minimum CPU	8088/4.77	486DX/66	486SX/25	Pentium /166	486SX/33	Pentium /60	386SX/25	386SX/25

When available, figures are from the manufacturer's documentation. Recommended minimum disk space value is author's estimate, as are most of the recommended RAM values. Linux requirements vary from one distribution to another. MS-DOS, DR-DOS, and FreeDOS have requirements similar to those of PC-DOS.

In most cases, it is impossible to install an OS if the available disk space doesn't meet the official requirements. If you attempt to do so, you might encounter a message stating that disk space is inadequate and the installer might refuse to proceed further. In some cases, though, the installer might issue a warning and then try to install, or not warn you about the problem at all. Some Linux distributions, for example, provide only minimal disk space checks and might attempt to install and perhaps even lead you to believe that your installation was successful, but then fail to boot, or behave oddly when booted because of inadequate free disk space.

You can sometimes reduce the need for disk space by using disk compression. This feature applies a compression algorithm, similar to those used in zip files, to every file you save on a hard disk. Although effective at reducing disk space requirements, filesystem compression slows disk accesses. Given that today's hard disks are quite inexpensive, it is usually better to buy a new hard disk rather than resort to disk compression.

Part
VIII

Ch
21

Creating a Minimal OS Installation In some cases it is possible to create special stripped-down installations that consume less than the minimum stated disk space. For example

- All versions of DOS enable you to create a DOS boot floppy by typing SYS A: or FORMAT A: /S. You can then copy critical DOS files, such as FDISK.EXE and MSCDEX.EXE, to the floppy to make it a useful system for emergency access to your computer or to perform tasks using DOS even on computers on which DOS isn't installed. Some DOS versions even include special installation options to create minimal floppy-based versions of the OS, in fact.

- Windows 9x, like DOS, includes the capability to create an emergency floppy using the Add/Remove Programs item in the Control Panel, as shown in Figure 21.1. In fact, the emergency Windows boot floppy *is* a DOS boot floppy—it uses the DOS core of Windows and omits the Windows GUI environment.

FIGURE 21.1

The Windows 9x Add/Remove Programs object enables you to create what is essentially a DOS boot floppy.

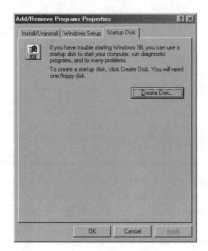

NOTE Windows NT (including Windows 2000) has an option to create an emergency disk. Unlike the Windows 9x emergency disk, the Windows NT emergency disk isn't a minimal boot disk for the OS without its GUI; it is a disk that contains backups of some of the most critical OS configuration files. You can use the emergency disk in conjunction with the OS installation floppies to recover the system in the event these critical files are damaged, but you can't boot Windows NT from the emergency disk, even in a reduced GUI-less capacity. ■

- Iomega and Symantec have produced a product called *Norton Zip Rescue* (http://www.symantec.com/specprog/nzr/ or http://www.iomega.com/software/featured/nzr.html). This product creates a floppy disk and a Zip disk that, when used together, boot the computer into a minimal Windows 9x system, complete with GUI environment, that fits on a 100MB Zip disk. You must have a working Windows 9x system to create the rescue disk set.

- The Boot-OS/2 utility, available from many OS/2 FTP sites, can create compact bootable OS/2 systems, either on a floppy disk or on a small partition. This utility includes options to create an extremely minimal text-only system or a more complete setup with minimal GUI support.

- An assortment of specialized Linux distributions exist to fit Linux on small media—as small as a single floppy disk. Examples include muLinux (`http://sunsite.auc.dk/mulinux/`) and the Linux Router Project (`http://www.linuxrouter.org`). Most of these projects aim to meet specific needs, such as Linux emergency recovery or converting old hardware into inexpensive network routers. By selecting minimal options, you can also fit a Linux system, complete with the X Window System GUI environment, on a Zip disk or similar removable medium. (The ZipSlack variant of the Slackware distribution, available from `ftp://ftp.cdrom.com/pub/linux/slackware/zipslack/`, was designed with this purpose in mind, although it lacks XFree86.) You must normally place your Linux kernel on a floppy disk to boot from such a disk.

Whenever your OS supports it, I recommend you create or obtain at least one method of booting your OS from a floppy or other removable medium. This practice enables you to gain access to your OS's files if the OS fails to boot. In many cases, such tools can also be used in complete emergency recovery operations, such as when your hard disk fails. Be sure to test your emergency boot procedures, both as soon as you create them and after making changes to your system configuration. Some mini-configurations are highly dependent on factors such as drive letter assignments and video hardware and might fail after a hardware upgrade unless you make appropriate changes.

 TIP If your OS can't boot from a floppy, you might nonetheless be able to use nonnative tools for at least some emergency recovery procedures. For example, an NTFS read/write driver on a DOS or Linux boot floppy can help you recover from some problems with Windows NT installations on NTFS partitions.

▶ To learn more about drivers for nonnative filesystems, **see** Chapter 13, "Tools for Accessing Foreign Filesystems."

Using Shared Space to Minimize Wasted Disk Space

When designing your partition layout, you should probably allocate at least one partition as space to be shared across OSs. Not only does such a practice aid in sharing data across OSs, but it can sometimes reduce wasted disk space. Examples of using shared space include shared temporary directories, shared directories for emulation or multiple installations of similar OSs, and shared swap space.

Sharing Temporary Space Most OSs set aside a directory to be used as temporary storage space. If you place that directory on a shared partition, the relevant disk space effectively does duty for both OSs, reducing the total disk space requirements.

CAUTION

UNIX programs often use UNIX filesystem features in temporary files. This fact makes sharing of temporary space impossible between many UNIX systems and non-UNIX OSs. You can share temporary space between Linux and any FAT-using OS, however, by using the Linux UMSDOS filesystem to mount the relevant partition. UMSDOS is slower than native Linux filesystems, however, and might be a poor choice if your programs frequently access their temporary files.

Sharing temporary space across OSs has an extra benefit in the form of reduced administration effort. It is common for temporary files to build up in temporary space, requiring your intervention sooner or later to clean out old files. If all your OSs use the same temporary space, this task becomes simpler because it is necessary to do it less often. Also, some OSs include some method of automatically clearing old data out of temporary space. Many UNIX-like OSs, for example, do so at regular intervals. You might be able to harness this feature to reduce the effort required to administer other OSs, if a common filesystem is available that meets both OSs needs.

TIP

You can add commands in your system startup or shutdown files to clear out temporary space. For example, in DOS or Windows, you can use the DELTREE command in your AUTOEXEC.BAT file, as in DELTREE /Y C:\WINDOWS\TMP*.*, to clear out the contents of the C:\WINDOWS\TMP directory. I recommend placing such commands in the shutdown script; that way, they'll leave temporary files intact on system startup after a system crash, which might be extremely important in recovering data from any programs you happened to be using at the time of a crash.

Sharing Files for Emulation or Related OSs   Sharing disk space is particularly helpful when you want to run the same programs across several OSs, either through emulation or because two or more OSs can run the same programs (such as Windows 98 and Windows 2000). The key to successful file sharing in such situations is to use a filesystem that both OSs understand. For example, in the case of Windows 98 and Windows 2000, you could use FAT-32; but if you use Windows NT 4.0 instead of Windows 2000, you would need to either use FAT-16 or add a third-party driver to one or the other OS to accomplish the file sharing goal. Another alternative would be to use a shared network filesystem hosted on another computer.

▶ To learn more about accessing one OS's filesystems from another OS, **see** Chapter 13, "Tools for Accessing Foreign Filesystems."

In the case of the VMware emulator (http://www.vmware.com), you can point it to a raw disk partition rather than use a virtual hard disk file. When you do so, VMware boots using the same files that you use when you boot the OS directly. You should read the instructions on VMware's Web site concerning hardware profiles, however, to ensure that you do this safely: http://www.vmware.com/support/hardwareprofiles.html. Alternatively, you can boot VMware from a small virtual disk and then use networking features to provide it with access to your OS's regular files.

▶ To learn more about VMware, **see** "VMware," **p. 466**.

▶ To learn more about sharing filesystems via networking, **see** Chapter 20, "File and Printer Sharing."

Sharing a Swap Partition   Many modern OSs use *swap space*—a file or disk partition set aside to serve as an adjunct to RAM. Using swap space, you can run programs that consume more RAM than exists in your computer. The downside to this operation is that the use of swap space greatly slows memory accesses involving the swap space. Nonetheless, swap space is extremely useful, and because most OSs use swap space, you might be tempted to use the same disk space for this function across several OSs.

When you share swap space, it is often desirable to configure your system to use a separate swap partition. Many OSs, including all varieties of Microsoft Windows and IBM's OS/2, use swap files on their boot partitions (or potentially on other partitions accessible to the OS); but many UNIX versions favor separate swap partitions.

The key to sharing swap space is for each OS to clear out all other OSs' swap files at boot time. For example, OS/2 creates a swap file called SWAPPER.DAT but doesn't delete this file when it shuts down. Likewise, Windows 9x's swap file is called WIN386.SWP. If you share swap space between Windows and OS/2, therefore, you should include an appropriate line in your Windows AUTOEXEC.BAT file to delete the SWAPPER.DAT file and a line in OS/2's CONFIG.SYS file to delete WIN386.SWP.

When using a UNIX-like OS, it is often necessary to initialize the swap partition as such, using a command such as mkswap. You should find the initialization file that issues the swapon command and add the mkswap command before the swapon command. You should then include an appropriate command to reformat the swap partition for your other OS or OSs in your system shutdown scripts, just after the swapoff command. You can then instruct your other OSs to use that partition for their swap files. In Windows 9x, for example, you can click the Virtual Memory button on the Performance tab of the System Properties dialog box to get the Virtual Memory dialog box shown in Figure 21.2. You can then adjust the hard disk on which Windows places the swap file. In OS/2, you can adjust the swap file location by setting the SWAPPATH variable in OS/2's CONFIG.SYS file. The mkswap and partition formatting commands will increase your startup and shutdown times.

CAUTION

Issuing mkswap and mkfs commands in startup and shutdown scripts can be convenient and helpful, but if your device identifiers ever change, these commands can wreak havoc. For example, suppose your swap partition is /dev/hda7 in Linux and it is followed by a BFS partition. If you consolidate two earlier partitions into one, the BFS partition will become /dev/hda7, and the next time you boot, you'll wipe it out unless you remembered before modifying the partitions to remove or change the mkswap command.

Part VIII

Ch 21

FIGURE 21.2
You can change the location of a swap file to share swap space between OSs.

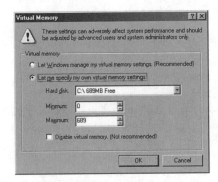

Tips when Adding Disk Space

You might discover that you need to expand your hard disk space, either because you're outgrowing a hard disk with your current set of OSs or because you need more space in which to place a new OS. When this happens, you have two options:

■ **Replace a small hard disk with a larger one**—You can buy one hard disk as a replacement for an old one. The problem with this approach is that it requires you to copy your existing files from the old hard disk to the new one. This task can be particularly tedious if any OSs boot off of the hard disk you're replacing. A disk replacement might be your only choice, however, particularly if you use only EIDE devices and already have four or if you have no room in your computer's case for another hard disk.

▶ To learn more about backing up and copying files between partitions and disks, **see** Chapter 8, "Modifying Partitions After the Fact," and "Cross-Platform Backup Needs," **p. 548**.

■ **Add a hard disk**—If you have the space in your case and haven't filled out your EIDE or SCSI adapter's capacity, you can add a drive and leave your old one intact. This approach is generally more convenient than replacing an old drive and has the advantage of enabling you to install an OS across both drives, which can improve system performance.

▶ To learn more about using two disks to improve performance, **see** "Splitting OSs Across Multiple Hard Disks," **p. 172**.

Whether you add disk space by replacing an old drive with a larger one or by adding a new drive, you should consider several factors to help ensure that you get the most out of the new disk space. These factors include

■ **OS placement requirements**—Be aware of the boot requirements of each OS. Microsoft OSs require a primary partition on the first physical disk, for example, whereas Linux can reside just about anywhere. Unless you use a rare LBA-enabled boot loader, all OSs must reside at least partly below the 1024-cylinder mark.

- **Allocation block sizes**—Some filesystems (most notably FAT-16) allocate space with increasing inefficiency as partition size increases. Plan your partition sizes appropriately.

  ▶ To learn more about allocation block sizes for various filesystems, **see** Chapter 12, "Filesystems for Assorted OSs."

- **Primary versus logical partitions**—Whenever possible, you should use logical partitions rather than primary partitions because primary partitions are both limited in number per disk and required by certain OSs.

  ▶ To learn more about partition types, **see** "Partition Types," **p. 119**.

- **Choice of partitioning tool**—If you use the wrong tool to partition a new disk, you might run into incompatibilities down the line. If you have it, I recommend you use PartitionMagic to create all your partitions. My second choice is OS/2's FDISK, followed by DOS's or Windows 9*x*'s FDISK. Another option is to use each OS's partitioning tool to create that OS's partitions.

  ▶ To learn more about partitioning tools, **see** Chapter 6, "Tools for Disk Partitioning."

- **Partition placement**—Placement of partitions, both in absolute location on the hard disk and relative to other partitions, can greatly affect the speed of your OSs.

  ▶ To learn more about improving OS performance by appropriate partition placement, **see** Chapter 7, "Tips for Optimizing System Performance."

OS Memory Requirements

Random access memory (RAM) is a limited resource that is taken over by one OS when that OS runs. Therefore, there is no need to add more RAM when you add a new OS unless your new OS requires more RAM than does your old OS.

As I mentioned earlier in this chapter, it is possible to supplement RAM with disk space by using an OS's support for swap space (which is also known as *virtual memory*). Swap space is slow, however, so all other things being equal, it is better to have more memory than less memory with more available swap space.

Memory Requirements for Various OSs

Table 21.1 summarizes the memory requirements of various OSs. Most modern OSs require a minimum of somewhere between 8MB and 16MB of RAM, but these minimum values are generally quite optimistic. When run with their minimum amounts of memory, modern OSs tend to be quite slow because they rely on swap space far too much. Most modern OSs become truly usable with 32MB of memory or more.

Part
VIII

Ch
21

Keep in mind that your computer's memory requirements depend not just on the OS you run, but on the applications you use—both their type and their number. For example, if you only run a handful of lightweight applications, you might be happy with the minimum recommended amount of RAM for an OS; but if you run several memory-intensive programs such as image editors for processing large graphics files, you'll need much more RAM. You should consider your applications' memory needs when deciding how much memory you require.

Getting By with Reduced Memory

Some OSs can run on less memory than is specified in Table 21.1. For example, the FreeBSD 5MB figure represents a requirement for the installation program. When installed, FreeBSD can run on as little as 4MB of RAM. Others, such as Windows 2000, can install and run on less than their manufacturer-claimed minimums reported in Table 21.1, but such a procedure results in painfully slow operation as the OS uses its disk-based swap space for the most basic tasks.

For any OS, there are steps you can take to enhance your computing experience on a low-memory computer. These include

- **Run in text mode**—Some OSs, and particularly the UNIX-like OSs, can run without any GUI environment. Because GUIs chew up several megabytes of RAM, running an OS without its GUI can help you get by on reduced RAM. In fact, the minimum RAM figures for Linux and FreeBSD reflect operation in text mode only. You can also strip Windows 9*x* and OS/2 of their GUI environments, but doing so reduces their utility more than does running a UNIX-like OS in text mode.

- **Use basic GUI tools**—Even if you require a GUI environment, you might be able to use only the most basic GUI tools. As with running in text mode, this procedure is easiest to accomplish with UNIX-like OSs because you control the window manager and desktop environment you run. In OS/2, you can specify a shell to run other than the WPS by replacing the reference to PMSHELL.EXE in CONFIG.SYS with a replacement GUI shell of your choice.

- **Avoid use of GUI add-ons**—Programs and utilities such as those discussed in Chapter 17, "Modifying GUI Look and Feel," can be amusing and even helpful in many situations, but when you're short on RAM, they're more likely to cause frustration by slowing down your computer.

- **Limit multitasking**—The more programs you load into memory at once, the more RAM those programs consume. If you run as few programs as possible at once, you'll reduce this memory load. The effect of running few programs at once might not be as substantial as you might initially think, however. If two programs are loaded but you work with only one at a time, the program with which you're not working is likely to be swapped out to disk and dormant, so it won't consume any actual RAM. Only if two or more programs are actively engaged in computations will they compete for physical RAM.

- **Choose programs carefully**—Competing products often require substantially different amounts of RAM. If you're writing a half-page note, you probably don't need a full office suite such as StarOffice or ApplixWare; any of dozens of smaller word processors or even plain text editors will likely do the job. You might also want to consider using an older version of a program because applications often increase their resource requirements as their version numbers increase.

People did useful work on computers with 1MB or less of RAM, albeit not with OSs anywhere near as sophisticated as those available today. By choosing your OS and tools carefully, you might be able to squeeze more life out of a RAM-challenged computer or put off adding RAM to it. On the other hand, RAM isn't very expensive these days—certainly not compared to the cost of RAM when people used 1MB computers—so investing a few dollars in a memory upgrade might be very worthwhile.

Motherboard Memory Support

If you decide you want to upgrade your computer's memory, you should know something about the different types of memory required by different motherboards. There are several different ways to classify memory. One is by speed and location in the computer. The three main types when measured by this yardstick are

- **Level 1 cache**—A *cache* is a small but fast storage area that holds a subset of a larger but slower storage area's contents for quick access. One important type of memory cache is the level 1 (L1) cache located on the CPU. Typically a few tens or hundreds of kilobytes in size, the L1 cache is not upgradable except by replacing the CPU.

- **Level 2 cache**—Also referred to as the L2 cache, this storage area is located on some CPU's modules, but not in the chip that comprises the CPU proper. Other systems place the L2 cache on the motherboard, and some omit it entirely. In early 2000, L2 cache sizes typically hover around 1MB. L2 caches aren't normally upgradable, although sometimes they are.

> **CAUTION**
>
> The amount of L2 cache, in conjunction with other design features of the motherboard or CPU module, determines how much RAM is cacheable. If you install more RAM in a computer than the cache can handle, overall system performance can degrade. You should check your motherboard's documentation to determine not just how much RAM the computer can use, but how much RAM the motherboard can cache. Do not exceed this cacheable RAM limit.

- **RAM**—RAM is usually what is meant when computer memory is discussed, and it is the type of memory to which I have referred earlier in this chapter. RAM comes in various forms, but mostly in single inline memory modules (SIMMs) or dual inline memory modules (DIMMs) that you plug into sockets in your computer. Because most computers have several SIMM or DIMM sockets, you can often upgrade a computer's RAM without replacing existing RAM.

Over the past several years, a plethora of RAM types has come and gone. Depending on the age of your computer, you might encounter any of the following:

- **DRAM**—Dynamic RAM is the oldest and most generic type of RAM. You're unlikely to encounter ordinary DRAM except in old 386 systems.

- **FPM DRAM**—Fast Page Mode DRAM is an improvement on ordinary DRAM that was used on many 486 systems. It is available in 30- and 72-pin SIMM format.

- **EDO DRAM**—Extended Data Out DRAM is an extension on FPM DRAM design principles. It is available in 72-pin SIMMs and 168-pin DIMMs and was commonly used on Pentium-class systems.

- **SDRAM**—Synchronous DRAM is substantially faster than EDO DRAM. It is usually distributed as 168-pin DIMMs and is used in high-end Pentium systems and above.

- **PC-100 and PC-133**—The PC-100 and PC-133 specifications apply to SDRAM that meets timing requirements for computers with 100MHz and 133MHz bus speeds, respectively.

- **RDRAM**—Rambus DRAM uses a design that is substantially different from previous RAM designs in order to increase the speed of RAM. RDRAM is available on a new type of memory module known as a RIMM (Rambus inline memory module). This technology is likely to become important as motherboard speeds increase past 133MHz in 2000 and beyond.

Many of these memory technologies come in an assortment of subtypes and variants, such as

- **Parity**—Some memory modules include a *parity* bit, which helps the motherboard locate memory errors. The parity bit means that the memory module has nine bits to the byte instead of eight.

- **Sides**—Some memory module types support minor interface variants that are often associated with the physical placement of chips on one or both sides of the module. Some motherboards don't work well with single-sided or double-sided memory types, but work fine with the other type.

- **Speed**—The faster the motherboard runs, the faster the memory must run. Older memory is incapable of keeping up with the speeds required by modern motherboards, and in fact this factor has pushed the development of new memory types, such as RDRAM. Even within a type, though, memory speed often varies.

- **Number of chips**—Even for a module of a specific capacity, it is often possible to produce the product using differing numbers of chips. These differences can produce subtle electronic effects that occasionally cause problems, particularly in older 386 and 486 motherboards that use 30-pin SIMMs.

Part of the difficulty of upgrading memory, especially if your computer is more than a few months old, is in locating the appropriate memory type—both the technology in use (EDO DRAM, SDRAM, and so on) and the physical format for the RAM modules themselves (30-pin SIMM, 72-pin SIMM, 168-pin DIMM, or something more exotic). Figure 21.3 shows an old 30-pin SIMM and a newer 168-pin DIMM for comparison. You should consult the documentation that came with your computer to determine what type of RAM you need.

FIGURE 21.3
RAM modules have gotten larger over the years, both in capacity and in physical size.

Ironically, it is often more expensive to upgrade the RAM of an older computer than to do the same for a newer computer because manufacturers frequently abandon older RAM technologies, leading to a limited supply of older products. If you need to perform major memory upgrades, therefore, you might want to consider upgrading your motherboard to a type that supports newer memory—but this might entail a need to upgrade the CPU and even add-on cards, which might make this approach much less appealing.

Depending on the type of CPU you use and the type of RAM module your motherboard accepts, you might need to add memory modules in groups ranging in size from one to eight. For example, most Pentium-class motherboards accept 72-pin SIMMs in groups of two, or 168-pin DIMMs one at a time. Consult your motherboard's manual for details.

Fortunately, RAM seldom presents problems for one OS but not another, unless there is not enough RAM in a computer for a given OS. On rare occasions, though, one OS might behave erratically with certain memory modules whereas another works fine. This problem was somewhat common when 32-bit OSs such as UNIX and OS/2 competed against the 16-bit DOS. The patterns of memory access imposed by 32-bit OSs are different than those imposed by 16-bit DOS, and some RAM in years past failed to work correctly when confronted with 32-bit memory access patterns. With the ubiquity of the (mostly) 32-bit Windows 9x in today's computer marketplace, such problems are now rarer than they were in the mid-1990s, but they aren't quite completely nonexistent. If you experience bizarre lockups in one OS but not another, one possible, albeit unlikely, explanation is RAM. If such a pattern of problems begins after a RAM upgrade, this explanation is more likely.

Part
VIII

Ch
21

CPU Speed Requirements

Like RAM, your computer's CPU is a resource that each OS monopolizes when running, so adding a new OS won't make an old OS any slower. You might need to consider a CPU upgrade if you add a new OS with substantially higher CPU requirements than an old OS, however.

The CPU arena changes frequently, so if you need to buy a new CPU, you should research what is available at the time you read these words. In general, the very fastest CPUs cost twice or more what a CPU just a few percent slower costs, so the best values typically come in something a bit less than cutting-edge performance. You might also find better value, and possibly better performance, with Intel-compatible CPUs (such as the AMD K6-III and Athlon processors) than with Intel CPUs, but this isn't always true.

CPU Speed Requirements for Various OSs

Most OSs don't really require extraordinarily speedy CPUs for basic functionality. Table 21.1 summarizes official CPU speed requirements for several OSs. In some cases it is possible to run an OS with a lesser CPU than is officially supported, but this practice is generally inadvisable. With the exception of DOS, all major OSs available for x86 hardware today use 32-bit addressing modes introduced with the 386 CPU. These OSs therefore don't run on 286 or lesser computers. Some OSs use CPU features introduced on 486 or Pentium computers, as well, but others are simply optimized to use these CPU's instructions rather than those of earlier CPUs.

Beyond basic OS functionality, however, faster CPUs might be required to use certain OS or application features. For example, IBM's OS/2 4.0 officially requires a 486/33 CPU, but to use its built-in speech recognition features, you must have a Pentium 75 or higher. An increasing number of games for Windows OSs require CPUs with multimedia extension (MMX) features. Of course, any new computer sold today more than meets the CPU requirements for all the OSs listed in Table 21.1. These limits might be important if you want to use a new OS on an older computer, however. Also, CPU speed can be a limiting factor in certain applications, such as high-end scientific or engineering work, or even for playing the latest games.

Intel-Compatible CPUs

x86 computers can use CPUs from any of several manufacturers. Intel is the largest supplier of such CPUs in 2000 and has been since the introduction of the original IBM PC. For this reason, most OS manufacturers state their OSs' CPU requirements in terms of the minimum Intel CPU needed to run the OS. If you have a non-Intel CPU, therefore, you might need to do some translation to discover what CPU is adequate. In this section I provide an overview of the CPUs available from various manufacturers and provide rough guidelines on CPU equivalencies to help you make the Intel-to-competitor translation.

N O T E It is critical to remember, when comparing CPUs, that the clock speed alone isn't an adequate measurement of speed. For example, Cyrix 6x86 CPUs run at a given speed routinely outperform Pentium CPUs run at the same speed, at least for integer operations. Some manufacturers therefore label their CPUs with numbers they believe to be equivalent to an Intel CPU run at the same clock speed. ▪

When comparing CPUs, and particularly CPUs from different manufacturers, be aware that CPU speed varies depending on the type of operation being performed. For example, floating-point math operations use a particular part of the CPU known as the *floating-point unit (FPU)*, and CPUs with otherwise similar speed might have different FPU speed. Until recently, Intel had the best FPU speed of any x86 CPUs, but AMD's Athlon now provides very strong FPU performance.

Intel   Intel originated the design of CPUs used in modern x86 computers and continues to lead its competitors in the introduction of many new features—at least, in features that influence the design of programs. In years past, Intel, like most CPU manufacturers, gave its CPUs numbers of the form 80x86, or x86 for short, where *x* was a value from 1 up. (The first x86 CPU had no x—it was the 8086. The 80186 was never commonly used in PCs. The 8088 used in the first IBM PC was a further exception to Intel's naming rules.) Intel changed to a CPU name in order to trademark the name, with the CPU that would have been known as the 586. The name Intel chose was *Pentium*, and Intel has used that name in conjunction with Roman numerals to identify most subsequent CPUs in the line (Pentium II and Pentium III). The *Celeron* line is an offshoot that strips away certain features from Pentium II and above CPUs. Table 21.2 summarizes the features and improvements in the x86 line of CPUs from Intel.

Table 21.2   Intel CPU Features

CPU	Features	Minimum for OSs
8088	8086 with reduced-width data bus	All versions of DOS
8086	16-bit CPU; first in x86 line	
80286	16-bit CPU with extra memory addressing modes to expand memory space from 1MB to 16MB	OS/2 1.*x*
80386	32-bit CPU. SX versions had 16MB memory limit; DX versions had 4GB memory limit	Windows 95 & NT 3.*x*; OS/2 2.*x* & 3.0; FreeBSD; Linux
80486	Speed enhancements to 386; all versions have 4GB memory limit; DX versions were first to incorporate FPUs	Windows 98 & NT 4.0; OS/2 4.0

continues

Part
VIII

Ch
21

Table 21.2   Continued

CPU	Features	Minimum for OSs
Pentium	Speed enhancement and extra instructions; 64-bit data bus, but still 32-bit internally	Windows 2000; BeOS 4.*x*
Pentium MMX	Pentium with multimedia extensions	
Pentium Pro	Pentium better optimized for 32-bit code; no MMX; 64GB memory limit; L2 cache on CPU package	
Pentium II	Pentium Pro with MMX and speed enhancements	
Pentium III	Pentium II with speed enhancements	
Celeron	Pentium II with no or smaller L2 cache on CPU package (models with cache run it at core speed rather than bus speed)	

In general, Intel CPUs are safe bets for use with any x86 OS, assuming the CPU meets the minimum architectural requirements of the OS. In early 2000, the Pentium III is used on midrange and high-end systems, whereas the Celeron is used on low-cost introductory computers. Earlier x86 models are difficult to find.

Developments in the Intel CPU line in 2000 are likely to include an increase in the bus speed (the speed at which the CPU interfaces to the motherboard) from 100MHz to 133MHz and likely increases of core speed past 1000MHz (1GHz). It is possible that Intel will apply the *Pentium IV* moniker to a CPU incorporating these changes. Intel is also preparing the release of a true 64-bit CPU that should be compatible with 32-bit OSs such as those discussed in this book. To take best advantage of this CPU, new OSs—or at least new variants of existing OSs—will be required.

AMD   Advanced Micro Devices (AMD; http://www.amd.com) is Intel's largest competitor in the x86 arena. Intel originally licensed the design of its x86 CPUs to AMD in order to gain contracts that required a second source for all products. Later, Intel revoked that license, forcing AMD to independently develop an x86 clone CPU, which was known as the K5. AMD then purchased a smaller company, NexGen, and used its technology as the basis for the K6 and later AMD CPUs. The K6 series CPUs continue to use a socketed design such as that of the Pentium CPU, which is less expensive to produce but that produces slower L2 cache performance than the design used by Pentium II CPUs. The Athlon uses a proprietary slotted design similar to that of the Pentium II and later CPUs. This history and features are outlined in Table 21.3.

Table 21.3   AMD CPU Features

CPU	Features	Drop-in Replacement for Intel CPU
80386 & 80486	Near-identical clones of like-named Intel CPUs	Equivalently named Intel CPUs
K5	Pentium-like performance	Pentium
K6	Performance near Pentium II levels, but uses older motherboard types; MMX extensions	Pentium MMX
K6-2	Improved speed over K6	Pentium MMX
K6-III	Improved speed over K6-2	Pentium MMX
Athlon	Improved speed over K6-III; L2 cache on CPU package	None; uses Alpha EV6 interface

In late 1999, the fastest available x86 systems were built on high-end Athlon CPUs. The Athlon and Intel's Pentium III are both worthy of serious consideration for high-end systems. As I write this, the K6 series is still worth consideration for lower-end systems, but that situation might not last long into 2000. AMD is expected to break the 1GHz speed barrier sometime in 2000.

In terms of OS compatibility, AMD's line is as capable as Intel's. You shouldn't try running an OS with heavy CPU requirements, such as Windows 2000, on an underpowered AMD CPU, of course, but so long as you get an AMD CPU equivalent to or better than the Intel CPU listed by the OS manufacturer, you should be fine. I've run most of the OSs discussed in this book on systems with AMD CPUs up to the K6-2. The Athlon does pose installation problems with a few OSs, however. If you run into a problem using an Athlon, check the OS manufacturer for an update. There is an updated installation floppy for SuSE Linux 6.2 (http://www.suse.com), for example, to fix problems installing on Athlon systems. These problems are fixed in the newer 6.3 release of SuSE Linux.

VIA   VIA (http://www.via.com.tw) has long been a manufacturer of chipsets for motherboards and other components. In 1999, VIA purchased Cyrix and IDT's x86 CPU designs. VIA has continued CPU development, basing its latest product on extensions of the old Cyrix designs. Cyrix and IDT, and hence now VIA, use unique designs for their CPUs, but they implement the same features as do Intel's x86 CPUs and are compatible with x86 OSs and software. Table 21.4 summarizes the VIA, Cyrix, and IDT CPU families.

Table 21.4   VIA/Cyrix/IDT CPU Features

CPU	Features	Drop-in Replacement for Intel CPU
Cyrix 80386 & 80486	Near-identical clones of like-named Intel CPUs. SL models were stripped-down versions to fit in previous-generation motherboards.	Equivalently named Intel CPUs
Cyrix 5x86	Souped-up 486 to produce Pentium-like performance on 486 motherboards.	486
Cyrix 6x86	Roughly equivalent to Intel Pentium in speed and features.	Pentium
Cyrix 6x86MX	Roughly equivalent to Pentium MMX in speed and features.	Pentium MMX
Cyrix MII	6x86 run at higher clock speeds.	Pentium MMX
IDT WinChip C6	Roughly equivalent to Intel Pentium MMX.	Pentium MMX
IDT WinChip 2	Roughly equivalent to Intel Pentium MMX.	Pentium MMX
VIA Joshua	Roughly equivalent to Pentium II/III or Celeron.	Pentium II/III/Celeron

The latest CPU in Table 2.4, the Joshua, is not yet available as I write these words, and in fact *Joshua* is a code name—the final CPU will likely be called something else. The exact details of this CPU's performance are therefore uncertain.

Earlier Cyrix and IDT CPUs have tended to fall at the low end of the performance spectrum when compared to Intel's CPUs. The IDT offerings, in particular, are architecturally simpler than are Intel's or AMD's equivalent CPUs. In early 2000, these CPUs compete well in the low end of the CPU marketplace, but you shouldn't consider them for high-end systems.

The Cyrix and IDT CPUs are highly compatible with x86 OSs. In fact, Nessus, my multi-OS system, runs on a Cyrix MII CPU.

▶ To learn more about the hardware in Nessus, **see** "Nessus: The Eight-OS Computer," **p. 21**.

When Cyrix was a separate company, it owned no manufacturing facilities and entered into agreements with other companies to manufacture its CPUs. In some cases, these companies obtained the right to sell Cyrix CPUs under their own names. Most notably, IBM sells 6x86 and 6x86MX CPUs (IBM hasn't picked up the MII moniker, but sells those CPUs under the 6x86MX name). Some third parties also sell Cyrix CPUs repackaged as upgrades for older systems.

Transmeta   The latest entrant to the x86 arena is Transmeta (http://www.transmeta.com). This company's Crusoe processor line is designed to be used in mobile and embedded applications, such as notebook computers and PDAs. It is distinguished from other x86 designs in its low power consumption and its unusual design—it uses low-level software to implement much of the x86 functionality.

The Crusoe CPU was unveiled in early 2000, and as I write these words it is not yet available in any shipping product. It is therefore too early to say how well it handles multiple OSs. Transmeta does, however, employ Linus Torvalds, the originator of Linux, and a version of Linux optimized for the CPU was announced along with the CPU.

Defunct and Obscure Manufacturers   The x86 marketplace is brutal and has seen the coming and going of several manufacturers. Some of these include

- **NexGen**—This company produced the first Pentium clone CPU, the Nx586. NexGen was bought by AMD, which developed its technology into the K6 CPU.
- **Cyrix**—As I just noted, Cyrix has been bought by VIA, which still uses the Cyrix name on its CPUs at the start of 2000.
- **IDT**—IDT entered an agreement in late 1999 to sell its CPU technology to VIA.
- **NEC**—NEC produced (and still produces) a line of 8086-compatible CPUs such as the V30. These are generally used in embedded products today, but in the mid-1980s they were found in some PC-compatible computers. Because these CPUs are based on the earliest available x86 CPUs, they can't run any modern 32-bit x86 OS, although they can run DOS.

Non-x86 CPUs for the Daring

This book focuses on OSs for x86-based PCs. If you want to expand your horizons still further, however, there are other alternatives, such as

- **PowerPC**—The PowerPC (or PPC) line of CPUs was designed in a joint venture by Apple, IBM, and Motorola. It is currently used mostly in Apple Macintosh computers, although both Motorola and IBM have offered computers built around this CPU. Apple's Mac OS runs on its PPC systems, but you can also run Linux and some BSD variants on these computers. Older Macintoshes and some non-Apple hardware can run BeOS. For a time, IBM offered a PPC version of OS/2, but it is no longer supported.
- **680x0**—Motorola's 680x0 line was used in older Macintosh computers, as well as in computers from a variety of other manufacturers. It is not used in many current computers, however. Depending on the specific computer, you can run older versions of Mac OS, Linux, certain BSD variants, and more obscure OSs on such hardware.
- **Alpha**—The Digital (now Compaq) Alpha CPU is a high-performance CPU that has been used in several UNIX workstations. You can also run Windows NT, Linux, and some BSD variants on it.
- **SPARC**—Sun's UNIX workstations are built around the SPARC CPU. These computers run Solaris and can also run Linux.

A plethora of other CPUs are used in everything from hand-held PDAs to supercomputers. In most cases, the computers that use these obscure CPUs run only the OS provided by the device's manufacturer—usually a custom OS or some variety of UNIX. For most of these computers, though, one cross-platform OS is available, albeit often in a very crude form: Linux. Linux enthusiasts have ported that OS to a wide range of improbable platforms, such as 3Com's PalmPilot. In many cases (including that of the PalmPilot), Linux isn't really usable on the target platform, but if you like low-level OS programming, you might want to look into such projects.

Cross-Platform Backup Needs

When you run a multi-OS computer, it is critically important that you have adequate backup hardware and that you use this hardware on a regular basis. A hard disk crash in a multi-OS environment can take out untold hours of work in configuring your system. Lest you think such an occurrence is unlikely, consider this: While writing this book, Nessus (my multi-OS computer) suffered just such a disk crash. The fact that I had backups turned what might have been a setback costing me a week or more of work into an annoyance that took less than a day to correct. I therefore present some information on how to select and use a tape backup drive to obtain maximal OS functionality.

> **N O T E** If you check the list of hardware contained in Nessus that I present in Chapter 1, "The Trials and Triumphs of a Multi-OS Computer," you'll note that no tape backup drive is listed. This is because my tape backup drive is on another computer on my network, and I'm able to use network file sharing, as described in Chapter 20, to back up Nessus. You can learn more about network backups in my book *Linux: Networking for Your Office*, published by Sams. ■

Selecting a Tape Drive

One of the most widely used backup media is magnetic tape. Tapes are inexpensive on a per-megabyte basis, and both the drives and media are inexpensive. Although you can use other devices, such as CD recordable (CD-R) drives or removable hard disks, tapes generally have higher capacities or lower costs than their competition. It is possible to use a combination of tape backup with other backup media, as I outline shortly.

Four basic types of tape drives are marketed for x86 PCs, as defined by the way they interface to the computer:

■ **Parallel port drives**—Some drives connect to a computer through the parallel port. These external devices are easy to connect, but they tend to be slow, and they require special drivers in the host OS. This last fact makes them a poor choice in many multi-OS environments because appropriate drivers often don't exist.

- **Floppy port drives**—Some tape drives attach to the computer's floppy controller. These devices tend to be slow and unreliable, but they're inexpensive. Their popularity has faded in recent years as higher-capacity drives have abandoned this interface method. Support for these drives across OSs is common but not universal.

- **EIDE drives**—Many popular tape drives in 2000 connect to the EIDE port, along with hard disks and CD-ROM drives. These devices are often inexpensive, reasonably speedy, and reasonably reliable. Cross-OS support is good. The drawback is that a typical PC can support only four EIDE devices.

- **SCSI drives**—SCSI drives can be internal or external. They tend to be more expensive than other varieties, but they come in higher-capacity models and have unparalleled cross-OS support.

As a general rule, I favor SCSI tape drives, but you might find an EIDE drive to be adequate for your needs. You should confirm that all your host OSs can use the particular type of drive you select before you buy it, though. In most cases you don't need to use a driver for your specific model device. Like hard disks or CD-ROM drives, tape drives work from generic drivers for the broad class of device (SCSI, EIDE, and so on). There are a few exceptions to this rule, though. For example, the minimal backup tools that come with most versions of Windows don't work with all drives.

Each interface type can be used with any of a number of tape formats. Like cassettes or eight-track tapes, each tape type is incompatible with others and has different characteristics in terms of price, speed, capacity, and so on. Common examples include

- **QIC-80**—This was a common tape format in the early 1990s, but its capacity isn't sufficient for modern computer systems. QIC-80 drives were generally parallel-port or floppy-interfaced devices.

- **Travan**—There are several subvarieties of Travan drive. Older and lower-capacity forms generally used the floppy port, but newer and higher-capacity varieties use the EIDE or SCSI port. Travan drives tend to be inexpensive, but the tapes are relatively costly. Capacities range from 400MB to 10GB (uncompressed). Higher-capacity Travan drives can usually read from, but not write to, lower-capacity Travan and QIC-80 tapes.

- **DAT**—4mm digital audio tape (DAT) has been adapted for use in computer backup devices. DAT drives generally use the SCSI interface. The drives are relatively expensive, but tapes are inexpensive. Capacities range from 2GB to 20GB (uncompressed). Higher-capacity DAT drives can both read and write lower-capacity DAT tapes.

The high end also supports a range of additional formats, such as digital linear tape (DLT) and 8mm DAT. Because multi-OS computers often require large hard disks, it is best to purchase a high-end Travan or DAT system. You might need several tapes to back up your multiple OSs, so DAT's pricing system might prove beneficial.

Depending on the capacity and type, tape backup devices for desktop computers in 2000 generally cost between $200 and $1500, with extra high-capacity changers or network server tape backups going for $5000 or more. Tapes range from $5 to $40.

Part

VIII

Ch

21

Determining a Backup Schedule

How often you back up your system depends on how much you use it and what you do with it. For example, if you use your computer every day for vital work, you might want to consider daily backups. Most users can get by with weekly backups, and some can get by with monthly backups. Keep in mind that you might need different backup schedules for your different OSs.

TIP No matter what backup schedule you use, it is a good idea to keep at least two backups. For example, you can use two tapes, rotating which one you use for backup. This way, if a restoration fails, you'll still have the older backup to use in its place.

One important distinction to understand in dealing with backups is the difference between *full* and *incremental* backups. A full backup backs up all of an OS's files. If you've made a full backup, in theory you should be able to restore your system to a working state by restoring those files, even if your hard drive is completely destroyed—you just need a new hard disk, your backup tape, appropriate software, and, of course, the rest of your computer. An incremental backup, on the other hand, backs up only those files that have changed since the last backup. Incremental backups can therefore proceed much more quickly than can a full backup, but restoring data in the case of a full restore is more involved because you must first restore the full backup and then restore files from one or more incremental backups.

It is often desirable to follow a schedule that mixes both full and incremental backups. For example, you could do a full backup once a week and an incremental backup on nights when you don't do a full backup.

Most OSs come with a basic tape backup utility, such as the Microsoft Backup program shown in Figure 21.4; you can also obtain such a program from a third party.

FIGURE 21.4
Most backup utilities enable you to select the files to back up through a browser with check boxes next to drives or files.

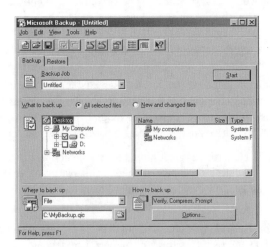

The following are examples of third-party backup utilities:

- **tar**—The UNIX `tar` program is a basic backup program for UNIX-like OSs. It is also available on many other platforms, including OS/2 (as `GTAK`).
- **BeB**—BeB is a backup utility for BeOS. You can find more on the Bald Mountain Web site, `http://www.bald-mountain.com/`.
- **NovaBACKUP**—NovaSTOR's (`http://www.novastor.com`) backup software is available for all versions of Windows and OS/2.
- **BRU**—Enhanced Software Technologies (EST; `http://www.bru.com`) produces the Backup and Recover Utility (BRU) for many UNIX systems, including Linux and FreeBSD.

N O T E There is no standardized data format for tape backup utilities. That is, if you create a backup tape using one utility, chances are that another won't be able to read that backup. You should therefore use one tape backup program exclusively or clearly mark each tape as to which backup utility you used to create it. If you want the flexibility of reading backup tapes in OSs other than those that created the tapes, your best bet is a cross-platform program like `tar` or NovaBACKUP. ■

When you obtain a backup utility, you should be sure to read its documentation. After you've found a need to recover files is the wrong time to discover that you've been using the software incorrectly!

What to Back Up and from Which OS

In general, full backups provide the best protection of your investment in your OSs. If you lack the hardware capacity to perform regular full backups, you can get by with backing up critical files. Most important, of course, are your own data files. If you design your directory structure properly, you can back up all your data files merely by selecting a single directory in your backup program. Backing up applications can help you restore your system if and when you need to do so, but in many OSs—particularly Windows—applications tend to store critical files mingled in with OS files, so backing up applications might not do much good. On restoration, the applications might not work because of the missing OS files, so you must reinstall them anyway. If you're lucky, though, the reinstallation will leave your configuration files in place if you restore the applications from a tape backup.

As a general rule, it is best to back up each OS using its own native tools because each OS is usually best at reading and writing its own filesystems. Even when two OSs share the capability to read and write a filesystem, one OS might use the filesystem in an unusual way. For example, OS/2 stores Extended Attributes (EAs) on FAT partitions in a way that other OSs can't process properly. Similarly, any OS that can't handle VFAT long filenames won't back up Windows 9*x* or NT on a FAT partition properly.

N O T E   Some OSs provide a means to back up their unusual methods of using filesystem features. In OS/2, the EABACKUP utility, available from OS/2 FTP sites, backs up EAs so that they can be restored after using a non-OS/2 backup utility. Similarly, the LFN Backup and Restore utility (http://www.mslm.com/free.htm) can back up and restore VFAT long filenames for Windows. ◼

There are exceptions to the rule of using only native utilities for backup, however. For example, Linux does a good job of backing up DOS and Windows 9x systems. After a full restore of such an OS from Linux, however, you might need to use an emergency floppy disk from the restored OS and run the SYS.EXE program on the C: partition to make it bootable.

CAUTION

Windows 9x stores some directory information in its Registry using truncated 8.3 filenames. It is possible to restore a system in such a way that it gets different 8.3 filenames than it had to begin with. For example, if you created two files, longfilename1.txt and longfilename2.txt, in that order, these files will acquire the 8.3 filenames LONGFI~1.TXT and LONGFI~2.TXT, respectively. If you subsequently delete longfilename1.txt, back up, and restore, longfilename2.txt's short filename will change to LONGFI~1.TXT. Such changes can cause subtle and not-so-subtle problems if they occur with critical files. This problem can occur when backing up Windows from another OS or even with some Windows native backup utilities.

You can reduce the chance of such problems by using short directory names whenever possible for program installations. Changing short filenames isn't normally a problem for data files, just for programs that have Registry entries. If you use Linux, you should also be sure not to use the nonumtail option when you access a VFAT filesystem.

File and Disk Image Backups

Most backup software operates on a file-by-file basis, transferring data one file at a time to tape. Such software has the advantage that you can restore a single file if the need arises. You can also restore data to a different filesystem than you used originally. For example, you can back up a FAT partition and restore it to HPFS or NTFS.

File backups have a drawback, however, in that they make it more difficult to restore a working system in the event of a catastrophic failure. Some backup software, such as PowerQuest's (http://www.powerquest.com) DriveImage or the dd utility that comes with most UNIX-like OSs, can back up a partition by creating an *image copy*—the contents of the partition, including filesystem structures, copied directly to a tape or other medium. It is generally difficult to recover individual files from an image copy, but if you need to restore a bootable system, an image copy can be much easier to deal with than a file copy. Cruder image copies, such as those created by dd, depend heavily on the exact size of the partition, however, which makes this technique less useful when you need to restore to a partition of a new size—possibly including a restore to a new hard disk. DriveImage and some other commercial products can adjust the size of the restored image to fit a new partition, however.

> **TIP**
>
> You might want to use image copies for bootable partitions and file copies for data and program partitions. If your bootable partitions are 650MB or smaller, it is easy to place image copies of your bootable partitions on CD-R discs from Linux or other UNIX-like OSs. You can then quickly restore a bootable partition by using dd, and if Linux supports the filesystem, you can even read files by mounting the CD-R disc.

Developing an Emergency Restore Procedure

Restoring files can be much more tedious than backing them up. If your system suffers a catastrophic failure—for example, if your hard disk stops working—you might need to restore everything from your backup to recover a working system. Such emergency restores are tedious because you must have a working copy of each OS on a floppy disk or some other way to recover a working system. If you lack such an emergency recovery disk, you might need to do a minimal installation of the target OS and use that to restore your main system from the backup tape.

> **TIP**
>
> If you need to do a minimal installation, try to do it on a different partition than you plan to use for the final restore. Failing that, use a different directory structure (for example, install Windows NT to C:\WIN-TMP rather than C:\WINNT). Placing the minimal installation in an odd location lets you restore the complete original backup, including all system files. If you try to restore over the freshly installed system, the restore program might be incapable of replacing certain key files, resulting in an OS that fails to boot or that behaves strangely after booting.

Most backup programs come with instructions for creating an emergency recovery disk, or at least for a procedure to follow in the event of an emergency restoration. If your software doesn't include such instructions, you should create a minimal OS installation of your own, preferably on a floppy or other removable disk, to serve in case of an emergency. Be sure to test your emergency disks for each OS, and test them whenever you make any major changes to your computer.

▶ To learn more about creating stripped-down OS installations, **see** "Creating a Minimal OS Installation," **p. 532**.

If you need to restore only a few files, you can generally use your backup software to do so from your regular OS installation. The software generally provides a means to select files stored on the tape for restoration.

Summary

OSs have varying needs with respect to hardware resources. Although adding a new OS necessarily removes some of your available disk space from use by other OSs, a new OS won't detract from an existing OS's capability to use your computer's memory or CPU (unless you run an OS under an emulator such as VMware). Nonetheless, it is important to understand the resource requirements of each OS you use; you might need to expand your RAM or upgrade your CPU for a new OS, simply because the new OS requires more of these resources than does your old OS.

One hardware resource that many people overlook is a backup device. It is important that you have—and use!—a backup device such as a tape drive on a multi-OS computer. Sooner or later, you *will* need it to recover from a hardware failure, a software failure, or even human error. ●

Finding Drivers

Tracking Down Drivers

One of the greatest challenges of running a multi-OS system is in locating *drivers* for your hardware. A driver is a program that is used by the OS to control hardware. Modern x86 PCs are a conglomeration of varied components from dozens of manufacturers. Devices such as video cards, sound cards, and SCSI host adapters all come in dozens of makes and models, and each OS you use must have drivers for each of these components. A single missing or buggy driver for a critical component can render an OS installation useless.

The task of finding drivers for your OS is often turned around: When it comes time to upgrade your hardware, you must evaluate each new component based on the availability of drivers for all your OSs. You might be forced to use a less-sophisticated device to obtain adequate driver support in all your OSs. Alternatively, you might be faced with an unpleasant trade-off between two or more OSs, in which driver quality varies such that the device with the best driver in one OS has a poor driver in a second OS, and vice versa.

I can't provide any magical solution to driver problems, but I can provide information on how to track down information about drivers and the drivers themselves. Armed with this information, you might be able to locate drivers superior to those that came with your OS or hardware device.

Determining Your Hardware's Chipsets

Most hardware in use in x86 computers today is built around one or more *chipsets*. A chipset is one or more chips that provide most of the electronic functionality of the device. As I describe shortly, understanding what chipset a device uses is often critical to coaxing the device into a functioning state on an OS.

NOTE It is not always necessary to know the chipset used in your hardware. Manufacturers often include drivers for several OSs with their products. As a general rule, knowing the chipset is more critical for unusual OSs that aren't supported by the product's manufacturer than for more common OSs. You should probably check for support by product name before you try to determine the chipset a board uses. When you need to know it, though, knowing the chipset used on a product is critically important. ▨

The Importance of Chipsets and Drivers

In terms of driver support, a hardware component can be classified into one of several different categories:

- **Generic devices**—Some components, such as keyboards, serial ports, and RAM chips, either require no drivers or are so well standardized that you need not locate drivers

for them, because these drivers are always included in the OS. Most of the devices provided on most motherboards fall into this category.

N O T E Some motherboards come with built-in video, audio, SCSI, network interface card (NIC),
or other devices that require specialized drivers. Such designs are especially common in
low-cost PCs (which integrate audio and video to cut costs) and in high-end motherboards (which
sometimes integrate SCSI and NIC). Although often a convenience, integrated components can turn
into an albatross quickly if unsupported in even one OS, or if you need to upgrade a component. You
can often disable on-board devices by changing an appropriate BIOS setting. ▪

- **Plug-in cards**—Most cards that plug in to your motherboard use a chipset made by
  the same or, more often, different company than the one that made the board. Drivers
  for the device are written to function with that chipset. Card manufacturers sometimes
  tweak the drivers for their boards to hide the chipset's manufacturer or take advantage
  of features unique to their products, but fundamentally the products use drivers written
  for a given chipset.

- **SCSI and EIDE devices**—Hard disks, CD-ROM drives, tape drives, and other SCSI
  and EIDE devices generally require drivers that are essentially generic drivers. Aside
  from some very old devices, SCSI and EIDE components all respond to the same command sets and function with generic drivers for the device type. SCSI host adapters,
  however, require their own drivers, and EIDE interfaces increasingly benefit from specialized drivers but usually don't require them for basic functionality.

- **External devices**—Printers, mice, scanners, and other external devices often require
  their own drivers. Some of these devices, such as mice, are quite well standardized so
  they do not require unusual drivers, but others, such as printers, often sport unique features that might require specialized drivers.

N O T E External devices necessarily interface through some sort of connection, such as a serial or
parallel port, which itself requires drivers. Sometimes these ports use generic drivers that
come with any OS, but other times they don't. An external SCSI device, for example, requires support
for the SCSI host adapter in use on the computer, in addition to whatever drivers are needed for the
specific SCSI device in use. ▪

The preceding classification is imperfect. Some devices might not fit neatly into any given category, and some devices might function in a minimal fashion without specialized drivers but
might benefit when you add such drivers. For example, any modern video card supports
basic text mode and VGA (640×480 16-color) functionality without board- or chipset-specific
drivers, but to use high resolutions and accelerated graphics, it needs specialized drivers.

In general, drivers function with privileged access to the hardware—that is, they can manipulate the computer's hardware on a low level. Such drivers typically reside in *kernel space*,
meaning that they're part of the kernel, either in a very literal sense (compiled into a Linux

kernel, say) or somewhat peripherally (run from a separate file). Some drivers, however, have less direct access to low-level hardware. Printer drivers in UNIX-like OSs, for example, often reside in the Ghostscript program, which doesn't have privileged access to the hardware; it only must be capable of sending data down the port to which a printer is connected, and other drivers handle the low-level manipulations involved in that transmission. Thus, using one device might actually involve several drivers working together in a hierarchical fashion.

For example, when you print using WordPerfect 8 for UNIX or Linux, WordPerfect uses its own built-in printer driver to create PostScript output. That output might go through a Ghostscript driver to convert PostScript into a form understandable by your printer. Ghostscript's output then traverses the parallel port via the kernel's parallel port driver, which might itself consist of several layers internally.

Using Device Information in Windows

One of the best ways to find out what hardware you have on your system is to use an existing OS's configuration or hardware probing tools to uncover this information. Microsoft's Windows OSs include utilities to help you locate this information.

In Windows 98, follow these steps:

1. Open the System item in the Control Panel.

2. Click the Device Manager tab. The display resembles that shown in Figure 22.1.

FIGURE 22.1
Windows categorizes devices by type, and you can often have more than one device of a given type on one computer.

3. Click the plus sign next to a device type to see all the devices of that type installed on your system. Double-click a specific device to learn more about the resources it consumes, its driver, and so on.

4. Click Properties or View Devices by Connection in the System Properties dialog box to change how you browse for devices. For example, you can examine devices by the interrupt requests (IRQs) they use.

Windows NT 4.0 and earlier have comparatively weak hardware browsing tools. You can use the Devices item in the Control Panel in Windows NT 4.0 to learn something about the drivers installed, but the information provided by this tool is comparatively cryptic. If you use Windows 2000, you have a tool more like that provided by Windows 98, but the steps you follow to find information on your hardware are somewhat different:

1. Open the System item in the Control Panel.

2. Click the Hardware tab in the System Properties dialog box.

3. Click the Device Manager button. Windows responds by displaying the Device Manager window shown in Figure 22.2.

FIGURE 22.2

The Windows 2000 Device Manager works much like its Windows 98 counterpart.

4. You can expand any device type by clicking the plus sign to see all devices, and double-click a specific device to find details about its driver and the resources it uses.

5. If you prefer to browse your devices by some other criterion, such as the IRQs they use, you can select a new view method from the View menu.

Whichever OS you use to view hardware device information, you might or might not obtain information on the chipsets used; instead, the drivers might identify the board's model. For example, Figure 22.1 shows the Windows 98 System Properties dialog box, which identifies the Ethernet adapter in the computer as a Linksys LNE100TX. This identification is correct but tells you nothing about the chipset used on the board. On the other hand, also in Figure 22.1, the system correctly identifies the EIDE controller as a VIA Bus Master PCI device (this controller is built into the motherboard of that computer), which can point you to the appropriate chipset drivers—in this case, available from VIA's Web site at http://www.via.com.tw.

Sometimes, you can install a driver for one product on a system that uses another (but related) product. It is also common for the same product to be sold under two different names—for example, under one name to computer manufacturers and under another name to end users. In such cases, the product name as reported by Windows might be incorrect, but it is always incorrect in a way that is not misleading with respect to the chipset in use. For example, if Windows identifies your product as a Linksys LNE100TX network card, but you really have a NetGear FA310TX, you can be sure that both boards use the same chipset. Therefore, if you can track down the chipset used by the Linksys LNE100TX, drivers for that chipset in your other OSs will almost certainly work on your NetGear FA310TX. (In fact, both these products use a Lite-On PNIC 82c168, which is a popular clone of the Digital "Tulip" Ethernet chipset.)

When Windows identifies the board model rather than the chipset, you must try to find what chipset the board uses. There are several ways you can do so:

- **Ask the manufacturer**—Although some manufacturers are loathe to part with information concerning the chipsets used by their products, others aren't. In fact, some manufacturers place this information on their Web pages.

- **Check Deja News**—The Deja News Web site (http://www.deja.com) can be an important source of information. Type chipset or drivers and the name of the product and you might find the information you need.

- **Ask on an appropriate Usenet newsgroup**—Ask about your hardware on a newsgroup such as one for your OS or for the type of product you're researching. Be sure to do a Deja News search first, though, because driver questions are quite common, so there is a good chance you'll find the answer on Deja News.

  ▶ To learn more about Usenet newsgroups, **see** "Reading Usenet Newsgroups," **p. 282**.

If these steps fail, you might need to resort to further methods of locating drivers for your device.

Visually Inspecting the Board

One of the best ways to determine what chipset a product uses is to visually inspect the board. Figure 22.3 shows a typical PCI card (a J-Bond JDC5010 SCSI host adapter). Like many cards, this one has one dominant chip, on which is printed an identifying code. This particular card's main chip clearly identifies it as a Symbios Logic 53c860, which is enough information to lead you to an appropriate driver, either by selecting it in an OS's configuration screens or by doing a quick Deja News or Web site search.

Sometimes, a manufacturer places a sticker over the main chip in a board. This practice obscures the markings of the chip's manufacturer and usually serves no other function. You can peel back such stickers to reveal the manufacturer's markings.

FIGURE 22.3
Most internal cards are dominated by one or two chips; check them for markings to identify the board's chipset.

The main chip

CAUTION

Erasable Programmable Read-Only Memory (EPROM) chips have small glass windows to expose a portion of the chip. These chips contain information, such as device firmware code, and the window exists so that the chip can be erased by exposure to ultraviolet light. Removing such stickers is therefore inadvisable, although a brief removal won't cause any problems. If you peel back a sticker and find a glass window, replace the sticker or place a new one over the window to reduce the chance of inadvertent erasure of an EPROM.

Increasingly, board manufacturers are removing the chip manufacturer's markings and replacing them with their own. As with a chip manufacturer's sticker, this practice obscures the fact that the board manufacturer merely assembles off-the-shelf components. This practice also makes it difficult for you to determine what drivers are appropriate for a device, assuming the manufacturer doesn't provide them for one or more of your OSs.

Some high-performance cards, including many new video cards, have chips that run at such high speeds that they require heat sinks much like those for CPUs. These heat sinks have the unfortunate characteristic of obscuring the chipset markings. If you can temporarily remove the heat sink, you might be able to check the markings, but many plug-in board heat sinks are permanently bonded to their chips. Do not attempt to remove such heat sinks.

Snooping in Driver Files

If other methods of investigation fail, you might be able to discover something about your device's chipset by examining the driver files provided by the manufacturer, even for an OS other than the one you intend to use. Of particular interest are files that provide information to the OS about the driver files to be installed. In Windows, these files have extensions of .INF; in OS/2, they're .INI or .DDP files. You might also want to check the driver files themselves, but you'll need a binary file editor or viewer to do so, or some other tool, such as the UNIX strings command, which extracts text strings from binary files.

When you browse in driver files, you probably won't find an extremely obvious statement of the chipset in use—these files seldom contain text that reads "this driver handles the Macronix MX98713 Ethernet chipset" or anything equally obvious. Instead, you'll find a chipset model number. For example, the NETFE100.INF driver configuration file for an NDC SOHOware Ethernet adapter includes the following line:

```
0512.DeviceDesc=  "NDC 10/100 Fast Ethernet PCI Adapter (MX-A)[MX98713]"
```

The chipset model number *MX98713* appears at the end of this line. It takes a keen eye to spot this information, and by itself it might not do you much good. If you notice something that looks like a chipset model number, however, you can try doing a Deja News (http://www.deja.com) search using it and your OS's name as keywords. You might also be able to use grep to search for the same string in a collection of drivers for your OS. This option is particularly viable for Linux. For example, searching for *MX98713* on all the .c (C source code) files in the /usr/src/linux/net directory (where Linux networking device driver source code resides) reveals hits in the tulip.c file and no others. In fact, the NDC SOHOware Ethernet board uses a Tulip clone chipset from Macronix, so in this case this procedure would lead to the correct driver. (In fact, a simpler solution in the case of Linux drivers for this board is to check the manufacturer's Web site, which hosts the appropriate drivers.)

TIP If you can find Linux drivers for your product, you can examine the source code itself to find what chipset the product uses. This information generally appears in comments near the start of the .c file, so you can locate it even if you don't know how to program. The driver filename might provide a clue, too, although manufacturers sometimes change this to reflect their product name rather than the chipset name. So even if you don't use Linux, checking any Linux driver files provided by the board's manufacturer can be quite informative.

Checking for Drivers from the Manufacturer

Hardware manufacturers almost always include drivers for their products on a CD or floppy disk that is bundled with the hardware. Manufacturers generally support popular OSs the best—it is the rare hardware indeed that doesn't include Windows 9*x* drivers, for example.

Drivers for relatively rare OSs, such as FreeBSD or BeOS, are less common from the manufacturer.

N O T E Especially if you frequent computer shows or purchase hardware from cut-rate Internet dealers, you might end up with *generic* or *OEM* hardware. Such products frequently come with limited or even no drivers. Such products often cost less than their fully branded and in-box counterparts, but you might need to hunt a bit more to locate drivers for these boards, especially for the OSs that are most often supported, such as Windows. ■

In general, the drivers you use with a product were written by the chipset manufacturer and might have been modified by the board manufacturer to specify the board manufacturer's name rather than the chipset manufacturer's name. In some cases, and particularly for boards made by small manufacturers or drivers for less-popular OSs, the manufacturer might distribute unmodified drivers from the chipset manufacturer or some other source (such as from the Linux kernel, in the case of Linux drivers).

There are two main sources for drivers from the manufacturer:

- **Media distributed with the product**—Check the floppy or CD-ROM that came with the product. Drivers generally appear in subdirectories named after the OS in question, such as os2 for OS/2 drivers or Win2000 for Windows 2000 drivers.

- **The manufacturer's Web site**—Check the Web site for the manufacturer. If you don't know the URL, check your product's documentation, perform a Web search, or just type likely URLs (such as www.*companyname*.com).

It is worth checking the company's Web site even if there is no driver on the disk that came with the board. Manufacturers often add drivers after packaging a product or update their drivers to add features or fix bugs.

 TIP Even if you don't find a driver for your OS on the distribution media or board manufacturer's Web site, it is worth checking the chipset manufacturer's Web site, if you can determine who this is. Chipset manufacturers sometimes distribute a wider range of drivers than do specific hardware manufacturers.

When you look for a driver for your OS, keep in mind that drivers might be compatible across OS versions. For example, if you want to find a Windows 2000 driver, it might be possible to use Windows NT 4.0 drivers on Windows 2000, because Windows 2000 is the next version of Windows NT. If the hardware manufacturer hasn't updated the driver's documentation, it might not reflect compatibility with newer versions of an OS. It is possible that a driver for a newer or older version of an OS won't work, though, so use some caution when trying to use such a driver—back up your system before you install the driver, and have a plan to recover should the driver crash your system on boot, which is the worst-case scenario for such incompatibility.

Checking for Drivers from the OS Publisher

Particularly for less-common OSs such as BeOS, one critical source for drivers is the OS's publisher. Indeed, despite the fact that Linux is rising in popularity, most Linux drivers come not from the hardware manufacturers but from Linux enthusiasts who write the drivers and then donate them for inclusion in the Linux kernel. Most manufacturers who make Linux drivers available simply provide a specific version of the standard Linux drivers that are known to work with the manufacturer's hardware. An increasing number of hardware manufacturers, however, write Linux drivers themselves. These generally find their way into the Linux kernel.

As with drivers provided by the hardware manufacturer, there are two common sources to check for drivers provided by the OS publisher: the OS's distribution CD-ROM and the publisher's Web site.

N O T E You might find that both the hardware manufacturer and the OS publisher produce drivers that work with your hardware. In some cases, the OS publisher provides a relatively generic driver that works with a wide range of hardware (based on the hardware's chipset, although it might identify your hardware by board name). Other times, the OS manufacturer might simply distribute the driver produced by the hardware manufacturer. In general, you're better off using the hardware manufacturer's driver, because that driver is likely to include extra features. If you obtain the hardware manufacturer's driver from the manufacturer's Web site, that driver is also likely to be more up to date than the OS publisher's driver for the same hardware. ▣

Checking the OS Distribution CD-ROM

Each OS has its own way of supplying drivers on the distribution medium. Some common methods of providing these drivers include

- **Driver install utility**—Some OSs, such as Windows and OS/2, provide GUI install utilities for drivers. Figure 22.4, for example, shows the Windows 2000 Add/Remove Hardware Wizard dialog box. Such installers typically auto-detect your hardware or enable you to specify your device by hand. They then locate the drivers on the installation CD and install them on your system.

- **Linux or BSD modules**—Linux and the BSD variants provide a large number of drivers, either compiled into the kernel file itself or compiled as separate modules. These OSs typically install all available modules when you install the OS, so you don't need to install a new driver per se. You might need to edit a configuration file, however, such as /etc/conf.modules, in order to use the file. Some distributions provide GUI tools similar to the hardware wizards of Windows to aid in this process. In some cases, you might need to recompile a kernel to get a driver to work properly, particularly if you need the driver to run from within the kernel file rather than as a module (as is necessary for the boot hard disk's driver).

FIGURE 22.4
The Add/Remove Hardware Wizard locates available hardware and lets you install appropriate drivers.

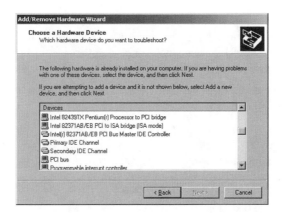

- **Stand-alone driver files**—Sometimes an OS provides additional drivers in a separate directory, typically called `drivers` or something similar. For example, Windows 9*x* includes a few unusual drivers in this form rather than as part of the normal device driver installation routines.

Checking the OS's Official Web Site

OS publishers frequently make updated and additional drivers available on their Web sites. You can check these Web sites for drivers if your OS doesn't come with a driver for a given piece of hardware. Specific sites you might want to check include

- **Windows**—Check the main Microsoft Web site at `http://www.microsoft.com`. Click links to your specific OS version, and then go to the downloads page. Many driver updates come bundled with *service packs*—collections of bug fixes, updates, and extensions for a given OS or product.

- **OS/2**—IBM maintains an online database of OS/2 drivers at `http://service.software.ibm.com/os2ddpak/html/index.htm`. The list of drivers is organized by category and includes links to both IBM-supported drivers and those from third parties.

- **BeOS**—Like IBM, Be maintains a list of driver updates on its Web site, at `http://www.be.com/software/beware/drivers.html`. Many of the drivers listed on this Web site are actually provided by third-party developers.

- **Linux**—Check with your Linux distribution maintainer or on `http://www.kernel.org` for updated Linux kernels. All low-level Linux drivers are part of the kernel, either directly and officially or by patching a new or third-party driver into the kernel. You can also try to find a Web site devoted to a specific driver you want to update; check the kernel source code or do a Web search to find an appropriate Web site. Printer and video card drivers are parts of the Ghostscript and XFree86 packages, respectively, which I describe shortly.

- **The BSD versions**—Like Linux, the BSD kernels are the source of official low-level drivers for the OS. Check your BSD version's Web page for information on kernel updates. The BSD versions use Ghostscript and XFree86 for printing and video display, just as does Linux.

    ▷ To learn more about Linux and BSD distribution Web sites, **see** "Useful Official Contact Information," **p. 264**.

OS manufacturers often want you to upgrade to a newer version of the OS to get new drivers. This isn't always necessary, though; as with drivers provided by hardware manufacturers, drivers provided by OS publishers can often be used across several versions of the OS. If the drivers are available for public download, therefore, you might be able to use a driver from a later release of your OS in an earlier version. Using an older driver is usually not necessary or desirable, but on rare occasion it might be if a new driver has a bug.

CAUTION

Windows 95 and 98 are in one line of Windows products, whereas Windows NT 3.1 through 4.0 and Windows 2000 are in another. These two lines (which I refer to as *Windows 9x* and *Windows NT* in this book) use fundamentally different driver designs, so you shouldn't attempt to use a driver written for one line on the other. There are a few exceptions to this rule—generally in the form of an installer program that detects which OS is running and installs the appropriate driver automatically. The result is something that looks like it is using one driver for both OS lines but really it isn't.

Checking for Third-Party Drivers

Hardware manufacturers and OS publishers aren't the only sources of drivers, although they're the most important sources. In some cases, third parties provide drivers for hardware, particularly for the combination of rare hardware with unusual OSs. Sometimes these drivers are provided as shareware, but other times they're available free.

In the case of open-source OSs such as Linux, most drivers start out as third-party implementations. Such drivers usually find their way into the official OS distribution, however. If you have particularly new hardware or want to use features of your hardware that aren't officially supported, you might want to track down these not-yet-official drivers or updates before they make their way into the official OS releases.

Freeware and Shareware Drivers

You can obtain freeware and shareware drivers for many OSs from the usual sources for programs for those OSs, such as

- **Windows**—http://www.winfiles.com and http://www.cnet.com/downloads are good sources for Windows files of all varieties. You'll find relatively few third-party drivers for

Windows, however, because Windows (and particularly Windows 9x) has such strong driver support from Microsoft and from hardware manufacturers, so there is little demand for third-party drivers.

■ **OS/2**—The OS/2 FTP sites, `ftp://ftp-os2.nmsu.edu/pub/os2/system/drivers` and `ftp://ftp-os2.cdrom.com/pub/os2/drivers`, both contain a wide array of drivers. Most of these drivers are available from hardware manufacturer Web sites, but a few are not. The IBM-maintained driver index at `http://service.software.ibm.com/os2ddpak/html/index.htm` is also well worth investigating.

■ **BeOS**—As I mentioned earlier, Be maintains a Web site at `http://www.be.com/software/beware/drivers.html` with links to drivers for BeOS, many of which were written by third-party developers.

Keep in mind that third-party drivers might not have been tested very extensively and are almost certainly not supported by either the OS publisher or your hardware manufacturer. Therefore, you might be on your own if you encounter problems. If you're uncomfortable with this state of affairs, you might want to consider replacing the hardware in question with a product that is supported under all your OSs.

Not-Yet-Official Linux Drivers

Linux drivers that have yet to appear in the official Linux kernel can be difficult to track down. Some methods you might want to pursue to locate such drivers include

■ **Linux information sites**—Check for links on Linux information sites, such as `http://www.linux.com` or `http://www.linux.org`. You might be able to locate a link to an appropriate project.

■ **Development kernels**—Check the latest development kernel (one with an odd-numbered second number, such as one in the 2.3.x series). These might have drivers that are currently being incorporated into the main kernel.

■ **Updated drivers**—If the driver you seek is an update to an existing driver, check the kernel source code (both the source files themselves and any documentation files in the `/usr/src/linux/Documentation` directory) for a Web or FTP site maintained by the developer.

■ **Web searches**—Try using a Web search engine such as `http://www.altavista.com` or `http://www.excite.com` to locate a Web page devoted to your hardware under Linux. Alternatively, you can try a Deja News search, at `http://www.deja.com`.

In addition to these general strategies, there are a few specific sites you might want to check for specific types of drivers:

■ **Sound drivers**—The *Advanced Linux Sound Architecture (ALSA)* project is dedicated to developing new sound card drivers for Linux. They maintain a Web page at http://www.alsa-project.org. The shareware Open Sound System is another source of sound drivers for Linux. You can find out more at http://www.4front-tech.com. 4Front also develops sound drivers for other UNIX OSs.

■ **Video drivers**—Under Linux, video card drivers are built into an X server. Most Linux systems use XFree86 (http://www.xfree86.org) as the X server, and you might be able to find an updated X server from that site. SuSE (http://www.suse.com) is on the forefront of developing XFree86 X servers for new hardware, and they often make early versions available for new hardware. Alternatives to XFree86 include the Xi Graphics (http://www.xig.com) Accelerated-X and the Metrolink (http://www.metrolink.com) Metro-X. Both also produce X servers for other UNIX-like OSs.

■ **Windows-only modems**—Linux drivers for a few formerly Windows-only modems are beginning to appear. You can find out more at http://www.linmodems.org/.

■ **USB devices**—In the 2.2.*x* kernel series, Universal Serial Bus (USB) devices have little support. This support is being added in the 2.3.*x* kernel series, but even after kernels in the 2.4.*x* series appear, developments in USB are likely to continue. You can check http://www.linux-usb.org/ for the latest information on this support.

■ **Printer drivers**—Printer drivers under Linux are part of the Ghostscript package, hosted at http://www.cs.wisc.edu/~ghost. The printer compatibility document on that site includes a great deal of information, including links to a few third-party drivers at the bottom of the page. If you use an RPM-based Linux distribution, you might also want to check http://www.users.dircon.co.uk/~typhoon/html/ghostscript.html, which has a version of Ghostscript that includes several drivers that aren't compiled into most binary distributions. (The Ghostscript source code includes several drivers that are not, by default, compiled into the program.)

If you want to contribute to Linux by helping to develop a new driver, you're more than welcome to do so. You should probably post a query to an appropriate newsgroup, though, to try to ascertain whether anybody else is currently working on such a project. If so, you might be able to collaborate, thus producing a better driver faster. Note that driver development is not for the novice programmer, so don't undertake such a project unless you're familiar with driver programming or are willing to invest substantial time and effort in learning about it.

Summary

Locating drivers for a multitude of OSs can be a challenging task, particularly if your OSs or hardware devices are exotic. Much of the challenge in locating drivers comes in tracking down all the possible sources of drivers. Although some OS manufacturers, such as IBM and Be, maintain Web pages that aim to help you in this task, with others you might be forced to perform Web or Deja News searches to locate drivers. You're also often faced with the challenge of converting information on the make and model of the product you have into information on the chipset it uses. Particularly for rarer OSs, drivers are often identified by chipset rather than by device manufacturer.

If you plan to upgrade your existing computer or build a new one with an eye to multi-OS use, you should conduct your driver research before making any new purchases. If you're diligent in this research, you shouldn't have any unpleasant driver-related surprises when your new hardware arrives. If you're installing a new OS on existing hardware, you might be faced with the prospect of replacing hardware for which no drivers exist in the new OS or suffering through reduced functionality with your existing hardware. If you decide to upgrade your hardware, you'll find the next chapter, "Performing Hardware Upgrades," to be of interest. ●

Part

VIII

Ch

22

Performing Hardware Upgrades

The Upgrade Process

Performing a hardware upgrade on a multi-OS computer can be quite an adventure. Unless the upgrade is to some device that requires no unusual drivers (such as a keyboard), you must normally perform several steps:

1. Research driver availability for all your OSs.
2. Obtain drivers for all your OSs. These might come with the hardware.
3. Uninstall existing drivers or change drivers to generic drivers that work with any device of a type, such as plain VGA for video cards. You must perform this step in every OS you run.
4. Swap out the old hardware for the new hardware.
5. Install the new drivers. You must perform this step in every OS.

In truth, you must perform similar steps when upgrading hardware even in a single-OS environment. The difference is that many of these steps are more challenging for a multi-OS computer, simply because the procedure entails work in each OS. Steps 3 and 5, in particular, can each take more than an hour on a computer with more than two or three OSs. Step 1 is critically important; if you pick the wrong hardware, you might end up screaming at your computer more than you use it.

This chapter helps guide you through this process, although I don't cover all these steps in this chapter. In particular, locating drivers is covered in Chapter 22, "Finding Drivers."

N O T E I've written this chapter with an eye toward what might be called "nontrivial" upgrades and additions—those that require the installation of major new drivers. Many hardware replacements and additions, such as external modems, keyboards, and monitors, require few or no OS changes. You might need to change a configuration or two, such as a default dialing string in your modem software or the resolution setting for your display, but that is all. Such minor upgrades seldom require much OS-specific research, even when the product is a major purchase, such as a 21-inch monitor. As a general rule, if a device comes with drivers for an OS, you must research drivers for that device in all your OSs. A few devices might come with drivers to enable special functionality but can work without drivers in other OSs, but at the cost of access to that special functionality. Keyboards with special keys to launch specific programs in Windows 9x are an example. ▪

Locating Suitable Hardware

The first two steps in performing a hardware upgrade (researching and obtaining drivers) are actions you can perform without making any changes to your computer. You can entertain the possibility of replacing an old video card with one model and then decide to switch your focus to another if you decide your initial choice isn't really suitable. Your emphasis at this point should be on digging up as much information as possible about your hardware for each of the OSs you run. You might also want to investigate the hardware's suitability to run with other OSs, in case you should later decide to add another OS to your computer.

In many respects, the issues involved in locating hardware are the same as those discussed in Chapter 22. The difference is largely one of your goals—when you need to locate a driver for a specific OS, your search has a single, clearly defined goal. When you want to add or upgrade hardware, however, the goal is more vague; you might be satisfied with any of several competing products. Therefore, you must find the best fit between your needs and the available hardware, rather than a single driver.

Researching OS Requirements

One good way to begin a search for a new hardware component is to study the approved hardware lists maintained by many OS manufacturers. Look for hardware that is supported in all your OSs. Depending on your OSs and the type of hardware in question, this might narrow the field slightly or dramatically. For example, most OSs don't support a particular type of internal modem (often referred to as "Windows modems"), but among conventional internal modems, few models aren't supported by all x86 PC OSs.

▶ To learn more about OS publisher Web sites, most of which have hardware compatibility listings, **see** "Useful Official Contact Information," **p. 264**.

Keep in mind that different OS publishers might list hardware support in different ways. For example, some might attempt to enumerate boards by brand name, whereas others might list devices by the chipsets used. Also remember that manufacturers might produce radically different products; one component might be compatible across a wide range of OSs, whereas another might work only in Windows 98. Sometimes these products might bear remarkably similar, or even identical, names.

Such cases of multiple personality disorder among hardware components are the result of a manufacturer changing the design of a product without changing its name. The products might be distinguished only by a revision code. For example, many low-cost PCI Ethernet boards in 1998 and early 1999 used the Tulip chipset produced by Digital Equipment Corporation (DEC). When DEC folded, however, manufacturers changed their designs, usually without changing their products' names. In most cases, manufacturers switched to Tulip clone chipsets, but in a few cases they switched to entirely unrelated designs. Even the Tulip clone boards, however, don't function quite the same way their earlier counterparts did, and sometimes they require different drivers than do their older namesakes.

▶ To learn more about chipsets, **see** "Sight and Sound for Today's Multimedia," **p. 16**.

In addition to checking OS publisher Web sites, you can learn more about OS requirements by using other Internet resources, including

- http://www.xfree86.org—This is the home page for the XFree86 Project, which produces the GUI and video drivers used by open-source UNIX-like OSs such as Linux and FreeBSD. XFree86 is also available for OS/2, so if you plan to use a video board under OS/2, you might want to check on XFree86 compatibility. Commercial alternatives to XFree86 include Accelerated-X (http://www.xig.com) and Metro-X (http://www.metrolink.com).

Part
VIII

Ch
23

▪ `http://www.picante.com/~gtaylor/pht/printer_list.cgi`—This Web site maintains a printer compatibility listing for Ghostscript. Ghostscript is a tool for converting PostScript files into other formats, including formats that can be printed by a variety of non-PostScript printers. Ghostscript is used by many UNIX-like OSs to print to non-PostScript printers, so Ghostscript compatibility is a must for a non-PostScript printer in such an environment. You can also configure Ghostscript under other OSs to serve a similar function, so even if a printer lacks drivers under, say, BeOS or OS/2, you might be able to get it to work via Ghostscript. I don't recommend relying on Ghostscript in such a situation in your primary OS, but it might make a reasonable workaround if an otherwise good printer lacks support in one or two OSs.

▪ **OS newsgroups**—Many OS newsgroup hierarchies include hardware groups or groups dedicated to specific hardware-related topics such as networking or storage (hard disks, tape drives, and so on).

▶ To learn more about Usenet newsgroups, **see** "Reading Usenet Newsgroups," **p. 282**.

▪ **DOS program needs**—In the case of DOS, many hardware issues are tied to specific programs. For example, DOS programs often include drivers for printers, sound cards, and video display. Therefore, if you want to use a new component in DOS, you might need to consult the requirements of the programs from which that component will be used. If you intend to run Windows 3.11 or earlier atop DOS, you need drivers for that version of Windows.

In most cases, you must be most concerned with driver availability for your most obscure OSs, such as BeOS or UnixWare. All consumer-oriented hardware (video cards, modems, sound cards, and so on) is well supported in Windows 9x. However, some exotic devices, such as scientific or industrial data collection boards, might have unusual specific OS requirements.

Checking Claimed Compatibility

You should now have a list of hardware that is suitable for use with all your OSs. This list might contain many ancient products you wouldn't want to use in any event, so you can prune it to current products that meet whatever performance requirements you have. With any luck this will leave you with a manageable number of products to research more fully. Your challenge now is to ascertain, without shelling out money for each of these products, which of them provides the best compatibility and performance across your OSs. Sadly, just because a product is listed under a "supported" column on an OS publisher's Web site doesn't mean that the product performs well. Keep in mind that a poorly written driver can produce unending trouble, including but not limited to slow performance, heavy CPU loads, and system crashes. In some cases you might be better off with a product that is theoretically slower because the drivers for the faster product are so poor in your most important OSs.

NOTE For use in a multi-OS computer, take performance figures such as video card benchmarks published in magazines or online with a grain of salt. These figures are the result of the combination of the hardware and the drivers, and in a multi-OS environment, the latter factor won't always be the same as what was used for the tests. Similar comments apply to any rating that relies on drivers or application programs, such as print speed and quality ratings for printers, sound card features (particularly for MIDI functions), and CD-recordable (CD-R) drive performance. Hard disk speed, CD-ROM drive speed, and modem performance aren't likely to vary as much from one OS to another, but even in these cases there might be exceptions. For example, if the filesystems used by two OSs use a hard disk in different ways, that fact can influence effective hard disk speed. ▪

Part
VIII

Ch
23

Unfortunately, short of purchasing several products and evaluating each one yourself, your only choice in evaluating product compatibility is to rely on the judgment of others. You can consult several sources, which vary in their reliability:

- **The hardware manufacturer**—The manufacturer's Web page might include information on compatibility of their products across multiple OSs. Such Web pages are likely to downplay difficulties, of course, but you might be able to find an errata page or judge something of the manufacturer's level of commitment to an OS from a Web page.

- **The chipset manufacturer**—Like the component manufacturer, the chipset manufacturer might have a Web page. Try to locate a chipset manufacturer's Web page when you buy a video card, sound card, Ethernet board, or SCSI host adapter. In some cases, the chipset and board manufacturers are the same, but in many cases they're different.

  ▶ To learn how to identify a product's chipset, **see** "Determining Your Hardware's Chipsets," **p. 556**.

- **Deja News**—Try entering the name of the product you're considering in conjunction with your OS's name in the Deja News (http://www.deja.com) search field. With luck, you'll get helpful reports of successes and problems, perhaps even with workarounds for the problems. Because Deja News is an archive of recent Usenet news postings, you'll be reading the experiences of real people. Keep in mind that people tend to post problems more than successes to Usenet news, so don't be surprised if your hits turn up more problems than success stories. Also, remember that you'll see more postings about popular products than less-popular ones. This fact shouldn't deter you from buying a less-popular product, though, unless it is so unpopular that you can't find adequate information about it.

- **Usenet news**—If a Deja News search doesn't turn up anything useful, you can try to spark a discussion on Usenet by making a posting to an appropriate newsgroup.

  ▶ To learn more about Usenet newsgroups, **see** "Reading Usenet Newsgroups," **p. 282**.

I recommend that you research two or three products at once. This procedure should give you good comparative information on these products. Also, be sure to research the product for every OS you intend to run. Although basic drivers exist for just about all hardware in Windows 9x, those drivers vary in quality.

Contacting the Manufacturer

In addition to checking the manufacturer's Web site, you might want to initiate closer contact, either to obtain information or to ascertain the manufacturer's level of support. Most hardware manufacturers' Web pages include contact information in the form of telephone numbers, email addresses, or Web forms on which you can submit queries. If you have unanswered questions about the product, you should definitely use one or more of these methods of contact to try to obtain answers to your questions.

In general, hardware manufacturers have very limited technical support staff, and they're most used to dealing with common questions for common OSs. You should therefore not be disappointed if your query about support for OS/2, BeOS, or some other exotic OS garners little in the way of helpful information. If you do get a helpful response, though, that can be a major plus because it means you might not be on your own if you purchase the product and find you need help getting the drivers to function correctly.

Obtaining Drivers

I recommend that you collect drivers for your chosen product and possibly for your top one or two competing products before you make a purchase. Doing so enables you to read the driver documentation, which sometimes includes vitally important information such as limitations or extra functionality beyond that normally present in drivers of that type. For example, video and especially audio drivers for OS/2 often have quirks when used with Win-OS/2 or don't work at all with Windows programs.

In the course of your research to this point, you should already have stumbled across drivers for all your OSs. If one still eludes you, you might want to read Chapter 22, which can help you locate an errant driver. On rare occasions, a driver might be available only in a package from the manufacturer. This is most often true when the manufacturer wrote the driver and has not updated it since releasing the product. Unless the product is very new, this can be a bad sign because it might indicate a lack of interest on the manufacturer's part in supporting that OS. On the other hand, it could mean that they got the driver right the first time, so no updates are necessary.

> **CAUTION**
>
> In most cases, you should not attempt to install a driver until you've installed the product. Installing the wrong video driver, for example, might render your system unusable. A few drivers, such as those for printers, can often be installed before you buy the device itself. I recommend against installing such drivers before you buy the product, however, because doing so and then removing the device driver might leave files and configuration changes behind, which might cause problems down the line.

Part
VIII

Ch
23

Preparing a Zoo of OSs for an Upgrade

After you've decided on a new hardware component and purchased it, you should prepare your computer to receive the new hardware. This is step 3 of the procedure I outlined at the beginning of the chapter. In many cases, you must alter configurations in all your OSs. In some cases, though, you might not need to change one or more OSs at all. For example, if you use only text-mode applications in DOS or a UNIX-like OS, you don't need to do anything to prepare these OSs for a change in a video board.

In preparing your OSs, you must consider the current configuration and strip away drivers for any components you plan to remove. If you're adding a new device and not replacing an old one, you probably don't need to do anything to prepare for the new hardware installation. In some cases, though, you might still need to cope with changes the new hardware will create in your system's configuration because of changes to interrupt request (IRQ) numbers or other configuration options.

Checking the Existing Hardware Settings

If you plan to install an internal device, such as a new SCSI host adapter, it is important to record the state of your computer prior to making any changes. Doing so provides you with a baseline for comparison, both after installation and in case you run into problems and want to restore the computer to its original state.

OSs vary in how easily you can obtain information on the resources used by hardware. Because Windows 98 provides good access to this information and because Windows 98 is quite common, I describe how to obtain hardware information with it. Note that obtaining this information is most important if you want to install an older industry standard architecture (ISA) card. Peripheral component interconnect (PCI) cards and newer Plug-and-Play (PnP) ISA cards are assigned resources by the motherboard or OS. Even for PCI and PnP ISA cards, though, resource conflicts occasionally arise, so you might want to record information on resources used before changing your hardware. Follow these steps to record this information for either ISA or PCI cards:

1. Open the Windows Control Panel from within the My Computer window.
2. Open the System item in the Control Panel and click the Device Manager tab. The result should resemble Figure 23.1.

FIGURE 23.1
By default, Windows 9x
displays device infor-
mation categorized by
type, but you can
change the categoriza-
tion by clicking View
Devices by Connection.

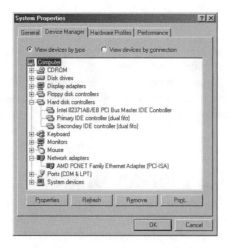

3. Click the Computer object in the list of devices.

4. Click Properties. Windows displays the Computer Properties dialog box shown in
Figure 23.2.

FIGURE 23.2
The Computer
Properties dialog box
enables you to view
which resources are
used by your hardware.

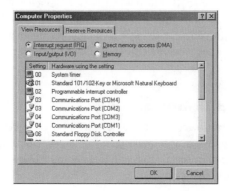

5. Write down which hardware uses which resources. IRQs are the most important of the
resources, but you might want to record the others, as well. If you record resources
indexed by resource rather than by device, you can easily locate unused resources for
a new piece of hardware if you need to do so.

 TIP Instead of writing down all the information, you can use the Print button in the System Properties
dialog box (refer to Figure 23.1) to record it all on paper for you.

If your computer doesn't have Windows 98 installed, you might be able to locate a similar utility in your preferred OS. In Windows 2000, the procedure is similar to what I've just
described, but the Device Manager is a separate window you open by clicking a button on the

Hardware tab in the System Properties dialog box. Some Linux GUI environments can provide some hardware information. For example, the K Desktop Environment (KDE) includes hardware information in the Information section of its KDE Control Center, as shown in Figure 23.3. You can find the most useful information in any distribution by examining the contents of files in the /proc directory tree. In particular, /proc/interrupts lists IRQs in use, /proc/ioports lists I/O ports, and /proc/dma lists direct memory access (DMA) channels. Linux might not assign a resource until the associated device has been used, however. For example, if you've rebooted but not yet used your sound card, its resources might not show up in the /proc directory tree or in resource viewers based on that tree, such as the KDE Control Center.

FIGURE 23.3
The KDE Control Center lets you view information from the /proc directory tree in a comparatively easy-to-access form.

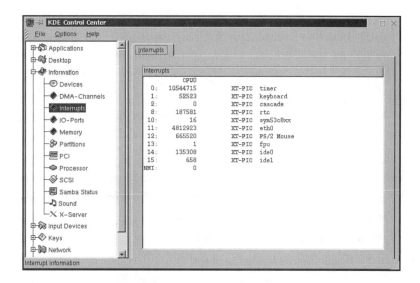

NOTE It is possible for two OSs to assign resources to the same device in different ways. For example, your Ethernet board and SCSI host adapter might use IRQs 10 and 11 in Windows 98 but 11 and 12 in Linux. In general, Windows is one of the fussiest when it comes to resource assignments, so it is best to record the Windows resource usage. If you want to record others, no harm will come of it. ■

Preparing Your OSs for the New Hardware

If you're replacing a component, it is often necessary to take some preparatory steps for this replacement. Specifically, it might be necessary to replace a driver for the old hardware with a generic driver that works with both the old and new hardware or to remove old drivers entirely. Unfortunately, it is impossible for me to provide information on all hardware and OSs, so you might need to rely on the documentation provided with your new hardware's drivers in deciding how to proceed. I can, however, provide a few guidelines and examples to help you prepare your system for new hardware.

> **CAUTION**
>
> Before you alter your OS driver configurations, you should back up your OS boot partitions. That way, if the attempt to upgrade a driver causes massive problems, as such attempts occasionally do, you can restore everything to a known working state and begin again.

Setting a Lowest-Common-Denominator Configuration   Some types of devices can work using drivers for a broad class of devices. Such drivers are typically slow and limited in capabilities compared to a driver customized for your particular device, but it might be necessary to use these drivers for a brief period while changing hardware. The classic example of such lowest-common-denominator configurations is VGA mode graphics. All modern video cards can handle VGA mode graphics—a 640×480 display with 16 colors. Such a display is woefully inadequate for serious use with modern OSs, but most GUI OSs can use VGA mode if nothing else is available. It is therefore sometimes helpful to switch an OS over to use VGA mode just before you remove the old video card or by using an emergency procedure when you first boot with the new video card. You might also want to install a lowest-common-denominator IDE driver when installing a new EIDE controller because many modern EIDE controllers come with custom drivers but work with generic drivers, albeit at slower speeds.

In fact, one OS (OS/2) requires you to "downgrade" to VGA mode when you replace your video card. To do so, follow these steps:

1. Install your new video hardware.
2. Turn on the computer and select OS/2 in your boot loader program.
3. Very soon after starting to boot, OS/2 displays a white square and the word *OS/2* in the upper-left corner of the screen. This appears before any OS/2 logo. Press Alt+F1 when the square and *OS/2* appear. OS/2 responds by presenting several special recovery options. If you're not fast enough, OS/2 displays its bootup splash screen. Press Ctrl+Alt+Del to reboot if this happens because you must boot in VGA mode after replacing the video hardware.
4. Pick option F3 (Reset Primary Video Display to VGA and Reboot) by pressing F3. OS/2 now boots the computer using VGA drivers.

After you've booted OS/2 into VGA mode, you can install the drivers for your new video card. (You should follow these instructions after installing the new board.)

In the case of UNIX-like OSs such as Linux, you can configure the computer to boot into text mode rather than graphics mode. This is generally done through the use of the /etc/inittab file, which contains a line such as the following:

```
id:5:initdefault:
```

The digit (5 in this example) represents the computer's runlevel. Precisely which runlevel corresponds to a text-mode boot and which to a full GUI boot varies from one OS to another. For example, on Red Hat Linux, 5 is a GUI login; but on SuSE Linux, 3 is the GUI login. There should be comments above or below the runlevel line that describe what the different values represent. Temporarily setting your system to boot into text mode enables you to experiment with starting X manually (via the `startx` command) without rebooting the computer, after you install a new X server for your new hardware.

> **CAUTION**
>
> If X can't start but the computer is set to run X automatically, the system falls into an infinite loop of trying, thus blocking access to the computer from the console. If your system is networked and has the appropriate daemons enabled, you can usually get in via Telnet or secure shell (SSH) login to set the runlevel manually using the `telinit` command, thus breaking out of the loop. Otherwise, you might need to use an emergency boot floppy to change `/etc/inittab`.

It is possible to assign a lowest-common-denominator configuration to a Windows system, but when you reboot, Windows (especially Windows 9x and Windows 2000) tends to redetect your hardware and install—or try to install—updated drivers. Therefore, lowest-common-denominator configurations usually don't accomplish much in Windows.

Uninstalling Existing Drivers   You might need or want to entirely uninstall old drivers before installing new hardware. I recommend doing this only when the hardware in question isn't critical to the basic functioning of the computer. Good examples include sound cards, network adapters, and SCSI host adapters that are not being used for a boot disk or a CD-ROM from which you intend to install drivers. There are three methods you can use to remove a driver from your system, depending on the OS:

- **GUI tools**—In Windows 9x, you can remove a device from your system by using the System Properties dialog box (refer to Figure 23.1). Select the device whose driver you want to remove and click Remove. Windows warns you that you're about to remove a device driver. Click OK to proceed. Similar procedures work in Windows 2000. In BeOS, many device types can be configured from dialog boxes accessible from the Be, Preferences menu. For example, Figure 23.4 shows the Network dialog box, in which you can add, remove, or configure drivers for your network cards.

- **Configuration files**—In DOS and OS/2, you can remove drivers by removing or commenting out their lines in the `CONFIG.SYS` file or sometimes the `AUTOEXEC.BAT` file for DOS. You must know which lines represent which drivers in order to do this. Similarly, Linux uses the `/etc/conf.modules` file to control the loading of kernel modules, which are Linux's driver files. The Linux `/etc/isapnp.conf` file controls the configuration of ISA PnP boards, but not the drivers per se.

FIGURE 23.4

Change your network device configuration, and then click Restart Networking to enable the changes immediately.

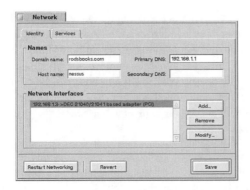

■ **Recompiling a kernel**—You can remove a driver by recompiling a Linux or BSD kernel if that driver was compiled directly into the kernel. In most cases, this effort is not justified unless you need to add a driver for the new hardware. Extra kernel drivers seldom do damage, although they do consume a few kilobytes of RAM. On rare occasions you might need to remove an old driver from a kernel to prevent probes from that driver from causing problems with other hardware.

In most OSs, you must reboot your computer to get it to function without the old driver. In most cases when installing new hardware, you would remove the old hardware, install the new hardware at the time of this reboot, and then proceed to install the new driver. A few OSs, such as Linux when using kernel modules and BeOS, support dynamic driver loading and unloading, so you need not reboot to remove a driver. Consult your OS's documentation for details.

Running Two Sets of Drivers   You can often run drivers for two devices simultaneously, even if one device isn't installed. This procedure works best on OSs that give the user full control over driver configuration, such as DOS, OS/2, and Linux. OSs with strong PnP features, such as Windows 9x and Windows 2000, tend to discard drivers that don't correspond to installed hardware.

If you try it, the usual consequence of running two drivers—one for hardware that doesn't exist—is that one simply doesn't work. Some OSs pause during the boot process to inform you of the fact that a driver couldn't find its hardware, but others roll blithely on. When you're finished reconfiguring your system, you can remove the old drivers, leaving only the new ones.

Installing multiple drivers works well for UNIX X servers—you can install two X servers, configure your system to boot into text mode, and start X manually using whichever server is appropriate for the hardware you have installed at the moment. This approach also often works well when upgrading SCSI host adapters and Ethernet adapters in many OSs. I recommend not trying this when upgrading video adapters in most non-UNIX OSs, however, because display systems are so critical to GUI OSs and many OSs become confused when you install two display drivers.

Taking Precautions Against Disaster

If you're like me, you'll underestimate the amount of time it will take to perform a hardware upgrade. When I upgrade hardware, I generally lay out in my mind the series of steps I must perform to carry out an upgrade, estimate the time for each step, and arrive at an estimate of the total time requirements. Unfortunately, there is invariably some complication along the way, particularly on a multi-OS computer. Perhaps a driver refuses to acknowledge that appropriate hardware is installed, or perhaps one driver interferes with another. I've even encountered situations where one failure leads to another, which leads to another, resulting in a completely useless OS installation. Lest such tales scare you off, I've written this section with advice on how to protect yourself from such worst-case situations, as well as from more minor problems, in your hardware upgrades.

Part

VIII

Ch

23

Proper Handling of Computer Hardware

Rule 1 in performing a hardware upgrade is to handle the equipment properly. If you fail to do this, the equipment might be damaged or might work unreliably because of poor connections between components. There are two main threats to hardware's well-being that you can mitigate by proper handling:

- **Dirt**—Computer components plug together like pieces of a child's puzzle, and it is vital that the connections between components be free of dirt (see Figure 23.5). In particular, oils from your hands can contaminate the metals in circuit boards' edge connectors, if you handle these connectors directly. Therefore, it is best to handle circuit boards along the sides that don't make contact with the motherboard. Similarly, it is best not to touch the portions of a circuit board on which chips and circuit traces reside, so as not to accidentally damage a component. Hard disks and other devices that attach via cables typically have recessed connectors, so it is easier to handle these devices properly. Although not an issue of cleanliness, it is also important to handle circuit boards gently; if you flex them, they will break. Sometimes you might not be able to see the damage, but it will manifest in unreliable operation or no operation at all.

- **Electrostatic discharge**—Computer components are quite sensitive to static electricity. When you walk across a carpet in winter and touch a doorknob, you will likely feel the effects of an electrostatic discharge. A discharge of that magnitude can destroy many computer components, so you should take pains to ensure that it happens with the doorknob rather than to your new $200 video adapter. Most computer components ship in special antistatic plastic bags, and you shouldn't remove the components from those bags until it is time to use them. When you handle components, you should do so while wearing an antistatic wrist strap, which you can obtain from most computer or electronics stores. Such straps ground you as long as you wear the strap, thus preventing a static buildup in your body. If you lack an antistatic wrist strap, at least ground yourself frequently and don't move around much (walking across carpets is a good way to build up a static charge in your body). You can ground yourself by touching a metal component on your computer, if it is plugged in, or a radiator or metal plumbing fixture.

FIGURE 23.5
The connection points on computer components should be kept free of dirt for trouble-free operation.

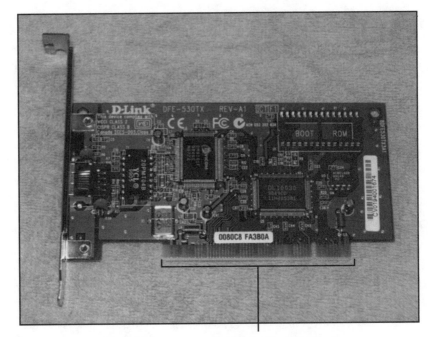

The edge connector

CAUTION

Older computers had on/off switches that cut all current to the computer's circuits, but newer models with ATX cases have on/off switches that leave some current flowing even when the computer is powered down. When using old-style computers, it is best to leave them plugged in when you work on them so that you can easily ground yourself by touching the case or by connecting a grounding strap to the case. For your own safety, however, it is best to unplug newer computers and find another way to ground yourself when you work on them. One exception is if the computer has an old-style on/off switch in addition to the main power button, as some do, typically accessible from the back of the power supply. You can then use the power supply's on/off switch to cut all power to internal components while you work on the computer.

It is unfair to leave you with the impression that computer hardware is so delicate that it breaks at the lightest touch. In fact, you often have to apply moderate force to install a card, and even a mild static discharge isn't guaranteed to destroy equipment, although it is the most serious danger to hardware in typical handling. The key is to take sensible precautions, as I've outlined in this section.

Backing Up Before an Upgrade

One of the most important precautions you can take in performing a hardware upgrade is to back up your boot partitions. In my experience, software failures are far more common than are hardware failures, so if you encounter problems when you upgrade your hardware, chances are those problems will be software related. As such, if all else fails, you can use a recent backup to restore your system to a state that works with your old hardware. You can then try again, starting with the old hardware, if necessary, to acquire a new set of drivers or follow a variant procedure for installing the new hardware's drivers.

▶ To learn more about backing up your computer, **see** "Cross-Platform Backup Needs," **p. 548**.

Part

VIII

Ch

23

Precisely what you must back up depends very much on what sort of hardware you're adding or replacing. In my experience, video card drivers, sound card drivers, and drivers for SCSI host adapters are the most likely to cause problems, especially in the case of OSs in which these services are tightly integrated into the OS, such as Windows and OS/2. Printer drivers are unlikely to cause an irreparable mess of things in any OS. In UNIX-like OSs, video drivers are part of the X server, which can be upgraded relatively cleanly without impacting other parts of the OS. If you're careful about setting your system to boot into text mode rather than directly into X, a complete backup might be unnecessary. If you recompile a Linux or BSD kernel, your backup should consist of keeping a copy of your old kernel in a format that enables you to boot it if the need arises.

 TIP

Do your backup first in any upgrade procedure. Particularly when recompiling a Linux kernel, it is easy to leave the backup of the working kernel until last, but then it becomes easy to forget to do it. If you find that you're partway through a procedure and have forgotten the backup, stop or use the OS's multitasking capability to do the backup immediately.

In addition to backing up your entire boot partition or affected files such as a Linux or BSD kernel, you should back up important configuration files, such as CONFIG.SYS, /etc/conf.modules, and /etc/X11/XF86Config. Depending on your driver changes, keeping these files might enable you to revert completely to an old configuration or just copy key lines from an old configuration if a driver installation utility becomes over-enthusiastic about making changes to your system.

Keeping Your Driver Options Open

One key principle in performing a hardware upgrade is to refrain from burning your figurative bridges until you're sure your new hardware works correctly in all your OSs. There are several steps you can take to help ensure your flexibility before, during, and after a hardware upgrade:

- **Keep backups**—As I've just described, keeping backups is important. If you can revert to a previous configuration, you can back out of an otherwise disastrous situation.

- **Keep copies of drivers**—Be sure you have on hand copies of drivers for both your new and old hardware. It is sometimes necessary to reinstall an old driver if the new hardware doesn't work out. Be sure the drivers are on a medium that will be accessible if no driver is available. For example, copy SCSI host adapter drivers from CD-ROM to floppy if your CD-ROM drive runs through the SCSI host adapter.

- **Keep emergency disks handy**—You might need to access your hard disk using an emergency boot disk or an alternative OS to repair a damaged configuration file, read documentation files, or perform some other action. Be prepared for this eventuality.

  ▶ To learn more about accessing one OS's filesystem from another OS, **see** Chapter 13, "Tools for Accessing Foreign Filesystems."

- **Don't delete drivers until all OSs work**—You might have no problems installing drivers for your first OS or two but then run into problems with a later OS. In fact, if Murphy's Law operates as usual, your problems will occur on the last OS you try to modify. Therefore, you should be sure to keep all the relevant files for both the old and the new hardware on hand until you're sure everything works in all your OSs.

After you're sure everything works correctly with the new hardware and drivers, you can burn a few bridges. I recommend using your upgraded system for a few days before you discard old drivers or your old hardware. Reverting to old hardware can be a drag, but sometimes it is the only option if you have problems with the new hardware.

What to Do If the New Hardware Doesn't Work

If your new hardware doesn't live up to your expectations, you must find some way to diagnose the problem. After you've discovered the cause of the problem, you can decide what sort of action to take.

Your first action should be to determine whether the problem is hardware or software related. A multi-OS configuration can be very helpful in determining this—if a problem occurs in all your OSs, it is almost certainly a hardware problem, but if it is isolated to just one or two OSs, it is almost certainly a software problem.

Whether the problem is isolated to one OS or is common to all of them, one potential source of problems is hardware resource conflicts. This is where the information you collected on resource use can come in handy. You can repeat the steps I described earlier to locate the resources used by your new device and try to determine whether those resources conflict with those used by other devices. If they do, try to reassign those resources. You might be able to do so using a GUI utility such as the Windows Device Manager or by using a text-mode configuration tool such as the /etc/isapnp.conf or /etc/conf.modules files in Linux. Consult your OS's documentation for details. With older ISA products, you might need to set jumpers or DIP switches on the hardware itself. Consult the product's documentation for details.

If you suspect your hardware is defective, one obvious solution is to return the hardware for a refund or exchange. If you exchange the product for an identical model, you don't need to reinstall the drivers you've already installed; the hardware should work just fine when you swap in the new board.

In general, if you suspect a hardware problem and contact the manufacturer about it, you should attempt to use the product under an OS that the manufacturer supports and ideally under Windows 9x because that is the OS with which the manufacturer's tech support people are most familiar. I suggest that you don't even mention you have other OSs installed because this fact might cause confusion. An exception, of course, would be if the problem manifests itself differently in different OSs.

In the event of a software problem, you should retrace the steps you took to locate drivers for the product and attempt to locate information on configuration settings, bug fixes, or alternative drivers. If you're using your OS's standard drivers for a device, see whether the manufacturer offers its own drivers; the two might be different, and in most cases the manufacturer's drivers are more up-to-date, particularly if you get them from the manufacturer's Web page.

▶ To learn more about locating drivers, **see** Chapter 22, "Finding Drivers."

Suggested Sequence of Updates

After you've completed all your research, made appropriate backups, and prepared your OSs for the change of hardware, it is time to implement that change. That is, it is time to perform the fourth and fifth steps of the procedure outlined at the beginning of this chapter.

The biggest question in performing these updates is in the sequence—which OS do you update first, which last, and which go in between? To some extent the ordering doesn't really matter as long as they all get finished; but there are a few reasons to do one OS before another.

Basic Hardware Checks

Before you install the hardware at all, though, you should perform some basic checks on it. You cannot do much to check the functionality of most hardware, of course, short of installing it and trying it out. For plug-in boards, you're restricted to a visual inspection, possibly coupled with a test to see that any connectors on the board (for SCSI cables, external audio jacks, and so on) accept the connectors they should. There is no point in installing the hardware and configuring drivers only to discover that you can't plug speakers into your sound card, after all.

Some devices—including SCSI host adapters, EIDE controllers, and the disks and other devices used with these boards—have internal connectors with a large number of pins (see Figure 23.6). Before you plug any cable into these connectors, you should inspect the connectors to be sure that no pins are bent. Some connector types, such as the connectors on floppy drives, are missing one or more pins, so this might be normal, but you might want to consult the documentation on this point just to be sure, if you find missing pins. Many connectors are *keyed*, meaning that a special notch prevents you from inserting a cable backward. Some cables and connectors lack these keys, however, so cables can be inserted backward. Be sure you insert the cable correctly with such devices—typically, a red stripe on one end of the cable marks pin 1, which you should align with an appropriate marking on the board or device. External SCSI connectors place the pins on the cable, so you must examine the pins there rather than on the host adapter.

FIGURE 23.6
Pins on SCSI and EIDE connectors can be bent or broken; be sure yours aren't before you try to use such a board.

Internal SCSI connector   External SCSI connector

Easy to Configure First, Difficult to Change Last

As a general rule, I recommend installing drivers first for those OSs that have the easiest and most easily reversed driver installation procedures and reserving for last those that are the most difficult to change. This policy can save you time if you encounter problems with one of the easier OSs. For example, recompiling a Linux kernel for a new SCSI host adapter is something of a nuisance compared to dropping in a driver file and modifying CONFIG.SYS in DOS or OS/2. When you're adding a SCSI driver for those three OSs, I recommend doing DOS first (before OS/2 simply because DOS boots more quickly), then OS/2, and then Linux. If the OS/2 driver crashes your system, you can return the board and need not bother with recompiling the Linux kernel.

The preceding example deserves a couple of caveats, however:

■ If you use Linux kernel modules for the SCSI host adapter, you need not recompile the entire kernel, so Linux configuration becomes much simpler, especially if the appropriate kernel module is already compiled, as is likely if you haven't recompiled the kernel provided by your distribution.

■ If you're replacing a SCSI host adapter that controls your boot disk, you must recompile the Linux kernel while the old hardware is installed, so that fact means you will have done most of the work of changing your configuration before installing the new hardware. Only a boot to Linux and a run of lilo is required to completely reconfigure Linux for the new hardware.

Part
VIII

Ch
23

Which OS is easiest to configure varies a great deal depending on the device and even on how you intend to configure your system, as illustrated by the question of where you put a SCSI driver in your Linux system (in the kernel or as a separate module). I therefore can't provide hard-and-fast rules on this matter. I do have some comments on specific OSs, however:

■ **DOS**—Some hardware doesn't work under DOS at all or requires no reconfiguration. You configure most other hardware by changing your CONFIG.SYS or AUTOEXEC.BAT files, either directly or by running an installation program. DOS configuration is therefore usually pretty simple if you understand how DOS handles such things. If you're used to Windows-style automatic hardware detection, editing DOS's configuration files can be intimidating.

■ **Windows 9x**—Windows 95 was the first x86 OS to implement strong PnP functionality, and Windows 98 improves on this matter. In theory, then, Windows 9x should be very easy to configure. In practice, it usually is, but the installation procedures sometimes derail themselves, causing serious problems.

■ **Windows NT**—Through version 4.0, Windows NT implemented only very weak PnP functionality, and hardware driver installation could be somewhat challenging at times. Windows 2000 improves matters substantially, adding Windows 9x–style wizards for hardware installation.

■ **OS/2**—OS/2 uses a variety of methods for driver installation, ranging from adding a line or two to CONFIG.SYS to installation scripts that make changes to a variety of files. How easy these methods are depends on the particular driver and your own inclinations (that is, whether you prefer a GUI installer or manual editing of configuration files).

■ **BeOS**—Adding drivers to BeOS often involves manually copying files to a directory and then letting the system detect their presence. The procedure is generally fairly easy, although you might need to know what BeOS utility to use to configure the new drivers (such as the network configuration tool shown in Figure 23.4).

■ **Linux and other UNIX versions**—Linux supports drivers in a variety of locations, depending on the driver type. Locations include the Linux kernel file, separate kernel modules, the X server file, and the Ghostscript executable. Device configuration can range from automatic as the kernel loads to tedious editing of complex configuration files such as XF86Config. You can often use a configuration program to help with the more tedious of these procedures. Linux driver installation therefore ranges from quite easy to quite complex compared to other OSs. Details differ from one UNIX-like OS to another, but similar comments apply to all of them.

Most Likely to Cause Problems First—Or Last

Earlier, I alluded to Windows 9*x*'s propensity to cause problems for itself when installing new drivers. This problem is certainly not unique to Windows 9*x*, but that OS's strong PnP orientation tends to lead it down disastrously wrong paths occasionally, which can be a problem if your hardware configuration is unusual or if you change it often. In my experience, Windows 9*x* is most likely to get things wrong when replacing existing hardware; it is much better at detecting and correctly configuring new hardware.

In general, if you think that an OS is likely to have problems with a hardware upgrade, you might want to tackle that OS first. This advice applies especially if you have doubts about the capability of an OS to handle a device; it is better to find out that a component is useless in one OS before you install drivers for that device in your other OSs. If, by contrast, you expect the hardware can be made to work but that you might need to try the driver installation several times or work around several glitches before getting acceptable results, you might prefer to leave the installation until last, simply because you can then still use your computer in your other OSs.

Most Important First

One final principle you might want to consider when deciding on an order of installation is to configure your most important OS first. If you do most of your work in Windows 2000 but keep BeOS and Linux on the system for non-critical work, you should probably install drivers in Windows 2000 first. That way, if driver installation takes longer than you expect, you can put off the installation in the non-critical OSs until some later time and use the most important OS with the new hardware in the meantime.

One variant on this principle is to configure an OS that provides access to other OSs' tools first. For example, Linux includes filesystem drivers and emulators that enable you to access many other OSs' tools, so you might favor Linux over other OSs because doing so enables you to edit other OSs' files and perhaps even run their programs through an emulator if the need arises.

▶ To learn more about emulators, **see** Chapter 18, "OSs Within OSs: Emulators."

This advice applies to hardware replacements that make an OS useless or almost useless until a new driver has been installed, such as video card upgrades. If a device is strictly an add-on that is not required to use a computer, such as a new Zip drive, it is much less critical whether you install the driver in an important or unimportant OS first.

Overall Suggestions

Some of the order of installation advice I've presented might lead in contradictory ways. For example, if the OS that is likely to take the longest on an upgrade is also your most important OS, you must decide which piece of advice to follow. You'll have to make that call yourself. Fortunately, you're unlikely to run into problems in one OS because of a driver installation in another. One possible exception to this rule is if you run two or more OSs—particularly related OSs, such as DR-DOS and MS-DOS—on a single partition. In such a situation, it is conceivable that a driver upgrade in one OS will cause problems in another, particularly if you delete a driver directory that had been used by both OSs. A bit of caution in locating driver files can help immensely—for example, don't use the same directory for both DOS and Windows 9x drivers unless you're sure there are no duplicate filenames.

 TIP If two OSs use the exact same driver files, as might DR-DOS and MS-DOS, you can often install the driver files once and use them in both OSs by making appropriate configuration changes to the second OS.

It is critically important that you follow the instructions provided by the driver's author when installing the driver. Unless you have a very good reason to do so (such as an adjustment that you know is required because you're using a more recent version of your OS), you shouldn't deviate from the installation instructions provided by the driver's author.

Summary

Performing hardware upgrades can be a challenging task, even on a single-OS computer. Doing the same on a multi-OS machine multiplies the challenge by the number of OSs installed. Fortunately, OS publishers have been slowly improving driver installation methods for years, so the task is usually manageable on modern OSs. The main keys to successfully performing such an upgrade are to carefully research the products for OS compatibility before making a purchase and to be careful and diligent when performing the upgrade. Give yourself enough time, and be sure to read the documentation for every OS. A poorly installed driver can result in erratic OS behavior or even an incapability to boot, so don't take shortcuts on driver installation. ●

Index

Other Related Titles

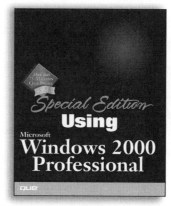

Special Edition Using Microsoft Windows 2000 Professional
Robert Cowart and Brian Knittel
ISBN: 0-7897-2125-2
$39.99 U.S./
$59.95 CAN

Special Edition Using MS-DOS 6.22, Second Edition
Allen Wyatt
ISBN: 0-7897-2040-X
$34.99 U.S./$52.95 CAN

Practical UNIX
Steve Moritsugu
ISBN: 0-7897-2250-X
$29.99 U.S./$44.95 CAN

Special Edition Using Microsoft Windows 98, Second Edition
Ed Bott
ISBN: 0-7897-2203-8
$39.99 U.S./$52.95 CAN

Upgrading and Repairing PCs, Eleventh Edition
Scott Mueller
ISBN: 0-7897-1903-7
$59.99 U.S./$81.95 CAN

SuSE Linux Installation and Configuration Handbook
Nazeeh Amin
ISBN: 0-7897-2355-7
$39.99 U.S./$52.95 CAN

Special Edition Using Linux System Administration
Arman Danesh
ISBN: 0-7897-2352-2
$39.99 U.S./$74.95 CAN

www.quecorp.com

Special Edition Using Red Hat Linux
Alan Simpson
ISBN: 0-7897-2258-5
$39.99 U.S./
$59.95 CAN

Special Edition Using Samba
Richard Sharpe
ISBN: 0-7897-2319-0
$39.99 U.S./
$59.95 CAN

All prices are subject to change.

Installation Instructions

Windows 95/NT 4

1. Insert the CD-ROM into your CD-ROM drive.

2. From the Windows desktop, double-click the My Computer icon.

3. Double-click the icon representing your CD-ROM drive.

4. Double-click the icon titled START.EXE to run the installation program.

NOTE If Windows 95/NT 4.0 is installed on your computer and you have the AutoPlay feature enabled, the START.EXE program starts automatically whenever you insert the disc into your CD-ROM drive. ▓

UNIX, BeOS, OS/2, and MS-DOS

Look in the individual directories for software and associated documentation.

GNU GENERAL PUBLIC LICENSE

Version 2, June 1991

Preamble

The licenses for most software are designed to take away your freedom to share and change it. By contrast, the GNU General Public License is intended to guarantee your freedom to share and change free software—to make sure the software is free for all its users. This General Public License applies to most of the Free Software Foundation's software and to any other program whose authors commit to using it. (Some other Free Software Foundation software is covered by the GNU Library General Public License instead.) You can apply it to your programs, too.

When we speak of free software, we are referring to freedom, not price. Our General Public Licenses are designed to make sure that you have the freedom to distribute copies of free software (and charge for this service if you wish), that you receive source code or can get it if you want it, that you can change the software or use pieces of it in new free programs; and that you know you can do these things.

To protect your rights, we need to make restrictions that forbid anyone to deny you these rights or to ask you to surrender the rights. These restrictions translate to certain responsibilities for you if you distribute copies of the software or if you modify it.

For example, if you distribute copies of such a program, whether gratis or for a fee, you must give the recipients all the rights that you have. You must make sure that they, too, receive or can get the source code. And you must show them these terms so they know their rights.

We protect your rights with two steps: (1) copyright the software, and (2) offer you this license, which gives you legal permission to copy, distribute and/or modify the software.

Also, for each author's protection and ours, we want to make certain that everyone understands that there is no warranty for this free software. If the software is modified by someone else and passed on, we want its recipients to know that what they have is not the original, so that any problems introduced by others will not reflect on the original authors' reputations.

Finally, any free program is threatened constantly by software patents. We wish to avoid the danger that redistributors of a free program will individually obtain patent licenses, in effect making the program proprietary. To prevent this, we have made it clear that any patent must be licensed for everyone's free use or not licensed at all.

The precise terms and conditions for copying, distribution and modification follow.

GNU GENERAL PUBLIC LICENSE

TERMS AND CONDITIONS FOR COPYING, DISTRIBUTION AND MODIFICATION

0. This License applies to any program or other work which contains a notice placed by the copyright holder saying it may be distributed under the terms of this General Public License. The "Program," below, refers to any such program or work, and a "work based on the Program" means either the Program or any derivative work under copyright law: that is to say, a work containing the Program or a portion of it, either verbatim or with modifications and/or translated into another language. (Hereinafter, translation is included without limitation in the term "modification.") Each licensee is addressed as "you."

Activities other than copying, distribution and modification are not covered by this License; they are outside its scope. The act of running the Program is not restricted, and the output from the Program is covered only if its contents constitute a work based on the Program (independent of having been made by running the Program). Whether that is true depends on what the Program does.

1. You may copy and distribute verbatim copies of the Program's source code as you receive it, in any medium, provided that you conspicuously and appropriately publish on each copy an appropriate copyright notice and disclaimer of warranty; keep intact all the notices that refer to this License and to the absence of any warranty; and give any other recipients of the Program a copy of this License along with the Program.

You may charge a fee for the physical act of transferring a copy, and you may at your option offer warranty protection in exchange for a fee.

2. You may modify your copy or copies of the Program or any portion of it, thus forming a work based on the Program, and copy and distribute such modifications or work under the terms of Section 1 above, provided that you also meet all of these conditions:

   a) You must cause the modified files to carry prominent notices stating that you changed the files and the date of any change.

   b) You must cause any work that you distribute or publish, that in whole or in part contains or is derived from the Program or any part thereof, to be licensed as a whole at no charge to all third parties under the terms of this License.

   c) If the modified program normally reads commands interactively when run, you must cause it, when started running for such interactive use in the most ordinary way, to print or display an announcement including an appropriate copyright notice and a notice that there is no warranty (or else, saying that you provide a warranty) and that users may redistribute the program under these conditions, and telling the user how to view a copy of this License. (Exception: If the Program itself is interactive but does not normally print such an announcement, your work based on the Program is not required to print an announcement.)

These requirements apply to the modified work as a whole. If identifiable sections of that work are not derived from the Program, and can be reasonably considered independent and separate works in themselves, then this License, and its terms, do not apply to those sections when you distribute them as separate works. But when you distribute the same sections as part of a whole which is a work based on the Program, the distribution of the whole must be on the terms of this License, whose permissions for other licensees extend to the entire whole, and thus to each and every part regardless of who wrote it.

Thus, it is not the intent of this section to claim rights or contest your rights to work written entirely by you; rather, the intent is to exercise the right to control the distribution of derivative or collective works based on the Program.

In addition, mere aggregation of another work not based on the Program with the Program (or with a work based on the Program) on a volume of a storage or distribution medium does not bring the other work under the scope of this License.

3. You may copy and distribute the Program (or a work based on it, under Section 2 in object code or executable form under the terms of Sections 1 and 2 above provided that you also do one of the following:

   a) Accompany it with the complete corresponding machine-readable source code, which must be distributed under the terms of Sections 1 and 2 above on a medium customarily used for software interchange; or,

   b) Accompany it with a written offer, valid for at least three years, to give any third party, for a charge no more than your cost of physically performing source distribution, a complete machine-readable copy of the corresponding source code, to be distributed under the terms of Sections 1 and 2 above on a medium customarily used for software interchange; or,

   c) Accompany it with the information you received as to the offer to distribute corresponding source code. (This alternative is allowed only for noncommercial distribution and only if you received the program in object code or executable form with such an offer, in accord with Subsection b above.)

The source code for a work means the preferred form of the work for making modifications to it. For an executable work, complete source code means all the source code for all modules it contains, plus any associated interface definition files, plus the scripts used to control compilation and installation of the executable. However, as a special exception, the source code distributed need not include anything that is normally distributed (in either source or binary form) with the major components (compiler, kernel, and so on) of the operating system on which the executable runs, unless that component itself accompanies the executable.

If distribution of executable or object code is made by offering access to copy from a designated place, then offering equivalent access to copy the source code from the same place counts as distribution of the source code, even though third parties are not compelled to copy the source along with the object code.

4. You may not copy, modify, sublicense, or distribute the Program except as expressly provided under this License. Any attempt otherwise to copy, modify, sublicense or distribute the Program is void, and will automatically terminate your rights under this License. However, parties who have received copies, or rights, from you under this License will not have their licenses terminated so long as such parties remain in full compliance.

5. You are not required to accept this License, since you have not signed it. However, nothing else grants you permission to modify or distribute the Program or its derivative works. These actions are prohibited by law if you do not accept this License. Therefore, by modifying or distributing the Program (or any work based on the Program), you indicate your acceptance of this License to do so, and all its terms and conditions for copying, distributing or modifying the Program or works based on it.

6. Each time you redistribute the Program (or any work based on the Program), the recipient automatically receives a license from the original licensor to copy, distribute or modify the Program subject to these terms and conditions. You may not impose any further restrictions on the recipients' exercise of the rights granted herein. You are not responsible for enforcing compliance by third parties to this License.

7. If, as a consequence of a court judgment or allegation of patent infringement or for any other reason (not limited to patent issues), conditions are imposed on you (whether by court order, agreement or otherwise) that contradict the conditions of this License, they do not excuse you from the conditions of this License. If you cannot distribute so as to satisfy simultaneously your obligations under this License and any other pertinent obligations, then as a consequence you may not distribute the Program at all. For example, if a patent license would not permit royalty-free redistribution of the Program by all those who receive copies directly or indirectly through you, then the only way you could satisfy both it and this License would be to refrain entirely from distribution of the Program.

If any portion of this section is held invalid or unenforceable under any particular circumstance, the balance of the section is intended to apply and the section as a whole is intended to apply in other circumstances.

It is not the purpose of this section to induce you to infringe any patents or other property right claims or to contest validity of any such claims; this section has the sole purpose of protecting the integrity of the free software distribution system, which is implemented by public license practices. Many people have made generous contributions to the wide range of software distributed through that system in reliance on consistent application of that system; it is up to the author/donor to decide if he or she is willing to distribute software through any other system, and a licensee cannot impose that choice.

This section is intended to make thoroughly clear what is believed to be a consequence of the rest of this License.

8. If the distribution and/or use of the Program is restricted in certain countries either by patents or by copyrighted interfaces, the original copyright holder who places the Program under this License may add an explicit geographical distribution limitation excluding those countries, so that distribution is permitted only in or among countries not thus excluded. In such case, this License incorporates the limitation as if written in the body of this License.

9. The Free Software Foundation may publish revised and/or new versions of the General Public License from time to time. Such new versions will be similar in spirit to the present version, but may differ in detail to address new problems or concerns.

   Each version is given a distinguishing version number. If the Program specifies a version number of this License which applies to it and "any later version," you have the option of following the terms and conditions either of that version or of any later version published by the Free Software Foundation. If the Program does not specify a version number of this License, you may choose any version ever published by the Free Software Foundation.

10. If you wish to incorporate parts of the Program into other free programs whose distribution conditions are different, write to the author to ask for permission. For software which is copyrighted by the Free Software Foundation, write to the Free Software Foundation; we sometimes make exceptions for this. Our decision will be guided by the two goals of preserving the free status of all derivatives of our free software and of promoting the sharing and reuse of software generally.

NO WARRANTY

11. BECAUSE THE PROGRAM IS LICENSED FREE OF CHARGE, THERE IS NO WARRANTY FOR THE PROGRAM, TO THE EXTENT PERMITTED BY APPLICABLE LAW. EXCEPT WHEN OTHERWISE STATED IN WRITING THE COPYRIGHT HOLDERS AND/OR OTHER PARTIES PROVIDE THE PROGRAM "AS IS" WITHOUT WARRANTY OF ANY KIND, EITHER EXPRESSED OR IMPLIED, INCLUDING, BUT NOT LIMITED TO, THE IMPLIED WARRANTIES OF MERCHANTABILITY AND FITNESS FOR A PARTICULAR PURPOSE. THE ENTIRE RISK AS TO THE QUALITY AND PERFORMANCE OF THE PROGRAM IS WITH YOU. SHOULD THE PROGRAM PROVE DEFECTIVE, YOU ASSUME THE COST OF ALL NECESSARY SERVICING, REPAIR OR CORRECTION.

12. IN NO EVENT UNLESS REQUIRED BY APPLICABLE LAW OR AGREED TO IN WRITING WILL ANY COPYRIGHT HOLDER, OR ANY OTHER PARTY WHO MAY MODIFY AND/OR REDISTRIBUTE THE PROGRAM AS PERMITTED ABOVE, BE LIABLE TO YOU FOR DAMAGES, INCLUDING ANY GENERAL, SPECIAL, INCIDENTAL OR CONSEQUENTIAL DAMAGES ARISING OUT OF THE USE OR INABILITY TO USE THE PROGRAM (INCLUDING BUT NOT LIMITED TO LOSS

OF DATA OR DATA BEING RENDERED INACCURATE OR LOSSES SUSTAINED
BY YOU OR THIRD PARTIES OR A FAILURE OF THE PROGRAM TO OPERATE
WITH ANY OTHER PROGRAMS), EVEN IF SUCH HOLDER OR OTHER PARTY HAS
BEEN ADVISED OF THE POSSIBILITY OF SUCH DAMAGES.

END OF TERMS AND CONDITIONS

Linux and the GNU System

The GNU project started 12 years ago with the goal of developing a complete free Unix-like operating system. "Free" refers to freedom, not price; it means you are free to run, copy, distribute, study, change, and improve the software.

A Unix-like system consists of many different programs. We found some components already available as free software—for example, X Windows and TeX. We obtained other components by helping to convince their developers to make them free—for example, the Berkeley network utilities. Other components we wrote specifically for GNU—for example, GNU Emacs, the GNU C compiler, the GNU C library, Bash, and Ghostscript. The components in this last category are "GNU software".

The GNU system consists of all three categories together. The GNU project is not just about developing and distributing free software. The heart of the GNU project is an idea: that software should be free, and that the users' freedom is worth defending. For if people have freedom but do not value it, they will not keep it for long. In order to make freedom last, we have to teach people to value it.

The GNU project's method is that free software and the idea of users' freedom support each other. We develop GNU software, and as people encounter GNU programs or the GNU system and start to use them, they also think about the GNU idea. The software shows that the idea can work in practice. People who come to agree with the idea are likely to write additional free software. Thus, the software embodies the idea, spreads the idea, and grows from the idea.

This method was working well—until someone combined the Linux kernel with the GNU system (which still lacked a kernel), and called the combination a "Linux system."

The Linux kernel is a free Unix-compatible kernel written by Linus Torvalds. It was not written specifically for the GNU project, but the Linux kernel and the GNU system work together well. In fact, adding Linux to the GNU system brought the system to completion: It made a free Unix-compatible operating system available for use.

But ironically, the practice of calling it a "Linux system" undermines our method of communicating the GNU idea. At first impression, a "Linux system" sounds like something completely distinct from the "GNU system." And that is what most users think it is.

Most introductions to the "Linux system" acknowledge the role played by the GNU software components. But they don't say that the system as a whole is more or less the same GNU system that the GNU project has been compiling for a decade. They don't say that the idea of a free Unix-like system originates from the GNU project. So most users don't know these things.

This leads many of those users to identify themselves as a separate community of "Linux users," distinct from the GNU user community. They use all of the GNU software; in fact, they use almost all of the GNU system; but they don't think of themselves as GNU users, and they may not think about the GNU idea.

It leads to other problems as well—even hampering cooperation on software maintenance. Normally when users change a GNU program to make it work better on a particular system, they send the change to the maintainer of that program; then they work with the maintainer, explaining the change, arguing for it and sometimes rewriting it, to get it installed.

But people who think of themselves as "Linux users" are more likely to release a forked "Linux-only" version of the GNU program, and consider the job done. We want each and every GNU program to work "out of the box" on Linux-based systems; but if the users do not help, that goal becomes much harder to achieve.

So how should the GNU project respond? What should we do now to spread the idea that freedom for computer users is important?

We should continue to talk about the freedom to share and change software—and to teach other users to value these freedoms. If we enjoy having a free operating system, it makes sense for us to think about preserving those freedoms for the long term. If we enjoy having a variety of free software, it makes sense for to think about encouraging others to write additional free software, instead of additional proprietary software.

We should not accept the splitting of the community in two. Instead we should spread the word that "Linux systems" are variant GNU systems—that users of these systems are GNU users, and that they ought to consider the GNU philosophy which brought these systems into existence.

This article is one way of doing that. Another way is to use the terms "Linux-based GNU system" (or "GNU/Linux system" or "Lignux" for short) to refer to the combination of the Linux kernel and the GNU system.

The FreeBSD Copyright

All of the documentation and software included in the 4.4BSD and 4.4BSD-Lite Releases is copyrighted by The Regents of the University of California.

Copyright 1979, 1980, 1983, 1986, 1988, 1989, 1991, 1992, 1993, 1994 The Regents of the University of California. All rights reserved.

Redistribution and use in source and binary forms, with or without modification, are permitted provided that the following conditions are met:

1. Redistributions of source code must retain the above copyright notice, this list of conditions and the following disclaimer.

2. Redistributions in binary form must reproduce the above copyright notice, this list of conditions and the following disclaimer in the documentation and/or other materials provided with the distribution.

3. All advertising materials mentioning features or use of this software must display the following acknowledgement:

    This product includes software developed by the University of California, Berkeley and its contributors.

4. Neither the name of the University nor the names of its contributors may be used to endorse or promote products derived from this software without specific prior written permission.

THIS SOFTWARE IS PROVIDED BY THE REGENTS AND CONTRIBUTORS "AS IS" AND ANY EXPRESS OR IMPLIED WARRANTIES, INCLUDING, BUT NOT LIMITED TO, THE IMPLIED WARRANTIES OF MERCHANTABILITY AND FITNESS FOR A PARTICULAR PURPOSE ARE DISCLAIMED. IN NO EVENT SHALL THE REGENTS OR CONTRIBUTORS BE LIABLE FOR ANY DIRECT, INDIRECT, INCIDENTAL, SPECIAL, EXEMPLARY, OR CONSEQUENTIAL DAMAGES (INCLUDING, BUT NOT LIMITED TO, PROCUREMENT OF SUBSTITUTE GOODS OR SERVICES; LOSS OF USE, DATA, OR PROFITS; OR BUSINESS INTERRUPTION) HOWEVER CAUSED AND ON ANY THEORY OF LIABILITY, WHETHER IN CONTRACT, STRICT LIABILITY, OR TORT (INCLUDING NEGLIGENCE OR OTHERWISE) ARISING IN ANY WAY OUT OF THE USE OF THIS SOFTWARE, EVEN IF ADVISED OF THE POSSIBILITY OF SUCH DAMAGE.

The Institute of Electrical and Electronics Engineers and the American National Standards Committee X3, on Information Processing Systems have given us permission to reprint portions of their documentation.

In the following statement, the phrase "this text" refers to portions of the system documentation.

Portions of this text are reprinted and reproduced in electronic form in the second BSD Networking Software Release, from IEEE Std 1003.1-1988, IEEE Standard Portable Operating

System Interface for Computer Environments (POSIX), copyright (c) 1988 by the Institute of Electrical and Electronics Engineers, Inc. In the event of any discrepancy between these versions and the original IEEE Standard, the original IEEE Standard is the referee document.

In the following statement, the phrase "This material" refers to portions of the system documentation.

This material is reproduced with permission from American National Standards Committee X3, on Information Processing Systems. Computer and Business Equipment Manufacturers Association (CBEMA), 311 First St., NW, Suite 500, Washington, DC 20001-2178. The developmental work of Programming Language C was completed by the X3J11 Technical Committee.

The views and conclusions contained in the software and documentation are those of the authors and should not be interpreted as representing official policies, either expressed or implied, of the Regents of the University of California.

www@FreeBSD.ORG

$Date: 1997/07/01 03:52:05 $

Read This Before Opening the Software